SECOND EDITION

# Administrative Justice

## IN SOUTH AFRICA

*An Introduction*

PUBLIC LAW

SECOND EDITION

# Administrative Justice IN SOUTH AFRICA

## *An Introduction*

PUBLIC LAW

GEO QUINOT | ALLISON ANTHONY
JANICE BLEAZARD | STEVEN BUDLENDER
RAISA CACHALIA | HUGH CORDER
MEGHAN FINN | MICHAEL KIDD
THULI MADONSELA | PETRUS MAREE
MELANIE MURCOTT | MFUNDO SALUKAZANA
EMMA WEBBER

OXFORD UNIVERSITY PRESS
SOUTH AFRICA

OXFORD
UNIVERSITY PRESS

Oxford University Press is a department of the University of Oxford. It furthers the University's objective of excellence in research, scholarship, and education by publishing worldwide. Oxford is a registered trade mark of Oxford University Press in the UK and in certain other countries

Published in South Africa by
Oxford University Press Southern Africa (Pty) Limited

Vasco Boulevard, Goodwood, N1 City, Cape Town, South Africa, 7460
P O Box 12119, N1 City, Cape Town, South Africa, 7463



First published 2015
Second Edition published in 2020



**Administrative Justice in South Africa: An Introduction**

ISBN 978 0 19 074424 3

Third impression 2022

Typeset in Utopia 9.5pt on 12pt
Printed on 70gsm wood-free paper

**Acknowledgements**
Publisher: Penny Lane
Development editor: Edward Ndiloseh
Project manager: Lindsay-Jane Lucks
Copy editor: Allison Lamb
Proofreader: Lee-Ann Ashcroft
Indexer: Clifford Perusset
Typesetter: Nazley Samsodien
Cover: Design Studio
Printed and bound by: Shumani RSA, Parow, Cape Town
WT081518

*To my big brother Jacques:*

*Thanks for showing me the realities of public administration,*
*I'll miss you.*

***Geo Quinot***

# Contents in brief

# Contents

# Preface

Although a late bloomer, administrative law became a key field of law in pursuit of justice in South Africa prior to democratisation in 1994. In the absence of a Bill of Rights and under parliamentary supremacy, administrative law often offered the only avenue to challenge bureaucratic decisions in law through the process of judicial review.

As with all law, the advent of constitutional democracy in 1994 ushered in a new paradigm for administrative law. The adoption of a supreme Constitution with a justiciable Bill of Rights shifted administrative law from a common-law based field to one premised on a fundamental right: the right to administrative justice. Today, administrative law in South Africa should thus be understood as a set of legal rules aimed at realising administrative justice.

The Constitution of the Republic of South Africa, 1996 defines administrative justice in section 33 in terms of a trio of principles as the right to administrative action that is lawful, reasonable and procedurally fair. It further provides that the right to reasons for administrative action is included in these principles. Section 33(3) gives Parliament the mandate of fleshing out this right with the particular instruction to balance efficient administration against control of administrative action in protection of affected persons. The Promotion of Administrative Justice Act 3 of 2000, generally known as PAJA, was the product of this mandate. Together, section 33 and PAJA form the backbone of administrative law in South Africa and hence the primary legal tools to pursue administrative justice. Over the past two decades, the courts have created a rich jurisprudence on this new constitutionalised administrative law in South Africa.

Two key differences between administrative law as understood at common law and administrative law in service of administrative justice in South Africa today pervade this book. The first is that administrative justice is about much more than simply judicial review. Although judicial review remains an important, and certainly still dominant, process in pursuit of administrative justice in South Africa, there are a host of other legal mechanisms that are just as important in realising administrative justice today. The development of these mechanisms in terms of administrative law is thus an important objective for the field. Second, administrative justice is not only about curbing the administration in order to protect those affected by administrative action, in other words, it is not only about control of the administration. Administrative justice is also concerned with facilitating good and efficient public decision-making in order to support the extensive social justice mandate of the public administration under the Constitution. Administrative justice is thus closely linked to social justice in South Africa – it is about promoting the type of public administration that can deliver on and reflect the social justice promises of the Constitution. In this perspective, administrative law takes on both an instrumental and intrinsic value. It is instrumental in pursuit of social justice, but it also carries intrinsic value by reflecting in itself the values of the society that the Constitution envisages.

This book aims to provide an introduction to administrative justice in South Africa through an analysis of administrative law. It uses section 33 and PAJA as the framework to structure the analysis. The book is intended to serve as a first introduction to the field and thus aims to present the relevant legal rules in a clear and accessible manner. To this purpose, lengthy and complex theoretical discussions are avoided, although the existence of critical (theoretical) debates about particular rules is highlighted for the reader to consider, often with an indication of further reading. The book also strives to present the rules in a practical context by extensive discussion of relevant case law and by providing hypothetical scenarios to illustrate the application of the rules.

The book starts out by sketching the field of administrative law and its development in South Africa in broad terms. The first chapter thus frames the rest of the book by positioning administrative law within its historical and contemporary context.

Chapter Two sets out the institutional landscape within which administrative law operates in South Africa. It pays particular attention to the administration as the primary actor in this field of law, which is often neglected in the study of administrative law. As the chapter indicates, an understanding of what the administration is and the function it is meant to fulfil within the state provides important further context to the study of administrative law. Chapter Three turns to the key concept in administrative law, namely that of administrative action. Since the most basic definition of administrative law is the law that governs administrative action, it is critical to understand what an administrative action is and how to identify it. These are questions that have become even more important under PAJA than under common law, given the highly conceptual nature of the Act in adopting a complicated definition of administrative action.

Chapters Four and Five discuss the ways in which the law regulates administrative action, that is through what mechanisms the rules of administrative law are brought to bear on administrative action. Chapter Four focuses specifically on the non-judicial mechanisms to enforce administrative law, while Chapter Five focuses on the still dominant mechanism of judicial review. Combined, these chapters pay particular attention to the need to develop mechanisms other than judicial review and to view the various mechanisms in relation to each other within the paradigm of administrative justice.

The following three chapters analyse in some detail the legal rules constituting the three pillars of administrative justice, namely lawfulness, procedural fairness and reasonableness respectively.

Chapter Nine focuses on the right to reasons as a major development in administrative law under the Constitution in contrast to the position at common law. It also explores the relationship between reason-giving and the other principles of administrative justice.

Chapter Ten is a completely new chapter in this second edition and aims to shift the attention away from judicial review and a reactive perspective on administrative law to a proactive focus. The chapter aims to explore the way in which administrative justice is relevant when administrative decision-making is mandated. The chapter thus provides a proactive perspective on administrative justice, that is, a perspective on what the implications of administrative justice are when legislatures (and other rule-makers) formulate mandates to take administrative action.

The final two chapters focus on the practical aspects of enforcing the rules of administrative law in courts by means of the process of judicial review. Chapter Eleven explores when a person can approach a court for judicial review, that is the rules of standing in administrative law judicial review, as well as the procedures to follow in bringing a review application before a court. Chapter Twelve sets out the relief that a court can grant in an application for judicial review. The chapter shows that the area of remedies is one of particular ongoing development in administrative law, with the Constitution and PAJA having introduced new remedial options that remain unexplored.

**Geo Quinot**

*Stellenbosch*

*April 2020*

# About the book

*Administrative Justice in South Africa: An Introduction*, second edition, offers a clear and applied explanation of the principles and framework of administrative justice in South Africa. It provides valuable focus on the application of principles to case law, problem-solving methodology, and specific procedural aspects of administrative justice. The text offers a clear pedagogical framework that develops independent, critical and reflective engagement with the subject matter. A strong conceptual and enquiring approach enriches knowledge, and engages readers in an interactive, topical and challenging manner.

***Brief description of the features:***

**Pause for reflection:** This feature instils a broader and deeper understanding of the subject matter. It invites readers to reflect upon specific questions and issues, thereby stimulating discussion, supporting independent thought, and developing the ability to analyse and engage meaningfully with relevant issues.

**Counterpoint:** This feature supports the reader's ability to engage critically and flexibly with concepts and perspectives that are discussed in the text. This feature might highlight areas of controversy, specific criticisms of the law, or possible options for law reform. It builds an awareness of various opinions about a particular principle, encourages readers to engage with issues and debates from different perspectives, and assists to develop skills in formulating and analysing legal argument.

**Reframing:** This feature introduces legal concepts through the lens of familiar experience, developing understanding through a graduated approach.

**Example:** This feature profiles extracts of legislation and case law underpinning critical case discussions. Such illustration broadens the reader's understanding, and encourages independent insight.

**This chapter in essence:** Primarily directed at supporting the reader's orientation, this feature maps, in a succinct paragraph, the key areas and core topics covered within each chapter.

**Further reading:** At the end of each chapter, a concise list of recommended reading suggests further material, primarily journal articles and book chapters, on the main themes discussed. This endows the reader's independent engagement with the subject matter.

**Diagrams:** These figures provide visual overviews for some specific concepts in the book. This feature reinforces understanding, helps to clarify key concepts, and illustrates the inter-relationship between distinct legal concepts.

**Tables:** These distinguish content, assisting with information management and conceptualisation.

**List of references:** This feature appears at the end of the book. The list of reference works covers the most important South African sources, as well as relevant international and comparative sources.

**Glossary:** The text is supported by a comprehensive glossary that succinctly explains and contextualises the key terms and concepts appearing in the text.

# List of authors

**Geo Quinot**
BA (Law) LLB (Stellenbosch), LLM (Virginia), MA (Free State), MPA (Birmingham) LLD (Stellenbosch)
Geo Quinot is Professor in the Department of Public Law at Stellenbosch University, where he presents courses in administrative justice and public procurement law. He is the founding Director of the African Procurement Law Unit (APLU). In 2012, Geo was awarded the National Excellence in Teaching and Learning Award by the South African Council for Higher Education (CHE) and the Higher Education Learning and Teaching Association of Southern Africa (HELTASA). He has since served as a member of the CHE's standards development expert working group, which was tasked with drafting national standards for the LLB educational qualification. He is also a past president of the Administrative Justice Association of South Africa and continues to serve on its executive committee. Geo is an editor of the *African Public Procurement Law Journal.* He publishes research within the fields of legal education and general administrative law, the latter focusing particularly on the commercial conduct of the state, including the regulation of public procurement processes.

**Allison Anthony**
BA (Law), LLB, LLM, LLD (Stellenbosch)
Allison Anthony is a senior lecturer in the Department of Public, Constitutional and International Law at the College of Law, University of South Africa (UNISA), where she presents courses in administrative law at undergraduate and postgraduate level. She is also Deputy Director of the African Procurement Law Unit at Stellenbosch University and co-editor of the *African Public Procurement Law Journal.* She publishes research in the areas of administrative law and public procurement law. Allison is also an admitted attorney and has been involved in training lawyers in the field of administrative law.

**Janice Bleazard**
BA (Hons), LLB (Cape Town), LLM (New York)
Janice Bleazard is an Advocate of the High Court of South Africa and a practising member of the Cape Bar, who specialises in administrative law and constitutional law.

**Steven Budlender SC**
BA LLB (Witwatersrand), LLM (New York)
Steven Budlender is a Senior Counsel and Advocate of the High Court of South Africa and a member of the Pan African Bar Association of South Africa. He has a varied practice with a particular focus on constitutional law and administrative law. He has appeared in more than 100 matters in the Constitutional Court and Supreme Court of Appeal.

**Raisa Cachalia**
BA, LLB, LLM (Witwatersrand)
Raisa Cachalia is a lecturer in the Faculty of Law at the University of Johannesburg where she teaches administrative law and legal skills at undergraduate level. Her research interests include administrative law and constitutional law, as well as the developing field of digital privacy and the role of regulation in an age of disruptive technologies. She is an editor at the *Constitutional Court Review* journal and sits on a panel of legal consultants at Caveat Legal

(Pty) Ltd where she provides advice on a broad range of regulatory issues, particularly in the areas of public procurement and data protection. Raisa was formerly a researcher at the South African Institute for Advanced Constitutional, Public, Human Rights and International Law (SAIFAC), a centre of the University of Johannesburg. She also served as a Clerk at the Constitutional Court of South Africa, to Deputy Chief Justice Zondo and then Justice Froneman. Prior to her research and teaching career, Raisa was admitted as an Attorney of the High Court after completing her articles at Bowman Gilfillan Inc.

**Hugh Corder**
BCom LLB (Cape Town), LLB (Cantab), DPhil (Oxon)
Hugh Corder is Professor Emeritus of Public Law at the University of Cape Town, and a Fellow of this University. He serves currently as the Interim Director of the Graduate School of Business. He taught administrative law (at LLB and LLM levels) for 35 years, including a course in comparative administrative law in the Commonwealth for the LLM programme at Melbourne University in the early 2000s. Hugh is an Advocate of the High Court of South Africa. He has played a leading role in the reform of administrative law in South Africa since 1991, and served as a technical adviser in the drafting of the transitional Bill of Rights. Hugh has published widely in the fields of constitutional and administrative law, with a particular focus on judicial appointment and accountability, and mechanisms for furthering administrative accountability. Hugh has contributed over many decades to the rule of law and social justice, through community work and service on the boards of non-governmental organisations.

**Meghan Finn**
BSocSci Honours (Cape Town), LLB (Cape Town), BCL (Oxon)
Meghan Finn is an nGAP lecturer in the Department of Public Law of the University of Johannesburg. She is an Advocate of the High Court of South Africa, practised at the Johannesburg Bar, and previously served as a Clerk of the Constitutional Court of South Africa. Meghan is currently pursuing her PhD with the SARChI Chair on Equality, Law and Social Justice at the University of Witwatersrand. She has broad research interests in constitutional and administrative law, and is an editor of *Constitutional Court Review*.

**Michael Kidd**
BCom, LLB, LLM, PhD (Natal)
Michael Kidd is Professor in the School of Law, University of KwaZulu-Natal, where he has lectured administrative law and environmental law at undergraduate and postgraduate level for 30 years. Michael is the author of one of the leading South African textbooks in environmental law and has published almost 100 peer-reviewed papers within the fields of administrative law, environmental law, and water law, all of which are underpinned by administrative decision-making. He is also Principal Editor of the *South African Journal of Environmental Law and Policy*.

**Thuli Madonsela**
BA (Law) (Swaziland), LLB (Witwatersrand)
Thuli Madonsela is Chair in Social Justice at Stellenbosch University and founder of the Thuma Foundation for Democracy Leadership and Literacy. As the former Public Protector of South Africa and full-time Law Commissioner in the South African Law Reform Commission, Prof Madonsela has an extensive background in applied administrative law

principles, mainly based on her public service years and investigations into improper conduct in state affairs. She was one of the drafters of the Constitution and a key participant in the conceptualisation and drafting of several laws, including the Promotion of Administrative Justice Act. She also helped draft several international rights instruments and country reports. She currently teaches constitutional law, administrative law, social justice law, democracy and governance and has written and published extensively on these matters. An Advocate of the High Court of South Africa and honorary member of the Botswana Bar, Prof Madonsela has eight honorary law doctorates in addition to her law degrees. A mother of two, she is an avid mountaineer who has summited Kilimanjaro under #Trek4Mandela to promote the Social Justice M-Plan.

**Petrus Maree**

BA (Law), LLD (Stellenbosch)

Petrus Maree is an artist and independent researcher based in Berlin and Cape Town. He obtained his LLD at Stellenbosch University, where he was also a post-doctoral fellow and taught introduction to law, constitutional law and administrative law. Between 2009 and 2016, he served as a member of the Overarching Strategic Plan (OSP) Project (on Combating Poverty, Homelessness and Socio-Economic Vulnerability under the Constitution) and of the Socio-Economic Rights and Administrative Justice Research (SERAJ) Project. Petrus's publications focus on critical, principle-based approaches to freedom, administrative law, deference, and the separation of powers.

**Melanie Murcott**

LLB (Cape Town), LLM (Pretoria), LLD (North-West)

Melanie Murcott is a Senior Lecturer in the Department of Public Law at the University of Pretoria, where she lectures administrative and environmental law. Her scholarly interests also include constitutional law and socio-economic rights. Melanie is a practising Attorney of the High Court of South Africa, and a Solicitor of England and Wales (non-practising roll). Prior to her academic career, her practice in commercial litigation included a focus on public procurement. Melanie's doctoral research concerned the ways in which the courts can, in the adjudication of environmental law disputes, more effectively contribute towards South Africa's project of transformative constitutionalism and its pursuit of social justice.

**Mfundo Salukazana**

LLB (Witwatersrand), LLM (London)

Mfundo Salukazana is an Advocate of the High Court and a member of the Johannesburg Bar. He formerly served as a Clerk of the Constitutional Court of South Africa, to Justice Edwin Cameron. Mfundo is developing a broad practice with his core areas of practice being in administrative law, banking and financial services, commercial litigation and constitutional law.

**Emma Webber**

BSocSci (PPE), LLB (Cape Town), BCL (Oxon)

Emma Webber is an Advocate of the High Court of South Africa and a member of the Pan African Bar Association of South Africa and the Johannesburg Bar. She formerly served as a Clerk of the Constitutional Court of South Africa, to Justice Edwin Cameron. Emma has a varied practice, which includes public interest, regulatory and commercial litigation. Her area of particular expertise is administrative law and constitutional law.

# Chapter 1

# The development of administrative law in South Africa

*Hugh Corder*

## 1.1 Introduction

Administrative law is everywhere. The cellphone service that you use, the public transport system that brings you to your class, work or home, the preparation and packaging of the food you buy in a supermarket, and so on, are all regulated by government agencies, whose actions are subject to administrative law.

Administrative law is concerned with the exercise of public power or the performance of a public function: it is indisputably part of 'public law'. An effective system of administrative law is a fundamental element in the idea of the 'rule of law', and thus critical to the transformative nature of constitutional democracy in South Africa. Perhaps one of the most-quoted statements in judgments of the courts is that written by Professor Mureinik[1] in 1994, that the Constitution demands that we must move from a 'culture of authority to a culture of justification'. Mureinik was a leading administrative lawyer, and he argued strongly that administrative law was a key element in transformative constitutionalism.[2]

The purpose of this chapter is to provide the context for all the chapters that follow in this book.[3] The scene will be set by defining administrative law, by describing critically its origins and development over the past century or so, and by outlining briefly the basic building blocks of this area of the law as we know it today.

Before considering the above matters, however, think about the following situation.

REFRAMING

**Losing your ID card and administrative law**

Imagine that you lose your new ID card. You need it urgently in order to register a cellphone contract. You go to the nearest office of the Department of Home Affairs, fill in the forms, pay the prescribed fee of R140, then present your application to the official at the counter. She responds that it will take a month to process, but if you give her an extra R150, you could have your ID within a week.

You are angry; this is an attempt to solicit a bribe for the provision of a public service and in any event, you have no extra cash. What steps can you take to remedy the situation? Do you shout out loud and accuse the official of corruption? Do you demand to see the supervisor? Do you walk away quietly and report this conduct at the nearest police station? Do you approach your political representative (councillor or MP) or your community/religious leader and ask them to intervene? Do you go to a friend who is a law student or to a lawyer and ask for legal advice? Do you approach the Office of the Public Protector?

CONTINUED >>>

1 Mureinik, E (1994) A Bridge to Where? Introducing the Interim Bill of Rights *SAJHR* 10(1):31 at 38–44.
2 Mureinik, E (1993) Reconsidering Review: Participation and Accountability *Acta Juridica* 35.
3 The leading texts in this field are listed at the end of this chapter, and provide essential context.

Think about answers to all these questions, each of which points to an aspect of administrative justice. Write your answers down and once you have completed your study of this book, return to your answers and consider how your newly developed knowledge of administrative justice impacts on your responses to these everyday events.

## 1.2 Defining administrative law

As you will see, the drawing of boundaries around what falls within the scope of administrative law is one of the most important issues in this area of the law. A good way to assist in developing an understanding of the subject is to start with a working definition and then to refine that definition by analysing more closely key aspects of it, by describing what administrative law is *not* concerned with, and by isolating a few areas of difficulty.

This raises a theme which will be referred to repeatedly throughout this chapter: you should not seek (or perhaps better, you are unlikely to find) absolute clarity or certainty on many rules of administrative law. Most often there is neither an absolutely correct nor wrong answer to a question, but rather an attempt to find that point on a spectrum or a range of factors which most comfortably fits the circumstances and demands of the applicable legal framework. So there is often (but not always) no 'one right answer', but rather a few acceptable solutions. I like to think of administrative law as predominantly grey in colour, with few points of sharp distinction between black and white.

Administrative law is ultimately all about a **quest for balancing rights, interests and obligations, in the determination of which public and legal policy play a central role**. I hope that this fundamental principle will become clear as you read through this book.

**PAUSE FOR REFLECTION**

**Law as compromise**

Does this characterisation of administrative law make it different from all other parts of law, or most of them? In other words, is all law not something of a compromise? Think of the other areas of law that you have already studied: did you come across areas where no one particular rule definitively governed a practical problem or where a rule was not absolutely clear, so that different interpretations or perspectives may lead to different outcomes in the application of the rule? Many would argue that there needs to be a degree of certainty about the applicability of a rule of law, especially in the criminal law, otherwise there would be chaos in society. In other words, we must readily concede that a substantial measure of certainty is a desirable quality to expect of all legal rules, also of administrative law. At the same time, we should be conscious of the imprecise edges of uncertainty in many parts of law, because that is often the most interesting part, ripe for creative lawyering and development.

### 1.2.1 A working definition

This is as good a start as any in seeking to define administrative law:

> Administrative law is that part of constitutional law which both empowers those exercising public authority or performing public functions through the law, and

which holds accountable to rules of law all those who exercise public power or perform public functions.

Let us take note of several key aspects of the above working definition.

#### 1.2.1.1 Administrative law as constitutional law

Administrative law is properly part of constitutional law, because it seeks to regulate the power of the executive branch of government through the law. As we will see in the next section, however, administrative law was regarded until about seventy years ago as a relatively minor aspect of constitutional law. In fact, it only became a separate subject in the LLB curriculum at most law faculties in South Africa in the late 1980s, and at some is still taught as a section of a course in 'constitutional and administrative law'.

#### 1.2.1.2 Two sides of public power

Administrative law deals with two sides of public power: its *authorisation* and its *regulation*. These aspects are often described as the 'empowerment' and 'accountability' elements of the subject. Too often, however, again for historical reasons which will be described later in this chapter, the emphasis falls on the 'accountability' and not on the 'empowerment' of the public administration. While such a focus may have been appropriate under apartheid, when public authority was frequently a threat to fairness and justice, now that public authority is based in a constitutional democracy, the empowerment of the public administration to do good by the fair and just provision of social goods and services should become a priority.

#### 1.2.1.3 Administrative justice

Administrative 'law' can be seen as the narrower foundation of the rapidly developing notion of administrative 'justice'. While administrative law tends to concentrate more narrowly on judicial review through the courts, administrative justice widens the view to encompass alternative methods of scrutinising the fairness and justice of administrative conduct. There are many potential avenues for the pursuit of administrative justice, among them appeals tribunals (either separate from or part of the administrative body whose action is being reviewed), ombuds offices (in South Africa the Public Protector), the use of alternative methods of dispute resolution (conciliation, mediation and arbitration) to resolve differences, the role of human rights commissions, and so on. The existence of protection through the law for a degree of transparent or open government is a critical and closely connected adjunct to all such alternative methods of review of administrative conduct.

#### 1.2.1.4 The role of the legislature

Although not usually thought of in this manner, the ultimate guarantee of the effectiveness of any administrative law system is the right of every citizen freely and fairly to vote for the highest representative law-making institution, and the role of that legislator (usually called Parliament) as the watchdog over the exercise of executive authority by government at all levels. Parliament holds Ministers to account by asking questions about decisions made in the state department for which they are responsible, by scrutiny of a state department's performance and budget through Parliamentary standing (or portfolio) committees, by critical evaluation of a Ministry's annual budget request, through the work of the office of the Auditor-General, a servant of Parliament whose onerous responsibility is the annual financial audit of all government expenditure, and, perhaps most fundamentally, by creating the statutory powers in terms of which administrative agencies fulfil their public functions. Supporting all these functions is the role of a free media, which investigates and publicises unfair, irregular and unlawful administrative conduct. So these are all effective methods of scrutinising administrative action, and ultimately could be regarded as an essential context for the narrower field of administrative law.

#### 1.2.1.5 Public authority and functions

Administrative law is concerned with *public* authority and functions. As you will see in the following section of this chapter, it used to be much easier to demarcate clearly the limits of the public from the private spheres. Over the past forty years or so, the boundary line between what is regarded as public and what is private has become very blurred, for many different reasons. As the role of the state developed in the last part of the twentieth century, bodies which were nominally private or privately owned increasingly began to wield public power, which raised the question whether the rules of administrative law applied to them in doing so. South African administrative law has always recognised this reality, which is why the definition above refers to the *nature* of the power exercised, rather than the *type* of body which is exercising it. So in all your involvement with administrative law you must recognise that the public/private divide might be an element, a 'gateway' question that you must ask at the outset of the consideration of any question.

**PAUSE FOR REFLECTION**

**Actions of private parties rendering public services**

Consider the following situation: The DFG Municipal Council outsources the collection of household refuse to a private company, Garbage Gobblers. The Garbage Gobblers truck is busy loading your wheelie-bin one morning when the driver forgets to put on the handbrake while taking a cellphone call, and the truck hits your vehicle gate, breaking it completely, and damaging your car in the process. Do you have an action for damages against the municipality or against Garbage Gobblers, or both of them in the alternative? If you do have such recourse to law, do you found your action in public law (which is likely to afford you greater scope to sue) or in the private law of contract or delict? Does it make any difference which party you sue?

#### 1.2.1.6 Administrative law as rules of law

Administrative law is primarily based in rules of law, just like any other part of our legal system. This means that, like all rules expressed in language, the possibility of more than one meaning being ascribed to such rules is likely, especially where competent and skilled lawyers are seeking to do their best for their clients, relying on interpretations of those rules in judgments of the courts. This indeterminate quality of our administrative law was accentuated by the fact that it was overwhelmingly 'judge-made', it became part of South African law as part of our 'common-law heritage' arising from our status as a British colony, at least from 1910, although the foundation stones had been laid many decades before. Thus you will find no traces in administrative law of the Roman-Dutch origins, which are so much a part of other areas of our 'mixed legal system', our administrative law is overwhelmingly English in its historical character.

#### 1.2.1.7 Rule of law

Allied to its grounding in 'rules of law', administrative law as a discipline fits neatly with the widely acknowledged and universal ideal of the 'rule of law'. The prominence of this concept within modern constitutional democracies and institutions of global governance is frequently traced to the work of the leading English constitutional lawyer of the late nineteenth century, AV Dicey. Dicey formulated the rule of law in three principles:[4] that everyone was subject to and equal before the law, appearing before the ordinary courts of the land (no special courts for specific groups of people), and that the rule of law represented the hard-won victories of the ordinary people through court proceedings, it had developed organically from below, and was not imposed by authority from above. Although many aspects of this definition were criticised, the 'rule of law' gained further prominence after World War II when it was championed by the Western allied forces to contrast their systems of government with those prevalent in the Soviet Union and its allied states.[5] A further important dimension was added to its definition when the emergence of post-colonial states in the developing world caused the international community to add an emphasis on socio-economic rights to the definition of the 'rule of law'.[6] Given that one of the main features of the rule of law (often called its 'rule by law' aspect) overlaps extensively with the administrative-law principle that no public power may be exercised without lawful grant (the *ultra vires* principle) and in an acceptably lawful manner, the close relationship between these two concepts is clear.

With this explanation of some of the key elements in any definition of administrative law in mind, let us turn our attention to how this part of our law has developed over the past century or so.

## 1.3 The development of South African administrative law

South African administrative law, in common with those like it in countries of the British Empire/Commonwealth during the twentieth century, underwent great growth and substantial revision during this period. Like all aspects of law, it is important to view administrative law in both its historical and social contexts, in order better to understand not only the past, but also the present. Those administering and adjudicating in this field of law are predominantly the products of that past system, and legal doctrines and approaches to basic principles can generally be traced to practices of the past. Law is overwhelmingly a conservative force in society, it mostly reflects established interests, and seeks to perpetuate those. This is not necessarily a bad thing, we just need to recognise this reality, and factor it into our thinking about law.

There is another important reason to know about the past: to avoid a repetition of errors committed in history, and to be sensitive to signs of similar practices rearing their heads in the present, so that speedy action can be taken to combat what may be unfair or unjust.

What were the factors that shaped the development of our administrative law in South Africa? I suggest that we need to examine in a little detail the following six forces for an answer to this question: the consequences of administrative law being 'judge-made', the shifting boundaries between public and private power and their impact on administrative

4 Dicey, AV (1924) *Introduction to the Study of the Law of the Constitution* (8th ed) at 198–199.

5 See the International Commission of Jurists (ICJ) *The Rule of Law in a Free Society: A Report on the International Congress of Jurists*, New Delhi India, January 5–10 1959, for the founding statement of its principles.

6 See the International Commission of Jurists (ICJ) *The Dynamic Aspects of the Rule of Law: A Report on the International Congress of Jurists*, Bangkok Thailand, 1965.

law, the growth of discretionary power allocated to the executive in a state, the division between executive and administrative authority, the formal distinction between review and appeal, and the particularly damaging effect of segregation and apartheid on administrative law in South Africa.

### 1.3.1 The consequences of 'judge-made law'

Given the British imperial stranglehold on the country from 1910, particularly in public law, it is not surprising that the judgments of the superior courts of South Africa reflected developments in English administrative law. Its 'common-law/judge-made' character also meant that, over time, the judicial 'track record' (that is, any discernible pattern in how judges decided similar cases) influenced the pace and path of development. In other words, individual judges or groups of judges were able directly to influence the course of development of administrative law because 'judicial review of administrative action' was almost the sole means available for an individual to seek to constrain the exercise of public power. This judicial authority was grounded in the 'inherent jurisdiction' of the Supreme Court of South Africa after 1910,[7] and its exercise was affected by at least two important factors:

1. **Judicial policy**, the unwritten but widely accepted common understanding of social-economic-political relationships of the parties before the court in a particular dispute, the possibility or indeed likelihood that the judge/s is/are more likely to understand and be sympathetic to one side rather than the other, and that this identification may affect their decisions in individual cases. Furthermore, over time and in retrospect, trends in judicial decision-making in like cases may appear to assume a pattern, varying broadly between the contrasting end-points of 'executive-mindedness' and concern for the individual in the face of the exercise of public power.[8] So, for example, judicial policy is said to have shifted overwhelmingly towards the interests of the executive branch of government from the late 1950s, especially as the judicial appointments made by the apartheid government worked though the court hierarchy.[9]
2. The second substantial variable, related to the first, is the judicial understanding of and adherence to **the doctrine of the 'separation of powers'**. In its most basic form, this doctrine requires (1) a degree of separation of both personnel and functions between the three branches of government (the executive, the judiciary and the legislature) and (2) a system of mutual checking and balancing of the exercise of governmental power by each such branch. In South African constitutional history, based as it was on the doctrine of parliamentary sovereignty, this meant that there was a substantial blurring of the separation as regards those who served in each branch, every member of the Cabinet being by definition a Member of Parliament. The judiciary, however, was at least formally independent, although the executive had an almost unrestricted authority to appoint judges. As a matter of historical fact, the dominance of Parliament over the other two branches of government in the first half of the twentieth century gave way rapidly to executive autocracy by the mid-1970s. The judicial response varied over time: judicial attitudes were initially hostile to Parliament giving away too much discretionary authority to the executive,[10] but by the 1930s the

7 For the most extensive treatment of this aspect, see Taitz, J (1985) *The Inherent Jurisdiction of the Supreme Court.*

8 See Dugard (1978) *Human Rights and the South African Legal Order*.

9 See Forsyth, CF (1985) *In Danger for their Talents: A Study of the Appellate Division of the Supreme Court of South Africa from 1950-80.*

10 See *Shidiack v Union Government (Minister of the Interior)* 1912 AD 642, especially in the judgments of Innes ACJ and Laurence J.

courts had come to terms with this new way of governing,[11] and judicial deference to the executive escalated to the point of servile submission by the 1980s.[12]

**PAUSE FOR REFLECTION**

**The concept of deference**

The concept of deference plays a key role in relation to the separation of powers. Essentially, a healthy democracy requires each branch of government to respect the legitimate spheres of operation of the other two branches.[13] So Parliament must respect the policy-making functions and executive roles of the Cabinet and the public administration, the Cabinet must in turn respect the law-making and regulatory roles of Parliament, and both these branches must respect judicial independence, while the courts in turn must not allow their judgments to stray into the mandated spheres of operation of the others. The critical principle here is 'mutual respect, each of the other', commonly known as deference. Sadly, under apartheid, both the courts and Parliament too easily submitted to the will of the executive, they became too deferential, a trend which is also to be seen in other countries.

## 1.3.2 The shifting line between the private and public spheres

Any examination of the history of the role of the state will alert you to the fact that the concept of what is properly within the scope of state power has shifted substantially over the past hundred years. It is widely accepted that 'the theory of administrative law reflects the theory of the state' within which it operates,[14] so any study of administrative law must take the structure and functions of the state into account.

It is fair to sum up the changes in the following manner: in 1900, the providers of most of the goods and services which we expect from the state today would have been privately owned. Mass transport (railways, buses, harbours), telecommunications (as far as they existed), education, health care, housing, roads, water, sanitation and electricity were not widely regarded as being part of the responsibility of the state, and so the ordinary private-law rules of the law of contract would have applied in this sector. Gradually, however, the demand arose for the government at all levels to step in to the breach and to begin to provide these goods and services in light of:

- the growth in popularity of social-democratic political parties,
- the decline of the idea of a completely free market,
- the imposition on employers of basic standards of health and safety at work,
- the consequences of the extreme horror of global wars and epidemics of fatal diseases,
- the steady rise in the population of the world and the consequent growth in urbanisation,
- the economic depressions of the 1920s and 1930s, and
- the developing need of the owners of capital for a more educated and skilled workforce.

11 Corder (1984) *Judges at Work* Chapter 9 and Postscript.

12 Ellmann (1992) *In a Time of Trouble Law and Liberty in South Africa's State of Emergency*.

13 For wider discussion, see Hoexter, C (2000) The Future of Judicial Review in South African Administrative Law *SALJ* 117(3):484; O'Regan, K (2004) Breaking Ground: Some Thoughts on the Seismic Shift in our Administrative Law *SALJ* 121(2):424; Corder, H (2004) Without Deference, with Respect: A Response to Justice O'Regan [comments] *SALJ* 121(2):438; and Davis, DM (2006) To Defer and Then When? Administrative Law and Constitutional Democracy *Acta Juridica* 23.

14 Harlow and Rawlings (2009) *Law and Administration* (3rd ed).

This trend was substantially strengthened by the extent of state regulation of the economy required during wartime (especially 1939 to 1945), and by the aftermath of World War II, with the foundation of international institutions like the United Nations Organisation and its many specialised agencies (such as UNESCO, UNDP, UNEP, UNHRC), all of which began to set minimum standards of human rights recognition and protection throughout the world. The process of decolonisation through which European countries after 1950 gave at least political independence to their former colonies, and the significant rise in the level of activity of non-governmental organisations which championed human rights, including socio-economic rights, also pushed expectations in this direction.

By the end of the 1960s, therefore, in most countries it was assumed that the government would supply at least basic levels of goods and services such as those above, to which could be added some form of social welfare support, such as old-age pensions and child grants. But this is not the end of the story, as we know, because the election of Margaret Thatcher and Ronald Reagan as political leaders of the United Kingdom and the United States of America in 1979/80 ushered in economic policies which threatened to reverse this trend, through the process of 'privatisation' of state resources. So the ports, railways, airports, state airlines, mines, telephone companies, and some gas/electricity and water providers were sold off to private owners, and the functions expected of the state were reduced. These national initiatives, which spread rapidly through the world, were also replicated at the private international level, by the foundation of bodies such as the World Trade Organization, and the renewed importance given to the programmes of the International Bank for Reconstruction and Development (World Bank) and the International Monetary Fund.

Thus far, I have set out a generalised account of global socio-economic development during the 1900s, but how did South Africa fare in this regard? Our national experience mirrored that described above, but with one vital difference. The state in South Africa started to provide public education, public health facilities, old-age pensions and disability grants, a telephone service, railway networks, harbours and airports, some low-cost housing, and so on. In some respects the South African state went further: it set up an insurance company (SANLAM) and a steel-processing plant (ISCOR) in the 1920s, and also established a national network of agricultural co-operatives and marketing boards to assist farmers to stay on the land profitably, and thus to provide adequate food for home consumption and export. These initiatives effectively pushed the role of the state substantially further than in many parts of the developed world. Some of these steps were reversed in the 1980s by the commercialisation and then privatisation of ISCOR (now Arcelor Mittal Steel), the railways and harbours (Transnet), the airports (ACSA), the telecommunications industry (TELKOM), the provision of electricity (ESKOM), and others.

So our own experience follows a similar pattern to that elsewhere throughout the world, but with one critical difference: the role of the state overwhelmingly favoured those classified 'white', with often no such goods and services provided at all to black South Africans.

**PAUSE FOR REFLECTION**

**Administrative law and changing patterns in society**

Why is this knowledge of developments in modern history relevant to our understanding of administrative law? Administrative law pursues both empowerment and accountability. Any exercise of public power needs lawful authority, and those who exercise public power are subject to more stringent regulation than those who operate using private power. This more intrusive degree of scrutiny is justified by the fact that public servants ought to be acting in the public interest. Therefore, it is absolutely vital that some workable form of defining what is *public* forms the entry point to review of administrative conduct through the law. It follows, then, that as the lawful limits of public power shift, in response to the changing patterns of demands on the state to intervene in society, the structures and processes of administrative review through the law must adapt to these changing circumstances.

One example will demonstrate this clearly. When the British government privatised British Telecom in the early 1980s, the type of regulation under administrative law which had previously been applied to the activities of the latter, because it was wholly owned by the government, fell away in principle. In order to provide some form of redress to replace this degree of regulation, the government established a specialist industry regulator, like an ombud, to investigate and resolve complaints about unfairness in the provision of the telecommunications services. This was known as the Office of Fair Telecommunications (OFTEL), and similar bodies were set up in other sectors of the economy which were privatised.

Thus the changing patterns of state intervention in the socio-economic sphere over time impact directly on the form and substance of administrative law, in myriad ways, because what is rightly regarded as 'public' really matters.

### 1.3.3 The growth of discretionary authority

This factor influencing the development of administrative law flows directly from the first two above (the consequences of administrative law being 'judge-made' and the shifting boundaries between public and private power and their impact on administrative law). A century ago, the source of all political power in a Westminster-style democracy was located in Parliament, which was deemed to represent the citizenry (although of course it did not, even in Britain at that stage, because women had no vote; the same point can be made as regards those not classified as 'white' in South Africa till 1994). Parliament made laws to regulate conduct and to authorise public officials to act, but Parliament was initially reluctant to hand over a great deal of discretion to such officials.

However, as the population grew and as more was expected of the state to exercise its authority in times of national emergency such as war or epidemics, in other words as the population needed to be controlled as well as benefits and services supplied, so it became more difficult for Parliament to foresee all the circumstances in which public officials would have to respond, often urgently. Acts of Parliament thus began to use phrases such as: 'when the Minister is satisfied ...' or 'in the opinion of the Minister' or, where a power was given to a Minister or some other senior official, it was in turn sub-delegated to someone lower down in the administrative hierarchy. In line with senior judges in the UK, South African judges expressed their misgivings of this trend, characterising it as an abdication of authority by

Parliament, and giving a strict interpretation of the common-law presumption against the implied sub-delegation of administrative authority.[15]

EXAMPLE

**Judicial misgivings of sub-delegation**

In *Shidiack v Union Government (Minister of the Interior)* 1912 AD 642 Innes ACJ stated:

> where the Legislature places upon any official the responsibility of exercising a discretion which the nature of the subject matter and the language of the section show can only be properly exercised in a judicial spirit, then that responsibility cannot be vicariously discharged. The persons concerned have a right to demand the judgment of the specially selected officer ... the Legislature has prescribed a test which is to be discharged 'to the satisfaction of the Minister', and that cannot mean to the satisfaction of anybody else.

However, as the calls for state intervention in the socio-economic sphere grew, the courts had to acknowledge the necessity for both the express as well as implied authority to sub-delegate power granted to the executive by Parliament, and this trend grew apace right through the twentieth century. In modern terms, the judicial stance against such delegations of a century ago, seems unthinkable.

Applying this phenomenon to South Africa, the exercise of discretion played a large administrative role in two key aspects of the apartheid era: the administrative process of race classification, which was the foundation stone of the whole system of race-based rule, and the increasingly broad discretion granted to police officers to act against those opposing apartheid. It was particularly in the last case that the courts were constantly confronted with challenges to the administrative decisions and conduct of the police force in detaining government opponents without trial and subjecting them to interrogation and torture.[16] Regrettably, with some noble exceptions, the courts too often acquiesced in such administrative injustice, using the rationale of the intention of Parliament to justify their judgments.

LEGAL THINKING

**What is delegation of authority?**

The short answer is that this occurs when someone or an institution to which a particular power is given by law hands it on to another body to act for it. The common law starts with Parliament as the original source of lawful power, which means that Parliament has in fact 'delegated' its authority when making the law which allows a member of the executive to exercise discretion on its behalf. Therefore, any further act of handing over of that authority to another body, be it on the same level of seniority, or much more frequently to an official lower down in the administrative hierarchy, is strictly regarded as 'sub-delegation', although this secondary action is most often described as 'delegation'.

CONTINUED >>>

15 See the remarks of Innes ACJ and Laurence J in *Shidiack*, referred to in note 10.

16 *Rossouw v Sachs* 1964 (2) SA 551 (A) and *Schermbrucker v Klindt NO* 1965 (4) SA 606 (A).

If such action has been expressly foreseen in and authorised by the legislation, then there is no difficulty in principle with it, but it is also possible, given compliance with a series of conditions, that such delegation can be impliedly lawful.[17] This approach has been effectively adopted in section 238 of the Constitution.[18]

EXAMPLE

**Statutory mandate for delegation of powers**

The Immigration Act[19] provides in the following terms for sub-delegation:

**3. Delegation of powers.–**

(1) The Minister may, subject to the terms and conditions that he or she may deem necessary, delegate any power conferred on him or her by this Act, excluding a power referred to in sections 3, 4, 5 and 7, to an officer or category of officers or an employee or category of employees or a person or category of persons in the Public Service, but shall not be divested of any power so delegated.

(2) The Director-General may, subject to the terms and conditions that he or she may deem necessary, delegate any power conferred on him or her by this Act to an officer or category of officers or an employee or category of employees or a person or category of persons in the Public Service, but shall not be divested of any power so delegated.

## 1.3.4 The distinction between executive and administrative authority

Every constitutional system which provides for the judiciary to exercise the power of review of the actions of the other two branches of government has to confront the question of how far such power extends. As part of the doctrine of the separation of powers and the notion of deference (both dealt with above), the constitution must stipulate in some manner what activities are so central to the functioning of each branch of government as almost to be protected from scrutiny by the other two branches. This is not easily done, as by the nature of government in a modern state, there will be many instances in which the answer to the question: 'is it reviewable?' is not obvious. So most constitutions lay down broad guiding principles, and leave it to the good sense of each branch of government to show mutual respect for the others.

In South African common law before 1994, the courts made extensive use of what was called the doctrine of the 'classification of functions', an approach which reflected the practice of courts elsewhere in the Commonwealth. Without going into detail, the judge on reviewing administrative conduct would informally classify the action taken by the public official in one of five categories – as **administrative action**:

1. **of a lawmaking nature** (such as the making of generally applicable regulations on health and safety at work by the Minister of Labour),

17 For detailed treatment of the development of the law relating to implied delegation of authority, see the judgment of Langa CJ in *AAA Investments (Pty) Ltd v Micro Finance Regulatory Council and Another* 2007 (1) SA 343 (CC) paras 74–91.

18 The Constitution of the Republic of South Africa, 1996.

19 13 of 2002.

2. **of a judicial nature** (such as a decision of an administrative appeals tribunal like the Commission for Conciliation, Mediation and Arbitration – the CCMA – today),
3. **of a quasi-judicial nature** (such as the granting of a licence to trade or of planning permission to build a house, after the consideration of representations and evidence presented by the interested parties),
4. **of a purely administrative nature** (such as the granting of a permit to catch crayfish as a recreation, not for a living, where the official exercises some but very limited discretion), and
5. **of a 'Ministerial' nature** (which paradoxically implied that the administrator had no discretion: on being presented with an application and the relevant fee to camp in a municipal campsite, the administrator had to issue a permit).

You may have noticed that the amount of discretion available to the administrator decreases as you read down this list, from a very high level in the first category to negligible in the last. This approach assisted the judge in determining the appropriate level of deference to display in his or her judgment, as the depth of judicial scrutiny varied according to the class of action being reviewed. In contrast to the extent of official discretion, the degree of judicial scrutiny on review becomes greater as you read down the list. In principle, the classification of functions was a very useful tool for judges to determine their approach, provided that it continued to facilitate predictability of judicial action and remained as a means to the end of administrative accountability, rather than as an end in itself. Regrettably, some judges tended to stray towards the latter approach, applying the classification of functions as a sort of formula which detracted from the true objective of judicial review of administrative action, a trend which Schreiner JA warned against in the 1950s in the following terms:[20]

> The classification of discretions and functions under the headings of 'administrative,' 'quasi-judicial' and 'judicial' has been much canvassed in modern judgments and juristic literature; there appears to be some difference of opinion, or of linguistic usage, as to the proper basis of classification, and even some disagreement as to the usefulness of the classification when achieved. I do not propose to enter into these interesting questions to a greater extent than is necessary for the decision of this case; one must be careful not to elevate what may be no more than a convenient classification into a source of legal rules.

As will be seen below, however, this type of tendency among judges is quite tenacious, and has reared its head again although in a different way over the past fifteen years.

Much of the jurisprudence of the Constitutional Court in developing administrative law after 1994 has been devoted to a case-by-case exploration of the appropriate limits of its authority to review administrative conduct, developing a nuanced understanding of the separation of powers in the process. In doing so, they have not referred specifically to the classification of functions as applied earlier, but have clearly been influenced by it indirectly, and in one particular way especially. You may have noticed in the scheme set out above that there is no reference to executive power as such, although all public administration falls by definition into the executive sphere of government. Executive power is a broader notion than the public administration, and is characterised by the availability of a very high level of discretion in the hands of the decision-maker. As a consequence, the courts review the exercise of such executive conduct with a much lighter touch, recognising the grant by

20 See *Pretoria North Town Council v A1 Electric Ice-Cream Factory (Pty) Ltd* 1953 (3) SA 1 (A) at 11.

Parliament of a much greater latitude to the official (usually a Minister or Director General of a government department) to act as he or she sees fit.

However, it is vital to note that, in the constitutional democracy provided for in the Constitution, the exercise of such authority is **not above the law**. Mandated by the provision for constitutional supremacy and the rule of law in section 1(*c*) of the Constitution, and faced with the restrictive and complex definition of the key phrase in modern South African administrative law, 'administrative action', the judiciary has over the past twenty years developed a parallel track for the review of executive conduct which does not amount to 'administrative action'. In doing so, the 'principle of legality' has been employed as the basis of such review, and the grounds for review included under this umbrella term have been gradually widened, although not so far as to be co-extensive with the grounds for review of administrative action (as will be seen below). Thus the distinction between 'executive' and 'administrative' action has become the new basis for classifying the exercise of public power or the performance of a public function in modern South African administrative law.

### 1.3.5 Distinguishing formally between review and appeal

A further direct consequence of the constitutional separation of powers is the principle that the judiciary 'reviews' the procedural regularity of the exercise of public power, and does not hear 'appeals' on the merits of such actions. Substantive decision-making on the facts or the merits is the proper territory of the executive branch of government, and it ought not to be for the courts to intrude on this sphere. What judges must do is to ensure that, in reaching its decisions or exercising the discretions granted to it, the executive and its public administration remain within the limits of the authority granted to them and comply with the processes prescribed by the law for its exercise.

In many ways, however, this distinction (between review and appeal) is easier to state than to carry out. There are of course easy cases, for example where the wrong official took the decision, or where the official acted procedurally unfairly, errors which can obviously be set right on review, but many cases which are brought to court to be 'reviewed' raise issues which sit uncomfortably on the unclear borderline between form and substance, and between lawful process and merits. This reality has been made more complex still by the constitutional guarantee since 1997 of administrative action that must not only be lawful and procedurally fair, but also 'reasonable'.

'Review for reasonableness' applies naturally to the process followed in taking the action, but it also manifestly necessitates a degree of consideration of the merits or facts, because the **reasonableness of the consequences** of the action taken also falls to be reviewed. So review for reasonableness requires the judge to consider both the form and the substance of the exercise of public power. The critical question which each judge needs to answer when called on to act in this way is 'how far does my enquiry go?' In other words, an investigation into the merits can stay comfortably within the notion of 'review' provided that the reviewing judge determines only that the action taken falls within the limits of a range of action which is reasonable, and does not seek to determine whether the action was correct or not (which would amount to an 'appeal').

Such a judicial decision demands wisdom, caution, respect, some sense of the politics of the question, and a good dose of common sense. These qualities are borne of experience and are often to be seen in leading judgments of the Constitutional Court or the Supreme Court of Appeal, which function as guidelines for the rest of the superior court judiciary. Some would describe this as 'due deference'. Rare decisions, in which the courts arguably exceed their jurisdiction and cross the line between review and appeal, always lead to public controversy, frequently damage relations between the courts and the executive, and on occasion lower the legitimacy of the judiciary in the eyes of the public. In learning about administrative law, the fundamental distinction between review and appeal must never be ignored, but the absence of a 'bright line' between the two notions must also not be forgotten.

**PAUSE FOR REFLECTION**

**Restricting courts to review**

Look back at the factual situation sketched at the outset, about the attempted bribe when applying for an ID. Is it appropriate that, in those circumstances, the remedial authority of the court is confined to review? Should there not be an opportunity for an appeal or some other form of remedy? Is it always right that the court should have no appellate authority? Think about these issues: there are no 'right answers' to these questions, but you need to be aware of them.

### 1.3.6 The peculiar character of South African administrative law

At several points above, mention was made of specific aspects of the development of administrative law in South Africa. In this last section describing factors affecting the development of this area of the law, the highly damaging effects of the racist policies of segregation and apartheid over at least the twentieth century need to be emphasised. I have already noted that the act of race classification was an administrative one, and decisions about which group a person belonged to gave rise on many occasions to applications for judicial review. In addition, because of the importance of the consequences which flowed from such classification, the apartheid regime even established specialised tribunals (Race Classification Appeal Boards) to hear appeals from such decisions on the facts.[21] The existence of a degree of official discretion in such classification meant that judicial review was forced to develop in this context.

Of much greater influence on the development of South African administrative law, however, was the fact that Parliament allocated ever greater tranches of discretion in terms of 'security legislation' to the executive and to police officers to act against those who opposed the implementation of apartheid. The foundation had in fact been laid as long ago as 1914 in the Riotous Assemblies and Criminal Law Amendment Act,[22] but the extent and frequency of allocation of almost unbounded discretion accelerated in and after the passage of the Suppression of Communism Act.[23] Even in the 'reformed' package of 'security' legislation consequent on the recommendations of the Rabie Commission in the early 1980s,[24] substantial discretion was allocated to the executive to act against opponents 'if they had reason to believe' or they were 'satisfied that' someone was a threat to law and order, to devastating effect on the lives of many. This use of official discretion, almost entirely free from judicial scrutiny, reached its highest point during the states of emergency rule from 1985 to 1990, which have justifiably been described as a time of 'state lawlessness'.[25]

The important consequence of all this for administrative law was that judicial review of administrative action provided the **only lawful avenue** to seek relief against such state oppression, because there was no Bill of Rights before 1994. Indeed, some have likened

21 Bamford, BR (1967) Race Reclassification *SALJ* 84(1):37, and the many cases cited there.

22 27 of 1914; *Sachs and Diamond v Minister of Justice* 1934 AD 11.

23 44 of 1950.

24 See the incisive analysis and critique of these laws in Mathews, AS (1986) *Freedom, State Security and the Rule of Law.*

25 Budlender, G (1988) Law and Lawlessness in South Africa *SAJHR* 4(2):139.

administrative law to our 'unwritten bill of rights' before freedom. So those desperate to gain some relief from the effects of apartheid and the exercise of state terror by the 'security forces' went to court typically to argue that the 'rules of natural justice' (that they had a right to a hearing before their rights were removed) had been violated by such administrative conduct[26] or that the official had exceeded his or her authority and had thus acted unlawfully (although this was very hard to prove), and thus that they should be released from detention without trial,[27] or that interrogation by torture should cease,[28] and so on. Some such litigants succeeded in their applications, but the overwhelming majority did not.[29]

The consequences for administrative law were highly damaging. Judges were forced into choosing between the needs of the 'state' and those of the individual, and too often preferred the former.[30] This stunted the development of administrative law, particularly in a period in which it was developing fast in similar jurisdictions within the British Commonwealth, from which South African judges were reluctant to borrow, for fear of being regarded as 'unpatriotic' or some such.

### 1.3.7 Conclusion and defining some basic terminology

At the end of this description of the factors which have exercised (and in many respects continue to exercise) an influence over the development of South African administrative law, it is time to turn our attention to the reform process which culminated in the inclusion of a constitutional right to administrative justice after 1994. Before doing so, however, it is vital to take note of some of the terminology and concepts which characterised administrative law by 1990, the better to understand the revolutionary significance of what follows throughout this book.

1. Highly restrictive rules about standing to sue (*locus standi in judicio*) prevented the wider reach of administrative law, in that only those directly affected in their legal rights by administrative action were entitled to approach a court for judicial review.
2. Further obstacles to judicial review came in the form of the frequent use of *ouster clauses*, legislative attempts to exclude the courts from exercising the power of judicial review, especially in the context of 'security legislation'.
3. The basic organising principle of judicial review was the *ultra vires doctrine*, which effectively stipulated that no public official could act 'beyond their powers' as laid down in the law (mainly in statute law, but also in the common law): this encapsulates the essential attribute of 'lawfulness'.
4. There were several precedent-setting statements of the grounds of review at the common law over the decades, the overriding emphasis in the most recent being 'the failure by the official concerned to apply the mind' to the decision-making process, as evidenced by one or more grounds of review.[31]
5. Over the centuries, the courts developed a number of *grounds of review*, which fell into two main categories, those which required lawfulness and those which insisted on

26 For example, see *R v Ngwevela* 1954 (1) SA 123 (A) and *Saliwa v Minister of Native Affairs* 1956 (2) SA 310 (A).
27 For example, see *Loza v Police Station Commander, Durbanville* 1964 (2) SA 545 (A).
28 For example, see *Schermbrucker v Klindt NO* 1965 (4) SA 606 (A).
29 The earlier cases in the 1950s witnessed more successful applications, but once the judicial personnel had changed, the general attitude towards the rights of those subjected to state action seemed to harden: see Dugard (1978) at 360–365, and Chapter 9 generally.
30 This approach reached its greatest extent during the states of emergency in the late 1980s: for the most extensive analysis of this issue, see Ellmann (1992).
31 The most authoritative restatement of which is to be found in *JSE and Another v Witwatersrand Nigel* 1988 (3) SA 132 (A) at 152 C ff.

procedural fairness (usually described as the 'rules of natural justice').[32] These grounds of review came to be rules of the common law, and included a commitment to rational conduct, but not reasonableness as a ground of review. As will be seen in the rest of this book, the courts in South Africa today draw a distinction between 'rationality' and 'reasonableness': in essence, the latter ground of review authorises a more invasive enquiry by the reviewing judge than the former. These terms must, however, be used with great care: in English law, for example, 'rationality' means 'reasonableness'.

6. Allied to this last point, the common law at no stage required an administrator to give reasons for their decision or action, although isolated statutes[33] required compliance with this duty.

## 1.4 The reform of South African administrative law 1990 to 2000

Although some planning for a post-apartheid South Africa had begun even in the late stages of the states of emergency in the 1980s, discussions about the constitution to replace apartheid began in earnest after the freeing up of political activity, the release of political prisoners and the return of exiles from 1990. At least four stages of reform[34] of the administrative-law system can be readily identified, as set out in the next sections.

### 1.4.1 First stage of reform

Without a doubt, the most important event which set the agenda for reform was a three-day workshop held at the Breakwater campus of the University of Cape Town in February 1993. It was attended by about 100 delegates from throughout the country (including most of those who would be influential figures in the Ministry of Justice and the senior ranks of the judiciary after 1994) and several leading administrative lawyers from abroad, and at its conclusion the *Breakwater Declaration* was unanimously adopted.[35] This two-page document listed points of agreement as well as areas requiring further work in order to ensure a properly revised and nuanced system of administrative review which could take its place as one of the pillars of a constitutional democracy in South Africa. Vitally, one of the key proposals was the inclusion of a right to administrative justice in a future constitution, a rather unusual proposal in international terms, but the example of the 1990 Namibian Constitution's Article 18 was fresh in the minds of the delegates.

### 1.4.2 Second stage of reform

Such a right was duly included in the transitional Constitution of 1993, in section 24. There was unanimity among the delegations at the Multi-Party Negotiating Process that such a right was necessary: those in government belatedly recognised the value of administrative law safeguards, especially as they were likely to be in opposition after 1994, while those who had always opposed apartheid had seen the damage which could be inflicted as the result of the unbridled exercise of power and appreciated the role played by judicial review during

32 These rules, usually expressed in their Latin format as *audi alteram partem* (hear the other side) and *nemo judex in sua causa esse debet* (no one should be a judge in their own cause/interest), are regarded as 'natural' because they are said to be inalienable rights under the common law.

33 Such as the Riotous Assemblies and Criminal Law Amendment Act 27 of 1914, section 1(13).

34 For further details of this process, see Corder, H. 'Reviewing Review: Much Achieved, Much More to Do' in Corder, H and van der Vijver, L (Eds) (2002) *Realising Administrative Justice* at 1–19.

35 See Corder, H (1993) Introduction: Administrative Law Reform *Acta Juridica* 1 for a report on the event and for a copy of the Declaration, at 17–20. Most of the papers delivered on that occasion are included in that same volume.

apartheid. The formulation of the right (or better, bundle of rights) was however much more controversial, leading to a relatively complex set of guarantees of fair administrative action, as follows:

> **Section 24 Administrative Justice**
> Every person shall have the right to –
> (*a*) lawful administrative action where any of his or her rights or interests is affected or threatened;
> (*b*) procedurally fair administrative action where any of his or her rights or legitimate expectations is affected or threatened;
> (*c*) be furnished with reasons in writing for administrative action which affects any of his or her rights or interests unless such reasons have been made public; and
> (*d*) administrative action which is justifiable in relation to the reasons given for it where any of his or her rights is affected or threatened.

Key elements of this provision were:

- the requirement of achieving varying 'thresholds' before the different rights (to lawful, procedurally fair, and justifiable administrative action, and to obtain written reasons for such action) became available, which depended on proving that one's 'rights, legitimate expectations and/or interests' had been 'affected or threatened',
- the remarkable elevation to constitutional status of the right to receive written reasons, from being completely absent in the common law before that,
- the endorsement of the notion of 'procedural fairness' rather than continued reference to the 'rules of natural justice' as was the practice in the courts and as proposed by some negotiators, and
- the introduction of the right to 'justifiable' administrative action, rather than constitutionalising 'reasonableness' as the standard of review. The adoption of this term is largely attributed to the influence of Mureinik in the drafting process, and that 'justifiability' was a compromise term acceptable to all parties, especially those who felt apprehensive about the misuse of such a concept in the hands of a recalcitrant judiciary after apartheid.[36]

### 1.4.3 Third stage of reform

This interim provision came into force on 27 April 1994, but practising lawyers and judges proved slow to rely on its remarkably generous and innovative provisions. In the process of drafting the final Constitution, the ANC-led government proposed the scrapping of the right to administrative justice and its replacement with a more comprehensive statutory regime. The opposition parties and civil society resisted strongly, and a compromise was reached: a new right would be adopted, but it would not come into force for a period of three years, or until Parliament approved a statute especially drafted to give effect to such a right, but also to limit its scope, whichever event came first. The new right in section 33 is remarkable for its breadth and the elegant simplicity of its wording:

> (1) Everyone has the right to administrative action which is lawful, reasonable and procedurally fair.
> (2) Everyone has the right to written reasons for administrative action which affects their rights.

36 For a fuller account of this drafting history, see Du Plessis, LM and Corder, H (1994) *Understanding South Africa's Transitional Bill of Rights* at 165–170.

Subsection (3) contained the compromise to suit government:

> National legislation must be enacted to give effect to these rights, and must
> (*a*) provide for the review of administrative action by a court or, where appropriate, an independent and impartial tribunal;
> (*b*) impose a duty on the state to give effect to the rights in subsections (1) and (2); and
> (*c*) promote an efficient administration.

Item 23 in Schedule 6 of the final Constitution provided that, until the envisaged legislation had been drafted, section 33 would be taken to read like a 'plain language' version of section 24 of the transitional Constitution. Thus the transitional Constitutional provision effectively applied to all causes of action which arose in the period from 27 April 1994 to early February 2000.

### 1.4.4 Fourth stage of reform

The Minister of Justice was slow to initiate the drafting of the legislation envisaged in section 33(3), and the working committee of the South African Law Commission which was mandated to research this issue and to produce a draft bill on administrative justice was only convened late in 1998. It set to work early in the following year, and after a series of workshops around the country, it produced a draft bill by August 1999. This bill then served before the Portfolio Committee on Justice in Parliament, which made extensive changes to what had been proposed. In the views of one of the members of the Law Commission committee,[37] much of the progressive substance of the bill was removed, and an important opportunity to advance the quality, flexibility and accessibility of administrative review in South Africa was lost. The bill was duly approved as the Promotion of Administrative Justice Act 3 of 2000 (PAJA), by both houses of Parliament in time for the Presidential assent on 3 February 2000, a day before the expiry of the three-year period prescribed for its drafting and passage into law.

The Act was only brought into force on 30 November 2000, which meant that section 33(1) and (2) could have been relied on in an uninhibited fashion for those ten months. Since December 2000, however, PAJA has provided a statutory cloak to the bare framework of administrative justice rights in section 33, effectively limiting its scope. Such limitations must, naturally, comply with the tests prescribed by the general limitations clause in section 36; some have argued[38] that there are crucial aspects of PAJA which do not satisfy these tests, but no court has yet pronounced on this question. Given its prominence in modern administrative law, it is vital to note in superficial terms an outline of its main provisions and their purpose, which follows in section 1.5 of this chapter below.

### 1.4.5 Superstructural reform

The account of this thorough process of reform of the constitutional and legislative framework within which administrative law must function in South Africa represents a remarkable achievement. Although Australia undertook a complete and similar overhaul of its system in the 1970s, the South African process occurred at the same time as other momentous changes were being made to almost every aspect of the Constitution, and at a time of great tumult in society. The success of this reform process is due to the committed

37 See Hoexter (2000) at 484–519.

38 See the authors referred to in note 48 below.

initiative and energy of a few individuals, both in government, legal practice and academic life. It is probably not surprising that these changes have taken time to be translated into changed patterns of behaviour, both by lawyers seeking to review, and public servants engaged in, the exercise of public power. This last sphere provides both the challenge as well as the interest in the study of administrative law in this country.

## 1.5 Outline of the general structure of the Promotion of Administrative Justice Act 3 of 2000 (PAJA)

The Promotion of Administrative Justice Act (PAJA) is a short statute barely ten sections in length. It starts, however, with an extraordinarily long set of definitions, the most important of which is in section 1(*i*), which attempts to define one of the key phrases in the Act, 'administrative action'. Now any system of administrative law must define the kind of conduct subject to review, as a 'gatekeeping device', otherwise the reviewing body (such as a court or tribunal) will not be able to cope with the demand on its services, the administration will become snowed under with having to respond to reviews, and its ability to do its day-to-day work, its efficiency, will suffer. This was the main purpose behind the inclusion of section 33(3)(*c*) in the Constitution: the message to the drafters of PAJA was not to be too demanding on the public administration, giving it time to adapt to the new standards expected of it, which contrasted so strongly with those under apartheid: in other words, **to balance accountability with efficiency**. Therefore the inclusion of a definition of 'administrative action' was to be expected, but not quite the degree of complexity that eventuated.

The essential elements of this definition are as follows:

- a decision (or failure to take one),
- by an organ of state (itself very broadly defined in section 239 of the Constitution) when acting in terms of the Constitution or when exercising a public power or performing a public function in terms of legislation,
- or by a natural or juristic person when exercising a public power or performing a public function in terms of an 'empowering provision' (this term is also defined in section 1, but so widely as to be of little practical effect),
- which adversely affects the rights of any person, and
- which has a direct, external legal effect.

The definition goes on to list nine instances in which the official conduct is **expressly excluded** from the definition of administrative action. In summary, these are the 'executive' and 'legislative' functions of government at national, provincial and local levels, the actions of judges, magistrates and traditional leaders when dispensing justice, 'a decision to institute or continue a prosecution', a decision of the Judicial Service Commission in any part of the **appointment** process of judges, and two other relatively minor but specific acts of administration.

As you will see in the rest of this book, this definition has assumed great importance in post-2000 administrative law.[39] Of course the exclusion of certain categories of public decision-making does not render them immune from constitutional scrutiny, again as will be explained in due course. This definition has, however, become the subject of great attention from the courts on review, such that it has almost served to distract attention from

39 For a summary treatment, see Hoexter, C (2006) 'Administrative Action' in the Courts *Acta Juridica* 303.

the main purpose of section 33 and PAJA, much as the doctrine of the classification of functions did under apartheid. Notice several significant aspects of the definition: 'action' includes an omission, administrative action can be taken by a private body, the requirement of an 'adverse effect on rights' clearly is intended as a limitation on the rights in section 33, nowhere is the crucial word 'public' defined, and the reference to a 'direct, external legal effect' is an attempt to require finality in a decision-making process before an aggrieved party can seek judicial review.

The only other element of section 1 that should be noted is the provision that a magistrate's court will have jurisdiction to hear an application for review of administrative action provided that the court has been designated by the Minister to do so, and provided that the presiding magistrate has undergone appropriate training and also been so designated.[40] While this has the potential substantially to widen access to judicial review of administrative action, the Department of Justice and Constitutional Development has been very slow in initiating this jurisdictional development with the result that there has been little meaningful broadening of access to administrative review.[41]

Section 2 of PAJA marks an important gesture in the direction of the balance needed between accountability and efficiency, because it allows specified groups of administrative action to be exempt from the provisions of the Act or for some administrators to vary their compliance with the Act, provided that it is 'reasonable and justifiable' in the circumstances. This is an important safety valve for administrative frustration with the strictures of PAJA, but it has yet to be used.

Sections 3, 4 and 5 of PAJA give greater detail on what is required from the administrator in the area of procedural fairness: first in regard to administrative action affecting an individual, then where administrative action affects the public at large, and finally what steps need to be taken to give expression to the duty to give reasons for administrative action. Sections 3 and 4 follow a similar pattern: they require compliance with certain steps as a minimum level of procedural fairness, then some steps which it would be desirable to take, and finally they provide for a 'different but fair' escape route, where an administrator effectively complies with the obligations under PAJA, but in a different manner from that laid down in the Act. Section 5 requires those who seek reasons for administrative action to apply for them within 90 days of hearing about the action, to which the administrator must respond in writing, again within 90 days of the request, with 'adequate' reasons. This last set of obligations is naturally of great assistance to those who seek to challenge the reasonableness of administrative action, for to do so without knowing why the administrator acted is rather like shooting in the dark. In general, commentators are agreed that this set of steps relating to procedural fairness marks a significant advance on the common law.

Section 6 is the heart of PAJA for, in setting out the possible grounds of review on which the validity of administrative action may be challenged, it draws together and codifies the grounds which existed at common law. Noteworthy aspects of this section are the fact that administrative action will frequently be challengeable under more than one such ground; that the attempt at giving greater clarity to the idea of review of 'reasonableness' (section 6(2)(*h*))

40 In fact, PAJA has been amended to facilitate this process: see the addition of section 9A Designation and Training of Judicial Officers.

41 In Government Notice (GN) No. 1216 in *Government Gazette (GG)* 42717 of 19.09.2019, the Minister of Justice purports to designate all regional and magistrates' courts as 'courts' for purposes of review under PAJA. This arrangement came into effect on 1 October 2019, so it is too early to assess its impact in the widening of access to administrative justice.

was extremely unhelpful, and has been effectively sidelined by the courts;[42] and finally that section 6(2)(*i*) keeps the list of grounds open for further development as courts push the boundaries of review: it provides that any action which is 'otherwise unconstitutional or unlawful' may be set aside on that ground, thus preserving a degree of flexibility for the reviewing judges to develop the law, much as was done under the common law.[43]

Section 7 of PAJA lays down certain procedures which must be followed in seeking to review administrative action, one of which requires such action to have been launched within 180 days of the action having been taken.[44] Section 8 outlines the various remedies which a court can order if it has found administrative action to have failed to comply with the law, under the broad cloak of enhancing justice and equity. The innovation here is the authority granted to the court to order the payment of financial compensation to those who have suffered because of the unlawfulness of the action, a power which did not exist before, and which effectively allows a judge to order the executive to spend money.

Section 9 authorises a court on application to allow a variation of any of the time periods stipulated in the Act, while section 9A provides guidance in respect of the training of magistrates to preside over judicial review applications. Finally (section 11 merely specifies the short title of the Act), section 10 requires the Minister (of Justice and Constitutional Development) to make certain regulations, and mandates him or her to make others. The only point worth mentioning here is that the Minister has not yet accepted the invitation in section 10(2)(*a*) to establish an administrative justice advisory council, to monitor and continue the process of administrative law reform.[45] A set of *Regulations on Fair Administrative Procedures* was duly approved and promulgated in July 2002,[46] and these give yet further detail in support of the proper implementation of sections 3 and 4.

What effect has the existence of PAJA had on the development of administrative justice?[47] In the first place, it has inhibited the growth of alternatives to judicial review, through its failure to address the wider scope of and mechanisms to achieve administrative *justice*. Second, the problems attendant on the complex definition of the key phrase (administrative action) have limited its usefulness. Third, some have argued[48] that PAJA unduly and unjustifiably (and therefore unconstitutionally) limits the rights to administrative justice by, for example, prescribing strict time periods within which steps must be taken, and by requiring internal remedies to have been exhausted before applying for review. On the other hand, the renewal contained in the provisions relating to procedural fairness, and several other aspects, mark advances on the common law. On balance, therefore, I would argue that PAJA, although an 'opportunity lost', has had a positive influence on the level of administrative justice in South Africa.

---

42 See the judgment of O'Regan J in *Bato Star Fishing (Pty) Ltd v Minister of Environmental Affairs and Others* 2004 (4) SA 490 (CC).

43 Thus, have the courts been able still to hold that 'vagueness' and 'acting under dictation' are valid grounds of review in the constitutional era.

44 Rules for applying for judicial review of administrative action in a High Court were promulgated in the *GG* No. 42740 of 04.10.19; they came into effect on 1 November 2019.

45 The SA Law Reform Commission recommended that the establishment of such a body be mandatory.

46 GN R 1022 (*GG* 23764 of 31.07.2002).

47 For a provocative view of the impact of PAJA, see Currie, I (2006) What Difference Does the Promotion of Administrative Justice Act Make to Administrative Law *Acta Juridica* 325.

48 See, for example, Plasket, C (2002) The Exhaustion of Internal Remedies and Section 7(2) of the Promotion of Administrative Justice Act 3 of 2000 *SALJ* 119(1):50, and Hoexter, C (2012) *Administrative Law in South Africa* (2nd ed), at 532–543.

## 1.6 Outline of the various avenues to judicial review of administrative action in South Africa

The rest of this book examines the state of our administrative law in some detail. The purpose of this short overview is to allow the reader to situate their reading and study of what follows within a framework, by outlining the main avenues through which the process of judicial review has developed over the past twenty years.[49] Judicial review is the mechanism through which a court scrutinises an administrative action to determine whether it meets the standards of administrative justice as set out in the Constitution, PAJA and the common law and grants a remedy where it does not. In considering this summary account, you should recall that, a mere twenty-five years ago, only two such avenues to judicial review existed, being resort to the common law of judicial review and the use of such special statutory processes as may have existed in isolated areas of law (such as labour law). Using the image of 'avenues' is an attempt to make sense of the several possible routes available to a court when approached by a party challenging the validity of administrative conduct. There are at least five avenues through which the review of administrative conduct can be sought. I use the word 'conduct' in order to cover as wide a range of behaviour by the administration as possible: within it, one can find decisions, actions, omissions and so on.

- Whether the administrative conduct being challenged falls within the definition of '**administrative action**' or not is the first question which needs to be answered, or at least it ought to be so. If the conduct concerned can be classified as such, then the provisions of PAJA apply, and must be followed. This avenue is likely by far to be the one most commonly used, and it provides the widest range of grounds of review and remedies of all the avenues.
- If the conduct does not fall within PAJA definition of administrative action, but rather within the broad compass of '**executive action**', for example where a Minister lays down policy for the guidance of public officials, or the President appoints someone to public office at his discretion or decides to pardon a prisoner, then the conduct is clearly reviewable, but this time against the demands of the 'principle of legality', which is enshrined as an aspect of the 'rule of law' as one of the founding values of the Constitution, in section 1(*c*). Here the grounds on which the challenger can rely are lawfulness, rationality and honesty,[50] with the duty to show procedural fairness in very limited circumstances. It seems, too, that the duty to give reasons for this conduct, at least so that the rationality of the conduct can be assessed, is required by law.[51] However, in the past five years, the courts have increasingly pushed the boundaries of the grounds of review under the principle of legality, especially in their interpretation of what is required by review for 'rationality'. Applicants for judicial review also prefer often to proceed under this avenue because the procedural obstacles thrown up by PAJA (such as the 180-day limit) are not present in the same way under this avenue. Similarly, judges sometimes prefer to hear a review under the principle of legality, because they then do not have to grapple with the difficulties attendant on the

49 Hoexter calls these 'pathways' to review, and is chiefly responsible for identifying them as such in her work over the past decade: see Hoexter (2000), and also Hoexter, C 'The Rule of Law and the Principle of Legality in South African Administrative Law Today' in Carnelly, M and Hoctor, S (Eds) (2011) *Law, Order and Liberty Essays in Honour of Tony Mathews* at 55–74.

50 The founding authority for such a view is to be seen in *President of the Republic of South Africa and Others v South African Rugby Football Union and Others* 2000 (1) SA 1 (CC).

51 See *Judicial Service Commission and Another v Cape Bar Council and Another* 2013 (1) SA 170 (SCA).

definition of 'administrative action' in PAJA. This trend in litigation undermines the overall scheme of administrative review contemplated in the Constitution.

- In certain circumstances where the conduct can be defined as 'administrative action' in terms of PAJA, because of the existence of structures and processes established by legislation which applies to a particular sphere of the public administration or a particular type of economic activity, the courts will insist that the 'special statutory' review mechanisms be used, rather than PAJA. The only exception to this rule seems to be where the public impact of the conduct justifies resort to PAJA.[52] The best-known examples of this route are to be seen where the complaint relates to employment by government, to which both the Labour Relations Act[53] and PAJA both potentially apply.
- Again, where the conduct complies with PAJA definition, but for example it raises doubts about the constitutionality of one or more of the provisions of PAJA itself, the court on review will use as its benchmark the terms of section 33 of the Constitution itself, which of course uses the term 'administrative action', and gives it an interpretation uninfluenced by the definition in PAJA. This route will very rarely be resorted to, but will allow the court a greater degree of latitude to develop the law without reference to PAJA.[54]
- Finally, although it has been emphatically and repeatedly emphasised that the common law avenue no longer exists as some kind of parallel review process, nevertheless where a private body such as a voluntary association (be it of a charitable, sporting, religious or other nature) acts to discipline a member, or in some way acts as if it is exercising regulatory power, the rules of procedural fairness and rationality at least will apply to its conduct. Of course, it will also be bound by the terms of its constitution, so will have to act lawfully in that sense. This avenue is not the one followed where a private body exercises public power or performs a public function, perhaps as an outsourced service provider for government. In this last case it will be subject to the ordinary review process as laid down in PAJA as if it was an organ of state.

## 1.7 Concluding remarks about the current state of administrative law, and some challenges

The purpose of this chapter has been to describe the development of administrative law in South Africa and some of the basic concepts and principles which underlie its development. This final section of the chapter attempts to summarise the main features of the current administrative law jurisprudence, and to list briefly some of the challenges facing it. The remaining chapters in the book will take all of these issues much further, but it is appropriate to be aware of the structure of the whole subject from the outset.

**PAUSE FOR REFLECTION**

**Main features of pre-constitutional administrative law**

Before proceeding, look back at the summary of the main features of administrative law before the advent of the Constitution, set out above at section 1.3.7. This will demonstrate the relatively far-reaching shifts which have occurred in this part of the law.

52 See *Gcaba v Minister for Safety and Security and Others* 2010 (1) SA 238 (CC).

53 66 of 1995.

54 See *Zondi v MEC for Traditional and Local Government Affairs and Others* 2005 (3) SA 589 (CC).

### 1.7.1 The current state of administrative law

Most of the features which characterise judicial review of administrative action at present have been established authoritatively only in the past twenty years (since the passage into law and coming into force of PAJA), although as explained previously, the roots of most of them can be traced back many decades. The main characteristics of the law are as follows:

- The foundation of the exercise of the jurisdiction to review administrative action by the courts is to be found in the Constitution, particularly sections 1(*c*), 33 and 195. So there is now little reference to the *ultra vires* doctrine as the basis of review.
- Review according to the general tenets of PAJA is by far the most frequent type of regulation of the exercise of public power, because most acts done by the public administration fall within the bounds of the definition of administrative action in PAJA.
- One of the earliest decisions found that putting goods and services out to tender by government (what is called 'public procurement') qualified as administrative action,[55] so that much litigation has centred on the lawfulness and procedural fairness of the tender process.[56] The status of the subsequent contractual relationship between government and the service provider as being governed by private law or public law has also generated a fair degree of judicial disagreement.[57]
- The applicability of PAJA where a specialised statutory regime exists (for example, in the labour relations field) has been a source of several high-profile decisions, with the outcome appearing to be that the special statutory regime will apply, unless the outcome of the decision will have a substantial public impact.[58]
- A significant number of cases has focused on the importance of administrative fairness to the provision of socio-economic rights, many litigants electing to rely on the failure of government to follow the prescripts of administrative justice as the basis for arguing that socio-economic rights should be granted to them.[59]
- Perhaps the most significant development in this period has been the creation of a parallel avenue for review of executive action, that is the exercise of public power by government which does not qualify as administrative action in terms of PAJA.[60] Here the courts have concluded that review can occur on many of the grounds which could have been relied on were it administrative action, while being constrained by a due degree of deference needing to be shown to the executive branch of government.

---

55 See *Umfolozi Transport (Edms) Bpk v Minister van Vervoer* [1997] 2 All SA 548 (A).

56 See, for example, *Cape Metropolitan Council v Metro Inspection Services (Western Cape) CC and Others* 2001 (3) SA 1013 (SCA) and *Logbro Properties CC v Bedderson NO and Others* 2003 (2) SA 460 (SCA).

57 See *Steenkamp NO v Provincial Tender Board, Eastern Cape* 2007 (3) SA 121 (CC).

58 Among the chief cases in this regard, see *Fredericks v MEC for Education and Training, Eastern Cape* 2002 (2) SA 693 (CC), *Chirwa v Transnet Ltd and Others* 2008 (4) SA 367 (CC), and *Gcaba v Minister for Safety and Security and Others* 2010 (1) SA 238 (CC).

59 See, for example, *Joseph and Others v City of Johannesburg and Others* 2010 (4) SA 55 (CC), and *Mazibuko and Others v City of Johannesburg and Others* 2010 (4) SA 1 (CC).

60 See the excellent explanation of this development in Hoexter (2011) 55, note 49 above. For a recent example in the case law, see *Albutt v Centre for the Study of Violence and Reconciliation and Others* 2010 (3) SA 293 (CC).

- Some advances have been made in the creative use of the wide authority granted to the courts in the ordering of a 'just and equitable' remedy having found administrative action to be unlawful,[61] including on occasion the refusal by a court to set aside the action, even though it is invalid in law.[62]
- Unlike before 1994, almost no questions are raised currently about litigants' standing to sue, and direct ouster clauses are effectively eliminated because of the existence of the right of access to court in section 34 of the Constitution; although the broad grant of discretionary authority without sufficient guidelines for its implementation may be seen to be an indirect ouster.

### 1.7.2 Some challenges facing administrative law

As far as the challenges are concerned, the following areas of administrative law present most of the potential dangers for the achievement of administrative justice:

1. The seemingly endless disputes about whether the administrative conduct being challenged falls under PAJA or not. These often serve to distract the court from its fundamental task, which is to achieve the greatest degree of compliance with administrative justice.
2. The delimitation of the grounds of review under the 'principle of legality', the basis of review where PAJA definition has not been satisfied. In many ways it seems that it will be just a matter of time before the gap between the grounds of review available under the two separate avenues will converge, which defeats the intention of the Constitution in section 33.
3. The courts have not been able to reach a sufficiently predictable approach to the deference which they must show to the other branches of government.[63] Although this is a highly-charged area of law, or because it is, the urgency of some authoritative statement in this regard from the Constitutional Court is imperative.
4. The exaggerated prominence of judicial review as the main avenue to review, despite all its many and serious drawbacks, means that access to administrative justice is available to only very few. It also means that insufficient attention is being paid to the development of alternative avenues for achieving administrative justice, such as appeals tribunals, specialised ombuds offices, greater transparency, and so on.

Despite these challenges, the level of administrative justice in South African law today has increased enormously over the past twenty-five years, and there is no reason to suppose that this trajectory will not continue, albeit at a slower pace. In fact, if one returns to the objectives set in the *Breakwater Declaration* of just twenty-six years ago, you will see that they have been reached in almost every respect. That in itself is of great significance for our participative democracy.

61 For example, see *Millennium Waste Management (Pty) Ltd v Chairperson, Tender Board: Limpopo Province and Others* 2008 (2) SA 481 (SCA).

62 See *Allpay Consolidated Investment Holdings (Pty) Ltd and Others v Chief Executive Officer, South African Social Security Agency and Others* 2013 (4) SA 557 (SCA), referring to the judgment of Matojane J *a quo* in the North Gauteng High Court, at para 2, who had found the tender process to be invalid, but had refused to set it aside. This matter was then appealed to the Constitutional Court, under the same name, which overruled the SCA judgment (*Allpay Consolidated Investment Holdings (Pty) Ltd and Others v Chief Executive Officer, South African Social Security Agency and Others* 2014 (1) SA 604 (CC)), and set aside the tender award in contention, but postponed granting any further remedy, pending a further hearing some months later.

63 See the treatment of this area of the law in the works referred to in note 13 above.

## THIS CHAPTER IN ESSENCE

This chapter seeks to provide a broad outline of the field of the regulation through law of power relations covered by administrative law. This is done within the historical, socio-economic and democratic governance contexts within which this area of law has both developed and operates today. The meaning of the concept of the 'exercise of public power or the performance of a public function', phrases central to the scope of administrative law, is explored. The several avenues to review of administrative and executive conduct in the public domain are outlined. This chapter provides, therefore, the essential skeleton of concepts and rules on which the rest of the chapters in this book will build.

## FURTHER READING

- 1993 *Acta Juridica*
- Baxter, L (1984) *Administrative Law* Cape Town: Juta
- Currie, I (2007) *The Promotion of Administrative Justice Act A Commentary* (2nd ed) Cape Town: Siber Ink
- De Ville, JR (2003) *Judicial Review of Administrative Action in South Africa* Durban: LexisNexis Butterworth
- Hoexter, C (2012) *Administrative Law in South Africa* (2nd ed) Cape Town: Juta
- Quinot, G (2008) *Administrative Law Cases & Materials* Cape Town: Juta

# Chapter 2

# Administrative authorities in legal context

*Petrus Maree*

## 2.1 Introduction

What is the administration? What is administrative law? To whom does administrative law apply? These are not straightforward questions: they do not lead to straightforward answers and they prove challenging because they are often neglected and cannot be addressed in a vacuum. However, an awareness of context and complexity is essential to appreciating administrative justice. Therefore, this chapter sketches the broad contours of the conceptual framework and context within which these questions are posed.

Defining the concepts and nomenclature necessary for a discussion on public authorities and administrative law serves as the chapter's point of departure. Subsequently the constitutional framework within which the administration operates is discussed. Normative imperatives imposed by the Constitution, such as democracy, and institutional principles, such as the separation of powers, are always relevant to an understanding or analysis of administrative authorities. Therefore any response to the question 'what is the administration?' must be based on these constitutional provisions.

On the basis of the constitutional and conceptual framework, specific examples of administrative authorities are discussed. The examples include national departments, a Chapter 9 institution and a state-owned company. The legislative framework and the institutional nature of each institution are set out in order to illustrate the diversity of administrative authorities. However, there are shared characteristics: for instance, administrative authorities are typically concerned with the implementation of legislation and the performance of public functions.

Finally, the relationship between institutions that can be described as administrative authorities and administrative law is explained.

## 2.2 Concepts and nomenclature

Public law relies on a number of concepts and terms, which bear several meanings. For example, the word 'state' can be employed in a technical sense,[1] but also in a more general sense, colloquially.[2] Thus the term 'state' has more than one definition, but not all definitions are necessarily relevant to administrative law. Definitions for terms such as 'state', 'executive' and 'government' are discussed in this section, in order to identify those definitions relevant to administrative law and to distinguish these terms from one another.

### 2.2.1 State

The word 'state' is a broad term bearing a number of meanings. Although the Constitution refers to 'state' consistently, it is not defined. The Oxford English Dictionary lists the definitions of state relevant to this discussion under the heading of 'commonwealth or

1 Section 1 of the Companies Act 71 of 2008 defines 'state-owned companies' as 'a public entity in Schedule 2 or 3 of the Public Finance Management Act [1 of 1999]', such as Eskom. A public entity, in turn, refers to 'a juristic person under the ownership control of the national executive' (from the definitions of national public entity, national government business enterprise, section 1 PFMA). Thus 'state', in this context, denotes the executive, rather than constitutional and political institutions in their totality.

2 For instance, Dr Matebesi, referring to his research on service-delivery protests, explains that '[w]ith the increase of violence, the space for building trust between *the state* and civil society is decreasing' (University of the Free State 'UFS Research Sheds Light on Service Delivery Protests in South Africa' (03.02.2015) *Mail & Guardian* https://www.ufs.ac.za/templates/news-archive/campus-news/2019/february/worldmothertongueday-celebrating-your-native-langue-mother-tongue?NewsItemID=5231 (emphasis added)). In this context, 'state' can be read in a broad sense, referring to a range of national, political institutions comprising the policy branch, the public administration and legislative organs.

polity'.[3] In this sense, state can refer to a community, living in a specified geographical area with its own political organisation, or a nation. For example, the Freedom Charter provides that 'South Africa shall be a fully independent state which respects the rights and sovereignty of all nations'. In this sense state signifies the nation in a broad sense, comprising political, economic, cultural and private entities and activities.

State can also refer to the geographical area inhabited by such a community. For example, article 12 of the African Charter on Human and Peoples' Rights provides that '[e]very individual shall have the right to freedom of movement and residence within the borders of a State ...'. 'The state', often with a capital S, refers to '[t]he body politic as organized for supreme civil rule and government'.[4] Thus the state refers to the apparatus of a nation endowed with public authority, including the executive, legislature, judiciary, police etc. In this sense, the term serves as a collective noun describing the totality of entities endowed with public authority. Louis XIV famously declared 'I am the State'[5] to mean the monarch wields absolute power. In other words, the monarch is the ultimate authority on all forms of public power (legislative, executive, judicial and administrative) and the embodiment of that power; thus the body politic, the state, is the monarch. The Constitution provides a more recent example of this usage of 'state' as body politic: section 26(2) of the right to housing holds that '[t]he state must take reasonable legislative and other measures ... to achieve the progressive realisation of this right'. Similarly, criminal law cases employ the word state in this sense: consider the designation *S v Makwanyane and Another*,[6] where S designates 'the State'.

Finally, state can also signify the type of constitution operating in a country. For example, section 1 of the Constitution reads '[t]he Republic of South Africa is one, sovereign, democratic state'; article 1 of the 1977 Soviet Constitution reads as follows:

> The Union of Soviet Socialist Republics is a socialist state of the whole people, expressing the will and interests of the workers, peasants, and intelligentsia, the working people of all the nations and nationalities of the country.

'State' can be used in more than one sense in a given context and, evidently, all of these definitions can overlap.

## 2.2.2 Executive

'Executive', as a noun, is a more technical term than 'state'. Executive generally refers to that branch within the separation of powers primarily concerned with the formulation of policy and the implementation of legislation and policy. This term is crucial to the study of administrative law.

In the South African context, executive is defined by section 85 of the Constitution:

> (1) The executive authority of the Republic is vested in the President.
> (2) The President exercises the executive authority, together with the other members of the Cabinet ...

3 'state, n.' OED *Oxford English Dictionary: The Definitive Record of the English Language*, Oxford University Press 2019 Online available at: http://www.oed.com/ (accessed 23.10.2019). Reproduced with permission of OUP (Book) through PLSclear.

4 OED (2019) 'state'.

5 *'L'état, c'est moi'*.

6 1995 (3) SA 391 (CC).

Thus, broadly speaking, the executive performs two functions: formulating policy and implementing policy and legislation. In *Permanent Secretary, Department of Education and Welfare, Eastern Cape and Another v Ed-U-College (PE) (Section21) Inc.*[7] O'Regan J elaborated on this distinction, with reference to *President of the Republic of South Africa and Others v South African Rugby Football Union and Others*:[8]

> It should be noted that the distinction drawn ... is between the implementation of legislation, on the one hand, and the formulation of policy on the other. Policy may be formulated by the executive outside of a legislative framework. For example, the executive may determine a policy on road and rail transportation, or on tertiary education. The formulation of such policy involves a political decision and will generally not constitute administrative action. However, policy may also be formulated in a narrower sense where a member of the executive is implementing legislation. The formulation of policy in the exercise of such powers may often constitute administrative action.[9]

It is essential to bear in mind the dual nature of the executive, in both the institutional and functional sense: on the one hand the executive is concerned with formulating policy and, on the other, with implementing legislation. From an institutional perspective, the public administration specifically is primarily concerned with the latter, rather than the executive proper. In a sense, most state decisions or acts entail an element of policy. Therefore, policy in the wide sense and policy in the narrow sense are distinguished, as explained in *Ed-U-College*. The executive can also be subdivided into the national, provincial and local spheres.[10] In order to facilitate accuracy, Vile proposes referring to the public administration and the 'policy branch' as divisions within the executive.[11] This appellation acknowledges the dual nature of the executive.

### 2.2.3 Government

The term government is also employed in several ways. On occasion, 'government' is synonymous with 'executive' in the wide sense, comprising both politicians and administrators.[12] Sometimes government refers to the high executive, that is, Cabinet, and sometimes the ruling or majority party is referred to as the government.

### 2.2.4 Public administration

As indicated, the public administration forms part of the executive. The term public administration is not clearly defined, but section 195 of the Constitution expressly identifies the constitutional role of the administration. In a general sense, the public administration is that part of the executive concerned with the implementation of legislation and of policy, rather than their initiation and formulation.

7 2001 (2) SA 1 (CC).
8 2000 (1) SA 1 (CC).
9 *Permanent Secretary, Department of Education and Welfare, Eastern Cape and Another v Ed-U-College (PE) (Section21) Inc* 2001 (2) SA 1 (CC) para 18. Cf. the approach followed in *Mazibuko and Others v City of Johannesburg* 2010 (4) SA 1 (CC).
10 See sections 125 and 151(2) of the Constitution.
11 Vile, MJC (1998) *Constitutionalism and the Separation of Powers* (2nd ed) 400.
12 Currie, I & De Waal, J (2001) *The New Constitutional and Administrative Law Volume One Constitutional Law* 228.

### 2.2.5 Civil service

The civil service is a division of the public administration.[13] Chapter 197(1) of the Constitution provides the following:

> Within public administration there is a public service for the Republic, which must function, and be structured, in terms of national legislation, and which must loyally execute the lawful policies of the government of the day.

The Constitution also establishes a Public Service Commission,[14] tasked with safeguarding the values and principles listed in section 195. The Constitution establishes the Commission's independence and grants it investigative powers.[15] The Public Service Commission is accountable to the National Assembly.[16]

## 2.3 Constitutional supremacy

Section 2 of the Constitution establishes the supremacy of the Constitution:

> This Constitution is the supreme law of the Republic; law or conduct inconsistent with it is invalid, and the obligations imposed by it must be fulfilled.

Therefore, the Constitution in general and provisions concerned with the administration or administrative law in particular are always relevant and should inform any corresponding determination. Evidently, the status of the Constitution has far-reaching implications, also for the administration and for administrative law.

An overview of the constitutional framework within which the administration and administrative law operate is provided in this section. The scope of constitutional supremacy is encompassing. Section 2 of the Constitution applies not only to conduct and the content of legal rules, but also imposes obligations. Thus the Constitution not only entrenches certain values, but obliges the state to take positive steps. This is illustrated by section 7(2): '[t]he state must respect, protect, promote and fulfil the rights in the Bill of Rights'. Section 8 states that '[t]he Bill of Rights applies to all law, and binds the legislature, the executive, the judiciary and all organs of state'.[17] The Bill of Rights includes socio-economic rights such as the right to housing and the right to education,[18] which themselves oblige the state to take positive steps.[19] Therefore, according to the unqualified wording of section 8, the Bill of Rights applies to all branches of state, including the administration. The public administration, in turn, is specifically recognised by sections 195 and 239. Finally, the Constitution, in general, and the Bill of Rights, in particular, are justiciable and enforceable: section 172(1)(*a*) provides that the courts 'must declare that any law or conduct that is inconsistent with the Constitution is invalid' and 'may make any order that is just and equitable'.[20] The supremacy of the Constitution is reflected in context of judicial review: the Promotion of Administrative

---

13 Section 197 of the Constitution.

14 Section 196 of the Constitution.

15 Section 196(2) and section 196(4)(*b*) of the Constitution, respectively.

16 Section 196(5) of the Constitution.

17 Section 239 of the Constitution defines 'organs of state'.

18 Sections 26 and 29, respectively.

19 Section 26(2) provides that '[t]he state must take reasonable legislative and other measures, within its available resources, to achieve the progressive realisation of this right'.

20 Sections 172(1)(*a*) and (*b*), respectively. In Chapter 12 sections 12.3–12.4 the implications of section 172 for administrative law remedies are discussed.

Justice Act (PAJA)[21] provides that 'a court ... has the power to judicially review an administrative action'[22] if it is unlawful, procedurally unfair, or unreasonable and 'may grant any order that is just and equitable'.[23] Thus the rule of law as the supremacy of the Constitution is established in relation to the state as a whole, in a radical departure from the system of parliamentary sovereignty within which the administration functioned prior to 1994 as we noted in Chapter 1.[24]

### 2.3.1 Democracy

Democracy is repeatedly emphasised throughout the Constitution:[25] the Constitution entrenches general notions of democracy as well as more specific conceptions of democracy, such as participation. Since democracy is a founding constitutional principle, the public administration is also bound to uphold and promote it. Section 1 provides that South Africa is 'founded' on '[u]niversal adult suffrage, a national common voters roll, regular elections and a multi-party system of democratic government, to ensure accountability, responsiveness and openness'.[26] When read with the supremacy clause, the importance of democratic principles to the state as a whole, including the administration, is evident. More specifically, section 195(1) provides that the '[p]ublic administration must be governed by the democratic values and principles enshrined in the Constitution'.[27]

As mentioned, the Constitution entrenches various conceptions of democracy. Section 17 provides for a measure of direct democracy and section 34 provides for representative democracy. Section 57(1)(*b*), regulating the internal arrangements of the National Assembly, provides that the 'National Assembly may ... make rules and orders concerning its business, with due regard to representative and participatory democracy, accountability, transparency and public involvement.' Similarly, section 59(1)(*a*), regulating public access to and involvement in the National Assembly, provides that the 'National Assembly must facilitate public involvement in the legislative and other processes of the Assembly and its committees'.[28] These provisions are expressions of participatory democracy, confirmed by the Constitutional Court: '[o]ur Constitution contemplates a democracy that is representative, and that also contains elements of participatory democracy'.[29] Similarly, section 195 requires the administration to promote participation in policy-making.[30]

The importance of participation is revealed by the form of its protection: the Constitution safeguards participation at the legislative function, even where representation is strongest at national and provincial level. Thus, the Constitution requires, in express terms, participation at the formulation of generally applicable rules. In the South African context, given the traditional, tripartite understanding of the separation of powers, a history of unchecked parliamentary sovereignty and a Diceyan legacy on administrative law, it is not surprising that rule-making and its regulation are regarded as almost solely the purview of

21 3 of 2000.
22 Section 6(2) PAJA.
23 Section 8(1) PAJA.
24 See Chapter 1 section 1.4 above.
25 For instance, the constitutional prominence of democracy is illustrated in the Preamble; democracy is also included among the Founding Provisions. More specifically, section 36 provides that '[t]he rights in the Bill of Rights may be limited only ... to the extent that the limitation is reasonable and justifiable in an open and democratic society'. Thus, democracy is a general founding principle that informs all rights.
26 Section 1(*d*) of the Constitution.
27 Emphasis added.
28 Emphasis added. Section 118 provides the same protection at the provincial level.
29 *Matatiele Municipality and Others v President of the RSA and Others (No 2)* 2007 (6) SA 477 (CC) para 40.
30 Section 195(1)(*e*) of the Constitution.

the legislature.[31] Nevertheless, sections 3 and 4 of PAJA illustrate the importance of participation in the processes of branches of state other than the legislature.[32]

### 2.3.2 The Bill of Rights

The Bill of Rights lists a number of human rights protected by the Constitution and regulates their application. However, the list is not exhaustive:

> 39. (3) The Bill of Rights does not deny the existence of any other rights or freedoms that are recognised or conferred by common law, customary law or legislation, to the extent that they are consistent with the Bill.

Concerning the conceptual framework and context of the administration and of administrative law, section 33 is of particular significance. Bear in mind that section 33 is a human right listed in the Bill of Rights and therefore sections 7, 8 and 36 are applicable. Section 33 entrenches the right to 'just administrative action':

> (1) Everyone has the right to administrative action that is lawful, reasonable and procedurally fair.
> (2) Everyone whose rights have been adversely affected by administrative action has the right to be given written reasons.
> (3) National legislation must be enacted to give effect to these rights, and must -
> (*a*) provide for the review of administrative action by a court or, where appropriate, an independent and impartial tribunal;
> (*b*) impose a duty on the state to give effect to the rights in subsections (1) and (2); and
> (*c*) promote an efficient administration.

The promulgation of PAJA gives effect to section 33(3), but does not imply that that subsection is obsolete.

### 2.3.3 Section 195 of the Constitution

Section 195 recognises the constitutional role of the public administration as such. This section lists a range of values and principles to which the administration must adhere and makes it quite clear that a very high standard of conduct is expected of the administration. The public administration is not defined in this section, though.

The justiciability of section 195 is arguable. Hoexter, relying on Skweyiya J in *Chirwa v Transnet Ltd and Others*,[33] proffers that the values and principles of section 195:

> are comparable to the founding values in s 1 of the Constitution in that they appear to impose duties without giving rise to justiciable rights ... 'the Constitutional Court has upheld the view that the section provides valuable interpretive assistance but does not confer any directly enforceable rights.'[34]

31 See Chapter 3 section 3.7.1 below on the arguments about whether rule-making by the executive should be recognised as administrative action and thus be subject to administrative-law control.

32 See Chapter 7 section 7.3 below on the procedural requirements of sections 3 and 4 of PAJA.

33 2008 (4) SA 367 (CC) paras 74–76.

34 Hoexter, C (2012) *Administrative Law in South Africa* (2nd ed) 19 (footnotes omitted). Reprinted by permission of © Juta & Company Ltd.

The Constitutional Court has recently reiterated this approach to section 195:

> This Court has on a number of occasions stated that although these values underlie our Constitution they do not give rise to independent rights outside those set out in the Bill of Rights.[35]

However, the Constitution holds that the courts '*must* declare that any law or conduct that is inconsistent with the Constitution is invalid'.[36] Thus the courts are constrained to uphold the Constitution as a whole and not only the Bill of Rights.[37] In addition, legality, based on the rule of law in section 1, is directly enforceable [38] and the courts have, for example, consistently applied section 217 to instances of public procurement.[39]

## 2.4 The doctrine of the separation of powers[40]

The separation of powers is a mainstay of modern democratic constitutions. Formulated by Montesquieu, in his classic book *De l'esprit des lois*,[41] the separation of powers has since been recognised in numerous constitutions throughout the world. The administration, as a constitutional and state entity, operates within the framework of the separation of powers, since the doctrine encompasses all state institutions. Therefore, the administration must be classified in relation to the separation of powers in order to categorise the functional and institutional aspects of the administration.

Despite its widespread constitutional entrenchment, defining the doctrine remains challenging owing to a variety of variables, including differences of interpretation. Vile formulates a 'pure doctrine' to serve as a 'benchmark' for discussing the separation of powers.[42] This pure doctrine is circumscribed thus:

> It is essential for the establishment and maintenance of political liberty that the government be divided into three branches or departments, the legislature, the executive, and the judiciary. To each of these three branches there is a corresponding identifiable function of government, legislative, executive, or judicial. Each branch of the government must be confined to the exercise of its own function and not allowed to encroach upon the functions of the other branches. Furthermore, the persons who compose these three agencies of government must be kept separate and distinct, no individual being allowed to be at the same time a member of more than one branch. In this way each of the branches will be a check to the others and no single group of people will be able to control the machinery of the State.[43]

35 *Britannia Beach Estate (Pty) Ltd and Others v Saldanha Bay Municipality* 2013 (11) BCLR 1217 (CC) para 16.

36 Section 172(1)(*a*) of the Constitution (emphasis added).

37 See section 39(3) of the Constitution.

38 *Fedsure Life Assurance Ltd and Others v Greater Johannesburg Transitional Metropolitan Council and Others* 1999 (1) SA 374 (CC); *President of the RSA v SARFU* 1999 (4) SA 147 (CC) para 27.

39 See, for instance, *Rainbow Civils CC v Minister of Transport and Public Works, Western Cape and Others* (21158/2012) [2013] ZAWCHC 3 (6 February 2013).

40 The section on the separation of powers relies heavily on those sections discussing the doctrine in Chapters 2 and 3 of the doctoral dissertation by Maree, PJH (2013) *Investigating an Alternative Administrative-Law System in South Africa* Unpublished doctoral dissertation (US).

41 Published in 1748. Although the novelty of Montesquieu's contribution to separation-of-powers theory is disputed, he is generally cited as the father of the doctrine.

42 Vile (1998) 13–14.

43 Vile (1998) 14.

The 'pure doctrine' contains four elements.[44] First, all state institutions are classified under one of three branches. Second, all state functions are classified as either executive, legislative or judicial and each branch is restricted to a single function. Third, a separation of personnel is upheld between the branches. Finally, the maintenance of the separation between institutions, functions and personnel maintains liberty because the branches keep one another in check thereby avoiding a monopoly of power. This triadic categorisation of institutions and functions is also known as the *trias politica*.[45] In terms of the 'pure doctrine' each branch is absolutely independent, functionally and institutionally, and any interference is strictly forbidden. However, in practice, a system of checks and balances tempers such a strict, compartmentalised understanding of the separation of powers. Checks and balances allows for a 'partial separation', whether of functions or personnel,[46] which is widely considered compatible with the doctrine of the separation of powers.

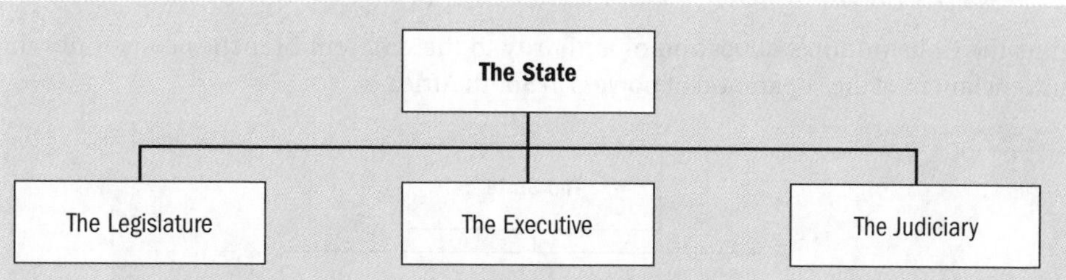


*Figure 2.1 The 'pure doctrine' of the separation of powers or* trias politica

## 2.4.1 The separation of powers in South Africa

The Constitution does not refer expressly to the separation of powers. Nevertheless, Constitutional Principle VI in Schedule 4 of the interim Constitution[47] required the inclusion of the separation of powers in the final Constitution,[48] which would not come into force without the entrenchment of the doctrine. Constitutional Principle VI provides that:

> There shall be a separation of powers between the legislature, executive and judiciary, with appropriate checks and balances to ensure accountability, responsiveness and openness.

The question whether the separation of powers was adequately entrenched in the final Constitution, despite not referring to the doctrine expressly, arose in *Ex Parte Chairperson of the Constitutional Assembly: In Re Certification of the Constitution of the Republic of South Africa, 1996*.[49] In a unanimous judgment the court found that:

> [w]hat CP VI requires is that there be a separation of powers between the legislature, executive and judiciary. It does not prescribe what form that separation should take. We have previously said that the CPs must not be interpreted with

44 Vile (1998) 14–17.
45 See Du Plessis, LM (1999) *An Introduction to Law* (3rd ed) 90; (2002) *Re-Interpretation of Statutes* 171.
46 Vile (1998) 20–21.
47 Schedule 4 of the Constitution of the Republic of South Africa Act 200 of 1993.
48 Thirty-four Constitutional Principles were agreed upon during the multiparty negotiations for the interim Constitution and the final Constitution's validity was contingent on compliance with these principles.
49 1996 (4) SA 744 (CC).

> technical rigidity. The language of CP VI is sufficiently wide to cover the type of separation required by the NT.[50]

The entrenchment of the separation of powers in the Constitution was confirmed again in *South African Association of Personal Injury Lawyers v Heath and Others.*[51] The court explained that:

> [t]he constitutions of the United States and Australia, like ours, make provision for the separation of powers by vesting the legislative authority in the legislature, the executive authority in the executive, and the judicial authority in the courts. The doctrine of separation of powers as applied in the United States is based on inferences drawn from the structure and provisions of the Constitution, rather than on an express entrenchment of the principle. In this respect, our Constitution is no different.[52]
>
> There can be no doubt that our Constitution provides for such a separation, and that laws inconsistent with what the Constitution requires in that regard, are invalid.[53]

Thus the Constitution's allocation of authority to the different branches constitutes the entrenchment of the separation of powers in South Africa.

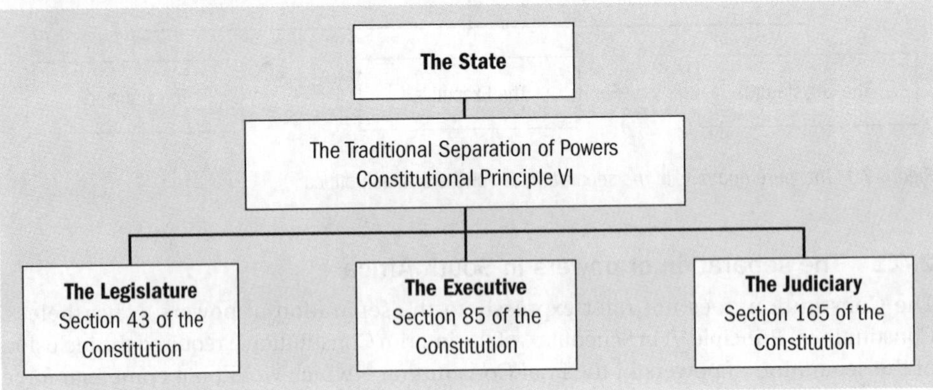


*Figure 2.2 The South African separation of powers*

**PAUSE FOR REFLECTION**

**Separation of powers in South Africa**

Consider the nature and characteristics of the separation of powers in South Africa. Which other institutions are, or should, fall under the separation of powers? Does the South African Reserve Bank fall under the separation of powers? Should it? Who holds the Reserve Bank accountable? Also consider the position of state-owned companies. Where would they fit into the scheme set out in Figure 2.2 above? Finally, consider the position of purely private entities that perform public functions on behalf of the state such as the private refuse removal company Garbage Gobblers that we noted in Chapter 1.[54] Should such companies be accommodated in Figure 2.2 above, and if so, where?

50 *Ex Parte Chairperson of the Constitutional Assembly: In Re Certification of the Constitution of the Republic of South Africa,* 1996 1996 (4) SA 744 (CC) para 113 (footnotes omitted). CP refers to Constitutional Principle; NT refers to New Text (i.e. a draft for the final Constitution).

51 See 2001 (1) SA 883 (CC) paras 21–22.

52 *Heath* para 21.

53 *Heath* para 22.

54 See Chapter 1 section 1.2.1.5.

### 2.4.2 The normative nature of the separation of powers

The wording of Constitutional Principle VI suggests that the separation of powers is not an end in itself. The purpose of the separation of powers seems to be 'to ensure accountability, responsiveness and openness'.[55]

Even Vile's pure doctrine is based on the preservation of liberty. Therefore the separation of powers is not concerned merely with realising a particular institutional structure, the *trias politica*, as an end in itself. Rather, the institutional structure prescribed by the separation of powers is a means to an end.

Gwyn describes the separation of powers in relation to 'certain desirable ends' that the doctrine aims to achieve.[56]

He identifies a number of normative objectives that have appealed to the separation of powers for protection:

> the separation of powers has been urged (1) to create greater governmental efficiency; (2) to assure that statutory law is made in the common interest; (3) to assure that the law is impartially administered and that all administrators are under the law; (4) to allow the people's representatives to call executive officials to account for the abuse of their power; and (5) to establish a balance of governmental powers.[57]

As mentioned, the 'pure doctrine' is concerned with securing liberty. Montesquieu himself reasons 'political liberty' can only be safeguarded 'when there is no abuse of power'; and '[t]o prevent this abuse, it is necessary from the very nature of things that power should be a check to power'.[58] Montesquieu argues that:

> [w]hen the legislative and executive powers are united in the same person, or in the same body of magistrates, there can be no liberty; because apprehensions may arise, lest the same monarch or senate should enact tyrannical laws, to execute them in a tyrannical manner.
>
> Again, there is no liberty, if the judiciary power be not separated from the legislative and the executive. Were it joined with the legislative, the life and liberty of the subject would be exposed to arbitrary control; for the judge would be then the legislator. Were it joined to the executive power, the judge might behave with violence and oppression.[59]

The normative nature of the separation of power provides a framework that assists the administration in structuring itself, internally and in relation to other branches of state, so as to promote accountability, efficiency and independence, without compromising rights unduly.

55 Constitutional Principle VI Schedule 4 of the Constitution of the Republic of South Africa Act 200 of 1993.

56 Gwyn, WB (1965) *The Meaning of the Separation of Powers: An Analysis of the Doctrine from its Origin to the Adoption of the United States Constitution* 5. Reprinted by permission of Tulane University. See Maree (2013) Chapter 2.

57 Gwyn (1965) 127–128 (footnote omitted).

58 Montesquieu (1959) *The Spirit of the Laws* tr Nugent, T 150. Reprinted by permission of Tulane University.

59 Montesquieu (1959) 151–152.

### 2.4.3 The public administration and the separation of powers

The administration forms part of the executive branch. Therefore the mechanisms that safeguard normative objectives, such as accountability and the balance of power, are those aimed at the executive as a whole, including the administration.

Section 85 of the Constitution vests the national executive authority in the President and the members of Cabinet. The core of the executive function, at least according to this provision, is the formulation of policy and legislation and their implementation, including the coordination of departments. However, the fundamental differences between the formulation of policy and legislation and their implementation are obscured by lumping them under one branch and function, not that the classification itself is the source of the problem.

The exponential growth of the administration is a relatively recent and sudden phenomenon. Quite simply, the classic separation of powers, including the basic architecture the doctrine has entailed, was settled well before this phenomenon. Modern conceptions of the administrative function, the administration and administrative law only made their appearance well after the classic formulation of the separation of powers. Montesquieu himself reasons 'political liberty' can only be safeguarded 'when there is no abuse of power'; and '[t]o prevent this abuse, it is necessary from the very nature of things that power should be a check to power'.[60] Ackerman adds that the separation of powers has not incorporated these developments and the administrative function, as mentioned, has simply been categorised as executive. Vile critiques this conflation of policy formulation and administration:

> The modern world is characterized by the development of what has been described as the 'administrative state.' Bureaucracy has been with us, of course, for more than two hundred years, but the modern administrative state exhibits such complexity of structures and such a proliferation of rules that the earlier conception of an "executive" consisting of a body of civil servants putting into effect, under the direction of ministers, the commands of the legislature is no longer tenable. The distinction between political leaders and bureaucrats has simultaneously become sharper and more confused. Sharper because the administrative state has taken on an autonomy of its own—it is only marginally under the control of its political masters at any point in time.[61]

Thus Vile questions the capacity of politicians to control the administration and suggests they are not actually accountable to parliament in this regard. This reality is exacerbated by strict adherence to a triadic separation of powers.

As a result, Ackerman contends that a reassesment of the *trias politica* is overdue.[62] He argues that new institutions, playing a significant role at state level, cannot be classified under the three functions of the separation of powers. This does not imply that the separation of powers is obsolete, though, but that the doctrine has to evolve to reflect these developments: state power and its control are distributed differently than in Montesquieu's day. Therefore, dogmatic adherence to three branches and functions must fall away; the number of branches in itself should be irrelevant.

---

60 Montesquieu (1959) *The Spirit of the Laws* tr Nugent, T 150. Reprinted by permission of Tulane University.

61 Vile (1998) 399–400.

62 Ackerman (2010) 129. Similarly, Harlow and Rawlings claim that 'given the present state of fusion between executive and Parliament, the idea of a constitution held in balance by triadic division of functions is quite simply untenable', Harlow, C & Rawlings, R (2009) *Law and Administration* (3rd ed) 23.

Therefore, Vile proposes adopting the term 'policy branch' to designate that part of the government or executive concerned primarily with the formulation of policy and legislation;[63] those institutions responsible for the implementation of legislation and policy are classified under the administration. Vile's proposition of a separation of at least four branches is adopted by the authors, in order to distinguish between the nature of policy formulation and implementation and to counter disproved assumptions of parliamentary control over the executive and administration, of ministerial or executive control over implementation, and of the adequacy of judicial review as the only, or even primary, form of administrative law.

Would a separation of powers accommodating at least four branches be inconsistent with the Constitution? Notably, the Constitution does not define the separation of powers. Constitutional Principle VI requires three branches, but this requirement can be regarded as a minimum configuration. Support for such a view can be found in the Constitution. Chapter 10 of the Constitution expressly recognises the constitutional role of the public administration and civil service. Section 195 requires that the administration 'be governed by the democractic values and principles enshrined in the Constitution'; more specifically section 195 imposes values and principles that govern the administration, including '[s]ervices must be provided impartially, fairly, equitably and without bias'[64] and '[p]ublic administration must be accountable'.[65] These principles are congruent with the normative objectives of the separation of powers.

In addition, the separation of powers per se is a flexible doctrine.[66] The Constitutional Court found, in response to the complaint that members of Cabinet simultaneously serving in the National Assembly infringes the separation of powers, that:

> [a]s the separation of powers doctrine is not a fixed or rigid constitutional doctrine, it is given expression in many different forms and made subject to checks and balances of many kinds.[67]

Therefore, the tripartite division is not set in stone. The content of the separation of powers is also contingent on context, including constitutional development:[68]

> The practical application of the doctrine of separation of powers is influenced by the history, conventions and circumstances of the different countries in which it is applied.[69]

On the whole, the separation of powers is normative, flexible and dynamic. Given the nature and scale of the modern administration, the South African separation of powers should incorporate the administration as a separate branch and function.

---

63 Vile (1998) 400.

64 Section 195(1)(*d*).

65 Section 195(1)(*f*).

66 'What CP VI requires is that there be a separation of powers between the legislature, executive and judiciary. It does not prescribe what form that separation should take. We have previously said that the CPs must not be interpreted with technical rigidity.' (*Certification of the Constitution* para 113).

67 *Certification of the Constitution* para 111.

68 'Within the broad requirement of separation of powers and appropriate checks and balances, the CA was afforded a large degree of latitude in shaping the independence and interdependence of government branches. The model adopted reflects the historical circumstances of our constitutional development.' (*Certification of the Constitution* para 112).

69 *Heath* para 24.

In *De Lange v Smuts*[70] Ackermann J said:

> I have no doubt that over time our Courts will develop a distinctively South African model of separation of powers, one that fits the particular system of government provided for in the Constitution and that reflects a delicate balancing, informed both by South Africa's history and its new dispensation, between the need, on the one hand, to control government by separating powers and enforcing checks and balances and, on the other, to avoid diffusing power so completely that the government is unable to take timely measures in the public interest.[71]

The essential concern of the separation of powers is not form and traditional classification, but rather a contextual, institutional arrangement that promotes the normative objectives imposed by the Constitution. Mechanisms that prevent the overconcentration of power and promote accountability and the rule of law are purposes of the separation of powers, rather than classifying new institutions performing new functions in changed circumstances under three categories formulated centuries ago. However, as Ackerman suggests, adding a fourth branch to the separation of powers does not resolve the doctrine's content once and for all. Consider, for instance, the role played by the so-called 'Chapter 9 institutions' in securing constitutional democracy, which have been described as the 'accountability branch'. The emphasis remains, not on the number of institutions, but on institutional design that promotes normative objectives.

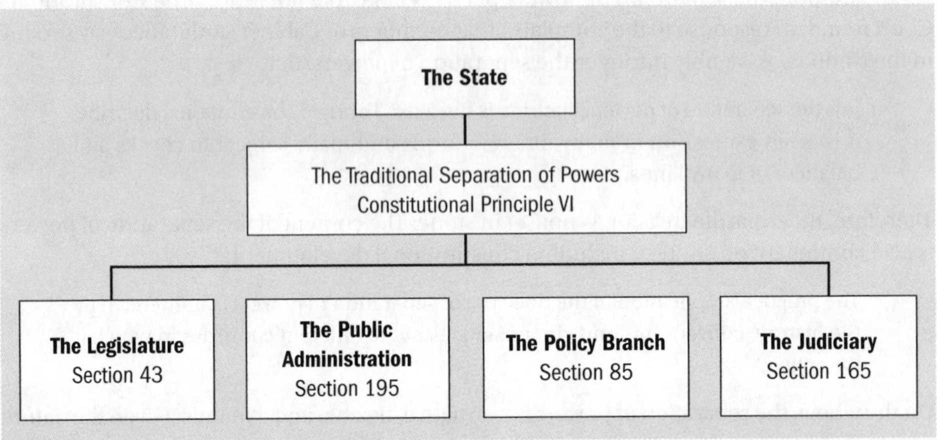


*Figure 2.3 A modern doctrine of the separation of powers*

## 2.5 Identifying the administration

With the proliferation of democratic states during the twentieth century, certain state institutions and arrangements became commonplace. National executives comprised of the majority political party, representative parliaments and independent judiciaries are no longer unusual or controversial; these branches of state are typically organised in terms of the doctrine of separation of powers. Thus each enjoys functional and institutional independence.

70 1998 (3) SA 785 (CC).

71 *De Lange v Smuts NO and Others* 1998 (3) SA 785 (CC) para 60.

Nevertheless, this seemingly simple and uncontested structure can obscure the nature of modern states, which is complex and continuously changing. Although the broad terms of the modern democratic state seem established, fundamental institutional vicissitudes also typify the twentieth century; these developments cannot all be reduced to the triadic narrative of the separation of powers, as explained in section 2.4.3 above.

The 'rise of the administrative state' is an apt and pertinent example of such fundamental change. Although the administrative state is not limited to the administration, the administration is certainly an essential component of the administrative state. Therefore, the nature of the administration, defining the administration, and identifying the South African administration are discussed in this section.

What is the administration? There is no definitive answer to this question. The term is neither defined by the Constitution nor general legislation, nor is it a technical legal term. Nevertheless, the absence of an incontrovertible definition for the administration does not imply that the term is not useful. Several approaches exist to identify administrative authorities. The first is the institutional approach. This approach holds that certain institutions are administrative authorities by virtue of the nature or identity of the institution. For example, certain institutions are traditionally described as part of the administration, such as national departments. Other institutions are regarded as administrative authorities in certain instances, such as Eskom, and as a private actor in other instances. Yet other institutions are not regarded as part of the administration, but are subject to administrative law. This reveals at least two approaches: the institutional approach and the functional approach. The institutional approach holds that certain institutions are in themselves subject to administrative law. The functional approach holds that the application of administrative law is subject to the nature of the function performed. Perhaps the simplest accurate definition for administrative authority is the following: administrative authorities are primarily concerned with the implementation of legislation.

This section attempts to identify the so-called 'administration', but the impossibility of providing an all-encompassing definition serves as the point of departure. The nature of the administration is discussed and since the administration has both institutional and functional characteristics[72] a list of institutions is inadequate. Certain institutions, such as departments, are typically regarded as part of the administration, though. Nevertheless, departments themselves differ from each other in functional, institutional and regulatory terms. For instance, the Public Protector will in certain circumstances qualify as an administrator, for the purposes of PAJA. In such circumstances, the administration will consist of an organ tasked with promoting accountability and constitutional democracy.[73] In many cases the subject of the Public Protector's investigations will be administrative authorities,[74] thus the administration itself. Therefore, appreciating that the administration consists of a conglomeration of widely divergent institutions and actors is essential to the study of administrative law.

## 2.5.1 The rise of the administrative state

During the twentieth century, the role of the nation state changed dramatically. Historically the state was primarily responsible for national security, the creation of law and the

72 See the definition for 'administrative action', section 1 of PAJA and the definition for 'organ of state', section 239 of the Constitution. Both public and private actors can perform administrative action and the definition of administrative action itself bears institutional and functional aspects.

73 Chapter 9 of the Constitution.

74 See 182(1)(*a*) of the Constitution.

maintenance of law and order within the state. This is reflected in John Locke and Montesquieu's classification of state functions. However, the Industrial Revolution served as a catalyst for a rapidly expanding, increasingly pro-active state. This process was already well on its way in 1941 when Sir Cecil Carr noted that:

> [w]e nod approvingly today when someone tells us that, whereas the State used to be merely policeman, judge and protector, it has now become schoolmaster, doctor, house-builder, road-maker, town-planner, public utility supplier and all the rest of it. The contrast is no recent discovery. De Tocqueville observed in 1866 that the State 'everywhere interferes more than it did; it regulates more undertakings, and undertakings of a lesser kind; and it gains a firmer footing every day, about, around and above all private persons, to assist, to advise, and to coerce them' (*Oeuvres*, III, 501). Nassau William Senior, a Benthamite ten years older than Chadwick, a colleague of his on the original Poor Law Commission, had justified this tendency. A government, he thinks, must do whatever conduces to the welfare of the governed (the utilitarian theory); it will make mistakes, but non-interference may be an error too; one can be passively wrong as well as actively wrong. One might go back much earlier still to Aristotle, who said that the city-state or partnership-community comes into existence to protect life and remains in existence to protect a proper way of living. What is the proper standard? That is an age-long issue which is still a burning question of political controversy. The problems of administrative law are approached in the light of that fire. Those who dislike the statutory delegation of legislative power or the statutory creation of a non-judicial tribunal will often be those who dislike the policy behind the statute and seek to fight it at every stage. On the one side are those who want to step on the accelerator, on the other those who want to apply the brake.[75]

In South Africa, the inclusion of socio-economic rights in the Constitution was hotly contested and the debate fits neatly into Carr's description of choosing to increase or decrease state interference. With their entrenchment in the final Constitution, the role of the state has increased once again. The state must now provide access to education, housing and health care. Extensive mandates are imposed by rights such as the right to housing, which have introduced positive obligations. Predominantly the administration is responsible for the realisation of these mandates. Thus the process identified by Carr in 1941 continues into the twenty-first century.

### 2.5.2 The term 'the administration'

Although one can assert confidently that the administration has expanded rapidly and extensively, this observation does not resolve the questions 'what is the administration?' and 'how does one identify the administration?'

The administration is not a technical legal term; there is no generally applicable definition of the administration.[76] Therefore, from a legal perspective this term is fraught with ambiguity, inconsistency and sometimes inaccuracy. Yet politicians, jurists and journalists refer to the administration on a daily basis. The term seems to refer to a single entity. Common usage of the term supports this view: consider 'the Obama administration'. However, in reality 'administration' is a collective noun, not for a collective of broadly similar

75 Carr, C (1941) *Concerning English Administrative Law* 10–11. London: Humphrey Milford, Oxford University Press. Reprinted by permission of Oxford University Press.

76 Baxter, L (1984) *Administrative Law* 98–99.

institutions, such as the courts constituting the judiciary for example, but for a vast number of organs, divergent in function, nature and size.

A distinction needs to be drawn between administrative law and the administration in an institutional sense. Broadly speaking, administrative law regulates the performance of public functions. Therefore, administrative law does not apply whenever the administration acts, though it often does. Furthermore, administrative law also often applies when the administration is not involved, but the function performed by a private entity has a public (administrative) nature. Similarly, private law often applies to actions performed by the administration. Nevertheless, historically the administration is at the heart of the development of administrative law and the administration merits close scrutiny regardless of the application of private or public, specifically administrative, law. In addition, on any particular occasion where the administration acts, a matrix of legal rules, both public and private, are operating. For example, where an administrative organ concludes a contract the legal instrument itself is traditionally classified as a private law instrument; however, administrative law may very well regulate the contractual relationship in addition to the private law of contract. The power of the administration to conclude a specific contract may stem from public law (for example, legislation empowers a particular entity to conclude contracts) and the very existence of the administrative organ is established by the operation of law. Thus even in a classic private law context, classifying a particular situation as purely private or purely public is rather artificial.

### 2.5.3 The South African administration

As indicated, the administration bears no general legal definition; the presence of the administration does not imply the application of administrative law. This is relevant since PAJA refers to 'administrator' which is defined as 'an organ of state or any natural or juristic person taking administrative action'.[77] 'Organ of state', in turn, is defined by section 239 of the Constitution which entrenches the functional approach. The functional approach operates in addition to the institutional approach: organ of state may also refer to 'any department of state or administration in the national, provincial or local sphere of government'.[78] Therefore, for the purposes of PAJA 'administrator' may refer to a private person. However, in this section national administration refers to the South African administration in an institutional sense, that is, those institutions primarily concerned with the implementation of legislation and policy as such and created for this very purpose.

The administration can be divided into three spheres: national, provincial and local.

#### 2.5.3.1 National departments

The term 'department' is ubiquitous. The President establishes departments as head of the national executive:

> The President has the powers entrusted by the Constitution and legislation, including those necessary to perform the functions of Head of State and head of the national executive.[79]

77 Section 1(*ii*) of PAJA.
78 Section 239(*a*) of the Constitution.
79 Section 84(1) of the Constitution.

More specifically, section 85 of the Constitution provides that:

> (1) The executive authority of the Republic is vested in the President.
> (2) The President exercises the executive authority, together with the other members of the Cabinet, by -
> (*a*) implementing national legislation except where the Constitution or an Act of Parliament provides otherwise;
> (*b*) developing and implementing national policy;
> (*c*) co-ordinating the functions of state departments and administrations;
> (*d*) preparing and initiating legislation; and
> (*e*) performing any other executive function provided for in the Constitution or in national legislation.

This section illustrates that the term executive, in its overarching sense, refers both to the formulation of policy as well as the implementation of policy and legislation. However, the question as to what constitutes the administration and its corresponding function is left unexplored.

The President lists the national departments in Schedule 1 of the Public Service Act, 1994 (Proclamation 103 of 1994).[80] The President is empowered by section 7(5)(*a*) to determine the number and functions of departments:

> (5) Subject to section 7A and the principles contained in section 195 of the Constitution, the President may by proclamation in the *Gazette*—
> (*a*) on the advice of the Minister amend Schedule 1 so as to establish or abolish any national department, designate such department and the head thereof or amend any such designation.

The list changes regularly: even though the ANC has been in power since South Africa's first democratic elections, the number of departments has varied continually. However, overall the number has been increasing steadily, in line with the 'rise of the administrative state'. With the promulgation of the Public Service Act, 1994 (Proclamation 103 of 1994), in terms of section 237(3) of the interim Constitution,[81] Schedule 1 listed twenty-six departments.[82] In 2009 shortly after Zuma's election as president, Schedule 1 was amended to list over forty departments.[83] Thus not only the number of departments changes regularly, but also the functions associated with each department. It is virtually impossible to formulate a pointed description of the nature of all departments, since some are concerned with providing services and others with regulation, for example. It is also beyond the scope of this chapter to provide a description of each. However, selected examples of departments are discussed below in order to identify those aspects relevant to understanding departments in general: the department's constitutional and legislative framework, its institutional structure, and its powers and functions.

80 Although referred to as an Act, the Public Service Act is not numbered. On MyLexisNexis the Public Service Act is listed as Act 103 of 1994, but this is erroneous as 103 refers to the number of the proclamation (see *GG* 15791 GN 103 of 03.06.1994).

81 Constitution of the Republic of South Africa Act 200 of 1993. Section 237 of Act 200 of 1993 is still in force.

82 The number twenty-six includes the National Defence Force, but does not count the Provincial Administrations which are also listed in Schedule 1.

83 Not counting the Offices of the Premier.

### 2.5.3.2 National department: The Department of Water and Sanitation

To discuss every department would be beyond the scope of this textbook. Therefore the Department of Water and Sanitation's structure and regulation are set out for illustrative purposes. It is listed in Schedule 1 of the Public Service Act and is a clear example of an administrative authority.

#### Constitutional and legislative framework

Section 27 of the Bill of Rights provides that:

> (1) Everyone has the right to have access to –
> (*a*) health care services, including reproductive health care;
> (*b*) sufficient food and water; and
> (*c*) social security, including, if they are unable to support themselves and their dependants, appropriate social assistance.
> (2) The state must take reasonable legislative and other measures, within its available resources, to achieve the progressive realisation of each of these rights.
> (3) No one may be refused emergency medical treatment.

Thus, access to 'sufficient' water is entrenched in the Constitution as a human right. Not only is the state[84] obliged not to interfere with citizens' access to water, but it must also take positive steps to promote access to water.[85] Specifically, a positive obligation is imposed upon Parliament to create legislation that safeguards the right to access to water. Failure to do so would be unconstitutional and invalid,[86] subject to the limitations clause.[87] Schedule 5 of the Constitution lists the functional areas of concurrent national and provincial legislative competence. Part B, setting out national and provincial legislative authority over local governments, lists water and sanitation services.

In terms of section 44:

> (2) Parliament may intervene, by passing legislation in accordance with section 76(1), with regard to a matter falling within a functional area listed in Schedule 4, when it is necessary –
> (*a*) to maintain national security;
> (*b*) to maintain economic unity;
> (*c*) to maintain essential national standards;
> (*d*) to establish minimum standards required for the rendering of services; or
> (*e*) to prevent unreasonable action taken by a province which is prejudicial to the interests of another province or to the country as a whole.

Thus, the Constitution affords Parliament the authorisation to interfere with provincial and local mandates in the public interest.

In line with section 27 of the Constitution, Parliament has created two statutes to regulate South Africa's water supply and distribution: the National Water Act[88] and the Water Services Act.[89]

---

84 Note the use of the word 'state', which is not defined by the Constitution. See Currie & De Waal (2001) 4–6, 228–229. In general, the state refers to a concept broader than executive, government or administration. In this sense the choice of the word state has far-reaching implications.

85 Sections 2, 7 and 27(2) of the Constitution.

86 Sections 2 and 172 of the Constitution.

87 Section 36 of the Constitution.

88 36 of 1998.

89 108 of 1997.

These statutes set out the corresponding powers and functions of the Minister and administrative authorities. Consistent with the principles of the rule of law and legality, which are constitutionally protected, these constitutional and statutory provisions provide the legal framework within which the Department of Water and Sanitation must act. Moreover, especially the constitutional provisions necessitate the existence of some administrative entity tasked with delivering water services to members of the public. Therefore, any departmental act or decision should always be evaluated in the light of these legal sources as a minimum requirement.

#### Institutional structure

The Department of Water and Sanitation,[90] its appellation since 2014, is a national department. The Ministry for Water and Sanitation heads the department. Therefore the political head of the department is the Minister for Water and Sanitation. The administrative head of the department is the Director-General for the department.[91]

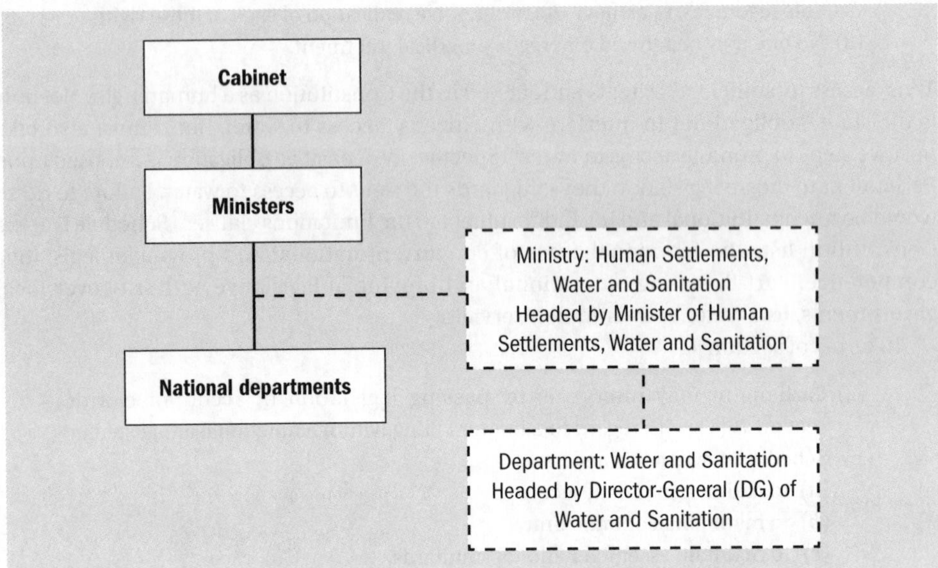


*Figure 2.4 The constitutional context and structure of the Department of Water and Sanitation*

Figure 2.4 illustrates the constitutional context and structure of the Department of Water and Sanitation. The top tier of Figure 2.4 consists of the Cabinet, which is formed by the President shortly after an election. The President decides which Ministries to create and each Ministry will be headed by a Minister responsible for that Ministry. In this case the Minister of Humans Settlements, Water and Sanitation is the political head of the Ministry of Humans Settlements, Water and Sanitation. These decisions are promulgated in Schedule 1 of the Public Service Act. The Minister is also the political head of the Department of Water and Sanitation, which falls within the corresponding Ministry. The administrative head of the Department is the Director-General of Water and Sanitation. In general, the Ministry

90 GN 43 in *GG* 37817 of 08.07.2014. Since 1994, this department has been known as the Department of Water Affairs and Forestry, the Department of Water and Environmental Affairs, and the Department of Water and Sanitation.

91 GN 43 in *GG* 37817 of 08.07.2014.

will formulate policies and propose legislation related to water affairs and the department will implement those policies and statutes. This illustrates the dual nature of the executive, which forms the basis of the rationale for Vile's call for a separation of powers of four branches: the executive is divided into the policy branch and the administration. The entire structure depicted by Figure 2.4 operates within the constitutional framework discussed above. Thus, section 27 of the Constitution, in particular, informs the functions performed by the Minister, the Ministry as a whole, the Director-General and the Department of Water and Sanitation.

### Power and functions

The department describes its role broadly as follows:

> The Department of Water and Sanitation is the custodian of South Africa's water resources. It is primarily responsible for the formulation and implementation of policy governing this sector. It also has an overriding responsibility for water services provided by local government.
>
> While striving to ensure that all South Africans gain access to clean water and safe sanitation, the water sector also promotes effective and efficient water resources management to ensure sustainable economic and social development.[92]

Thus, one sees the political and administrative dimensions of the department itself: on the one hand the department must formulate policy on South Africa's water resources; on the other hand, the department must implement that policy. For instance, in 1994 the Department of Water Affairs and Forestry, as it was then known, issued the White Paper on Water Supply and Sanitation Policy.[93]

The White Paper sets out guidelines for the provision of water services.[94] In the Basic Service Provision Policy the White Paper determines guidelines for water supply.[95] The basic water supply is a daily allowance of 25 litres per person.[96] Thus the guideline set by this policy document fixes a particular amount of water as a minimum for certain, identified needs. This illustrates the political role played by the administration in formulating policy, including the responsible Minister.

However, the administration also implements policy and legislation. Section 9 of the Water Services Act[97] empowers the Minister to 'prescribe compulsory national standards' on the management of water services; sections 49, 61, and 66 empower the Minister to issue regulations on various matters; the Minister may also issue directives and guidelines and

---

92 https://www.dwa.gov.za/about.aspx (accessed 07.08.2020).

93 Department of Water Affairs and Forestry *Water Supply and Sanitation Policy, White Paper: Water – An Indivisible National Asset* Cape Town, November 1994. Available at: https://www.dwa.gov.za/Documents/Policies/WSSP.pdf (accessed 07.08.2020).

94 According to the White Paper:
[g]uidelines are intended to assist decision making whilst standards are enforceable absolute limits. The rigid application of guidelines or inappropriate standards can have the opposite effect to that intended. An example would be the closure of 'sub-standard' water supplies which forced communities to revert to sources of even worse quality.
Given that they are chosen to be the minimum needed to ensure health, the levels of service presented below should be seen as minimum standards to be applied in publicly funded schemes unless a relaxation has been specifically approved. This does not mean that higher standards cannot be applied.

95 White Paper 14–15.

96 15. 'This is considered to be the minimum required for direct consumption, for the preparation of food and for personal hygiene. It is not considered to be adequate for a full, healthy and productive life which is why it is considered as a minimum.'

97 108 of 1997.

may delegate certain functions.[98] However, the Minister may not delegate the power to make regulations.[99] These are empowering provisions: they grant powers to the Minister, some of which must be implemented, others which may be implemented. In other words, the exercise of some powers is mandatory, others are discretionary.

The Minister has exercised the power to issue regulations in terms of the Water Services Act [100] on several occasions.[101] In the regulations issued by GNR. 509 of 8 June 2001, the Minister prescribed compulsory national standards in terms of section 9(1), mentioned above, and section 73(1)(*j*). Section 3 of the regulations reads:

> 3. The minimum standard for basic water supply services is—
> (*a*) the provision of appropriate education in respect of effective water use; and
> (*b*) *a minimum quantity of potable water of 25 litres per person per day* or 6 kilolitres per household per month—
> (i) at a minimum flow rate of not less than 10 litres per minute;
> (ii) within 200 metres of a household; and
> (iii) with an effectiveness such that no consumer is without a supply for more than seven full days in any year.[102]

Thus, the Minister gave legal force to the White Paper in issuing these regulations. Simultaneously the Minister implemented the legislation in issuing the regulations by exercising the powers granted by the statute. However, instead of formulating policy, the promulgation of regulations amounts to the implementation of legislation and, in this case, of policy also. The administration itself is then tasked with implementing those regulations, in this case the Department of Water and Sanitation and provincial and local administrations.

***Mazibuko and Others v City of Johannesburg* 2010 (4) SA 1 (CC)**

**From policy formulation to the implementation of legislation to litigation**

In the case of *Mazibuko*, a local authority, the City of Johannesburg, was the party responsible for implementing the Water Services Act[103] in Phiri, Soweto. The Act and its regulations came under scrutiny in the context of their application by the municipality. Thus we see the White Paper's impact: it was initially formulated at national level by a national department, then formalised by means of regulation and later applied by a local administrative authority in a particular context.

The legal question before the court in *Mazibuko* was whether the provision of 25 litres per person per day, or 6 kilolitres per household, by the City of Johannesburg to the residents of Phiri was reasonable.[104] The decision was challenged on the grounds of inconsistency with section 27 of the Constitution, lawfulness, procedural fairness, and administrative-law reasonableness.[105] The court had to decide whether or not the adoption of water plans by the Johannesburg City Council qualified as administrative action. The court found that:

> [w]hen the Johannesburg City Council adopted the Business Plan of Johannesburg Water which includes operation Gcin'amanzi, it was exercising executive powers to determine how services

98 Sections 41 and 73(1)(*h*) of the Water Services Act 108 of 1997, respectively.
99 Section 74(2)(*a*) of the Water Services Act 108 of 1997.
100 108 of 1997.
101 See GN R509 of 08.06.2001, GN R652 of 20.07.2001 and GN R980 of 19.07.2002.
102 Emphasis added.
103 108 of 1997.
104 See Liebenberg, S (2010) *Socio-Economic Rights Adjudication under a Transformative Constitution* 467.
105 Liebenberg (2010) 466; Quinot, G (2010) Substantive Reasoning in Administrative-Law Adjudication *Constitutional Court Review* 3:111 at 125–126.

> should be implemented in the City. The applicants' argument that that decision constituted administrative action cannot therefore be sustained.[106]

*Mazibuko* demonstrates the confluence of public administration, policy and legal regulation. The court characterises operation Gcin'amanzi as the exercise of an executive power, within the meaning of section 1(i)(*cc*) of PAJA. As discussed, the term 'executive' is not very useful in characterising particular incidences of public power. Regardless of the merits of the court's reasoning, the distinction between broad and narrow policy formulation does not appear to have been applied.

#### 2.5.3.3 The Ministry of Finance and its administrative authorities

The Department of Water and Sanitation serves as an illustration of a single department under the political supervision of a single Ministry. In the case of the Ministry of Finance, several departments[107] and administrative authorities are placed under one Ministry's oversight. This effectively illustrates the difference in institutional architecture between departments and ministries, with departments forming the core of the administration while ministries represent the executive from an institutional perspective.

The Ministry of Finance plays a crucial role in governing the economic affairs of South Africa:

> The Ministry of Finance is at the heart of South Africa's economic and fiscal policy development. The Minister of Finance and Deputy Minister of Finance are responsible for a range of state entities that aim to advance economic growth and development, and to strengthen South Africa's democracy.[108]

Strictly speaking, the Ministry of Finance is part of the executive in the political sense and therefore not an administrative authority. The Ministry is headed by the Minister of Finance and is typically involved in formulating policy, a function which is not subject to administrative law as we shall see in Chapter 3. However, the Ministry is also the political head of several administrative authorities and thus the ultimate authority for the administrative power exercised by those entities. Each institution is regulated by a dedicated statute. Although these institutions enjoy a large degree of independence it is important also to note their interdependence and position within the Finance Ministry. As an example, the Ministry of Finance illustrates that 'the administration', or that part of the state subject to administrative law, cannot be captured neatly within a single, institutional template.

##### Institutional structure

The administrative authorities that fall within the Ministry of Finance include the Treasury, the South African Revenue Service, the Public Investment Corporation, Statistics South Africa, the Financial Intelligence Centre and the Financial Services Board.

106 *Mazibuko* para 131. See Quinot (2010) 125–126, 135–136.

107 The Treasury and Statistics South Africa are both listed in Schedule 1 of the Public Service Act.

108 National Treasury 'Information about the Ministry' http://www.treasury.gov.za/ministry/info.aspx (accessed 07.08.2020).

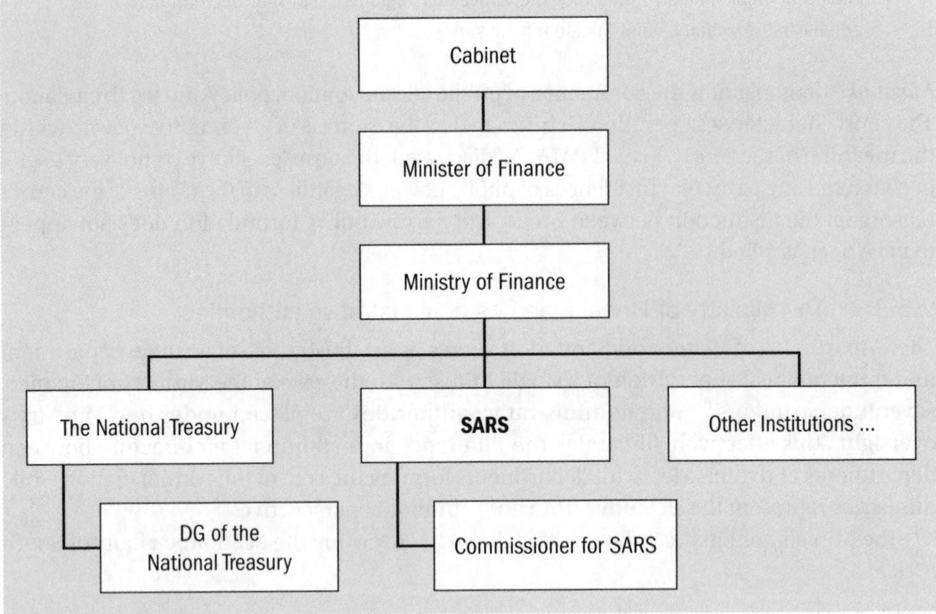


*Figure 2.5 The institutional structure of the Ministry of Finance*

### National Treasury

Section 216 of the Constitution provides that:

(1) National legislation must establish a National Treasury and prescribe measures to ensure both transparency and expenditure control in each sphere of government, by introducing -
   (*a*) generally recognised accounting practice;
   (*b*) uniform expenditure classifications; and
   (*c*) uniform treasury norms and standards.

(2) The National Treasury must enforce compliance with the measures established in terms of subsection (1), and may stop the transfer of funds to an organ of state if that organ of state commits a serious or persistent material breach of those measures.

The Treasury is responsible for ensuring that organs of state comply with sound financial practices as regulated by statute. Therefore the role of the Treasury is unique in the sense that it regulates the funding and expenditure of the state as a whole, of all spheres of government, including other national departments. In other words, this particular national department [109] has the critical function of overseeing the financial prudence of all national departments as well as all spheres of government. In addition, the Treasury has the discretionary power to withhold funds to sanction 'serious or persistent material [breaches]'.[110]

109 See Schedule 1 Public Service Act.
110 Section 216(2) of the Constitution.

As mentioned, the Constitution obliges Parliament to establish a National Treasury.[111] The Public Finance Management Act[112] (PFMA) gives effect to this constitutional duty.

Section 5 of the Act provides the following:

> 5(1) A National Treasury is hereby established, consisting of—
> (*a*) the Minister, who is the head of the Treasury; and
> (*b*) the national department or departments responsible for financial and fiscal matters.

The PFMA also provides that:

> [t]he National Treasury is in charge of the National Revenue Fund and must enforce compliance with the provisions of section 213 of the Constitution.[113]

In turn, section 213(1) of the Constitution provides that:

> [t]here is a National Revenue Fund into which all money received by the national government must be paid, except money reasonably excluded by an Act of Parliament.

All monies collected by SARS must be paid into the National Revenue Fund.[114]

According to section 2 of the PFMA the purpose of the statute:

> is to secure transparency, accountability, and sound management of the revenue, expenditure, assets and liabilities of the institutions to which this Act applies.

The wide scope of responsibility accorded to Treasury is illustrated by section 6, which lists the functions and powers of the National Treasury. The National Treasury must manage the government's fiscal and macroeconomic policy, prepare the budget, safeguard sound financial practice etc. Thus the PFMA creates the institution of the National Treasury and determines its nature and functions. As indicated, the Treasury has the unique function of overseeing the financial management of other departments. The powers and functions listed in section 6 include the management of financial and other resources, the formulation of rules and their implementation as well as 'anything further that is necessary to fulfil its responsibilities effectively'.[115] The wording of these powers and functions is very broad. However, more specific content is given to these provisions elsewhere in the Act.

Section 36(1) of the PFMA, for instance, requires that:

> [e]very department and every constitutional institution must have an accounting officer.

An accounting officer is defined as 'a person mentioned in section 36'.[116] Section 36(2) nominates the head of a department or the chief executive officer of a constitutional institution as accounting officers. Section 38 lists the functions of accounting officers. The functions allocated to accounting officers are numerous, significant and far-reaching: their general responsibilities include the management of their department's finances and assets in line with certain normative objectives such as efficiency, transparency and economical use of funds and assets. In effect, section 38 subsumes many of the tasks listed in section 6.

---

111 Section 216(1) of the Constitution.
112 1 of 1999.
113 Section 11(1) PFMA.
114 Section 12(1) PFMA.
115 Section 6(2)(*g*) PFMA.
116 Section 1 PFMA.

Thus, much of the responsibility imposed on the National Treasury is thereby channelled to individual departments, with the National Treasury overseeing these functions.

The Local Government: Municipal Finance Management Act [117] identifies accounting officers at the local level. The definition in section 1 of the Act provides that the accounting officer:

> (*a*) in relation to a municipality, means the municipal official referred to in section 60; or
> (*b*) in relation to a municipal entity, means the official of the entity referred to in section 93, and includes a person acting as the accounting officer.[118]

Section 60 of the Local Government: Municipal Finance Management Act [119] provides that:

> [t]he municipal manager of a municipality is the accounting officer of the municipality for the purposes of this Act, and, as accounting officer, must—
> (*a*) exercise the functions and powers assigned to an accounting officer in terms of this Act; and
> (*b*) provide guidance and advice on compliance with this Act to—
> (i) the political structures, political office-bearers and officials of the municipality; and
> (ii) any municipal entity under the sole or shared control of the municipality.

Section 93 of this Act provides that:

> [t]he chief executive officer of a municipal entity appointed in terms of section 93J of the Municipal Systems Act is the accounting officer of the entity.

### The South African Revenue Service

SARS is not listed in Schedule 1 of the Public Service Act. Therefore SARS is not a national department. However, SARS performs a critical national function of a quintessentially public nature: collecting taxes.

SARS was established by the South African Revenue Service Act [120] and is therefore a so-called 'creature of statute'.[121] SARS is largely autonomous.[122] The head of SARS is the Commissioner for the South African Revenue Service;[123] the Commissioner is accountable to the Minister of Finance.

SARS is primarily concerned with the collection of taxation and administering the tax system by means of the implementation of statutes, such as the Public Finance Management Act.[124] The monies collected by SARS are paid into the National Revenue Fund.[125] Since SARS

117 56 of 2003.
118 Section 1 of the Local Government: Municipal Finance Management Act 56 of 2003.
119 56 of 2003.
120 34 of 1997.
121 Section 2 of the South African Revenue Service Act 34 of 1997 reads as follows: 'The South African Revenue Service is hereby established as an organ of state within the public administration, but as an institution outside the public service.'
122 See section 5 of the South African Revenue Service Act 34 of 1997.
123 Section 6(1) of the South African Revenue Service Act 34 of 1997.
124 1 of 1999. See Schedule 1 to the South African Revenue Service Act 34 of 1997, which lists the statutes administered by the Commissioner.
125 See section 213 of the Constitution.

is primarily concerned with the implementation of legislation and policy SARS can be regarded as an administrative authority, even if it is not classified as a department.[126]

The functions and powers of SARS and the Commissioner are set out in the South African Revenue Service Act.[127] Section 3 provides that:

> SARS's objectives are the efficient and effective—
> (*a*) collection of revenue; and
> (*b*) control over the import, export, manufacture, movement, storage or use of certain goods.

SARS administers a number of statutes including the South African Revenue Service Act,[128] the Value-Added Tax Act,[129] and the Customs and Excise Act.[130] The example of SARS demonstrates that a narrow focus on the national departments listed in Schedule 1 of the Public Service Act is a limited approach to determining which institutions form part of the public administration or qualify as administrative authorities. In fact, should one follow that approach only, one would exclude the institution that collects the state's revenue from the purview of the public administration, an absurd outcome.

#### 2.5.3.4 State-owned company: Eskom SOC Ltd.[131]

Eskom is a public utility responsible for the provision of electricity. In terms of the Eskom Conversion Act,[132] Eskom was converted from a statutory body to a public company.[133] Although Eskom is described as a public company having a share capital in terms of the Companies Act,[134] the state is the sole shareholder.[135] In terms of the Act, Eskom is a state-owned company (SOC), a category of profit company.[136] Section 11(3)(*c*)(iv) requires every state-owned company to append 'SOC Ltd.' at the end of its name.

Section 1 of the Companies Act[137] defines 'state-owned companies' as 'a public entity in Schedule 2 or 3 of the Public Finance Management Act [1 of 1999]', such as Eskom. A public entity, in turn, refers to 'a juristic person under the ownership control of the national executive'.[138]

The shareholding of Eskom requires elaboration. Even though Eskom is defined as a public company its shares are not traded and the state is the only shareholder, as mentioned. Thus, despite the institution's private-law form, suggesting that Eskom is primarily a free-market player would be misleading: the South African government owns and controls Eskom. Eskom was established, through statute, by the government which maintains

---

126 See also section 2 of the South African Revenue Service Act 34 of 1997 which classifies SARS as an organ of state within the administration.

127 34 of 1997.

128 34 of 1997.

129 89 of 1991.

130 91 of 1964.

131 The name 'Eskom' combines two acronyms, ESCOM (Electricity Supply Commission) and EVKOM (Elektrisiteitsvoorsieningskommissie).

132 13 of 2001.

133 Section 2 Eskom Conversion Act 13 of 2001.

134 71 of 2008.

135 Section 2 Eskom Conversion Act 13 of 2001. Section 2 refers to section 19(1)(*a*) of the Companies Act 61 of 1973 (see the definition for 'Companies Act', section 1 Eskom Conversion Act 16 of 2001) which has been repealed by the Companies Act 71 of 2008.

136 Section 8 Companies Act 71 of 2008.

137 71 of 2008.

138 The definitions of national public entity and national government business enterprise, section 1 of PFMA.

ownership control. The Minister of Public Enterprises is the government's shareholder representative.

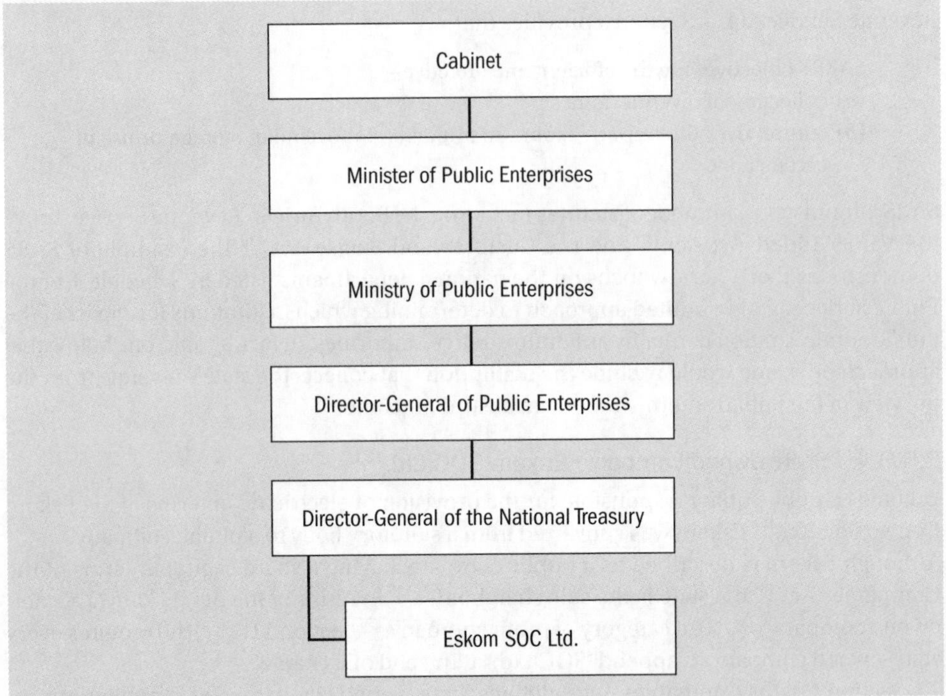


*Figure 2.6 Institutional position of Eskom*

The Public Finance Management Act[139] applies to Eskom.[140] The accounting authority of Eskom is the board of directors[141] and the Minister of Public Enterprises represents the government.[142]

According to Eskom:

> [t]he Board is responsible for providing strategic direction and leadership, ensuring good corporate governance and ethics, determining policy, agreeing on performance criteria and delegating the detailed planning and implementation of policy to the Executive Management Committee (EXCO).[143]

### 2.5.3.5 The Public Protector

Chapter 9 of the Constitution creates six state institutions that support constitutional democracy in South Africa. The Public Protector is one of the six Chapter 9 institutions.[144] Specifically, sections 181–183 of the Constitution establish and regulate the Public Protector.

139 1 of 1999.
140 Schedule 2 PFMA.
141 Section 49 PFMA.
142 Section 6(4) Eskom Conversion Act 13 of 2001.
143 Eskom: Powering Your World available at: <http://www.eskom.co.za/OurCompany/CompanyInformation/Pages/Legislation.aspx> (accessed 07.08.2020).
144 Section 181 of the Constitution of the Republic of South Africa, 1996.

Section 181(2)-(5) identifies the principles that govern the so-called Chapter 9 institutions, including the Public Protector:

> (2) These institutions are independent, and subject only to the Constitution and the law, and they must be impartial and must exercise their powers and perform their functions without fear, favour or prejudice.
> (3) Other organs of state, through legislative and other measures, must assist and protect these institutions to ensure the independence, impartiality, dignity and effectiveness of these institutions.
> (4) No person or organ of state may interfere with the functioning of these institutions.
> (5) These institutions are accountable to the National Assembly, and must report on their activities and the performance of their functions to the Assembly at least once a year.

Section 182 lists the functions of the Public Protector, including:

> (1) The Public Protector has the power, as regulated by national legislation -
> (*a*) to investigate any conduct in state affairs, or in the public administration in any sphere of government, that is alleged or suspected to be improper or to result in any impropriety or prejudice;
> (*b*) to report on that conduct; and
> (*c*) to take appropriate remedial action.
> (2) The Public Protector has the additional powers and functions prescribed by national legislation.

Thus the Public Protector is primarily concerned with the investigation of conduct that is allegedly improper, reporting her findings and taking remedial action. However, the Public Protector is not limited to these functions, because section 182(2) indicates that legislation may prescribe additional powers and functions. The Public Protector Act [145] regulates the office of the Public Protector, of which section 6 sets out additional powers. Overall, the Public Protector is designed to safeguard the accountability of actors exercising public power.

Evidently, the Public Protector is a constitutional body. The Public Protector is not an 'organ of state' in terms of section 239(*a*) of the Constitution because it is not a 'department of state or administration in the national, provincial or local sphere of government'. However, depending on the function performed by the Public Protector, the institution may qualify as an organ of state in terms of section 239(*b*) of the Constitution.

The Supreme Court of Appeal, referring to the Public Protector Act,[146] states that:

> [t]he Act makes it clear that while the functions of the Public Protector include those that are ordinarily associated with an ombudsman they also go much beyond that. The Public Protector is not a passive adjudicator between citizens and the state, relying upon evidence that is placed before him or her before acting. His or her mandate is an investigatory one, requiring proaction in appropriate circumstances.[147]

145 23 of 1994.
146 23 of 1994.
147 *The Public Protector v Mail & Guardian Ltd and Others* 2011 (4) SA 420 (SCA) para 9 (footnote omitted).

The Constitution emphasises the functional and institutional independence of the Public Protector, an important consideration in relation to the nature of the Public Protector. First, section 181(2) of the Constitution declares that the Public Protector is:

> independent, and subject only to the Constitution and the law, and [it] must be impartial and must exercise [its] powers and perform [its] functions without fear, favour or prejudice.

Second, section 181(3) provides that:

> [o]ther organs of state, through legislative and other measures, must assist and protect these institutions to ensure the independence, impartiality, dignity and effectiveness of these institutions.

Finally, 'no person or organ of state may interfere with the functioning of [the public protector]'.

Evidently, the independence of Chapter 9 institutions is secured in language similar to those sections which establish the independence of the judiciary.[148] Nevertheless, the Public Protector is not a judicial institution.

**PAUSE FOR REFLECTION**

**The Public Protector in action**

In March 2014 Adv. Thuli Madonsela, the Public Protector at the time, released her findings on the alleged irregular expenditure on President Zuma's Nkandla compound, his private residence.[149] These findings and remedial steps to be taken were published in the report *Secure in Comfort.*

Madonsela found that a proportion of the expenditure 'went beyond what was reasonably required for the President's security, was unconscionable, excessive, and caused a misappropriation of public funds'.[150] In fact, 'the expenditure [constituted] opulence at a grand scale'.[151]

Regarding President Zuma's role, he:

> improperly benefited from the measures implemented in the name of security which include non-security comforts such as the Visitors' Centre, such as the swimming pool, amphitheatre, cattle kraal with culvert and chicken run. The private medical clinic at the family's doorstep will also benefit the family forever. The acts and omissions that allowed this to happen constitute unlawful and improper conduct and maladministration.[152]

CONTINUED >>>

148 Section 165(2): 'The courts are independent and subject only to the Constitution and the law, which they must apply impartially and without fear, favour or prejudice.' Section 165(4) is couched in language virtually identical to section 181(3): 'Organs of state, through legislative and other measures, must assist and protect the courts to ensure the independence, impartiality, dignity, accessibility and effectiveness of the courts.' The Public Protector and judiciary also have a prohibition against interference in common: 'No person or organ of state may interfere with the functioning of the courts.'

149 Public Protector *Secure in Comfort: Report on an investigation into allegations of impropriety and unethical conduct relating to the installation and implementation of security measures by the Department of Public Works at and in respect of the private residence of President Jacob Zuma at Nkandla in the KwaZulu-Natal province* Report No. 25 of 2013/2014.

150 *Public Protector Secure in Comfort Report* 430.

151 *Public Protector Secure in Comfort Report* 430–431.

152 *Public Protector Secure in Comfort Report* 431.

Therefore, the Public Protector 'ordered' that several remedial steps be taken under section 182(1)(*c*) of the Constitution, including the payment of:

> a reasonable percentage of the cost of the measures as determined with the assistance of National Treasury, also considering the DPW [Department of Public Works] apportionment document.

In this case, the Public Protector reacted to complaints from members of the public and politicians who, in turn, were prompted by newspaper reports alleging improper expenditure to lodge these complaints. This is in line with section 182(1)(*a*) of the Constitution. Section 182(1)(*c*) empowers the Public Protector 'to *take* appropriate remedial action'. The *Secure in Comfort* report includes a section entitled 'Remedial Action', which sets out steps to be taken by the President and others.

The preceding section on the nature of the Public Protector points out the clear language securing the independence of the Public Protector, which is similar to the provisions establishing the independence of the judiciary. However, section 165 and section 181 differ in one important respect. Section 165(5) provides that:

> [a]n order or decision issued by a court binds all persons to whom and organs of state to which it applies.

Although section 182(1)(*c*) provides that the Public Protector can 'take appropriate remedial action', the wording of this section is not that same as that of section 165(5). Whether or not this implies that the Public Protector's findings have binding force is unclear.

This section illustrates how a large proportion of legal activity and dispute takes place out of the courts, even assuming that the dispute may at some stage go to court. It is important to note that administrative law operates outside of judicial review, as explained by green-light theories discussed further below.

### 2.5.3.6 Commissions

Commissions are a regular feature in the political and legal landscape of South Africa. However, a wide variety of institutions performing different functions are called commissions and therefore it is important to bear in mind that commissions are not homogenous institutions. For instance, some commissions are permanent institutions and others are created for a limited period of time to perform a particular function. Whether commissions are subject to administrative law will depend on the nature of the function performed,[153] but generally they are concerned with the implementation of legislation. Therefore, commissions serve as another example of institutions that can be classified as public authorities (often performing a public function).

153 PAJA does not exclude the decisions of commissions in general, or of the Public Service Commission specifically, in the definition of administrative action. See *Corruption Watch and Another v Arms Procurement Commission and Others* [2019] 4 All SA 53 (GP) where the Seriti Commission's report was set aside on the basis of legality and rationality, without referring to PAJA, however.

One example of a permanent institutional body named a commission is the Public Service Commission. Section 196 of the Constitution establishes the Public Service Commission and determines its institutional status:

> 196. Public Service Commission. –
> (1) There is a single Public Service Commission for the Republic.
> (2) The Commission is independent and must be impartial, and must exercise its powers and perform its functions without fear, favour or prejudice in the interest of the maintenance of effective and efficient public administration and a high standard of professional ethics in the public service. The Commission must be regulated by national legislation.
> (3) Other organs of state, through legislative and other measures, must assist and protect the Commission to ensure the independence, impartiality, dignity and effectiveness of the Commission. No person or organ of state may interfere with the functioning of the Commission.

The language is reminiscent of the Chapter 9 institutions, especially insofar as the Public Service Commission is also independent.

Section 196(4) lists the powers and functions of the Public Service Commission:

> 196(4) The powers and functions of the Commission are –
> (*a*) to promote the values and principles set out in section 195, throughout the public service;
> (*b*) to investigate, monitor and evaluate the organisation and administration, and the personnel practices, of the public service;
> (*c*) to propose measures to ensure effective and efficient performance within the public service;
> (*d*) to give directions aimed at ensuring that personnel procedures relating to recruitment, transfers, promotions and dismissals comply with the values and principles set out in section 195;
> (*e*) to report in respect of its activities and the performance of its functions, including any finding it may make and directions and advice it may give, and to provide an evaluation of the extent to which the values and principles set out in section 195 are complied with; and
> (*f*) either of its own accord or on receipt of any complaint -
> (i) to investigate and evaluate the application of personnel and public administration practices, and to report to the relevant executive authority and legislature;
> (ii) to investigate grievances of employees in the public service concerning official acts or omissions, and recommend appropriate remedies;
> (iii) to monitor and investigate adherence to applicable procedures in the public service; and
> (iv) to advise national and provincial organs of state regarding personnel practices in the public service, including those relating to the recruitment, appointment, transfer, discharge and other aspects of the careers of employees in the public service; and
> (*g*) to exercise or perform the additional powers or functions prescribed by an Act of Parliament.

Evidently, the Public Service Commission's remit is extensive.

In contrast to the Public Service Commission, that is established by the Constitution and that is a permanent institution, section 84(2)(*f*) of the Constitution empowers the President to appoint commissions of inquiry. A recent example is the Judicial Commission of Inquiry into Allegations of State Capture, Corruption and Fraud in The Public Sector including Organs of State. By Proclamation, President Ramaphosa appointed the commission:

> In terms of section 84(2)(*f*) of the Constitution of the Republic of South Africa of1996, I hereby appoint a Commission of Inquiry to investigate allegations of state capture, corruption and fraud in the Public Sector including organs of state with the terms of reference in the Schedule attached hereto and appoint Honourable Mr Justice Raymond Mnyamezeli Mlungisi Zondo, Deputy Chief Justice of the Republic of South Africa, as its Chairperson.[154]

In the mentioned Proclamation, the commission is required 'to investigate matters of public and national interest concerning allegations of state capture, corruption, and fraud', which are specified, and to 'submit its report and recommendations to the President within 180 days of the commencement of the Commission'. Thus, the remit is limited in scope and the commission exists only for a limited period of time.

## 2.6 Administrative law: A discipline steeped in controversy

Administrative law has only been acknowledged as a legitimate legal discipline in South African relatively recently. The slow start of administrative law can be attributed to the influence and legacy of Dicey. Dicey advocated a 'red light'[155] approach to judicial review and denied the existence of administrative law, deeming it unnecessary under the rule of law.

Although Dicey's approach is now widely considered outdated, administrative law remains controversial. The subject of administrative law is the exercise of public power and whether this imposition on power is legitimate or not, the exercise of power will always remain contested. Administrative law also influences and operates at the juncture of overlapping concerns such as democratic legitimacy, the separation of powers and party politics. Other concerns such as the courts' supposed inability to resolve polycentric issues or its interference with the executive function have also been raised. The judiciary is also expected to exhibit a degree of deference to executive decisions.

As we have seen in Chapter 1, administrative law is pervasive, diverse and dynamic, rendering any short definition limited and temporary. In 1984 Baxter defined administrative law as:

> that branch of public law which regulates the legal relations of public authorities, whether with private individuals and organizations, or with other public authorities.
>
> Precisely because it is so pervasive, administrative law is seldom identified as such. It permeates virtually every facet of the legal system.[156]

154 Proclamation No. 3 of 2018 in *GG* 41403 of 25.01.2018.

155 See 2.6.1 below.

156 Baxter (1984) 2. Reprinted by permission of © Juta & Company Ltd.

Baxter's definition reveals an institutional approach to administrative law: administrative law is concerned with a particular set of institutions, namely public authorities.[157] In 2007 Hoexter, in response to Baxter's definition, claimed that:

> it is more accurate to regard administrative law as regulating the activities of bodies that *exercise public powers or perform public functions*, irrespective of whether those bodies are public authorities in a strict sense.[158]

Hoexter's definition is indicative of a shift from an institutional to a functional approach. Thus, from a theoretical perspective, administrative law is not so much concerned with the nature of the institution performing a particular function than the nature of the function itself. This observation does not imply at all that the nature of an institution is irrelevant, but it does suggest a significant shift in emphasis.

Administrative law can be categorised under two, broad categories: general administrative law or particular administrative law.[159] General administrative law refers to those rules of administrative law that are applicable to all incidences of administrative action. For instance, section 33 of the Constitution, a source of administrative law, requires that all administrative action be lawful, reasonable and procedurally fair. Particular administrative law applies to a particular type of administrative action.

**PAUSE FOR REFLECTION**

**Different instances of particular administrative law**

In light of the large range of different areas in which the state and accordingly the public administration play a key role in modern societies, the range of different areas of law that can be viewed as examples of particular administrative law, or that contain dimensions that are examples of administrative law, is quite extensive. You have most probably already studied some of these areas and hence particular administrative law without realising it.

Examples of particular administrative law include the following:

- The law pertaining to tax administration
- Planning law, which includes the law governing decisions on whether to approve building plans or zoning applications
- The law governing decisions to expropriate land
- Competition law, especially those parts dealing with the powers of competition authorities to investigate and take action in response to anti-competitive behaviour
- Environmental law focusing on the control of conduct that poses environmental risks
- Aspects of labour law governing dispute-resolution processes of the CCMA
- Law of succession focusing on the role of the Master of the High Court in relation to wills
- Company law governing the registration of companies.

157 However, it is not clear what would constitute a public authority.

158 Hoexter, C (2007) *Administrative Law in South Africa* 2. Reprinted by permission of © Juta & Company Ltd.

159 Particular administrative law is also referred to as specific administrative law.

### 2.6.1 The dual nature of administrative law

The nature of administrative law can be described as twofold: on the one hand, administrative law aims to restrict public power; on the other hand, administrative law aims to enable and facilitate the exercise of public power.[160] The former concerns control and the latter empowerment of the administration. Although these competing concerns certainly stand in opposition to one another, they are not mutually exclusive. For example, section 38J of the Higher Education Act [161] provides for intervention by the Minister of Education [162] in certain circumstances. Section 38J(1)(*a*) reads:

> 38J(1) The Minister may issue a directive to the board of a national institute for higher education to take such action specified by the Minister if the national institute for higher education—
>
> (*a*) is involved in financial impropriety or is being otherwise mismanaged.[163]

Note that this provision is not a source of administrative law, but of administrative power. However, administrative law determines how the provision or administrative power can be understood: lawfulness, an administrative-law principle, requires that the decision-maker may only act in terms of the empowering provision. Thus, administrative law implies that the decision-maker's actions are limited to the content of the authorising provision, thereby shaping the nature of the source of administrative power. In this case, the Minister *may* issue directives, which is a discretionary power. This illustrates the enabling or empowering aspect of administrative law. However, the decision-maker may only exercise that particular power in a particular manner; the Minister cannot perform any other act whatsoever. The Minister must issue a directive to a national institute of higher education and only if there is financial impropriety or mismanagement. In this way the power is limited in several ways: the Minister is restricted to issuing a directive, the Minister must issue the directive to the board of a national institute, and the Minister may only do so in certain circumstances. The empowering provision illustrates that a source of administrative power both empowers the decision-maker to act, thereby enabling the decision-maker to exercise public power, and restricts that power. Thus one observes the simultaneous operation of these two features of administrative law.

Harlow and Rawlings articulate the dual nature of administrative law in their seminal work *Law and Administration*.[164] They identify two schools of thought, both reacting to the exigencies of the welfare state: 'red light theory' and 'green light theory'.[165] Red light theory regards administrative law primarily as a form of control of public power, enforced by the courts through judicial review.[166] Green light theory also recognises the need for control, but 'prefers democratic or political forms of accountability'.[167] In addition, while red light theory regards the exercise of public power as a potential threat to liberty, 'green light theory sees

160 Cf. the dual nature of the executive branch and of the executive function.

161 101 of 1997.

162 See section 1 'Minister' of the Higher Education Act 101 of 1997.

163 Emphasis added.

164 The first edition of *Law and Administration* was published in 1984. In 2009 the third edition was published.

165 Harlow, C & Rawlings, R (2009) *Law and Administration* (3rd ed) Ch 1.

166 Harlow & Rawlings (2009) 23.

167 Harlow & Rawlings (2009) 38.

in administrative law a vehicle for political progress and welcomes the "administrative state"'.[168] The differences between the two schools of thought can be summarised thus:

> Red light theorists believed that law was autonomous to and superior over politics; that the administrative state was dangerous and should be kept in check by law; that the preferred way of doing this was through adjudication; and that the goal should be to enhance liberty, conceived in terms of the absence of external constraints. Green light theorists ... believed that law was not autonomous from politics; that the administrative state was not a necessary evil, but a positive attribute to be welcomed; that administrative law should seek not merely to stop bad administrative practice, and that there might be better ways to achieve this than adjudication; and that the goal was to enhance individual and collective liberty conceived in positive and not just negative terms.[169]

Administrative law and administrative power were distinguished in the preceding example. Likewise, the *sources* of administrative law and administrative power ought to be distinguished. The sources of administrative law for the preceding example are section 33 of the Constitution and PAJA, which gives effect to section 33. The source of administrative power is the empowering provision, namely, section 38J(1)(*a*) of the Higher Education Act.[170]

## 2.6.2 Administrative law and administrative power distinguished

As explained in the preceding section administrative law refers to the body of legal rules that regulate incidences of public power or the exercise of public functions. However, administrative power refers to the legal authorisation for a particular function. Thus administrative power is concerned with the source of power or authorisation that allows the performance of a function. Baxter explains:

> Since all public authorities, offices and powers are institutional creations of the law, when we talk of administrative 'power' we refer only to *authorized* power: what is really meant is administrative authority.[171]

Bear in mind that Baxter is writing from an institutional perspective and that the emphasis has shifted to a functional approach. Administrative law and administrative power can be distinguished by means of an example.

The Local Government: Municipal Systems Act[172] is a statute issued by Parliament that regulates municipalities, or local government. Section 75A of the Act authorises municipalities to impose and collect fees:

> 75A(1) A municipality may—
> (*a*) levy and recover fees, charges or tariffs in respect of any function or service of the municipality; and
> (*b*) recover collection charges and interest on any outstanding amount.

The legal authorisation for this function is an example of administrative power, as opposed to administrative law. Thus Parliament bestows this power or capacity upon municipalities

168 Harlow & Rawlings (2009) 31.

169 Tomkins, A (2002) In Defence of the Political Constitution *Oxford Journal of Legal Studies* 22(1):157. By permission of Oxford University Press.

170 101 of 1997.

171 Baxter (1984) 75–76 (footnote omitted). Reprinted by permission of © Juta & Company Ltd.

172 32 of 2000.

without which municipalities cannot perform such a function. Administrative law remains relevant, though. Whenever a municipality exercises its power to impose fees and collect them, corresponding decisions would have to be lawful, reasonable and procedurally fair, so long as those decisions qualify as administrative action under administrative law.[173]

### 2.6.3 Administrative law and administrative authorities distinguished

Administrative law and administrative authorities should not be confused. On a superficial level administrative law refers to a set of legally binding rules and administrative authorities refer to a number of public institutions. This chapter is primarily concerned with the institutional dimension of administration.[174] Despite the terms 'administrative law' and 'administrative authorities' sharing the same adjective, administrative law cannot be reduced to the law applicable to administrative authorities, nor can it be said that administrative law alone regulates administrative authorities. Virtually all law is applicable to the administration. Consider section 8(1) of the Constitution, for instance:

> The Bill of Rights applies to all law, and binds the legislature, the executive, the judiciary and all organs of state.

Thus the Bill of Rights clearly applies to administrative authorities, since administrative authorities are part of the executive or qualify as organs of state. The Bill of Rights is not administrative law, though. Similarly, administrative authorities often perform private acts such as concluding contracts and then the private law of contract applies.[175] In addition, administrative law does not only bind administrative authorities; depending on the circumstances, administrative law can apply to natural persons, juristic persons, organs of state and every branch of state, including the judiciary.[176] Two dicta, stated in negative terms, map the reach of administrative law and the extent of its association with administrative authorities: administrative law does not apply only to administrative authorities and administrative authorities are not subject only to administrative law. These observations do not detract from the fact that in a large majority of cases administrative law is applied to administrative authorities.

### 2.6.4 Sources of administrative law

South Africa has four primary sources of administrative law: the Constitution, legislation, the common law and case law. As explained above, administrative law can be divided into general administrative law and particular administrative law.[177] General administrative law denotes those legal rules and principles that apply to all types of administrative action; every administrative action is subject to general administrative law. Section 33 of the Constitution and PAJA are examples of general administrative law. Therefore, every administrative action must be reasonable, procedurally fair and lawful, in line with the requirements of section 33. In addition, any rule of particular administrative law is subject to general administrative law.

---

173 Section 33 of the Constitution; section 6 of PAJA.

174 See para (*a*) of the definition of 'organ of state', section 239 of the Constitution.

175 However, the fact that contract law applies in a particular instance does imply that other fields do not also apply. It may well be that contract law in addition to administrative law is applicable to a set of facts. See *Logbro Properties CC v Bedderson NO and Others* 2003 (2) SA 460 (SCA).

176 Note that section 1 of PAJA excludes a number of functions from PAJA's purview, i.e. PAJA does not apply to certain functions such as 'the judicial functions of a judicial officer of a court referred to in section 166 of the Constitution'. However, the exclusion refers to the judicial function and not the judiciary as an institution.

177 Hoexter (2012) 8.

Particular administrative law denotes the legal rules and principles that apply only to certain types of administrative action as we also noted above. Tax law, labour law and public procurement law are all examples of particular administrative law, which:

> deals with the rules and principles that have developed in specific and specialised areas of administration.[178]

For instance, public procurement is regulated directly by the Preferential Procurement Policy Framework Act.[179] In *Steenkamp NO v Provincial Tender Board, Eastern Cape*[180] the Constitutional Court confirmed that public procurement qualifies as administrative action.

Therefore, the rules set out in the Preferential Procurement Policy Framework Act[181] apply to all public procurement processes, and those rules themselves are subject to the Constitution and PAJA, by implication.[182]

Thus, a hierarchy of administrative law rules can be identified: the Constitution is supreme and supersedes all administrative law, both general and particular. Section 33 is an example of general administrative law with constitutional status. Consequently, legislation, including PAJA, and the common law are subject to section 33. Since PAJA gives effect to section 33, all administrative-law statutes, such as the Income Tax Act,[183] are subject to it in the sense that they must be interpreted in a manner that takes PAJA into account. Finally, specific types of administrative action must conform to the relevant, particular administrative law. The reasoning of judgments must reflect this normative hierarchy.

### 2.6.5 Sources of administrative power

The rule of law implies that public power must be authorised by law. Where the law empowers an individual or institution to perform a public power, the provision amounts to a source of administrative power. PAJA elaborates on sources of administrative power. The definition of 'administrative action' refers to an organ of state exercising a power in terms of the Constitution, a provincial constitution or legislation.[184] Where 'a natural or juristic person, other than an organ of state' exercises a power in terms of an 'empowering provision' the corresponding decision can also qualify as administrative action. An 'empowering division'[185] is defined as 'a law, a rule of common law, customary law, or an agreement, instrument or other document in terms of which an administrative action was purportedly taken'.[186] Thus the sources of administrative power are extremely divergent. Even though administrative functions are typically characterised as the implementation of legislation, other sources of law, or even contracts, can amount to a source of administrative power.

---

178 Hoexter (2012) 8. Reprinted by permission of © Juta & Company Ltd.

179 5 of 2000. This does not mean that the Preferential Procurement Policy Framework Act 5 of 2000 is the only statute that applies directly to public procurement. Other statutes, such as the Public Finance Management Act 1 of 1999 and the Broad-Based Black Economic Empowerment Act 53 of 2003 also regulate public procurement.

180 2007 (3) SA 121 (CC).

181 5 of 2000.

182 See *Zondi v MEC for Traditional and Local Government Affairs and Others* 2005 (3) SA 589 (CC).

183 58 of 1962.

184 Section 1 of PAJA.

185 'Empowering provision' is defined by section 1 of PAJA, but this definition is only relevant to 'a natural or juristic person, other than an organ of state', i.e. an organ of state is not permitted to act in terms of an empowering provision for the purposes of PAJA to the extent that the definition includes sources other than the Constitution, provincial constitutions, and legislation.

186 Section 1 of PAJA.

Hoexter points out that:

> [i]n South Africa, as in most countries, the bulk of legislation is produced not by original lawmaking authorities but by administrative authorities. An array of terms is used for different types of delegated legislation: regulations, proclamations, rules, orders, declarations, directives, decrees and schemes.[187]

To this one could add 'less formal' sources of administrative power such as standards, practice notes, circulars etc.[188] Thus the origins of administrative power, as well the rules governing the exercise of that power, are diverse. This raises concerns of democratic legitimacy and the counter-majoritarian dilemma where the administration has formulated a rule, rather than the legislature.

## THIS CHAPTER IN ESSENCE

An awareness of the importance and diversity of administrative authorities is critical to the study of administrative law. Despite the shift to a functional approach, institutions are important; they exist for a reason. Administrative authorities play a decisive and expansive role in society: they collect taxes, regulate institutions such as national departments and are principally responsible for the implementation of policy and legislation. In a country witnessing protests against poor service delivery on a daily basis, the implementation of socio-economic rights is evidently urgent, complex and obligatory, legally speaking. The failure of government and of parliament to play their part is often mooted as the source of these protests. However, as we have seen, administrative authorities are primarily responsible for 'getting the job done'. This statement in no way trivialises the importance of the government and legislature to the project of transformation. An awareness of administrative authorities and their nature provides a different perspective on the architecture of the state, so to speak. This chapter furnishes a template for analysing incidences of public authority, from an institutional perspective.

## FURTHER READING

- Ackerman, B 'Good-bye, Montesquieu' in Rose-Ackerman, S, Lindseth, PL and Emerson, B (Eds) (2017) *Comparative Administrative Law* (2nd ed) Cheltenham, UK & Northampton, MA: Edward Elgar Publishing
- Harlow, C and Rawlings, R (2009) *Law and Administration* (3rd ed) Cambridge: Cambridge University Press, Chapter 1
- Maree, PJH (2013) *Investigating an Alternative Administrative-Law System in South Africa* Unpublished doctoral dissertation (US) Chapter 2 (http://hdl.handle.net/10019.1/85591)
- Vile, MJC (1998) *Constitutionalism and the Separation of Powers* (2nd ed) Oxford: Clarendon Publishers

187 Hoexter (2012) 52. Reprinted by permission of © Juta & Company Ltd.

188 Hoexter (2012) 32. For examples of practice notes issued under the Public Finance Management Act 1 of 1999, consult the website of the National Treasury at <http://www.treasury.gov.za/legislation/pfma/practice%20notes/default.aspx> (accessed 07.08.2020).

# Chapter 3

# Administrative action

*Geo Quinot & Petrus Maree*

## 3.1 Introduction

This chapter introduces the concept of administrative action and explains how to identify an administrative action among a vast array of state activities.

Administrative action bears several meanings and its definition has changed over time; in fact, it is a concept that continues to develop. Therefore, despite this chapter's focus on the definition of administrative action in the Promotion of Administrative Justice Act,[1] the nature of administrative action in general is discussed too.

The importance of administrative action to administrative law warrants emphasis from the onset. The presence of an administrative action is decisive for the application of administrative law: section 33 and PAJA only apply to administrative action. Therefore, the preliminary question to any administrative law inquiry would be 'is there an administrative action?' If the answer to this question is 'no', administrative law does not apply; if the answer is 'yes', administrative law applies.

However, one first has to understand what constitutes administrative action and how to identify administrative action before attempting to classify any given act.

## 3.2 The separation of powers and the classification of state functions

The separation of powers provides a useful reference point for contextualising and describing administrative action, because administrative action has both institutional and functional aspects. Administrative action, though defined by statute, does not exist in a vacuum: it stands in a dynamic and interactive relationship with other state functions and activities. Thus administrative action is informed by the nature and content of all state functions. In other words, administrative action is given meaning in relation to the functions under the separation of powers.[2]

In terms of the separation of powers all state institutions and functions can be classified under three categories: executive, legislative and judicial. Accordingly, administrative action should be classified as executive, legislative or judicial in nature, at least in theory. However, these functions are neither completely distinct in a conceptual sense nor completely separated in practice, owing to checks and balances.[3]

Executive power is derived from the Constitution[4] and is exercised at national, provincial and local level. The executive function as a whole is concerned primarily with the formulation of policy and the implementation of legislation. Executive functions are not automatically administrative actions. Legislative power is also derived from the Constitution[5] and is exercised at national, provincial and local level. The legislative function implies the creation of legislation. Legislative acts as such do not qualify as administrative action. Judicial power is also derived from the Constitution, but the judiciary is a unitary system, unlike the executive and legislature, which are federal.[6] Thus we observe the classification of all state functions and institutions into three categories and the allocation of one function to each

1 3 of 2000 (PAJA); section 1 PAJA.
2 Consider, for example, the exclusions listed in the definition of 'administrative action' (section 1 PAJA), discussed below at 3.7.7.
3 As mentioned in Chapter 2, the executive function conflates policy formulation with public administration.
4 Sections 83–85 of the Constitution.
5 Sections 43, 44 of the Constitution.
6 Section 165 of the Constitution.

of the three branches. Where does administrative action fit in, though? Is it associated with a particular institution or function? There are no absolute answers to these questions.

Administrative law is largely concerned with the activities of the executive branch, that is, the formulation of policy and the implementation of legislation. However, the separation of powers cannot specify which functions qualify as administrative action, despite suggesting that a majority of administrative acts will be performed by the executive branch. In fact, acts performed by the executive, legislature or judiciary may qualify as administrative action. Thus, the fact that a particular act was performed by the legislature does not preclude that act from qualifying as an administrative action. Administrative action cannot be reduced to a single state function or to the activities performed by a particular branch. Therefore, a more nuanced standard for identifying administrative action is required.

Note that the executive has a dual nature: the President and the other members of Cabinet are primarily concerned with the formulation of policy as opposed to the public administration that implements policy as well as legislation. The distinction between the two is significant: the executive as an institutional whole is not the more useful indicator of the presence of administrative action; rather, the public administration is typically involved with the implementation of policy and legislation.

## 3.3 Branches capable of performing administrative action

When we focus more closely on the various branches of the state, we can find examples of administrative action under each one. We can also see how the actions of the executive are best understood in terms of a distinction between the 'policy branch' and the administration. The identification of administrative action taken by each of these branches is illustrated by the judgments discussed below.

### 3.3.1 The 'policy branch'[7]

***Permanent Secretary, Department of Education and Welfare, Eastern Cape and Another v Ed-U-College (PE)(Section21) Inc* 2001 (2) SA 1 (CC)**

In this matter, an independent school challenged the annual subsidy amount paid to the school by the Provincial Department of Education in 1997. The subsidy amount was determined by the MEC for Education by means of an allocation formula.

(Note that the MEC should be regarded as a politician rather than an administrator. Therefore the MEC falls under the policy branch within the executive.)

One of the legal questions before the court was whether the determination of a formula by the MEC amounted to administrative action. The court found that the decision qualified as administrative action on the ground that the determination of the subsidy amounted to policy formulation in a narrow sense, that is, within a legislative framework.[8]

***Pharmaceutical Manufacturers Association of South Africa and Another: In Re Ex Parte President of the Republic of South Africa and Others* 2000 (2) SA 674 (CC)**

In this case, the President's action of issuing a proclamation to bring the South African Medicines and Medical Devices Regulatory Authority Act[9] into operation was challenged upon review. The President heads the executive in the political sense of the word and can be classified as part of

---

7 Vile, MJC (1998) *Constitutionalism and the Separation of Powers* (2nd ed) Chapter 13.

8 *Permanent Secretary, Department of Education and Welfare, Eastern Cape and Another v Ed-U-College (PE)(Section21) Inc* 2001 (2) SA 1 (CC) paras 18, 21, 24.

9 132 of 1998.

the policy branch. The court classified the President's capacity to issue proclamations that bring statutes into operation as a power:

> between the law-making process and the administrative process. The exercise of that power requires a political judgment as to when the legislation should be brought into force, a decision that is necessarily antecedent to the implementation of the legislation which comes into force only when the power is exercised. In substance the exercise of the power is closer to the legislative process than the administrative process.[10]

Therefore, the decision could not qualify as administrative action.

### 3.3.2 The public administration

***Government of the Republic of South Africa v Thabiso Chemicals (Pty) Ltd* 2009 (1) SA 163 (SCA)**

The State Tender Board, an organ of state within the public administration, purported to cancel a contract concluded with the respondent. The respondent claimed damages, arguing that the cancellation was wrongful. Brand JA found that administrative law was not applicable, even though the Board's power to cancel derived from statute and regulation.[11] The implication is that the cancellation did not amount to administrative action.

***Earthlife Africa (Cape Town) v Director-General: Department of Environmental Affairs and Tourism and Another* 2005 (3) SA 156 (C)**

The Director-General (first respondent), which is the head administrator for the national department, authorised Eskom to construct a pebble bed modular (nuclear) reactor. In a challenge to this decision, Griesel J found that the decision qualified as administrative action,[12] rendering it susceptible to judicial review.

### 3.3.3 The legislature

***Fedsure Life Assurance Ltd and Others v Greater Johannesburg Transitional Metropolitan Council and Others* 1999 (1) SA 374 (CC)**

The Greater Johannesburg Transitional Metropolitan Council, 'a deliberative legislative body whose members are elected',[13] adopted several resolutions providing for levies and subsidies. These were challenged by the appellants as administrative action. However, the court found that '[t]he enactment of legislation by an elected local council acting in accordance with the Constitution is, in the ordinary sense of the words, a legislative and not an administrative act'.[14]

***Economic Freedom Fighters v Speaker of the National Assembly* [2018] 2 All SA 116 (WCC)**

Subsequent to disciplinary proceedings, members of the applicant opposition party in Parliament, were suspended from Parliament by the National Assembly following recommendations of the standing Powers and Privileges Committee. In considering a challenge against the suspension, the court held that the approach taken by the committee had to be understood within the context of the procedural fairness requirements set out in PAJA, implying that such conduct amounts to administrative action.

10 *Pharmaceutical Manufacturers Association of SA and Another: In Re Ex Parte President of the RSA and Others* 2000 (2) SA 674 (CC) para 79.

11 *Government of the Republic of South Africa v Thabiso Chemicals (Pty) Ltd* 2009 (1) SA 163 (SCA) para 18.

12 *Earthlife Africa (Cape Town) v Director-General: Department of Environmental Affairs and Tourism and Another* 2005 (3) SA 156 (C) para 21.

13 *Fedsure* para 41.

14 *Fedsure* para 42.

### 3.3.4 The judiciary

***Le Roux and Others v Honourable Magistrate and Others* (16013/05) [2006] ZAGPHC 63 (22 June 2006)**

In this matter, the applicants applied to court for the review of a search warrant issued by a magistrate in terms of the Insolvency Act.[15] The court found that the magistrate's authorisation of the search warrant amounted not to an administrative, but a judicial function.

***President of the Republic of South Africa and Others v South African Rugby Football Union and Others* 2000 (1) SA 1 (CC)**

The Constitutional Court has acknowledged that the court could perform administrative functions:

> It may well be, as contemplated in ***Fedsure***, that some acts of a legislature may constitute 'administrative action'. Similarly, judicial officers may, from time to time, carry out administrative tasks.[16]

The judgments discussed above illustrate that the institution performing a particular function is not decisive when determining whether an administrative action has been performed. In principle, any branch of the separation of powers is capable of performing administrative action; the nature of the function itself is the critical consideration. This basic point was confirmed in *Nkabinde and Another v Judicial Service Commission President of the Judicial Conduct Tribunal and Others*[17] where the court had to decide whether it was objectionable for a member of the National Prosecuting Authority (NPA) to participate in the work of a Judicial Conduct Tribunal in terms of the Judicial Service Commission Act.[18] In holding that it was not, the judge stated as follows:

> As already stated, just as Judges are required to undertake certain non-curial functions, such as commissions of inquiry, the functions of members of the NPA on a day to day basis go beyond merely prosecuting, and could include other functions, including of course, mundane administrative functions which are implicit in every role in every branch of government.

## 3.4 The meaning of administrative action understood within the phases of development of administrative law

The meaning of the concept of administrative action must be understood within the developmental phases of administrative law in general, as its meaning has changed over time and continues to develop.[19]

The development of South African administrative law can be divided into three, broad periods: first, the pre-constitutional period; second, the constitutional period prior to the enactment of PAJA; and, finally, the constitutional period subsequent to the enactment of PAJA. During the pre-constitutional period, administrative law operated within the common-law tradition and a framework of parliamentary sovereignty. The power of judicial review under the common law derived from the courts' inherent jurisdiction. In this period, the

15 24 of 1936.

16 *President of the Republic of South Africa and Others v South African Rugby Football Union and Others* 2000 (1) SA 1 (CC) para 131 (footnotes omitted).

17 2015 (1) SA 279 (GJ) para 111.

18 9 of 1994.

19 See generally Chapter 1 on the historical development of administrative law.

meaning of administrative action was dominated by the question of the extent of the courts' review powers over actions of the executive in implementing the mandate of the sovereign parliament acting as a restraining force of the ambit of administrative law. However, this period also saw deliberate attempts to extend the scope of administrative law and thus a broader meaning of administrative action in response to the absence of a justiciable bill of rights that could serve as a check on state power.

The promulgation of the interim Constitution ushered in the constitutional period of administrative law. The primary source of administrative law was no longer the common law, but section 24 of the interim Constitution. Thus the common law was not replaced, but became a source of administrative law additional to and subject to the Constitution.[20] The constitutional period continued with the repeal of the interim Constitution and the promulgation of the final Constitution, which entrenched the right to just administrative action in section 33. However, section 33 did not come into operation with the final Constitution. Item 23 of Schedule 6 to the Constitution provided that the right to just administrative action would be set out in Item 23(2)(*b*) of Schedule 6, temporarily. The wording of that right was virtually identical to section 24 of the interim Constitution. Section 33 would only become operational once national legislation giving effect to the right to just administrative action had been enacted. National legislation had to be enacted within three years. During this three-year period and under the interim Constitution the courts had to formulate a new approach to the meaning of administrative action in light of a justiciable, supreme Constitution and an extensive bill of rights providing a range of different mechanisms to regulate state power as well as significantly different public institutional arrangements.

In February of 2000, PAJA was promulgated, before the expiration of the three-year period. In November 2000, PAJA came into force, introducing the third and final period. The Act introduced, for the first time, a statutory definition of administrative action.

## 3.5 Administrative action during the pre-constitutional period

Under the common law, governmental functions were classified for the purposes of judicial review.[21] Only certain types of administrative action were reviewable under administrative law; therefore the classification of functions had far-reaching effects. Note, however, that the term administrative action as such was not the main criterion for the application of administrative law; the emphasis was on the identity of the institution performing the function.[22]

Administrative functions were categorised as pure, legislative, judicial or quasi-judicial administrative action. The intensity of judicial review depended on the classification of administrative action.[23] Pure administrative action was unsusceptible to review; legislative administrative action could be subjected to reasonableness review but not the principles of natural justice; quasi-judicial administrative action was subject to the principles of natural justice.[24] Nevertheless, despite the classificatory and formalistic approach of the common

20 See *Pharmaceutical Manufacturers of SA*; Chapter 2 section 2.6.4 above.
21 See Rose Innes, LA (1963) *Judicial Review of Administrative Tribunals in South Africa* 39; *Fedsure* para 23 and Chapter 1 section 1.3.4 above.
22 Hoexter (2012) *Administrative Law in South Africa* (2nd ed) 173.
23 Hoexter (2012) 174.
24 Hoexter (2012) 174.

law, '[b]y the end of the pre-democratic era the realm of administrative action at common law was a very broad one'.[25]

## 3.6 Administrative action during the pre-PAJA constitutional period

Section 33 entrenches the right to just administrative action. Therefore, the conception of administrative action is central to the operation of section 33 and the application of administrative law. *Administrative action* must be lawful, reasonable and procedurally fair; where rights have been negatively affected by *administrative action*, the aggrieved party is entitled to written reasons. However, even though the Constitution establishes the centrality of administrative action, the Constitution has left the concept undefined. Therefore, knowledge of the development of the concept is necessary. Case law concerning the content of administrative law also precedes the Constitution's promulgation and therefore retains relevance. As we will see below, there is still divergence today, after the promulgation of PAJA with its definition of administrative action, about the most appropriate methodology to identify administrative action. One approach starts with the definition in PAJA and only turns to the meaning of administrative action under the Constitution to supplement or challenge PAJA's definition. Another approach starts with the meaning of administrative action under the Constitution and only thereafter moves on to the definition in PAJA.[26]

The right to just administrative action is a human right expressly recognised in the Bill of Rights (not that this is decisive, since the Bill of Rights is not an exhaustive list). It is subject to section 36.

As mentioned, administrative action as such is not defined in the Constitution. However, the wording of this particular right is significant: it is not expressly a right to administrative justice, but a right to just administrative action. The adjective 'just' refers to the lawfulness, reasonableness and procedural fairness of the action; that is, if an action is lawful, reasonable and procedurally fair it will be just in terms of section 33.

The operation of section 33 is dependent on the presence of an administrative action. Likewise, the operation of PAJA is dependent on the presence of an administrative action. In other words, without an administrative action neither section 33 nor PAJA applies. Thus administrative action plays a decisive role in administrative law: administrative action serves as the key to the application of administrative law. This explains why the starting point for questions concerning the application of section 33 of the Constitution and of PAJA is administrative action.[27]

### 3.6.1 The *SARFU* judgment[28]

#### 3.6.1.1 A new approach: from institutional to functional

The Constitutional Court confirmed the predominance of a new approach to public power in the *SARFU* case; *SARFU* is central not only to the interpretation of section 33, but also to the operation of administrative law in general. Thus the very nature of administrative action is characterised by the *SARFU* judgment as is the legal regulation of all public power.

25 Hoexter (2012) 173.
26 See section 3.7 below.
27 See Hoexter (2012) 172.
28 *President of the Republic of South Africa and Others v South African Rugby Football Union and Others* 2000 (1) SA 1 (CC).

Therefore one should note that administrative action is an incidence of the exercise of public power.

The court had to determine the scope of 'administrative action' in response to the legal question: does the appointment of a commission of inquiry by the President, in terms of section 84(2)(*f*) of the Constitution, qualify as administrative action?[29] Section 84 lists the President's Head-of-State functions, as opposed to the President's functions as Head of the Executive.

In determining the content of administrative action, the court notes that '[t]he administration is that part of government which is primarily concerned with the implementation of legislation'[30] and that the public administration forms part of the executive.[31] Thus the institutional and functional nature of the public administration is clarified. Section 33 of the Constitution entrenches the right to just administrative action, but does not amount to 'a mere codification of common-law principles'.[32] Therefore the constitutional meaning of administrative action is not limited to the common law.

The court identifies the variety of functions performed by the executive as a whole; importantly, the distinctive role of the executive in developing and initiating policy and legislation, in contrast to the tasks of the administration, is recognised.[33] The court emphasises the fact that section 33 refers to *administrative*, not executive, action.[34] This leads the court to reason that:

> [w]hat matters is not so much the functionary as the function. The question is whether the task itself is administrative or not.[35]

This does not resolve the matter, however, but leads to a new inquiry: what does 'administrative' imply? Several factors can assist in determining whether an action is administrative: the power's source, nature and subject matter, whether the power relates to exercising a public duty, and whether the power can be associated more closely to policy matters or the implementation of policy.[36] In addition, the Constitution as a whole and the 'overall constitutional purpose of an efficient, equitable and ethical public administration' inform the scope of administrative action.[37] The court concedes that '[d]etermining whether an action should be characterised as the implementation of legislation or the formulation of policy may be difficult'.[38]

On the whole, the *SARFU* judgment entrenches the functional approach and that characterises the regulation of public power generally. The shift from an institutional to a functional approach is reflected in the Constitution's definition of 'organ of state'[39] and PAJA's definition of 'administrative action' and 'decision'.[40]

---

29 *President of RSA v SARFU* paras 136–137.
30 *President of RSA v SARFU* para 138.
31 *President of RSA v SARFU* para 133.
32 *President of RSA v SARFU* para 136 (footnote omitted).
33 *President of RSA v SARFU* paras 139, 142.
34 *President of RSA v SARFU* para 141.
35 *President of RSA v SARFU* para 141. In other words, '[t]he focus of the enquiry as to whether conduct is "administrative action" is not on the arm of government to which the relevant actor belongs, but on the nature of the power he or she is exercising' (para 141).
36 *President of RSA v SARFU* para 143.
37 *President of RSA v SARFU* para 143.
38 *President of RSA v SARFU* para 143.
39 Section 239 of the Constitution.
40 Section 1 of PAJA, see section 3.7 below.

### 3.6.1.2 The Constitution and prerogative powers

The powers listed in section 84(2) are conferred on the President acting in the capacity of Head of State, as opposed to Head of the Executive.[41] Historically, these powers were derived from the royal prerogative. However, the Head of State is constrained to constitutional powers only and the royal prerogative no longer exists.[42] Head of State powers do not qualify as administrative action, since they are 'closely related' to policy and do not involve the implementation of legislation.[43] They are in function thus not administrative.

> **PAUSE FOR REFLECTION**
>
> **Classifying a section 84 function**
>
> Given the court's theoretical understanding of section 84(2), classify the nature of a decision to appoint a commission of inquiry and rationalise your answer.[44] Is the decision administrative action, a prerogative function, an executive function, a function of the Head of State or a private function?

Finally, even Head of State powers are subject to judicial scrutiny.[45] Thus, even where the President's conduct does not qualify as administrative action, implying that section 33 does not apply and the decision does not have to be lawful, reasonable and procedurally fair as a matter of administrative law, that decision will always be subject to the requirements of legality.

### 3.6.1.3 The scope of the functional approach

*SARFU* confirmed the predominance of the functional approach in relation to the institutional approach. Thus, where any branch of state (whether the policy branch, public administration, legislature or judiciary) performs a public function, the identity or nature of the institution is not decisive for the application of public-law principles, including administrative law, but the nature of the function.

In the *SARFU* case, the Constitutional Court confirmed that the executive branch's exercise of public power must conform to the requirements of legality, even where the action does not qualify as administrative action. Nevertheless, the functional approach is not limited to the branches of state.

## 3.6.2 The *AAA Investments* judgment

*AAA Investments (Pty) Ltd v Micro Finance Regulatory Council and Another*[46] illustrates the scope of the functional approach, which encompasses the activities of private entities too. In this matter, the Minister of Trade and Industry issued an exemption notice in terms of section 15A of the Usury Act[47] thereby exempting a category of lenders from compliance with the Act upon the condition that those lenders register with the respondent Council. The Council was a pre-existing, private company incorporated in terms of the Companies Act[48] that was tasked with the regulation of the exempt class of lenders. The applicants challenged the legality of rules made by the Council and the court had to decide whether the Council's

41 As opposed to Head of the Executive. See sections 83, 85 of the Constitution.
42 *President of RSA v SARFU* para 144.
43 *President of RSA v SARFU* paras 145–146.
44 See, especially, *President of RSA v SARFU* para 147 and 148.
45 *President of RSA v SARFU* para 148.
46 2007 (1) SA 343 (CC).
47 73 of 1968.
48 71 of 2008.

actions were subject to public-law regulation. The court explained that during the pre-constitutional period the nature of an institution played a crucial role in determining whether a decision was susceptible to judicial review,[49] in line with the institutional approach:

> In the pre-constitutional era in South Africa the nature of institutions and the way in which they exercised their power became relevant in the context of determining whether particular decisions were subject to judicial review.

The court referred to *Dawnlaan Beleggings (Edms) Bpk v Johannesburg Stock Exchange and Others*[50] where a High Court had to determine:

> the correctness of the contention that the decisions of the JSE were not subject to judicial review because the JSE was a private body.[51]

The High Court found that the JSE's decisions were susceptible to review owing to the public impact of its decisions and the legislative obligation to act in the public interest, *inter alia*:[52]

> The Court concluded that, to regard the JSE as a private entity would be to ignore the commercial reality and the very public interest that the Legislature sought to protect.[53]

The court considered the legal role of the 'exercise of power' in foreign jurisdictions and noted that both functional and institutional approaches determine its reviewability.[54] In the South African context:

> the exercise of all public power ... is constrained by the legality principle. It is therefore not necessary, for the purpose of determining whether the legality principle applies, to decide whether the power is governmental.[55]

What was relevant was whether the Council qualified as an organ of state in terms of section 239 of the Constitution,[56] which was largely concerned with the question of whether a public function had been performed.

*In casu*, the purpose of the legislation was for regulation by the executive branch of exempted transactions[57] and the court found that:

> [t]he extent of the control exercised by the Minister over the functioning of the Council ... shows that the function is public rather than private.[58]

Therefore, even though the Council was relatively autonomous in relation to some of its functions:

> [t]he fact that the Minister passed on the regulatory duty means that the function performed must, at least, be a public function.[59]

49 *AAA Investments* para 31 ('In the pre-constitutional era in South Africa the nature of institutions and the way in which they exercised their power became relevant in the context of determining whether particular decisions were subject to judicial review.').
50 1983 (3) SA 344 (W).
51 *AAA Investments* para 31.
52 *AAA Investments* para 31.
53 *AAA Investments* para 31 (footnote omitted).
54 *AAA Investments* para 38.
55 *AAA Investments* para 39.
56 *AAA Investments* paras 40–42.
57 *AAA Investments* para 43.
58 *AAA Investments* para 44.
59 *AAA Investments* para 43.

The Minister also formulated rules which the Council had to apply.[60]

COUNTER POINT

**Executive control over a private institution**

Identify six forms of control that led to the finding in *AAA Investments (Pty) Ltd v Micro Finance Regulatory Council and Another*[61] that the Minister exercised control over the Council. Focus in particular on paragraphs 39 to 45 of the judgment.

How does the court's approach in *AAA Investments* compare to the approach of the SCA in *Calibre Clinical Consultants (Pty) Ltd and Another v National Bargaining Council for the Road Freight Industry and Another*?[62] In the latter matter the SCA also grappled with the question of when an ostensibly private entity (a bargaining council in this instance) should be subjected to public-law norms, including administrative law. The SCA interpreted the judgment in *AAA Investments* to have held:

> that the Micro Finance Regulatory Council indeed performed a 'governmental' function, so far as it was the instrument through which the Minister exercised regulatory control over the industry.[63]

The SCA thus focused its own analysis on categorising the action before it as 'governmental' or not. Note in particular the court's reasoning in paragraphs 34 to 40. Is it the same thing to ask whether a function is public in nature and whether the function is governmental in nature? If we have truly made a shift from an institutional approach to a functional approach in identifying public power and thus administrative action, should the control of government over a function/functionary or the involvement of government in that function play such a major role in the analysis?

## 3.7 Administrative action under PAJA

PAJA contains an extensive definition of administrative action in section 1(i). This definition has rightly been described by the courts as 'unwieldy',[64] 'cumbersome' and serving 'not so much to attribute meaning to the term as to limit its meaning by surrounding it within a palisade of qualifications'.[65] The definition is furthermore difficult to work with because a number of terms in the definition are defined separately in PAJA and the Constitution. One thus has to read all these definitions together to get a full picture of what an administrative action is under PAJA.

As stated in the introduction to this chapter, the definition of administrative action in PAJA serves a key gatekeeping function. The rest of the Act ostensibly only applies to administrative action as defined. Thus, you can only approach a court for relief under PAJA if you can first show that the public conduct you wish to complain about amounts to administrative action as defined. Viewed differently, an administrator must only comply with the requirements set out in PAJA, for example the procedural steps set out in section 4 of the

60 *AAA Investments* para 44.
61 2007 (1) SA 343 (CC).
62 2010 (5) SA 457 (SCA).
63 *Calibre Clinical Consultants (Pty) Ltd and Another v National Bargaining Council for the Road Freight Industry and Another* 2010 (5) SA 457 (SCA) para 33.
64 *Minister of Defence and Military Veterans v Motau and Others* 2014 (5) SA 69 (CC) para 33.
65 *Grey's Marine Hout Bay (Pty) Ltd and Others v Minister of Public Works and Others* 2005 (6) SA 313 (SCA) para 21.

Act, when taking an action if that action will constitute administrative action. This means that you must be able to determine whether something *will* amount to administrative action even before the action is taken.

At this point it is important to remember the general rule of statutory interpretation which states that a term must be understood in 'its statutorily defined meaning unless that meaning would lead to an injustice or absurdity not contemplated by the [statute]'.[66] In the context of PAJA this means that where the Act refers to 'administrative action' it must be understood to refer to the term as defined in section 1(i), unless the context within the particular section indicates that the legislature did not intend the section 1 definition to apply. This is arguably the case in relation to section 3 of PAJA as we shall see in Chapter 7.

COUNTER POINT

**The Constitution or PAJA as the starting point**

Different views have emerged about the appropriate starting point in establishing whether particular action amounts to administrative action.

One view is that the starting point is section 33 of the Constitution. In *Minister of Health and Another NO v New Clicks South Africa (Pty) Ltd and Others*,[67] Ngcobo J formulated this approach as follows:

> The starting point in determining whether PAJA is applicable to the exercise of the power conferred by [the empowering provision] is section 33(1) of the Constitution. The meaning of administrative action must be determined by reference to section 33 of the Constitution and not PAJA. Once it is determined that the exercise of the executive power authorised by [the empowering provision] is administrative action within the meaning of section 33, the next question to consider is whether PAJA nevertheless excludes it.

In following this approach, the court in *Majake v Commission for Gender Equality and Others*[68] stated:

> The application of 'PAJA' is triggered once it is determined that the conduct in question constitutes administrative action under [section 33].

A different view is that the definition in section 1 of PAJA is the starting point and that one should only turn to section 33 if the definition in PAJA is found wanting or needs clarification. An example of this approach is *Minister of Defence and Military Veterans v Motau and Others*[69] where the court stated:

> PAJA gives content to the right to just administrative action in s 33 of the Constitution. The Act categorises certain powers as administrative (through a rather complex taxonomy) and thereby determines the appropriate standard of review and the concept of 'administrative action', *as defined in s 1(i) of PAJA*, is the threshold for engaging in administrative-law review.[70]

CONTINUED >>>

66 *Minister of Mineral Resources and Others v Sishen Iron Ore Co (Pty) Ltd and Another* 2014 (2) SA 603 (CC) para 59.

67 *Minister of Health and Another NO v New Clicks (Pty) Ltd and Others (Treatment Action Campaign and Another as Amici Curiae)* 2006 (2) SA 311 (CC) para 446.

68 2010 (1) SA 87 (GSJ) para 48.

69 2014 (5) SA 69 (CC) para 29 (footnotes omitted).

70 *Motau* para 33 (emphasis added).

The role of section 33 is thus secondary (in sequence, not authority) or a background one in determining whether action amounts to administrative action. The court continued to state in *Motau*:[71]

> As a starting point, in *New Clicks* Chaskalson CJ suggested that the definition of 'administrative action' under PAJA must be 'construed consistently' with the right to administrative justice in s 33 of the Constitution. As s 33 itself contains no express attempt to delimit the scope of 'administrative action', it is helpful to have reference to jurisprudence regarding the interpretation of that section.

Where the definition of administrative action under PAJA provides no interpretative difficulties, there would be no need to turn to section 33. There are accordingly many examples of cases where the courts have decided whether the action at issue constitutes administrative action purely with reference to PAJA and with no reference to section 33.

Since both these approaches have been used by the Constitutional Court, it is difficult to say which is the most appropriate one. However, it is worth bearing in mind the relationship between the different sources of administrative law in grappling with this question.[72] The Constitutional Court has made it clear that it is impermissible to rely on a constitutional right directly where specific legislation has been enacted to give effect to that right. Section 33 and PAJA provide one example of such a case. The court has stated:

> This court has repeatedly held that where legislation has been enacted to give effect to a right, a litigant should rely on that legislation in order to give effect to the right or alternatively challenge the legislation as being inconsistent with the Constitution.[73]

It arguably follows that reliance must first be placed on PAJA in identifying administrative action rather than going behind PAJA to section 33. This would support the second of the approaches outlined above.

The complicated nature of the definition of administrative action in PAJA has led South African courts to develop a useful analytical framework to break the definition of administrative action down into constituent parts and to test for compliance with each part in determining whether a particular action amounts to administrative action. In *Minister of Defence and Military Veterans v Motau and Others*[74] the Constitutional Court identified the following seven elements:

> there must be
> (*a*) a decision of an administrative nature;
> (*b*) *by* an organ of state or a natural or juristic person;
> (*c*) exercising a public power or performing a public function;
> (*d*) *in* terms of any legislation or an empowering provision;
> (*e*) that adversely affects rights;

71 *Motau* para 35 (footnotes omitted).
72 See Chapter 2 section 2.6.4.
73 *Mazibuko and Others v City of Johannesburg and Others* 2010 (4) SA 1 (CC) para 73.
74 2014 (5) SA 69 (CC) para 33.

(*f*) that has a direct, external legal effect; and
(*g*) that does not fall under any of the listed exclusions.

The order of analysis set out in this list follows the definition itself and is also the order followed in the discussion below. However, from a strategic point of view it would be sensible to start with the last element, since an action can never qualify as administrative action if it is expressly excluded by the definition regardless of whether it complies with all the other elements. Starting with the exclusions is thus an efficient way to filter out those actions that cannot be administrative action under PAJA.

### 3.7.1 A decision of an administrative nature

Section 1(i) defines an administrative action as a 'decision' or a 'failure to take a decision' and section 1(v) provides a separate definition of 'decision'. This is immediately an important clue as to the type of conduct in which administrative law is interested. Administrative law focuses on decision-making by those exercising public power. It is thus not interested in steps that follow automatically from earlier conduct, even where such later steps may have legal consequences. A good example is when a disability grant is awarded to a person with a temporary disability under the Social Assistance Act[75] for a set period. Once that period comes to an end the payment of the grant will terminate automatically. Such termination will not constitute administrative action since no decision was taken to bring the grant to an end even though such termination will have significant implications for the beneficiary. The only administrative action in this scenario will be the original decision to approve the grant for a particular period.

The element of a decision implies a measure of finality in administrative action. Administrative law thus applies to an entire administrative process leading to a final decision as a whole. It does not apply in a piecemeal fashion to parts of a multistage administrative process. This means that one cannot determine whether an administrative action is, say, procedurally fair by looking only at a part of the process leading to the decision. It also means that one cannot challenge the process in court before the final decision is taken. It is only once the final decision is taken that the process constitutes a complete administrative action and one can evaluate it against the requirements of PAJA. In this respect the element of decision overlaps largely with the later element requiring a direct, external legal effect.[76]

**PAUSE FOR REFLECTION**

**Final decisions**

While section 1(i) refers to a 'decision taken' thereby implying finality in the process, the separate definition of 'decision' refers to 'any decision ... proposed to be made, or required to be made'. These phrases may seem to qualify the finality characteristic of what constitutes a decision. Something that is still 'proposed to be made' is arguably not final. However, one should remember that the later element requiring a direct, external legal effect before the action will constitute administrative action reinforces the notion of finality as a requirement. A mere proposal arguably cannot have this requisite effect and will thus never qualify as administrative action.

CONTINUED >>>

75 13 of 2004.
76 See section 3.4.6 below.

> One has to follow an interpretation of the definition that reconciles these ostensibly contradictory parts. This may be achieved if the phrase 'proposed to be made' is read as only referring to the timing of the decision and not the substantive conditionality thereof. In other words, conduct will be included as a decision 'proposed to be made' where it is only a matter of time before the final decision is taken, but the content of the final decision is no longer in doubt. Such content (once the decision becomes operational) will furthermore have to comply with the effect requirement in order to qualify as administrative action.
>
> In whatever way one interprets the definition of 'decision' it seems that the real work in either including or excluding preliminary steps in an administrative process under the definition of administrative action is done by the effect requirement of the definition (element (*f*) in the list above).

The definition expressly includes omissions in the definition of administrative action. The main definition in section 1(i) thus talks of 'any failure to take a decision' and the separate definition of 'decision' in section 1(v) likewise includes 'a failure to take a decision' as one instance of 'a decision'. The effect is that when an administrator does nothing it could constitute an administrative action! This part of the definition should be understood alongside section 6(2)(*g*) and 6(3) of PAJA, which creates the possibility for someone to challenge an administrator's conduct in court where the administrator fails to act.[77] As is clear from section 6(3), this does not mean that any non-action by an administrator will be open to challenge as administrative action. The same is true for a failure to act as part of the definition of administrative action. Not all failures to act (that is, not taking a decision) will qualify as administrative action.

In *Offit Enterprises (Pty) Ltd and Another v Coega Development Corporation and Others*[78] the Supreme Court of Appeal explained that a failure that would be relevant under PAJA:

> refers to a decision that the administrator in question is under some obligation to take, not simply to indecisiveness in planning on policy issues. It is directed at dilatoriness in taking decisions that the administrator is supposed to take ...

It follows that something will only constitute a 'failure to take a decision' and thus potentially qualify as administrative action under PAJA if there is a duty on the administrator to take the decision and the administrator has not done so.

The definition of 'decision' further qualifies the concept by requiring that it must be a decision 'of an administrative nature'. It is of course somewhat tautological to define a term, 'administrative action', by repeating the same word, 'administrative'.

The question remains: what is administrative? In grappling with this element of the definition, the courts have relied heavily on the meaning attributed to administrative action under section 33 of the Constitution. Especially in *Grey's Marine Hout Bay (Pty) Ltd and Others v Minister of Public Works and Others*[79] and again in *Minister of Home Affairs and Others v Scalabrini Centre and Others*[80] the Supreme Court of Appeal aligned this part of the definition with the typical separation of powers exclusions from the ambit of administrative law.

---

77 See Chapter 6 section 6.2.1.2 below.

78 2010 (4) SA 242 (SCA) para 43.

79 2005 (6) SA 313 (SCA) para 24.

80 2013 (6) SA 421 (SCA) paras 54–57.

These are primarily the legislative decisions of original legislatures, judicial decisions of courts and pure executive or policy decisions of the executive. None of these are 'administrative' in nature and are thus disqualified as administrative action under this element in addition to the specific exclusions listed in section 1(i). The court stated in *Grey's Marine* that conduct 'of an administrative nature' is generally understood as:

> the conduct of the bureaucracy (whoever the bureaucratic functionary might be) in carrying out the daily functions of the State, which necessarily involves the application of policy, usually after its translation into law ...[81]

The Constitutional Court has endorsed this formulation and held that this part of the definition fulfils two functions. First, it requires a reviewing court to make a positive determination that the action complained of involves the exercise of public power 'of an administrative character'.[82] Second, it indicates that a larger category of decisions is excluded from the definition than those listed in the exclusions. The court added to the *Grey's Marine* formulation that 'administrative powers usually entail the application of formulated policy to particular factual circumstances' that the 'exercise of administrative powers is policy brought into effect, rather than its creation'[83] and that a 'decision or action that is administrative in nature is therefore operational, for it is about carrying out what has already been prescribed often in some detail'.[84] From the *Motau* judgment it would seem that the closer a decision is to the policy function of especially a politically elected official, the less likely it is that such decision will be of an administrative nature. Likewise, in *Scalabrini* the court stated that 'decisions heavily influenced by policy generally belong in the domain of the executive' and the 'more a decision is to be driven by considerations of executive policy the further it moves from being reviewable under PAJA and vice versa'.[85]

The definition of 'decision' in section 1(v) includes a list of types of actions that would qualify as decisions under the definition. It is, however, not an exhaustive list as the word 'including' preceding the list indicates.[86] The final item on the list is furthermore a 'catch-all' provision in that it includes 'a decision relating to ... doing or refusing to do any other act or thing of an administrative nature'.

**COUNTER POINT**

**Rule-making**

One area of administrative action that has resulted in considerable controversy under PAJA's definition of administrative action is that of executive rule-making or what was referred to as legislative administrative action at common law.

As we have noted, the making of rules by administrators (primarily members of the executive) in terms of a legislative mandate has long been recognised as subject to some administrative law controls.[87] The typical example is the making of regulations aimed at implementing a particular statute. Other examples include the issuing of practice notes and circulars by various public bodies. The distinctive feature of these

CONTINUED >>>

81 *Grey's Marine Hout Bay* para 24.
82 *Motau* para 34.
83 *Motau* para 34.
84 *AfriForum v University of the Free State* 2018 (2) SA 185 (CC) para 34.
85 *Minister of Home Affairs and Others v Scalabrini Centre and Others* 2013 (6) SA 421 (SCA) para 57.
86 *Van Zyl v New National Party and Others* [2003] 3 All SA 737 (C) para 87.
87 See Chapter 1 section 1.3.4 above.

types of public actions is that they are not aimed at one particular instance of state administration, but are aimed at governing generally a category of cases. The application of these actions is thus general rather than specific.

Under PAJA the question has emerged whether the act of rule-making can be viewed as 'a decision of an administrative nature'. The definition of 'decision' in PAJA does not seem to cater specifically for rule-making and it is not clear that rule-making can even be viewed as 'a decision'. The question also arises whether rule-making is not rather of a legislative nature as opposed to an administrative nature.

The case that was set to bring clarity on this matter, *Minister of Health and Another NO v New Clicks South Africa (Pty) Ltd and Others*,[88] unfortunately failed to provide a definitive answer. In this matter the Minister issued regulations on a pricing system for the sale of medicine in terms of section 22G of the Medicines and Related Substances Act.[89] The relevant part of the empowering provision stated that:

> [t]he Minister may, on the recommendation of the pricing committee, make regulations ... on the introduction of a transparent pricing system for all medicines and Scheduled substances sold in the Republic.

Various entities challenged the validity of the Minister's conduct *inter alia* in terms of administrative law. When the matter reached the Constitutional Court, the court was split on whether the making of the regulations amounted to administrative action as defined in PAJA and was thus subject to PAJA. Five justices held that the making of regulations (at least in this instance) did qualify as administrative action as defined; five justices held that it was not necessary to decide the issue and one justice held that the making of regulations did not constitute administrative action. There was accordingly no majority view on this issue and it remained unresolved.

Chaskalson CJ presented strong reasoning in favour of the (minority) view that all regulation-making constitutes administrative action under PAJA. He noted *inter alia* that the making of delegated legislation was recognised as administrative action under common law and that nothing in either the interim Constitution or the Constitution indicated a departure from that position.[90] To the contrary, there is much in the Constitution that indicates a commitment to 'open and transparent government' that would require the making of regulations to be subject to administrative justice rights.[91] Chaskalson CJ held that the 'making of delegated legislation by members of the Executive is an essential part of public administration', implying that it is of an administrative nature.[92] He also held that the absence of specific mention of rule-making in the definition of 'decision' in section 1(v) is not definitive, since that section includes '*any* decision of an administrative nature' and contains a catch-all sub-provision in subsection (g) which recognises 'doing or refusing to do *any* other act or thing of an administrative nature' as a qualifying decision.[93] In the Chief Justice's view, these formulations included rule-making.

CONTINUED >>>

88 2006 (2) SA 311 (CC).
89 101 of 1965.
90 *New Clicks* para 109.
91 *New Clicks* paras 110–113.
92 *New Clicks* para 113.
93 *New Clicks* para 128 (original emphasis).

In the subsequent judgment in *City of Tshwane Metropolitan Municipality v Cable City (Pty) Ltd*[94] the Supreme Court of Appeal simply stated, without any reasoning, that it

> agree[d] with the appellant's contention that the making of regulations by a Minister constitutes administrative action within the meaning of [PAJA].

The court relied solely on Chaskalson CJ's judgment in *New Clicks* as authority for this statement. However, as we noted above, Chaskalson CJ's judgment was a minority view and thus cannot be relied upon as authority for the statement that all executive rule-making constitutes administrative action under PAJA. The Supreme Court of Appeal judgment in *Cable City* has in turn been relied upon by the High Court as authority for the statement that rule-making is administrative action under PAJA. In *Mobile Telephone Networks (Pty) Ltd v Chairperson of the Independent Communications Authority of South Africa and Others, In Re: Vodacom (Pty) Ltd v Chairperson of the Independent Communications Authority of South Africa and Others*[95] the court stated:

> Although there was some controversy in the past, the Supreme Court of Appeal has now confirmed that the act of making regulations amounts to administrative action as contemplated in PAJA.

However, in *Mostert NO v Registrar of Pension Funds and Others*,[96] the Supreme Court of Appeal revisited its earlier statement, noting that:

> in ... *Cable City* ... the position was also stated too widely.

The court correctly pointed out that Chaskalson CJ's judgment was not a majority view on this point in *New Clicks* and is accordingly not authority for a general statement that all rule-making amount to administrative action under PAJA. The court furthermore highlighted that Chaskalson CJ in any case did not aver that all rule-making qualified as administrative action under PAJA, but only that the particular instance of rule-making before the court in *New Clicks* amounted to administrative action. The inquiry thus remains a contextual one, to establish in each case whether the rule-making in that case qualifies as administrative action or not. This reasoning of the Supreme Court of Appeal suggests that the answer to whether a particular instance of rule-making amounts to administrative action under PAJA or not, does not primarily turn on whether such action is conceptually 'of an administrative nature', but rather on other elements of the definition such as the impact requirements, which may or may not be met in particular cases. As the court pointed out in *Mostert*:

> the final word on regulation-making and the applicability of PAJA to it may therefore not have been spoken.[97]

### 3.7.2 By an organ of state or a natural or juristic person

This element of the definition emphasises that administrative action is not only taken by public bodies, but also by private entities. This confirms the functional approach to the

94 2010 (3) SA 589 (SCA) para 10.
95 [2014] 3 All SA 171 (GJ) para 71 (footnotes omitted).
96 2018 (2) SA 53 (SCA) para 10.
97 *Mostert* para 10.

application of administrative law, where the key question is what the nature of the function is that is being performed, rather than an institutional approach, which asks who is taking the action.[98]

PAJA defines 'organ of state' with reference to the definition of that term in section 239 of the Constitution. The constitutional definition includes, in addition to state departments:

> any other functionary or institution ... exercising a public power or performing a public function.

This already opens the door to non-public entities to be recognised as organs of state and hence come under the scope of the definition of administrative action in PAJA.

The inclusion of actions of non-public entities is further strengthened by the addition of 'natural or juristic person' to the list of actors that can perform administrative action under PAJA.

**REFRAMING**

**Refuse collection by private companies**

Recall the example in Chapter 1 about the private company Garbage Gobblers that was appointed by a municipality to collect household refuse.[99] When one applies the second element of the definition of administrative action to the scenario, one can see that it makes no difference to the applicability of PAJA that it is a private company performing the work of refuse collection. The key question will be what the nature of the function is. One will thus focus on the nature of refuse collection rather than *who* is collecting the refuse.

The importance of this point in practical terms can be illustrated by the following extension of the scenario sketched in Chapter 1. Consider that Garbage Gobblers is only contracted to collect refuse in your suburb, while the municipality itself collects the refuse in a neighbouring suburb where one of your friends lives. Your friend has a very similar experience when the municipal refuse truck hits his front gate, causing damage. Would it make sense to view your friend's legal recourse differently from yours simply on the basis that his refuse was collected by the municipality while yours was collected by a private company?

One can think of many similar examples raised by the modern trend to involve private entities in performing public functions. Think of prisons, hospitals or schools that are operated by private companies. Think of private providers of water or electricity. Think of professions and entire industries, like accounting, engineering, various sports – soccer, rugby and athletics for example – or advertising that are regulated by bodies that do not form part of the state. In all these cases the identity of the body tells us very little about whether the action itself should be subject to administrative law.

It is important to note the expansive view of the actor that may take administrative action *inter alia* because, as the Constitutional Court stated in *AAA Investments (Pty) Ltd v Micro Finance Regulatory Council and Another*:[100]

> Our Constitution ensures ... that government cannot be released from its human rights and rule of law obligations simply because it employs the strategy of delegating its functions to another entity.

98 See *President of RSA v SARFU.*
99 See Chapter 1 section 1.2.1.5 above.
100 2007 (1) SA 343 (CC) para 40.

### 3.7.3 Exercising a public power or performing a public function

As we have seen in the examples above, the nature of the action stands at the core of the definition of administrative action. Administrative action is thus action of a public nature. We already noted in Chapter 1, when defining *administrative law*, that public authority is a key defining feature of this part of the law. The definition in PAJA expresses this by including as an element that the action must amount to the exercise of a public power or the performance of a public function. Again, this puts the focus on *what* is being done rather than *who* is acting: a functional approach rather than an institutional one.

**PAUSE FOR REFLECTION**

**Public functions as contextual**

The notion of a public function is not a fixed one. What a society views as a public function can change over time. It can also differ between societies.

Good examples of how our perceptions of what constitute public functions change over time are broadcasting and telecommunications. Thirty years ago, most people in South Africa would instinctively have said that the function of broadcasting, especially television, and providing a telecommunications network by way of landline telephone services are public functions. The state exclusively provided these services to society and people generally accepted it as the natural state of affairs. However, today we would not as easily regard either broadcasting or telecommunications as the primary responsibility of the state or something that is inherently a function of the state. Major private players such as MultiChoice's DSTV and MidiTV's e.TV have come to dominate the broadcasting sector, while the major cellular phone companies, Vodacom, MTN and CellC, are certainly the first ones most people would think of in terms of telecommunications service providers in South Africa.

An example of how public functions differ between societies is rail services. In South Africa rail services are largely considered to be a public function, something that the state is responsible for through Transnet. In Great Britain, however, rail services are provided by private companies, of which there are more than 20, so that the British would not consider rail services to be inherently public, that is something that the state is providing to citizens.

A final example of the contextual nature of public functions is the changes that South Africans are currently witnessing in the energy sector. The provision of energy, primarily electricity, has been the exclusive function of the state through Eskom. South Africans would consequently consider this to be an inherently public function. In many other parts of the world private companies play a major role in providing energy to users with the state only fulfilling a regulatory function, rather than providing energy. Changes to the regulation of energy provision in South Africa at present may also lead to changes in perceptions about whose responsibility it is to provide users with energy as more private providers enter the market. It is thus quite possible that South Africans will in thirty years' time no longer think of energy provision as an inherently public function.

It is not an easy matter to define what a 'public power' or a 'public function' is. In his minority judgment in *Chirwa v Transnet Ltd and Others*[101] Langa CJ stated:

> Determining whether a power or function is 'public' is a notoriously difficult exercise. There is no simple definition or clear test to be applied.

The Chief Justice continued to list a number of useful factors that can give one an indication of whether a particular power or function is public. These are:

(*a*) the relationship of coercion or power that the actor has in its capacity as a public institution;
(*b*) the impact of the decision on the public;
(*c*) the source of the power; and
(*d*) whether there is a need for the decision to be exercised in the public interest.

Langa CJ's remarks were quoted with approval by the court in *Association of Mineworkers and Construction Union v Chamber of Mines of South Africa*.[102] Cameron J listed the following 'pointers' in determining whether a particular power is public. These are:

(*a*) the source of the power;
(*b*) the nature of the power;
(*c*) its subject matter; and
(*d*) whether it involves the exercise of a public duty.[103]

No single one of these factors will on its own determine whether a particular action is public, but may in combination point in one direction or another.

In *AMCU v Chamber of Mines*, the court highlighted the first of Langa CJ's factors in *Chirwa* as particularly important in its analysis. The conduct under scrutiny in this case was the conclusion of a collective agreement between employers and unions in the mining industry, which, by virtue of the Labour Relations Act,[104] applied to all employees of the employers regardless of whether they were members of the particular unions or not. The applicant challenged the constitutionality of the extension of the agreement to all employees, *inter alia* on the basis that it authorised 'private actors the right to effectively exercise public power arbitrarily'.[105] The court held that the extension of the collective agreement to non-parties entailed the exercise of public power based on the following reasoning:

> Features pointing to 'public' are: (a) the decision is rooted in legislation and its effects are circumscribed by the statute; (b) the effect of the decision is mandatory on non-parties and coercive on their constitutional entitlements; (c) the decision results in binding consequences without those parties' acquiescence; and (d) the rationale for extension is a plainly public goal, namely the improvement of workers' conditions through collectively agreed bargains.[106]

The public impact of the recall of a permanent member of the National Council of Provinces by her political party was held to be an important factor pointing to the public nature of such

101 2008 (4) SA 367 (CC) para 186.
102 2017 (3) SA 242 (CC) para 75.
103 *AMCU v Chamber of Mines* para 74.
104 66 of 1995; section 23(1)(*d*).
105 *AMCU v Chamber of Mines* para 62.
106 *AMCU v Chamber of Mines* para 81.

action in *Van Zyl v New National Party and Others.*[107] The court held that such recall impacted on the functioning of a public institution (the NCOP) and subsequently on the public generally whose interests are served by this body. In contrast, in *Dube v Zikalala,*[108] the court held that decisions taken at an elective conference of a political party, including the election of provincial leaders, were not public in nature since they did not concern the public, but only the members of the party. Langa CJ adopted similar reasoning in his minority judgment in *Chirwa,* holding that the appellant fulfilled a purely internal function within Transnet and was not involved in Transnet's public functions with the result that the appellant's dismissal by Transnet did not have any impact on the public.

In a number of cases the presence or absence of a statutory source of the relevant power played a major role in deciding whether the action is public or not. In *Cape Metropolitan Council v Metro Inspection Services (Western Cape) CC and Others*[109] the court held that had the organ of state relied upon its statutory powers to cancel the agreement at issue it would have amounted to the exercise of public power, but since the organ of state relied upon its contractual rights to cancel, the exercise of the power was private. As Plasket J rightly pointed out in *Police and Prisons Civil Rights Union and Others v Minister of Correctional Services and Others (No 1)*:[110]

> a statutory source of power is significant because 'it places the existence of public power largely, if not completely, beyond contention'.

Finally, and perhaps the most general of all the factors listed by Langa CJ in *Chirwa,* the public interest in the relevant decision has long been a key factor in identifying public power. Public interest in the functioning of the Johannesburg Stock Exchange, formally a private company, was determinative in the common-law cases that held actions of that body to be public in nature[111] as well as under PAJA.[112] Under PAJA in *Police and Prisons Civil Rights Union*[113] Plasket J held that:

> the pre-eminence of the public interest in the proper administration of prisons and the attainment of the purposes specified in ... the Correctional Services Act all strengthen my view that the powers that are sought to be reviewed in this matter are public powers as envisaged by ... PAJA

Similarly, in *AMCU v Chamber of Mines*[114] the Constitutional Court noted that the 'rationale for the power and its exercise is the public interest in improving workers' conditions through collectively agreed bargains', indicating that the power was public in nature.

The public interest element should, however, be treated with caution. In respect of this element it is particularly important to bear in mind that the elements (and all other relevant factors) must be viewed together, rather than just relying on one factor. In a number of cases the courts have thus cautioned that a decision will not necessarily be public in nature merely because the public has an interest in it. In *Calibre Clinical Consultants (Pty) Ltd and Another*

107 [2003] 3 All SA 737 (C) para 75.
108 [2017] 4 All SA 365 (KZP) para 131.
109 2001 (3) SA 1013 (SCA) para 20.
110 2008 (3) SA 91 (E) para 54 fn 55 with reference to the unreported High Court judgment in *Chirwa v Transnet Ltd and Others* (Case No 03/01052, WLD).
111 *Johannesburg Stock Exchange and Another v Witwatersrand Nigel Ltd and Another* 1988 (3) SA 132 (A) at 152; *Dawnlaan Beleggings (Edms) Bpk v Johannesburg Stock Exchange and Others* 1983 (3) SA 344 (W) at 361–362.
112 *Absa Bank Ltd v Ukwanda Leisure Holdings (Pty) Ltd* 2014 (1) SA 550 (GSJ) paras 51–52.
113 2008 (3) SA 91 (E) para 54.
114 Para 79.

*v National Bargaining Council for the Road Freight Industry and Another*[115] Nugent JA for the Supreme Court of Appeal thus stated:

> I have considerable doubt whether a body can be said to exercise 'public powers' or perform a 'public function' only because the public has an interest in the manner in which its powers are exercised or its functions are performed, and I find no support for that approach in other cases in this country or abroad.

Other factors that the courts have pointed to as indicative of public power, either as variants of the elements set out above or as distinct factors, are the use of public funds in exercising the relevant power,[116] the control of government over the exercise of the power or the function (primarily by looking at government control over the entity performing the function in relation to that function),[117] the monopolistic regulatory nature of the function[118] and whether government would have had to step in and perform the function had it not been for the actions of the entity at stake.[119]

**COUNTER POINT**

**Is the control of sport administrative action?**

South African courts have not been consistent in their treatment of the actions of sporting bodies in terms of administrative law.[120] These are private bodies established to regulate the affairs of a particular sporting code, with little or no involvement by the state. Typical examples are the South African Football Association (SAFA), the South African Rugby Union (SARU formerly South African Rugby Football Union SARFU)), Cricket South Africa (CSA) (which includes the former United Cricket Board of South Africa (UCB)), Athletics South Africa (ASA) and the National Horseracing Authority of Southern Africa (NHA). In some instances, courts have treated such conduct as purely private and accordingly not subject to principles of administrative law, whereas in other instances courts have viewed the conduct as public and subjected it to administrative-law scrutiny.

Thus, in *Cronje v United Cricket Board of SA*,[121] the court held that the UCB was not a public body and that its action in banning a former player from the sport was not subject to the rules of natural justice under administrative law. By contrast, in *Dr. Nyoka v Cricket South Africa*,[122] the court held that the decision by CSA to remove its president was subject to administrative law rules of natural justice given CSA's public function in respect of cricket in South Africa.

CONTINUED >>>

115 2010 (5) SA 457 (SCA) para 36.

116 *Calibre Clinical Consultants* para 42; *Airports Company South Africa Ltd and Another v ISO Leisure OR Tambo (Pty) Ltd* 2011 (4) SA 642 (GSJ) para 59.

117 *Calibre Clinical Consultants* para 42; *Airports Company SA* para 47; *Khan v Ansur NO and Others* 2009 (3) SA 258 (D) para 32.

118 *National Horseracing Authority of Southern Africa v Naidoo and Another* 2010 (3) SA 182 (N) para 23 (minority judgment of Wallis J).

119 *Calibre Clinical Consultants* para 42; *Airports Company SA* para 59.

120 See Plasket, C (2016) The fundamental principles of justice and legal vacuums: the regulatory powers of national sporting bodies *SALJ* 133(3):569.

121 2001 (4) SA 1361 (T).

122 2011 JDR 0460 (GSJ).

In *Ndoro v South African Football Association*,[123] Unterhalter J provided a useful summary of the principles at issue in these instances:

> First, private entities may discharge public functions by recourse to powers that do not have a statutory source. Powers of this kind may be characterized as public powers. So characterized, actions that issue from their exercise may constitute administrative action. Second, a private entity may exercise public powers, but this does not entail that all its conduct issues from the exercise of a public power or the performing of a public function – all depends on the relevant power or function. Finally, while there are broad criteria for making an evaluation as to whether a competence enjoyed by a private entity is a public power or public function, there is no warrant to conclude that simply because a private entity is powerful and may do things that are of great interest to the public that it discharges a public power or function. Rather, it is the assumption of exclusive, compulsory, coercive regulatory competence to secure public goods that reach beyond mere private advancement that attract the supervisory disciplines of public law.

In *Ndoro*, the court was called upon to determine whether the resolution of a dispute between Ajax Cape Town Football Club and one of its players against SAFA and the National Soccer League (NSL), one of SAFA's members, by way of arbitration under the SAFA Arbitration Tribunal constituted administrative action open to judicial review. In finding that the resolution of the dispute and the regulatory powers of SAFA and the NSL more generally do constitute administrative action, Unterhalter J placed emphasis on the following factors:

> These bodies, (FIFA, SAFA and the NSL) constitute an institutional framework within which a comprehensive scheme of regulations is administered and enforced. Each entity is a private organization. Neither the entities nor their rules derive from public statutes. These associations and their relationships with their members are founded upon contracts.

But for all this, as a general matter, it is hard to escape the conclusion that what these bodies do and the objects they strive after are public in nature. First, the regulatory scheme constituted by the statutes and regulations [of FIFA, SAFA and NSL] is exclusive, comprehensive, compulsory and coercive. There is no other way to conduct professional football, save in compliance with this regulatory scheme. FIFA and its progeny are the singular source of professional football regulation. Second, compliance is not optional and the rules are backed by coercive sanctions. Third, although many actors participate in football for great private reward, football is not the sum of these private actions. Rather it is a sport so widely enjoyed and passionately engaged by large sections of the public that the flourishing of the game is a public good, and one that is often understood to be bound up with the well-being of the nation.

> Once this is so, private associations that regulate football exercise public functions because they oversee a public good, and do not simply regulate private interests. And importantly, this is precisely how FIFA and SAFA see themselves. They seek to promote football as a public good and not as organisations simply furthering the private interests of their members.[124]

123 2018 (5) SA 630 (GJ) para 23.

124 Paras 29–31.

### 3.7.4 In terms of a constitution, any legislation or an empowering provision

Another key characteristic of administrative law is that it deals with delegated powers. In other words, it deals with the exercise of powers granted to the administrator by another authority in an instrument. The stereotypical case is of the legislature that has granted the administrator the power in a statute to take an action. The definition of administrative action reflects this characteristic by requiring the presence of a source for the decision.

For organs of state that source can be either a constitution (the national constitution or a provincial constitution) or legislation. Accordingly, in *Mostert v Nash,*[125] the court held that a decision taken by the Financial Services Board, an organ of state, in respect of the remuneration of a curator of a pension fund, was not an administrative action, *inter alia* because the source of the power exercised was the court order under which the curator was appointed and not legislation.

For non-organs of state, that source can be an 'empowering provision', which has its own extremely wide definition in section 1(vi) and includes any 'instrument or other document in terms of which an administrative action was purportedly taken'. Examples of empowering provisions may thus include the constitution of a voluntary association such as a political party or a church, the code of conduct of a school or university, circulars or practice notes issued by state departments as well as guideline documents and manuals.

### 3.7.5 That adversely affects rights

The fifth element of the definition of administrative action, read with the sixth element, is probably the most problematic aspect of the definition. If this element is to be taken literally it would imply that only those decisions that in fact result in rights being negatively affected can ever qualify as administrative action. This is problematic for a number of reasons. First, there is no similar restriction in section 33(1) of the Constitution, but only in section 33(2) in relation to the right to reasons. Since PAJA is meant to give effect to the whole of section 33, this element may elevate the restriction found only in section 33(2) to the entire section. If this element of the definition is interpreted literally it may very well render the definition unconstitutional. Second, PAJA is meant to provide guidance to administrators *before* they act as much as it is meant to provide redress to affected persons *after* an administrative action has been taken. However, a logical conundrum emerges if an administrator must know whether his or her decision will impact adversely on rights *before* that decision is taken in order to know whether it is administrative action and would thus require the prescripts of PAJA (for example, the rules of procedure in sections 3 or 4) to be followed in reaching the conclusion in the first place!

**REFRAMING**

**Fracking in the Karoo**

Imagine that Shale of Africa (Pty) Ltd, a major player in the energy industry, wishes to conduct hydraulic fracturing (fracking) to extract natural gas from rocks deep underground in the Karoo, near a residential area. They apply to the Director-General (DG) of the Department of Environmental Affairs for an environmental authorisation allowing the fracking to take place. The DG needs to know whether he must take

CONTINUED >>>

125 2018 (5) SA 409 (SCA) para 34.

account of the procedural requirements in sections 3 and/or 4 of PAJA in deciding on the application. This will, for example, determine whether he must engage with the community of the adjacent residential area before taking his decision and what form that engagement will have to take. The first step in answering the DG's question is of course to determine whether his decision will amount to administrative action under section 1 of PAJA, which is the gateway to the rest of the Act.

On a literal reading of this fifth element of the definition, the DG will have to know whether he will grant the authorisation or not before he can determine whether his decision will amount to administrative action. However, the DG will in all likelihood not know whether he should grant the authorisation before he has received input from all interested parties. The DG thus finds himself in a circular argument: the application of the procedure depends on the outcome of the definition, but the definition depends on the outcome of the procedure.

In *Greys Marine Hout Bay (Pty) Ltd and Others v Minister of Public Works and Others*[126] Nugent JA held that a literal interpretation of this element cannot be accepted. Instead, the court ruled, the fifth and sixth elements were:

> probably intended rather to convey that administrative action is action that has the capacity to affect legal rights, the two qualifications in tandem serving to emphasise that administrative action impacts directly and immediately on individuals.

This interpretation has been endorsed by the Constitutional Court.[127] In applying this approach in *Greys Marine* the court held that the respondent's decision to lease a portion of state land to a private company was administrative action since it had 'immediate and direct legal consequences' for the lessee.[128] Not much is left of the 'adverse' part of this element of the definition following the judgment. In the later judgment in *Minister of Home Affairs and Others v Scalabrini Centre and Others*[129] Nugent JA noted that the adverse impact element may influence 'the actionability of the decision', but not the nature of the decision as administrative action.

The generous interpretation of the definition's impact requirement has been adopted to hold, for example, that the decision not to appoint a person to a public service position amounted to administrative action[130] and the same for a decision to appoint a person to such a position.[131] It is thus clear that *any* impact on rights, whether negative or positive, will satisfy this element. The judgment in *Wessels v Minister for Justice and Constitutional Development and Others*[132] is especially noteworthy since it expressly endorsed a

126 2005 (6) SA 313 (SCA) para 23.

127 *Allpay Consolidated Investment Holdings (Pty) Ltd and Others v Chief Executive Officer, South African Social Security Agency and Others* 2014 (1) SA 604 (CC) para 60; *Walele v City of Cape Town and Others* 2008 (6) SA 129 (CC) para 37; *Joseph and Others v City of Johannesburg and Others* 2010 (4) SA 55 (CC) para 27; *Viking Pony Africa Pumps (Pty) Ltd t/a Tricom Africa v Hidro-Tech Systems (Pty) Ltd and Another* 2011 (1) SA 327 (CC) para 37.

128 *Grey's Marine Hout Bay* para 28.

129 2013 (6) SA 421 (SCA) para 49.

130 *Minister of Defence and Others v Dunn* 2007 (6) SA 52 (SCA); *Kiva v Minister of Correctional Services and Another* (2007) 28 ILJ 597 (E).

131 *Wessels v Minister for Justice and Constitutional Development and Others* 2010 (1) SA 128 (GNP).

132 2010 (1) SA 128 (GNP).

determination approach to the impact element of the definition.[133] In terms of such an approach, the determination of rights is enough to satisfy the impact element, it is not required that rights be taken away, that is a deprivation approach.

The judgment in *Joseph and Others v City of Johannesburg and Others*[134] has also opened up the potentially restrictive influence of the definition's impact requirement. In this matter, the City terminated the electricity supply to an apartment building in which the applicant was a tenant. Electricity was supplied in bulk to the building so that only the landlord had a contract with the City for the supply of electricity. The tenants in turn only had their rental contracts with the landlord, which included the supply of electricity, but had no contractual relationship with the City. When the landlord failed to pay the City, it terminated supply. In challenging the termination decision of the City, the tenants argued that the decision amounted to administrative action, which attracted the procedural fairness obligations of PAJA towards them. The City argued in response that the decision did not amount to administrative action vis-à-vis the tenants *inter alia* because the decision did not impact on any rights of the tenants. The court rejected this argument, dealing with it as much under the definition's impact elements as the impact requirement under section 3(1).[135] The court held that the City had a general duty 'to provide municipal services' flowing from a collection of constitutional and statutory provisions.[136] It followed that:

> when City Power supplied electricity to [the apartment building], it did so in fulfilment of the constitutional and statutory duties of local government to provide basic municipal services to all persons living in its jurisdiction. When the applicants received electricity, they did so by virtue of their corresponding public-law right to receive this basic municipal service.[137]

As a result, the City's decision amounted to administrative action and the procedural obligations under section 3 of PAJA were activated, which means that the rights of the applicants were adversely affected for purposes of PAJA. This judgment is significant, because it shows that the impact element of the definition of administrative action should not be narrowly interpreted to refer only to private-law or common-law rights or to fundamental rights in the Bill of Rights, but also includes so-called 'public-law rights', which emerge from broad constitutional and statutory obligations placed on organs of state. This latter category of rights is obviously much broader than a traditional understanding of legal rights.

### 3.7.6 That has a direct, external legal effect

The sixth element of the definition is often read alongside the fifth element to constitute a single impact element, as is illustrated by the *Grey's Marine* judgment noted above. This approach was expressly endorsed by the Constitutional Court in *Joseph and Others v City of Johannesburg and Others.*[138] It seems to be common sense that a decision that has an adverse impact on rights will by implication also have a direct, external legal effect.

This element furthermore confirms the characteristic of finality in the definition of administrative action that we already noted under the first element above. A decision can

133 See *Wessels* para 137.
134 2010 (4) SA 55 (CC).
135 See Chapter 7 section 7.3 on the impact requirement for the application of rules of procedural fairness under PAJA.
136 *Joseph* paras 34–40.
137 *Joseph* para 47.
138 2010 (4) SA 55 (CC) para 27.

be viewed as final, and thus potentially an administrative action, if it manifests in a direct and external legal effect. Consequently, administrative conduct that is wholly internal to the administration, often as part of a larger multistage decision-making process, will not constitute administrative action on its own, but only as part of the administrative action that will emerge once a final decision is taken that has the requisite external effect.

One must be careful, however, of not simply excluding all conduct on the basis that further steps may follow that may have further effect. Under particular circumstances, a decision may have adequate external effect and thus amount to administrative action even though further action is to follow. A good example is the case of *Oosthuizen's Transport (Pty) Ltd and Others v MEC, Road Traffic Matters, Mpumalanga and Others*.[139] In this matter the MEC appointed an investigation team to look into alleged overloading practices of the applicant in contravention of the National Road Traffic Act.[140] Upon completion of their investigation, the team expressed the view in their report that the applicant had failed to meet its obligations under the Act and recommended to the MEC a suspension of the applicant's operations pending compliance with the Act. The applicants challenged the findings and recommendations of the investigation team on administrative-law grounds, but the respondents argued that there was no administrative action (yet) since the MEC had not taken any decision. The respondents relied directly on the impact requirements of the definition of administrative action. The court rejected the respondents' argument, holding that the investigation team's recommendation to the MEC was indeed administrative action. The court reasoned that it cannot be said that all recommendations lack the requisite finality and external effect to render them universally excluded from the definition of administrative action. The court held that a recommendation, even though it is still part of a larger multistage decision-making process, may on its own already have the necessary external effect to qualify as administrative action. The question in each case will be whether the particular decision has 'serious consequences' in its own right.[141] Furthermore, following the Supreme Court of Appeal's lead in *Grey's Marine*, the court held that an actual direct, external effect is not required. As long as the decision is aimed at generating such effect the present element will be satisfied, irrespective of whether that effect eventually follows or not.[142] This is in line with the general guidance that the Constitutional Court has given in *Viking Pony Africa Pumps (Pty) Ltd t/a Tricom Africa v Hidro-Tech Systems (Pty) Ltd and Another*[143] regarding investigations. It held that it is unlikely that the decision to investigate and the process of investigation itself would amount to distinct administrative action, but that a determination of culpability and a decision on what steps to take in response would constitute administrative action.

### 3.7.7 That does not fall under any of the listed exclusions

The final part of the definition is a list of nine particular actions or action types that are expressly excluded from the definition of administrative action. The effect is that these decisions are not subject to PAJA. It thus does not matter whether these actions satisfy the preceding six elements of the definition.

139 2008 (2) SA 570 (T).
140 93 of 1996.
141 *Oosthuizen's Transport* para 25.
142 *Oosthuizen's Transport* para 29.
143 2011 (1) SA 327 (CC) para 38.

The exclusions can be broadly placed in two categories. On the one hand there are what can be called the separation of powers exclusions.[144] These are the actions listed in subsections (*aa*) to (*ee*). These actions are all actions that are not administrative in nature, but rather executive, legislative or judicial. As such these actions are also excluded from the definition by the first element and in particular the requirement that the decision be of an administrative nature. These exclusions thus largely overlap with the first element. However, the exclusions are particularly useful in that they provide clear-cut examples of what would qualify as not of an administrative nature. Subsections (*aa*) and (*bb*) in particular provide references to powers granted in the Constitution that would qualify as executive and not administrative. This is helpful since the executive/administrative distinction is probably one of the most difficult to make in the current context, as we have noted a number of times in this chapter. Thus, when the President assents to a bill it is clearly not administrative action since the power to assent is granted in section 84(2)(*a*) of the Constitution, which is listed in subsection (*aa*) of the definition as an excluded executive action. However, it may not always be so easy to identify which actions would be executive and thus be excluded and which are administrative. Especially at local government level (exclusion (*cc*)), this may be problematic given that the municipal council acts as legislative, executive and administrative body and the exclusion lists no examples of clear-cut exclusions as with subsections (*aa*) and (*bb*). To determine whether a particular action falls inside the exclusion, the same approach to distinguishing between executive and administrative decisions set out in section 3.7.1 above, under the element of a decision of an administrative nature, would apply. Thus the closer the decision is to the policy function of an elected official, the more likely it will be that the decision is executive.

The second broad category of exclusions, comprising subsections (*ff*) to (*ii*), can be viewed as pragmatic exclusions. Many of these actions will probably qualify as administrative action under the first six elements of the definition, but are for practical reasons excluded from PAJA. The reasons for these exclusions differ between them. The exclusion of decisions to institute or continue a prosecution (*ff*), and decisions taken under the Promotion of Access to Information Act[145] (*hh*), should be viewed in light of the existence of alternative legal mechanisms in terms of which such decisions are structured and can be reviewed. Including them under PAJA will probably lead to duplication and hence administrative inefficiency.

**COUNTER POINT**

**To prosecute or not to prosecute**

The question of whether the exclusion of decisions 'to institute or continue a prosecution' under subsection (ff) of the definition also excludes decisions *not* to prosecute has become somewhat controversial in recent years, especially in light of a number of decisions to continue or withdraw prosecutions of high-profile individuals.

In *Kaunda and Others v President of the Republic of South Africa and Others*[146] Chaskalson CJ stated that unlike decisions to institute prosecutions, PAJA 'does not ... deal specifically with a decision not to prosecute'. He continued to state that he is prepared to assume that different considerations may apply in relation to the latter

CONTINUED >>>

144 On the role of the separation of powers in administrative law, see Chapter 2 section 2.4.
145 2 of 2000.
146 2005 (4) SA 235 (CC) para 84.

type of decisions and that there may be circumstances under which such decisions are reviewable. Academics have largely endorsed this view, *inter alia* based on the drafting history of PAJA.[147] Hoexter thus notes that there is less of a need to allow review of decisions to prosecute since these will be followed by a trial during which irregularities could be challenged, which is not the case for decisions not to prosecute.

However, this view was questioned in an *obiter dictum* in *Democratic Alliance and Others v Acting National Director of Public Prosecutions and Others*[148] where Navsa JA stated that:

> there appears to be some justification for the contention that the decision to discontinue a prosecution is of the same genus as a decision to institute or continue a prosecution.

This would mean that decisions not to prosecute would also be excluded under subsection (*ff*).

Subsequently, the Supreme Court of Appeal has endeavoured to 'put the issue to rest' in *National Director of Public Prosecutions and Others v Freedom Under Law.*[149] The court unequivocally held that decisions not to prosecute are of the same nature as decisions to prosecute so that the same policy considerations underlying the exclusion of the latter apply to the former. Decisions not to prosecute (which would include decisions to discontinue a prosecution) are consequently also excluded from the definition of administrative action under subsection (*ff*) of the definition. The main policy considerations for excluding both types of actions are 'safeguarding the independence of the prosecuting authority' and recognition of the broad discretionary nature of these decisions and their polycentricity. The court, however, acknowledged that this view is not necessarily supported by the text of the definition in PAJA.[150]

The exclusion of certain decisions of the Judicial Service Commission in subsection (*gg*) is to some extent tied to the separation of powers exclusions. These decisions are closely related to the judicial function, although they are not judicial in themselves. The proximity to the judicial function may explain the exclusion.

Finally, decisions taken in terms of section 4(1) of PAJA are excluded in subsection (*ii*). These are the choices made by administrators regarding which particular public participation process to follow in cases where the administrative action impacts on the public. It is important to note that it is only the choice itself that is excluded, not the subsequent action in implementing that choice or the proposed decision that is the subject of the procedure. The section 4(1) choice will most likely not qualify as administrative action on the basis of elements five and six of the definition as well. Such choices are largely internal, preliminary decisions on which procedure to follow, rather than decisions that will have an impact on their own.

147 Hoexter (2012) 241–242; De Ville, JR (2005) *Judicial Review of Administrative Action in South Africa* 64–65; Currie, I (2007) *The Promotion of Administrative Justice Act: A Commentary* (2nd ed).
148 2012 (3) SA 486 (SCA) para 27.
149 2014 (4) SA 298 (SCA).
150 *Freedom Under Law* para 27.

COUNTER POINT

**Public employment decisions**

One area of administration that has created significant difficulties under the definition of administrative action is that of public service employment decisions. These decisions result in an overlap between labour law and administrative law. Since labour law disputes are governed by a distinct regime of dispute resolution, including a separate court structure, jurisdictional difficulties arise when public employment decisions are challenged on administrative-law grounds. A key question is whether such decisions qualify as administrative action and can thus be challenged in the High Court, thereby circumventing the Labour Court system and resulting in parallel labour dispute jurisdictions.

Over time the courts have taken diametrically opposite views on this matter. In *South African Police Union and Another v National Commissioner of the South African Police Service and Another*[151] Murphy AJ held that the commissioner's decision to change a shift system for policemen does not amount to administrative action. He pointed to the contractual basis of the power exercised and held that the commissioner did not act from a position of superior power based on his public position. In contrast, Plasket J held in *Police and Prisons Civil Rights Union and Others v Minister of Correctional Services and Others (No 1)*[152] that the dismissal of correctional services employees was administrative action. He pointed to the public interest in the functioning of the department, the statutory source of the power and the constitutional obligations of the department as factors leading to his conclusion.

The Constitutional Court considered the labour-law–administrative-law overlap in a number of cases, the most significant of which for present purposes were the *Chirwa* judgment and *Gcaba v Minister for Safety and Security and Others*.[153] In both cases the court held that the relevant decision did not amount to administrative action. In the latter case the court seems to lay down the rule that '[g]enerally, employment and labour relationship issues do not amount to administrative action within the meaning of PAJA' and '[s]ection 33 does not regulate the relationship between the state as employer and its workers'.[154] As Cora Hoexter has argued, the reasoning of the court is particularly thin and not always persuasive.[155] It is also clear from subsequent High Court judgments that the Constitutional Court ruling has not wholly resolved the problems in this area with the overlap between labour law and administrative law continuing.[156]

151 (2005) 26 *ILJ* 2403 (LC).
152 2008 (3) SA 91 (E) para 54.
153 2010 (1) SA 238 (CC).
154 *Gcaba* para 64.
155 Hoexter (2012) 214–218.
156 See Quinot, G (2010) *Administrative Law Annual Survey of South African Law* 41 at 48–52; *Kwemaya v National Commissioner, Correctional Services* [2017] ZAKZDHC 33; *Mlokothi v Trollip* [2017] ZAECPEHC 43; *Notyawa v Makana Municipality* [2017] 4 All SA 533 (ECG); *Funani v MEC: Department of Education Eastern Cape Province* [2017] ZAECBHC 9.

## 3.8 Conclusion

Despite all the technicalities involved in the statutory definition in section 1(i) of PAJA, administrative action can broadly be understood as decisions ostensibly taken under empowering provisions in fulfilling the function of state administration and aimed at consequences outside of the administration.

Administrative action has become the key concept in administrative law under the Constitution and PAJA. Cora Hoexter has noted that the strong conceptualism of this approach, especially under PAJA, is regrettable since it diverts attention away from substantive questions about administrative justice.[157] In a sense PAJA's approach has continued the formalism that characterised our common-law administrative law in the form of the classification of functions. We are still spending a disproportionate amount of time trying to figure out whether we have administrative action rather than asking what the standards of administrative justice may require of public conduct. The development of the concept of legality, as a basis for judicial scrutiny over all forms of public conduct regardless of whether it qualifies as administrative action or not, can be seen as a response to the difficulties introduced by the 'cumbersome' definition of administrative action in PAJA. The dangers of this situation are of course the development of parallel systems of law – one under legality and another under section 33 of the Constitution – with different requirements that are ostensibly aimed at achieving the same purposes and regulating and facilitating the same public conduct.

### THIS CHAPTER IN ESSENCE

The Constitution introduced an important shift from an institutional approach, identifying which actions are subject to administrative law, to a functional approach. The institutional approach focused on the entity that is taking the action and its position as a state entity. The functional approach focuses on the particular function that is being performed by the action at hand and asks whether that function is public in nature.

The Constitution also introduced a distinct concept of administrative action, which has subsequently become the 'gateway' to administrative law. Administrative law only applies to administrative action. Thus, the first question in every administrative-law analysis is whether the action at hand qualifies as administrative action.

PAJA has introduced an extensive definition of administrative action in section 1 of the Act. This definition is best understood in terms of a number of elements, in terms of which administrative action is:

1. a decision of an administrative nature;
2. by an organ of state or a natural or juristic person;
3. exercising a public power or performing a public function;
4. in terms of any legislation or an empowering provision;
5. that adversely affects rights;
6. that has a direct, external legal effect; and
7. that does not fall under any of the listed exclusions.

157 Hoexter, C (2000) The Future of Judicial Review in South African Administrative Law *SALJ* 117(3):484 at 517; Hoexter (2012) 249–250.

## FURTHER READING


- Craig, PP 'What is Public Power' in Corder, H & Maluwa, T (Eds) (1997) *Administrative Justice in Southern Africa* Cape Town: Dept of Public Law UCT 25
- Hoexter, C 'From *Chirwa* to *Gcaba*: An Administrative Lawyer's View' in Kidd, M & Hoctor, S (Eds) (2010) *Stella Iuris: Celebrating 100 Years of Teaching Law in Pietermaritzburg* Cape Town: Juta 47
- Hoexter, C (2012) *Administrative Law in South Africa* (2nd ed) Cape Town: Juta 171–194
- Konstant, A (2015) Administrative action, the principle of legality and deference – The case of *Minister of Defence and Military Veterans v Motau, Constitutional Court Review VII*:68
- Penfold, G (2019) Substantive reasoning and the concept of 'administrative action' *SALJ* 136(1):84
- Pfaff, R & Schneider, H (2001) The Promotion of Administrative Justice Act from a German Perspective *SAJHR* 17:59
- Quinot, G (2008) *Administrative Law Cases and Materials* Cape Town: Juta 24–25, 41, 177–178
- Thornton, L (1999) The Constitutional Right to Just Administrative Action – Are Political Parties Bound? *SAJHR* 15(3):351
- Williams, RC (2011) The Concept of a 'Decision' as the Threshold Requirement for Judicial Review in Terms of the Promotion of Administrative Justice Act *PER* 14:230
- Wolf, L (2017) In search of a definition for administrative action *SAJHR* 33(2):314
- Wolf, L (2018) Implications of the 'direct, external legal effect' of administrative action for its purported validity *SALJ* 135(4):678

# Chapter 4

# Non-judicial regulation of administrative action

GEO QUINOT & THULI MADONSELA



## 4.1 Control and facilitation

The work of the state administration takes place within a broad range of different frameworks. Section 197 of the Constitution states that the public service 'must loyally execute the lawful policies of the government of the day'. Public administration is thus guided by the policies adopted by the government, that is by the governing executive. These include, for example, the *Batho Pele* principles aimed at transforming public service delivery[1] and the *Public Service Integrity Management Framework*.[2] There are various guidelines and official manuals that steer the public administration in fulfilling their functions, such as the National Treasury's *Supply Chain Management: A Guide for Accounting Officers/Authorities* and the Department of Public Service and Administration's *Senior Management Service (SMS) Handbook*. The work of various oversight entities, such as the Auditor-General's guidance on records management and the Public Service Commission's *Code of Conduct for Public Servants*, has a direct bearing on how the administration goes about its daily functions. While

1 See the White Paper on Transforming Public Service Delivery (*Batho Pele 'People First'* White Paper on Transforming Public Service Delivery), Dept. of Public Service and Administration 18 Sept 1997, Notice 1459 of 1997 in *GG* 18340 of 01.10.1997.

2 Department of Public Service and Administration RSA (2013) *Public Service Integrity Management Framework*.

these policies, principles, guidelines, codes and manuals play an important role in shaping administrative action, they differ in at least one important respect from the rules of administrative law. The rules are legally enforceable in contrast to these other instruments that are not (at least not without the help of administrative law). This means that the rules of administrative law constitute a normative framework for administrative action that can be enforced by means of a host of legal institutions. Administrative law thus plays an important role in ensuring that these policy frameworks and the decisions taken in terms of them adhere to the broad normative framework of the Constitution, such as the values and principles governing public administration in section 195, the core values of human dignity, equality and freedom contained in the Bill of Rights, the principles of cooperative government set out in chapter 3 of the Constitution and the inherent doctrine of separation of powers. As we have noted in preceding chapters, administrative justice is about enforceable principles of good public governance. To put the same point differently, administrative actions that do not comply, for example, with the principles of *Batho Pele* or Treasury's *SCM Guide* may be poor decisions, but may still be valid, whereas administrative actions that do not comply with the rules of administrative law are not only bad decisions, but can be invalidated in terms of legal mechanisms. Administrative action is thus regulated by means of the rules of administrative law.

When one thinks of the regulatory function of the rules of administrative law, one should guard against thinking of that function as purely one of control. Within the paradigm of administrative justice, the rules of administrative law are as much about facilitating administrative action as they are about controlling that action. When we say that administrative law regulates administrative action, we mean that the law tells a person affected by an administrative action whether the action is valid or whether such person can seek some form of legal redress in response to the administrative action and we mean that the law tells the administrator what he or she can or must do and how he or she must go about doing it. The regulatory function of administrative law should thus be viewed from both the perspectives of control and facilitation. This is what we called the dual nature of administrative law in Chapter 2 above and which was classically captured by Harlow and Rawlings's green light and red light theories of administrative law.[3]

We shall see in the following chapters that the rules of administrative justice in South Africa stand on three main pillars, namely lawfulness, procedural fairness and reasonableness. Each one of these pillars addresses a particular characteristic that an administrative action must have in order to be constitutionally valid. However, before we look at each one of these distinct elements of administrative justice, we must understand what the mechanisms are in terms of which these rules are enforced. Thus, before we look at the content of the rules, we must look at how the law brings these rules to bear on administrative action. As we shall also see in subsequent chapters, the way in which administrative action is regulated, that is the particular mechanism that is used to bring the rules to bear on the action, often holds important implications for the *content* of the rules. For example, our understanding of the content of reasonableness as one pillar of administrative justice in South Africa is greatly influenced by what is possible and desirable under the mechanism of judicial review as a way to regulate the reasonableness of administrative action.[4]

3 See Chapter 2 section 2.6.1 above and Harlow, C & Rawlings, R (2009) *Law and Administration* (3rd ed) Chapter 1.
4 See Chapter 8 below.

In South African administrative law, as in most other administrative-law systems based on English common law, one mechanism has dominated the administrative-law regulatory landscape, namely judicial review. In fact, the mechanism of judicial review has played such an important role in common-law administrative-law systems that this branch of law was often thought of as the law of judicial review.[5] However, today it is important to take a more balanced view of administrative law within the paradigm of administrative justice. As we noted in Chapters 1 and 2, the administration has a distinct and legitimate function under the Constitution as an integral part of constitutional democracy in South Africa. Administrative law as part of constitutional law should accordingly strive to support the administration in fulfilling this function. Furthermore, the Constitution introduced important innovations in South African public administration by creating a range of institutions that can steer administrative decision-making, such as the State Institutions Supporting Constitutional Democracy, primarily the Public Protector and Auditor-General, and the Public Service Commission. Administrators now have a wider range of legal mechanisms available to assist them in taking decisions than just legislation and case law. One should seek to understand the regulatory function of administrative law in terms of an integrated vision of the different ways in which the rules are applied to administrative action in pursuit of both the control and facilitative function of administrative justice. As we explore the different ways in which administrative-law rules are applied in this chapter, we should thus consider how they relate to each other and whether a coherent, integrated picture of the regulation of administrative action emerges.

This chapter will only focus on the regulatory function of non-judicial mechanisms aimed at realising administrative justice. In Chapter 5 we shall focus on judicial review as a specific form of regulation of administrative action.

## 4.2 Legislative regulation

The first, and often overlooked, way in which administrative action is regulated is through the work of legislatures. Legislative regulation precedes all other forms of regulation for the simple reason that the majority of administrative action is taken in terms of legislative provisions. This means that administrative action mostly has its origin in legislation enacted by a legislature. The legislature thus plays a key role in formulating the empowering provision in such a manner that both facilitates and controls the subsequent action. When the legislature formulates a source of administrative power it should do so mindful of the rules of administrative law and in a way that promotes administrative justice. The legislature can, for example, build in limits on the administrative power or other forms of control, such as procedures that must be followed or oversight mechanisms to check the exercise of the particular power. The legislature also exercises a form of regulation by framing the administrative power either widely or narrowly.

5 Hoexter, C (2000) The Future of Judicial Review in South African Administrative Law *SALJ* 117(3):484 at 485–488; Wade, HWR & Forsyth, CF (2014) *Administrative Law* (11th ed) 4, 8. The first book in South Africa to deal exclusively with administrative law, was Rose Innes, LA (1963) *Judicial Review of Administrative Tribunals in South Africa*.

**PAUSE FOR REFLECTION**

When the legislature formulates an empowering provision that grants power to an administrator to take administrative action, it has a fairly wide discretion in how to frame that power. The legislature may decide to grant the administrator a very wide discretion, which may make it much easier for the administrator to formulate an administrative action on a case-by-case basis, but which may make it much harder to control via other regulatory processes such as judicial review. Alternatively, the legislature may grant a very narrow power, which prescribes in much greater detail the circumstances under which the power is to be exercised and the limited number of options that an administrator has to act under that power. Such an approach may render control much easier, since there will be much more against which the administrative action can be measured, but may make it much more difficult for an administrator to respond to the particular circumstances of a given case.

Compare the following two empowering provisions and consider the regulatory function that the legislature has already played when formulating these provisions.

**National Building Regulations and Building Standards Act**[6]

7. Approval by local authorities in respect of erection of buildings.–

(1) If a local authority, having considered a recommendation referred to in section 6(1)(*a*)–

(*a*) is satisfied that the application in question complies with the requirements of this Act and any other applicable law, it shall grant its approval in respect thereof;

(*b*) (i) is not so satisfied; or

(ii) is satisfied that the building to which the application in question relates–

(*aa*) is to be erected in such manner or will be of such nature or appearance that–

(*aaa*) the area in which it is to be erected will probably or in fact be disfigured thereby;

(*bbb*) it will probably or in fact be unsightly or objectionable;

(*ccc*) it will probably or in fact derogate from the value of adjoining or neighbouring properties;

(*bb*) will probably or in fact be dangerous to life or property,

such local authority shall refuse to grant its approval in respect thereof and give written reasons for such refusal:

Provided that the local authority shall grant or refuse, as the case may be, its approval in respect of any application where the architectural area of the building to which the application relates is less than 500 $m^2$, within a period

CONTINUED >>>

6 103 of 1977.

of 30 days after receipt of the application and, where the architectural area of such building is 500 $m^2$ or larger, within a period of 60 days after receipt of the application.

**Collective Investment Schemes Control Act**[7]

22. Exemptions.–

When it is in the public interest, the registrar may exempt–

(*a*) a manager; or

(*b*) any category of persons,

from any provision of this Act on such conditions and to such extent as he or she may determine.

In recognition of the regulatory function of legislatures, the law places some restrictions on legislatures when formulating administrative powers. The fact that administrative justice is now included in section 33 of the Constitution as part of the Bill of Rights, means that the use of ouster clauses in empowering provisions is *prima facie* questionable. An ouster clause is a provision in a statute that attempts to shield the exercise of particular administrative power from legal scrutiny, particularly by courts. Prior to the constitutional dispensation, this type of clause was often used to insulate administrative power from challenge, especially in security legislation.[8] An ouster clause would mean that the administrative action taken under the particular empowering provision would be immune from control via administrative law. Today such a clause would almost certainly amount to a limitation of section 33 as well as section 34 (the right of access to courts) of the Constitution. As a result, an ouster clause could only be valid if it could meet the requirements for a justifiable limitation of a fundamental right under section 36 of the Constitution. This will not often be possible, given the test in section 36 that 'the limitation is reasonable and justifiable in an open and democratic society'. It is difficult to see how the exclusion of (judicial) scrutiny over administrative action, that is the possibility of measuring administrative action against the Constitution, could easily meet this test.

A second restriction on the legislature's freedom in formulating administrative power, was expressed in the judgment in *Dawood and Another v Minister of Home Affairs and Others; Shalabi and Another v Minister of Home Affairs and Others; Thomas and Another v Minister of Home Affairs and Others.*[9] In this matter the Constitutional Court held that the rule of law requires legislatures to provide guidance to administrators on what factors to take into account when wide discretionary powers are granted in empowering provisions.[10]

7 45 of 2002.

8 Examples could be found in sections 8, 11, 19, 28, 29 and 41 of the Internal Security Act 74 of 1982; section 5B of the Public Safety Act 3 of 1953; section 103 of the Defence Act 44 of 1957.

9 2000 (3) SA 936 (CC).

10 *Dawood* para 47.

The effect of the court's judgment in this matter is that legislatures cannot grant unfettered discretionary powers to administrators without providing any guidance on how such discretion is to be exercised. In this regard, the court stated:

> In a constitutional democracy such as ours the responsibility to protect constitutional rights in practice is imposed both on the legislature and on the executive and its officials. The legislature must take care when legislation is drafted to limit the risk of an unconstitutional exercise of the discretionary powers it confers.[11]

We shall return to this issue in Chapter 10 when we consider the implications of administrative justice in legislative drafting, that is, in the creation of legislative mandates.

A different form of regulation exercised by legislatures flows from the constitutional obligation of legislatures to provide oversight over the functions of the executive. In the national sphere this obligation is stated in section 55(2) of the Constitution, which reads:

> (2) The National Assembly must provide for mechanisms-
> (*a*) to ensure that all executive organs of state in the national sphere of government are accountable to it; and
> (*b*) to maintain oversight of-
> (i) the exercise of national executive authority, including the implementation of legislation; and
> (ii) any organ of state.

At provincial level, this obligation is contained in virtually identical terms in section 114 of the Constitution. Since administrative action largely amounts to the implementation of legislation, these constitutional provisions oblige legislatures to regulate the exercise of administrative action. Some of the mechanisms used by legislatures to fulfil this constitutional obligation are the direct accountability of members of the executive to the legislature through debate in the relevant legislature; the work of committees of the legislature in scrutinising the functions of particular state departments, including calling administrators to appear before committees to answer questions or to submit documents to such committees for scrutiny; and crucially through the power of the public purse. The exercise of administrative powers inevitably involves spending public money. Such money may only be spent in terms of a budget allocated to a particular department by the legislature. It is thus legislatures that ultimately decide on how much money is allocated to a particular state department. Members of the executive must annually present their departments' budgets to the relevant legislature for approval. This process provides an important mechanism in terms of which legislatures can control the administrative functions of the relevant department, but also facilitates such functions by allocating the necessary funds.

Finally, it is important to note the interaction between legislatures as mechanisms of regulating administrative action and other such mechanisms. The legislature's own conduct, especially in creating new legislation, is also subject to review by the courts. When the legislature thus exercises a form of regulation over administrative action by enacting legislation in a particular manner, the courts in turn may regulate the conduct of the legislature by reviewing that legislation, including assessing the legislation's compliance with section 33 of the Constitution. The Constitutional Court judgment in *Zondi v MEC for*

11 *Dawood* para 48.

*Traditional and Local Government Affairs and Others*[12] is a good example. In this matter, the applicant challenged the constitutionality of the Pound Ordinance (KwaZulu-Natal), 1947. This ordinance allowed the impoundment of trespassing animals by landowners under certain circumstances and the sale or destruction of such animals by pound keepers. The applicant challenged the constitutionality of the ordinance, *inter alia* on the basis that it allowed the impoundment and sale/destruction of the animals without notice to the owner in violation of section 33(1) of the Constitution that requires all administrative action to be procedurally fair. The challenge was not against any particular action impounding the applicant's animals, but against the statutory provisions themselves. The High court allowed the challenge, finding that the statutory provisions were unconstitutional in that they allowed administrative action to be taken that would adversely affect a person's rights without requiring procedural fairness, that is, without requiring notice to the owner and an opportunity to make representations. The Constitutional Court, however, found that the relevant statutory provisions did not exclude the right to procedural fairness. The court held that the ordinance should be interpreted as supplemented by the requirements of procedural fairness in the Constitution and Promotion of Administrative Justice Act (PAJA)[13] and should thus be read to require procedural fairness in taking action under the ordinance. This interpretation saved the ordinance from constitutional invalidity.

Many of the oversight bodies that we shall note below are obliged to report to Parliament so that Parliament fulfils an oversight function over the regulatory function of oversight bodies in respect of administrative action. As we will also note, the courts can also ensure that Parliament fulfils this function. These mechanisms thus all exist within a single framework that constitute the legal regulation of administrative action.

## 4.3 Internal controls

A second form of regulation of administrative action is that of internal controls. Internal controls, often referred to as internal remedies, are mechanisms within the administration aimed at addressing administrative failures. These provide the administration with the tools to correct their own mistakes.

In South Africa there is no uniform system of internal controls, unlike in some other countries where there are now extensive systems for internal controls. There is also no right to an internal remedy or conversely an obligation on a particular part of the administration to have internal remedies. It all depends on the particular legislative framework in terms of which the administrative action is taken. One thus finds an assortment of different mechanisms in various statutes that provide some form of internal redress to an aggrieved person.

12 2005 (3) SA 589 (CC).
13 3 of 2000.

REFRAMING

**Framing internal control mechanisms**

Compare, for example, the vast difference between the following two internal control mechanisms created under two separate legislative frameworks:

**Treasury Regulations under the Public Finance Management Act**[14]

16A9.3 The National Treasury and each provincial treasury must establish a mechanism:-

(*a*) to receive and consider complaints regarding alleged non-compliance with the prescribed minimum norms and standards; and

(*b*) to make recommendations for remedial actions to be taken if non-compliance of any norms and standards is established, including recommendations of criminal steps to be taken in the case of corruption, fraud or other criminal offences.

**Financial Services Board Act**[15]

26(1) A person who is aggrieved by a decision of a decision-maker may, subject to the provisions of another law, appeal against that decision to the appeal board in accordance with the provisions of this Act or such other law.

26B(15) The appeal board may-

(*a*) confirm, set aside or vary the decision under appeal, and order that any such decision of the appeal board be given effect to; or

(*b*) remit the matter for reconsideration by the decision-maker concerned in accordance with such directions, if any, as the appeal board may determine.

When PAJA was drafted, the possibility of creating a more coherent and uniform system of internal remedies was considered. However, it was left to the discretion of the Minister of Justice in the Act to establish an advisory council that may advise the Minister on 'any improvements that might be made in respect of internal complaints procedures, internal administrative appeals'.[16] No steps have yet been taken under this section to establish such an advisory council or to reform the fragmented South African internal remedies landscape.

14 1 of 1999.
15 97 of 1990.
16 PAJA section 10(2)(*a*)(ii).

**PAUSE FOR REFLECTION**

**A coherent system of internal control: The Australian Commonwealth Administrative Appeals Tribunal**

Since the late 1970s Australia has been at the forefront of reform of administrative justice systems in the common-law world. One of the major reforms introduced in Australia was the creation of a comprehensive administrative appeals tribunal system. The Commonwealth Administrative Appeals Tribunal (AAT) was introduced in 1976 as the most general administrative tribunal to hear appeals on a host of administrative decisions taken by the federal administration in Australia.[17] A number of further specialised tribunals were also introduced such as the Migration Review Tribunal, Refugee Review Tribunal and Social Security Appeals Tribunal. In 2015, these tribunals were amalgamated into the AAT to form a single appeals tribunal consisting of various divisions.[18]

In 2006, Robin Creyke noted that this system is clearly successful if one simply compares the amount of cases finalised by the tribunal system with administrative-law reviews by the courts. By 2004, the Federal Court of Australia had finalised less than 10 000 administrative-law cases since it was granted jurisdiction in such matters in 1976.[19] In the same period, the five major Australian tribunals[20] have finalised over 450 000 cases. The AAT has a wide appeal power, meaning that it may reconsider the merits of the relevant decision on either law or fact and reach a new decision. The AAT is statutorily obliged to conduct its proceedings 'with as little formality and technicality, and with as much expedition' as law and practice permit.[21]

PAJA does contain one important provision that strengthens the role of internal controls. Section 7(2) of PAJA defers the jurisdiction of the courts to review administrative action until all internal remedies have been exhausted. We shall return to this rule below when we consider judicial review.[22] For the moment it can be noted that this is a strong signal that our law favours reliance on internal controls prior to judicial controls.

It is not difficult to see why one would want to adopt such a position. Internal controls are mostly much more informal than judicial proceedings, can potentially be accessed much quicker and consequently with lower costs, and can address a wider range of issues regarding the administrative action.[23] Since internal controls function within the relevant administration, there is much less concern about the institutional ability of the internal control mechanisms to deal with the technical and often specialised substance of the relevant administrative action compared to courts that often lack such expertise.[24] For example, under the Genetically Modified Organisms Act,[25] the Executive Council for Genetically Modified Organisms must 'decide whether to approve an application ... for the use of facilities to conduct activities in

17 Administrative Appeals Tribunal Act 1975.

18 Tribunals Amalgamation Act 2015 (No 60, 2015).

19 Creyke, R (2006) Administrative Justice: Beyond the Courtroom Door *Acta Juridica* 257 at 262.

20 These were the AAT, the Refugee Review Tribunal, the Migration Review Tribunal, the Social Security Appeals Tribunal and the Veterans' Review Board. Creyke (2006) 262.

21 Administrative Appeals Tribunal Act 1975 section 33.

22 Section 4.6.2.3 below.

23 *Koyabe and Others v Minister for Home Affairs and Others (Lawyers for Human Rights as Amicus Curiae)* 2010 (4) SA 327 (CC) para 35.

24 See *Koyabe* para 37.

25 15 of 1997.

respect of genetically modified organisms'.[26] Any person that feels aggrieved by a decision of the Council, say the refusal to approve an application, may lodge an appeal against such decision to an appeal board appointed by the relevant Minister consisting of persons who 'have expert knowledge of the matter on appeal and who are otherwise suitable to make a decision on the appeal concerned'.[27] In the case of such an appeal, the appeal board will be in just as good a position to judge the merits of the application as the Council, whereas a court that may be faced with a challenge against the Council's decision will mostly not have the necessary expertise to judge 'activities in respect of genetically modified organisms'. In the absence of any coherence in the South African system of internal controls, these advantages of course depend largely on how the particular mechanism is set up in the legislation and (as with all regulatory mechanisms) how well it is implemented. A common mechanism in South African law is an appeal to the relevant Minister or MEC who is responsible for the department within which the administrative action was taken. The advantages of internal mechanisms set out above will evidently be less in such a case given that Ministers will not necessarily be more accessible than courts or even have higher levels of expertise in the technical matter at issue.

## 4.4 Specialised oversight bodies

A third distinct mechanism to regulate administrative action is the work of specialised bodies created to provide oversight over various aspects of government. The most important of these are created in Chapter 9 of the Constitution, the State Institutions Supporting Constitutional Democracy or as they have become known colloquially, Chapter 9 institutions. These are:

- the Public Protector,
- the South African Human Rights Commission,
- the Auditor-General,
- the Commission for the Promotion and Protection of the Rights of Cultural, Religious and Linguistic Communities,
- the Commission for Gender Equality,
- the Electoral Commission, and
- the Independent Authority to Regulate Broadcasting.

While these institutions are all important in supporting constitutional democracy in South Africa, the first three are the most relevant for administrative justice.

Another key oversight body for administrative law is the Public Service Commission, created in Chapter 10 of the Constitution.

In Chapter 2 above, we have already noted one of these institutions, the Public Protector, and the role that it plays in administrative justice.[28] We also noted that these institutions do not easily fit into the classical separation of powers doctrine and that they are both administrative and judicial in nature. As a mechanism of regulation, this is one of their main advantages. These institutions are independent from the government and the state administration like courts, but are not constrained by the formal judicial structure in which courts operate. Unlike courts, these oversight institutions can do their own investigations and appoint experts to assess conduct of the administration before reaching conclusions.

---

26 Section 5(1)(*b*) and 5(1)(*b*)(i).
27 Section 19(2)(*a*).
28 Chapter 2 section 2.5.3.5.

While all these bodies have the general mandate of supporting constitutional democracy in South Africa, they each have specific areas of focus and different powers in executing their functions. As we shall see in the following sections, these powers range from purely investigatory to issuing binding remedies. The various institutions were designed to function in a complementary manner rather than to duplicate the same functions and it is thus important to keep the particular focus area of a specific institution in mind when considering the role of that institution in the pursuit of administrative justice. As we shall also see in the following sections, this design is not static, but continues to evolve.

The jurisdiction of quite a number of these oversight bodies includes conduct that may qualify as administrative action or that is closely linked to administrative action.

### 4.4.1 The Public Protector[29]

The Public Protector's mandate is:

(*a*) to investigate any conduct in state affairs, or in the public administration in any sphere of government, that is alleged or suspected to be improper or to result in any impropriety or prejudice;
(*b*) to report on that conduct; and
(*c*) to take appropriate remedial action.[30]

This constitutional mandate clearly includes oversight over administrative action. The constitutional powers of the Public Protector are supplemented by the Public Protector Act[31] and other statutes.[32] In the key judgment in *Economic Freedom Fighters v Speaker of the National Assembly and Others; Democratic Alliance v Speaker of the National Assembly and Others,*[33] the Constitutional Court emphasised the importance of bearing in mind that the Public Protector's powers flow directly from the Constitution and that the Public Protector Act and other statutes are secondary sources, fleshing out those constitutional powers.

In recent years, the Public Protector has become a key institution in pursuit of administrative justice. An overview of reports issued by the Public Protector over the last five years, shows that a significant number of matters investigated and reported on involve administrative action. For example, the Public Protector has found irregularities in public contracts at many different organs of state,[34] wrongful disconnection of public services,[35] delays and failures in home affairs decisions such as relating to citizenship,[36] improper

29 Also note the discussion of the Public Protector in Chapter 2 section 2.5.3.5 above.

30 Constitution section 182(1).

31 23 of 1994.

32 For example, the Executive Members' Ethics Act 82 of 1998, the Prevention and Combating of Corrupt Activities Act 12 of 2004, the Promotion of Access to Information Act 2 of 2000, the Protected Disclosures Act 26 of 2000 and the Promotion of Equality and Prevention of Unfair Discrimination Act 4 of 2000.

33 2016 (3) SA 580 (CC) para 71.

34 See, for example, Public Protector Report No. 3 of 2015/6 reporting on contracting irregularities at PRASA; Report No. 5 of 2015/6 on irregularities in lease and other procurement decisions at the South African Post Office; Report No. 13 of 2016/2017 on an irregular procurement in appointing a security tender by the Kagisano-Molopo Local Municipality; Report No. 5 of 2017/18 on irregular payment of professional and legal fees by the North West Department of Local Government and Traditional Affairs; Report No. 8 of 2018/19 on the irregular appointment of a service provider to render academic consultancy services to the University of Limpopo; Report No. 116 of 2019/20 on irregular tenders for rehabilitation of streets by the Greater Letaba Local Municipality.

35 See Report No. 1 of 2016/17 on disconnection of electricity services by Eskom.

36 See Report No. 8 of 2016/17 on the Department of Home Affairs' failures in finalising a citizenship application; Report No. 32 of 2017/18 on the Department of Home Affairs' undue delay to finalise and the improper adjudication of applications for naturalisation.

management of tax administration,[37] and educational matters,[38] failures to manage conflicts and in the administration of social services such as social grants and social housing.[39] In these matters, the Public Protector thus provided a mechanism to assess whether the relevant administrative action complied with the principles of administrative justice and to provide redress where it did not.

The Constitutional Court aptly captured the key role of the Public Protector within the constitutional system as follows:

> The Public Protector is thus one of the most invaluable constitutional gifts to our nation in the fight against corruption, unlawful enrichment, prejudice and impropriety in State affairs and for the betterment of good governance. The tentacles of poverty run far, wide and deep in our nation. Litigation is prohibitively expensive and therefore not an easily exercisable constitutional option for an average citizen. For this reason, the fathers and mothers of our Constitution conceived of a way to give even to the poor and marginalised a voice, and teeth that would bite corruption and abuse excruciatingly. And that is the Public Protector. She is the embodiment of a biblical David, that the public is, who fights the most powerful and very well resourced Goliath, that impropriety and corruption by government officials are. The Public Protector is one of the true crusaders and champions of anti-corruption and clean governance.[40]

Under section 182(1)(*a*) of the Constitution, as given effect to in the Public Protector Act,[41] the Public Protector has wide investigatory powers. As noted above, the Constitution mandates the Public Protector 'to investigate any conduct in state affairs, or in the public administration in any sphere of government, that is alleged or suspected to be improper or to result in any impropriety or prejudice'. Section 7 of the Act implements this power by stating that the Public Protector may conduct investigations 'on his or her own initiative or on receipt of a complaint or an allegation or on the ground of information that has come to his or her knowledge'. The Public Protector determines the format and procedure of the investigation himself or herself and may request any person performing a public function to assist him or her, may designate any person to conduct the investigation, may direct any person to give evidence by affidavit and to produce any document, may examine any person and may request any person to provide an explanation having a bearing on a matter being investigated. In exercising these investigatory powers, the Public Protector may subpoena a person to appear before the Public Protector, may require the person to evidence under oath and may, having obtained a warrant, enter any premises and seize anything bearing on an investigation. These are extensive powers and as the Constitutional Court has noted, the Public Protector's 'investigative powers are not supposed to bow down to anybody, not even at the door of the highest chambers of raw State power'.[42]

37 See Report No. 14 of 2017/18 on failures by SARS to consider representations and objections before levying additional taxes.

38 See Report No. 9 of 2017/18 on the North West Department of Education and Sports Development's failures in dealing with the death of a learner while playing rugby for a public school; Report No. 39 of 2018/19 on the Eastern Cape Department of Rural Development and Agrarian Reform's failures pertaining to the placement of learners.

39 See Report No. 11 of 2014/15 on the City of Johannesburg's failures in respect of providing emergency housing; Report No. 6 of 2014/15 on failures to timeously deal with social assistance appeals.

40 *Economic Freedom Fighters* para 52 (footnotes omitted).

41 23 of 1994.

42 *Economic Freedom Fighters* para 55.

Following an investigation, the Public Protector has wide powers to remedy any failures in administration. In terms of section 182(1)(*c*) of the Constitution, the Public Protector has the power 'to take appropriate remedial action'. Under the Public Protector Act,[43] these powers are further described as the power to:

> endeavour, in his or her sole discretion, to resolve any dispute or rectify any act or omission by—
> (i) mediation, conciliation or negotiation;
> (ii) advising, where necessary, any complainant regarding appropriate remedies; or
> (iii) any other means that may be expedient in the circumstances.[44]

The Public Protector differs from the other Chapter 9 institutions in respect of remedies. It is the only one of these institutions that is explicitly granted remedial powers in the Constitution. In the important judgment in *Economic Freedom Fighters*,[45] the Constitutional Court accordingly held that the Public Protector's remedial power is premised on the Constitution. In interpreting this power, the court held that 'one cannot really talk about remedial action unless a remedy in the true sense is provided to address a complaint in a meaningful way'.[46] Accordingly, the court held that 'the words "take appropriate remedial action" do point to a realistic expectation that binding and enforceable remedial steps might frequently be the route open to the Public Protector to take'.[47] The judgment thus confirmed that the Public Protector may take binding legal action in remedying an administrative injustice, that is, the Public Protector may issue binding legal remedies. This does not mean that all remedial action issued by the Public Protector will be binding. The court held that 'the nature of the issues under investigation and the findings made' will dictate whether binding legal remedies are appropriate in the given case. The court helpfully summarised the position regarding the Public Protector's remedial powers as follows:

> (a) The primary source of the power to take appropriate remedial action is the supreme law itself, whereas the Public Protector Act is but a secondary source;
> (b) It is exercisable only against those that she is constitutionally and statutorily empowered to investigate;
> (c) Implicit in the words 'take action' is that the Public Protector is herself empowered to decide on and determine the appropriate remedial measure. And 'action' presupposes, obviously where appropriate, concrete or meaningful steps. Nothing in these words suggests that she necessarily has to leave the exercise of the power to take remedial action to other institutions or that it is power that is by its nature of no consequence;
> (d) She has the power to determine the appropriate remedy and prescribe the manner of its implementation;
> (e) 'Appropriate' means nothing less than effective, suitable, proper or fitting to redress or undo the prejudice, impropriety, unlawful enrichment or corruption, in a particular case;

43 23 of 1994.
44 Public Protector Act 23 of 1994, section 6(4)(*b*).
45 Para 64.
46 Para 65.
47 Para 67.

(f) Only when it is appropriate and practicable to effectively remedy or undo the complaint would a legally binding remedial action be taken;
(g) Also informed by the appropriateness of the remedial measure to deal properly with the subject-matter of investigation, and in line with the findings made would a non-binding recommendation be made or measure be taken; and
(h) Whether a particular action taken or measure employed by the Public Protector in terms of her constitutionally allocated remedial power is binding or not or what its legal effect is, would be a matter of interpretation aided by context, nature and language. [48]

The Public Protector's powers, including his or her remedial powers, are not unfettered. Like all other exercises of public power, the Public Protector's actions are subject to judicial scrutiny by way of judicial review.

COUNTER POINT

**Are the Public Protector's actions themselves administrative action?**

While the Public Protector clearly plays an important role in regulating administrative action taken by other organs of state, the question emerges whether the Public Protector's own actions, including her remedial actions, amount to administrative action. This is an important question, because it will determine, as we will see in Chapter 5, whether the Public Protector's actions should be judicially reviewed in terms of administrative law (including PAJA) or whether it can only be reviewed in terms of the constitutional principle of legality.

In a number of High Court judgments, the courts held that the Public Protector is generally subject to administrative-law scrutiny when investigating and reporting on alleged maladministration, including the remedial action taken. In *Minister of Home Affairs v Public Protector*,[49] the High Court found that 'as a general proposition, the decisions and actions of the Public Protector amount to administrative action as intended by PAJA'. The court focused on the status of the Public Protector as an organ of state, the constitutional and statutory sources of her powers and the potential impact of her decisions in reaching this conclusion. This approach was followed in *South African Reserve Bank v Public Protector*[50] and in *Absa Bank Limited and Others v Public Protector*.[51] However, in *Minister of Home Affairs and Another v Public Protector of the Republic of South Africa*,[52] the Supreme Court of Appeal came to the opposite conclusion. The SCA focused specifically on the nature of the Public Protector's actions and held that decisions taken by the Public Protector were not administrative in nature. The SCA listed the following considerations in reaching this conclusion:

> First, the Office of the Public Protector is a unique institution designed to strengthen constitutional democracy. It does not fit into the institutions of public administration but stands apart from them. Secondly, it is a purpose-built watch-dog that is independent and answerable not to the executive branch of government but to the

CONTINUED >>>

48 Para 71.
49 2017 (2) SA 597 (GP).
50 2017 (6) SA 198 (GP).
51 2018 JDR 0190 (GP).
52 2018 (3) SA 380 (SCA).

> National Assembly. Thirdly, although the State Liability Act 20 of 1957 applies to the Office of the Public Protector to enable it to sue and be sued, it is not a department of state and is functionally separate from the state administration: it is only an organ of state because it exercises constitutional powers and other statutory powers of a public nature. Fourthly, its function is not to administer but to investigate, report on and remedy maladministration. Fifthly, the Public Protector is given broad discretionary powers as to what complaints to accept, what allegations of maladministration to investigate, how to investigate them and what remedial action to order – as close as one can get to a free hand to fulfil the mandate of the Constitution. These factors point away from decisions of the Public Protector being of an administrative nature, and hence constituting administrative action. That being so, the PAJA does not apply to the review of exercises of power by the Public Protector in terms of s 182 of the Constitution and s 6 of the Public Protector Act. That means that the principle of legality applies to the review of the decisions in issue in this case.[53]

While the SCA's pronouncement reflects the current law, these factors can be critically considered. The first three factors listed by the SCA are all institutional in nature, that is relate to the institutional framework within which the Public Protector functions. Care must be taken in placing too much emphasis on institutional factors, since, as the Constitutional Court warned in the *SARFU* judgment:

> the test for determining whether conduct constitutes 'administrative action' is not the question whether the action concerned is performed by a member of the executive arm of government. What matters is not so much the functionary as the function ... The focus of the enquiry as to whether conduct is 'administrative action' is not on the arm of government to which the relevant actor belongs, but on the nature of the power he or she is exercising.[54]

As we noted in Chapter 2, South African administrative law now largely adopts a functional approach to the identification of administrative action as opposed to an institutional approach.[55] The fourth and fifth factors also do not seem to take the inquiry much further. There are many examples of administrators exercising investigatory functions as part of their administrative work, such as investigations by tax administrators, or competition authorities, or home affairs administrators (for example, in relation to refugee applications), or health and safety officials, or police officials. The fact that the work of these core administrators involves some form of investigation and consequent remedial action based on the conclusions reached during such investigations, hardly takes them out of the realm of administrative law. Likewise, wide discretionary powers are very common among administrative decision-makers. It would be very surprising if the existence of a wide discretion could point away from the power being administrative.

53 Para 37 (footnotes omitted).

54 *President of the Republic of South Africa and Others v South African Rugby Football Union and Others* 2000 (1) SA 1 (CC) para 141. *President of RSA v SARFU* para 141.

55 See Chapter 2 section 3.6.1.

### 4.4.2 The Human Rights Commission

The South African Human Rights Commission has a broad mandate to promote and protect human rights. It must:

(*a*) promote respect for human rights and a culture of human rights;
(*b*) promote the protection, development and attainment of human rights; and
(*c*) monitor and assess the observance of human rights in the Republic.[56]

Since administrative justice is included in the Bill of Rights, it follows that the whole of administrative law falls within the jurisdiction of the Human Rights Commission.

The Commission's powers under the Constitution and as given further effect to in the South African Human Rights Commission Act[57] are largely restricted to investigation and reporting. The Commission is competent to investigate 'on its own initiative or on receipt of a complaint, any alleged violation of human rights'.[58] Unlike the Public Protector, the Commission does not have the power to issue binding remedial action. If it finds a violation of any human rights, the Commission must assist any person adversely affected to secure redress, which may include approaching a court for relief. The Commission may also make recommendations to any organ of state on action to be taken in pursuit of human rights.

The Commission has, however, not been particularly active in respect of the right to administrative justice. There are only a very few examples of where the Commission has investigated matters involving a breach of section 33 of the Constitution. One such example is the Commission's report on the matter between a private party and the Refugee Appeal Board and others in 2017. In this matter, the complainant lodged a complaint to the Commission that his application for asylum seeker status had been unduly delayed by the Refugee Appeal Board. Following its investigation, the Commission found that the complainant's right to lawful administrative action was infringed due to the unreasonably long delay in finalising his application. The Commission recommended that the Refugee Appeal Board issue an apology to the complainant, that it report to the Commission on the back-log of appeal matters and the steps it intends to take to address the back-log and to provide facilities to enable efficient appeals.

### 4.4.3 The Auditor-General

Section 188 of the Constitution sets out the functions of the Auditor-General, which are 'to audit and report on the accounts, financial statements and financial management' of public entities. The Auditor-General's functions thus focus on scrutinising financial management within the state. Given that public spending flows to a large extent from administrative action, such action also falls within the ambit of the Auditor-General's work. The Auditor-General's functions are given detailed content in the Public Audit Act.[59]

The Auditor-General annually audits the accounts and financial management of all national and provincial government departments, all municipalities and all legislatures. In addition, it also audits the accounts of a number of state-owned entities (in the 2018/19

56 Constitution section 184.
57 40 of 2013.
58 South African Human Rights Commission Act 40 of 2013 section 13(3)(*a*).
59 25 of 2004.

financial year, the Auditor-General was responsible for the external audit of 67% of state-owned entities). In respect of each audit conducted, the Auditor-General must issue an audit report, which is tabled in Parliament, in which it expresses a view on:

(*a*) the financial statements of the auditee in accordance with the applicable financial reporting framework and legislation;
(*b*) compliance with any applicable legislation relating to financial matters, financial management and other related matters; and
(*c*) reported performance of the auditee against its predetermined objectives.[60]

The Auditor-General's audits and reports thus go beyond simply expressing a view on the financial standing of organs of state. As is evident from the Public Audit Act,[61] the reports also express a view on compliance with legislation. This is a core administrative-law function. When the Auditor-General thus reports on instances where organs of state did not comply with legislation in their spending, it is in effect expressing a view on unlawful administrative action. This part of the Auditor-General's work utilises a number of key concepts to express misalignment between public spending and the regulatory regime. The most important of these are:

- overspending,
- unauthorised expenditure,
- irregular expenditure,
- fruitless and wasteful expenditure, and
- material irregularity.

The first four of these concepts are defined in the Public Finance Management Act[62] and Local Government: Municipal Finance Management Act[63] whereas the last concept is defined in the Public Audit Act.[64] It is important to distinguish between these concepts since they express different notions of non-compliance with the regulatory framework and will have different consequences. The concept of *irregular expenditure* has become the most commonly noted one of the four. As we shall note below, this concept refers to expenditure not in line with legislative prescripts. It is important to keep in mind that this does not necessarily imply that the expenditure amounts to corruption or an abuse of public funds. Irregular expenditure could have been incurred in a completely *bona fide* manner.

These concepts are closely related to the budgetary process. Annually, government departments are awarded a share of the total budget by the legislature. That is, national departments are awarded a share of the national budget by Parliament and provincial departments are awarded a share of the provincial budget by the relevant provincial legislature. Each department must submit its proposed budget to the relevant legislature in what is called a budget vote, that is the legislature's vote on that department's annual budget. A budget vote is divided into main divisions, setting out the part of the department's budget allocated to each of its main programmes. At local government level, the municipality's annual budget is approved by the municipal council.

60 Public Audit Act 25 of 2004 section 20(2).
61 25 of 2004.
62 1 of 1999.
63 56 of 2003.
64 25 of 2004.

The concept of *overspending* refers to expenditure that exceeds the annual budget. This can be either in relation to an entity's entire budget, that is its budget vote, or a main division within that entity's budget. In other words, overspending refers to total expenditure by a department that exceeds its total budget allocated or to expenditure within a particular main segment of its budget that exceeds the amount allocated for that particular segment in its approved budget. Overspending thus refers to expenditure by an entity that exceeds the amount authorised by the legislature to be spent on a particular programme.

*Unauthorised expenditure* includes overspending, but also includes expenditure that is not in accordance with the purpose of a budget vote or a main division within that vote, regardless of whether it amounts to overspending. Spending can thus be unauthorised even if it is within the amount budgeted, but for a purpose that does not accord with the purpose of that main division of its budget vote.

*Irregular expenditure* refers to expenditure that was incurred in a manner not in line with applicable legislation, but does not include unauthorised expenditure. Irregular expenditure and unauthorised expenditure are thus mutually exclusive concepts. Expenditure will be irregular if the action leading to the expenditure did not comply with applicable legislation.

*Fruitless and wasteful expenditure* is expenditure that, as the label suggests, is wasteful, that is, was made in vain. Importantly, expenditure can only be viewed as fruitless and wasteful if it would have been avoided had reasonable care been taken. For expenditure to be noted as fruitless and wasteful, two conditions must thus be met. It must, factually, have amounted to a waste, that is made in vain, and reasonable care would have avoided it, that is there must be a lack of reasonable care accompanying the expenditure. The concept of *fruitless and wasteful expenditure* may overlap with any of the preceding concepts, that is overspending, unauthorised expenditure or irregular expenditure may also be fruitless and wasteful expenditure. This will be the case if the conditions for both concepts are met in a given case. However, this will depend on the circumstances of the particular case as there is no necessary overlap, that is overspending or unauthorised expenditure or irregular expenditure is not necessarily fruitless and wasteful. For example, a department may conclude a contract for services to be rendered to it based on two quotations instead of the statutorily required three quotations. When those services are rendered at a market price and the department pays the contractor, the expenditure will be irregular, because the department did not adhere to the statutory rule about quotations, but the expenditure will not be fruitless and wasteful, because the department did receive the services.

*Material irregularity* is a concept that was fairly recently introduced by way of an amendment to the Public Audit Act.[65] This concept refers to irregularities identified during an audit that meet two conditions. Firstly, the irregularity must amount to a transgression. This transgression can be in the form of noncompliance/contravention of legislation, fraud, theft or a breach of a fiduciary duty. Secondly, that transgression must have or be likely to have certain consequences. These consequences must be material financial loss, misuse or loss of a material public resource or substantial harm to a public sector institution or the general public. A causal connection is required between the transgression and the consequence, either in fact or in likelihood. It is also important to note the degree of consequence required – it is not any financial loss, but only a material one; not misuse/loss of any public resource, but only a material public resource and the harm must be substantial. In essence, a material irregularity will exist when an organ of state failed to comply with legal prescripts and that failure resulted in serious financial harm.

65 Public Audit Amendment Act 5 of 2018 amended the Public Audit Act 25 of 2004.

All of the concepts noted above can be seen as expressing a view on administrative justice in some form. The Auditor-General thus reports on whether organs of state are adhering to principles of administrative justice, primarily in the form of lawfulness, when they incur expenditure in their daily functions.

The Auditor-General traditionally only played an investigatory and reporting role, much like the Human Rights Commission. It did not have any remedial powers to take steps when it found irregularities. The result was that even though the Auditor-General's work was comprehensive in testing compliance with the law, it was fairly weak since it could not take any action to remedy non-compliance itself. This changed dramatically with the 2018 amendments to the Public Audit Act,[66] which came into effect in April 2019. The Public Audit Amendment Act of 2018 augmented the Auditor-General's powers by providing it with binding remedial power. Under these new powers, the Auditor-General can issue recommendations to organs of state on how to address material irregularities found in an audit. Organs of state are now obliged to report to the Auditor-General on compliance with those recommendations, while the Auditor-General is also obliged to follow up on his or her recommendations.[67] If the Auditor-General finds that an organ of state did not adhere to the recommendations, the Auditor-General must take appropriate remedial action to address the failure.[68] This may include an instruction to the organ of state to recover any losses that resulted from material irregularities from the responsible official. If the administrative head of the organ of state (referred to as the accounting officer or accounting authority) fails to recover such losses, the Auditor-General may issue a certificate of debt against the head of the organ of state, obliging that person to repay the losses himself or herself.

The Auditor-General's work has become a key driver in the pursuit of administrative justice. Given the regularity of public audits, the publication of the results and the detailed findings on each and every public entity's conduct and the new powers to enforce compliance with recommendations, the Auditor-General's work is a very powerful mechanism to compel public entities to pay specific attention to their compliance with legislative requirements, which means in essence paying special attention to what administrative justice requires.[69] The Auditor-General's reports also fulfil further important functions in regulating administrative action. They facilitate Parliament's role of oversight over the state administration by providing Parliament with the necessary information on public spending by individual organs of state to enable Parliament to hold those organs of state to account. Organs of state thus commonly have to appear before Parliament's Standing Committee on Public Accounts (SCOPA) to explain their financial management conduct as reported on in the Auditor-General's reports. It is also clear that the Auditor-General's findings play an important role in public discourse regarding the state administrations' work. It is common to find significant engagement with findings of overspending or irregular expenditure or fruitless and wasteful expenditure in the popular media when the Auditor-General releases reports.

---

66 25 of 2004.

67 Public Audit Act 25 of 2004 section 5A.

68 Public Audit Act 25 of 2004 section 5B.

69 See Auditor-General of South Africa (2014). *Consolidated General Report on National and Provincial Audit Outcomes PFMA 2013–14* at 30, 57–65 where it is reported that 72% of national and provincial entities audited had findings of material non-compliance with legislation.

COUNTER POINT

**Can the Auditor-General's findings be challenged in court?**

We discussed above the issue of whether the Public Protector's decisions amount to administrative action and would thus be subject to scrutiny in terms of administrative law in judicial review proceedings. We noted that the SCA has held that this is not the case, but that the Public Protector's decisions are subject to judicial scrutiny in terms of the constitutional principle of legality.

A very similar question can be asked of the decisions of the Auditor-General. That is, can an organ of state that disagrees with a finding of the Auditor-General approach a court to review those findings and set them aside? The Western Cape High Court judgment in *Member of the Executive Council for Economic Opportunities, Western Cape v Auditor General of South Africa and Another*[70] was the first case in which this question was addressed. In this matter, the applicant applied for the review and setting aside of the Auditor-General's findings in his audit report on the financial statements of the Western Cape Department of Agriculture.

In analysing the legal nature of the Auditor-General's findings, the court distinguished these findings from those of the Public Protector and accordingly the present case from the SCA judgment holding that the Public Protector's actions do not amount to administrative action. The difference, according to the court, lies in the administrative nature of the Auditor-General's work compared to that of the Public Protector. The court held that the Auditor-General 'fits squarely into the institutions of the public administration' and that its function is 'indeed to administer, by auditing the accounts and financial statements of the relevant organs of state'.[71] On this basis, the court concluded that the Auditor-General does take administrative action when making audit findings. The result is that those findings can be challenged by way of judicial review in administrative law. However, the court also noted that even if it is mistaken in its view that the findings amount to administrative action, the Auditor-General's findings would still be subject to judicial review in terms of the principle of legality.

### 4.4.4 The Public Service Commission

As noted in Chapter 2 above, the civil or public service exists within the public administration and is the personnel of the state.[72] The Public Service Commission is created in Chapter 10 of the Constitution to provide oversight over the work of the public service. Section 196 of the Constitution lists the following functions of the Public Service Commission:

> (4) The powers and functions of the Commission are-
> (*a*) to promote the values and principles set out in section 195, throughout the public service;
> (*b*) to investigate, monitor and evaluate the organisation and administration, and the personnel practices, of the public service;
> (*c*) to propose measures to ensure effective and efficient performance within the public service;

70 (19259/2018) [2020] ZAWCHC 50 (8 June 2020).
71 Para 17.
72 Chapter 2 section 2.2.5.

(*d*) to give directions aimed at ensuring that personnel procedures relating to recruitment, transfers, promotions and dismissals comply with the values and principles set out in section 195;

(*e*) to report in respect of its activities and the performance of its functions, including any finding it may make and directions and advice it may give, and to provide an evaluation of the extent to which the values and principles set out in section 195 are complied with; and

(*f*) either of its own accord or on receipt of any complaint-

  (i) to investigate and evaluate the application of personnel and public administration practices, and to report to the relevant executive authority and legislature;

  (ii) to investigate grievances of employees in the public service concerning official acts or omissions, and recommend appropriate remedies;

  (iii) to monitor and investigate adherence to applicable procedures in the public service; and

  (iv) to advise national and provincial organs of state regarding personnel practices in the public service, including those relating to the recruitment, appointment, transfer, discharge and other aspects of the careers of employees in the public service.

These are clearly wide powers involving significant oversight over administrative action. An important hallmark of the Public Service Commission is its proactive role in promoting good administration as opposed to simply investigating administrative failures and attempting to rectify such failures. In fulfilling this function, the Public Service Commission has thus published various reports and guidelines to promote good decision-making, such as its *Template for Developing Guidelines on Public Participation* and its *Code of Conduct for Public Servants*. While these documents are not sources of administrative law, they do clearly promote decision-making that adheres to administrative law. They can thus be viewed as mechanisms in bringing rules of administrative law to bear on the conduct of the public service.

There is some uncertainty regarding the Public Service Commission's authority over members of the executive. This stems mainly from the specific reference to 'public service' within its mandate. Conceptually, the term 'public service' excludes members of the executive.[73] To the extent that the Public Service Commission's mandate relates to conduct of the public service, it thus does not have authority over conduct of members of the executive. However, this view should be carefully considered. Insofar as the Public Service Commission has a constitutional mandate to monitor the functioning of the public service, conduct of members of the executive in steering the public service may quite likely fall within the Commission's mandate. For example, in terms of section 196(4)(*d*) of the Constitution, the Commission has the power 'to give directions aimed at ensuring that personnel procedures relating to recruitment, transfers, promotions and dismissals comply with the values and principles set out in section 195'. Members of the executive are quite often involved in these personnel decisions and conduct would be subject to the powers of the Commission.

73 See Chapter 2 section 2.2.

## 4.5 Alternative dispute resolution (ADR) in administrative law

An interesting question that has emerged in recent years is what role alternative dispute resolution processes (ADR) can play as a mechanism to regulate administrative action. In many other areas of law, ADR has become a major route to resolving disputes and thus enforcing legal rules. ADR typically involves processes of negotiation, mediation and/or arbitration to resolve a dispute.

There are some statutory and regulatory indications that ADR may be used in addressing administrative-law disputes. Section 6(4) of the Public Protector Act[74] provides that the Public Protector shall have the power:

> (*b*) to endeavour, in his or her sole discretion, to resolve any dispute or rectify any act or omission by ... (i) mediation, conciliation or negotiation.

As is clear from the Annual Reports of the Public Protector, a very significant proportion of complaints brought to the Public Protector are resolved by means of alternative dispute resolution.

In terms of the Supply Chain Management Regulations under the Local Government: Municipal Finance Management Act[75] bid documents for public tenders at local government level must 'stipulate that disputes must be settled by means of mutual consultation, mediation (with or without legal representation), or, when unsuccessful, in a South African court of law'.[76] Given that our courts have long held that decisions taken in adjudicating and awarding public tenders are administrative action, it would seem that this provision contemplates using mediation to resolve administrative-law disputes in a public tender at local government level. The Tax Administration Act[77] provides that '[b]y mutual agreement, SARS and the taxpayer making the appeal [against an assessment or "decision" by SARS] may attempt to resolve the dispute through alternative dispute resolution under procedures specified in the "rules"'. Since most of the decisions taken by SARS will amount to administrative action, this provision thus expressly allows for settling administrative-law disputes by way of ADR in the tax context.

The judgment in *Airports Company South Africa Ltd and Another v ISO Leisure OR Tambo (Pty) Ltd*[78] has, however, cast some doubt as to whether ADR can be utilised in the administrative-law context. In this matter the judge found that an arbitrator did not have the jurisdiction to deal with a dispute between a public entity and a bidder for a public tender relating to an administrative decision taken as part of the tender adjudication process. The judge stated:

> I, therefore, hold that s 7(4) of PAJA precludes any forum, apart from the High Court and the Constitutional Court, to adjudicate over claims brought in terms of PAJA. The parties cannot, in my view, confer jurisdiction upon a private arbitrator to decide a claim brought in terms of PAJA. To allow such would be to allow parties to privatise constitutional disputes, and this bears the risk of allowing a parallel constitutional jurisprudence to develop in this country — one that is separate and independent from that developed by the Constitutional Court. Such a development

74 23 of 1994.
75 56 of 2003.
76 Regulation 21(e) GN 868 in *GG* 27636 of 30.05.2005.
77 Tax Administration Act 28 of 2011 section 107(5).
78 2011 (4) SA 642 (GSJ).

> goes against the entire grain of our constitutional system, which is based on recognising the Constitutional Court as the highest and, in some respects, the only court that can make pronouncements on constitutional matters. The privatisation of disputes involving constitutional matters is anathema to our Constitution, and rightly so, in my view.[79]

On one reading of the judgment, it may only be authority for the narrow point that claims expressly brought under PAJA cannot be submitted to ADR processes, which is what happened on the facts in this case. Such a result would not be particularly problematic given that PAJA expressly provides for *judicial* review. ADR procedures are clearly not judicial processes and would thus not qualify as the type of fora contemplated by PAJA. However, the judge's remarks towards the end of the paragraph quoted above and particularly in the last sentence, suggests a broader view, namely that since administrative-law disputes are by implication constitutional-law disputes (which is beyond doubt) they will never be amenable to resolution through ADR processes. Such an interpretation of the judgment clearly has a much further impact and would effectively remove ADR altogether as a mechanism to regulate administrative law.

COUNTER POINT

**ADR, 'privatisation of disputes' and constitutional matters**

Consider the court's statement in *ISO Leisure OR Tambo* quoted above that 'the privatisation of disputes involving constitutional matters is anathema to our Constitution'. This ostensible principle underlies the court's rejection of recourse to ADR in the administrative-law dispute at issue in that case. Does this reasoning hold true in all areas of law? Think of a dispute between a private landlord and tenant where, say, discrimination is at issue and the lease agreement includes an ADR clause. Would the court's reasoning forbid these parties from submitting their dispute to arbitration under their ADR clause, because equality is inevitably a constitutional matter? If we accept ADR in this context, how do we draw a line between such cases and administrative-law disputes, assuming that we can find a basis for the ADR in the latter cases, for example where there is an agreement between the parties?

Perhaps the resistance to ADR in administrative-law disputes signals the courts' adherence to the dominance of judicial review as a mechanism of regulating administrative action. Such resistance may, however, be to the detriment of developing an integrated system of regulation where different types of regulation, including ADR, can play complementary roles.

79 *ISO Leisure OR Tambo* para 68.

## THIS CHAPTER IN ESSENCE

Administrative law is different from other frameworks that guide the work of the public administration in that administrative law can be enforced by means of various legal mechanisms. This is a hallmark of administrative justice, namely the enforceable normative character of the rules constituting this field. In South African law, one mechanism has dominated the regulatory landscape, namely judicial review, but there are actually a range of different mechanisms that can ensure compliance with administrative-law principles. These include legislative oversight, internal controls, the work of specialised bodies such as Chapter 9 institutions and possibly ADR. Many of these non-judicial forms of regulation over administrative action can enhance administrative justice in a manner that courts cannot. A more integrated and coherent approach to regulating administrative action in terms of which the various distinct regulatory mechanisms are aligned and play distinct, but complementary roles remains an important challenge for South African administrative law.

## FURTHER READING


- Creyke, R (2006) Administrative Justice: Beyond the Courtroom Door *Acta Juridica* 257
- Govender, K 'Administrative Appeals Tribunals' in Bennett, TW & Corder, H (Eds) (1993) *Administrative Law Reform* Cape Town: Juta
- Hoexter, C (2000) The Future of Judicial Review in South African Administrative Law *SALJ* 117(3):484
- Theophilopoulos, C and De Matos Ala, C (2019) An Analysis of the Public Protector's Investigatory and Decision-Making Procedural Powers *PER / PELJ* 22
- Venter, R (2017) The Executive, the Public Protector and the Legislature: The Lion, the Witch and the Wardrobe *TSAR* 176

## Chapter 5

# Judicial regulation of administrative action

*Geo Quinot & Raisa Cachalia*



## 5.1 The primacy of judicial review

In South African administrative law, as in many other common-law systems, the courts have been viewed as the primary mechanism of regulating administrative action. The way in which administrative law has developed, as discussed in Chapter 1, was premised on judicial oversight of the work of the administration. This is clear, for example, from the original pillars of administrative law, namely the *ultra vires* doctrine and the rules of natural justice, which were judicially developed and enforced principles. As a discipline, at least in the common-law tradition, administrative law is thus closely tied to judicial enforcement. As we shall see in the following chapters, the rules of administrative law are consequently often formulated in a negative way, called grounds of review, which are essentially descriptions of when courts may interfere with administrative action.

In this chapter, we focus on judicial review of administrative action as distinct from other forms of regulation of administrative action noted in Chapter 4. It is important to bear the relationship between judicial review and other forms of regulation of administrative action in mind when considering the complete administrative-justice system. In Chapter 11 we will look in more detail at the procedural aspects of utilising the primary mechanism of review and in Chapter 12 we will see what relief a court can grant a party in terms of the mechanism of judicial review.

**PAUSE FOR REFLECTION**

**A limited role for courts in administrative law**

In her influential 2000 article, Cora Hoexter has accurately described two of the biggest challenges facing modern South African administrative law as relating to the role of courts in this area:

> South African administrative law of the twentieth century cried out for two things. First, it called for completion. There was a need to develop an integrated system of administrative law in which judicial review could play a more suitable and more limited role. Secondly, it called for the construction of an appropriate theory of deference. There was a need to identify principles to guide the courts' intervention and non-intervention in administrative matters.[1]

As we explore the role of the courts as regulators of administrative action in this section, it is important to consider that role in relation to the other mechanisms already discussed in the preceding chapter. One should ask how the role of the courts on particular points can be understood as part of a larger, integrated system of regulation with other mechanisms fulfilling distinct, but complementary roles. For example, when one argues that a court should not be able to do something in administrative law that should not mean that it cannot be done in administrative law. It could simply mean that the courts may not be the best or appropriate mechanism to achieve the particular function of administrative law, but some other mechanism may be better suited to do so. A good illustration is in respect of appeals against administrative decisions. Unlike administrative reviews, which are concerned with the manner in which decisions are taken, appeals involve an assessment of the appropriateness or correctness of a decision itself. For the reasons that are given more detailed attention in section 5.2 below, the courts are generally not well-placed to adjudicate the latter questions given their lack of expertise in the technical matters of running a complex modern bureaucracy. The responsibility for deciding administrative appeals thus, more often than not, resides with the administration itself rather than the courts.

## 5.2 Review and appeal

The above-mentioned distinction between review and appeal has always been an important one in administrative law. This is largely because of the separation of powers doctrine.[2] As we noted in Chapter 2, the courts are generally not allowed to take over the work of the administration, because that is the function specifically allocated to the administrative branch of state. The courts' role in administrative law is thus restricted to ensuring that the administration keeps within its mandate and exercises its function in a manner that complies with all law. As a result, the courts are not tasked with asking whether the administration took the correct decision, but whether the decision taken was a legal one. The vital point is that there may be many different decisions that can achieve the same administrative purpose and all of them may be legal. The fact that some may be better than others is largely irrelevant for the courts' purpose in adjudicating administrative reviews. This essentially sums up the

1 Hoexter, C (2000) The Future of Judicial Review in South African Administrative Law *SALJ* 117(3):484. Reprinted by permission of © Juta & Company Ltd.

2 *Carephone (Pty) Ltd v Marcus NO and Others* 1999 (3) SA 304 (LAC) para 34.

distinction between review and appeal. Review is concerned with 'how' the decision was taken, and specifically whether it is a decision that complies with all law. Appeal, in contrast, is concerned with whether the correct or best decision was taken in the circumstances.

In South African law, courts have the constitutional mandate to review administrative action based on sections 33 (just administrative action) and 34 (access to courts) of the Constitution. All affected persons thus have the right to approach a court for the review of administrative action. Any attempt to limit the exercise of these rights would need to meet the requirements of section 36 of the Constitution as a reasonable and justifiable limitation of fundamental rights to be constitutionally valid. In contrast, there is no general mandate for the courts to hear appeals against administrative action. In a few instances, statutory provisions provide for courts to entertain such appeals[3] and it would only be in cases where such specific mandate for appeal is created that a person can appeal to a court against an administrative action.

The distinction between review and appeal has come under increasing pressure as the grounds of review have extended to include scrutiny of matters of substance, that is grounds of review that have inevitably resulted in judges having to consider the merits of a particular action. It is sometimes very difficult to draw a clear line between judging whether the decision was taken in a correct manner and judging whether the correct decision was taken when the ground upon which the administrative action is challenged involves matters of reasonableness[4] or mistake of fact or law.[5]

Despite the evident and growing difficulty in maintaining a line between review and appeal, South African courts have remained steadfast in insisting on the distinction. In a key judgment delivered by the Labour Appeal Court and dealing with the requirement of justifiable administrative action,[6] Froneman J stated in *Carephone (Pty) Ltd v Marcus NO and Others*[7] that:

> It appears from a number of decisions of the High Court that the effect of, particularly, the administrative justice section in the Bill of Rights is seen as broadening the scope of judicial review of administrative action ...
> The peg on which the extended scope of review has been hung is the constitutional provision that administrative action must be justifiable in relation to the reasons given for it (sections 33 and item 23(*b*) of Schedule 6 to the Constitution). This provision introduces a requirement of rationality in the *merit* or outcome of the administrative decision. This goes beyond mere procedural impropriety as a ground for review or irrationality only as evidence of procedural impropriety.
> But it would be wrong to read into this section an attempt to abolish the distinction between review and appeal. According to the *New Shorter Oxford English Dictionary* 'justifiable' means 'able to be legally or morally justified, able to be shown to be just, reasonable, or correct; defensible'. It does not mean 'just', 'justified' or 'correct'. On its plain meaning the use of the word 'justifiable' does not ask for the obliteration of the difference between review and appeal ...

3 For example, under section 28 of the Planning Profession Act 36 of 2002 either an aggrieved person or the South African Council for Planners may appeal against a decision of the Appeal Board created under that Act to the High Court.

4 We will see what reasonableness entails in Chapter 8 below and note there the extent to which the merits of the particular action are relevant in scrutinising reasonableness.

5 We will explore mistakes in Chapter 6 below and see that administrators can err in respect of their mandate either by an incorrect interpretation of the law involved or by basing their decisions on the wrong facts.

6 This was in terms of the interim wording of section 33 of the Constitution pending the enactment of PAJA as set out in item 23(2)(*b*) of Schedule 6 to the Constitution.

7 1999 (3) SA 304 (LAC) paras 30–32, 36.

> In determining whether administrative action is justifiable in terms of the reasons given for it, value judgments will have to be made which will, almost inevitably, involve the consideration of the 'merits' of the matter in some way or another. As long as the judge determining this issue is aware that he or she enters the merits not in order to substitute his or her own opinion on the correctness thereof, but to determine whether the outcome is rationally justifiable, the process will be in order.

This reasoning was confirmed by the Constitutional Court in *Bel Porto School Governing Body and Others v Premier, Western Cape and Another*.[8] Subsequently, in *Bato Star Fishing (Pty) Ltd v Minister of Environmental Affairs and Others*[9] the Constitutional Court adopted the same reasoning in respect of the broader requirement of reasonableness in section 33 of the Constitution where O'Regan J stated for the court:

> Although the review functions of the court now have a substantive as well as a procedural ingredient, the distinction between appeals and reviews continues to be significant. The court should take care not to usurp the functions of administrative agencies.

The point of departure for judicial oversight over administrative action is thus that the courts can only ask a limited number of questions. While the substance or merits of the particular action is not irrelevant for the purpose of judicial oversight, the purpose for which the courts engage with the merits of the action is strictly limited to ascertaining whether the decision falls within the scope of actions that could legally be taken and not whether it is the correct or best decision.

## 5.3 Judicial review

Judicial review is the specific procedure that developed under our in common law in terms of which a court scrutinises administrative action against the rules of administrative law. In South Africa the basis for this procedure was authoritatively established in the two judgments of Innes CJ in *Johannesburg Consolidated Investment Co v Johannesburg Town Council*[10] and *Shidiack v Union Government (Minister of the Interior)*.[11] In the first judgment the court formulated the power of the court to engage in judicial review of administrative action as follows:

> Whenever a public body has a duty imposed upon it by statute, and disregards important provisions of the statute, or is guilty of gross irregularity or clear illegality in the performance of the duty, this Court may be asked to review the proceedings complained of and set aside or correct them. This is no special machinery created by the Legislature; it is a right inherent in the Court, which has jurisdiction to entertain all civil causes and proceedings arising within the Transvaal. The non-performance or wrong performance of a statutory duty by which third persons are injured or aggrieved is such a cause as falls within the ordinary jurisdiction of the Court.[12]

8 2002 (3) SA 265 (CC) para 89.
9 2004 (4) SA 490 (CC) para 45.
10 1903 TS 111.
11 1912 AD 642.
12 *Johannesburg Consolidated Investment Co* para 115.

For the better part of the twentieth century this remained the basis for judicial review in South Africa. It was of course a fairly weak basis given that the courts' reviewing powers were restricted to narrow procedural grounds and limited to cases where a serious decisional defect or illegality was shown to be present. A further constraint on judicial power in this regard was the fact that the legislature, which had superior power to the courts in terms of the doctrine of parliamentary supremacy, could simply oust the courts' reviewing jurisdiction and thus insulate particular administrative action from judicial scrutiny.[13]

With the advent of constitutional democracy in South Africa in 1994 the basis for judicial review of administrative action also changed radically. Rather than arising from the inherent (and self-proclaimed) common-law jurisdiction of the courts, judicial review was now founded expressly on fundamental rights protected in the supreme Constitution.

In its judgment in *Pharmaceutical Manufacturers Association of SA*[14] the Constitutional Court confirmed this shift to a single, constitutional foundation for judicial review of administrative action. It also follows from this judgment that all instances of judicial review of administrative action automatically amount to constitutional matters, since they all involve the enforcement of the Constitution regardless of the specific arguments presented in the particular review. In what has become one of the most important dicta in South African constitutional law pertaining to the nature of the constitutional law system, the court stated:

> There are not two systems of law, each dealing with the same subject-matter, each having similar requirements, each operating in its own field with its own highest Court. There is only one system of law. It is shaped by the Constitution which is the supreme law, and all law, including the common law, derives its force from the Constitution and is subject to constitutional control.
>
> Whilst there is no bright line between public and private law, administrative law, which forms the core of public law, occupies a special place in our jurisprudence. It is an incident of the separation of powers under which courts regulate and control the exercise of public power by the other branches of government. It is built on constitutional principles which define the authority of each branch of government, their inter-relationship and the boundaries between them. Prior to the coming into force of the interim Constitution, the common law was 'the main crucible' for the development of these principles of constitutional law. The interim Constitution which came into force in April 1994 was a legal watershed. It shifted constitutionalism, and with it all aspects of public law, from the realm of common law to the prescripts of a written constitution which is the supreme law. That is not to say that the principles of common law have ceased to be material to the development of public law. These well-established principles will continue to inform the content of administrative law and other aspects of public law, and will contribute to their future development. But there has been a fundamental change. Courts no longer have to claim space and push boundaries to find means of controlling public power. That control is vested in them under the Constitution, which defines the role of the courts, their powers in relation to other arms of government and the constraints subject to which public power has to be exercised. Whereas previously constitutional law formed part of and was developed consistently with the common law, the roles have been reversed. The written

---

13 See Chapter 4 paragraph 4.2.

14 *Pharmaceutical Manufacturers Association of South Africa and Another: In Re: Ex Parte Application of the President of the Republic of South Africa and Others* 2000 (2) SA 674 (CC).

> Constitution articulates and gives effect to the governing principles of constitutional law. Even if the common law constitutional principles continue to have application in matters not expressly dealt with by the Constitution (and that need not be decided in this case), the Constitution is the supreme law and the common law, insofar as it has any application, must be developed consistently with it and subject to constitutional control.[15]

Judicial review of administrative action is thus today simply the enforcement of section 33 of the Constitution. However, as we have noted in Chapters 1 and 2 above, it was never contemplated that the courts will fulfil this function directly in terms of section 33. Thus, section 33(3) prescribed that legislation must be enacted to *inter alia* 'provide for the review of administrative action by a court'. PAJA is this legislation and it thus follows that judicial review is today primarily premised on PAJA. In *Bato Star Fishing* the Constitutional Court confirmed that the cause of action for judicial review of administrative action today arises from PAJA on the authority of the Constitution.[16]

**PAUSE FOR REFLECTION**

**Judicial review under the constitutional principle of legality**

While the advent of constitutional democracy shifted judicial review of administrative action from a common-law system to one founded on constitutional rights, as recent developments show, it did not end there. The triptych of judgments – *Fedsure*,[17] *SARFU*[18] and *Pharmaceutical Manufacturers Association of SA* – are largely credited with having developed the deeper constitutional principle of legality as an aspect of the rule of law in section 1(c) of the Constitution. In so doing, these judgments broadened the powers of our courts to review all exercises of public power, including those that do not qualify as administrative action for the purposes of section 33 of the Constitution, as given legislative effect to in PAJA. While this development may be positively regarded as ensuring that all exercises of public power are not insulated from judicial scrutiny, with the growth and expansion of the courts' reviewing powers under the mandate of legality, the flipside has been the relegation of judicial review of administrative action under PAJA in favour of the more flexible and open-ended system of review under the legality principle.[19] This proliferation of possible avenues to review, which receives more detailed attention in section 5.3.2 below, has also undermined the goal of creating a more limited role for the courts in exercising their review functions in the constitutional era.

---

15 *Pharmaceutical Manufacturers Association of SA* paras 44–45.

16 *Bato Star Fishing* para 25.

17 *Fedsure Life Assurance Ltd and Others v Greater Johannesburg Transitional Metropolitan Council and Others* 1999 (1) SA 374 (CC) paras 56–59.

18 *President of the Republic of South Africa and Others v South African Rugby Football Union and Others* 2000 (1) SA 1 (CC) ('*SARFU*') para 148.

19 The most recent example of this trend in favour of relying on legality review at the expense of PAJA is seen in the developing body of law on state self-reviews. See in this regard *State Information Technology Agency SOC Ltd v Gijima Holdings (Pty) Ltd* 2018 (2) SA 23 (CC), subsequently affirmed in *Buffalo City Metropolitan Municipality v Asla Construction (Pty) Limited* 2019 (4) SA 331 (CC) and *BW Bright Water Way Props (Pty) Ltd v Eastern Cape Development Corporation* 2019 (6) SA 443 (ECG). These cases involve decisions that clearly qualify as administrative actions under PAJA and would, for this reason, ordinarily be reviewed under that legislation.

### 5.3.1 Grounds of review

Unlike appeal, judicial review is not an open-ended procedure in terms of which an applicant can make any argument to show that the administrator erred in taking the decision. In review there are a limited number of causes of action on which an applicant can approach a court to scrutinise an administrative action. An applicant must frame his or her case in terms of one or more of these causes of action, called grounds of review. In *Bato Star Fishing* the Constitutional Court also held that PAJA amounts to a codification of the grounds of review.[20] This means that an applicant must argue his or her case on review in terms of one or more of the grounds set out in section 6(2) of PAJA. Put differently, judicial review of administrative action involves proving that the administrator made one or more of the mistakes described in section 6(2) of PAJA. While this is clearly a limitation on the type of arguments that can be made upon review, it must be noted that the final subsection of section 6(2) allows for the argument that the administrative action 'is otherwise unconstitutional or unlawful'. This very broad formulation thus allows scope for arguments that cannot be brought under one of the more specific other grounds of review in section 6(2) to be presented as long as it can be shown that such argument has a constitutional dimension or is broadly linked to lawfulness.

As was stated above, the grounds of review can be viewed as the rules of administrative law formulated in the negative. When a court thus scrutinises an administrative action on a ground of review, the court is testing whether the action adhered to the particular rule of administrative law.

The list of grounds of review in section 6(2) of PAJA unfortunately does not follow a logical structure. The ideal would have been for section 6(2) to follow the structure of section 33(1) of the Constitution and to align particular grounds of review with each of the three main pillars of administrative justice, namely lawfulness, reasonableness and procedural fairness. This is not the case. The subsections of section 6(2) are a jumble of grounds addressing particular aspects of the three main pillars with some overlap between them. While the Constitution attempted to provide a clean break with the common-law approach to judicial review, the grounds of review in section 6(2) of PAJA unfortunately largely reflect the common-law position. Table 5.1 below attempts to provide a broad structure to the grounds of review in terms of the pillars of administrative justice. However, since there is certain overlap between some grounds these categories cannot be viewed as clearly demarcated.

*Table 5.1* *Grounds of review and principles of administrative justice*

| Section 33(1) principle of administrative justice | Sections with corresponding grounds of review in PAJA |
|---|---|
| Lawfulness | 6(2)(*a*)(i), (ii)<br>6(2)(*b*)<br>6(2)(*d*)<br>6(2)(*e*)<br>6(2)(*f*)(i)<br>6(2)(*g*)<br>6(2)(*i*) |

20 *Bato Star Fishing* para 25.

| Section 33(1) principle of administrative justice | Sections with corresponding grounds of review in PAJA |
|---|---|
| Reasonableness | 6(2)(*f*)(ii)<br>6(2)(*h*)<br>6(2)(e)(vi) |
| Procedural fairness | 6(2)(*a*)(iii)<br>6(2)(*c*) |

### 5.3.2 Avenues to review

Despite the ostensible clarity brought about by judgments such as *Pharmaceutical Manufacturers* and *Bato Star Fishing* about the status and approach to judicial review of administrative action under the Constitution as set out in the sections above, there have been parallel developments in the law that have resulted in fairly significant fragmentation of judicial oversight of administrative action. Hoexter has termed these 'different pathways to administrative-law review' and has identified five such pathways as we noted in Chapter 1 above.[21] They are:

- Review under PAJA where the action qualifies as administrative action as defined in the Act.
- Review in terms of special statutory provisions other than PAJA where the action qualifies as administrative action as defined, but for policy reasons is reviewed along a separate avenue from PAJA. The primary example is review of decisions of the Commission for Conciliation, Mediation and Arbitration (CCMA), which may qualify as administrative action under PAJA, but is reviewed in terms of the Labour Relations Act (LRA)[22] and not in terms of PAJA.[23]
- Review directly in terms of section 33 of the Constitution where there is action that may qualify as administrative action, but the challenge is mounted at either PAJA itself or another statutory provision rather than the action.[24]
- Review in terms of the common law without reliance on PAJA or section 33 of the Constitution in cases of private actions that do not qualify as administrative action as defined, but that were subjected to administrative-law principles at common law. Examples would be where private bodies such as a voluntary association (be it of a charitable, sporting, religious or other nature) acts to discipline members. Importantly, this does not include cases where private bodies exercise public functions, which would be subject to review under PAJA or the principle of legality.
- Review in terms of the constitutional principle of legality without reliance on PAJA or section 33 of the Constitution where the action is public, but not administrative action as defined. Alternatively, and more controversially, this avenue is now available where the review is sought by the decision-maker itself against its own decision in the fast-developing area of 'state self-reviews'.[25]

21 Hoexter, C (2012) *Administrative Law in South Africa* (2nd ed) 131.
22 66 of 1995.
23 *Sidumo and Another v Rustenburg Platinum Mines Ltd and Others* 2008 (2) SA 24 (CC).
24 See *Zondi v MEC for Traditional and Local Government Affairs and Others* 2005 (3) SA 589 (CC).
25 *Buffalo City* para 112.

The picture of five different avenues to review reveals significant and in fact growing fragmentation in the system of judicial oversight of the exercise of different forms of power and even within particular forms of public power – a reality which runs contrary to the goal, alluded to in section 5.1 above, of creating an integrated system of administrative-law review in the constitutional era.

Although the Constitutional Court in *Bato Star Fishing* seems to have contemplated the multiplicity of avenues when it did not close the door to the existence of grounds of review outside of PAJA, O'Regan J was adamant that the 'cause of action for the judicial review of administrative action now *ordinarily* arises from PAJA'.[26] On this approach, the question whether the particular action qualifies as administrative action as defined in PAJA thus remains a key consideration. When the action does amount to administrative action, the number of avenues is immediately reduced to the first three above. In principle, having the first two avenues to review is not particularly problematic since one can understand them in terms of a general avenue (PAJA) and a more specific avenue (other statutes, for example the LRA). Such an approach is in line with established principles of subsidiarity given expression in, for instance, the Latin maxim *generalia specialibus non derogant* that applies to statutory interpretation. This maxim holds that general statutes must be read as not interfering with more specific statutes,[27] thereby affirming the distinction between general and specific administrative law.[28] Such an understanding of the difference between the first two avenues set out above would imply that the second avenue cannot be in conflict with the first, that is PAJA. When such a conflict does arise, the third avenue set out above may come into play to allow for the particular statutory provision to be tested against section 33 bearing in mind that PAJA is intended to give effect to this constitutional provision.

The most problematic of the five avenues listed above is the fourth one, namely review in terms of the constitutional principle of legality, which we traversed briefly in the introductory section of 5.3 above. In theory this option should not be available where the conduct that is challenged in review amounts to administrative action. The Constitutional Court has explained that it is impermissible to rely directly on constitutional provisions when particular legislation has been enacted to give effect to the Constitution as this would amount to bypassing the relevant legislation.[29] Ngcobo J stated the position clearly as follows:

> Where, as here, the Constitution requires Parliament to enact legislation to give effect to the constitutional rights guaranteed in the Constitution, and Parliament enacts such legislation, it will ordinarily be impermissible for a litigant to found a cause of action directly on the Constitution without alleging that the statute in question is deficient in the remedies that it provides. Legislation enacted by Parliament to give effect to a constitutional right ought not to be ignored.[30]

It follows that where action amounts to administrative action a person wanting to challenge such action in review proceedings *must* do so under PAJA and cannot rely on the legality principle. Unfortunately, the courts have not been consistent in following this logic and have increasingly side-stepped PAJA in favour of reliance on the less cumbersome and apparently

26 *Bato Star Fishing* para 25 (emphasis added).

27 See Du Plessis, LM (2002) *Re-interpretation of Statutes.*

28 See Chapter 2 section 2.6.

29 *Minister of Health and Another NO v New Clicks South Africa (Pty) Ltd and Others (Treatment Action Campaign and Another as Amici Curiae)* 2006 (2) SA 311 (CC) paras 96 (per Chaskalson CJ) and 436–437 (per Ngcobo J) concurred at paras 586 (Sachs J), 842 (Langa DCJ), 846 (O'Regan J), 851 (Van der Westhuizen J).

30 *New Clicks* para 437 (references omitted).

more flexible legality principle. There is thus a growing trend in administrative-review judgments where judges do not engage with the threshold question whether the relevant action amounts to administrative action with the consequence that PAJA must be followed[31] or where judges expressly state that it does not matter whether the action amounts to administrative action, because the principle of legality would nevertheless apply.[32] Given the position expressed in the *New Clicks* judgments, following either of these approaches is incorrect.

The problem of expansion of legality review has been compounded following the Constitutional Court judgment in *State Information Technology Agency SOC Ltd v Gijima Holdings (Pty) Ltd*[33] where the court created a 'special exception' from PAJA in respect of reviews brought by state organs reviewing their own unlawful decisions. In this case, the court held that an organ of state cannot rely on section 33 of the Constitution or PAJA when challenging its own decisions in judicial review proceedings, irrespective of whether such action amounts to administrative action. The court found that section 33 (and hence PAJA) only affords protection to private persons and that only private persons could accordingly rely on the provision in enforcement proceedings. While an organ of state has standing to challenge its own administrative action, what is now referred to as state self-review,[34] it cannot do so on the basis of section 33 or PAJA. It must bring its review in terms of the legality principle. This is a problematic approach since it implies, for the first time, that the difference between review in terms of PAJA and review in terms of legality no longer lies in the nature of power being exercised but, rather, on the identity of the reviewing party. Put differently, while it was understood that if the action amounts to administrative action review *had* to be sought under PAJA whereas if the action did not amount to administrative action review could not be sought under PAJA and *had* to be sought under legality. The difference thus turned on the conceptualisation of the relevant action as being of an administrative character or not and had nothing to do with the identity of the party seeking review. Following *Gijima*, that is no longer the case. The very same action could now be subject to PAJA review and legality review, depending on who brings the review application as opposed to what the nature of the action itself is. The *Gijima* approach has been severely criticised in academic

31 See, for example, *Electronic Media Network Limited and Others v e.tv (Pty) Limited and Others* 2017 (9) BCLR 1108 (CC) where Mogoeng CJ, writing for the majority of the Constitutional Court, concluded that an amendment to a broadcasting policy introduced by the Minister of Communications under the Electronic Communications Act 36 of 2005 was reviewable under the principle of legality. In reaching this conclusion the court did not, however, engage in the mandated threshold enquiry whether the decision in question qualified as administrative action but proceeded on the narrow basis that all policy formulation by the executive arm is automatically governed by the legality principle (para 26). This approach is inconsistent with judicial precedent, which calls for a more a nuanced approach to determining the nature and character of public power (see, for example, *Minister of Defence and Military Veterans v Motau and Others* 2014 (5) SA 69 (CC) paras 37–44).

32 For example, in *Malema and Another v Chairman of the National Council of Provinces and Another* 2015 (4) SA 145 (WCC) the court stated at para 47: 'The parties were not in agreement as to whether first respondent's rulings could be challenged under the provisions of PAJA. This issue raises two constituent questions: firstly, whether first respondent's rulings constituted "administrative action" as defined in sec 1 of PAJA or whether they were excluded from this definition by virtue of the exemption provided in the Act for "the legislative functions of Parliament"; secondly, it raises the question of whether first respondent's rulings had "a direct external legal effect". In the view that I take of this matter, however, I consider that it is unnecessary to determine the applicability of PAJA since it was common cause that first respondent's rulings were, at the very least, subject to review under the principle of legality' (references omitted).

33 2018 (2) SA 23 (CC).

34 See Chapter 11 on standing in self-review cases.

commentary[35] and even though the Constitutional Court confirmed the approach in *Buffalo City Metropolitan Municipality v Asla Construction (Pty) Limited,*[36] a dissenting minority noted that 'It may in due course become necessary to reconsider whether the legality review pathway chosen in Gijima withstands the test of time'.[37]

Finally, the fifth avenue listed above is of course not strictly-speaking a matter of administrative law. As we noted in Chapter 3 above, action that does not constitute the exercise of public power is not administrative action and thus falls outside the scope of administrative law. At common law, principles of administrative law were nevertheless at times applied to actions of private entities that did not amount to administrative action, but that exhibited similar characteristics such as the exercise of coercive power over an individual. The courts were as a result prepared to apply administrative-law principles to such relationships on policy grounds.[38] It is evident that neither PAJA nor section 33 of the Constitution can be the basis for the continued application of administrative-law principles to these private actions through judicial review. The courts have, however, continued to subject private coercive powers to judicial review on administrative-law grounds after 1994 ostensibly on the basis of the common law. In *Klein v Dainfern College and Another*[39] the judge stated:

> I am therefore of the view that the principles of natural justice have not been excluded by the Constitution as far as the coercive actions are concerned of domestic tribunals established by contract which impliedly or expressly include such principles of justice.

The construction adopted in *Dainfern* is thus that administrative-law rules were incorporated into the contract between the parties (a contract of employment in this case) and that the court could review the actions of the more powerful party (the employer) in a judicial review proceeding. This approach was rejected by the Supreme Court of Appeal in *Transman (Pty) Ltd v Dick and Another,*[40] at least in the context of disciplinary action taken in the employment context. The SCA held that the court in *Dainfern* erred in reasoning that the incorporation of administrative-law rules into the contract between the parties resulted in the mechanism of judicial review being available.[41] The court held that such incorporation cannot change the nature of the enforcement proceedings available in contractual relationships to that of administrative-law relationships. Thus, when administrative-law rules are incorporated into a contract between parties either party would be able to enforce such rules in a contractual action, but not in a judicial review. The SCA succinctly stated: 'The incorporated requirements cannot convert what is essentially a contractual claim into an entitlement to judicial review on any of the grounds recognised in law.'[42] The SCA restricted its reasoning to the employment context and also distinguished the common-law authority that *Dainfern* relied upon, which indicated that domestic tribunals may be subject

35 See Boonzaier, L (2018) A Decision to Undo *SALJ* 135(4):642; De Beer, MN (2018) A New Role for the Principle of Legality in Administrative Law: *State Information Technology Agency Soc Ltd v Gijima Holdings (Pty) Ltd SALJ* 135(4):613–630; Quinot, G & Van der Sijde, E (2019) Opening at the Close: Clarity From the Constitutional Court on the Legal Cause of Action and Regulatory Framework for an Organ of State Seeking to Review its Own Decisions? *TSAR* 324.

36 2019 (4) SA 331 (CC).

37 Para 112.

38 *Theron en Andere v Ring van Wellington van die NG Sendingkerk in Suid-Afrika en Andere* 1976 (2) SA 1 (A); *Turner v Jockey Club of South Africa* 1974 (3) SA 633 (A).

39 2006 (3) SA 73 (T) para 25.

40 2009 (4) SA 22 (SCA).

41 *Klein* paras 14, 24, 27.

42 *Transman* para 24.

to administrative-law rules via judicial review generally on the basis that none of those dealt with employment relationships. The judgment in *Transman* does not close down the fifth avenue to judicial review listed above in relation to private power, but at least narrows it to non-employment contexts. The generality of the reasoning in *Transman* may yet have a broader impact in further narrowing judicial review of private power.

**PAUSE FOR REFLECTION**

It is interesting to compare the approach adopted by the SCA in *Transman* with that of the Constitutional Court in *AMCU*. The latter case concerned a decision to extend a collective bargaining agreement in terms of section 23(1)(*d*) of the LRA between certain (private) mining enterprises, represented by the Chamber of Mines South Africa, and the unions representing the majority of workers at those companies.[43] Rather than interrogating whether this extension qualified as an exercise of private power with coercive attributes that ought to be reviewable on common-law grounds (the fourth avenue to review), the Constitutional Court concluded that what was at stake was an exercise of public power susceptible to a legality challenge (the fifth avenue to review).[44] This was because relying on section 23 to extend their collective agreement 'ha[d] a coercive effect' in that 'it [bound] non-parties to the agreement, willy-nilly ... with just about industry-wide effects'.[45] In this regard Cameron J reasoned that the extension had 'extensive implications for members of the public' because 'for its duration, non-member employees [were] bound' and would 'forfeit the right to strike' in circumstances where the collective agreement regulates the dispute in question.[46] This is an interesting development for two reasons. The first is that it affirms the narrow basis upon which the courts are generally willing to invoke the common law as a justification for reviewing what are ostensibly private powers. The second is what it reveals about the principle of legality and the increasing willingness on the part of courts to stretch our understanding of public power to invoke it as a basis for review.

### 5.3.3 Review and internal remedies

As we noted when we looked at internal controls in Chapter 4, there is a distinct relationship between judicial oversight and internal oversight. PAJA adopts a strict stance in section 7(2) by stating that a court may not entertain an application for judicial review as long as all internal remedies have not been exhausted. PAJA thus sets out expressly the relationship between internal controls and judicial oversight by preferencing internal remedies. This is the most deliberate attempt in PAJA to advance an integrated system of regulation of administrative action.

In *Koyabe* the Constitutional Court noted that it is only proper that courts should allow the administration to complete its own processes in relation to administrative action before entertaining a challenge against the administration's actions.[47] This includes internal control mechanisms. The court added in *Dengetenge Holdings (Pty) Ltd v Southern Sphere Mining & Development Co Ltd and Others*[48] that section 7(2) obliges all involved, the courts, the

43 National Union of Mineworkers (NUM), Solidarity, and United Association of South Africa (UASA).
44 *AMCU* para 72.
45 *AMCU* para 78.
46 *AMCU* para 78.
47 *Koyabe* para 36.
48 2014 (5) SA 138 (CC) paras 127–133.

person wanting to challenge the administrative action as well as the administrator to exhaust the internal remedy before proceeding with review. The administrator thus cannot waive pursuit of the internal remedy in favour of judicial review.

Section 7(2) only applies to a particular type of internal remedy. First, it must be a remedy provided for 'in any other law'.[49] This implies that it is only internal remedies provided for in statute that are at issue here. However, it seems that internal remedies created in regulations under a statute would also qualify.[50] Second, the remedy must be internal to the administration. This means that remedies provided for in other statutes, but that are not internal to the particular administration taking the administrative action, are not included under section 7(2).[51] Third, the internal remedy must be available to the complainant and be effective.[52] To be effective, the remedy must be capable of providing the complainant with appropriate relief, which must at least be equivalent to the relief that a court can grant upon review.[53] If these conditions are met, an aggrieved person will have no choice but to pursue the internal remedy before he or she may approach a court for judicial review. Conversely, a court will be obliged under section 7(2)(*b*) to refuse to entertain the review and to direct the applicant to exhaust the internal remedy first.

The duty to exhaust internal remedies under section 7(2) is, however, not absolute. Section 7(2)(*c*) allows a court to hear a review even though internal remedies have not been exhausted if there are exceptional circumstances and it is in the interest of justice to hear the review immediately. The courts have provided some guidance on when these two conditions will be met. [54] For example, in *Nichol* the court said that exceptional circumstances will be present when the applicant's case is different from the typical case for which the internal remedy was created.[55] It seems that the ineffectiveness of the internal remedy will (again) be a factor that may show exceptional circumstances.[56] However, arguments relating to the grounds of review upon which the applicant wants to bring the review cannot serve to prove exceptional circumstances. As the court rightly noted in *Nichol*, this would amount to circumventing the bar to hearing the review before internal remedies had been exhausted.[57] If a court were to entertain grounds of review arguments as part of the argument under section 7(2)(*c*) it would in effect already be hearing the review application, which it is not allowed to do until it has decided on the section 7(2) issue. Finally, the court indicated in *Koyabe* that the lapse of the time period for instituting the internal remedy cannot, without more, constitute exceptional circumstances under section 7(2)(*c*).[58] A person cannot thus simply wait out the period for bringing the internal remedy and then approach a court. All reasonable steps to exhaust the internal remedy must first be taken.

---

49 PAJA section 7(2)(*a*).

50 *Road Accident Fund v Duma and Three Similar Cases* 2013 (6) SA 9 (SCA) para 25.

51 *Reed and Others v Master of the High Court of South Africa and Others* [2005] 2 All SA 429 (E) para 25; Hoexter (2012) 540–541.

52 *Koyabe* para 44.

53 *Reed* paras 20–25; *Koyabe* para 44.

54 *Koyabe* para 44 where the court mentioned lack of availability and ineffectiveness of an internal remedy as factors relevant to determining whether 'exceptional circumstances' for the purposes of section 7(2)(*c*) of PAJA are present.

55 *Nichol and Another v Registrar of Pension Funds and Others* 2008 (1) SA 383 (SCA) para 16; *Earthlife Africa (Cape Town) v Director-General: Department of Environmental Affairs and Tourism and Another* 2005 (3) SA 156 (C) para 33.

56 *Nichol* para 18; *Koyabe* para 45.

57 *Nichol* para 24.

58 *Koyabe* para 47.

## 5.4 Deference

The relationship between courts exercising their oversight function and the administration fulfilling its constitutional mandate in taking administrative action has become a major point of debate in South African law. While this debate is inherent to the separation of powers, as we noted in Chapter 2 above, and has thus always been part of the discipline of administrative law, the current debate has gained prominence following the influential article of Cora Hoexter published in 2000.[59]

In her article Hoexter called for debate on the development of a theory of deference. This she understood to mean developing principles that can guide courts in intervention and non-intervention when scrutinising administrative action.[60] In what has become a classic formulation of the issues at stake, Hoexter stated:

> the sort of deference we should be aspiring to consists of a judicial willingness to appreciate the legitimate and constitutionally-ordained province of administrative agencies; to admit the expertise of those agencies in policy-laden or polycentric issues; to accord their interpretations of fact and law due respect; and to be sensitive in general to the interests legitimately pursued by administrative bodies and the practical and financial constraints under which they operate. This type of deference is perfectly consistent with a concern for individual rights and a refusal to tolerate corruption and maladministration. It ought to be shaped not by an unwillingness to scrutinize administrative action, but by a careful weighing up of the need for – and the consequences of – judicial intervention.[61]

Hoexter's notion of deference has been taken up by the courts. In *Logbro Properties CC v Bedderson NO and Others*[62] the Supreme Court of Appeal expressly endorsed her description and held it to be an appropriate approach given that the administrative action under scrutiny involved complex issues of policy and interests that had to be balanced by the administrator in reaching a decision. In such cases, the SCA held that a court should be careful to interfere with the decision-maker's judgment given that the decision-maker will generally be in a better position than a court to evaluate all the relevant considerations. Subsequently, the Constitutional Court utilised Hoexter's notion of deference to similar effect. In the leading case of *Bato Star Fishing*, O'Regan J explained that deference does not entail submission by the courts to the administration, but rather respect by the courts for the constitutionally ordained function of the administration. She stated it as follows:

> A decision that requires an equilibrium to be struck between a range of competing interests or considerations and which is to be taken by a person or institution with specific expertise in that area must be shown respect by the courts. Often a power will identify a goal to be achieved, but will not dictate which route should be followed to achieve that goal. In such circumstances a court should pay due respect to the route selected by the decision-maker. This does not mean however that where the decision is one which will not reasonably result in the achievement

59 Hoexter (2000) 484. See the Pause for reflection box in section 4.6 above.
60 Hoexter (2000) 500.
61 Hoexter, C (2000) The Future of Judicial Review in South African Administrative Law *SALJ* 117(3):501–502 (footnotes omitted). Reprinted by permission of © Juta & Company Ltd.
62 2003 (2) SA 460 (SCA).

of the goal, or which is not reasonably supported on the facts or not reasonable in the light of the reasons given for it, a court may not review that decision.[63]

Deference is thus about respect for the role of another branch of state within the separation of powers. It is partly based on the constitutional mandate of various public entities: it is simply not the function of the courts to administer and they should not attempt to do so via their oversight of the administration. However, it is also clear that deference is about the *ability* of courts to judge certain types of decisions made by administrators. As the SCA noted in *Logbro Properties* some decisions are of such a nature that it is very difficult or even impossible for a court, with limited expertise and ability to investigate matters, to judge on substance. These concerns are to a large extent accentuated by the increasing substantive dimension of review, which we noted in section 5.2 above when we looked at the distinction between review and appeal. The more the courts engage in matters of substance as part of their oversight function over administrative action, the bigger the concerns of constitutional mandate and institutional capacity become.

COUNTER POINT

**The need for deference**

The notion of judicial deference is not universally accepted.

A lighter form of resistance to deference is premised on two different understandings of what deference may entail, largely flowing from the word 'deference' itself. The fear is that deference may be understood to mean submission.[64] In this understanding deference would thus mean that the courts play a secondary and inferior role to the administration in administrative law. The dangers of a judiciary adopting an executive-minded stance towards its oversight functions, where the executive, including the administration, is treated lightly and allowed a wide margin of discretion are well-known in South Africa. Such an understanding would also not accord with the Constitution, which grants the power to courts to provide oversight over administrative action. An alternative understanding of deference is as respect. This is the understanding adopted by O'Regan J in *Bato Star Fishing*, discussed above, and renders deference less objectionable.

There are also more stringent forms of criticism against deference. The English scholar TRS Allan has, for example, criticised the notion of deference as unnecessary and only causing confusion.[65] He argues that everything that is ostensibly addressed through a notion of deference is already incorporated in the normal rules and principles of administrative law such as the grounds of review and the distinction between review and appeal. This view is one shared by some judges in South Africa too. In a recent article, Clive Plasket writing extra-curially has also questioned the utility of the concept of deference,[66] arguing that in fact it has served 'no separate, standalone function'[67] having not ever made any difference to a court's decision in a given case.

CONTINUED >>>

63 *Bato Star Fishing* para 48.

64 See Corder, H (2004) Without Deference, With Respect: A Response to Justice O'Regan *SALJ* 121(2):438 at 441.

65 Allan, TRS (2006) Human Rights and Judicial Review: A Critique of 'Due Deference' *Cambridge Law Journal* 65(3):671.

66 Plasket, C (2018) Judicial Review, Administrative Power and Deference: A View from the Bench *SALJ* 135(3):502.

67 Plasket (2018) at 502.

This, he explains, is because 'respect for the decisions of properly empowered primary decision-makers is already embedded in the review function of courts, principally as part of the doctrine of the separation of powers'.[68]

Malcolm Wallis, also in his extra-curial writings, positions his critique slightly differently.[69] He insists that deference as a concept offers little value in and of itself and cannot therefore be relied on as an independent justification for non-intervention in a particular case. The primary duty of South African judges is 'reasoned decision-making'[70] and deference in his view 'adds nothing to judicial reasons in the absence of expansion and explanation'.[71] Wallis also disapproves of the fact that South Africa has simply adopted the 'immigrant'[72] concept of deference from foreign jurisdictions in a way that he deems inappropriate to the unique function of reviewing courts in our country. There is accordingly no further need for a free-standing notion of deference according to these authors.

In a different vein, Dennis Davis has also criticised the endorsement of deference especially by the courts.[73] Davis's criticism is, however, premised on what he perceives to be a failure in South Africa to understand administrative law within a new rights-based paradigm. He thus charges that deference does very little to help us develop new ways of viewing administrative law that is primarily aimed at facilitating the fundamental right to administrative justice.

## THIS CHAPTER IN ESSENCE

Administrative law is different from other frameworks that guide the work of the public administration in that this branch of law can be enforced by courts. This is a hallmark of administrative justice, namely the enforceable normative character of the rules constituting this field. In South African law, one mechanism has dominated the regulatory landscape, namely judicial review. Like most common-law systems, South African administrative law, both under common law and under PAJA, is often viewed as the law of judicial review of administrative action (or, increasingly judicial review of public power under the auspices of the legality principle). While the Constitutional Court has given a clear indication early on in the constitutional dispensation that there is only one system of law, flowing from the Constitution, there has been significant fragmentation in approaches to judicial review of various forms of public action. Today one can identify at least five different avenues to the challenge of public action, three of which could potentially be used to judicially review administrative action (and even four, in cases where the legality principle is inappropriately invoked). Finally, the expanded scope of judicial review under the constitutional dispensation, especially given the increased substantive character of review introduced by review for reasonableness, has created debate about judicial deference, which is a debate about the limits of the courts' power of intervention in public decision-making.

68 Plasket (2018) at 502.
69 Wallis, M (2018) Do We Need Deference? *SAJEI* 1(1):97.
70 Wallis (2018) at 107.
71 Wallis (2018) at 107.
72 Wallis (2018) at 97.
73 Davis, DM (2006) To Defer and then When? Administrative Law and Constitutional Democracy *Acta Juridica* 23; Davis, DM (2006) Adjudicating the Socio-Economic Rights in the South African Constitution: Towards 'Deference Lite'? *South African Journal on Human Rights* 22(2):301.

## FURTHER READING


- Boonzaier, L (2018) A Decision to Undo *SALJ* 135(4):642-677
- De Beer, MN (2018) A New Role for the Principle of Legality in Administrative Law: *State Information Technology Agency Soc Ltd v Gijima Holdings (Pty) Ltd SALJ* 135(4):613-630
- Hoexter, C (2000) The Future of Judicial Review in South African Administrative Law *SALJ* 117(3):484
- Maree, PJH & Quinot, G (2016) A Decade and a Half of Deference (Part I) (2016) *Journal of South African Law* 268-280
- Maree, PJH & Quinot, G (2016) A Decade and a Half of Deference (Part II) (2016) *Journal of South African Law* 447-466
- Plasket, C (2002) The Exhaustion of Internal Remedies and Section 7(2) of the Promotion of Administrative Justice Act 3 of 2000 *SALJ* 119(1):50
- Plasket, C (2018) Judicial Review, Administrative Power and Deference: A View from the Bench *SALJ* 135(3):502
- Quinot, G & Van der Sijde, E (2019) Opening at the Close: Clarity from the Constitutional Court on the Legal Cause of Action and Regulatory Framework for an Organ of State Seeking to Review Its Own Decisions? *Journal of South African Law* 324-336
- Saunders, C 'Appeal or Review: The Experience of Administrative Appeals in Australia' in Bennett, TW & Corder, H (Eds) (1993) *Administrative Law Reform* Cape Town: Juta
- Wallis, M (2018) Do We Need Deference? *SAJEI* 1(1):97

# Chapter 6

# Lawfulness

GEO QUINOT & ALLISON ANTHONY



## 6.1 Introduction

A key feature of administrative law is that it deals with actions taken in terms of some form of authorisation. In fact, as we noted in Chapter 3, administrative action is defined by reference to the existence of an empowering provision, that is a source in terms of which the action was purportedly taken.[1] This characteristic of administrative law reflects an important element of the rule of law, which we have also noted is a key aspect of administrative law.[2] In *Fedsure Life Assurance Ltd and Others v Greater Johannesburg Transitional Metropolitan*

1 See Chapter 3 section 3.7.4.
2 See Chapter 1 section 1.2.1.7.

*Council and Others*[3] the Constitutional Court recognised this important aspect of the rule of law as follows:

> [I]t is a fundamental principle of the rule of law, recognised widely, that the exercise of public power is only legitimate where lawful. The rule of law – to the extent at least that it expresses this principle of legality – is generally understood to be a fundamental principle of constitutional law.

Lawfulness thus stands at the core of the general constitutional-law principle of legality and applies to all public actions. It is not surprising that it is also stated as the first requirement of administrative justice in section 33(1) of the Constitution: 'Everyone has the right to administrative action that is lawful ...'

At its most basic meaning, lawfulness simply means that the administrative action and the authorisation for that action must be aligned. This is illustrated in Figure 6.1 below.

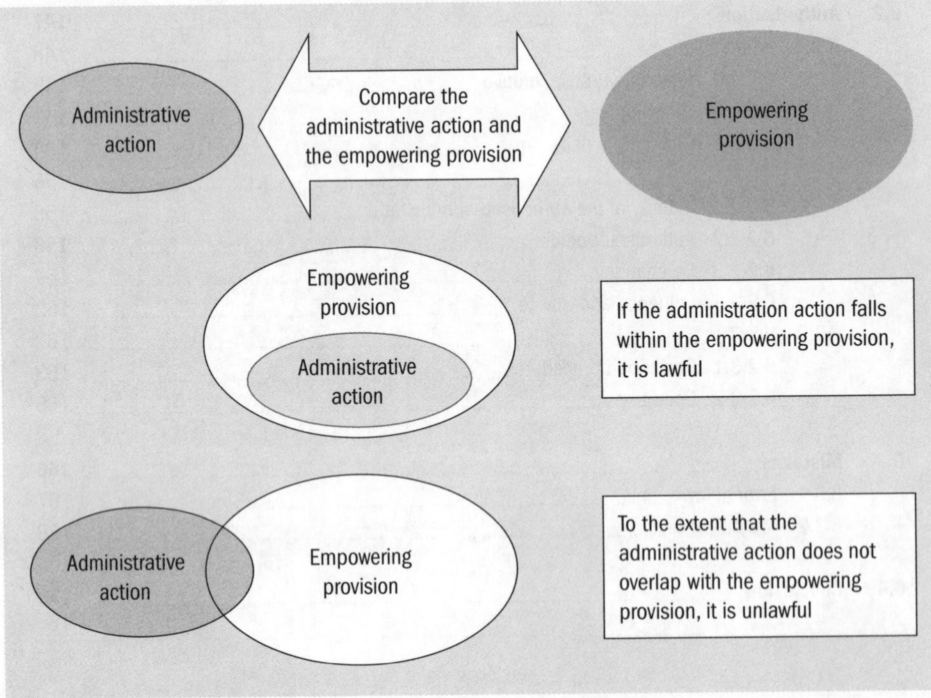


***Figure 6.1*** *The basic lawfulness enquiry*

An analysis of lawfulness in administrative law thus always involves comparing the administrative action to the authorisation for that action in the relevant empowering provision. The goal of the analysis is to determine whether the action and the empowering provision overlap. Any areas of non-overlap point to potential lawfulness problems. Viewed from a facilitative perspective, lawfulness provides administrators with the tools to identify specifically what they are entitled to do.

3 1999 (1) SA 374 (CC) para 56 (footnotes omitted).

The Promotion of Administrative Justice Act (PAJA)[4] unfortunately does not provide a clear statement of lawfulness despite the prominence of the concept in administrative justice and the broader notion of legality. PAJA only deals with lawfulness as a matter of grounds of review. That is to say, PAJA tells one when an administrative action can be taken upon review to court based on the non-overlap between action and authorisation. At its most basic, PAJA captures the principle established in the *Fedsure* judgment in section 6(2)(*i*), which states that administrative action can be reviewed if 'the action is ... unlawful'.

**PAUSE FOR REFLECTION**

**The elements and limits of administrative power**

Consider the following hypothetical statutory provision:

**Western Cape Disasters Act**

5(1) The Premier must by notice in the *Gazette* designate land, owned or leased by the state, for the purpose of constructing temporary shelter to house people who have been left without shelter due to a natural disaster in the province.

If you had to advise the provincial government on the use of this provision, what would you point out? Consider the following questions in formulating your advice:

- Who may act under this provision?
- What specific action may be taken in terms of this provision?
- For what purpose may action be taken under this provision?
- How must action be taken under this provision?
- For whose benefit may action be taken under this provision?
- Under what circumstances may action be taken under this provision?

All these questions point to different elements of the power that is granted in this provision. They all limit the power in some way. Teasing out those elements or limitations allows one to formulate administrative action in terms of this provision that will be lawful.

When you have completed your study of this chapter, return to this exercise and identify the aspects of lawfulness that are raised by the questions above. Can you align them to particular grounds of review in PAJA?

## 6.2 Authorisation

The first requirement of lawfulness is the basic one of authorisation. For every action that an administrator takes, there must be a valid authorisation in an empowering provision. In the absence of such authorisation the administrative action will be unlawful. The Constitutional Court confirmed this basic notion of authorisation in *Fedsure*[5] when it stated:

> It seems central to the conception of our constitutional order that the Legislature and Executive in every sphere are constrained by the principle that they may exercise no power and perform no function beyond that conferred upon them by law.

4 3 of 2000.

5 *Fedsure* para 58.

The court continued to confirm that this basic principle is captured in the lawfulness requirement of administrative justice.[6] It held that the constitutional requirement of lawfulness includes the common-law principles of *ultra vires* (meaning, beyond the conferred power), but underpins it with a constitutional foundation and supplements it. Today, PAJA thus tells us that an administrative action can be reviewed if the action itself was not authorised.[7]

However, it is not often that administrators act in the complete absence of authorisation or an empowering provision. In fact, the complete absence of an empowering provision may be a good indication that the action is not administrative at all, but rather of a policy nature and hence excluded from administrative law. In *Permanent Secretary, Department of Education and Welfare, Eastern Cape and Another v Ed-U-College (PE) (Section 21) Inc*[8] O'Regan J held that when executive action is taken 'outside of a legislative framework' it may be a good indication that it is of a policy nature and not administrative. The question of lawfulness in terms of administrative law would not even arise.

Lawfulness problems in administrative law more often arise from a lack of overlap between the empowering provision and the administrative action as illustrated in Figure 6.1 above. The issue is thus typically not that there is no authorisation, but rather that some aspect of the authorisation (as expressed in the empowering provision) does not align with the action. It is thus essential to analyse an empowering provision in terms of the various elements of the authorisation that it grants and to compare each element with the administrative action. A useful way to approach this exercise is to ask the questions: what was authorised, who was authorised, and how did the authorisation prescribe the action to be taken? The what, who and how questions can serve as a structure in terms of which one can determine the lawfulness of any action, whether already taken or only contemplated.

### 6.2.1 What?

The what question is perhaps the most fundamental of the three questions since the answer tells us exactly what it is that an administrator can do under the relevant authorisation. Essentially, if an administrator is authorised to do A, he or she must do A and not B. If his or her action amounts to B it will be unlawful. Section 6(2)(*f*)(i) of PAJA is the primary provision capturing this element of lawfulness.

This basic notion is well illustrated by the judgment in *Minister of Education v Harris*.[9] In this matter the Minister of Education was empowered by section 3(4) of the National Education Policy Act[10] to 'determine national policy' for the education system, including 'national policy for ... the admission of students to education institutions which shall include the determination of the age of admission to schools'. The Minister, acting in terms of this authorisation, published a notice stating that a learner must be admitted to Grade 1 in the year he or she turns seven and may not be admitted at a younger age. The court held that this notice amounted to a binding legal rule, which is something different from 'national policy'. It followed that the Minister's action was unlawful, because he attempted to do something (make a rule) while something else (make a policy) was authorised.

6 *Fedsure* para 59.
7 PAJA section 6(2)(*f*)(i).
8 2001 (2) SA 1 (CC) para 18.
9 2001 (4) SA 1297 (CC)
10 27 of 1996.

**PAUSE FOR REFLECTION**

**Authorisation in more than one place**

The *Harris* case also raised the issue of authorisation flowing from more than one empowering provision. It is not uncommon to find an empowering provision that grants different powers to the same administrator in different sections or of course to find completely different empowering provisions (for example, different statutes) that grant powers to the same administrator that may be exercised in the same context. In the *Harris* matter the Minister was authorised in the National Education Policy Act[11] to 'determine national policy' and was authorised under the Schools Act[12] to 'determine age requirements for the admission of learners to a school'. Following the court's finding that the Minister's notice in this matter amounted to a binding rule on admission rather than policy and thus was not authorised by the National Education Policy Act,[13] the question arose as to whether the Minister's actions were nevertheless lawful because they were authorised under the Schools Act.[14] The court held that the Minister's actions could not be rescued by reference to the alternative authorisation in the Schools Act,[15] because the Minister relied deliberately and expressly on the National Education Policy Act[16] and not the Schools Act.[17] The Minister thus purported to exercise his powers under the National Education Policy Act,[18] which turned out not to cover the particular action. Under such circumstances it is not open to an administrator to point to an alternative authorisation that may nevertheless serve as a basis for the action. Such a scenario is to be distinguished from one where an administrator does not rely deliberately on one particular empowering provision, but reference is mistakenly made to an empowering provision that subsequently turns out not to provide authority for the action. If there is, in such a case, an alternative provision that provides the necessary authority for the action, unlawfulness may be avoided.

When one considers a grant of power to an administrator in an empowering provision, one can mostly identify a range of elements that define what it is that the administrator may do in terms of that authorisation. In addition to the substance of the authorised action, as illustrated in the *Harris* matter, these elements may include the time and/or place at which the action may be taken and the reason or purpose for which it may be taken. Any action that does not align with these prescripts will be unlawful.

#### 6.2.1.1 Reason, purpose, motive

A particularly challenging part of lawfulness relates to the reason, purpose or motive for which action is taken. This is especially the case where the empowering provision grants a wide discretion to the administrator. In such instances the primary role of lawfulness is to ensure that the administrator does in fact have a discretion, that is, freedom of choice, and exercises a discretion when taking the action. Anything that results in the discretion being

11 27 of 1996.
12 84 of 1996.
13 27 of 1996.
14 84 of 1996.
15 84 of 1996.
16 27 of 1996.
17 84 of 1996.
18 27 of 1996.

curtailed may lead to unlawfulness as we shall see below. In the context of wide discretionary powers lawfulness thus serves to protect the freedom of the administrator to take action within that discretion as much as it serves to restrict the administrator's actions to what is authorised. The what question accordingly becomes difficult as the answer may simply be freedom: the administrator is authorised to exercise his or her discretion in making a choice, whatever that choice may be. However, one manner in which even the widest of discretionary powers may be limited is by means of the purpose for which the power was given. No administrative power is given without a reason or purpose, doing so would breach the principle of rationality which is a requirement for all public action including legislation.[19] Whatever the administrator's choice may be in exercising his or her (wide) discretionary powers, the administrator's purpose in making that choice or his or her reasons for doing so must be aligned to what is authorised in the empowering provision.

This principle is illustrated by the judgment in *Gauteng Gambling Board and Another v MEC for Economic Development, Gauteng.*[20] In this matter the MEC had the wide discretionary statutory power to 'terminate the term of office of any member of the [applicant] board or the entire board if in the responsible Member's opinion there are good reasons for doing so'.[21] The MEC instructed the board to make available office space in its own building to a private company and when the board refused, she instructed the board to relocate the entire operation of the board to her department's offices and lease the board's building to the private company. When the board still refused, relying on its statutory obligations *inter alia* in terms of public finance regulation, the MEC terminated the term of office of the entire board. In a challenge to the MEC's action in dissolving the board, the court found that even though the MEC had the discretionary power to terminate the board's term and could do so for any 'good reasons', her actions were still unlawful because of her motive in taking the action. The court held that the MEC took the decision 'to compel compliance with the prior instruction to accommodate [the private company]'.[22] This was clearly not an authorised motive.

PAJA recognises the importance of the purpose for which the action is taken by listing three different grounds of review in this regard. Administrative action can thus be reviewed if it was taken for an unauthorised reason (section 6(2)(*e*)(i)), ulterior purpose or motive (section 6(2)(*e*)(ii)) or in bad faith (section 6(2)(*e*)(v)). Under the first two of these provisions it is not necessary to show that the administrator had a bad motive in taking the action to show that the action was unlawful. As long as the motive, purpose or reason for the action is not authorised it makes no difference to the lawfulness enquiry that the action was taken with the best of intentions. This position was already recognised in common law where, in *Van Eck, NO, and Van Rensburg, NO, v Etna Stores,*[23] the judge stated that the court's findings about the unlawfulness of the action due to the unauthorised motive should not be read as 'attaching any moral obliquity to the appellants or their officers; doubtless they were acting in what they conceived to be the public interest'. However, Hoexter rightly points out that the existence of dishonesty is still relevant in assessing the action against the standards of administrative justice as a sinister motive infringes on a wider range of constitutional values,

19 *Pharmaceutical Manufacturers Association of South Africa and Another: In Re Ex Parte President of the Republic of South Africa and Others* 2000 (2) SA 674 (CC) para 90.
20 2013 (5) SA 24 (SCA).
21 Gauteng Gambling Act 4 of 1995 section 18B(7).
22 *Gauteng Gambling Board* para 41.
23 1947 (2) SA 984 (A) at 997.

such as transparency and accountability, and should certainly attract more stringent censure.[24]

COUNTER POINT

**Changing the motive**

It is an interesting question whether an administrator can take an action for one purpose and then later attempt to change the purpose. This is illustrated by the judgment in *Harvey v Umhlatuze Municipality and Others*.[25] In this matter the administrator expropriated land for a particular purpose, that is, to create a recreational open space and a conservation area. When that purpose could no longer be achieved, because no viable development plan could be found, the administrator decided to use the expropriated land for a different purpose, namely residential development. In a challenge to the decision to use the land for a different purpose, the court held that the administrator was entitled to change the purpose once the original purpose turned out not to be viable as long as the administrator acted with *bona fides* throughout. In its judgment the court implies that the purpose should only be assessed at the time of the action and then becomes irrelevant. The purpose for which the action was originally taken is thus not a continuous condition on that action. This is a problematic view from a lawfulness perspective since the key aim of the lawfulness requirement is to keep administrators within the bounds of their authority. If an administrator is thus allowed to change a purpose once the action has already been taken, the door is opened for an unlawful purpose and for administrators to extend their own powers.[26]

### 6.2.1.2 Omission

We have noted in Chapter 3 that an omission can constitute administrative action.[27] However, as we also noted, not all omissions will constitute administrative action. An omission will only be an administrative action if it amounts to a failure to act, that is when there is a duty on the administrator to act and the administrator does not act. It should be immediately evident that the recognition of administrative action and the lawfulness requirement attaching to such administrative action are closely tied in such a scenario. It is the administrator's failure in light of the duty to act that results in the omission being administrative action, while it is that very same failure in light of the duty to act that constitutes the unlawfulness of the action.

This is nothing more than a particular form of the what question of lawfulness. Under these scenarios the administrator is mandated (indeed obliged) to do something (act), but does something else (does not act). The omission and the empowering provision do not align, making the omission both an administrative action and an unlawful one at that.

The key question in such cases is when the omission will turn into an administrative action and be unlawful. That is, when will the administrator's supine attitude turn into a legally relevant action under administrative law. PAJA provides the answer in sections 6(2)(*g*) and 6(3). The former contains a ground of review for failures to take decisions and the latter provides the time frame in terms of which non-action will become a failure to act. The easy case is where the relevant empowering provision contains an express timeline within which

24 Hoexter, C (2012) *Administrative Law in South Africa* (2nd ed) 312.

25 2011 (1) SA 601 (KZP).

26 See Quinot, G (2010) *Administrative Law Annual Survey of South African Law* 56–57; Hoexter (2012) 309.

27 See Chapter 3 section 3.7.1 above.

the action must be taken. Once that timeline had lapsed without any action by the administrator there is a failure to act and hence an unlawful administrative action. However, much more difficult is the case where the empowering provision contains no express timeline in terms of which the administrator must act. In such a case section 6(3)(*a*) of PAJA states that a person can institute proceedings after a reasonable time had lapsed. It will thus be up to a court to judge whether the time that had lapsed is indeed unreasonably long thus resulting in the administrator's non-action being a failure to act.

**PAUSE FOR REFLECTION**

**Applications for grants and ID documents**

Unlawfulness in the form of omissions has been especially common in the areas of welfare grants and identity documents. Both these contexts involve a fairly standard application process with a limited number of potential outcomes. The Social Assistance Act,[28] for example, provides in relevant part that:

> **14. Application for social assistance.** –
>
> (1) Any person who wishes to apply for social assistance ... must do so in the prescribed manner.
>
> (2) In considering an application made in terms of subsection (1), the Agency may conduct an investigation and request additional information.
>
> (3) (*a*) If the applicant qualifies for social assistance in terms of this Act, the Agency must render the relevant social assistance.
>
> (*b*) If the applicant does not qualify for social assistance in terms of this Act, the Agency must ... inform the applicant –
>
> (i) that he or she does not qualify for social assistance in terms of this Act ...

However, many applicants for grants, ID documents or other registration documents such as (late) birth registrations have been faced with long delays in getting any decision taken on their applications. They thus face the dilemma of the relevant administrator neither granting nor refusing their applications, but simply doing nothing. This has resulted in a number of applications to court on the basis of the relevant administrators' delay in taking a decision. These applications are typically pursued as applications for the review of the administrator's omission on lawfulness grounds.

In *Thusi v Minister of Home Affairs and Another and 71 Other Cases*[29] Wallis J noted a 'steady stream of cases' against the Department of Home Affairs for failures to take decisions and quoted the following as a typical example of this type of application:

> (2) That the second respondent's failure to take decisions on:
>
> (*a*) the applicant's application for the late registration of birth made in terms of section 9(3)(A) of the Births and Deaths Registration Act 51 of 1992 (the Births Act);

CONTINUED >>>

28 13 of 2004.
29 2011 (2) SA 561 (KZP) para 3.

(*b*) the applicant's application for an Identity Document, made in terms of section 15 of the Identification Act 68 of 1997 (the Identification Act); be reviewed, in terms of section 6(3)(*a*) of PAJA and declared unlawful.

(3) That the second respondent be ordered in terms of section 8(2) of PAJA to:

(*a*) register the applicant's birth; and

(*b*) issue an identity document to the applicant within 10 (ten) days of date of this Order.

(4) That the respondents be ordered to furnish written proof of the registration of the applicant's birth and issue of the identity document and written details as to when and where such may be collected to the applicant's Attorney within 10 days of the issue thereof.[30]

The judge noted an affidavit on behalf of the respondent in which it was stated that between August 2007 and September 2010, '12 631 applications similar to those under consideration in this judgment were served upon the State Attorney, KwaZulu-Natal'.[31]

In the context of social assistance, Plasket J noted in *Vumazonke v MEC for Social Development, Eastern Cape, and Three Similar Cases*[32] that 'literally thousands of orders have been made against the respondent's department over the past number of years'[33] and that:

> If this volume of social assistance cases had been unique to one week's Motion Court roll, it would have been cause for concern. Unfortunately, it is a phenomenon that is now common: the Judges of this Division, as well as those in the other two Divisions in the Eastern Cape, have grown accustomed to the depressing tales of misery and privation contained in an ever-increasing volume of cases that clog their Motion Court rolls, in which applicants complain about administrative torpor in the processing of their applications for social assistance. To make matters worse, this situation is not new. Over the last four or five years, Judges have commented, often in strident terms, about the unsatisfactory performance of the respondent's department in the administration of the social assistance system in the province.[34]

In this particular matter, the applicants all applied for social grants in 2003. When the matter was heard in November 2004, three of the applicants had no response from the respondent department on their applications. Plasket J held that on the respondent's own account three months was a reasonable period to take a decision and the delay on the respondent's part amounted to an omission, which was reviewable as unlawful administrative action under PAJA.

30 *Thusi* para 13.
31 *Thusi* para 29.
32 2005 (6) SA 229 (SE).
33 *Vumazonke* para 10.
34 *Vumazonke* para 2.

### 6.2.1.3 Changing a decision

The final issue to consider under the what question is that of changing a decision that has already been taken. Under common law, this issue arose within the context of the *functus officio* doctrine, which dictated when an administrator could vary a decision.[35]

The simple answer to this issue is that an administrator can vary a decision already taken if the administrator is authorised to do so. It is thus merely an application of the standard what question. When an administrator varies a decision that he or she is not authorised to vary, the administrator is taking unlawful action, which can be reviewed under section 6(2)(*f*)(i) of PAJA. A prime example of typical statutory authority to vary decisions is to be found in tax law. As the judgment in *Carlson Investments Share Block (Pty) Ltd v Commissioner, SARS*[36] indicates, the power to vary tax decisions is fairly commonly found in legal systems.

In South Africa, sections 92, 98 and 150 of the Tax Administration Act[37] provide, for example, as follows:

> 92 If at any time SARS is satisfied that an assessment does not reflect the correct application of a tax Act to the prejudice of SARS or the *fiscus*, SARS must make an additional assessment to correct the prejudice.
>
> 98 (1) SARS may, despite the fact that no objection has been lodged or appeal noted, withdraw an assessment which-
> (*a*) was issued to the incorrect taxpayer;
> (*b*) was issued in respect of the incorrect tax period;
> (*c*) was issued as a result of an incorrect payment allocation; or
> (*d*) in respect of which the Commissioner is satisfied that-
> (i) it was based on-
> (*aa*) an undisputed factual error by the taxpayer in a return; or
> (*bb*) a processing error by SARS; or
> (*cc*) a return fraudulently submitted by a person not authorised by the taxpayer;
> (ii) it imposes an unintended tax debt in respect of an amount that the taxpayer should not have been taxed on;
> (iii) the recovery of the tax debt under the assessment would produce an anomalous or inequitable result;
> (iv) there is no other remedy available to the taxpayer; and
> (v) it is in the interest of the good management of the tax system
>
> (2) An assessment withdrawn under this section is regarded not to have been issued, unless a senior SARS official agrees in writing with the taxpayer as to the amount of tax properly chargeable for the relevant tax period and accordingly issues a revised original, additional or reduced assessment, as the case may be, which assessment is not subject to objection or appeal.
>
> 150 (1) If a 'dispute' between SARS and the person aggrieved by an assessment or 'decision' is 'settled' under this Part, SARS may, despite anything to the contrary contained in a tax Act, alter the assessment or 'decision' to give effect to the 'settlement'.

35 See Pretorius, DM (2005) The Origins of the *Functus Officio* Doctrine, with Specific Reference to its Application in Administrative Law *SALJ* 122(4):832.

36 2001 (3) SA 210 (W).

37 28 of 2011.

In its judgment in *MEC for Health, Eastern Cape and Another v Kirland Investments (Pty) Ltd t/a Eye and Lazer Institute*[38] the Constitutional Court confirmed the basic position that an administrator is bound to an administrative action once taken and cannot vary or ignore such action without approaching a court for an order to set the action aside. In this matter the administrator had approved an application to establish a private hospital, but attempted later to reverse that decision, taking the view that the original approval was defective and that the administrator could subsequently 'withdraw' it and further refuse to implement it. The applicant challenged the administrator's conduct and sought an order that the original decision was still valid and the administrator bound to it. The court explained the position as follows:

> When government errs by issuing a defective decision, the subject affected by it is entitled to proper notice, and to be afforded a proper hearing, on whether the decision should be set aside. Government should not be allowed to take shortcuts. Generally, this means that government must apply formally to set aside the decision. Once the subject has relied on a decision, government cannot, barring specific statutory authority, simply ignore what it has done. The decision, despite being defective, may have consequences that make it undesirable or even impossible to set it aside. That demands a proper process, in which all factors for and against are properly weighed.[39]

In the context of legislative administrative action, that is rule-making by administrators, the Interpretation Act[40] provides a special regime. Section 10(3) states that:

> [w]here a law confers a power to make rules, regulations or by-laws, the power shall, unless the contrary intention appears, be construed as including a power exercisable in like manner and subject to the like consent and conditions (if any) to rescind, revoke, amend or vary the rules, regulations or by-laws.

The Interpretation Act[41] thus provides the authority to vary legislative administrative action, unless the particular empowering provision excludes such power.

## 6.2.2 Who?

The second major aspect of the authorisation that one can interrogate as part of the lawfulness inquiry relates to the administrator that is authorised to act: the who question.

### 6.2.2.1 Identity of the authorised administrator

In most cases the empowering provision will indicate specifically which administrator is given a particular power. The way in which this is done varies between empowering provisions. A statutory provision may thus identify the particular office holder or the entity that must take the action. Alternatively, the empowering provision may identify the qualifications or characteristics of the authorised administrator without stating specifically the identity of the administrator.

38 2014 (3) SA 481 (CC).
39 *Kirland* para 65.
40 33 of 1957.
41 33 of 1957.

EXAMPLE

**Different ways of identifying the authorised administrator**

As noted above, there are different ways in which an empowering provision may indicate who the authorised administrator is.

The empowering provision may name the specific authorised administrator as illustrated in the following sections from the Ship Registration Act:[42]

> 8(1) There must be an officer for the Republic, called the Registrar of Ships, who, subject to the directions of the Authority, is responsible for the maintenance of the Register and has chief control of the Registration Office.
>
> 10(2) In addition to any other duty imposed by this Act or any other law, the Registrar must maintain the Register and must for that purpose ...
>
> (*b*) grant, issue, vary or revoke the certificates and other documents that are required or permitted to be granted or issued in terms of this Act

In this example one can identify the particular individual, the Registrar of Ships, that is authorised to act.

The empowering provision may grant authority to a particular position, but which may not amount to any specific individual. The following section from the National Building Regulations and Building Standards Act[43] provides an example:

> 6(1) A building control officer shall –
>
> (*a*) make recommendations to the local authority in question, regarding any plans, specifications, documents and information submitted to such local authority

In terms of this section, power is granted to a particular office within a local authority, namely that of a building control officer, of which there will be one in each local authority.

Empowering provisions may authorise entities rather than individuals. As with the examples above, such empowering provisions may be specific or general. The following are examples:

**Scientific Research Council Act**[44]

> 4(6) The CSIR [Council for Scientific and Industrial Research] shall, subject to its other functions in terms of this Act or any other Act-
>
> (*a*) undertake the investigations or research which the Minister may require; and
>
> (*b*) advise the Minister on research in general.

CONTINUED >>>

42 58 of 1998 (emphasis added).
43 103 of 1977.
44 46 of 1988 (emphasis added).

**Nursing Act**[45]

57(1) A person aggrieved by a decision of the Council may within the prescribed period and in the prescribed manner appeal against such decision to an appeal committee contemplated in subsection (2) and appointed by the Minister ...

(7) The appeal committee may after hearing the appeal –

(*a*) confirm, set aside or vary the relevant decision of the Council

**National Land Transport Act**[46]

49(2) The holder of a permit or operating licence for a vehicle authorising minibus taxi-type services who has not yet done so may apply in the prescribed manner for recapitalisation of the vehicle and may choose either to –

(*a*) leave the industry, in which case the Department must cancel the permit or operating licence

In each of these examples a body is empowered to act rather than an individual ranging from the specific (the Council for Scientific and Industrial Research) to the less specific (appeal committee) to the general (the Department).

An empowering provision may identify the authorised administrator by way of qualifications, rather than specifically identifying such administrator by name or office. The following section from the National Health Act[47] illustrates this approach:

58(1) A person may not remove tissue from a living person for transplantation in another living person or carry out the transplantation of such tissue except ...

(*b*) on the written authority of-

(i) the medical practitioner in charge of clinical services in that hospital or authorised institution, or any other medical practitioner authorised by him or her

In this example, both administrators that are authorised must be medical practitioners.

PAJA section 6(2)(*a*)(i) contains the requirement that only the authorised administrator may act. The ambit of this subsection is sometimes confused with that of section 6(2)(*f*)(i). The latter, as we have noted above, is the most general lawfulness requirement in PAJA, requiring the action itself to be authorised. Section 6(2)(*a*) in contrast focuses on a specific aspect of the authorisation, namely the administrator that is authorised, that is, the *who* question. This is clear from the structure of the latter subsection, which starts with 'the administrator who took it', and then continues to list a number of problems that may flow from that aspect of the authorisation. This indicates that the focus of subsection (*a*) is on the administrator rather than the action itself.

45 33 of 2005 (emphasis added).
46 5 of 2009 (emphasis added).
47 61 of 2003 (emphasis added).

Thus, when the Minister is authorised to take action X, but he or she takes action Y, the applicable lawfulness rule will be found in section 6(2)(*f*)(i), because the nature of the issue lies in what was authorised compared to what was done. In contrast, if the Minister is authorised to take action X, but the Director-General takes action X, the relevant rule will be found in section 6(2)(*a*), since the nature of the issue in this scenario lies not in what is authorised, but in who is authorised compared to who acted.

#### 6.2.2.2 Authorised bodies

Apart from the general rule that the administrator who is authorised by name should be the one that acts, one can ask a number of further questions about the authorised administrator as part of the who question, depending on the nature of the empowering provision. Thus, where an entity, especially a council or committee, is authorised rather than an individual, a pertinent question will be whether that entity was correctly constituted when it acted. As a general rule, if the entity is incorrectly constituted, it will not amount to the authorised administrator and any action taken by such body will be unlawful.[48] For example, section 57 of the Nursing Act[49] that authorises an appeal committee, quoted in the box above, states in subsection (2) that:

> The appeal committee referred to in subsection (1) consists of –
> (*a*) a retired judge or magistrate or an advocate or attorney of the High Court of South Africa who has practised as such for a period of at least five years, and who must be the chairperson of such committee; and
> (*b*) a nurse.

If a committee that does not include a nurse attempts to decide an appeal under section 57, such decision will be unlawful on the grounds that the administrator that took the action, that is, the ostensible appeal committee, was not authorised. To be precise, the entity that acted in such a case will not *be* an appeal committee as authorised by section 57 given the absence of one of its constituents (a nurse). The same reasoning applies to any requirements in how the entity must be created. A failure to comply with such requirements may result in the body not being properly constituted and thus not being the authorised administrator. For example, section 57(1) of the Nursing Act,[50] quoted above, states that the appeal committee must be appointed by the Minister. If the appeal committee is not appointed by the Minister, it will not be properly constituted and any subsequent decision by such committee may be unlawful on the basis that the administrator who acted was not authorised.

A more difficult question is whether all members of an entity must always be present during the process leading to administrative action. The argument can of course be made that when one member is not present during deliberations, the deliberations are not those of the entity, but only of a few members of the entity. In the 1919 judgment of *Schierhout v The Union Government*[51] it was thus stated that 'whenever a number of individuals, were empowered by Statute to deal with any matter as one body; the action taken would have to be the joint action of all of them ... for otherwise they would not be acting in accordance with the provisions of the Statute'. However, at the same time the practical difficulties that may emerge from strict adherence to such an approach should be acknowledged.

48 *Premier, Western Cape v Acting Chairperson, Judicial Services Commission* 2010 (5) SA 634 (WCC) paras 17–18; *Judicial Service Commission and Another v Cape Bar Council and Another* 2013 (1) SA 170 (SCA) para 27.

49 33 of 2005.

50 33 of 2005.

51 1919 AD 30 at 44.

Especially larger bodies may be significantly hamstrung in their functioning if all members must always be present for all activities. Thus, in *S v Naudé*[52] the court stated:

> [I]t must be conceded that a commission is, in general, the master of its own procedures. Within the bare framework provided by the Act and such modifications and regulations as may have been made by the State President in terms of s 1(1) of the Act, it is free to determine how it shall function. There is no doubt that a commission, particularly where it consists of a substantial number of persons, may operate without every member participating personally in every activity. Were it otherwise, a commission would be hamstrung from the start.[53]

In *New Clicks* the Constitutional Court held that in 'each case what will be required will depend on the interpretation of the empowering legislation and relevant regulations, prescribing how a commission should function'.[54] In the absence of clear instructions in the empowering provisions that prescribe the procedure for the entity to follow, that entity will be able to formulate its own procedure, including quorum rules stating how many members must be present for the entity to take valid decisions, implying that not all members must always be present. The key is the provisions of the relevant empowering provision and how it contemplates the body will function.[55]

### 6.2.2.3 Delegation

Empowering provisions often identify the particular administrator that must take a decision as we have noted above. This will typically be the chief administrator in a given organ of state. One thus finds that empowering provisions routinely authorise the relevant Minister or MEC to take particular decisions. At the same time one does not in practice expect the Minister or the MEC to take all decisions him- or herself. For one reason, it is simply not practically feasible to think that one person at the head of an organ of state can personally take all decisions. There is accordingly a need to recognise that authorised administrators can get someone else to be involved in taking a decision. The primary way in which the rules of administrative law provide for this reality is through delegation.

**PAUSE FOR REFLECTION**

**Practical necessity of delegation**

Consider the following powers that are granted to the Director-General of the Department of Home Affairs in the Identification Act:[56]

> 7. Assignment of identity numbers. –(1) The Director General shall assign an identity number to every person whose particulars are included in the population register ...

CONTINUED >>>

52 1975 (1) SA 681 (A) at 704.

53 Quoted with approval in *Minister of Health and Another NO v New Clicks South Africa (Pty) Ltd and Others (Treatment Action Campaign and Another as Amici Curiae)* 2006 (2) SA 311 (CC) para 171.

54 *New Clicks* para 171.

55 *Judicial Service Commission and Another v Cape Bar Council and Another* 2013 (1) SA 170 (SCA) paras 23–26.

56 68 of 1997.

> 13. Certificates of certain particulars included in population register. –(1) The Director General shall as soon as practicable after the receipt by him or her of an application, issue a birth, marriage or death certificate in the prescribed form after the particulars of such birth, marriage or death were included in the register in terms of section 8 of this Act.
>
> Is it practically feasible to think that the Director-General will be able to assign identity numbers to all citizens and to issue relevant certificates to all applicants him- or herself?
>
> It is fairly self-evident that the Director-General will not be able to fulfil these functions personally. There is accordingly a clear need in cases such as these to enable someone other than the specifically authorised administrator to exercise the powers granted to the administrator.

In section 6(2)(*a*)(ii) PAJA recognises that someone other than the administrator that is authorised in the empowering provision to take a decision can lawfully take the decision by means of delegation. To establish whether delegation is possible, one must ask the standard lawfulness question: is it authorised? An authorised administrator can delegate his or her power to take a decision to another person if such delegation is authorised.

In common law there was a presumption against delegation, expressed in the maxim *delegatus delegare non potest*.[57] This meant that an administrator had to be able to point to specific authorisation to justify a delegation of power to another person if the administrator wanted such other person to lawfully take a decision in his or her stead. In the absence of such authorisation the law would presume the decision by the person other than the originally authorised administrator to be unlawful.

The Constitution and PAJA do not work with any presumptions in respect of delegation. Section 238 of the Constitution states that executive authority may be delegated where authorised and section 6(2)(*a*)(ii) of PAJA likewise states that administrative decisions taken under delegated authority will only be reviewable if the delegation is not authorised. The question is simply one of authorisation, similar to all other lawfulness questions. The law now recognises that delegation is not an exception to lawfulness rules governing who is authorised, but part of those rules.

When deciding whether a particular decision taken in terms of delegated power is lawful, one must in effect ask the who lawfulness question twice. First, one must ask who the authorised administrator is, that is who is identified in the empowering provision as the administrator that must take the decision. If the administrator that actually took the decision is not that authorised one, the second question is whether the originally authorised administrator was authorised to delegate his or her powers to the actual decision-maker. This second question involves a full lawfulness analysis, that is asking what the empowering provision authorises and whether it was followed, but this time only in relation to the delegation of power.

As with the authorisation of all administrative power, delegation can be authorised either expressly or tacitly. The easy case is where the empowering legislation contains a section

57 *Chairman, Board on Tariffs and Trade and Others v Teltron (Pty) Ltd* 1997 (2) SA 25 (A) at 34.

allowing for delegation. An example is section 4 of the Identification Act[58] (which we also noted in the box above), which provides that:

> (1) The Director General may – (*a*) delegate any power granted to him or her by or under this Act, except the power referred to in this section and section 6, to an officer in the public service ...

Somewhat more problematic are cases where the empowering legislation does not contain a provision expressly allowing for delegation, but where authorisation for delegation can be inferred, or stated differently, where the power to delegate is tacitly granted. Under common law a number of factors have emerged that can serve as indicators that a statute tacitly allows for delegation. While these factors are specific to the question of whether delegation is tacitly authorised, it must be kept in mind that this remains a standard exercise in statutory interpretation aimed at establishing what the empowering provision entails that is not expressly stated. In *Minister of Trade and Industry and Others v Nieuwoudt and Another*[59] the court endorsed the following list of factors identified by Baxter:[60]

(i) the degree of devolution of the power;
(ii) the importance of the original delegee;
(iii) the complexity and breadth of discretion;
(iv) the impact of the power; and
(v) practical necessities.

Generally a court will more readily accept tacit authority to delegate only a part of the power, while the original holder of the power retains some control. The more important the original holder of the power is and particularly the more deliberate the legislature's choice of that original administrator as the holder of the power seems to be, the less likely it is that a court will find tacit authorisation to delegate. More complex decisions and decisions involving the exercise of broad discretion will be less likely to be subject to tacitly authorised delegation. Delegation will also not easily be inferred where the exercise of the power has a significant impact. Finally, practical necessities may provide a strong case for finding tacit authority for delegation, especially where it can be argued that it is simply not feasible for the original holder of the power to exercise that power individually in every case, particularly where that administrator is a fairly high-ranking administrator or member of the executive such as a Minister or MEC.

To this list one can add the existence of express authority for delegation in the relevant statute. It is highly unlikely that tacit authority for delegation will be found in a statute that grants express authority for delegation in limited terms.

The possibility of delegation must be distinguished from scenarios where the administrator that is authorised by name takes the decision, but under the influence of another person or body. The question of delegation is not activated where the administrator that is expressly authorised to act ostensibly takes the decision, regardless of who else may also be involved in taking that decision. Thus where the empowering provision authorises administrator A and administrator B takes the decision, then we need to establish whether A could possibly have delegated his or her power to B. However, if A is authorised and A acts

58 68 of 1997.

59 1985 (2) SA 1 (C) at 13. Also see the minority judgment of Langa CJ in *AAA Investments (Pty) Ltd v Micro Finance Regulatory Council and Another* 2007 (1) SA 343 (CC) para 85.

60 Baxter, L (1984) *Administrative Law* 435. Reprinted by permission of © Juta & Company Ltd.

under the influence of B, the question of delegation does not arise, but the question of influence may arise to which we now turn.

#### 6.2.2.4 Influence and advice

The basis of the *who* question of lawfulness is that the authorised administrator must take the relevant decision him- or herself. This rule applies not only in form, but also in substance. The authorised administrator must not only be the one that formally takes the decision, but also be the one that applies his or her mind and comes to the relevant decision, that is, takes the decision in substance. Where an administrator takes a decision under the influence of another there is thus a lawfulness problem.[61] This problem is often referred to as dictates, fettering or rubberstamping: the authorised administrator is acting under the dictates of another, his or her discretion is fettered by another, or he or she is simply rubberstamping the decision of another, rather than applying his or her own mind. Section 6(2)(*e*)(iv) of PAJA provides that administrative action will be unlawful if it was taken because of unauthorised dictates of another person or body.

Dictates or fettering is not restricted to the influence of other persons on the administrator, but may also come in the form of a document. When an administrator thus blindly follows a policy document, his or her discretion is similarly fettered.[62] The problem is the same as above, the authorised administrator is not making the decision him- or herself. In *Cape Town City v South African National Roads Agency Ltd*[63] the court reasoned that the broad notion of fettering as an established ground of review in common law can be understood as part of the residual lawfulness ground of review in PAJA in section 6(2)(*i*), which allows administrative action to be reviewed if it is 'otherwise ... unlawful'.

While administrative law protects the discretion of the authorised administrator by holding decisions taken under the dictates of another unlawful, administrators should not be discouraged from seeking advice or using guidelines that may result in better and more consistent decision-making.[64] The line between fettering and advice or guidance should thus be carefully determined in every case. The key question in every instance is whether the administrator him- or herself took the relevant decision after forming his or her own view on the relevant considerations.

### 6.2.3 How?

The third basic question that we can ask in a lawfulness inquiry is the how question. The issue here is whether the administrator followed the process set out in the empowering provision for taking the relevant decision. The focus is on how the decision must be taken in terms of the empowering provision.

PAJA requires in section 6(2)(*b*) that all mandatory and material procedures and conditions must be followed in taking administrative action. The *how* question thus relates to both purely procedural prescripts and substantive preconditions that must be met in order for the administrator to exercise the power lawfully.

In common law, these statutory requirements were referred to as jurisdictional facts. They were viewed as facts that had to exist for the administrator to have jurisdiction to act. Under the Constitution, this terminology is no longer accurate. This is mainly because the

---

61 *Minister of Environmental Affairs and Tourism and Another v Scenematic Fourteen (Pty) Ltd* 2005 (6) SA 182 (SCA) para 20.

62 *Kemp NO v Van Wyk* 2005 (6) SA 519 (SCA).

63 2015 (6) SA 535 (WCC) para 247.

64 *Scenematic Fourteen* para 20; *Kemp* para 1.

justification for testing the lawfulness of an administrator's conduct, including testing for compliance with prescribed procedures and conditions, is premised on section 33(1) of the Constitution. It is no longer based on a common-law notion of adherence to the will of a sovereign parliament as expressed in the empowering provision. The Constitutional Court explained this shift in our law as follows in *MEC for Health, Eastern Cape and Another v Kirland Investments (Pty) Ltd t/a Eye and Lazer Institute*:[65]

> Jurisdictional facts refer broadly to preconditions or conditions precedent that must exist before the exercise of power, and the procedures to be followed when exercising that power. It is true that we sometimes refer to lawfulness requirements as 'jurisdictional facts.' But that derives from terminology used in a very different, and now defunct, context (namely where all errors, if they were to be capable of being reviewed at all, had to be construed as affecting the functionary's 'jurisdiction'). In our post-constitutional administrative law, there is no need to find that an administrator lacks jurisdiction whenever she fails to comply with the preconditions for lawfully exercising her powers. She acts, but she acts wrongly, and her decision is capable of being set aside by proper process of law.

#### 6.2.3.1 Prescribed procedures

Many empowering provisions prescribe the steps that an administrator must follow when taking a decision. An example is the following procedural prescriptions for appeals against decisions of the Nursing Council as set out in section 57 of the Nursing Act[66] (which we also noted above):

> (3) An appeal under subsection (1) must be heard on the date, place and time fixed by the appeal committee.
>
> (4) The appeal committee must ensure that the appellant as well as the Council are informed of the date, place and time contemplated in subsection (3) at least 14 days before such appeal is heard.
>
> (8) (*a*) The decision of the appeal committee must be in writing, and a copy must be furnished to the appellant as well as to the Council.
>
> (*b*) The decision of the appeal committee contemplated in paragraph (*a*) must be conveyed to the appellant and the Council within 14 days of the decision being reached.

If the appeal committee notified the appellant and the Council of the date and time of the appeal hearing only five days before such hearing, the subsequent decision of the appeal committee could be challenged on lawfulness grounds for a failure to follow section 57(4) of the Nursing Act.[67] The use of the word 'must' in the section is a good indication that the procedure set out in that section is mandatory, following normal rules of statutory interpretation.

Compliance with procedures in empowering provisions should not, however, be judged formalistically. The courts have held that a deviation from a prescribed procedure will not necessarily result in the administrative action being unlawful. The question that must be answered in every case is whether the administrator complied sufficiently with the

65 2014 (3) SA 481 (CC) para 98 (footnotes omitted).

66 33 of 2005.

67 33 of 2005.

prescribed procedure to achieve the purpose of the particular provision.[68] In *Allpay Consolidated Investment Holdings (Pty) Ltd and Others v Chief Executive Officer, South African Social Security Agency and Others*[69] the Constitutional Court stated:

> The proper approach is to establish, factually, whether an irregularity occurred. Then the irregularity must be legally evaluated to determine whether it amounts to a ground of review under PAJA. This legal evaluation must, where appropriate, take into account the materiality of any deviance from legal requirements, by linking the question of compliance to the purpose of the provision, before concluding that a review ground under PAJA has been established …
>
> Assessing the materiality of compliance with legal requirements in our administrative law is, fortunately, an exercise unencumbered by excessive formality. It was not always so. Formal distinctions were drawn between 'mandatory' or 'peremptory' provisions on the one hand and 'directory' ones on the other, the former needing strict compliance on pain of non-validity, and the latter only substantial compliance or even non-compliance. That strict mechanical approach has been discarded. Although a number of factors need to be considered in this kind of enquiry, the central element is to link the question of compliance to the purpose of the provision.

**PAUSE FOR REFLECTION**

**Distinguishing between PAJA section 6(2)(*b*) and section 6(2)(*c*)**

Problems with procedure in taking administrative action can be challenged under either section 6(2)(*b*) or section 6(2)(*c*) of PAJA. However, the one deals with procedure as a matter of lawfulness (6(2)(*b*)) while the other deals with procedure as a matter of procedural fairness (6(2)(*c*)). The key difference in practice between these different grounds of review is the origin of the particular procedure at issue. Procedure as a matter of lawfulness and as set out in this chapter, focuses on the procedural requirements set out in the empowering provision. It is thus the procedure that forms part of the authorisation that is relevant from a lawfulness perspective. Procedure as a matter of procedural fairness is mostly premised on the procedural requirements set out in PAJA itself in sections 3 and 4. This is dealt with in Chapter 7 below. There is also a conceptual difference in testing for compliance with these different procedural aspects of administrative decision-making. As a matter of lawfulness the procedural inquiry is whether there was compliance with the authorisation, that is, did the administrator act within the limits of his or her powers? As a matter of procedural fairness the procedural inquiry focuses not on compliance or the limits of power, but on the fairness of decision-making. The latter thus allows for much more variability and contextual influence in the inquiry than the former.

CONTINUED >>>

68 *Weenen Transitional Local Council v Van Dyk* 2002 (4) SA 653 (SCA) para 13; *African Christian Democratic Party v Electoral Commission and Others* 2006 (3) SA 305 (CC) paras 24–25.

69 2014 (1) SA 604 (CC) paras 28 and 30.

> However, there is not a watertight distinction between these different procedural dimensions of an administrative action. It is quite possible to find that the exact same facts may support arguments on both these grounds of review. For example, giving only five days' notice of the time and date of an appeal hearing under section 57 of the Nursing Act,[70] noted above, may render the appeal decision unlawful on the basis of non-compliance with section 57(4). At the same time, five days' notice may not be 'adequate notice of the nature and purpose of the proposed administrative action' and may result in a party not receiving 'a reasonable opportunity to make representations' as required by section 3(2)(*b*) of PAJA as a matter of procedural fairness.
>
> Conversely, compliance with the procedure set out in the empowering provision, that is satisfying the lawfulness inquiry, may simultaneously satisfy the requirements of procedural fairness under section 3(5) for example, which allows for a fair but different procedure mandated by an empowering provision to be followed instead of the standard procedures set out in section 3.[71]

### 6.2.3.2 Conditions

Apart from pure procedures, the empowering provision may also prescribe (substantive) conditions for the exercise of a particular power. At its most basic, this takes the following form: in the case of A, the administrator may do B, where A is the condition and B the administrative action. The administrator's power to take action B is thus dependent on the existence of A.

Conditions can broadly be categorised as either subjective or objective.[72] Examples of both types are found in the following provision from the South African Police Service Act:[73]

> 17D(2) If, during the course of an investigation by the Directorate, evidence of any other crime is detected and the Head of the Directorate considers it in the interests of justice, or in the public interest, he or she may extend the investigation so as to include any offence which he or she suspects to be connected with the subject of the investigation.

In this example, the Head of the Directorate of Priority Crime Investigation may extend an investigation if two distinct sets of conditions are met. The first condition is objective: evidence of any other crime is detected. The existence of this condition can be objectively determined, that is, the condition simply refers to a fact. The second set of conditions is subjective: the Head of the Directorate must consider it in the interest of justice or in the public interest to take the action. This condition does not refer to a fact that can be objectively determined. It rather refers to the subjective view of a particular person. Note that this second condition is not that it must in fact be in the interest of justice or in the public interest to extend the investigation. The condition is that the Head must consider it so, that is, his or her subjective view is the condition.

70 33 of 2005.

71 See Chapter 7 section 7.3.1.2 below on the option of following a fair but different procedure under the requirements of procedural fairness.

72 *South African Defence and Aid Fund and Another v Minister of Justice* 1967 (1) SA 31 (A) at 34.

73 68 of 1995.

The establishment of compliance with objective conditions are of course fairly unproblematic. One can simply investigate whether the relevant facts pertaining to the condition exist. If they do not exist, the condition is not met and the administrator cannot lawfully take the action.

Subjective conditions are much more difficult to test. Since it is the subjective view of a particular person that is the basis of the condition, it would seem that the objective existence of the matter on which a view must be formed is irrelevant. In the example above, it is thus ostensibly irrelevant, at least from a lawfulness perspective, whether extending an investigation is indeed in the public interest or not. The only relevant question is whether the Head formed the view that it is. As a result, it is thus fairly easy for an administrator to simply assert that he or she did indeed form the view, thereby fulfilling the condition. In the old classic case of *South African Defence and Aid Fund and Another v Minister of Justice*[74] the court held that in the case of a subjective condition a court may only interfere if 'it is shown that the repository of the power, in deciding that the pre-requisite fact or state of affairs existed, acted *mala fide* or from ulterior motive or failed to apply his mind to the matter'.[75]

Today, scrutiny of subjective conditions is less problematic than under common law, because of the constitutional requirement that administrative action must also be reasonable. While, following the approach set out in the *South African Defence and Aid Fund* case above, subjective conditions cannot be significantly scrutinised as a matter of lawfulness, an administrator's subjective conclusion under the condition can be much more closely assessed as a matter of reasonableness.[76] In *Walele v City of Cape Town and Others*[77] the Constitutional Court thus stated:

> In the past, when reasonableness was not taken as a self-standing ground for review, the City's *ipse dixit* could have been adequate. But that is no longer the position in our law. More is now required if the decision-maker's opinion is challenged on the basis that the subjective precondition did not exist. The decision-maker must now show that the subjective opinion it relied on for exercising power was based on reasonable grounds.

Furthermore, the requirement that an administrator take all relevant considerations into account when taking administrative action in section 6(2)(*e*)(iii) of PAJA also undermines the highly deferential approach of the *South African Defence and Aid Fund* case to subjectively framed conditions. On the strength of this section of PAJA it is now competent to argue that an administrator acted unlawfully when he or she formed the view that the condition was satisfied while there are considerations pointing to the opposite conclusion.

## 6.3 Mistakes

The final aspect of lawfulness to consider is that of mistake. An administrator's action may be unlawful if he or she makes a mistake in either law or fact pertaining to his or her authorisation. It is particularly important to remember that we are not talking about a

74 1967 (1) SA 31 (A) at 35; confirmed by the Constitutional Court as still the leading authority in this area in *President of the Republic of South Africa and Others v South African Rugby Football Union and Others* 2000 (1) SA 1 (CC) para 168 fn 132.

75 Also see *Kimberley Junior School and Another v Head, Northern Cape Education Department and Others* 2010 (1) SA 217 (SCA) paras 12–13.

76 See Chapter 8 below on the substantive dimension of the reasonableness standard.

77 2008 (6) SA 129 (CC) para 60 (footnotes omitted).

mistake in relation to the content of the administrator's decision. In other words, we are not saying that the administrator took the wrong administrative action. We are still focusing on the lawfulness of the administrative action, which means that we are still only focusing on the authorisation of the action. The mistake we are talking about here is thus purely in relation to the authorisation.

### 6.3.1 Error of law

The most established form of mistake that may lead to unlawfulness is in relation to the empowering provision, commonly referred to as error of law. In section 6(2)(*d*) PAJA states that an administrative action will be unlawful if it was materially influenced by an error of law.

Administrative law requires that the administrator must take the administrative action upon a correct interpretation of the applicable law, particularly the empowering provision. If the action is taken on the basis of an incorrect interpretation of the law, it may be unlawful. The ground of review should not be interpreted narrowly as only referring to errors in relation to the empowering provision. Any error in relation to law that materially impacts the decision could result in the decision being set aside as unlawful. In *Genesis Medical Scheme v Registrar of Medical Schemes*,[78] the court held that it may be a reviewable error of law where an administrator relied on an incorrect judicial pronouncement.

A classic example is found in *Tseleng v Chairman, Unemployment Insurance Board and Another*.[79] In this case Mr Tseleng was employed from 26 March 1990 until 6 November 1992, during which time he contributed to the Unemployment Insurance Fund. In April 1993 he applied for unemployment benefits under the Unemployment Insurance Act,[80] which was granted. On 18 April 1994, Mr Tseleng applied for further benefits. This application was rejected with reference to section 35(13)(*a*) of the Act, which states that:

> a contributor shall not be entitled to unemployment benefits - (*a*) unless he has been employed as a contributor or otherwise in employment for at least 13 weeks ... during the 52 weeks immediately preceding the date upon which a period of unemployment is deemed to have commenced.

Section 35(7)(*a*) of the Act further states that 'a period of unemployment shall not be deemed to have commenced until the contributor has lodged an application'.

The board interpreted these sections as meaning that an applicant for further benefits had to be employed for at least 13 weeks during the 52 weeks immediately preceding the date of application for further benefits. Since Mr Tseleng was last employed in November 1992 and applied for further benefits in April 1994, he did not meet this requirement and the board thus rejected the application for further benefits. Mr Tseleng challenged this decision as unlawful, arguing that it was made on a mistaken interpretation of the applicable statute. The court upheld this argument finding that the correct interpretation of the Act is that 'the reference to a "period of unemployment" in ss (13)(*a*) is intended to refer to the single period of unemployment which is deemed to commence on the lodging of the initial application for unemployment benefits'.[81] The administrator thus made an error in interpreting the period of unemployment to have commenced when the application for further benefits was lodged, rather than the original application for benefits. Upon a correct

78 2017 (6) SA 1 (CC) para 21.
79 1995 (3) SA 162 (T).
80 30 of 1966.
81 *Tseleng* 171.

interpretation of the statute, which would take the period of unemployment to have commenced in April 1993, Mr Tseleng was not disqualified under section 35(13)(*a*) of the Act. The administrator's particular decision was thus taken *because* of the error of law and was hence unlawful.

The leading case on errors of law in South African common law is *Hira and Another v Booysen and Another*.[82] In this case Corbett CJ exhaustively analysed the relevant case law and held that an error of law will be reviewable, that is, lead to unlawfulness of the administrative action, if it was material.[83] Materiality is determined by asking if the same decision would be reached if the administrator had adopted the correct interpretation of the applicable law. If the answer is yes, the error of law will not be material and not lead to the unlawfulness of the administrative action. Conversely, if the answer is no, as in the *Tseleng* case, the error will be material and the decision unlawful. This is the approach also adopted in section 6(2)(*d*) of PAJA.[84]

### 6.3.2 Mistake of fact

A more recent development in South African administrative law relates to mistakes of fact. In common law these types of mistake were generally not considered to impact on the lawfulness of a particular administrative action,[85] that is apart from jurisdictional facts as prescribed conditions or procedures were known in common law.

In the key judgment of *Pepcor Retirement Fund v Financial Services Board*,[86] the Supreme Court of Appeal broke with the common-law position and held, in terms of the Constitution, but prior to PAJA, that mistake of fact should be considered a ground of review going to the lawfulness of an administrator's action. The court held that:

> a material mistake of fact should be a basis upon which a Court can review an administrative decision. If legislation has empowered a functionary to make a decision, in the public interest, the decision should be made on the material facts which should have been available for the decision properly to be made. And if a decision has been made in ignorance of facts material to the decision and which therefore should have been before the functionary, the decision should ... be reviewable at the suit of, *inter alios*, the functionary who made it - even although the functionary may have been guilty of negligence and even where a person who is not guilty of fraudulent conduct has benefited by the decision. The doctrine of legality which was the basis of the decisions in *Fedsure, Sarfu* and *Pharmaceutical Manufacturers* requires that the power conferred on a functionary to make decisions in the public interest, should be exercised properly, ie on the basis of the true facts; it should not be confined to cases where the common law would categorise the decision as *ultra vires*.

In this matter, the Registrar of Pension Funds decided to allow the transfer of business from one pension fund to a number of other funds. This decision was taken on the basis of actuarial calculations, which later turned out to be incorrect. Upon a challenge, the court

82 1992 (4) SA 69 (A).

83 *Hira* 93.

84 *Johannesburg Metropolitan Municipality v Gauteng Development Tribunal and Others* 2010 (6) SA 182 (CC) para 91; *Security Industry Alliance v Private Security Industry Regulatory Authority and Others* 2015 (1) SA 169 (SCA) para 26.

85 *Pepcor Retirement Fund and Another v Financial Services Board and Another* 2003 (6) SA 38 (SCA) para 32.

86 2003 (6) SA 38 (SCA) para 47.

found the decision of the Registrar to be unlawful, because of the mistaken facts on which it was premised.

PAJA recognises mistake of fact as an element of lawfulness in section 6(2)(*e*)(iii), which requires an administrator to take all relevant considerations into account and ignore all irrelevant considerations when taking administrative action.[87] The mistaken facts would of course constitute irrelevant considerations and the correct facts relevant considerations. Alternatively mistake of fact can be reviewed in terms of section 6(2)(*i*), which captures the general ground of review for instances of unlawfulness that do not neatly fit into any of the other grounds of review.

As with error of law, the mistake of fact must also be material before it will impact on the lawfulness of the administrative action. In *Chairman, State Tender Board v Digital Voice Processing* Plasket AJA thus held that an error of fact will only justify a finding of invalidity if that error 'was the direct cause of the decision' at issue.[88]

## 6.4 Conclusion

Lawfulness is one of the most basic requirements of administrative justice. It is directly linked to the overarching constitutional principle of legality, premised on the rule of law. At its simplest this notion requires all public action to be based on a valid source of power. Beyond simply requiring that administrative action must be based on authorisation, that is an empowering provision, lawfulness further requires that the action be aligned to the empowering provision. The action should fall within the four corners of the empowering provision.

PAJA does not contain a consolidated statement of what lawfulness in terms of section 33(1) of the Constitution entails. The Act only contains various grounds of review in section 6 that can be labelled as lawfulness grounds of review. These are listed in Table 6.1 below. From these negatively stated grounds of review, one can extrapolate the rules of lawfulness in administrative justice.

***Table 6.1** Lawfulness grounds of review*

| **Lawfulness rules in PAJA** | |
|---|---|
| **PAJA section** | **Lawfulness rule** |
| 6(2)(*a*)(i) | The authorised administrator must act |
| 6(2)(*a*)(ii) | Delegation can only occur as authorised |
| 6(2)(*b*) | Mandatory and material conditions and procedures in the empowering provision must be followed |
| 6(2)(*d*) | The decision must be taken on a correct interpretation of the applicable law |
| 6(2)(e)(i) | The reason for the action must be authorised |
| 6(2)(e)(ii) | The motive and purpose of the action must be authorised |

87 *Chairman, State Tender Board v Digital Voice Processing (Pty) Ltd; Chairman, State Tender Board v Sneller Digital (Pty) Ltd and Others* 2012 (2) SA 16 (SCA) para 34; *Dumani v Nair and Another* 2013 (2) SA 274 (SCA) para 30.

88 *Chairman State Tender Board* para 36.

| Lawfulness rules in PAJA | |
|---|---|
| 6(2)(e)(iii) | All relevant considerations must be taken into account and all irrelevant considerations must be ignored in taking the action |
| 6(2)(e)(iv) | The administrator must take the decision him- or herself and not follow the prescripts of another |
| 6(2)(e)(v) | The decision must not be taken in bad faith |
| 6(2)(*f*)(i) | The action itself must be authorised |
| 6(2)(*g*) - read with section 6(3) | A decision must be taken when there is a duty to decide |
| 6(2)(i) | The action must comply with all legal rules |

## THIS CHAPTER IN ESSENCE

Lawfulness is one of the most basic requirements of administrative justice. The core of lawfulness is authorisation. In essence it requires that all administrative action must be taken in terms of a valid source, called an empowering provision, and that the action must fit within the four corners of the empowering provision.

To determine the lawfulness of a particular administrative action one can ask a series of questions when comparing the action to the empowering provision:

- What was authorised versus what was done?
- Who was authorised versus who acted?
- How should the action have been taken versus how was it taken?

## FURTHER READING


- Forsyth, C & Dring, E 'The Final Frontier: The Emergence of Material Error of Fact as a Ground for Judicial Review' in Forsyth, C, Elliott, M, Jhaveri, S, Ramsden, M & Scully-Hill, A (Eds) (2010) *Effective Judicial Review: A Cornerstone of Good Governance* 245
- Hoexter, C (1994) Administrative Justice and Dishonesty *SALJ* 111:700
- Pretorius, DM (2005) The Origins of the *Functus Officio* Doctrine, with Specific Reference to its Application in Administrative Law *SALJ* 122:832

# Chapter 7

# Procedural fairness

*Melanie Murcott*



## 7.1 Introduction

Most of us can probably conjure a childhood memory of complaining to a parent that his or her decision was 'unfair'. More recently, you might have watched a sports match where you threw your hands up in the air at the 'unfairness' of a referee or umpire's decision. Perhaps, in these situations, you were upset by not being properly heard by a parent, or by a referee that appeared to favour one team over another. All of us probably have an intuitive sense of what fairness entails, but are there concrete factors or actions that render decision-making fair or unfair?

When it comes to administrative law, at common law before 1994, decisions were considered fair if they complied with the 'rules of natural justice', usually expressed in their Latin format as *audi alteram partem* (hear the other side) and *nemo judex in sua causa esse debet* (no one should be a judge in his or her own cause/interest). These rules of natural justice largely resemble what we would expect of decisions in other contexts, including on the sports field or in the household. They essentially ensured that people adversely affected by decisions would know about the decision and be able to participate in that decision, which entailed prior notice of the decision and an opportunity to state their case and influence the outcome of the decision to an unbiased decision-maker. For example, in *Heatherdale Farms (Pty) Ltd and Others v Deputy Minister of Agriculture and Another*[1] Colman J held that before the Deputy Minister could confiscate the poultry or eggs of companies engaged in large-scale chicken breeding, the companies had to be given an adequate opportunity to make representations to the Deputy Minister. As the companies concerned were not afforded such an opportunity, the Deputy Minister's conduct was found to be inconsistent with the maxim *audi alteram partem* and Colman J set aside the Deputy Minister's order of confiscation in respect of the companies' poultry and eggs. In *Barnard v Jockey Club of South Africa*[2] a decision of a domestic tribunal of the Jockey Club of South Africa to convict a racehorse trainer of contravening club rules was set aside by the court because a member of the tribunal was a partner of the firm of attorneys representing the club, such that he had a financial interest in the proceedings, which created a suspicion in the mind of a reasonable person that he was not impartial or that there was a likelihood of bias.

The requirements of fairness as demanded by the rules of natural justice remain in place post-apartheid, as they are protected by the right to just administrative action in section 33 of the Constitution and the Promotion of Administrative Justice Act[3] (PAJA). However, they have been supplemented, particularly in relation to administrative action affecting the public.[4] Further the requirements of fairness are now more generously applied than under the common law. At common law the rules of procedural fairness were applied in a restrictive manner with reliance on the 'classification of functions'.[5] Put very simplistically, the rule against bias was applied in judicial or quasi-judicial contexts, and not to other types of administrative conduct (that is, of a legislative or 'purely administrative' nature), while the maxim *audi alteram partem* was applied principally to cases where someone was deprived of a right, rather than cases concerning 'mere applicants', and also only to judicial or quasi-judicial conduct, in the absence of a legislative provision that demanded the application of the maxim to other types of administrative conduct. Under the Constitution and PAJA,[6] in contrast, the requirements of fairness apply to all administrative action, and sometimes even apply when the exercise of public power does not amount to administrative action, in terms of the principle of legality.[7]

Post-apartheid, the imposition of procedural fairness standards is particularly important because these standards serve to uphold principles and values that underpin our

1 1980 (3) SA 476 (T).
2 1984 (2) SA 35 (W).
3 3 of 2000.
4 See section 4 of PAJA.
5 See Chapter 1 section 1.3.4 above on the 'classification of functions'.
6 In terms of sections 3 and 4 of PAJA.
7 Section 1(*c*) of the Constitution. See, for example, *Albutt v Centre for the Study of Violence and Reconciliation and Others* 2010 (3) SA 293 (CC); *Minister of Home Affairs and Others v Scalabrini Centre and Others* 2013 (6) SA 421 (SCA) and *Law Society of South Africa and Others v President of the Republic of South Africa and Others* 2019 (3) BCLR 329 (CC).

Constitution: accountability, responsiveness and openness.[8] Moreover, our new constitutional dispensation envisages a participatory democracy,[9] in which '[t]he right to speak and be listened to is part of the right to be a citizen in the full sense of the word ... and the right to have a voice on public affairs is constitutive of dignity'.[10]

However, the problem with procedural fairness standards is that they take time and resources to uphold and fulfil, possibly to the extent of causing 'administrative paralysis' at the expense of efficiency.[11] Particularly in relation to decisions affecting large numbers of people, it is not difficult to imagine that it will be burdensome for administrative officials to give prior notice of an intended decision, listen to and consider representations, then give notice of the decision taken and notice of opportunities to appeal every time they take a decision. For this reason, as discussed below, what fairness demands will depend on the circumstances of each case.[12]

This chapter spells out in detail what it means for administrative action to be fair under section 33 of the Constitution and in terms of sections 3 and 4 of PAJA. PAJA gives greater detail on what is required from an administrator in the area of procedural fairness: first in section 3, in regard to administrative action affecting an individual (that is, decisions with a specific impact), then, in section 4, where administrative action affects the public at large (that is, decisions with a general impact). We then consider the rule against bias in more detail. We discuss the development of the principle of legality such that it demands that public power that is not administrative action may also, in certain situations, be subject to at least some of the demands of fairness. Lastly, the circumstances in which the exercise of private power may be subject to procedural fairness standards are briefly considered.

**PAUSE FOR REFLECTION**

**The practicality of procedure**

Consider an administrator in the Department of Environmental Affairs, who must decide whether or not to grant an environmental authorisation permitting the development of a new power plant on the outskirts of Soweto. The power plant is needed urgently to support the national grid and prevent load shedding in the future. To what extent is it practical for the administrator to be expected to give notice of her proposed decision to determine the application for an environmental authorisation, and listen to representations about whether or not she should do so? Even if it is impractical, what are some of the reasons why the administrator should nonetheless engage with people before she takes her decision?

CONTINUED >>>

8 Section 1(*d*) of the Constitution. See further section 195 of the Constitution, which demands, among other things, that the public administration must provide services in an impartial, fair and equitable manner, without bias (section 195(1)(*d*)), that people's needs must be responded to, and the public must be encouraged to participate in policy-making (section 195(1)(*e*)), that the public administration must be accountable (section 195(1)(*f*)) and that transparency must be fostered by providing the public with timely, accessible and accurate information.

9 *Minister of Health and Another NO v New Clicks (Pty) Ltd and Others (Treatment Action Campaign and Another as Amici Curiae)* 2006 (2) SA 311 (CC) paras 111 and 625.

10 *New Clicks* para 627.

11 *Joseph and Others v City of Johannesburg and Others* 2010 (4) SA 55 (CC) paras 28–29.

12 *Zondi v MEC for Traditional and Local Government Affairs and Others* 2005 (3) SA 589 (CC) paras 113–114. Although there are certain minimum requirements of fairness, according to *Joseph* paras 57–63 even these may be applied in a flexible manner.

> Compare this scenario with some of the others we have seen in earlier chapters. Look, for example, at the box in Chapter 1 section 1.1 with the ID card example. What form did participation in the contemplated decision (to issue an ID) take there? What are the practical differences between the scenario here and the one in Chapter 1 for purposes of procedure? Should these differences impact on how we view procedure as an aspect of administrative justice?

## 7.2 Procedural fairness in the constitutional era

As set out above, the common-law rules of natural justice (that is, *audi alteram partem*, which means hear the other side, and *nemo judex in sua causa esse debet*, which entails that no one should be a judge in their own cause/interest) ensured that people adversely affected by decisions would know about such decisions and be able to participate in the decision-making process, which entailed prior notice of the decisions, and an opportunity to state their case and influence the outcome of the decisions to an unbiased decision-maker. However, during apartheid these rules were typically applied in a restrictive, all-or-nothing manner: not to cases where a 'mere applicant' was adversely affected by a decision, but rather to cases where the holder of an existing right was so affected: where the decision was 'quasi-judicial' rather than 'legislative or purely administrative'.[13] Moreover, other than quasi-judicial decisions, there was a presumption against the application of the standards of procedural fairness unless there was a legislative provision that expressly or by necessary implication, demanded their application.

In a break from the restrictive application of procedural fairness standards of our apartheid past, section 33 of the Constitution demands that all administrative decisions are subject to procedural fairness standards. Now, where the exercise of public power amounts to 'administrative action', section 33 provides that such power must be 'procedurally fair'.[14] As we will discuss below, the provisions of section 3 and 4 of PAJA give detailed content as to what fairness demands whenever administrative action is taken. Where empowering legislation imposes specific procedural fairness standards, and those standards fall short of what PAJA demands, the empowering legislation must be read with PAJA.[15]

Below we will discuss first section 3 of PAJA, where decisions have a specific impact and affect a person, rather than the public at large. Second, we will discuss section 4 of PAJA, where decisions have a general impact and affect the public. Third, we will consider what the rule against bias entails. Next, we will consider the circumstances in which some of the requirements of fairness will be imposed in terms of the constitutional principle of legality, in relation to public power that is not administrative action. Finally, we will discuss the circumstances under which the requirements of procedural fairness may be imposed upon exercises of private power under the common law.

At the outset it is important to understand that when administrative action is taken in a manner that does not comply with the standards imposed by sections 3 or 4 (as applicable), or when it falls foul of the rule against bias, the action will be reviewable in terms of

13 See, for example, *R v Ngwevela* 1954 (1) SA 123 (A).
14 Previously, section 24(*b*) of the transitional Constitution of 1993 provided for a right to 'procedurally fair administrative action where any ... rights or legitimate expectations is affected or threatened'.
15 *Zondi* para 101.

section 6(2) of PAJA, and could be set aside as invalid in terms of section 8 of PAJA. Section 6(2) confers on the courts the power to judicially review administrative action that was procedurally unfair (in terms of subsection (*c*)), or that was biased or reasonably suspected of bias (in terms of subsection (*a*)(iii)).

## 7.3 Procedural fairness under PAJA

### 7.3.1 Section 3 of PAJA: Procedural fairness in respect of decisions that affect individuals

When Mr B applies for his passport at the Department of Home Affairs and is told that his application has been unsuccessful, or when a local municipality cuts off Mrs A's electricity supply, these are situations where administrative action 'affects a person'. Section 3(2)(*b*) of PAJA provides that in order to be procedurally fair, this kind of administrative action **must** comply with certain procedural requirements, essentially:

- adequate notice of proposed administrative action,
- a reasonable opportunity to make representations,
- a clear statement of the administrative action taken,
- adequate notice of any review or internal appeal, and
- adequate notice of the right to request reasons.

Section 3(3) provides that in some situations, more demanding procedures **may** be required in respect of administrative action that affects a person, such as:

- an opportunity for the affected person to obtain assistance and, in serious or complex cases, legal representation, and
- an opportunity for the affected person to present and dispute information and arguments, including in person (as opposed to in writing).

We will discuss each of the procedural requirements of section 3 in more detail below. First, however, we must consider under what circumstances section 3 is applicable to administrative action.

#### 7.3.1.1 When does section 3 apply?

Section 3(1) tells us that the procedural fairness requirements apply when the administrative action at issue:

1. 'affects **any person**',
2. has a '**material** and adverse affect', and
3. affects 'rights or **legitimate expectations**'.

Below we consider each of these aspects more carefully. At the outset it is important to understand that 'substantive values and factors that inform the need for administrative justice' in a particular case ought to determine whether section 3 applies, rather than 'highly technical and abstract conceptual analyses of terms such as "legal effect" and "rights"'.[16] These substantive values and factors include the 'the role of procedural fairness in affirming the dignity of all those affected by public action', 'raising the quality of decision-making',

16 Quinot, G (2010) Substantive Reasoning in Administrative-Law Adjudication *Constitutional Court Review* 3:111 at 121.

'achieving a culture of accountability, openness and transparency, especially in public administration' and fostering 'trust in state administration and more generally democracy'.[17]

### Any person

Administrative action affects 'any person', and attracts the fairness standards imposed by section 3 of PAJA, first when it has a specific impact, rather than a more general impact on the public at large, or a group or class of the public. For instance, a decision of an official of the Department of Social Development to reject an application for a disability grant affects the person who applied for the grant personally, and has a specific impact on him, rather than a more general impact on the public at large.

Bear in mind that 'person' includes juristic persons so that a decision by the Department of Basic Education to reduce the subsidy of a specific public school, for example, would still fall under section 3. The impact is still specific to the 'person', here the school, even though there may be many individuals (learners, teachers, and so on) that form part of the school. However, it may at times be difficult to draw the line between an impact on a person and an impact on a group as we shall see when we look at the field of application of section 4 of PAJA dealing with procedural fairness in cases where the administrative action impacts on the public.

### Materiality

At first glance, section 3 suggests that only administrative action that has a 'material' or significant impact on a person must comply with its procedural requirements: it seems to qualify or limit its application to conduct that '**materially** and adversely affects ... any person' (that is, a 'materiality qualification').[18] You will recall that the definition of 'administrative action' in section 1 of PAJA does not require that decisions must have a material impact in order to fall within its scope. Instead, section 1 requires that the impact of a decision must be adverse and sufficiently final. Section 3's 'materiality qualification' is potentially significant, as it could be interpreted so as to result in a substantial narrowing of the application of procedural fairness standards to a limited type of administrative decision-making. Although a narrowing of the application of procedural fairness standards would help reduce the burden imposed on the state administration that these standards entail, such a narrowing could also run counter to the constitutional values of accountability, responsiveness and openness applicable to the public administration. Fortunately, the Constitutional Court has interpreted the 'materiality qualification' in section 3 of PAJA to mean that administrative action will attract the standards of procedural fairness unless it has a 'trivial' affect.[19] The court took the view that rather than limit the application of section 3 to a narrow class of administrative action, administrators could tailor the content of procedural fairness depending on the circumstances of the case.

17 Quinot (2010).
18 Emphasis added.
19 *Joseph* para 31.

### Rights or legitimate expectations

*Rights*

The administrative action to which the standards of procedural fairness apply according to section 3(1) seems a wider category of conduct than the category 'administrative action' as defined in section 1 of PAJA. You will recall that 'administrative action' as defined in section 1 is only action that affects **rights**.[20] Rights include common-law rights, such as rights attaching to individuals under the law of property, contractual rights, as well as constitutional rights.[21]

In *Joseph,* the Constitutional Court further extended the meaning of 'rights' under section 3(1) of PAJA by holding that the term includes 'legal entitlements that have their basis in the constitutional and statutory obligations of government'.[22] The City had disconnected the electricity supply to an apartment building after the owner failed to pay his account. It was common cause that the City followed a fair procedure vis-à-vis the owner before taking the decision, including appropriate notices to him of arrears and the proposed disconnection. The residents of the building had no contractual relationship with the City for the supply of electricity since supply was in bulk to the building, rather than to the individual apartments. The resident tenants only had a contractual relationship with the owner for the supply of electricity, who in turn had a contractual relationship with the City. The question was consequently whether the City's decision to disconnect the power supply impacted on any of the rights of the tenants so that the City was obliged to act in a procedurally fair manner vis-à-vis the tenants in terms of section 3(1) of PAJA before taking the decision to disconnect their electricity. The court held that the tenants had no contractual rights vis-à-vis the City that were impacted by the decision to disconnect. The court also refrained from deciding whether any of the tenants' fundamental rights (like the right to housing or dignity) were infringed by the decision. Rather, the court found that the City had constitutional and legislative obligations to provide basic municipal services to everyone living in its jurisdiction, which included electricity supply.[23] The tenants had a 'correlative public law right' to receive such services.[24] The City's decision to disconnect the electricity supply impacted adversely on these rights, which resulted in section 3 of PAJA applying to the decision vis-à-vis the tenants. *Joseph* thus extends the scope of application of procedural fairness under section 3 of PAJA well beyond the traditional category of rights.

Curiously, unlike section 1, section 3(1) of PAJA determines that procedural fairness applies to conduct that affects rights or **legitimate expectations**.

*Legitimate expectations*

A legitimate expectation is something less than a right.[25] It entails the expectation of a fair procedure being followed or of a certain outcome being afforded the expectant party. The expectation must have a reasonable basis, having arisen from an undertaking given by an

20 See *Grey's Marine Hout Bay (Pty) Ltd and Others v Minister of Public Works and Others* 2005 (6) SA 313 (SCA) paras 29–33.

21 Refer to section 3.7.5 in Chapter 3 on the rights element of the definition of administrative action in section 1 of PAJA.

22 *Joseph* para 43.

23 *Joseph* para 35.

24 *Joseph* para 40.

25 See *Walele v City of Cape Town and Others* 2008 (6) SA 129 (CC) para 35, where the court held that a legitimate expectation can arise in respect of a mere 'privilege or benefit which it would be unfair to deny [a] person without giving him or her a hearing'.

administrator or an administrator's long-standing practice.[26] Legitimate expectations were first recognised under the common law in *Administrator, Transvaal and Others v Traub and Others*,[27] where doctors recommended for particular posts were refused appointment by an administrator, but claimed to have a legitimate expectation that they would be appointed or at the very least that they would be given a hearing before being refused appointment. The doctors argued that their expectation arose from the administrator's long-standing past practice of appointing all the doctors recommended for the particular post. The court recognised the doctors' legitimate expectation and afforded the expectation procedural protection by ordering that given their expectation the doctors were entitled to be heard if the administrator wished to depart from its long-standing past practice.

In our constitutional era, the requirements for a legitimate expectation were enumerated in *National Director of Public Prosecutions v Phillips and Others*[28] as follows:

- First, the expectation must be 'reasonable';
- Second, the representation giving rise to the expectation must be:
  - 'clear, unambiguous and devoid of relevant qualification',
  - 'induced by the decision-maker', and
  - 'one which it was competent and lawful for the decision-maker to make'.[29]

*Phillips* concerned an expectation that the owner of The Ranch, a brothel, would not be prosecuted in respect of offences related to the operation of the brothel. He asserted a legitimate expectation based on past practice of the police and prosecuting authorities, since they had allowed the owner to carry on criminal activities such as prostitution undisturbed for some time, and had been 'lax' in their enforcement of offences related to the operation of the brothel. The court held that the words and conduct of the authorities could not have given rise to a legitimate expectation in favour of the owner of the brothel. Any expectation arising from the conduct of the police and prosecuting authorities would be 'naïve, unreasonable and, consequently, not legitimate'.[30]

Under section 3(1) of PAJA where a legitimate expectation is disappointed without a fair procedure having been followed, the decision giving rise to the disappointment of the legitimate expectation may be set aside on the grounds of procedural unfairness. *Premier Mpumalanga and Another v Executive Committee, Association of State-Aided Schools, Eastern Transvaal*[31] is a pre-PAJA example of the court setting aside a decision that disappointed a legitimate expectation on the grounds of procedural unfairness. The Department of Education had issued a notice promising to pay bursaries to certain schools for tuition and transport for the 1995 school year. The practice of paying these bursaries to the schools had been in place for some years. Subsequently, the schools were informed that they would no longer receive the bursaries from the Department for the 1995 school year. The schools had budgeted and planned for 1995 on the basis that they would receive the bursaries. In the absence of a contract between the schools and the Department, the schools did not have a 'right' to receive the bursaries. They could not therefore assert that any contractual right had been affected that triggered the Department's procedural fairness obligations under administrative law. However,

26 Quinot, G (2004) The Developing Doctrine of Substantive Protection of Legitimate Expectations in South African Administrative Law *SAPL* 19:543 at 546–547. See further Pretorius, DM (2000) Ten Years After *Traub*: The Doctrine of Legitimate Expectation in South African Administrative Law *SALJ* 117(3):520.

27 1989 (4) SA 731 (A).

28 2002 (4) SA 60 (W).

29 2002 (4) SA 60 (W) para 28.

30 *Phillips* para 29.

31 1999 (2) SA 91 (CC).

they did have a legitimate expectation that the bursaries would be paid, and that the bursaries would not be terminated without reasonable notice first being given to the schools, that is, the expectation of a fair procedure in the form of reasonable notice, which stemmed from a reasonable basis in the form of the longstanding practice of paying the bursaries and the undertaking that the bursaries would be paid. The court ordered that in the absence of reasonable notice having been given to terminate the bursaries, the conduct of the Department was unfair and fell to be set aside.[32] Interestingly, although the school's legitimate expectation of a fair procedure had been disappointed, the effect of the court's order was to confer a substantive benefit on the schools in the form of payment of bursaries.

COUNTER POINT

**Procedural or substantive protection of legitimate expectations**

Although a legitimate expectation can be substantive or procedural in content, the protection of such expectations has typically been restricted to requiring that a procedure be followed, rather than ordering that a particular outcome materialise.[33] In other words, a person may legitimately expect a substantive benefit to materialise (for example, that a licence will be issued) or he or she may legitimately expect a particular procedure to be followed (for example, that he or she will be informed if the administrator intends to take certain steps). Both of these refer to the content of the expectation. Once the expectation has been established as legitimate, the protection that administrative law offers is traditionally procedural in nature, that is, the person should have the opportunity to participate in the decision leading to the disappointment of the expectation. This is also the case under PAJA where legitimate expectations are referred to in section 3, which deals with procedural fairness. As under common law, legitimate expectations serve under PAJA to trigger the rules of procedural fairness.

In South Africa, as in other common-law jurisdictions, the question has emerged whether legitimate expectations should also be protected substantively. In essence this would mean that where a person has a legitimate expectation, a court should be able to enforce the expectation itself, as opposed to simply force the administrator to follow a particular procedure if the expectation is to be disappointed. If the expectation was thus to receive a particular substantive benefit, say that a licence will be granted, the substantive protection of that expectation would entail a court ordering the administrator to issue the licence.

Different common-law countries have answered this question differently. In England it is now accepted that legitimate expectations can be enforced, that is, protected substantively. In the leading judgment in *R v North and East Devon Health Authority Ex Parte Coughlan (Secretary for Health and Another Intervening)*[34] the English Court of Appeal held that a legitimate expectation will be enforced except if there is 'sufficient overriding [public] interest' in not doing so. However, in Australia[35] and Canada[36] the courts have rejected the notion of substantive protection.

CONTINUED >>>

32 *Premier Mpumalanga* paras 45–46.

33 See Murcott, M (2015) A Future for the Doctrine of Substantive Legitimate Expectation? The Implications of *Kwazulu-Natal Joint Liaison Committee v MEC for Education, Kwazulu-Natal PER* (18)1:3133.

34 [2000] 3 All ER 850 (CA) para 58.

35 *Re Minister for Immigration and Multicultural Affairs; Ex Parte Lam* (2003) 214 CLR 1.

36 *Mount Sinai Hospital Centre v Quebec (Minister of Health and Social Services)* [2001] 2 SCR 281.

In South Africa the possibility of substantive protection of legitimate expectations remains undecided. A number of South African scholars have proposed ways in which substantive protection of legitimate expectations could be recognised in South African law.[37] However, in two judgments the Supreme Court of Appeal expressly left the question open: *Meyer v Iscor Pension Fund*[38] and *Duncan v Minister of Environmental Affairs and Tourism and Another.*[39] In the latter case the SCA, with reference to academic opinion, stated:

> Since *Meyer*, the results of extensive academic research and analysis have been published ... These publications will undoubtedly be of valuable assistance when eventually the time comes in an appropriate case, as it presumably will, for our courts to cut the Gordian knot. But this is not that case.

Subsequently, in *KwaZulu-Natal Joint Liaison Committee v MEC for Education, Kwazulu-Natal and Others*[40] the Constitutional Court had the opportunity to develop a doctrine of substantive legitimate expectation. However, the issue of substantive protection of a legitimate expectation had not been properly pleaded or argued before the court, so the court left the question of when substantive protection would be afforded a legitimate expectation open for future determination. In *Abbott v Overstrand Municipality*[41] reliance was expressly placed on the doctrine of legitimate expectation in pursuit of a substantive benefit, but the court held that even if one were to accept that the doctrine of legitimate expectation of a substantive benefit forms part of our law, the applicant had not proved objective facts giving rise to such an expectation.

The Constitutional Court has resolved the inconsistency between the protection afforded rights in section 1 and the protection afforded rights and legitimate expectations in 3 respectively, by determining that notwithstanding the narrower terms of section 1 of PAJA, section 3(1) of PAJA confers the rights to procedural fairness on persons whose legitimate expectations had been adversely affected, on the basis that the more specific provision, section 3(1), had to be read as supplementing the more general provision, section 1.[42]

### 7.3.1.2 The requirements of section 3, and how they apply

Once we have established that section 3 applies to a particular administrative action we can consider in more detail the specific requirements of fairness in terms of section 3 and how those requirements apply. First, it is important to understand that these requirements apply in a flexible manner.

#### Flexibility

Importantly, section 3(2)(*a*) tells us that the requirements of procedural fairness contained in section 3 must be applied in a flexible manner. It provides that 'a fair administrative

37 See Hoexter, C (2012) *Administrative Law in South Africa* (2nd ed) 427–436; Quinot (2004); Campbell, J (2003) Legitimate Expectations: The Potential and Limits of Substantive Protection in South Africa *SALJ* 120(2):292.
38 2003 (2) SA 715 (SCA).
39 2010 (6) SA 374 (SCA).
40 2013 (4) SA 262 (CC).
41 Unreported, referred to as [2016] ZASCA 68, 20 May 2016 paras 32–34.
42 *Walele* para 37.

procedure depends on the circumstances of each case'. Flexibility is crucial, as it allows a context-sensitive application of the requirements of procedural fairness on a case-by-case basis. In some situations, for example where there is an urgent matter that needs to be dealt with, such as a decision to erect temporary shelters for people affected by a flood, it might be fair to give one day's notice of a decision, whereas if the matter is not urgent, such as the approval of a shopping centre development, fairness would invariably demand much more notice. In complex decisions, involving a vast number of documents, fairness could require that legal representation be permitted at a hearing, whereas for everyday issues that confront the ordinary person on the street, such as the disconnection of water or electricity, fairness might simply require opportunity to send written representations in the form of a letter or notice to an official.

The flexibility inherent in section 3 has been interpreted to mean that although section 3(2)(*b*) appears to impose 'mandatory' or 'minimum' requirements of procedural fairness, whilst section 3(3) appears to impose 'discretionary' or 'additional' requirements of procedural fairness, the courts will have a discretion as to whether or not to enforce even section 3(2)(*b*)'s requirements in appropriate cases.[43] In other words, a court may find that an administrator's conduct is procedurally fair even if it does not comply with all the requirements of section 3(2)(*b*). However, administrators would be ill-advised to overlook the requirements of section 3(2)(*b*) in the normal course, and run the risk of the court finding in subsequent litigation that theirs was a case in which all of the section 3(2)(*b*) procedures ought to have been followed. Instead, if and to the extent an administrator believes that a departure from the requirements of section 3(2) is appropriate, he or she should expressly invoke section 3(4), which reinforces the idea of flexibility by allowing administrators to depart from the requirements of section 3(2)(*b*) where it is reasonable and justifiable to do so, taking into account all relevant factors. These factors include the likely effect or impact of the administrative action, the urgency of the matter, and the need to promote an efficient administration. We will now turn to consider what procedures section 3(2)(*b*) and 3(3) envisage, in order for administrative action to be fair.

### The requirements of section 3

#### *Adequate notice*

The first and most basic procedural requirement of section 3(2)(*b*) is that a person who will be affected by administrative action must be given adequate notice of the intended action. So, for example, before a municipality may terminate your electricity supply on the grounds that you failed to pay your bill, it must give you notice, usually in writing, that it intends to do so within a certain period of time. Such notice ensures that you have the opportunity to engage with the municipality before your electricity is cut off.

Adequacy of notice is a relative concept, such that what is 'adequate', both in relation to the form and timing of notice, will depend on the circumstances of the case. When a municipality wishes to evict residents from a block of flats in Johannesburg because the building is derelict and unsafe to live in, it may be appropriate to afford a short period of notice, and simply to put written notices up on notice boards at the entrance of the block of flats, as well as on notice boards around the block of flats. If the residents are predominantly isiZulu speaking, adequacy could entail that the written notice be published both in English and isiZulu. However, if illiterate residents of an informal settlement are to be relocated to

43 *Joseph* paras 56–59.

a new RDP housing estate, written notice of the intended decision alone may not be adequate. In such a case, the officials involved may be required to engage verbally with community leaders, in their home language over a long period of time, in order to satisfy the requirement of adequate notice.

In *Police and Prisons Civil Rights Union and Others v Minister of Correctional Services and Others (No 1)*[44] members of the Department of Correctional Services were informed that the Department contemplated dismissing them *inter alia* for unauthorised absence from work and were afforded 48 hours to make representations before the decision was taken. Plasket J held that 'the notice of 48 hours cannot, by any stretch of the imagination, be said to be adequate notice of the nature and purpose of the proposed administrative action, as envisaged by s 3(2)(*b*)(i) of PAJA'.[45]

*A reasonable opportunity to make representations*

The second requirement of section 3(2)(*b*) is that a person affected by administrative action must be given a reasonable opportunity to make representations, either to the administrator who will take the decision, or where this would be impractical, persons who will later fully apprise the decision-maker of the content of representations made by interested parties. The opportunity must ordinarily be afforded **before** a decision is taken. In *Sokhela and Others v MEC for Agriculture and Environmental Affairs (Kwazulu-Natal) and Others*[46] it was found that:

> Where a person has a right to be heard before a decision is taken it is important that whatever the form of the hearing, the subject matter of the hearing or opportunity to make representations is made clear to the affected parties in order that the right to make representations may be effective.

In *Sokhela* it was alleged that affected parties had been afforded an opportunity to be heard, because they had been called to a meeting before the decision adversely affecting them had been taken. However, the court reasoned that since the affected parties were not informed at that meeting that its purpose was to afford them an opportunity to make representations, and the decision-maker did not disclose concerns that might result in an adverse decision, the meeting did not amount to a reasonable opportunity to make representations.[47]

The reason for allowing an opportunity for representations to be made is not because the representations will necessarily be accepted. However, representations may have an important influence on the outcome of decision-making. For instance, in the context of a decision to grant a prospecting right in respect of minerals on land, where it is necessary first for the landowners to be given notice and consulted in terms of the Mineral and Petroleum Resources Development Act,[48] it has been held that 'the purpose of consultation is to ascertain if some sort of accommodation can be reached in respect of [the] impact' of a decision to grant a prospecting right. In other words, the purpose of an opportunity to make representations includes managing the impact of a decision on those adversely affected.[49] Another important reason for allowing an opportunity to make representations relates to

44 2008 (3) SA 91 (E).
45 *Police and Prisons Civil Rights Union* para 73.
46 2010 (5) SA 574 (KZP) para 53.
47 *Sokhela* para 55.
48 28 of 2002.
49 Van Wyk, J (2014) Fracking in the Karoo: Approvals Required (1) *Stellenbosch Law Review* 25(1):34 at 44–45 referring to *Bengwenyama Minerals (Pty) Ltd and Others v Genorah Resources (Pty) Ltd and Others* 2011 (4) SA 113 (CC) paras 63–64.

enabling the decision-maker to hear all points of view so as to arrive at 'an objectively justifiable conclusion'.

What is 'reasonable' will depend on the circumstances of the case, but typically, the opportunity afforded is to present representations **in writing**. This is because it would be unduly burdensome to expect administrators to speak and listen, in person, to each person affected by a decision, so as to consider their representations. Further, section 3(3) recognises that administrators 'may ... in [their] discretion' (that is, not in the normal course) give affected persons the opportunity to do more than just present written representations including: (*a*) obtaining assistance, and in serious or complex cases, legal representation, (*b*) presenting and disputing information and arguments and (*c*) appearing in person. One could expect a decision-maker to exercise the discretion conferred by section 3(3), for instance, for the benefit of someone who is illiterate, and thus cannot make written representations on their own, or where a decision turns on the interpretation of a complex legal document, such that a layperson would struggle to make representations without the assistance of legal representation.

As for the timing of the opportunity to make representations, in order to be 'reasonable', the more complex the matter, the longer the opportunity to make representations should be, especially where a decision will be made based on vast amounts of information. On the other hand, if a decision needs to be taken urgently, it could be reasonable to allow a short period of time for representations to be made. Note that urgency is a factor here to determine what the flexible standard of fairness in giving an opportunity to make representations requires under the circumstances, rather than a justification for a departure from the requirement to allow representations.

Finally, in order for the representations to be meaningful, it is accepted that the administrator must disclose to the affected persons information that will inform the administrator's decision-making. This would usually include:

- provisions in legislation or contracts that will inform the administrator's decision,
- policy considerations that will be relied upon in making the decision, and
- adverse or prejudicial information in the administrator's possession.

*A clear statement of the administrative action*

The third requirement of section 3(2)(*b*) is that after a decision has been taken, those affected by it should be advised, in clear terms, of the decision. A clear statement of administrative action ought to set out:

- what was decided,
- who the decision-makers were, and
- on what legal and factual basis the decision was taken.

A statement of this kind would enable a person affected to launch a meaningful appeal or review in respect of the administrative action taken.

*Notice of any right of review or internal appeal and notice of the right to request reasons*

The final requirements of procedural fairness in section 3(2)(*b*) of PAJA demand that decision-makers must inform affected persons that they are entitled to ask for reasons for the decision in terms of section 5 of PAJA, and of any internal or special statutory review procedures or any internal appeal procedures available in respect of the decision. Decision-makers do not need to inform affected persons that they can pursue a judicial review in terms of section 6 of PAJA. If some other review or internal appeal is available, however, the decision-maker ought to advise affected persons of how long they have to pursue the review or appeal, where and with whom the review or appeal should be pursued, and any other formal requirements of the review or appeal.

Note that these requirements do not expressly oblige the administrator to provide reasons for the administrative action. The only obligation under this section is that the affected person be informed of his or her right to request reasons. As we shall see in Chapter 9, dealing with the right to reasons, this obligation to inform a person of his or her right to request reasons is an important element of PAJA's reason-giving regime, under which a person has a right to request reasons rather than a right to reasons.

**PAUSE FOR REFLECTION**

**How to change an exam date**

The exam date for administrative law is recorded in the exam schedule published on the university's intranet as date X. Your lecturer wants to change the exam date to date Y. She mentions this in passing to a handful of students who she bumps into in the library, but doesn't notify the student body more generally, or make inquiries about whether date Y would be suitable for the students. The lecturer then changes the exam date from date X to date Y, but does not publish the new exam date on the university's intranet. Instead, your lecturer discusses the new date with a student that she believes to be one of the strongest in the class. On date Y, most of the students are absent from the exam. The lecturer's decision is clearly unfair, but what is it about her decision that renders it unfair? For instance, in order to be fair, ought the lecturer to have given prior notice of her proposed decision to the students, ought she to have engaged with representations on the new date, and then given notice of the decision taken? Did the lecturer demonstrate a preference for a particular student?

**A fair, but different procedure**

It is not unusual for the procedure that an administrator must follow in order to take a decision to be specifically prescribed by legislation empowering that administrator to act. Section 3(5) recognises this by allowing administrators to follow a 'fair but different procedures' from those set out in section 3(2).

In order for an administrator to rely on this provision, the following elements must be present:

- An empowering provision must provide for a procedure to be followed (note the broad definition of empowering provision in section 1 of PAJA).
- The contemplated procedure may differ from that set out in section 3(2) of PAJA.
- The different procedure must still be fair.
- The administrator must follow the different procedure.

Fairness under this subsection will be judged against the general requirement that the affected person must have a meaningful opportunity to influence the administrative decision.

Following a 'fair but different procedure' under section 3(5) amounts to compliance with section 3 of PAJA even though the procedure followed may look very different from that set out in PAJA. This is another way in which the flexibility of procedural fairness is manifested under PAJA.

EXAMPLE

**Example of a 'fair but different procedure'**

The provisions in the Refugees Act[50] dealing with applications for asylum provide an example of a procedure that is somewhat different from that set out in PAJA, but that can still be considered fair.

Refugees Act 130 of 1998

21. Application for asylum.–

(1) An application for asylum must be made in person in accordance with the prescribed procedures to a Refugee Reception Officer at any Refugee Reception Office.

(2) The Refugee Reception Officer concerned–

(*a*) must accept the application form from the applicant;

(*b*) must see to it that the application form is properly completed, and, where necessary, must assist the applicant in this regard;

(*c*) may conduct such enquiry as he or she deems necessary in order to verify the information furnished in the application; and

(*d*) must submit any application received by him or her, together with any information relating to the applicant which he or she may have obtained, to a Refugee Status Determination Officer, to deal with it in terms of section 24.

(3) When making an application for asylum, every applicant must have his or her fingerprints or other prints taken in the prescribed manner and every applicant who is 16 years old or older must furnish two recent photographs of himself or herself of such dimensions as may be prescribed.

24. Decision regarding application for asylum.–

(1) Upon receipt of an application for asylum the Refugee Status Determination Officer–

(*a*) in order to make a decision, may request any information or clarification he or she deems necessary from an applicant or Refugee Reception Officer;

(*b*) where necessary, may consult with and invite a UNHCR representative to furnish information on specified matters; and

(*c*) may, with the permission of the asylum seeker, provide the UNHCR representative with such information as may be requested.

(2) When considering an application the Refugee Status Determination Officer must have due regard for the rights set out in section 33 of the Constitution, and in particular, ensure that the applicant fully understands the procedures, his or her rights and responsibilities and the evidence presented.

CONTINUED >>>

50 130 of 1998.

(3) The Refugee Status Determination Officer must at the conclusion of the hearing–
   (*a*) grant asylum; or
   (*b*) reject the application as manifestly unfounded, abusive or fraudulent; or
   (*c*) reject the application as unfounded; or
   (*d*) refer any question of law to the Standing Committee.

(4) If an application is rejected in terms of subsection (3)(*b*)–
   (*a*) written reasons must be furnished to the applicant within five working days after the date of the rejection or referral;
   (*b*) the record of proceedings and a copy of the reasons referred to in paragraph (*a*) must be submitted to the Standing Committee within 10 working days after the date of the rejection or referral.

In essence there are thus three main types of procedural routes that an administrator may adopt under section 3 of PAJA:

1. The administrator may follow the procedure set out in section 3(2) supplemented by the procedural steps in section 3(3) where the circumstances require, or
2. the administrator may depart from the procedure in section 3(2) if the circumstances allow in terms of section 3(4) taking into account the factors listed in section 3(4)(*b*), or
3. the administrator may follow a 'fair but different' procedure provided for in an empowering provision.

### 7.3.2 Section 4 of PAJA: Procedural fairness in respect of decisions that have a general impact

A decision of the Department of Home Affairs to close an office for the processing of asylum-seeker permits for refugees living in the country, or a decision to increase tolls on national highways does not merely have a specific impact on individuals. These decisions also have a broader impact in the sense that their impact is, in relation to a group or class of people, equal and impersonal.[51] When these types of decisions are taken, the decision-makers concerned must comply with the procedural requirements of section 4 of PAJA.

Unlike the procedures provided for in section 3 of PAJA, the procedures envisaged by section 4 do not contemplate one-on-one engagement. For example, in some situations, section 4 demands inviting, by way of notice in a regional newspaper, a community to attend a meeting in a public forum, such as a town hall or local sports club, to make verbal or written representations to a panel of decision-makers about an issue that affects that community (that is, to hold a public inquiry).[52] In other situations, section 4 demands that administrators put a notice in a national newspaper, inviting written comments from the public generally on a proposed decision, rather than only inviting a select few to make comments (that is, to follow a notice and comment procedure).[53]

51 Currie, I & Klaaren, J (2001) *The Promotion of Administrative Justice Act Benchbook* 114. See also Burns, Y & Henrico, R (2020) *Administrative Law* (5th ed) 179, 324.
52 Section 4(1)(*a*).
53 Section 4(1)(*b*).

Certain decisions that affect a group or class of the public might demand both a public inquiry and a notice and comment procedure,[54] whilst in some situations it might be fair to follow another procedure, provided that approach is also fair.[55] The inclusion in PAJA of procedures applicable when decisions affect the public is a welcome extension to fairness under the common law, as these procedures foster accountability, openness and justifiable decisions.[56] Hoexter describes section 4 as 'a novel and significant provision' in our constitutional dispensation, since it introduces new forms of participation when decisions affect the public.[57] Before we consider what the procedures provided for in section 4 entail, we must understand when section 4 will be triggered.

#### 7.3.2.1 When does section 4 apply?

Like section 3, the requirements of section 4 are triggered when rights are 'materially and adversely' affected by administrative action. These aspects of section 4 ought to be understood as set out in relation to section 3 above. The distinguishing trigger in section 4 is that the impact on rights must be on 'the public' rather than on 'a person'. We will now consider the meaning of the term 'the public'.

**The public**

Section 1 provides that for purposes of section 4, 'public' includes any group or class of the public. It is argued that administrative action affects a group or class of the public when its impact is 'equal and impersonal', rather than merely specific.[58] In addition, administrative action that is 'general' and has a significant public effect will arguably trigger the procedures in section 4, even if the group or class of the public affected is not clearly identifiable or cannot give input itself.[59] It has been held that section 4 allows public interest groups and individuals to make representations on decisions in such situations, that is, where the people who might actually be affected are not able to give input or are not identifiable.[60] This is because:

> [w]here administrative action is proposed which will adversely affect the public, there may often be an extant group of people who will be immediately affected but often the proposed action will also have future effects on people who, at the time of the decision, are not yet in contemplation as persons who will be adversely affected. Often these 'future victims' of the proposed decision will be the more numerous group. While their identity will not be known (they themselves might not yet know that their circumstances will ever bring them within the purview of the proposed decision), we are fortunate to live in a society where there are many organisations which concern themselves with public causes and with the welfare of others and where there are altruistic individuals with the knowledge, experience and skill to make useful representations on matters affecting the public.[61]

54 Section 4(1)(*c*).
55 Section 4(1)(*d*) and (*e*).
56 Currie & Klaaren (2001) 108–109.
57 Hoexter (2012) 406.
58 Currie & Klaaren 114.
59 *Scalabrini Centre and Others, Cape Town and Others v Minister of Home Affairs and Others* 2013 (3) SA 531 (WCC) paras 82–86.
60 *Scalabrini Centre* WCC paras 85–86.
61 *Scalabrini Centre* WCC para 85.

#### 7.3.2.2 The requirements of section 4

We will now consider in more detail the procedures provided for in section 4 of PAJA when administrative action affects the public.

An administrator taking a decision that will have a material and adverse general impact on the public may:

- hold a public inquiry (section 4(1)(*a*) and section 4(2)),
- follow a notice and comment procedure (section 4(1)(*b*) and section 4(3)),
- hold a public inquiry **and** follow a notice and comment procedure (section 4(1)(*c*)),
- follow a different but fair procedure prescribed by an empowering provision (section 4(1)(*d*)), **or**
- follow any other procedure that gives effect to section 3 (section 4(1)(*e*)).

Like section 3, section 4 envisages that what is fair will depend on the circumstances of the case (that is, section 4 will apply in a flexible fashion, as spelt out in relation to section 3 above). To this end, section 4 affords administrators a number of procedures from which to choose when their decisions materially and adversely affect the public in a general sense. Section 1 excludes from the definition of 'administrative action' a decision or failure to take a decision in terms of section 4(1).[62] The result of this exclusion is that the administrator's choice as to which section 4 procedure to use when his or her decisions materially and adversely affect the public will not be reviewable in terms of section 6 of PAJA. An administrator's choice may, however, be reviewable in terms of the constitutional principle of legality, which regulates the exercise of all public power. Administrators may also depart from the procedures provided for in section 4(1), (2) and (3) where it is reasonable and justifiable to do so, taking into account factors such as efficiency, good governance and the urgency of the intended administrative action.[63] In the next section, we will consider what each of the procedures in section 4 entails.

##### The section 4 procedures

The procedures in section 4 of PAJA became operational only once detailed regulations on fair administrative procedures giving greater content to those procedures had been put in place. Thus the procedures provided for in section 4 must be read with the Regulations on Fair Administrative Procedures 2002.

*A public inquiry*

A public inquiry is a formal hearing, in a public forum, where an administrator or a panel of administrators receives representations (either in writing or verbally) in relation to a decision that will have a general impact.

In terms of section 4(2), when an administrator has chosen to hold a public inquiry in order to ensure the fairness of a decision with a general impact that he or she wishes to take, the administrator must first decide whether to conduct the public inquiry him- or herself, or appoint a panel of suitably qualified persons to conduct the inquiry. Then, the administrator must invite the public to attend and participate in the inquiry about the decision. The invitation must contain sufficient information so as to enable those affected to participate meaningfully, and enable them to ask for more information if necessary. In addition, the invitation must be publicised effectively, so as to be brought to the attention

62 Section 1(*i*)(ii) of PAJA.

63 Section 4(4) of PAJA.

of those affected, including by means of internet, radio, television, posters, newspapers, etc. At the inquiry, people must be given a hearing (that is, a proper opportunity to participate and be heard), having regard to matters such as their level of literacy, the languages they speak, and the possible need for assistance. After the inquiry, it is necessary for a written report to be compiled, recording the reasons for any decision to be taken or recommended. The report must be published in the *Gazette* and conveyed to those members of the public affected by a decision to be taken or recommended.

*A notice and comment procedure*

Before some decisions affecting the public are taken it may simply be impractical to convene inquiries with people to receive representations about the decision. In these cases, a notice and comment procedure will likely be pursued, instead of a public inquiry. Section 4(3) gives more information about how a notice and comment ought to be conducted. As in the case of a public inquiry, administrators must issue a proper invitation to participate in the procedure, which must be publicised effectively. The invitation in this case will be to give written comments on a proposed decision by a certain date, rather than to participate in a hearing. Once written comments have been received, the administrators concerned are required to consider the comments and decide whether or not to take the intended decision, with or without changes, in light of the comments received.

*Fair but different procedure*

In *Bengwenyama Minerals,* the court was concerned with the procedure contained in the Mineral and Petroleum Resources Development Act,[64] in the context of a challenge to a prospecting right granted under that Act. The court pointed out that in order to satisfy the demands of fairness, the consultation demanded by the Act could not be 'a mere formal process'. Rather the consultation had to amount to 'genuine and effective engagement of minds between the consulting and the consulted parties'.

### 7.3.3 Procedural fairness in respect of decisions that affect individuals and the public

Some decisions may have both a specific and a general impact. These decisions will attract the fairness standards imposed by section 3 in respect of their specific impact, as well those imposed by section 4, in respect of their general impact. For instance, the decision to build the Gautrain railway line in Gauteng had a general impact on all people in Gauteng, as well as a specific impact on some people, such as those whose properties were expropriated in order to make way for the construction of particular portions of the railway line. Accordingly, in order to act fairly, the officials involved in the approval of the Gautrain's railway line would have been required to follow certain procedures prescribed by section 4 in respect of the public in Gauteng, as well as to follow procedures prescribed by section 3 in respect of the specific individuals affected by expropriation.

64 28 of 2002.

**PAUSE FOR REFLECTION**

**Fracking in the Karoo**

Imagine that Shale of Africa (Pty) Ltd, a major player in the energy industry, wishes to conduct hydraulic fracturing (fracking) to extract natural gas from rocks deep underground in the Karoo, near a residential area, and that the Director-General of the Department of Environmental Affairs grants an environmental authorisation allowing the fracking to take place. Clean Energy, an environmental non-governmental organisation, argues that the Director-General ought to have conducted a public inquiry, a notice and comment procedure or any other fair procedure provided for in environmental law before granting the environmental authorisation to allow any fracking.

Are the rights or legitimate expectations of 'the public' materially and adversely affected by the Director-General's decision to grant an environmental authorisation? If so, which group or class of the public is affected? Which rights or legitimate expectations are affected? Could the Director-General's decision potentially have a specific impact on certain individuals, in addition to a more general impact on the public? Which procedures do you think the Director-General ought to have followed before granting the authorisation?

## 7.3.4 The consequences of a failure to follow a fair procedure as required by sections 3 and/or 4 of PAJA

In the event that an administrator performs administrative action without complying with the demands of sections 3 and/or 4 (as applicable), his or her conduct will be reviewable in terms of section 6(2)(*c*) of PAJA on the grounds that it was procedurally unfair, and will typically be set aside as invalid. For example, in *Earthlife Africa Johannesburg v Minister of Energy*[65] a decision of the National Energy Regulator of South Africa (NERSA) permitting the procurement of 9600MW of electricity through nuclear energy was reviewed and set aside, amongst other things on the basis that NERSA had acted in a manner that was procedurally unfair in terms of section 4 of PAJA. The decision would have far-reaching implications, not least because it would entail substantial expenditure on infrastructure (around R1 trillion) which would have to be paid for through taxes and increased electricity charges.[66] Given these and other implications, the court concluded that 'a rational and fair decision-making process would have made provision for public input' before NERSA acted.[67]

In *Allpay Consolidated Investment Holdings (Pty) Ltd v Chief Executive Officer, South African Social Security Agency and Others*[68] the court held that the determination of the procedural fairness of an administrative decision is independent of the outcome of the decision. This means that the administrative action can be found invalid because of procedural irregularities, regardless of whether the action would have been the same had a fair procedure been followed. The court rejected the contrary approach followed by the Supreme Court of Appeal in this matter, which involved a challenge to a procurement decision, stating that the SCA's approach 'undermines the role procedural requirements play in ensuring even treatment of all bidders' and 'overlooks that the purpose of a fair process is to ensure the best outcome; the two cannot be severed'. The court held that on the SCA's approach 'procedural requirements are not considered on their own merits, but

65 2017 (5) SA 227 (WCC) para 44.
66 *Earthlife Africa* para 44.
67 *Earthlife Africa* para 45.
68 2014 (1) SA 604 (CC) para 24.

instead through the lens of the final outcome'. This is a flawed approach, among other reasons, because if 'the process leading to the bid's success was compromised, it cannot be known with certainty what course the process might have taken had procedural requirements been properly observed'.

Diagrams A and B in Figure 7.1 on pages 192–193 illustrate the process of analysing whether a particular administrative action complied with the procedural fairness requirements of PAJA in a step-by-step manner. In all instances the analysis starts in Diagram A, which determines in the first phase of the process what the impact of the relevant administrative action entails in order to ascertain whether section 3 and/or section 4 of PAJA applies. If the impact of the action is individualised, the focus is on section 3 as set out in the remainder of Diagram A. If the impact of the action is general (on the public), then the focus is on section 4, which is set out in Diagram B. In considering the flow diagram in Figure 7.1 the inherent flexibility of procedural fairness must be remembered, which means that even the mandatory requirements of section 3(2)(*b*) of PAJA need not always be strictly followed.[69]

## 7.4 The rule against bias

As set out above, the rule against bias was, at common law, captured in the Latin maxim *nemo judex in sua causa esse debet*, which means that no one should be a judge in their own cause/interest. One can think again of a referee in a football or rugby match. If the referee is also a player in the game, this would detract from his or her ability to make impartial decisions in the match, when what is required is for the referee (decision-maker) to approach the match (decision) with an open mind, without having, for any reason, prejudged the match (decision).

In our constitutional era, the rule against bias is recognised by incorporating in section 6(2)(*a*)(iii) of PAJA, among the grounds of review of administrative action, that administrative action will be reviewable when the administrator who took it was biased or reasonably suspected of bias.

An administrator's conduct may be set aside in terms of section 6(2)(*a*)(iii) when he or she has in fact prejudged a decision and has thus actually failed to approach the decision with an open mind, or when he or she has created the impression, perception, apprehension or suspicion in the eyes of a reasonable person, on reasonable grounds, that he or she might have been biased.[70] It will often be difficult to prove that an administrator is actually biased, since bias manifests in the mind of an administrator.[71]

---

69 *Joseph* paras 56–59.

70 *BTR Industries South Africa (Pty) Ltd and Others v Metal and Allied Workers' Union and Another* 1992 (3) SA 673 (A) 688D–697; *Telkom SA Soc Limited v Mncube NO and Others; Mobile Telephone Networks (Pty) Ltd v Pillay NO and Others; Cell C (Pty) Limited v The Chairperson of ICASA and Others; Dimension Data Middle East & Africa (Pty) Ltd t.a Internet Solutions v ICASA and Others* unreported, referred to as [2016] ZAGPPHC 93, 26 February 2016 paras 52–55. See further *President of the RSA v SARFU* 1999 (4) SA 147 (CC) para 30 where the court preferred a reasonable apprehension of bias test, since a reasonable suspicion of bias test creates the impression that bias necessarily entails corruption or warrants suspicion, when in fact, bias simply entails a pre-judgment, which includes unintentional, innocent or inadvertent pre-judgment, and is not necessarily corrupt or malicious.

71 See C Okpaluba and L Juma(2011) 'The Problems of Proving Actual or Apparent Bias: An Analysis of Contemporary Developments in South Africa' *PER* 38. It was noted in *BTR Industries* 693C referring to *Council of Review, South African Defence Force v H J Mönnig and Others* 1992 (3) SA 482 (A) that 'bias is not only conscious but also subconscious'.

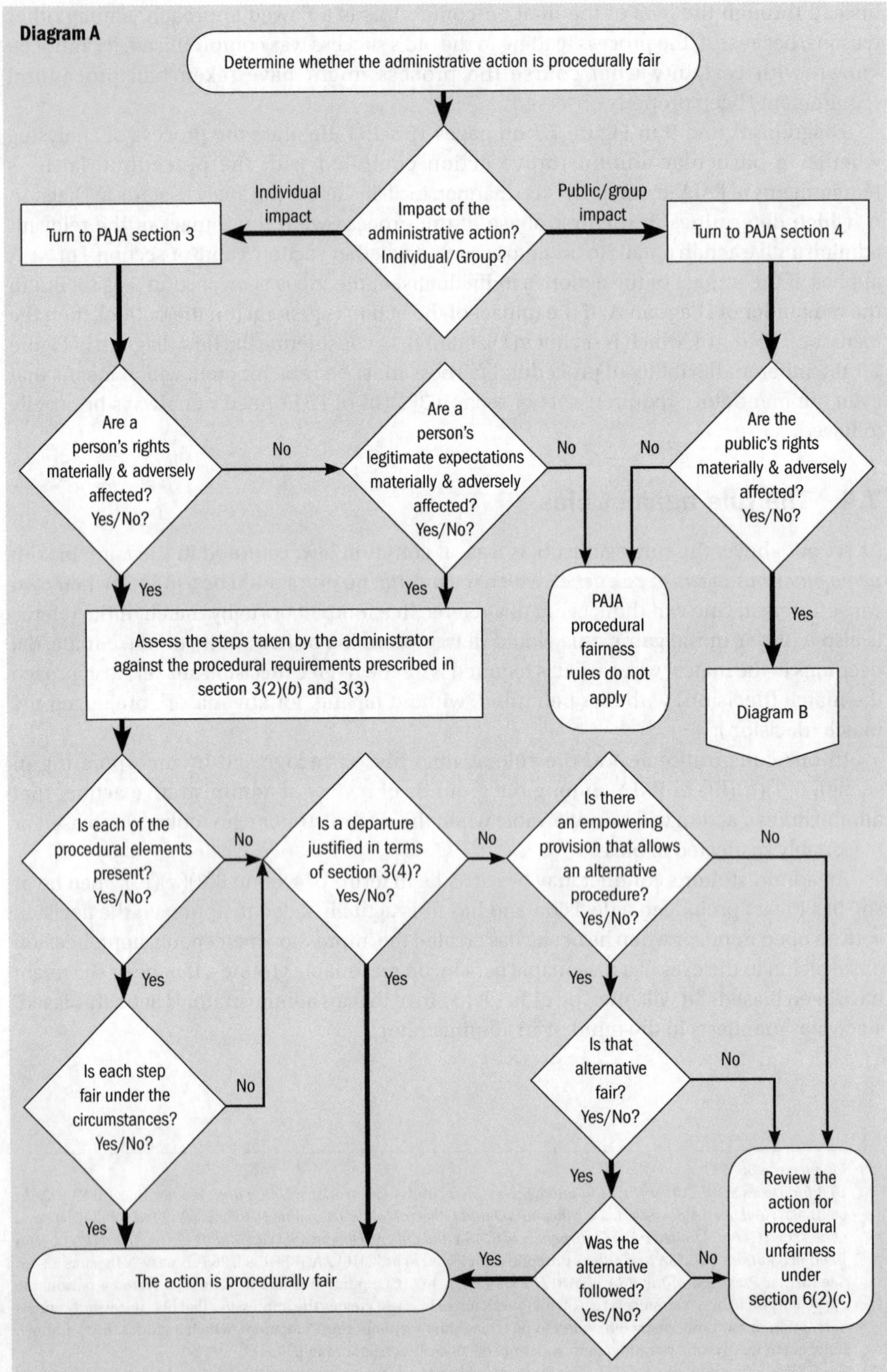


*Figure 7.1 Steps in analysing the procedural fairness of an administrative action: Diagram A*

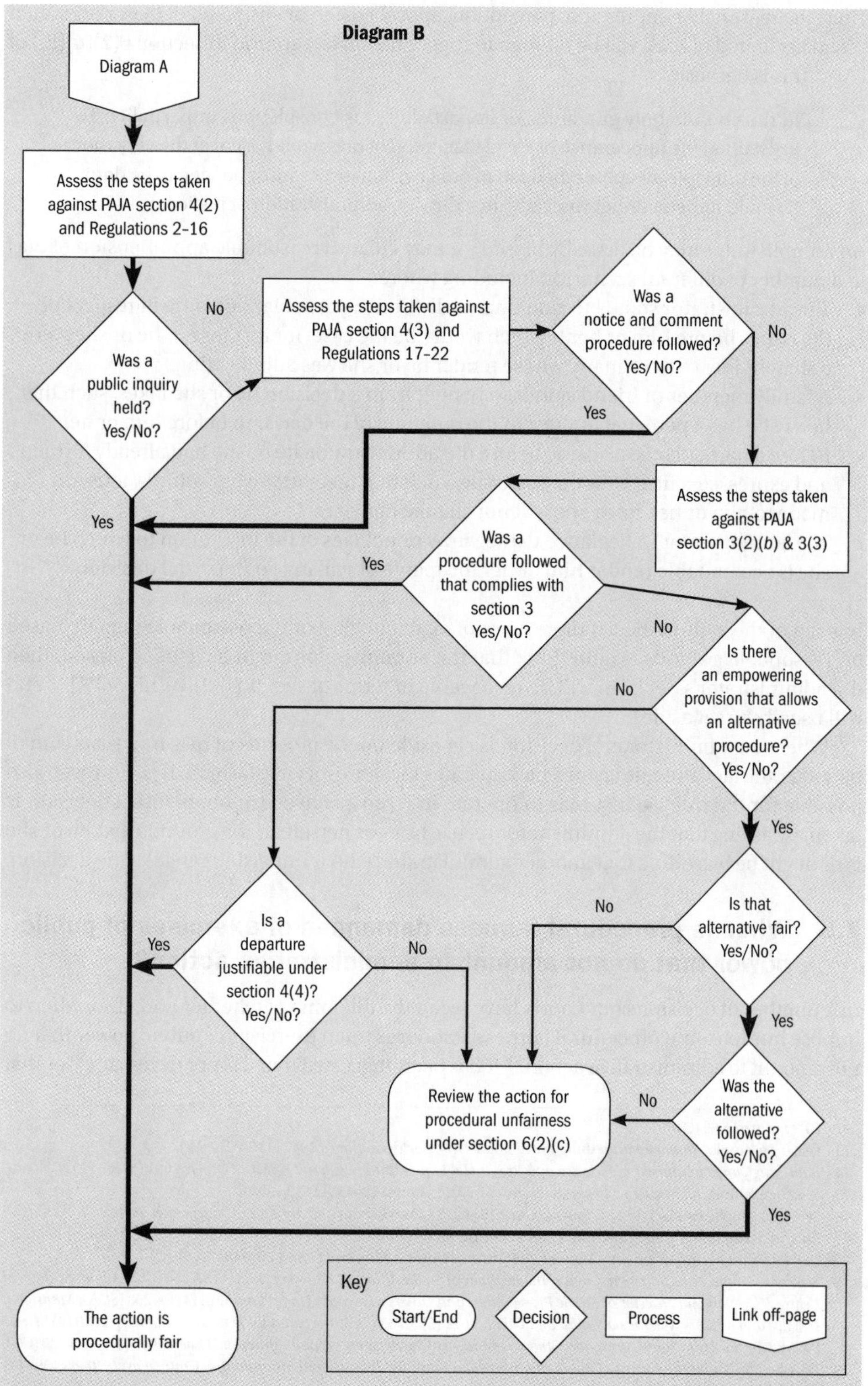


*Figure 7.1 Steps in analysing the procedural fairness of an administrative action: Diagram B*

Thus, the reasonable impression, perception, apprehension or suspicion of bias, rather than 'a real likelihood of bias' will be enough to trigger the review ground in section 6(2)(*a*)(iii) of PAJA. This is because:

> In the end the only guarantee of impartiality ... is conspicuous impartiality. To insist upon the appearance of a real likelihood of bias would ... cut at the very root of the principle, deeply embedded in our law, that justice must be seen to be done. It would impede rather than advance the due administration of justice.[72]

An administrator may be actually biased, or may create a reasonable apprehension of bias in a number of different scenarios, including where:

- The administrator stands to gain financially from a particular outcome in respect of the issues before him or her,[73] which would be the case, for instance, if he or she were a shareholder of a company whose tender he or she was adjudicating.[74]
- A family member or friend stands to benefit from a decision he or she takes, such that he or she has a personal interest in the outcome of the decision before him or her.[75]
- Before a particular issue came before the administrator, he or she had already formed and expressed a firm view on that issue, such that no matter what submissions are made to him or her, he or she will not change her view.[76]
- The administrator's allegiance to the views or policies of the institution to which he or she is accountable render him or her incapable of making an impartial decision.[77]

In each of these situations, if there is proof of actual bias, or if a reasonable person, based on reasonable grounds, would think that the administrator might have been biased, then the administrator's decision will be reviewable in terms of section 6(2)(*a*)(iii) of PAJA, and will usually be set aside.

Where an administrator's decision is set aside on the grounds of bias or a suspicion of bias after the fact, the rule against bias operates in a retrospective fashion. It is, however, also possible for the rule against bias to operate in a prospective fashion, before a decision is taken, by asking that the administrator recuse him- or herself on the grounds that he or she is or might be biased, so that another administrator, who is impartial, can take the decision.

## 7.5 When is procedural fairness demanded of exercises of public power that do not amount to administrative action?

In a number of decisions our courts have faced the dilemma of whether and, if so, when to impose burdensome procedural fairness standards upon exercises of public power that do not amount to administrative action.[78] It has been suggested that it is not necessary,[79] or that

72 *BTR Industries* 694G–694I.

73 See, for example, *Rose v Johannesburg Local Road Transportation Board* 1947 (4) SA 272 (W).

74 *Bam-Mugwanya v Minister of Finance and Provincial Expenditure, Eastern Cape and Others* 2001 (4) SA 120 (C).

75 See, for example, *Liebenberg v Brakpan Liquor Licensing Board* 1944 WLD 52.

76 See, for example, *Patel v Witbank Town Council* 1931 TPD 284; *Hamata and Another v Chairperson, Peninsula Technikon Internal Disciplinary Committee and Others* 2000 (4) SA 621 (C).

77 See, for example, *Ruyobeza and Another v Minister of Home Affairs and Others* 2003 (5) SA 51 (C).

78 See, for example, *Masetlha v President of the Republic of South Africa and Another* 2008 (1) SA 566 (CC); *Albutt*; *Scalabrini Centre SCA*; *National Director of Public Prosecutions and Others v Freedom Under Law* 2014 (4) SA 298 (SCA); *Minister of Defence and Military Veterans v Motau and Others* 2014 (5) SA 69 (CC); *The National Treasury v Kubukeli* 2016 (2) SA 507 (SCA); *Law Society of South Africa and Others v President of the Republic of South Africa and Others* 2019 (3) BCLR 329 (CC).

79 *Fedsure Life Assurance Ltd and Others v Greater Johannesburg Transitional Metropolitan Council and Others* 1999 (1) SA 374 (CC) paras 21–46.

it is not always appropriate,[80] to subject public power that is not administrative action to the rigours of notice and an opportunity to make representations. For instance, conduct that is judicial in nature, usually takes the form of the adjudication of disputes by application of law to facts in a public forum before an impartial decision-maker, such that the demands of procedural fairness are satisfied without having to apply PAJA (that is, it is not necessary to apply PAJA's procedural fairness standards to such conduct). Similarly, most law-making is regulated by a set of procedures contained in the Constitution, such that it is not necessary to impose PAJA's procedures to legislative conduct. Further, law-making typically occurs in a public, deliberative forum, which ensures transparency and accountability.[81]

In relation to conduct that is executive in nature the position is more complex. On the one hand, it may often be undesirable to impose procedural fairness standards on executive conduct, as to do so would fetter the political discretion of the decision-maker,[82] hinder effective governance, or could implicate issues of national security, which would be threatened by the transparency demanded by procedural fairness. For instance, a decision to fire the head of the National Intelligence Agency, arguably ought not to attract a fair hearing, as the decision is political in nature, and implicates issues of national security.[83] On the other hand, executive conduct that entails a decision to grant pardons to political prisoners arguably cannot rationally be taken without affording the victims of the crimes a hearing, and thus arguably ought to attract at least some of the demands of fairness.[84]

In essence, legality demands that all public power must be rationally and lawfully exercised.[85] Although there has been some uncertainty in relation to the requirements of legality, and whether and to what extent legality will require fairness, it is now clear that sometimes, in order to be rational or lawful, exercises of public power that are not administrative action must follow a fair process. For instance, the findings of a commission of inquiry have been set aside on the basis of the principle of legality, including on the basis that the commission did not follow a proper process. [86] The precise content of fairness in these situations remains unclear, however.[87] The Constitutional Court has distinguished between procedural fairness as a requirement for just administrative action, and procedural rationality as follows:

> Procedural fairness has to do with affording a party likely to be disadvantaged by the outcome the opportunity to be properly represented and fairly heard before an adverse decision is rendered. Not so with procedural irrationality. The latter is about testing whether, or ensuring that there is a rational connection between the exercise of power in relation to both process and the decision itself and the purpose sought to be achieved through the exercise of that power.[88]

80 *Masetlha* paras 42 and 77–78.

81 See *Fedsure Life Assurance.*

82 As was the case in *President of RSA v SARFU.*

83 This is arguably the principle reason why in *Masetlha* it was appropriate not to apply the standards of procedural fairness, which is to be contrasted with the reason actually relied upon by the majority of the Constitutional Court, namely that procedural fairness is not an aspect of legality. See further Murcott, M (2013) Procedural Fairness as a Component of Legality: Is a Reconciliation between *Albutt* and *Masetlha* Possible? *SALJ* 130(2):260 at 271–272.

84 This was the court's finding in *Albutt.*

85 See Hoexter, C 'The Rule of Law and the Principle of Legality in South African Administrative Law Today' in Carnelley, M & Hoctor, S (Eds) (2011) *Law, Order and Liberty, Essays in Honor of Tony Mathews* 55.

86 *Corruption Watch and Another v Arms Procurement Commission and Others* [2019] 4 All SA 53 (GP) paras 9–10, 14, 52–70.

87 See Murcott (2013) 269–270.

88 See *Law Society of South Africa and Others* para 64.

Legality imposes a duty to consult, first where the purpose of an exercise of public power cannot rationally be achieved without consultation with those affected by the decision.[89] Second, legality imposes a duty to consult where a failure to consult will amount to a failure to take into account information at the disposal of the decision-maker which ought rationally to be taken into account by the decision-maker.[90] Third, our courts have pointed out that sometimes a statutorily mandated procedure is required to be followed as a prerequisite for the lawful exercise of public power that is not administrative action, and that in such situations, legality will demand that a fair procedure as provided for in statute is followed.[91] At least in these situations, exercises of public power that are not administrative action will attract some of the procedural fairness standards that are typically the preserve of administrative action.

## 7.6 When is procedural fairness demanded of exercises of private power?

Under the common law, the rules of natural justice were sometimes applied in the context of the judicial review of private (as opposed to public) power.[92] Whilst on the face of it a voluntary association is a private body that exercises private power in terms of its constitution, which is a contract with its members, under the common law, punitive or coercive decisions of voluntary associations such as churches and sports clubs had to be not only consistent with their constitutions, but also unbiased and fair, in order to be valid.[93] Even with the introduction of the Constitution, these exercises of private power continue to be subject to review in terms of the common law rules of natural justice, as opposed to section 33 of the Constitution or PAJA. For instance, in *Fortuin v Church of Christ Mission of the Republic of South Africa*[94] the applicant successfully invoked the court's inherent review discretion under the common law to take on review a decision of the Church of Christ Mission of the Republic of South Africa (the church) to 'disfellowship' him from his pastoral duties based on the fact that he had divorced his wife and remarried a couple of months later. The court set aside the decision, ruling that the church was in violation of its own constitution when it failed to afford the applicant a fair process during his 'disfellowshipping', and confirming that the church's decision was subject to the rules of natural justice under the common law. In *Motswana v African National Congress*[95] branch members of the African National Congress (ANC) in the North West Province challenged a decision of the National Executive Committee of the ANC (NEC) to disband or dissolve the North West Province Executive Committee (PEC). The branch members argued that the decision fell to be reviewed and set aside in terms of the common law on the basis that it was procedurally unfair and substantively irrational.[96] The ANC argued that given that the ANC was a political party performing a discretionary function in terms of its own constitution, the court could

89 This was the case in *Albutt* and in *Scalabrini Centre* WCC, where it was held that consultation with those representing the interests of the victims of political crimes and asylum seekers respectively was required by legality.

90 See *Freedom Under Law v National Director of Public Prosecutions and Others* 2014 (1) SA 254 (GNP) paras 127 and 165, where a failure to consult with prosecutors and investigators before discontinuing criminal prosecution against an accused was found to be irrational.

91 See *Motau* which concerned the dismissal of a board member of a parastatal, an executive decision which attracted procedural fairness as demanded by provisions of the Companies Act 71 of 2008.

92 Hoexter (2012) 127–131.

93 *Theron en Andere v Ring van Wellington van die NG Sendingkerk in Suid-Afrika en Andere* 1976 (2) SA 1 (A); *Turner v Jockey Club of South Africa* 1974 (3) SA 633 (A).

94 Unreported, referred to as [2016] ZAECPEHC 18, 5 May 2016 para 17.

95 Unreported, referred to as [2019] ZAGPJHC 4, 6 February 2019.

96 *Motswana* paras 13–14.

only interfere if the ANC had acted capriciously or acted 'on a wrong principle'.[97] Finding in favour of the branch members, the court reasoned that it was 'well established in our law that the principles of natural justice can be implied from the express terms of the contract of a voluntary association'.[98] In this instance, requiring *audi alteram partem* was important, not only to ensure that the leadership of the political party could be provided with an opportunity to obtain information relevant for the proper exercise of its powers, but also to ensure that the political rights provided for in section 19 of the Constitution were fulfilled.[99] The court found that the ANC had failed to uphold the requirements of procedural fairness in a number of respects.[100] Under the circumstances, the court declared that the ANC's decision was unlawful. The court reviewed and set aside the decision and ordered the reinstatement of the disbanded PEC.[101]

## THIS CHAPTER IN ESSENCE

This chapter seeks to describe when and how the standards of procedural fairness as demanded by section 33 of the Constitution will apply to administrative action. It first examines section 3 of PAJA in relation to administrative action affecting a person, and second, section 4 of PAJA in relation to administrative action affecting the public. This chapter further describes the operation of the rule against bias, which is a key component of fair decision-making. Next, this chapter explains the circumstances in which the constitutional principle of legality demands that public power that is not necessarily administrative action will be subject to some of the demands of fairness. Finally, this chapter explains that private power can sometimes be susceptible to the demands of procedural fairness.

## FURTHER READING

- Hoexter, C (2011) 'The Rule of Law and the Principle of Legality in South African Administrative Law Today' in Carnelley, M & Hoctor, S (Eds) (2011) *Law, Order and Liberty, Essays in Honor of Tony Mathews* Scotsville: University of KwaZulu Natal Press 55
- Hoexter, C (2012) *Administrative Law in South Africa* (2nd ed) Cape Town: Juta, specifically Chapter 7: Procedural Fairness
- Murcott, M (2013) Procedural Fairness as a Component of Legality: Is a Reconciliation between *Albutt* and *Masetlha* Possible? *SALJ* 130:260
- Quinot, G (2010) Substantive Reasoning in Administrative-Law Adjudication *Constitutional Court Review* 3:111

97 *Motswana* para 16.
98 *Motswana* para 24.
99 *Motswana* paras 25–26.
100 *Motswana* paras 42–53.
101 *Motswana* para 59.

# Chapter 8

# Reasonableness

*Michael Kidd*

## 8.1 Introduction

Judges are not supposed to decide whether administrative decisions are correct or not. In other words, they are not to decide on the merits of administrative action. This is one of the cornerstones of the distinction between appeal and review. The principal reason for this is the separation of powers doctrine, which requires that different branches of government do not impermissibly intrude into the spheres of operation of other branches. A judge deciding on the merits of administrative action would be seen as an impermissible intrusion by the judiciary into the province of the executive. However, there is a more practical justification underpinning the broad principle of separation of powers. In most cases, judges are not *qualified* to make administrative decisions. They are not, for example, skilled in weighing the numerous facts and policy considerations required in deciding the allocation of fishing rights; issuing of water licences; environmental authorisations or trade licences. They *are,* however, skilled in weighing up evidence and settling disputes. Administrators, on the other hand, are (at least in theory) experts in their respective fields – whether it is immigration or income tax or the running of prisons – and their decisions in these fields ought to be respected by the judiciary for this reason.

The distinction between appeal and review and merits and regularity is not as clear as it might appear at first glance, however.[1] Probably the aspect that is primarily responsible for the blurring of the distinction is reasonableness as a ground of review. There has historically been resistance to permitting judges to decide on the reasonableness of administrative action because of concerns that this would entail judges scrutinising the merits of those decisions. While it is true that deciding whether an administrative decision is reasonable would inevitably involve considering the merits of the decision, it ought not to involve impermissible intrusion into the administrator's discretion, and it does not involve deciding whether the decision is right or wrong. This will be explored in more detail in this chapter.

**REFRAMING**

**What type of energy?**

Imagine that the National Energy Regulator of South Africa (NERSA – a statutory body created to regulate all aspects relating to energy in South Africa) grants a licence to Eskom to build and operate a new nuclear power plant in the Karoo. Likely opposition to such a decision would include arguments in favour of other forms of energy, in particular from renewable energy sources such as solar, wind and water-generated power facilities. How would one go about scrutinising, in legal terms, the reasonableness of NERSA's decision in light of such opposition? Would it, for example, be appropriate to allow a court to ask whether other forms of energy should not rather have been chosen e.g. solar/wind/coal/hydraulic fracturing (fracking)?

A second reason why reasonableness is often controversial is that it does not operate in an absolute fashion. Some grounds of review are either present or they are not; in other words, they operate in an absolute manner. There is either unlawful delegation or there is not. There is either compliance with the mandatory requirements of the empowering legislation or there is not. These are not matters of degree. It is easy to draw a line between what is unlawful and what is not. Reasonableness operates differently, however. Why is this?

1 See Chapter 5 section 5.2 above.

Let us consider the typical challenge to administrative action. A person will decide to challenge administrative action because he or she feels that the action was wrongly decided. In most cases, the affected person will have attempted to challenge the merits (correctness or otherwise) of the decision in an applicable appeal process. Once that avenue is exhausted, however, it is not open to him or her to challenge the merits of the decision in the courts. He or she will have to find some other ground upon which to challenge the decision. If he or she argues that the decision is unreasonable, the court will be faced with determining the reasonableness of the decision in the circumstances of that particular case. In other words, reasonableness is context-specific. The line between what is reasonable and unreasonable will have to be drawn differently depending on the different circumstances of individual cases. There are numerous factors that influence this line-drawing exercise, which are discussed below. It is worth mentioning that one of the most important of these factors is that the judge ought to *respect* the constitutionally ordained functions of the administrator and not lightly interfere in the latter's decision. The idea of respect is discussed in section 8.8.

**PAUSE FOR REFLECTION**

**Different types of unreasonableness cases**

The esteemed English academic Sir Jeffrey Jowell, writing more than 20 years ago, said the following:

> It is possible to discern three categories of case that fall under the general rubric of unreasonableness:
>
> (*a*) Where there has been an extreme defect in the **decision-making process**. The assessment here focuses upon the reasoning or justification for the decision; upon the quality of the argument supporting the decision. We see here: (i) decisions taken in bad faith; (ii) decisions based on considerations wrongly taken into account or ignored, or given inappropriate weight; and (iii) strictly 'irrational' decisions, namely those justified by inadequate evidence or reasoning;
>
> (*b*) Decisions taken in violation of common law **principles governing the exercise of official power**. In the absence of express intent to the contrary, these principles apply even where discretion has been conferred in the widest terms. The principles of (i) equality and (ii) legal certainty fall under this head.
>
> (*c*) **Oppressive decisions** are ones which have an unnecessarily onerous impact on affected persons or where the means employed (albeit for lawful ends) are excessive or disproportionate in their result.[2]

With some minor exceptions relating to the source of some of these observations, it is submitted that these categories would be relevant to the South African law of reasonableness today. Indeed, this passage was quoted with approval in the South African case of *Ehrlich v Minister of Correctional Services and Another*.[3] The categorisation of different forms of unreasonableness in this chapter is different from Jowell's, but it can be seen from the discussion of the various forms of unreasonableness below how the categorisation is consistent with the substance of Jowell's argument.

---

2 Jowell, J 'Judicial Review of the Substance of Official Decisions' in Bennett, TW & Corder, H (Eds) (1993) *Administrative Law Reform* 117–120, emphasis in original. Reprinted by permission of © Juta & Company Ltd.

3 2009 (2) SA 373 (E).

## 8.2 Reasonableness and related grounds of review

Before PAJA, reasonableness sometimes operated as an 'umbrella' concept under which other grounds of review, now individually identified in our law as separate grounds of review, were grouped. This chapter will deal with these grounds of review under the general heading of reasonableness, even though they may have obtained a separate identity, so to speak. The links between the grounds of review, however, will become evident as they are discussed. Ultimately, the concept of reasonableness entails the idea that a decision will be unreasonable if it is a decision that a reasonable decision-maker would not reach.[4] The various grounds briefly outlined below are discussed in detail further on in the chapter but are set out here to indicate what is covered in the chapter and to justify the order in which the concepts are discussed:

- **Symptomatic unreasonableness**. This type of unreasonableness manifests itself due to the presence of another flaw in the decision, usually an abuse of discretion. For example, a decision made with an ulterior purpose is thus unreasonable. We will start with this because it was the primary 'meaning' of unreasonableness under the common law.
- **Rationality**. Traditionally seen as part of reasonableness, this is now separately provided for in PAJA.
- **Proportionality**. Regarded as part of reasonableness in respect of only certain types of administrative action under the common law, this is not provided for explicitly in PAJA, but widely regarded as being covered by the concept of reasonableness.
- **Vagueness**. It is arguable that vagueness is out of place here. It is also not explicitly addressed in PAJA, but it can compellingly be argued that a reasonable decision-maker would not make a decision that is vague. This would justify its inclusion under this heading.
- **Reasonableness generally**. We will explore if there is any residual aspect of reasonableness that is not covered by the concepts listed above. This could also be called reasonableness per se.

## 8.3 Symptomatic unreasonableness

Prior to PAJA, our common-law approach to reasonableness was rather complex. It relied on the so-called classification of functions approach, whereby the test for reasonableness would differ depending on whether the administrative action was legislative, judicial (or quasi-judicial) or 'purely administrative' (that is, any action that fell into neither of the first two categories).[5] The test for 'purely administrative' actions (such as deciding permit applications or deciding to arrest and detain a person) was that set out in the case of *Union Government (Minister of Mines and Industries) Appellants v Union Steel Corporation (South Africa) Ltd Respondents*:[6]

> [N]owhere has it been held that unreasonableness is sufficient ground for interference; emphasis is always laid upon the necessity of the unreasonableness being so gross that something else can be inferred from it, either that it is

4 *Bato Star Fishing (Pty) Ltd v Minister of Environmental Affairs and Others* 2004 (4) SA 490 (CC), discussed in further detail below.

5 See Chapter 1 section 1.3.4.

6 1928 AD 220 at 237.

> 'inexplicable except on the assumption of *mala fides* or ulterior motive' ... or that it amounts to proof that the person on whom the discretion is conferred has not applied his mind to the matter.

**PAUSE FOR REFLECTION**

**Reasonableness under the common law**

Reasonableness under the common law was applied on the basis of a 'classification of functions' approach.

In legislative administrative action (for example, the making of regulations or municipal by-laws), the test for reasonableness was based on the English decision of *Kruse v Johnson*:[7]

> If, for instance, ... [by-laws] were found to be partial and unequal in their operation as between different classes; if they were manifestly unjust; if they disclosed bad faith; if they involved such oppressive or gratuitous interference with the rights of those subject to them as could find no justification in the minds of reasonable men, the Court might well say, 'Parliament never intended to give authority to make such rules; they are unreasonable and *ultra vires*'.

In addition, delegated legislation that was vague or uncertain was also set aside on that basis in various cases.

For judicial administrative action, the test was that laid down in *Theron en Andere v Ring van Wellington van die NG Sendingkerk in Suid-Afrika en Andere*.[8] Such decisions could be declared unreasonable if they are not reasonably supported by the evidence available. It was stressed that this test applied only in 'purely judicial' cases, such as this one (a disciplinary inquiry), involving the same sort of discretion exercised by courts of law.

All other administrative action was reviewable on the basis of gross unreasonableness (discussed in the main text).

Whereas the classification of functions approach was jettisoned by the Appellate Division in respect of procedural fairness before the onset of the constitutional era, there was not a similar decision in respect of reasonableness. The common law would not continue to apply on this basis post-1994 because of the requirements of the Constitution.

Section 33 of the Constitution requires administrative action that is 'lawful, reasonable and procedurally fair'. It is clear that the requirement of 'reasonableness' is not qualified in any way, but the legislature provided for reasonableness in rather a curious manner when it enacted PAJA in 2000:[9] administrative action is reviewable if 'the exercise of the power or the performance of the function authorised by the empowering provision, in pursuance of which the administrative action was purportedly taken, is so unreasonable that no reasonable person could have so exercised the power or performed the function'.[10]

7 [1898] 2 QB 91 99–100.

8 1976 (2) SA 1 (A) 20D–21C.

9 The provision in PAJA may be 'curious', but it is not inexplicable. See De Ville, JR (2005) *Judicial Review of Administrative Action in South Africa* 196–7 and 209–10 and Currie, I (2007) *The Promotion of Administrative Justice Act: A Commentary* (2nd ed) 169–70 for explanation of the drafting history of this clause.

10 PAJA section 6(2)(*h*).

Initially, concern was expressed that this section was remarkably similar to the English test for unreasonableness which has come to be referred to as the *Wednesbury* test after the case of its origin:[11] 'a decision so unreasonable that no reasonable authority could ever come to it'.[12] The problem with this approach would be that it sets the bar for unreasonableness so high that the presence of such unreasonableness would inevitably be accompanied by some other ground of review relating to abuse of discretion (most of which are explicitly provided for in PAJA as grounds of review under section 6),[13] rendering the reasonableness ground of review superfluous. In the light of the Constitutional requirement of reasonableness, it was suggested that the section be interpreted purposively to mean that 'simple' (as opposed to gross) unreasonableness be a ground of review.[14]

It was not long after the enactment of PAJA that the Constitutional Court had an opportunity to provide some clarity on the reasonableness requirement in *Bato Star Fishing (Pty) Ltd v Minister of Environmental Affairs and Others.*[15] O' Regan J, for a unanimous court, citing the English judgment of Lord Cooke in *R v Chief Constable of Sussex, Ex Parte International Trader's Ferry Ltd,*[16] decided that:

> Even if it be thought that the language of section 6(2)(*h*), if taken literally, might set a standard such that a decision would rarely if ever be found unreasonable, that is not the proper constitutional meaning which should be attached to the subsection. The subsection must be construed consistently with the Constitution and in particular section 33 which requires administrative action to be 'reasonable'. Section 6(2)(*h*) should then be understood to require a simple test, namely, that an administrative decision will be reviewable if ... it is one that a reasonable decision-maker could not reach.[17]

This clearly rejects the notion that section 6(2)(*h*) requires gross (or symptomatic) unreasonableness. This test is somewhat circular – a decision is unreasonable if it is one that a reasonable decision-maker could not reach. In other words, the unreasonableness of the decision depends on a decision as to the reasonableness of the decision-maker in the circumstances. The court, however, did provide some pointers, indicating that the determination of a reasonable decision will depend on the circumstances of each case,[18]

---

11 *Associated Provincial Picture Houses Ltd v Wednesbury Corporation* [1948] 1 KB 223 at 230. See Wade, HWR & Forsyth, CF (2014) *Administrative Law* (11th ed) at 302.

12 Hoexter, C with Lyster, R and Currie, I (Eds) (2002) *The New Constitutional and Administrative Law Vol II Administrative Law* 186; Currie, I & Klaaren, J (2001) *The Promotion of Administrative Justice Act Benchbook* 172.

13 In terms of s 6(2), administrative action is reviewable if –
(*e*) the action was taken –
(i) for a reason not authorised by the empowering provision;
(ii) for an ulterior purpose or motive;
(iii) because irrelevant considerations were taken into account or relevant considerations were not considered;
(v) in bad faith; or
(vi) arbitrarily or capriciously;
(*g*) the action concerned consists of a failure to take a decision;
(*i*) the action is otherwise unconstitutional or unlawful.
Unlawful fettering is not expressly provided for in PAJA.

14 Hoexter (2002) 186.

15 2004 (4) SA 490 (CC).

16 [1999] 1 All ER 129 (HL) at 157.

17 *Bato Star Fishing* para 44, references omitted.

18 *Bato Star Fishing* para 45.

and that there are various factors which will be relevant in determining whether a decision is reasonable or not:

- the nature of the decision,
- the identity and expertise of the decision-maker,
- the range of factors relevant to the decision,
- the reasons given for the decision,
- the nature of the competing interests involved, and
- the impact of the decision on the lives and well-being of those affected.[19]

These factors are discussed further below.

For purposes of dispensing with symptomatic unreasonableness, it goes without saying that if the correct test in South African law is what could be called 'simple' unreasonableness, any decision displaying unreasonableness of such a degree that it was indicative of abuse of discretion would be reviewable. Such a decision would not only be reviewable in terms of reasonableness but also by using the individual grounds which collectively make up the abuse of discretion grounds.

## 8.4 Rationality

Even though rationality is not explicitly provided for in the Bill of Rights, it is central to the rule of law: a 'minimum threshold requirement applicable to the exercise of all public power by members of the Executive and other functionaries'.[20] Prior to PAJA, the test for rationality in respect of administrative action was held to be whether there is 'a rational objective basis justifying the connection made by the administrative decision-maker between the material properly available to him and the conclusion he or she eventually arrived at'.[21] The Supreme Court of Appeal confirmed this test, post PAJA, in *Trinity Broadcasting (Ciskei) v Independent Communications Authority of South Africa*.[22] It is important to note that the justification for the connection must be *objectively* rational. This means that a reasonable observer must regard the connection as rational – it is not sufficient if the decision-maker thinks the decision is rational.

### 8.4.1 Rationality under PAJA

PAJA provides that administrative action is reviewable if:

> the action itself is not rationally connected to –
> (*aa*) the purpose for which it was taken;
> (*bb*) the purpose of the empowering provision;
> (*cc*) the information before the administrator; or
> (*dd*) the reasons given for it by the administrator.[23]

19 *Bato Star Fishing* para 45.

20 *Pharmaceutical Manufacturers Association of SA and Another: In Re Ex Parte President of the Republic of South Africa and Others* 2000 (2) SA 674 (CC) para 90.

21 *Carephone (Pty) Ltd v Marcus NO and Others* 1998 (11) BLLR 1093 (LAC) para 37.

22 2004 (3) SA 346 (SCA) para 21.

23 Section 6(2)(*f*)(ii).

This provision envisages four 'connections' or 'links' that must have a rational objective basis, as follows:

- **A rational connection between the decision and the purpose for which it was taken**. The purpose for which the decision was taken would usually be evident from the reasons given for the decision. The purpose would have to be consistent with the purpose of the legislation, or it could be set aside on the basis of ulterior purpose.[24] For example, if the Department of Water and Sanitation indicated in its reason for a decision to grant a water use licence to a white male applicant that the decision had been taken to further the Department's transformation agenda (meaning that there is a goal to produce more black and women water users), this decision would clearly not be rationally connected to the purpose for which it was taken. This would overlap with the fourth type, and would probably also be aimed at those cases where the real purpose would not be explicitly stated in the reasons, but could be inferred from the circumstances (including the reasons actually supplied).
- **A rational connection between the decision and the purpose of the empowering provision**. In the event of such a connection being absent, the decision would probably be reviewable on the basis of ulterior purpose as well. An example would be a decision to authorise the hunting of a rare species of animal for the purpose of generating a large amount of money, when the legislation in terms of which such authorisation was given empowers the decision-maker to take into account only factors relating to the conservation of that species. Another example of this 'basis' of rationality is found in the *Trinity Broadcasting* decision, discussed below.
- **A rational connection between the decision and the information before the administrator**. This is probably the most frequently encountered form of irrationality. 'Information' would include both the evidence before the administrator (the factual material or submissions which the administrator would consider in the process) and the administrator's findings on the evidence.[25] The decision (the conclusion) must be rationally connected to these. There are a number of examples of this type of case discussed below.
- **A rational connection between the decision and the reasons for which it was taken**. This would more than likely refer to the reasons that have been provided to the affected individual. The example given for the first 'connection' would be relevant here too.

There are several cases where rationality has been invoked. In *Trinity Broadcasting (Ciskei) v Independent Communications Authority of South Africa*,[26] several conditions imposed on a broadcasting licence were held to be irrational. Some were found to be so because there was no rational connection between the decision and the information before the administrator. For example, a decision to impose a language breakdown involving a minimum of 40% isiXhosa and Afrikaans collectively was justified by the respondent on the basis that the applicant had undertaken in its application to do so. The court, however, held that there had been no such undertaking, because the applicant had explained that 75% of its content was foreign programming.[27]

24 See Chapter 6 section 6.2.1.1.

25 For more on the meaning of 'information' and 'findings', see Chapter 9 section 9.1 below.

26 2004 (3) SA 346 (SCA) para 21.

27 *Trinity Broadcasting (Ciskei)* para 36. Other irrationality findings relating to the connection with the information are at paras 48 and 50.

The court also found one of the licence conditions irrational because the condition was not rationally connected to the purpose of the empowering provision. The condition requiring compulsory news broadcasts was not required by the applicable Act, which provides that broadcasting services, viewed collectively, must provide for news.[28] This condition was also not rationally connected to the information available (the application).

Other matters in which courts have found no objective rational connection between the facts (information) and the decision are *Radio Pretoria v Chairperson, Independent Communications Authority of South Africa and Another*[29] (the decision was made on the basis of a broadcasting 'target area' different from that for which the applicant had applied) and *Total Computer Services (Pty) Ltd v Municipal Manager, Potchefstroom Local Municipality, and Others*[30] (a tender 'points score' was not justified by the information relating to 'price, company profile, preference and reference sites').[31]

*WWF South Africa v Minister of Agriculture, Forestry and Fisheries*[32] was a particularly striking example of the lack of a rational link between the evidence before the decision-maker and the decision. The Deputy Director-General (DDG) of the respondent Department (DAFF) was responsible for determining the total allowable catch (TAC) of West Coast rock lobster in terms of the Marine Living Resources Act.[33] The decision is supposed to entail a balancing of environmental, economic and social considerations and is advised by a recommendation from the Scientific Working Group (SWG) of the Department. In the face of a critical shortage of stocks (the lobster stocks were at a level of 1,9% of the population before human exploitation), the SWG recommended a large cut in the quota, as it had for several years before this one (2016–2017). Despite the recommendation and the related evidence, the DDG relied on social and economic considerations to decide on a TAC far larger than that recommended. The court, correctly, concluded that, in:

> setting the TAC at the previous season's level of 1 924,08 tons, rather than at a level no higher than 1 167 tons, [the DDG] acted arbitrarily and irrationally, failed to observe the mandated precautionary approach, and made a decision which no reasonable person could have made.[34]

This case is a good example of the overlap between irrationality and unreasonableness.

Another example illustrating this overlap is *FNM v Refugee Appeal Board and Others.*[35] In this case, the Refugee Appeal Board, in the same document, both condoned and refused to condone a late filing of an appeal. This, the court understandably held, was:

> not rationally connected to the reasons given for it, as contemplated in s 6(2)*(f)*(ii)*(dd)* of [PAJA]; and so unreasonable that no reasonable person could have so exercised the power, as contemplated in s 6(2)*(h)* of PAJA.[36]

28 *Trinity Broadcasting (Ciskei)* para 43.
29 2008 (2) SA 164 (SCA).
30 2008 (4) SA 346 (T).
31 *Total Computer Services* para 55.
32 [2018] 4 All SA 889 (WCC).
33 18 of 1998.
34 *WWF South Africa* para 117(g).
35 2019 (1) SA 468 (GP).
36 *FNM* para 44. For further examples, see *Cape Gate (Pty) Ltd and Others v Eskom Holdings (Soc) Ltd and Others* 2019 (4) SA 14 (GJ).

In *Ocean Ecological Adventures (Pty) Ltd v Minister of Environmental Affairs*[37] the irrationality involved the absence of links both between the information before the decision-maker and the purpose of the guiding policy. The decision involved adjudicating bids to award a permit for boat-based whale watching (BBWW). The applicant, an existing permit holder, was unsuccessful and the permit was granted to a new entrant. The problem with the decision was that the official used separate scoring systems for existing permit holders and new entrants, and then considered the applications through the lens of transformation objectives, which had the effect of considering this aspect (transformation) twice in the case of new applicants, which the court found to be irrational.

A case that does not fit into any of the four 'connections' set out above is *Minister of Safety and Security v Moodley*.[38] The Supreme Court of Appeal, in considering the administrator's inflexible application of a policy, stated that:

> The inflexibility ... effectively precluded a proper consideration of Moodley's circumstances. The decision as a result of the Committee's absolute inflexibility is also arguably, on the face of it, irrational and can on that basis alone be impugned.

It has been suggested that the court in this quote found that an inflexible application of policy 'amounted to irrationality'.[39] If this is what the court held, then it is a novel way of applying rationality – essentially that a rational decision cannot be made in the absence of considering all the relevant information. It is not beyond doubt that this is what the court actually meant, since the court states that the decision is *also* irrational, suggesting that this may be a separate holding. This conclusion is not explained, however.

Often the absence of a rational connection will be found by a court without much difficulty, because judges are experienced in the use of logic in order to solve disputes. Sometimes, however, the technical or scientific nature of the information on which the decision is based may make it more difficult for judges, without scientific backgrounds, to assess its connection with the decision. In *SA Predator Breeders Association and Others v Minister of Environmental Affairs and Tourism*,[40] a challenge to regulations purporting to regulate the practice of 'canned lion hunting', the court was prepared to find the regulations irrational. This was, first, because the regulations were not rationally connected to the purposes of the Act. The relevant statutory purpose in this regard was the conservation of endangered or threatened species, and these regulations had not been made with that end in mind.[41] The second reason was that the regulations envisaged lawful hunting of lions once a period of 24 months had elapsed after a captive-bred lion had been rehabilitated. Not only did the 24-month period have no foundation in the facts, but the expert opinion relied upon by the court suggested that it was highly unlikely that such lions would ever be rehabilitated. Consequently, there was no rational connection between the information and the decision.[42] It is submitted that the link in this case between the 'scientific' fact and the administrator's conclusion was relatively straightforward for a non-scientist to assess.

Two decisions in a single matter relating to the granting of fishing rights may not have been justified, however. In *Foodcorp (Pty) Ltd v Deputy Director-General, Department of*

37 (6744/2018) [2019] ZAWCHC 42.

38 [2011] 4 All SA 47 (SCA). See also *Samons v Turnaround Management Association Southern Africa NPC and Another* 2019 (2) SA 596 (GJ), where the rationale for the court's finding of rationality is not clear from the judgment.

39 Quinot, G (2011) Administrative Law *Annual Survey of South African Law* 49 at 53.

40 [2011] 2 All SA 529 (SCA).

41 *SA Predator Breeders Association* para 45.

42 *SA Predator Breeders Association* para 45. Note that the court did not explicitly rely on PAJA for this decision.

*Environmental Affairs and Tourism: Branch Marine and Coastal Management and Others,*[43] the court was considering a challenge to the allocation of fishing rights based on the application of a mathematical formula by the respondent authority. In the light of certain 'glaring anomalies' that the court identified in the allocation decisions, it concluded (on the basis of a reasonableness argument) that:

> One does not need to understand the 'complex processes, mathematical or otherwise' ... to realise that at least some of the results produced by the simple application of the formula were irrational and inexplicable and consequently unreasonable.[44]

The court does not explain further on what basis the decision was irrational. Seemingly on its reasoning process, the irrationality arose because of the lack of what it regarded as a rational connection between the rights allocated in the previous rights allocation process and the one under scrutiny in this case. This conceivably falls under a link between the information and the decision. The court did not refer to the rationality provision in PAJA, but rather the reasonableness one (section 6(2)(*h*)).

Because of this adverse decision, the Department made a new decision, using a revised mathematical formula. This new allocation was also challenged and, once again, the court found it irrational. Relying on section 6(2)(*h*), the court held that the new decision was 'no less irrational, inexplicable and unreasonable' than the first one and set it aside as well.[45] It has been argued that these decisions failed to appreciate the scientific rationale for the decisions and that the allocations were, in fact, not irrational.[46] If this argument is correct, it suggests that courts ought to be cautious in interfering with administrative decisions that are technically complex, without at least adequate explanation of the process (which seems to have been absent in this case).

**PAUSE FOR REFLECTION**

**The relationship between rationality and reasonableness**

Willis J in *Thebe Ya Bophelo Healthcare Administrators (Pty) Ltd and Others v National Bargaining Council for the Road Freight Industry and Another*[47] observed that it seemed to him that 'in regard to administrative action, at least, the Constitutional Court may have taken the decision to suffuse "rationality" into "reasonableness"'. He based this observation on the fact that the Constitutional Court in the case of *Sidumo and Another v Rustenberg Platinum Mines Ltd and Others*[48] declined to decide the matter on the basis of rationality, which had been the basis of the decision in the same case in the Supreme Court of Appeal.[49] The reason for this is that the Constitutional Court did not categorise the matter as qualifying as administrative action, and consequently had to deal with the issue under applicable labour legislation that did not provide for rationality as a ground of review.

CONTINUED >>>

43 2006 (2) SA 191 (SCA).

44 *Foodcorp* para 203.

45 *Foodcorp (Pty) Ltd v Deputy Director-General, Department of Environmental Affairs and Tourism: Branch Marine and Coastal Management and Others* 2006 (2) SA 199 (C) para 209.

46 Butterworth, D, De Oliviera, JAA & De Moor, CL (2012) Are South African Administrative Law Procedures Adequate for the Evaluation of Issues Resting on Scientific Analyses? *SALJ* 129(3):461.

47 2009 (3) SA 187 (W) para 23.

48 2008 (2) SA 24 (CC).

49 *Rustenburg Platinum Mines Ltd (Rustenburg Section) v Commission for Conciliation, Mediation and Arbitration* 2007 (1) SA 576 (SCA).

Willis J's observation may lead one to ask what the difference is between reasonableness and rationality. First, the two grounds of review are explicitly provided for, separately, in PAJA: rationality in section 6(2)(*f*)(ii) and reasonableness in section 6(2)(*h*). Second, the two concepts do not mean the same thing conceptually. It is probably correct to note that rationality is a subset of reasonableness. This is because an irrational decision will inevitably be a decision that a reasonable decision-maker could not reach. An irrational decision will never be reasonable. The converse, however, is not true. A decision may be rational and yet still unreasonable for at least two reasons: either on the basis of proportionality or on the basis of infringing the right to equality. Unreasonableness may also manifest itself as a symptom of abuse of discretion, but most cases involving abuse of discretion would probably fall foul of the rationality test as well.

In short, rationality is part of reasonableness but reasonableness covers other concepts as well. The fact that both grounds of review are provided for in PAJA means that rationality should be specifically invoked where a decision's rationality is in question, rather than relying on the broader ground of unreasonableness.

### 8.4.2 Rationality and legality

It is well-established that the principle of legality requires decisions of public authorities, even if not administrative action under PAJA, to be rational. The courts have applied so-called rationality review in a number of such cases.[50] It seems clear that there is some inconsistency in the way in which this has been applied and, consequently, some concerns have been expressed about the possible erosion of the separation of powers doctrine by some of these judgments.[51] Further discussion of this aspect, other than the topic covered in the next section, is beyond the scope of this work. It is worth noting that the concept of rationality invoked in a legality review as opposed to one under PAJA is different to the concept under PAJA and has been described as 'a narrow one, not necessarily the same as that applied in a review under s 6(2)(*f*)(ii) of PAJA'.[52]

### 8.4.3 Rationality of process

The rationality provision in PAJA[53] focuses on the decision of the administrator.[54] A question that has arisen is whether review of the rationality of a decision can (or must) include the consideration of the rationality of the process taken in reaching that decision. This question has been answered in the affirmative (albeit wrongly) by the Constitutional Court in *National Energy Regulator of South Africa and Another v PG Group (Pty) Limited and Others.*[55]

50 See, for example, *Merafong Demarcation Forum and Others v President of the Republic of South Africa and Others* 2008 (5) SA 171 (CC); *Zealand v Minister of Justice and Constitutional Development and Another* 2008 (4) SA 458 (CC); *Albutt v Centre for the Study of Violence and Reconciliation and Others* 2010 (3) SA 293 (CC); *Poverty Alleviation Network and Others v President of the Republic of South Africa and Others* 2010 (6) BCLR 520 (CC); *Judicial Service Commission and Another v Cape Bar Council and Another* 2013 (1) SA 170 (SCA); *Democratic Alliance v The President of the Republic of South Africa and Others* 2013 (1) SA 248 (CC).

51 See Du Plessis, M & Scott, S (2013) The Variable Standard of Rationality Review: Suggestions for Improved Legality Jurisprudence *SALJ* 130(3):597; Kohn, L (2013) The Burgeoning Constitutional Requirement of Rationality and the Separation of Powers: Has Rationality Review Gone too Far? *SALJ* 130(4):810.

52 *Minister of Defence and Another v Xulu* 2018 (6) SA 460 (SCA) para 50.

53 Section 6(2)(*f*)(ii).

54 The subsection itself speaks of 'action', but 'action' is defined in section 1 as a decision.

55 2019 ZACC 28.

This case involved the setting of a maximum gas price in terms of the Gas Act.[56] The National Energy Regulator (NERSA) is required to set a maximum price of gas in a situation where the seller of gas has a monopoly (as in this case in respect of Sasol Gas, the second respondent). The purpose of this power is for NERSA to set a price that equates as far as possible with the price that would be charged in a competitive market.

In the Supreme Court of Appeal,[57] the court found that NERSA's price determination was irrational because, in essence, the price determined was higher than the monopolistic price that the determination process was intended to adjust, let alone one which would mimic a competitive market.

On appeal to the Constitutional Court, the majority[58] largely agreed with the result (the price determination was irrational) but for different reasons. Following the decision in *Democratic Alliance v President of the Republic of South Africa*[59] (a decision based on legality, not on PAJA), the court proceeded on the basis that it may not 'separate process rationality and substantive rationality' because it must determine 'whether the means (including the process of making a decision) are linked to the purpose or ends'.[60] This, the court held, is the case in dealing with rationality under PAJA 'or anywhere else'.[61] In *Democratic Alliance*, the court had stated:

> The means for achieving the purpose for which the power was conferred must include everything that is done to achieve the purpose. Not only the decision employed to achieve the purpose, but also everything done in the process of taking that decision, constitutes means towards the attainment of the purpose for which the power was conferred.[62]

The majority in *NERSA* were of the view that the central shortcoming of NERSA's decision had been the latter's failure to take into account Sasol's marginal costs in its determination. Such a flaw may easily be addressed by means of the ground of review requiring an administrator to take into account relevant considerations, but the court used the notion of procedural rationality (previously used only in legality cases) to address this defect. This reasoning has been criticised as being contrary to the clear provisions of PAJA. There is no linking of the finding of irrationality by the majority in *NERSA* and the provisions of section 6(2)(*f*)(ii) of PAJA.[63] It is also not necessary to use procedural rationality (whereas it might be in a legality review), because there is an available ground of review in PAJA already. It would appear, though, that this decision will now be binding.

If this is the case, the test for procedural rationality set out in *Democratic Alliance* will be relevant in PAJA cases too. The test involves:

> a three-stage enquiry ...when a court is faced with an executive decision where certain factors were ignored. The first is whether the factors ignored are relevant; the second requires us to consider whether the failure to consider the material concerned (the means) is rationally related to the purpose for which the power

56 48 of 2001.

57 *PG Group (Pty) Ltd v National Energy Regulator of South Africa* [2018] ZASCA 56.

58 Majority judgment delivered by Khampepe J, Jafta J dissenting.

59 [2012] ZACC 24.

60 *NERSA* para 48.

61 *NERSA* para 48.

62 *Democratic Alliance* para 36.

63 See the minority judgment of Jafta J in *NERSA* paras 94–120 and Tsele, M (2019) Rationalising Judicial Review: Towards Refining the "Rational Basis" Review Test(s) *SALJ* 136(2):328 at 359–360.

> was conferred; and the third, which arises only if the answer to the second stage of the enquiry is negative, is whether ignoring relevant facts is of a kind that colours the entire process with irrationality and thus renders the final decision irrational.[64]

Yacoob J in this passage clearly envisages this approach applying to an 'executive decision', and this view is supported by the discussion in the judgment containing this passage. The unfortunate precedent set in *NERSA* may be avoided by reliance on the ground relating to relevant and irrelevant considerations; rationality need not be invoked in such cases.

### 8.4.4 Rationality and common-law review

Private acts carried out by private bodies are not subject to review under PAJA because the act would not qualify as administrative action.[65] Disciplinary hearings carried out by private bodies have for some time under the common law been subject to the requirements of procedural fairness.[66] In *National Horseracing Authority of Southern Africa v Naidoo and Another,*[67] the majority extended this principle with reference to section 39 of the Constitution and held that such decisions are subject to the requirements of rationality as well. On the facts, the court held that the decision was rationally connected to the evidence.

## 8.5 Proportionality

Not only is proportionality 'inherent in the Bill of Rights',[68] but it 'will always be a significant element of reasonableness', stated Sachs J in *Minister of Health and Another NO v New Clicks South Africa (Pty) Ltd and Others (Treatment Action Campaign and Another as Amici Curiae).*[69] Jowell argued that one category of unreasonableness consists of 'oppressive decisions ... which have an unnecessarily onerous impact on affected persons or where the means employed (albeit for lawful ends) are excessive or disproportionate in their result'.[70] Proportionality is not explicitly provided for in PAJA (although in earlier drafts of the Act it was), but if proportionality were not regarded as part of reasonableness, the latter concept, provided for in section 6(2)(*h*), would not cover much. This is because rationality is covered separately (as described above) and symptomatic unreasonableness is largely redundant because the flaws on which this concept are based are all separately provided for as well.[71] The statements in *Bato Star Fishing* also support the idea that reasonableness review in terms of PAJA also includes proportionality.

In that case, the Constitutional Court set out various factors that would be relevant in determining whether a decision is reasonable or not.[72] Two of these factors are relevant to the concept of proportionality. The first is the 'nature of the competing interests involved'. If the court must consider the competing interests involved, it will invariably take into account the extent to which the decision impacts on the interests of affected individuals, which is the second of the two *Bato Star Fishing* factors relevant in this regard: 'the impact

64 *Democratic Alliance* para 39.
65 See Chapter 1 sections 1.2.1.5, 1.3.2; Chapter 2 section 2.5; Chapter 3 sections 3.6.2, 3.7.2, 3.7.3.
66 See *Turner v Jockey Club of South Africa* 1974 (3) SA 633 (A).
67 2010 (3) SA 182 (N).
68 *Minister of Public Works and Others v Kyalami Ridge Environmental Association and Another (Mukhwevho Intervening)* 2001 (3) SA 1151 (CC) para 101.
69 2006 (2) SA 311 (CC) para 637.
70 Quote appearing in box above, section 8.1.
71 See discussion above in section 8.3.
72 See the discussion below in section 8.8.1.

of the decision on the lives and well-being of those affected'. This raises the possibility of proportionality being seen as part of reasonableness under PAJA. Proportionality has been described by an English court as follows: 'a measure which interferes with a ... human right must not only be authorized by law but must correspond to a pressing social need and go no further than strictly necessary in a pluralistic society to achieve its permitted purpose; or, more shortly, must be appropriate and necessary to its legitimate aim'.[73] In other words, oppressive decisions may be 'impugned ... because of the unnecessarily onerous impact they have on the rights or interests of persons affected by them'.[74] More prosaically, proportionality can be seen as the proposition that 'one ought not to use a sledgehammer to crack a nut'.[75]

Hoexter describes the status of proportionality as a ground of review in South African law as 'controversial'.[76] In assessing how proportionality may operate in South African administrative law, the use of the concept in the courts will be considered, followed by an evaluation, conceptually, of how the principle may be applied.

### 8.5.1 Proportionality in South African courts

*Roman v Williams NO*[77] was, according to De Ville, the first case that explicitly recognised proportionality as an 'unqualified requirement for valid administrative action'.[78] The court, applying the requirements of the interim Constitution, stated that administrative action 'in order to qualify as justifiable in relation to the reasons given must meet the three requirements of suitability, necessity and proportionality'.[79] The judgment itself does not explain these aspects further and the administrative action under challenge was held to be valid without express application of this 'test' for proportionality.

In *Bel Porto School Governing Body and Others v Premier, Western Cape and Another*,[80] the minority of Mokgoro J and Sachs J stated that the 'right to administrative action that is justifiable in relation to the reasons given incorporates the principle of proportionality'.[81] This judgment also explicitly refers to the requirement of the 'suitability and necessity' of the decision as being relevant to a determination of whether the decision is justifiable.[82] The judges added that it 'might be relevant to consider whether or not there are manifestly less restrictive means to achieve the purpose'.[83]

In *Schoonbee and Others v MEC for Education, Mpumalanga and Another*,[84] the MEC's decision to suspend a School Governing Body (SGB) and the principal and deputy was under challenge. The court held, *inter alia*, that:

> there is no proportionality between the acts or conduct of the SGB which in the view of the second respondent compelled him to take certain administrative action on the one side and the administrative action which was actually taken; the action

73 *B v Secretary of State for the Home Department* [2000] UKHRR 498 (CA).
74 Woolf, H et al (2013) *De Smith's Judicial Review* (7th ed) 600.
75 Hoexter, C (2012) *Administrative Law in South Africa* (2nd ed) 344.
76 Hoexter (2012) 344.
77 1997 (2) SACR 754 (C).
78 De Ville (2005) 207.
79 *Roman v Williams NO* 765C.
80 2002 (3) SA 265 (CC).
81 *Bel Porto School Governing Body* para 162. This, of course, refers to the right to administrative justice in the interim Constitution.
82 *Bel Porto School Governing Body* para 165.
83 *Bel Porto School Governing Body* para 165.
84 2002 (4) SA 877 (T).

> of the wielder of power in dissolving the SGB is disproportionate to the conduct which was intended to be corrected or the result aimed at.[85]

This was part of the reason why the court found in favour of the applicants.

In *Ehrlich v Minister of Correctional Services and Another*,[86] Plasket J expressly mentioned proportionality in the judgment as, first, being a 'constitutional foundation'[87] and as 'embedded' in section 6(2)(*h*) of PAJA,[88] ultimately holding that the decision of the administrator to stop a karate development programme in a prison was:

> *disproportionate in the sense that it has entirely destroyed the* ... programme when, by simply ensuring that the programme was supervised by his staff, as he was required to do all along, it could have proceeded as before. In this sense the decision was what Professor Jowell called oppressive in that its impact on the karate development programme's participants was unduly and unjustifiably onerous.[89]

In *Medirite v South African Pharmacy Council*,[90] Leach JA linked the statement in *Bato Star* relating to 'the impact of the decision on the lives and well-being of those affected' (discussed above) to proportionality. The court found that the respondent's amendment to the Rule of Good Pharmacy Practice requiring supermarkets that contained pharmacies to demarcate the latter from the rest of the supermarket by means of a floor-to-ceiling wall to be 'wholly disproportional to the end it sought to achieve'.[91] This conclusion was facilitated by the respondent's concession that there were other less invasive alternatives available.[92] The court clearly located the idea of proportionality within section 6(2)(*h*) of PAJA.[93]

These judgments invoked proportionality explicitly. As Plasket notes, proportionality has been recognised 'sometimes expressly and sometimes implicitly'.[94] In *South African Shore Angling Association and Another v Minister of Environmental Affairs*,[95] regulations prohibiting the use of off-road vehicles on the sea shore were under challenge. The grounds of review raised included an argument that the effect (impact) of the ban on the applicants' use and enjoyment of the coastal zone was unreasonable.[96] Although the term 'proportionality' is not used at all in the judgment, this was essentially a proportionality argument. The court, however, found that the regulations were not unreasonable on this ground because 'the impact is softened by various and wide-ranging automatic exemptions'.[97]

Another case in which the term 'proportionality' was not used was *Ferucci and Others v Commissioner, South African Revenue Service and Another*,[98] an application relating to a search and seizure warrant issued in terms of the Income Tax Act[99] and the Value-Added Tax

85 *Schoonbee* 885E.
86 2009 (2) SA 373 (E).
87 *Ehrlich* para 11.
88 *Ehrlich* para 42.
89 *Ehrlich* para 43, referring to the Jowell quote in the box above, section 8.1.
90 [2015] ZASCA 27.
91 *Medirite* para 22.
92 *Medirite* para 22.
93 *Medirite* para 20. See Plasket, C (2019) Disproportionality — The hidden ground of review: *Medirite (Pty) Ltd v South African Pharmacy Council & Another SALJ* 136(1):15 at 26.
94 Plasket, C 'Administrative Justice in South Africa: A Snapshot Survey of Developments Since 1994' in Kidd, M & Hoctor, S (Eds) (2010) *Stella Iuris: Celebrating 100 Years of Teaching Law in Pietermaritzburg* 205–224.
95 2002 (5) SA 511 (SE).
96 *South African Shore Angling Association* 522H.
97 *South African Shore Angling Association* 525G.
98 2002 (6) SA 219 (C).
99 58 of 1962.

Act.[100] Relying on section 36 of the Constitution, specifically that fundamental rights in the Bill of Rights may be limited only to the extent that such limitation is reasonable and justifiable having regard, *inter alia*, to the availability of less restrictive means to achieve the purpose in question, the court was of the view that 'the contention that a search and seizure should not be permitted where the objective sought to be achieved thereby could be attained by other less drastic means is, generally speaking, correct'.[101] Consequently, the court held that a judge issuing a warrant in terms of the two Acts in question 'should consider whether one of the less drastic mechanisms contained in those Acts could not be utilised in order to attain the objective sought'.[102] Once again, proportionality was the basis of this decision without being expressly referred to.

In the unanimous Constitutional Court judgment in *Bato Star Fishing*,[103] O' Regan J observed that:

> Often a power will identify a goal to be achieved, but will not dictate which route should be followed to achieve that goal. In such circumstances a Court should pay due respect to the route selected by the decision-maker. This does not mean, however, that where the decision is one which will not reasonably result in the achievement of the goal, or which is not reasonably supported on the facts or not reasonable in the light of the reasons given for it, a Court may not review that decision.

The comment that a court should pay 'due respect' to the 'route selected by the decision maker' would be relevant in the context of deciding whether there were less onerous means to achieve the statutory purpose. The court does, however, open the door to proportionality (bearing in mind that earlier statements in the same judgment did more than merely open the door) by suggesting that a decision that does not 'reasonably result in the achievement of the goal' is open to review. A disproportionate decision would meet this description.

This discussion indicates that proportionality has played a role in judicial decision-making in the post-1994 era. None of these judgments, however, has spelt out a test for proportionality or what the requirements for such a test should be. The closest a court came to this was in *Roman v Williams NO*, where the court simply listed the requirements (for reasonableness) of suitability, necessity and proportionality, without more.

In the next section, the question of what such a test might look like is considered.

### 8.5.2 A test for proportionality in South African administrative law?

De Ville suggests that proportionality is usually said to entail three enquiries:

(*a*) was the measure in question suitable or effective to achieve the desired aim;
(*b*) was the measure necessary in the sense that no lesser form of interference with the rights of a person was possible in order to achieve the desired aim (such alternative measure being equally effective to the measure taken);

---

100 89 of 1991.
101 *Ferucci* 235B.
102 *Ferucci* 235G.
103 *Bato Star Fishing* para 48.

(c) does the measure (even though it may be suitable and necessary) not place an excessive burden on the individual which is disproportionate in relation to the public interest at stake? [104]

These three enquiries appear to equate with the three aspects mentioned in *Roman v Williams NO*. Hoexter, on the other hand, suggests that there are three 'essential elements' of proportionality: balance, necessity and suitability.[105] Suitability refers to 'lawful and appropriate means' and would be equivalent, in essence, to De Ville's first enquiry set out above. Necessity would be De Ville's second, and his third could be described as balance. In English law, 'balance' is expressed to involve (in this context), 'whether there has been a disproportionate *interference* with the claimant's rights or interests'.[106] This is substantively the same notion as that in the third of De Ville's inquiries.

The cases that were discussed above do not provide much, if any, guidance as to how these three elements of proportionality apply. In those cases where administrative action was found to be disproportionate (expressly or in effect), there is no explicit reference or application of these three elements. In *Schoonbee* [107] the decision was made on the basis of necessity only: 'it is not necessary to dissolve the entire school governing body in order to be able to raise and deal with, as the second respondent wanted to, the matters or accounting concerns raised by the report of the auditor-general'.[108] In *Ehrlich*[109] the decision was set aside because it was 'oppressive'. The court's observation that the object could have been achieved by less onerous means ties in with the idea of necessity. In *Ferucci*[110] the court set aside the decision on the basis that less onerous alternative measures were available. Once again, this is the test of necessity. In not one of these cases were the other elements invoked, certainly not expressly. Does proportionality require all three elements to be satisfied and, if so, is there a hierarchy of the elements?

In European Community Law, the so-called 'structured proportionality' test requires the first question to be whether the measure under challenge is suitable to attaining the identified ends (the test of suitability), which includes the question of whether there is a rational connection between means and ends.[111] The second step is the test of necessity: whether the measure is necessary and whether a less onerous alternative method could have been used. The test of necessity in this context requires 'minimum impairment of the right or interest in question'.[112] If both of these tests are satisfied, then the court considers whether the measure attains a 'fair balance of means and ends'.[113] In these cases, the onus rests on the public authority to justify the measure. This would be different from a challenge to administrative action under PAJA using proportionality (reasonableness), where the applicant would bear the onus of satisfying the court that the decision was unreasonable. South African courts have not adopted such a three-part test, however, and it is not clear

104 De Ville (2005) 203. Reprinted by permission of © LexisNexis. De Ville essentially reinforces this at 206, where he observes that 'a court can ... test administrative action with regard to its effectiveness (in achieving its purpose), less restrictive means to achieve the desired purpose and the appropriate balance to be achieved between the different interests affected'.

105 Hoexter (2012) 344.

106 Woolf et al (2013) 585.

107 2002 (4) SA 877 (T).

108 *Schoonbee* 885D.

109 2009 (2) SA 373 (E).

110 2002 (6) SA 219 (C).

111 Woolf et al (2013) 587.

112 Woolf et al (2013) 587.

113 Woolf et al (2013) 587.

whether such a test would be appropriate if the applicant bore the onus of satisfying it. In summary, our current jurisprudence does not indicate precisely how the three elements of proportionality apply.

A further matter to consider is that De Ville also suggests that in cases of administrative action that do not infringe 'fundamental rights':

> it becomes more difficult to make out a strong argument for the application of the principle of proportionality. The balancing required as part of the proportionality exercise and the consideration of alternative policy choices simply cannot be done effectively in every case involving the exercise of administrative discretion. The courts do not have the required expertise, knowledge and training to do this in every administrative law case. ... [T]he courts will necessarily be hesitant in judging the appropriateness of decisions involving social and economic policy and in other instances where they do not have comparable experience.[114]

If proportionality is applicable, says De Ville, it can be applied 'with different standards of scrutiny'.[115] The standards used will depend on a variety of factors, including the 'nature of the power and the objects to be achieved by its exercise, the specific rights or interests affected and the relative expertise of the court as compared to that of the decision-maker'.[116] These observations are, however, relevant to the application of reasonableness generally, not just proportionality and echo, in essence, statements to similar effect by the Constitutional Court in *Bato Star Fishing*.[117] This is discussed in more detail in section 8.8 below.

**COUNTER POINT**

**Confining proportionality review**

As noted above, De Ville argues that proportionality review should be confined to instances where administrative action infringes on fundamental rights. However, one can argue that if courts show appropriate respect for administrative decisions, then it is not necessary to confine proportionality review to cases involving infringement of fundamental rights, as De Ville prefers. The nature of the right or interest being adversely affected by the administrative action is one of several relevant factors to take into account by a court in deciding whether to interfere with such a decision, as will be seen from the discussion below in section 8.8. Elevating the infringement of a right to a single decisive factor in deciding whether to apply proportionality or not is not justified. Proportionality may well be justified in cases not involving infringement of rights if the other applicable factors support it.

One final aspect to note about proportionality is one that has not been expressly invoked by South African courts, but is likely to be relevant to the ground of review of relevant and irrelevant considerations.[118] Despite the Supreme Court of Appeal's holding in *MEC for Environmental Affairs and Development Planning v Clairison's CC*[119] that it 'has always been the law, and we see no reason to think that PAJA has altered the position that the weight or

114 De Ville (2005) 205–206. Reprinted by permission of © LexisNexis. Currie (2007) 172 seems to agree with this.
115 De Ville (2005) 206.
116 De Ville (2005) 206.
117 See *Bato Star Fishing*.
118 PAJA section 6(2)(*e*)(iii).
119 2013 (6) SA 235 (SCA).

lack of it to be attached to the various considerations that go to making up a decision, is that given by the decision-maker',[120] the court may indeed consider the relative weight of the considerations taken into account. In one of the leading cases dealing with this, *Bangtoo Bros and Others v National Transport Commission and Others*,[121] the court stated:

> Take a case, for example, where a factor which is obviously of paramount importance is relegated to one of insignificance, and another factor, though relevant, is given weight far in excess of its true value. Accepting that the tribunal is the sole judge of the facts, can it be said that it has in the circumstances postulated properly applied its mind to the matter in the sense required by law? After much anxious consideration I have come to the conclusion that the answer must be in the negative.[122]

Proportionality is relevant to this assessment in that the courts 'evaluate whether manifestly disproportionate weight has been attached to one or other considerations relevant to the decision'.[123]

**PAUSE FOR REFLECTION**

**English law and oppressive decisions**

English law distinguishes between, on the one hand, oppressive decisions as a category of unreasonableness and, on the other, proportionality as essentially a separate ground of review, even though they operate very similarly. Administrative decisions may be held to be 'unreasonable when they are unduly oppressive because they subject the complainant to an excessive hardship or an unnecessarily onerous infringement of his rights or interests'.[124] This clearly is concerned with the impact of the decision and not with the way in which the decision was reached. An argument that a decision is oppressive is essentially a claim of 'abuse of power, in the sense of excessive use of power'.[125] Because of this, every case must be considered 'in the context of the nature of the decision, the function of the particular power and the nature of the interests or rights affected'.[126]

Woolf et al provide various illustrative categories of oppressive decisions: those that impose an uneven burden (which may relate also to the question of equality, discussed below), those for which implementation is impossible, and a decision which has been unreasonably delayed.[127] The latter example is now expressly provided for as a ground of review in PAJA.[128]

Oppressive decisions would, it is submitted, be addressed by the 'balance' requirement of proportionality in South African law.

120 *MEC for Environmental Affairs and Development Planning v Clairison's CC* 2013 (6) SA 235 (SCA) para 20.
121 1973 (4) SA 667 (N).
122 *Bangtoo Bros* 685D.
123 Woolf et al (2013) 585 (emphasis omitted).
124 Woolf et al (2013) 578.
125 Woolf et al (2013) 579.
126 Woolf et al (2013) 579.
127 Woolf et al (2013) 579–584.
128 See Chapter 6 section 6.2.1.2.

## 8.6 Vagueness

Under the common law, even though vagueness was not mentioned in the grounds of reasonableness review applicable to legislative administrative action,[129] clarity was regarded as a requirement of delegated legislation. The courts extended this requirement in one case to a notice requiring a person to behave in a particular way (a 'banning order').[130]

Post 1994, the Constitutional Court has rightly stressed that the legislature 'is under a duty to pass legislation that is reasonably clear and precise, enabling citizens and officials to understand what it expected of them'.[131] In light of this, the courts have made it clear that 'the doctrine of vagueness is based on the rule of law':[132]

> [L]aws must be written in a clear and accessible manner. What is required is reasonable certainty and not perfect lucidity. The doctrine of vagueness does not require absolute certainty of laws. The law must indicate with reasonable certainty to those who are bound by it what is required of them so that they may regulate their conduct accordingly. The doctrine of vagueness must recognise the role of government to further legitimate social and economic objectives. And should not be used unduly to impede or prevent the furtherance of such objectives.[133]

Vagueness as a ground of review is not mentioned specifically in PAJA. It could be regarded as being covered by section 6(2)(*i*), which deals with action reviewable because it is 'otherwise unconstitutional or unlawful'.[134] Alternatively, and consistently with the common law, it could be regarded as encompassed by the concept of reasonableness. Jowell regards it as being a type of unreasonableness (his reference to 'legal certainty')[135] and it is difficult to argue against the idea that a reasonable decision-maker would not make a decision that is vague. The statements at the beginning of this section would suggest that vagueness is a concept that is relevant only in respect of legislation, but it goes further than that: it would apply to all administrative decisions which require persons to act in a particular way. Delegated legislation (assuming it is administrative action, which is not beyond doubt)[136] would be the obvious arena in which clarity would be important. However, there are numerous other types of decision that require clarity as well. Legislation might provide for administrators to issue directives (or similar notices) to persons requiring them to take specified steps in order to comply with the law.[137] Moreover, most permits, licences or other

129 See section 8.3 above, and the grounds set out in *Kruse v Johnson*.

130 *S v Meer and Another* 1981 (1) SA 739 (N).

131 *Investigating Directorate: Serious Economic Offences and Others v Hyundai Motor Distributors (Pty) Ltd and Others: In Re Hyundai Motor Distributors (Pty) Ltd and Others v Smit NO and Others* 2001 (1) SA 545 (CC) para 24. See also, for similar sentiments, *President of the Republic of South Africa and Another v Hugo* 1997 (4) SA 1 (CC) para 102; *Dawood and Another v Minister of Home Affairs and Others; Shalabi and Another v Minister of Home Affairs and Others; Thomas and Another v Minister of Home Affairs and Others* 2000 (3) SA 936 (CC) para 47; *South African Liquor Traders' Association and Others v Chairperson, Gauteng Liquor Board and Others* 2009 (1) SA 565 (CC) para 27; *Bertie van Zyl (Pty) Ltd and Another v Minister for Safety and Security and Others* 2010 (2) SA 181 (CC) para 23.

132 *New Clicks* para 246.

133 *Affordable Medicines Trust and Others v Minister of Health of RSA and Another* 2005 (6) BCLR 529 (CC) para 108 (footnotes omitted).

134 See judgment of Chaskalson CJ in *New Clicks* para 246. See also *Allpay Consolidated Investment Holdings (Pty) Ltd and Others v Chief Executive Officer, South African Social Security Agency and Others* 2014 (1) SA 604 (CC) ('*Allpay (merits)*') para 87.

135 See Jowell quote in box above, section 8.1.

136 See Chapter 3 section 3.7.1.

137 See, for example, section 19 of the National Water Act 36 of 1998 and *Harmony Gold Mining Company Ltd v Regional Director: Free State Department of Water Affairs and Others* 2014 (3) SA 149 (SCA).

types of authorisations would require persons to comply with conditions stipulated in those authorisation documents. These would all have to be sufficiently clear in order that the affected person would know what was required of him or her.

REFRAMING

**Clarity in tax matters**

The South African Revenue Service (SARS) is empowered under a range of taxation laws (for example, the Income Tax Act,[138] Customs and Excise Act[139] and the Value-Added Tax Act[140]) to issue instructions and interpretations on how it will implement taxation requirements. These notes have a direct bearing on how ordinary taxpayers are required to complete their tax returns. It is accordingly important for these notes to be clear in order for taxpayers to know what to do in filing their tax returns.

In the *New Clicks* case, the court also observed that it is 'implicit in all empowering legislation that regulations must be consistent with, and not contradict, one another'.[141] In that case, the Constitutional Court dealt with arguments that various regulations relating to the pricing of medicines were vague and contradictory,[142] but the majority found that the regulations in question were not void for vagueness. There was, however, no disagreement in the court as regards vagueness being a valid ground of review.

In *Kruger v President of the Republic of South Africa and Others*,[143] the court held two proclamations relating to the commencement date of an Act invalid because they were vague and uncertain. The court noted that the public 'should not have to depend on lawyers to interpret the meaning and import of words in proclamations in order for them to know whether a particular piece of legislation passed by Parliament has taken effect'.[144] This case was not decided under PAJA.

The link between vagueness and procedural fairness was raised in *Allpay Consolidated Investment Holdings (Pty) Ltd v Chief Executive Officer, South African Social Security Agency*.[145] The court observed: [146]

> vagueness can render a procurement process, or an administrative action, procedurally unfair under s 6(2)(*c*) of PAJA. After all, an element of procedural fairness – which applies to the decision-making process – is that persons are entitled to know the case they must meet.

This is because section 3(2)(*b*)(i) of PAJA requires 'adequate notice of the nature and purpose of the proposed administrative action'. In regard to a tender process, such adequate notice would 'require sufficient information to enable prospective tenderers to make bids that cover all the requirements expected for the successful award of the tender'.[147] The court held that

138 58 of 1962.
139 91 of 1964.
140 89 of 1991.
141 *New Clicks* para 246.
142 *New Clicks* paras 246–277; 284–292; 487–491, 492–498; 814–821; 822–835; 848; 851.
143 2009 (1) SA 417 (CC).
144 *Kruger* para 66.
145 *Allpay (merits)* para 88.
146 *Allpay (merits)* para 88.
147 *Allpay (merits)* para 90.

the notice provided by the tender documents in this case was inadequate because it 'did not specify with sufficient clarity what was required of bidders'.[148]

## 8.7 Reasonableness generally

The discussion above has dealt with unreasonableness as manifested in abuse of discretion (symptomatic unreasonableness), irrationality, disproportionate decisions, and vagueness. Can unreasonableness cover anything else? Since the test is a decision that a reasonable decision-maker could not reach, there is probably a wider reach of reasonableness review than covered by the above-mentioned categories. In *Ehrlich v Minister of Correctional Services and Another*,[149] the court pointed out that members of the karate development programme were being treated differently from other prisoners (those involved in the band, for example). The court found that this pointed to the 'unreasonableness of the decision: its unreasonableness lies in its defiance of the constitutional value and fundamental right of equality'.[150] The court held that, because 'there is no justification for this differentiation, it is arbitrary and unreasonable on that account'.[151] This case is an example of one that Jowell had in mind when he described decisions 'taken in violation of common law principles governing the exercise of official power',[152] including those involving the principle of equality.[153]

In *Millennium Waste Management (Pty) Ltd v Chairperson, Tender Board: Limpopo Province and Others*,[154] the court held that the tender committee had acted 'unreasonably' in disqualifying the applicant's tender.[155] The court held that the committee had made an error of law in deciding that the absence of a signature on a form was fatal to the applicant's tender application. While grounds of review that are regarded as 'abuse of discretion' grounds often trigger unreasonableness, as discussed above,[156] an error of law is not usually regarded as necessarily being unreasonable. It is submitted that the court was correct in holding so in this case because of the trivial nature of the omission.

The ground of review involving relevant and irrelevant considerations is also not regarded as abuse of discretion, but in *Minister of Defence and Another v Xulu*[157] the court held that the decision not to renew the respondent's fixed-term contract was a 'classic case of irrelevant, or only marginally relevant, considerations being taken into account and all the relevant considerations being discounted or ignored completely' with the result that, from a 'substantive perspective it was not a reasonable decision in the sense of one that a reasonable decision-maker could make in the circumstances'.[158]

---

148 *Allpay (merits)* para 91.
149 2009 (2) SA 373 (E).
150 *Ehrlich* para 44.
151 *Ehrlich* para 44.
152 See box above, section 8.1.
153 See box above, section 8.1.
154 2008 (2) SA 481 (SCA).
155 *Millennium Waste* para 21.
156 At section 8.3 and section 8.4.1.
157 2018 (6) SA 460 (SCA).
158 *Minister of Defence v Xulu* para 51. See also *Cape Town City and Another v Da Cruz and Another* 2018 (3) SA 462 (WCC) which raises the link between relevant and irrelevant considerations and rationality, but without clearly explaining such link (para 73).

## 8.8 Reasonableness and respect

Reasonableness as a ground of review has often been distrusted on the basis that it raises the prospect of judges unacceptably interfering in the sphere of the executive by setting aside administrative decisions on this basis. Consequently, reasonableness review was greatly circumscribed under the common law. In the introduction to this chapter, the task of a judge in deciding reasonableness cases was described as drawing a line between decisions which are reasonable and those that are not. Another way of looking at this is that the judge asks 'should I interfere in this decision or should I leave it be?'

The answer to this question lies in the concept of judicial deference or respect.[159] Hoexter has described deference as follows, in a passage quoted with approval in our highest courts:

> judicial willingness to appreciate the legitimate and constitutionally-ordained province of administrative agencies; to admit the expertise of those agencies in policy-laden or polycentric issues; to accord their interpretation of fact and law due respect; and to be sensitive in general to the interests legitimately pursued by administrative bodies and the practical and financial constraints under which they operate. This type of deference is perfectly consistent with a concern for individual rights and a refusal to tolerate corruption and maladministration. It ought to be shaped not by an unwillingness to scrutinise administrative action, but by a careful weighing up of the need for – and the consequences of – judicial intervention. Above all, it ought to be shaped by a conscious determination not to usurp the functions of administrative agencies; not to cross over from review to appeal.[160]

In *Minister of Environmental Affairs and Tourism v Phambili Fisheries (Pty) Ltd,*[161] Schutz JA stated that:

> [j]udicial deference does not imply judicial timidity or an unreadiness to perform the judicial function. It simply manifests the recognition that the law itself places certain administrative actions in the hands of the Executive, not the Judiciary.

In the appeal against the *Phambili Fisheries decision, Bato Star Fishing (Pty) Ltd v Minister of Environmental Affairs and Others,*[162] O' Regan J suggested that the term 'deference' may be misinterpreted. Instead, she preferred the term 'respect', stating that 'the need for Courts to treat decision-makers with appropriate deference or respect flows not from judicial courtesy or etiquette but from the fundamental constitutional principle of the separation of powers itself'.[163]

In *Bato Star Fishing,* O' Regan J set out various factors which she indicated would be relevant in determining whether a decision is reasonable or not:

- The nature of the decision;
- The identity and expertise of the decision-maker;
- The range of factors relevant to the decision;

159 Also see Chapter 5 section 5.4.

160 Hoexter, C (2000) The Future of Judicial Review in South African Administrative Law *SALJ* 117(3):484 at 501–502; quoted in *Logbro Properties CC v Bedderson NO and Others* 2003 (2) SA 460 (SCA) paras 21 and 22; *Minister of Environmental Affairs and Tourism and Others v Phambili Fisheries (Pty) Ltd; Minister of Environmental Affairs and Tourism and Others v Bato Star Fishing (Pty) Ltd* 2003 (6) SA 407 (SCA) para 47; and *Bato Star Fishing* para 46. Cf Plasket, C (2018) Judicial Review, Administrative Power and Deference: A View from the Bench *SALJ* 502.

161 *Phambili Fisheries* para 50.

162 2004 (4) SA 490 (CC).

163 *Bato Star Fishing* para 46.

- The reasons given for the decision;
- The nature of the competing interests involved; and
- The impact of the decision on the lives and well-being of those affected.[164]

Another way to look at these factors, and which makes them relevant to consider at this juncture, is that these factors are those that will influence a court in its decision as to whether to interfere with the administrative decision or not. Let us consider them in more detail (which the court did not do).

## 8.8.1 Factors influencing reasonableness review

### 8.8.1.1 The nature of the decision

It is unlikely that this statement was aimed at resurrecting a 'classification of functions' approach.[165] It is possible, however, to place some emphasis on the nature of the decision without going as far as rigidly to classify functions. One aspect of this may be that cases involving interference with rights (as opposed to interests) warrant heightened scrutiny. This was an issue discussed under the proportionality heading above.

Another important aspect of the nature of the decision is the extent that it is what could be called a 'policy' decision. Traditionally, courts have been reluctant to interfere too much in policy-based and polycentric [166] decisions due to the notion that the functionary is better versed in the matters of that particular policy than are the courts. As Sir Thomas Bingham MR stated:

> The greater the policy content of the decision, and the more remote the subject matter of the decision from the ordinary judicial experience, the more hesitant the court must necessarily be in holding a decision to be irrational. That is good law, and like most good law, common sense.[167]

On the other hand, following the approach in the well-known case of *Theron en Andere v Ring van Wellington van die NG Sendingkerk in Suid-Afrika en Andere* [168] decisions 'involving the same sort of discretion as that normally exercised by courts of law; ... characterized by the application of legal rules or principles rather than ... policy content',[169] often referred to as 'purely judicial' decisions, would be more amenable to judicial scrutiny as to their reasonableness.

### 8.8.1.2 The identity and expertise of the decision-maker

It would appear, from statements made by O' Regan J elsewhere in the *Bato Star Fishing* judgment,[170] that this factor suggests that a decision by an expert member or body of the administration ('a person or institution with specific expertise') ought to be treated with appropriate respect, particularly when it is concerned with subject matter that is outside of the usual experience of the courts. While this is undoubtedly a valid consideration, it is

---

164 *Bato Star Fishing* para 45. The words used are direct quotes from the judgment, although the bullets are added.

165 See box at section 8.3.

166 Hoexter describes a polycentric decision as one which is many-centred. A decision made in relation to such an issue has multifarious consequences, meaning that polycentric issues cannot be decided in isolation from other issues: Hoexter (2012) 188. The 'other issues' referred to in the quote may not be before the court: Hoexter (2012) 148–149.

167 *R v Ministry of Defence Ex Parte Smith* [1996] QB 517.

168 1976 (2) SA 1 (A) 20D–21C.

169 Hoexter (2002) at 177.

170 *Bato Star Fishing* para 48.

important, however, that this not be given undue emphasis. As Kerans has noted, 'expertise commands deference only when the expert is coherent'.[171]

#### 8.8.1.3 The range of factors relevant to the decision

While it is clear that the various factors relevant to the decision would have to be taken into account in determining whether a decision is reasonable or not, this factor must not be taken to mean that a decision involving a wide range of factors, what could perhaps be called a complex decision, is more worthy of judicial deference than a decision involving only a few relevant factors. The complexity of a decision should only influence how much and how carefully a court should probe the decision in order to ascertain its reasonableness, which is not the same as saying that it should be accorded more deference. As O' Regan J states in *Bato Star Fishing*, 'a decision that requires an equilibrium to be struck between a range of competing interests or considerations and which is to be taken by a person or institution with specific expertise in that area must be shown respect by the courts'.[172] However, the judge qualifies this comment, importantly, by pointing out that a court 'should not rubber-stamp an unreasonable decision simply because of the complexity of the decision or the identity of the decision-maker'.[173]

#### 8.8.1.4 The reasons given for the decision

If the reasons given do not support the decision, this would be a clear indicator of unreasonableness or irrationality, and a court would be justified in interfering in such a decision.

#### 8.8.1.5 The nature of the competing interests involved

The first consideration this factor raises is that, if one of the competing interests is something more than an interest – a right in the Bill of Rights, for example – then it is probable, as pointed out above, that the decision will attract heightened scrutiny. On the other hand, the nature of the interest pursued by the organ of state would also be relevant to the degree of respect accorded the decision by the courts.

This factor is also relevant to proportionality in respect of the balance to be struck between competing interests: the state's on one hand and the individual's on the other.

#### 8.8.1.6 The impact of the decision on the lives and well-being of those affected

This factor raises proportionality as discussed above.

Ultimately, what respect requires is not a formulaic exercise. The court must appreciate that it is not concerned with whether the decision was correct or not. Correctness and reasonableness do not necessarily correspond – a decision may be incorrect but still reasonable. This was recognised in *Bato Star Fishing* when O' Regan J observed that the administrator's decision 'may or may not have been the best decision in the circumstances, but that is not for this Court to consider'.[174] In *Carephone (Pty) Ltd v Marcus NO*,[175] the court stated that '[a]s long as the judge determining [the] issue is aware that he or she enters the merits not in order to substitute his or her own opinion on the correctness thereof, but to determine whether the outcome is rationally justifiable, the process will be in order'. If one

171 Kerans, RP (1994) *Standards of Review Employed by Appellate Courts* at 17.
172 *Bato Star Fishing* para 48.
173 *Bato Star Fishing* para 48.
174 *Bato Star Fishing* para 54.
175 *Carephone* para 36.

regards this judicial statement as being equally apposite to reasonableness generally, this is the basis for judicial respect. The *Carephone* dictum ought, in most cases, to ensure that courts do not interfere in the merits of administrative decisions in an unwarranted manner.

## THIS CHAPTER IN ESSENCE

Section 33 of the Constitution requires administrative action to be reasonable. Reasonableness is explicitly provided for in PAJA, in a way that the courts have interpreted as requiring the decision to be one that a reasonable decision-maker would reach. Reasonableness can thus be seen as an 'umbrella' concept, under which hang various related concepts that are relevant in the context of valid administrative action. The first of these concepts is rationality, which is explicitly provided for in PAJA. The second is so-called 'symptomatic unreasonableness', arising usually because one of the grounds of review that amounts to an abuse of discretion is a symptom of unreasonableness. In some cases, the presence of grounds of review other than abuse of discretion have been regarded as a symptom of unreasonableness too. Vagueness is also regarded as related to unreasonableness. Finally, proportionality, although not explicitly referred to in PAJA, has been invoked in several cases and is an aspect of reasonableness. Judicial consideration of reasonableness inevitably involves a consideration of the merits of the decision and therefore courts will exercise some restraint in interfering in administrative decisions on the basis of unreasonableness, as reflected in the idea of judicial deference or respect.

## FURTHER READING


- Currie, I (2007) *The Promotion of Administrative Justice Act: A Commentary* (2nd ed) Siber Ink: Cape Town 169–170
- De Ville, JR (2005) *Judicial Review of Administrative Action in South Africa* LexisNexis: Durban 196–197, 207–210
- Du Plessis, M & Scott, S (2013) The Variable Standard of Rationality Review: Suggestions for Improved Legality Jurisprudence *SALJ* 130(3):597
- Hoexter, C (2012) *Administrative Law in South Africa* (2nd ed) Juta: Cape Town 329–335, 443–444
- Kohn, L (2013) The Burgeoning Constitutional Requirement of Rationality and Separation of Powers: Has Rationality Review Gone too Far? *SALJ* 130(4):810
- Plasket, C (2019) Disproportionality – The Hidden Ground of Review: *Medirite (Pty) Ltd v South African Pharmacy Council & Another SALJ* 136(1):15
- Price, A (2010) The Content and Justification of Rationality Review *SAPL* 25:346

# Chapter 9

# Reasons

MICHAEL KIDD



## 9.1 Introduction

Section 33(2) of the Constitution provides that '[e]veryone whose rights have been adversely affected by administrative action has the right to be given written reasons'. The right to reasons for administrative action, not generally required by South African law before 1994,[1] is a very important supporting element of the right to administrative justice. As Mureinik argued in 1994, South Africa moved with the onset of the new constitutional era into a 'culture of justification'.[2] One of the pivotal purposes of reasons is thus to justify administrative action, and by so doing to advance the constitutional requirements of 'fairness, accountability and transparency'.[3] An administration that justifies its actions by

1 There was no general requirement for reasons, save where specifically provided for by statute.

2 Mureinik, E (1994) A Bridge to Where? Introducing the Interim Bill of Rights *SAJHR* 10(1):31 at 38–44.

3 *Koyabe and Others v Minister for Home Affairs and Others (Lawyers for Human Rights as Amicus Curiae)* 2010 (4) SA 327 (CC) para 62. See also Currie, I (2007) *The Promotion of Administrative Justice Act: A Commentary* (2nd ed) 137.

giving reasons is 'likely to increase public confidence in the administrative process and thus enhance its legitimacy'.[4]

Even before the constitutional era, the importance of reasons was recognised by Baxter as follows:[5]

> In the first place, a duty to give reasons entails a duty to rationalize the decision. Reasons therefore help to structure the exercise of discretion, and the necessity of explaining why a decision is reached requires one to address one's mind to the decisional referents which ought to be taken into account. Secondly, furnishing reasons satisfies an important desire on the part of the affected individual to know why a decision was reached. This is not only fair: it is also conducive to public confidence in the administrative decision-making process. Thirdly – and probably a major reason for the reluctance to give reasons – rational criticism of a decision may only be made when the reasons for it are known. This subjects the administration to public scrutiny and it also provides an important basis for appeal or review. Finally, reasons may serve a genuine educative purpose, for example where an applicant has been refused on grounds which he is able to correct for the purpose of future applications.

Baxter's comments relating to structuring of the exercise of discretion feed into the idea that the giving of reasons improves the quality of administrative decision-making. If an administrator is required to give reasons, then the quality and rationality of those decisions is more likely to be stronger than in cases where reasons are not required.[6]

In line with the above observations, the right has also been referred to as a right that is 'intended to make judicial review effective'.[7] This is because, in most cases, a person adversely affected by administrative action will not know whether or how to proceed with the case unless he or she has adequate reasons for the decision. Reasons will put such a person in a position to decide whether to let the matter rest, or whether to make a new, revised application, or whether to make use of any administrative appeal facility provided by the relevant legislation, or, subsequently, whether to take the matter on review. Reasons will also reveal to the affected person the aspect or aspects of the decision that are open to challenge. The absence of reasons for a decision effectively prevents an affected person from protecting his or her administrative justice rights. The Promotion of Administrative Justice Act (PAJA),[8] for example, provides that an administrative action may be judicially reviewed if the action itself is not rationally connected to the reasons given for it by the administrator,[9] and may also be reviewed if the action was taken for a reason not authorised by the empowering provision.[10] In the absence of reasons for a decision, these grounds of review will be difficult, if not impossible, to invoke.

4 Hoexter, C (2012) *Administrative Law in South Africa* (2nd ed) 463 fn 14.
5 Baxter, L (1984) *Administrative Law* 228, footnotes excluded, emphases in original. Reprinted by permission of © Juta & Company Ltd.
6 Currie (2007) 138.
7 *Kiva v Minister of Correctional Services and Another* (2007) 28 ILJ 597 (E) para 31.
8 3 of 2000.
9 PAJA section 6(2)(*f*)(ii)(*dd*).
10 PAJA section 6(2)(*e*)(i).

REFRAMING

**Reasons informing appropriate reaction to administrative action**

Under the National Building Regulations and Building Standards Act[11] no building work may be done without the prior approval of the plans by a local authority.

Imagine that your family wants to build an extension to your house to accommodate a cousin that wants to attend a better school in your area. You submit plans to your local authority's building department. After some time you receive an SMS notification stating: 'Plans not approved, please collect at counter'. As a law student your immediate reaction is that the municipality will not stand in the way of your extension and that you will take their refusal to approve your plans to court and have it overturned.

When you collect the plans from the building department, a cover letter is attached stating that the plans were not approved since the proposed new structure (that is, the extension to the existing house) is not indicated in red on the plans. The letter also contains a reference to the applicable rules of the municipality requiring building extensions to be identified in red in order to distinguish it from existing structures, which must be indicated in black.

You ask the official at the counter whether he has a red pen that you can borrow, which he does. You proceed to colour all the proposed extensions in red on the plans and there-and-then resubmit the plans. The official tells you that you can wait for the plans if you wish. Thirty minutes later you walk out of the municipal building with your approved plans and call your builder to tell him that he can commence with the work as soon as possible.

This example illustrates how a clearly formulated reason for an administrative action (the refusal to approve your plans) enabled you to know what the most appropriate course of action was in response. It would have been ridiculous in this scenario to approach a court for relief against the municipality in order to get your plans approved. The clear reasons enabled you to get a favourable action (the approval of your plans) in the most efficient manner.

It is important to bear in mind, however, that the benefits of providing reasons are accompanied by some drawbacks. A duty on the administration to provide reasons undoubtedly imposes a burden on administrators. It is obviously far less work for an administrator simply to decline an application, for example, than to provide reasons for the negative decision. Formulating and communicating written reasons is a time-consuming exercise. Other drawbacks (perceived or real) – 'that it will stifle the exercise of discretion, that reasons cannot be furnished in all instances, that it will lead to the *ex post facto* fabrication of artificial reasons to justify the decision, and that it will lead to an increase in review applications'[12] – 'are either unconvincing or can be remedied',[13] and are outweighed by the benefits outlined above.

In this regard, when considering whether reasons in a particular case are adequate or not (discussed in detail below), one of the most important balances to be struck is between protecting the administrative justice rights of the individual (ensuring that he or she is appropriately apprised of the reasons for the decision) on the one hand and promoting

11 103 of 1977.

12 De Ville, JR (2005) *Judicial Review of Administrative Action in South Africa* 288–289.

13 De Ville (2005) 289.

administrative efficiency on the other.[14] In other words, the administrator ought not to be unreasonably overburdened by having to provide reasons.

PAJA sets out how effect is to be given to this right in section 5. Broadly, PAJA provides for a request-driven process – an affected person may request reasons, which the administrator must then provide within the prescribed time. An administrator does not have to provide reasons at the time the decision is communicated to the affected individual and, absent a request in terms of section 5, will not have to provide reasons at all.[15] Section 5 and this process are discussed in detail below. There is nothing to stop an administrator from providing reasons at the time the decision is communicated, but there is no compulsion to do so, unless the legislation authorising that particular decision requires the giving of reasons at that stage. On the other hand, it has been observed that 'it is not as a rule appropriate to ask for reasons for the promulgation of regulations'.[16]

**PAUSE FOR REFLECTION**

**Terminology: reasons, findings, information and evidence**

- *Reasons* are the explanation for a decision.
- *Findings* are 'findings of fact or law which are the essential background to a decision but that are not in themselves a complete explanation for it'.[17] In the USA, a distinction is drawn between 'basic' findings and 'ultimate' findings:[18] basic findings have been referred to as 'established facts'[19] whereas ultimate findings are inferences or conclusions drawn from the basic facts.[20] 'Established facts' should be interpreted as meaning the facts established by the administrator.
- *Information* is a term that has often been used in South African legislation and it means the same as 'findings'.[21]
- *Evidence* means the oral or documentary information provided to the administrator.[22]

Let us consider an example to illustrate these terms. In terms of the National Environmental Management Act,[23] persons carrying out certain activities require 'environmental authorisations' for such activities. These authorisations are issued by provincial environment departments, after consideration of environmental impact assessment (EIA) reports submitted by the person wishing to carry out the activity. In our example, Under Par (Pty) Ltd (UP) is intending to develop a residential estate with a golf course on land that is largely still covered with undisturbed natural vegetation. The application is submitted to the KwaZulu-Natal Department of Environment (ZDE).

CONTINUED >>>

14 See section 33(3) of the Constitution for the importance of administrative efficiency.
15 See, for example, *Mostert NO v Registrar of Pension Funds and Others* 2018 (2) SA 53 (SCA) para 50.
16 *Mostert* para 41.
17 Currie (2007) 139.
18 Baxter (1984) 228.
19 Hoexter (2012) 461 fn 1; Currie (2007) 146 fn 38.
20 Currie (2007) 146 fn 38.
21 Hoexter (2012) 461.
22 The fact that evidence consists of 'information' (as defined in the *Concise Oxford Dictionary* (1982) (7th ed)), leads to potential confusion between 'information' and 'evidence' (see Baxter (1984) 230 also fn 263). The confusion is best avoided if one prefers the terms 'findings' and 'evidence'.
23 107 of 1998.

The *evidence* in this case is contained in all of the documentation that the ZDE is required to consider in order to make a decision: the applicant's documentation, including the EIA report, submissions, including expert reports, from persons who are opposed to the development, and submissions and reports from various government bodies: the KwaZulu-Natal Department of Agriculture, provincial conservation agency and the local municipality. The evidence contains both statements of fact and expert opinion based on the factual observations (for example, an expert opinion that a portion of the development will not impact adversely on a colony of rare frogs in a pond on the land).

In this case, there is a dispute in regard to a particular tree on the land. Opponents to the development and the conservation agency allege in their evidence that this is the last truffula tree growing in the wild in South Africa. UP and its experts in their evidence allege that there is a small grove of truffula trees growing in a relatively inaccessible part of the Drakensberg mountains. Everyone agrees that there are numerous truffula trees growing in the wild in Lesotho. In regard to this factual element, the ZDE will have to decide which factual allegation is correct: its decision, following investigation, is that the truffula tree on the land is the last one growing in the wild in South Africa. This would be a *basic finding*. The ZDE will then have to decide how important it is to protect the last remaining truffula tree in South Africa. The ZDE decides that, since internationally the species of tree is not under threat, and that there are numerous specimens in a neighbouring country, that the preservation of this tree is not critical. This will be an *ultimate finding* (a conclusion drawn from evaluation of the evidence available). The ZDE will then take this finding, together with all the other findings it makes in respect of other factual elements of the application (for example, the contribution of the development to the economy and employment, other environmental impacts, cultural and heritage considerations), in order to come to a final decision. In this case, the decision is to authorise the development, subject to specified conditions.

The *reasons* for this decision will have to explain how and why the ZDE made the findings it did, based on the evidence, and explain the reasoning process whereby these findings were evaluated in such a way as to reach the conclusions, reflected in the decision.

## 9.2 The right to reasons in section 5 of PAJA

Section 5 of PAJA sets out initially what a person may do if he or she desires reasons for a decision and then stipulates what the administrator must do when such a request has been made. In discussing section 5, we will examine the section from the perspective of the requester first, followed by the duties imposed on the administrator.

### 9.2.1 Requesting reasons under section 5 of PAJA

Section 5(1) provides:

> Any person whose rights have been materially and adversely affected by administrative action and who has not been given reasons for the action may, within 90 days after the date on which that person became aware of the action or might reasonably have been expected to have become aware of the action, request that the administrator concerned furnish written reasons for the action.

This section provides answers (at least in broad terms) to two questions:

1. Who may request reasons?

   and,

2. What must that person do in order to obtain reasons?

We will examine each question in turn.

#### 9.2.1.1 Who may request reasons?

Section 33(2) of the Constitution applies the right to reasons to everyone 'whose rights have been adversely affected by administrative action'. Section 5(1) of PAJA echoes this and confines the right to reasons to any person 'whose rights have been materially and adversely affected by administrative action'. In addition, such person must be one 'who has not been given reasons for the action'.

**Any person 'whose rights have been materially and adversely affected by administrative action'**

Although this requirement mirrors the Constitutional right, it adds the requirement of materiality. This aspect of the section requires an understanding of what is meant by the terms 'rights', 'adversely affected' and 'materially'. The idea of 'adversely affected rights' is also part of the definition of administrative action, discussed above.[24] There is nothing to suggest that the term means anything different in the context of section 5. It would seem to be clear that section 5 would apply in respect of a person whose pre-existing right has been adversely affected by an administrative action. So, for example, the holder of a fishing right which allows that person to catch 100 tons of pelagic fish in terms of the Marine Living Resources Act[25] would be entitled to request reasons in terms of section 5 if the Minister decided to reduce the holder's allocation to 50 tons of fish, because the holder's existing right to fish would be adversely affected by that decision.

However, what would be the position if the person requesting reasons did not qualify as a holder of an existing right, such as an applicant for fishing rights? At first glance, section 5 does not provide an immediate answer. There is, however, a decision of the Supreme Court of Appeal that could provide an answer in favour of including an applicant as a person qualifying in terms of section 5 whose rights have been adversely affected.

The decision in *Transnet Ltd v Goodman Brothers (Pty) Ltd*[26] dealt with the right to reasons in terms of the interim Constitution (PAJA was not applicable), but the reasoning would be applicable to the position under PAJA. The respondent (Goodman Brothers) had tendered unsuccessfully to provide goods to the appellant (Transnet), and had applied to court for the provision of written reasons for the decision not to accept its tender. The court was faced with Transnet's argument that Goodman Brothers did not have the right to reasons because none of its rights, interests or legitimate expectations (all covered by the right to reasons in the interim Constitution) had been adversely affected by Transnet's conduct.[27] The majority decided, focusing only on the concept of 'right' (not interests or legitimate expectations), that the right that was adversely affected in this case was the 'right to obtain the information which the tenderer reasonably required in order to enable him to determine whether his right to lawful administrative action ... had been violated'.[28] As the majority

24 PAJA section 1(*i*).
25 18 of 1998.
26 2001 (1) SA 853 (SCA).
27 *Goodman Brothers*, Olivier JA's judgment at para 40.
28 *Goodman Brothers*, Schutz JA's judgment at para 10.

stated, without reasons the respondent 'is deprived of the opportunity, to which he is entitled, to consider further action'.[29]

Moreover, Olivier JA in the same case suggested that Goodman Brothers' right to equality was also adversely affected. He stated:

> The right to equal treatment pervades the whole field of administrative law, where the opportunity for nepotism and unfair discrimination lurks in every dark corner. How can such right be protected other than by insisting that reasons be given for an adverse decision? It is cynical to say to an individual: you have a constitutional right to equal treatment, but you are not allowed to know whether you have been treated equally. The right to be furnished with reasons for an administrative decision is the bulwark of the right to just administrative action.[30]

The reasoning in *Goodman Brothers,* although it can be criticised (see Counterpoint below), is applicable to the position under PAJA, because it focused on the *rights* of the applicant. It has not been explicitly followed as often as one might have expected, but the court in *Kiva v Minister of Correctional Services* used the *Goodman Brothers* reasoning to hold that an applicant's rights to both just administrative action and equality had been adversely affected by a decision not to promote him. The applicant was consequently entitled to reasons for the decision in terms of section 5 of PAJA.[31] In addition, the applicant's rights of access to court (section 34 of the Constitution) and to fair labour practices (section 23(1) of the Constitution) had also been adversely affected. *Kiva* is an example of how the *Goodman Brothers* reasoning can be applied to PAJA right to reasons, even though the latter judgment was dealing with the right to reasons under the interim Constitution.

COUNTER POINT

**Which right must be adversely affected in order to 'trigger' the right to reasons?**

Hoexter argues that the reasoning adopted in *Goodman Brothers* is 'suspiciously circular or "bootstraps" reasoning'[32] in that one right to administrative justice (the right in section 33(1) of the Constitution) inevitably entitles one to the right to reasons in section 33(2). *Goodman Brothers* reasoning has the effect that the section 33(1) right will *always* be adversely affected by the failure to give reasons. While this may be a logical flaw, Hoexter suggests that it has the benefit of furthering the values of participation and accountability.[33]

Section 5(1) of PAJA also requires that the adverse effect on the right must be *material,* which is not a requirement of section 33(2) of the Constitution. It is unlikely that this adds anything significant to the applicability of section 5(1). The main reason for this is that it is not likely that one could envisage a 'situation where a person's rights have been adversely affected but the effect is not material',[34] or, in other words, would be 'too trivial to bother about'.[35] The

29 *Goodman Brothers* para 12.
30 *Goodman Brothers,* Olivier JA's judgment at para 42.
31 2006 JDR 0820 (E) paras 21 and 23.
32 Hoexter (2012) 224. Reprinted by permission of © Juta & Company Ltd.
33 Hoexter (2012) 471.
34 *Kiva* para 23.
35 Hoexter (2012) 473.

Constitutional Court, in *Joseph and Others v City of Johannesburg and Others*,[36] adopted the approach that 'materially and adversely affects' 'simply [means] that the administrative action had a significant and not trivial effect' in deciding that, in the case before it dealing with the right to procedural fairness, any effects on the applicant's rights were material and adverse.

In practice, the requirement that a person's right must have been materially and adversely affected in order to qualify for the right to reasons is unlikely to present much of an obstacle to the applicability of section 5(1) of PAJA, but it cannot simply be ignored.[37]

#### Any person 'who has not been given reasons for the action'

The person entitled to request reasons in terms of section 5(1) of PAJA must be someone who has not already been given reasons for the action. This may seem to be stating the obvious, but it is important when a requester has been given something that purports to be reasons, but which are inadequate. It also raises certain questions relating to the manner in which a person may have already been given reasons. It is not infrequent that a person will be given 'reasons' for a decision that do not sufficiently explain why the decision was taken. In such a case, the administrator would take the view that it has already furnished reasons (and that consequently a person requesting reasons would not qualify as someone 'who has not been given reasons for the action'). The requester, on the other hand, would argue that what he or she has received from the administrator does not qualify as reasons. Resolution of this kind of dispute depends on the adequacy of the reasons, which is discussed in section 9.3 below.

Two further questions must be considered. First, if a requester has already been given oral reasons would he or she be a person 'who has not been given reasons'? While there is no case law in point, the section 33(2) constitutional right speaks of the right to 'written reasons', which suggests that oral reasons would not suffice. Moreover, if one considers that the primary role of reasons is to enable a person to decide whether his or her rights to just administrative action have been adversely affected and what he or she can do about remedying the situation, oral reasons would not enable him or her to assess this properly.[38] The second question is whether a person could be said to have been 'given' reasons if he or she has not been furnished with such reasons individually, but they have been made public? An example would be the publication in a newspaper of reasons for a decision. The answer to this question has also not been addressed in our courts, but, according to Hoexter, 'the answer must depend on the extent of the publication and the medium used'.[39] The important element in this regard would be, first, whether the affected person would have reasonable access to the published reasons and, second, whether the reasons published were adequate.

### 9.2.1.2 What must that person do in order to obtain reasons?

A person who qualifies to request reasons in terms of section 5(1) 'may within 90 days after the date on which that person became aware of the action or might reasonably have been expected to have become aware of the action, request that the administrator concerned furnish written reasons for the action'. The 90-day period runs from either the date on which

---

36 2010 (4) SA 55 (CC) para 31.

37 Draft 2009 'Rules of procedure for judicial review of administrative action' (which did not come Into effect) provide that the administrator may refuse a request for reasons if, *inter alia*, 'the requester is not a person whose rights are materially and adversely affected by the administrative action' (reg 3(5)(*c*) of GN R966 in *GG* 32622 of 09.10.2009).

38 See Hoexter (2012) 473.

39 See Hoexter (2012) 473.

the requester became aware of the action or the date on which he or she 'might reasonably have become aware of the action'. The first is a matter of fact, but the second would be ascertained on the basis of the particular circumstances of the administrative decision in question, and what would be reasonable to expect in those circumstances.

The 'Regulations on fair administrative procedures'[40] set out requirements for the request, which must be (a) in writing, (b) addressed to the administrator concerned, and (c) sent to the administrator by post, fax or electronic mail or delivered to the administrator by hand.[41] If an administrator receives an oral request for reasons from a person who cannot write or otherwise needs assistance, the administrator or a person designated by the administrator must give reasonable assistance to that person to submit such request in writing.[42] A request for reasons must indicate the administrative action which affected the rights of the person making the request; and which rights of that person were materially and adversely affected by the administrative action.[43] It must also state the full name and postal and, if available, electronic mail address of that person; and any telephone and fax numbers where that person may be contacted.[44] These requirements make practical sense for the most part but the requirement that the requester stipulate the right(s) that were adversely affected by the administrative action is probably asking too much of the average person.

Section 9(1) of PAJA provides that the period of 90 days referred to in section 5 may be reduced or extended for a fixed period, by agreement between the parties or, failing such agreement, by a court or tribunal on application by the person or administrator concerned. The court or tribunal may grant such an application where the interests of justice so require.[45]

### 9.2.2 Providing reasons under section 5 of PAJA

According to section 5(2) of PAJA, the administrator 'to whom the request is made must, within 90 days after receiving the request, give that person adequate reasons in writing for the administrative action'. Section 9 of PAJA applies to this 90-day period as well: it may be reduced or extended by agreement. It has been suggested that in assessing the 'interests of justice' referred to in section 9(2) in a particular case, 'regard no doubt will need to be given to the circumstances in which the request for reasons is made; the nature of the administrative action and the ease with which reasons can be formulated and provided, the effect of the decision on the person requesting reasons; and such other factors as may be relevant'.[46] The 'Regulations on fair administrative procedures'[47] require the administrator to whom a request for reasons is made to acknowledge receipt of the request; and either to accede to the request and furnish the reasons in writing; or decline the request.[48] The essential element of this duty is that the reasons, in writing as required by the Constitution, must be adequate. Adequacy is discussed in the next section.

40 GN R1022 in *GG* 23674 of 31.07.2002. PAJA requires, in section 10(1)(*d*), the Minister to make regulations relating to the procedures to be followed in connection with requests for reasons. These regulations are those that are required by section 10. The draft 2009 'Rules of procedure for judicial review of administrative action' supra (note 37), which did not come into effect, provide for somewhat different procedures (setting out a prescribed form for requesting reasons, for example).

41 Reg 27(1).

42 Reg 27(2).

43 Reg 27(3)(*a*).

44 Reg 27(3)(*b*).

45 PAJA section 9(2).

46 *Sikutshwa v MEC for Social Development, Eastern Cape and Others* 2009 (3) SA 47 (TkH).

47 GN R1022 in *GG* 23674 of 31.07.2002.

48 Reg 28.

An interesting question is whether the 90-day period may be reduced in the absence of an agreement or court order in terms of section 9. Two cases have dealt with this issue. In *Sikutshwa v MEC for Social Development, Eastern Cape and Others*,[49] the administrator argued that the applicant's application to be given reasons was premature because it had been brought prior to the 90-day period prescribed in section 5(2). The court held that:

> an administrator cannot with impunity wait until the 90-day period has all but expired before furnishing the reasons that she is obliged to provide. On the contrary, the administrator must furnish the reasons sought as soon as they are available.[50]

The court does not adequately explain why this is the case, but suggests that, even if this interpretation is wrong, the application was not premature in this particular case because the respondent department had, on its own admission, sent out reasons some time before the application had been brought (but the letter had not been received by the applicant).

A contrasting approach was adopted in *Jikeka v South African Social Security Agency*,[51] where the court stated:

> (*a*) The legislature intended the administrator to have a period of 90 days within which to furnish reasons when it promulgated s 5(2) of PAJA, unless circumstances warranted a reduction in terms of s 9, or else s 9 would not have been promulgated;
> (*b*) section 5(2) accordingly is a bar to the institution of proceedings prior to the expiration of the 90-day period unless by way of an application or by agreement;
> (*c*) the proceedings can accordingly only be instituted after the expiration of the 90-day period provided for in PAJA, unless an agreement has been reached to reduce the time period or an application has been brought in terms of s 9(1), failing which it can be dismissed on the basis of it being prematurely launched.[52]

The court went on to express the opinion that an administrator ought not to wait until the 90-day period has 'all but expired' before furnishing the reasons if it is possible to provide reasons within a shorter period, and 'should not hide behind the provisions of PAJA'.[53] If the applicant were able to establish this to be the case, 'the court would most certainly consider it to be just and equitable to grant an application for the reduction of the time periods in those instances'.[54] The important point would be that the correct procedure would be to apply to court in terms of section 9 for the 90-day period to be reduced, not to apply for reasons to be furnished before the 90-day period in the absence of an agreement in terms of section 9, or a court order to this effect. Accordingly, *Jikeka*, it is submitted, provides the correct approach.

49 2009 (3) SA 47 (TkH).
50 *Sikutshwa* para 76, reference excluded.
51 2011 (6) SA 628 (ECM).
52 *Jikeka* para 11.
53 *Jikeka* para 12.
54 *Jikeka* para 12.

**PAUSE FOR REFLECTION**

**How do the time frames in section 5 relate to other time frames in the Act?**

The most important consideration in this regard is section 7(1) which provides that any proceedings for judicial review in terms of section 6(1) must be instituted without unreasonable delay and not later than 180 days after the date –

> (*a*) ... on which any proceedings instituted in terms of internal remedies ... have been concluded;
>
> or
>
> (*b*) where no such remedies exist, on which the person concerned was informed of the administrative action, became aware of the action and the reasons for it or might reasonably have been expected to have become aware of the action and the reasons.

The periods prescribed in section 5 have no bearing on section 7(1), because the 180-day period in section 7(1) begins to run only when the affected person becomes aware of the action *and the reasons for it* or might reasonably have been expected to have become aware of them. So the 180-day period in section 7(1) runs only from after the 90-day period the administrator is given to furnish reasons. This means that an application for review may be lodged up to 360 days after the decision (without reasons) was communicated to the person concerned.[55]

### 9.2.3 Failure to give reasons

Before the onset of the constitutional era and the right to just administrative action, the common law did not recognise a general right to give reasons where the statute authorising the administrative action in question did not require the furnishing of reasons. The absence of such a provision was the norm. In some cases, however, courts were prepared to draw an adverse inference from the failure to give reasons even where there was no statutory duty to give them. In *National Transport Commission and Another v Chetty's Motor Transport (Pty) Ltd*,[56] the court emphasised that the failure or refusal to give reasons is an important element to be taken into account only where there is other evidence of a flaw in the decision (such as bad faith or ulterior purpose). Once all the evidence is before a court, it would take this all into account, 'and if an adverse inference can be drawn from the absence of reasons, such inference is weighed together with all the other factors in the totality of the case, in deciding whether there is proof' of the ground of judicial review averred against the administrator.[57]

55 On section 7(1) see Chapter 11 at section 11.3.2.

56 1972 (3) SA 726 (A) 736.

57 *Chetty's Motor Transport* 736G.

**PAUSE FOR REFLECTION**

**Drawing adverse inferences from absence of reasons**

In *Oskil Properties (Pty) Ltd v Chairman of the Rent Control Board and Others*,[58] the court observed that:

> Where, as here, none of the evidence supports the determination arrived at by the Control Board and where such evidence remains unchallenged and uncontradicted by other evidence, it seems to me that the failure of the Control Board to furnish reasons as to the basis on which it determined the 'reasonable rental value' ... tends to support the inference that the evidence before it was ignored.

Consequently, the court held that the valuation decision had been made in an 'arbitrary manner' and was invalid.

A second example is *Jeffery v President, South African Medical and Dental Council*,[59] where the court held that 'the absence of reasons for the disciplinary committee's finding weighs against the contention that its inquiry was fair or its judgment fairly arrived at' and the decision to find the applicant guilty of improper conduct was thus set aside.

There is a provision in PAJA that has a similar effect. Section 5(3) of PAJA provides that, if an administrator fails to furnish adequate reasons for an administrative action, it must, in the absence of proof to the contrary, be presumed in any proceedings for judicial review that the administrative action was taken without good reason. This goes further than the common-law position outlined above, because, in the absence of reasons, the onus will be shifted onto the administrator to justify his or her decision. This will apply irrespective of the existence of evidence of other flaws in the process.

In *Wessels v Minister for Justice and Constitutional Development and Others*,[60] the applicant had requested reasons in terms of section 5 of PAJA for the respondent's appointment of the second respondent to the position of Regional Court President Limpopo instead of the applicant, who had been shortlisted. In the absence of reasons being furnished, the applicant applied for the decision to be set aside. The court held that, in the circumstances, the 'responsible minister's failure to furnish reasons ... cannot be seen other than proof that the administrative action was taken without good reason',[61] and the court set aside the decision.

It was argued in *JH v Health Professions Council of South Africa*[62] that failure by an administrator to provide reasons within the 90-day period envisaged by section 5(2) precluded it from raising reasons when its decision was taken on review. The court, however, held that an administrator in such circumstances could put up reasons in the review process, but that it bore the onus of showing that the decision was taken with good reason. Were the applicant to decide to abandon the review once it received reasons in the answering papers, the court stated that it would 'ordinarily be entitled to costs'.[63]

58 1985 (2) SA 234 (SE) 246H.
59 1987 (1) SA 387 (C).
60 2010 (1) SA 128 (GNP).
61 *Wessels* 141E.
62 2016 (2) SA 93 (WCC).
63 *JH v Health Professions Council of South Africa* 2016 (2) SA 93 (WCC) para 14.

In another case decided post PAJA,[64] the court was faced with a decision of an MEC overturning a decision relating to an amendment of an exemption from the requirement of an environmental authorisation where he gave no reasons for doing so. This had been a particularly contentious case for about a decade, and the court held, without referring to PAJA, that the absence of reasons 'renders the amendment decision irrational, for there is no link between the outcome the MEC reached and the evidence before him'.[65]

### 9.2.4 Departure from requirements of section 5 of PAJA

There are various opportunities for an administrator to depart from the requirements of section 5. First, section 2 of PAJA allows the Minister to exempt an administrator from the requirements of section 5 or to vary such requirements 'in order to promote an efficient administration and if it is reasonable and justifiable in the circumstances'. This power has not yet been utilised. In section 5 itself, there is further scope for departures: section 5(4) provides that an administrator may depart from the requirement to furnish adequate reasons if it is reasonable and justifiable in the circumstances, and must forthwith inform the person making the request of such departure. In determining whether such a departure is reasonable and justifiable, an administrator must take into account all relevant factors, including:

(i) the objects of the empowering provision;
(ii) the nature, purpose and likely effect of the administrative action concerned;
(iii) the nature and the extent of the departure;
(iv) the relation between the departure and its purpose;
(v) the importance of the purpose of the departure; and
(vi) the need to promote an efficient administration and good governance.[66]

The 'Regulations on fair administrative procedures'[67] provide that, if an administrator declines a request for reasons in terms of section 5(4)(*a*) of the Act, the administrator must give reasons in writing to the person who made the request why the request was declined.[68] There may be reasons other than those contemplated in section 5(4) for an administrator declining to give reasons – for example, the requester is not a person whose rights have been adversely affected, or he or she has already been given reasons. The regulations do not, however, require the administrator to give reasons for declining a request for reasons on grounds other than those in section 5(4), which is rather odd.

Another departure is provided for in section 5(5), allowing an administrator, who is empowered by any empowering provision to follow a procedure which is fair but different from the provisions of section 5(2), to act in accordance with that different procedure. This means that a statutory right to reasons that is more onerous than PAJA, including one which requires the giving of automatic reasons, must be followed, rather than section 5 of PAJA overriding such provisions.[69]

---

64 *Black Eagle Project Roodekrans v MEC: Department of Agriculture, Conservation and Environment, Gauteng Provincial Department* (6085/07) [2019] ZAGPJHC 23; [2019] 2 All SA 322 (GJ).
65 *Black Eagle Project* para 43.
66 PAJA section 5(4)(*b*).
67 GN R1022 in *GG* 23674 of 31.07.2002.
68 Reg 28(2).
69 See Currie (2007) 149.

### 9.2.5 Decisions requiring reasons to be furnished automatically

Section 5(6) of PAJA provides that, in order to promote an efficient administration, the Minister may, at the request of an administrator, publish a list specifying any administrative action or a group or class of administrative actions in respect of which the administrator concerned will automatically furnish reasons to a person whose rights are adversely affected by such actions, without such person having to request reasons in terms of this section. This list must be published within 14 days of receipt of such request. At the time of writing, no such list has been published.

It is worth noting that there are various statutory provisions which require the automatic provision of reasons (see box below for some examples), and these would not have to be listed in terms of section 5(6), but would have to meet the requirements of the 'fair but different' provision in section 5(5).

EXAMPLE

**Examples of statutory provisions requiring provision of reasons**

The National Environmental Management Act,[70] in section 24H(3), dealing with application to the Minister to be authorised as registration authorities, provides:

> After considering an application, and any other additional information that the Minister may require, the Minister may-
>
> ...
>
> (*b*) in writing addressed to the association, refuse the application, giving reasons for such refusal.

The National Environmental Management: Biodiversity Act[71] requires permits for various activities. Section 88(5) provides that if an application (for a permit) is rejected, the issuing authority must give reasons for the decision in writing to the applicant.

In PAJA, if an administrator decides to hold a public inquiry in terms of section 4, the administrator must compile a written report on the inquiry and give reasons for any administrative action taken or recommended.[72]

In the Promotion of Access to Information Act,[73] section 25(3) provides that if a request for access to information is refused, the notice of decision must state adequate reasons for the refusal, including the provisions of the Act relied upon.

## 9.3 Adequacy of reasons

The adequacy of the reasons is central to two issues raised by section 5 of PAJA: whether the applicant has been given reasons already; and it is a requirement of the written reasons furnished by the administrator in receipt of a section 5(1) request. In short, reasons that are inadequate are not reasons at all. This means that a requester who has been furnished with inadequate reasons nevertheless qualifies as a person entitled to request reasons in terms of section 5(1) because he or she has not been given reasons (assuming his or her rights have

70 107 of 1998.
71 10 of 2004.
72 PAJA section 4(2)(*b*)(iii).
73 2 of 2000.

been adversely affected). An understanding of the right to reasons thus requires a clear understanding of what 'adequacy' means in relation to reasons.

In general, whether something is adequate would depend on the circumstances within which the question arises. It is not surprising that this is true of the adequacy of reasons as well: it is not possible to 'lay down a general rule of what could constitute adequate or proper reasons, for each case must depend upon its own facts'.[74] Adequacy, however, suggests a fitness for purpose,[75] so the concept is not completely open-ended. What is the purpose of reasons in the context of PAJA and section 33 of the Constitution? One of the primary purposes is aimed at ensuring that the person affected by an administrative decision knows *why* and *how* the decision was made, so that he or she can evaluate whether to let the matter rest, make another application, or challenge the decision if it contains an evident flaw. The adequacy of the reasons furnished must place the affected person in such a position (think of our building plan example at the beginning of this chapter). The courts and academic writers have suggested several essential characteristics of adequate reasons, together with factors that would determine the adequacy or otherwise of reasons. Let us attempt to distil some pointers from these sources.

**PAUSE FOR REFLECTION**

**What is the basic element of adequacy?**

The Australian judge Woodward J, in the case of *Ansett Transport Industries (Operations) (Pty) Ltd and Another v Wraith and Others*,[76] stated that the duty to give reasons:

> requires the decision-maker to explain his decision in a way which will enable a person aggrieved to say, in effect: 'Even though I may not agree with it, I now understand why the decision went against me. I am now in a position to decide whether that decision has involved an unwarranted finding of fact, or an error of law, which is worth challenging.'

Along similar lines, the court in *Commissioner, South African Police Service and Others v Maimela and Another*[77] stated:

> Whether brief or lengthy, reasons must, if they are read in their factual context, be intelligible and informative. They must be informative in the sense that they convey why the decision-maker thinks (or collectively think) that the administrative action is justified.

So, if the reasons in a given case meet this standard, they are adequate. If not, then they are not adequate.

74 *Rèan International Supply Company (Pty) Ltd and Others v Mpumalanga Gaming Board* 1999 (8) BCLR 918 (T) at 926.
75 According to the *Concise Oxford Dictionary*, 'adequate' means 'sufficient or satisfactory'.
76 (1983) 48 ALR 500, quoted in *Minister of Environmental Affairs and Tourism and Others v Phambili Fisheries (Pty) Ltd; Minister of Environmental Affairs and Tourism and Others v Bato Star Fishing (Pty) Ltd* 2003 (6) SA 407 (SCA) para 40.
77 2003 (5) SA 480 (T) at 486.

A good point of departure is *Minister of Environmental Affairs and Tourism and Others v Phambili Fisheries (Pty) Ltd; Minister of Environmental Affairs and Tourism and Others v Bato Star Fishing (Pty) Ltd.*[78] The Supreme Court of Appeal, per Schutz JA, stated that adequacy:

> requires that the decision-maker should set out his understanding of the relevant law, any findings of fact on which his conclusions depend (especially if those facts have been in dispute), and the reasoning processes which led him to those conclusions. He should do so in clear and unambiguous language, not in vague generalities or the formal language of legislation. The appropriate length of the statement covering such matters will depend upon considerations such as the nature and importance of the decision, its complexity and the time available to formulate the statement. Often those factors may suggest a brief statement of one or two pages only.[79]

From this quote, the following characteristics of adequate reasons can be derived:

- The **administrator's understanding (interpretation) of the relevant law** (that is, the law that authorises the decision). This would allow the affected individual to determine if the administrator has made an error of law.
- The administrator's **finding on the facts**. In some cases, the facts will not be in issue, so the administrator's findings in this regard would be particularly important where the facts are in dispute. It is, of course, important for the affected individual to know which version of the facts the administrator relied on in order to reach his or her decision. This would enable the affected person to judge whether there has been a mistake of fact, or whether there is a rational connection between the factual finding and the decision, amongst other possible flaws. Disputes over facts would typically arise in cases heard by tribunals (for example, disciplinary inquiries) and would often arise in cases where applicants are applying for certain permissions (such as environmental authorisations) where there are persons opposing the application who may put forward different factual arguments to those of the applicant. For example, an applicant for an environmental authorisation may argue and put forward expert opinion indicating that a development will have a minimal detrimental impact on the environment, whereas opponents of the development may put forward expert opinion to the contrary. In regard to the facts, the Constitutional Court observed in *Koyabe and Others v Minister for Home Affairs and Others (Lawyers for Human Rights as Amicus Curiae)*,[80] that reasons do not have to be 'specified in minute detail, nor is it necessary to show that every relevant fact weighed in the ultimate finding'.[81]
- The administrator's **reasoning process**. It is not sufficient for the reasons to consist solely of the administrator's conclusions (for example, 'the tribunal finds that your actions did contravene the provision', or 'we have decided that this development will not have an unacceptably adverse impact on the environment'). Conclusions alone will not put the aggrieved person in a position where he or she can determine whether the decision is lawful, reasonable or rational. The reasoning process leading to the conclusion is important for him or her to be able to make such an assessment.

78 *Phambili Fisheries* para 40.
79 Quoting the Australian case of *Ansett Transport Industries* 507.
80 2010 (4) SA 327 (CC) para 64.
81 *Koyabe* para 63.

In *Kiva v Minister of Correctional Services and Another*,[82] the applicant requested reasons for the failure to promote him. He had been sent a letter purportedly informing him why he had been unsuccessful. The court held that the letter contained 'nothing that can even vaguely be considered to be a reason'.[83] This was because the letter 'informed him of the result ... without furnishing any explanation as to how that result was arrived at'.[84] A second document responding to the applicant's grievance informed him of the type of factors that had been considered, but 'did not state how he fared in relation to those factors and why he was considered to be less suitable than the person who was promoted'.[85] The court regarded this as being an inadequate explanation or justification for the decision not to promote the applicant. An explanation of the reasoning process must, therefore, not only set out the factors (considerations) that the administrator took into account but must explain the role those factors took in the decision-making process.

In *Gavric v Refugee Status Determination Officer Cape Town and Others*,[86] an applicant for refugee status had been refused on the basis of section 4(1)(*b*) of the Refugees Act.[87] This provision prohibits a person from qualifying for refugee status 'if there is reason to believe that he has committed a crime which is not of a political nature and which, if committed in the Republic, would be punishable by imprisonment'. The court held that the reasons for the decision in this case, taken by the Refugee Status Determination Officer (RSDO), had not addressed the question of whether his crime was 'of a political nature' and in 'this matter the RSDO provided mere conclusions, not reasons'.[88] The 'paucity of the reasons provided by the RSDO' was consequently one of the grounds on which the decision was held to be invalid and set aside.[89]

In another refugee case decided just after *Gavric*,[90] the court set aside a refusal of an application for refugee status, calling the statement accompanying the decision 'disjointed' and stating that, on reading it, one 'simply does not know why the RSDO rejected the application'.[91] The decision here, according to the court, 'was neither intelligible nor informative and came nowhere near the required standard. It did not tell [the applicant] why his asylum application was rejected' and was accordingly declared invalid.[92]

- The reasons must be worded in **clear and unambiguous language**. Most recipients of administrative decisions are laypersons or, at least, not well versed in law and legal language. It is important for the person concerned to be able to understand the reasons. Using statutory language is often not conducive to this kind of understanding, and it goes without saying that ambiguity is undesirable. Similarly, vagueness detracts from understanding – clarity and lucidity are necessary. The court also mentions an

82 (2007) 28 ILJ 597 (E).
83 *Kiva* para 39.
84 *Kiva* para 39.
85 *Kiva* para 40.
86 2019 (1) SA 21 (CC).
87 130 of 1998.
88 *Gavric* para 69.
89 *Gavric* para 81.
90 *Refugee Appeal Board and Others v Mukungubila* 2019 (3) SA 141 (SCA).
91 *Mukungubila* para 25.
92 *Mukungubila* para 27.

**appropriate length** (which will go hand-in-hand with the **appropriate level of detail**), which will be determined by the following factors:

- **The complexity of the decision**.[93] This stands to reason: as pointed out above, the more complex a decision, the more likely that it will take more length or more detail to explain (and vice versa).
- **The time available to formulate the statement**. Once again, this is a logical consideration. If reasons have to be formulated in a short period of time (although PAJA gives a period of 90 days, there may be other legislation requiring reasons within shorter periods), then less detail can be expected than if there is a longer time for the administrator to formulate a decision. Bear in mind, though, that whatever the length or detail of the reasons, they still have to be adequate in the circumstances.
- **The nature and importance of the decision**.[94] In *Moletsane v Premier of the Free State and Another*,[95] the court suggested that the 'more drastic the action taken, the more detailed the reasons which are advanced should be. The degree of seriousness of the administrative act should therefore determine the particularity of the reasons given'.[96] This suggests that the 'consequences or effects'[97] of the decision determine the level of details in the reasons. The view adopted in *Moletsane* is, however, not without criticism. It is thus important to consider these factors collectively rather than in isolation.

**COUNTER POINT**

**Impact and detail of reasons**

Currie criticises *Moletsane* as too simplistic: there is no necessary connection between the degree of seriousness of a case and the detail of the reasons given for it. This is because a case with severe consequences can be relatively easy to decide and, therefore, require only a succinct explanation. Think of a person who applies for an old age grant under the Social Assistance Act,[98] but who has not reached the prescribed age to qualify for such a grant. The reason for refusing such an application is quite simple – the applicant is too young, but may have severe financial consequences for the applicant. On the other hand, a case with less serious consequences could be the outcome of a complex reasoning process, which will inevitably take more detail to explain.[99] Think of a refusal to allow building alterations to a historical building under the National Heritage Resources Act.[100] Such refusal may be inconvenient for the owner, but not necessarily severe while the reasoning behind the refusal may include a detailed assessment of the historical value of the building and the potential impact of the proposed work on such value.

93 See *Maimela* 485–486.

94 See also *Maimela* 485–486, where the court stated: 'The adequacy of reasons will depend on a variety of factors, such as the factual context of the administrative action, the nature and complexity of the action, the nature of the proceedings leading up to the action and the nature of the functionary taking the action'.

95 (1996) 17 ILJ 251 (O).

96 *Moletsane* 254F.

97 Currie (2007) 146.

98 13 of 2004.

99 Currie (2007) 146–147.

100 25 of 1999.

Further characteristics of adequate reasons from other sources are:

- **Statement of the decision.**[101] This almost goes without saying, but it is important that the decision be stated clearly. This is also reflected in section 3 of PAJA which provides that a mandatory element of procedural fairness is a 'clear statement of the administrative action'.[102]
- The reasons must **not merely be a reiteration of the empowering provisions.**[103] This is consistent with the requirement that the reasons include not only the conclusion(s) that the administrator reached, but also the reasoning process.
- 'Reasons must not be intelligible and informative with the benefit of hindsight ... They must **from the outset be intelligible and informative to the reasonable reader thereof** who has knowledge of the context of the administrative action.'[104] In the *Maimela* case, an applicant for a firearm licence had been given reasons for the refusal to grant the licence, to the effect that 'premises/residence does not comply to required standard'.[105] It was subsequently explained by the SAPS that one of the requirements for granting a firearm licence is that a safe for the safe-keeping of a firearm must 'to the satisfaction of the Commissioner ... be affixed flush to a floor, wall or other immovable structure or part thereof of the house ... or other dwelling place of an applicant concerned'.[106] The application was refused because the applicant lived in a 'shack' with no immovable structural components to which a safe could be affixed. The court held that the reasons were inadequate because they were not sufficiently informative 'from the outset'.
- 'If reasons refer to an extraneous source, that **extraneous source must be identifiable** to the reasonable reader.'[107] In *Maimela*, the decision was made on the basis of non-compliance with an applicable regulation. The purported reasons provided had not referred to this regulation. The court suggested that if the SAPS had provided the reason that 'applicant's dwelling structurally unsuitable to affix a safe in accordance with reg 28(3)', it may have been sufficiently intelligible and informative. It is submitted that this does not go far enough. The average person does not have ready access to regulations and reasons ought not only to refer to the regulation in question (as suggested by the court), but also to provide the text of the regulation(s) that are applicable. The same would apply in respect of any 'extraneous source' that is relevant to the decision. Not only must the source be referred to explicitly, but the source itself (or relevant sections of it) provided to the affected person as well. This is in keeping with the idea that a person be placed in a position where he or she can assess whether the decision is legally valid or whether, for example, there is an error of law in that the administrator has misinterpreted the legal requirement.

One should be mindful of the point made in *Koyabe v Minister for Home Affairs*,[108] that the list of factors relevant to the adequacy of reasons is 'not a closed one, [and] will hinge on the facts and circumstances of each case and the test for the adequacy of reasons must be an

---

101 See Currie (2007) 145.

102 PAJA section 3(2)(*b*)(iii).

103 *Gumede and Others v Minister of Law and Order and Another* 1984 (4) SA 915 (N), confirmed in *Nkondo and Others v Minister of Law and Order* 1986 (2) SA 756 (A).

104 *Maimela* 486F-G.

105 *Maimela* 483D.

106 Reg 28(3)(*a*) of regulations promulgated in terms of the Arms and Ammunition Act 75 of 1969 - see *Maimela* 486E.

107 *Maimela* 486G.

108 *Koyabe* para 64.

objective one'. Several further factors influencing adequacy have, nevertheless, been suggested in court decisions and academic writing. These have been, in almost all cases, mentioned without further explanation, so it will be useful to consider how these factors might apply, bearing in mind the ultimate purpose that reasons serve and how adequacy relates to this purpose:

- **The factual context of the administrative action.**[109] This would tie in with the requirement (mentioned above) that the administrator must set out the findings on the facts, particularly where these have been in dispute. So a statement of reasons that did not deal in detail with the facts in a case where the facts were not in dispute would not be defective for this reason.
- **The nature of the proceedings leading up to the action.**[110] Many administrative decisions are reached after what can be called a 'multistaged' process. For example, an initial investigation into a state of affairs may lead to a further decision-making process which results in the ultimate decision.[111] In such a case, the reasons provided would probably have to outline the reasoning process in the preliminary step(s) as well.
- **The nature of the functionary taking the action.**[112] In the interests of promotion of administrative efficiency, one might expect that reasons provided by, for example, a Minister would be less detailed than those provided by a government functionary at a junior level.
- **The purpose for which reasons are intended.**[113] In many cases, this might be difficult for an administrator to assess because he or she will not necessarily know what the requester's use of the reasons is likely to be. This may, however, be determined by the nature of the decision – if, for example, it involves an application that may be revised by the applicant, then it would be important for the reasons to indicate how the applicant may alter his or her submission in order to stand a better chance of success in a second application. In cases where there is no opportunity for resubmission, it would be important to provide enough detail for the requester to consider possible grounds of appeal or review.
- **The stage at which these reasons are given.**[114] Usually, reasons would be given once a final decision is made. In multistaged decision-making processes, however, it may be necessary to give a person reasons after a preliminary decision in order to enable that person to exercise his or her rights of procedural fairness properly. The details provided at that stage may well be less detailed than reasons for the final decision.
- **Whether and what further remedies are available to contest the administrative decision.**[115] This ties in with the observations made in respect of the purpose for which reasons are intended (above).
- **Whether the issue involves an application for a benefit or a deprivation of a right.**[116] The rationale behind this suggestion is not immediately clear, but it may be that one would expect a higher standard of explanation and justification for a decision that adversely affects existing rights, than for one that involves determining rights.

109 *Maimela* 485–486.
110 *Maimela* 485–486.
111 See, for example, *Oosthuizen's Transport (Pty) Ltd and Others v MEC, Road Traffic Matters, Mpumalanga and Others* 2008 (2) SA 570 (T).
112 *Maimela* 485–486.
113 *Koyabe* para 64.
114 *Koyabe* para 64.
115 *Koyabe* para 64.
116 De Ville (2005) 294.

- **Administrative efficiency.**[117] This is a factor that will always be central. It is important that the duty on the administrator to provide reasons does not impose an unreasonable burden. What is reasonable will depend on the circumstances of the case and several of the other factors mentioned here. As Baxter observes, statements of 'reasons ought to be commensurate with the ... limits of administrative feasibility'.[118]

From the discussion above, we are able to distil what could be called 'prerequisites' for adequate reasons. These are itemised in Table 9.1 below.

*Table 9.1 Prerequisites for adequate reasons*

| **Prerequisites for adequate reasons** | |
|---|---|
| 1. | The reasons must contain the statement of decision. |
| 2. | The administrator's finding(s) on the facts must be provided. |
| 3. | The administrator's understanding (interpretation) of the relevant law must be provided. |
| 4. | The reasons must not consist solely of the administrator's conclusion(s), but the administrator's reasoning process must be explained. |
| 5. | The reasons must not merely be a reiteration of the empowering provision. |
| 6. | The reasons must be worded in clear and unambiguous language. |
| 7. | Reasons must be intelligible and informative from the outset; not only with the benefit of hindsight. |
| 8. | If reasons refer to an extraneous source (such as applicable statutory provisions), that extraneous source must be identifiable to the reasonable reader. |
| 9. | The reasons must be of an appropriate length and level of detail. |

Where the 'prerequisites' in Table 9.1 above are not absolute requirements, such as the last one (referring to 'appropriate length'), there are several factors that would influence this determination. These are set out in Table 9.2 below.

*Table 9.2 Factors influencing adequacy of reasons*

| **Factors influencing adequacy of reasons** | |
|---|---|
| 1. | The nature and importance of the decision |
| 2. | The complexity of the decision |
| 3. | The time available to formulate the statement |
| 4. | The factual context of the administrative action |
| 5. | The nature of the proceedings leading up to the action |
| 6. | The nature of the functionary taking the action |
| 7. | The purpose for which reasons are intended |

117 De Ville (2005) 294. See also the observations made in section 9.1 above.
118 Baxter (1984) 230.

| Factors influencing adequacy of reasons | |
|---|---|
| 8. | The stage at which these reasons are given |
| 9. | Whether and what further remedies are available to contest the administrative decision |
| 10. | Whether the issue involves an application for a benefit or a deprivation of a right |
| 11. | Administrative efficiency |

In *Minister of Environmental Affairs and Tourism v Phambili Fisheries (Pty) Ltd*,[119] the court suggested that the appropriate length of a statement of reasons may be 'a brief statement of one or two pages only'. In *Commissioner, South African Police Service and Others v Maimela and Another*,[120] on the other hand, the court suggested that, depending on the circumstances, 'the reasons need not always be "full written reasons"; the "briefest *pro forma* reasons may suffice".'

COUNTER POINT

**Standard form reasons**

There are two cases in which the adequacy of 'standard form' reasons have been considered.

In *Nomala v Permanent Secretary, Department of Welfare*,[121] the applicant was challenging the validity of reasons provided for refusal of a disability grant. The reasons provided were in a 'standard form reasons letter', which looked something like this:

**Application is rejected for the following reason:**

1. Not disabled [ ]
2. Condition is treatable [ ]
3. Specialist's report is required [ ]
4. Medical form incomplete [ ]
5. Not enough objective medical information [ ]

The administrator would place a tick in the appropriate square brackets on the form, indicating the 'reason' why the application had been rejected. The court held that the reasons were insufficient and invalid, deciding that the first two reasons 'disclose nothing of the reasoning process or the information upon which it is based'.[122] This would place an affected person in 'no better position' to appeal than had they been first-time applicants. The applicant argued that items 3 to 5, while also disclosing nothing of the reasoning process, indicate that 'by definition the decision maker admits that the information supplied is not sufficient for a proper decision to be taken'.[123]

CONTINUED >>>

119 *Phambili Fisheries* para 40.
120 *Maimela* 486A.
121 2001 (8) BCLR 844 (E).
122 *Nomala* 856.
123 *Nomala* 855.

The court agreed, finding that such a decision would be subject to review on this basis. The court added that:

> the reasons do not educate the beneficiary concerned about what to address specifically in an appeal or a new application. It does not instil confidence in the process, and certainly fails to improve the rational quality of the decisions arrived at.[124]

A seemingly contrary decision was reached in *Ngomana v CEO, South African Social Security Agency*.[125] The court in this case was considering whether reasons had been provided to social assistance applicants that complied with the requirements of the Social Assistance Act,[126] which required the provision of reasons. It did not consider PAJA in this context. The court was specifically concerned with written notice to unsuccessful applicants that their applications had been rejected because they were not supported by the required medical report. The court correctly recognised that the relevant legal provisions required the submission of a medical report and that, in the absence of such a report, the application was bound to fail.[127] The court suggested:

> The remedy of an applicant who took issue with the medical report furnished by a medical officer would be to seek to obtain an improved report, or to otherwise seek to impugn the report that had been furnished; it would not be to challenge or query the Agency's refusal to approve a grant application that self-evidently did not satisfy the eligibility requirements.[128]

The court proceeded to hold that:

> a notification to an applicant who had submitted an application for a disability grant that was not supported by a medical report confirming the disability, or was accompanied by a medical report negating the existence of a disability, which gave as a reason for the refusal of the application that it was not supported by the content of the submitted medical report would comply adequately with the requirement of ... [the Act].[129]

What is the correct approach? Starting with *Ngomana*, it is important to distinguish between the absence of a medical report and a medical report that does not support the application, a distinction that the court ignores. The absence of a medical report is a question of fact and it is clear that the decision-maker is not legally authorised to make a decision in such a case. Although the application would be rejected, it would be possible for the applicant to make a new submission accompanied by a report. What reasons ought to be given in this case, in accordance with the prerequisites and factors that were outlined above? It is submitted that it would be sufficient to notify the unsuccessful applicant that the application was rejected because of the absence of a medical certificate but to notify him or her that the applicable legislation requires the

CONTINUED >>>

124 *Nomala* 856.
125 (23036/09) [2010] ZAWCHC 172 (13 September 2010).
126 13 of 2004.
127 *Ngomana* para 48.
128 *Ngomana* para 48.
129 *Ngomana* para 49.

submission of a medical certificate supporting the application, accompanied by a copy of the relevant legislative requirements. This is in accordance with the requirement that the administrator must explicitly refer to extraneous sources. This would apply only in the case of the absence of a medical certificate, however.

Before examining the other scenarios raised in these two cases, it is worth mentioning that tender applications in the public procurement process are often rejected because of the applicants' failure to provide necessary information or other formalities. Tenders that are lacking in material requirements are essentially disqualified in an initial vetting process, which may be called the 'administrative compliance' stage. This means that only those that have complied with the formal requirements are then assessed substantively, in the 'technical compliance' assessment. This is illustrated in *Millennium Waste Management (Pty) Ltd v Chairperson, Tender Board: Limpopo Province and Others*.[130] In tender applications there is usually no second chance, but it is submitted that the reasons for rejection of tender applications that are lacking in formal requirements could be confined to notifying the applicant of the absence of a required detail accompanied by reference to the legal provisions requiring such item. This is essentially the same approach as outlined above in respect of an absent medical certificate. In both cases, the decision not to accept the application is one that is made by the exercise of very limited discretion – essentially a basic finding.

Returning to *Ngomana*, it is submitted that a medical certificate that does not support the application ought to be treated differently from an absent certificate. It is not enough for the administrator simply to notify the applicant that 'your certificate did not support your application', which the *Ngomana* court suggests would be acceptable. This is not a basic question of fact, but requires some judgment on the part of the administrator. The latter would have to explain *why* the certificate is inadequate. As the court suggests, it would then be the applicant's task to take the matter up with her doctor or another doctor in order to obtain an improved certificate (if the facts supported it).

Looking at the grounds supplied in the form mentioned in *Nomala*, item 3 is essentially the same as saying that there is no medical certificate. The others would all require some explanation on the part of the administrator: on what basis was the decision reached that the applicant is 'not disabled', how did the administrator decide that the condition is 'treatable', explain why the medical form is incomplete (what details are missing?) and, similarly, indicate what objective medical information is missing.

This discussion has been quite detailed, but it is a useful illustration of why, in some cases, the briefest pro-forma reasons may suffice, whereas more detail would be required in other cases.

The final observation to make in respect of the adequacy of reasons is an obvious one but should be stated in the interests of completeness: the reasons provided must be true.[131] In other words, the reasons must indicate the reasoning process actually followed and conclusions that were actually reached by the administrator.

130 2008 (2) SA 481 (SCA).

131 See *Minister of Social Development v Phoenix Cash & Carry-Pmb* CC [2007] 3 All SA 115 (SCA) para 23.

### 9.3.1 Are reasons revealing possible grounds of review 'adequate'?

As pointed out above, one of the requirements for adequacy is that the reasons must indicate how the administrator reached his or her decision, which includes the reasoning process leading up to the conclusion(s) reached. It is not necessary, for purposes of meeting the 'adequate reasons' standard, that such reasons have to be free from criticism. If the reasons reveal that there could be doubts as to the decision's reasonableness or rationality, or that the administrator failed to take into account relevant considerations (or any other possible ground of review), the reasons are not inadequate on that basis. On the contrary, if we bear in mind that one of the purposes of reasons is to allow the affected individual to decide whether to challenge the decision, reasons that reveal flaws in the decision-making process *will* be adequate. In short, what this means is that the adequacy of the reasons has no necessary bearing on the validity of the decision. They are two separate issues.

This was the essence of the court's finding in *Commissioner, South African Revenue Service v Sprigg Investment 117 CC t/a Global Investment*.[132] The respondent argued that reasons provided in this case were inadequate because they fell short of showing that the decision was rational and that the appellant had taken into account the relevant 'decisional referents'.[133] The court reasoned that, in essence, the respondent was putting the cart before the horse: assessing the adequacy of reasons was an inquiry that preceded a consideration of whether the decision was valid or not. As the court pointed out, 'the question ... is simply whether the respondent has sufficiently been furnished with the commissioner's actual reasons ... to enable it to formulate its objection thereto'.[134] The court accordingly concluded that there was 'absolutely no reason why the respondent would be unable to formulate its objection, if it has any, in the circumstances'.[135]

This issue is further canvassed in the following section, in respect of procedural matters.

## 9.4 Procedure and remedies

Prior to PAJA, the court in *Commissioner, South African Police Service and Others v Maimela and Another*[136] stated that:

> the order sought was one to furnish 'full and proper written reasons'. To the extent that the wording of the prayer conveys that the Court can direct an administrative decision-maker, who has furnished reasons, to give further or better reasons, an order could not have been made in those terms. A Court can make an order for reasons to be furnished only if it concludes that the decision-maker did not give reasons at all or that what are purported to be 'reasons' do not in law constitute reasons. A Court cannot prescribe to an administrative decision-maker what his/her/its reasons should be. Should the person whose rights or interests are affected by an administrative action contend that the reasons do not justify the action, the appropriate remedy is to have the action reviewed, not to attempt to force the decision-maker to provide better reasons or to supply particulars to the reasons.

132 2011 (4) SA 551 (SCA).
133 *Sprigg Investment* para 13.
134 *Sprigg Investment* para 14.
135 *Sprigg Investment* para 17.
136 *Maimela* 487B–D.

Currie contends that this is unlikely to be correct under PAJA, and that 'an appropriate remedy to cure an inadequate statement of reasons is an order compelling provision of reasons that are up to the required standard'.[137] If we can regard reasons that are inadequate as being reasons that 'do not in law constitute reasons', then there is no necessary disagreement between the *Maimela* court and Currie. To be sure, if we consider the requirement that a requester must not already have been given reasons, this would clearly cover the situation where he or she has been given inadequate reasons. In other words, if the requester has been given inadequate reasons, for purposes of section 5(1), he or she has, in law, not been given reasons at all. The adequacy of the reasons must be seen in the context of whether they explain how the administrator reached the decision (whether in a flawed way or not), allowing the requester to weigh up his or her options. 'Adequacy' in this sense does not mean that the reasons must justify the decision in a way that satisfies the requirements of lawfulness, reasonableness and procedural fairness in PAJA. This is what the court in *Maimela* seems to be suggesting – that a person alleging that the reasons are defective because they reveal a flaw in the decision-making process is not permitted to ask for improved reasons but he or she must take the matter on review, alleging that the decision is defective on the basis of the ground of review in question.

A requester faced with a refusal to give adequate reasons (or any reasons at all) may make an application to court for an order directing the administrator to give reasons. This is suggested by the remedy in section 8(1)(*a*) of PAJA which states that a court or tribunal, in proceedings for judicial review in terms of section 6(1), may grant any order that is just and equitable, including orders directing the administrator to give reasons.

The 2009 regulations, setting out rules of procedure for administrative action,[138] confirm this. They provide that, if an administrator fails to respond to a request for reasons or refuses to give reasons, the requester may apply to court for an order compelling the administrator to give reasons. Such application must be made on notice of motion supported by affidavit.[139]

## 9.5 Inconsistent sets of reasons

An administrator may provide further reasons on affidavit if an application for the review of the decision is brought.[140] Is there a problem if these reasons are different from those initially furnished? In *National Lotteries Board and Others v SA Education and Environment Project*,[141] the court referred to the rule in English law that a decision unsupported by adequate reasons would:

> ordinarily be void and cannot be validated by different reasons given afterwards – even if they show that the original decision may have been justified. For in truth the later reasons are not the true reasons for the decision, but rather an *ex post facto* rationalisation of a bad decision.[142]

137 Currie (2007) 150 fn 54.

138 Rules of procedure for judicial review of administrative action, Reg 3(5)(*c*) of GN R966 in *GG* 32622 of 09.10.2009 (not yet in operation).

139 Reg 6.

140 See Rule 53 of the Uniform Rules of Court.

141 2013 (1) SA 170.

142 *National Lotteries Board* para 27.

The court, however, found that it did not need to 'strictly' decide whether our courts are required to follow this approach,[143] but held, in the circumstances before it, the appellant had exercised its discretion unlawfully when it exercised its discretion, despite the fact that it may have had other reasons for reaching the decision.[144]

COUNTER POINT

**Supplementing reasons upon review**

De Ville suggests that the reasons furnished upon request and subsequent reasons furnished in the review proceedings or on affidavit must be 'consistent'.[145] There are several cases where there were differences in the reasons provided, but none of these decisions turned on this inconsistency.[146] This does not, presumably, mean that the reasons have to be formulated in exactly the same way. The latter reasons may be more detailed, but there should be no factual inconsistencies, including reasons mentioned for the first time at a later stage.

Currie, on the other hand, suggests that 'reasons given in satisfaction of the right to be given reasons may form part of the administration's case for justifying the reasonableness of the action taken, but do not necessarily exhaust that case'.[147]

It is submitted that the correct position is that suggested by De Ville. Currie asks why a single statement of reasons should limit the government's ability to justify a decision on review, seemingly basing this view on the grounds of administrative efficiency: the administrator is under pressure to provide initial reasons and may consequently leave something important out of the statement of reasons. In the light of the fact that PAJA gives an administrator 90 days in which to furnish reasons, it is submitted that this is enough time to ensure that the reasons supplied at that stage adequately justify the decision.

## 9.6 Reasons and legality

In *Judicial Service Commission and Another v Cape Bar Council and Another*,[148] the respondent Bar Council (CBC) was challenging the decision by the applicant (JSC) not to appoint nominees for the Western Cape bench and to leave two positions unfilled. The 'reasons' provided by the JSC for this was simply that none of the candidates had received a majority vote.[149] The CBC alleged that this was 'no reason at all', thus raising the inference that the decision was irrational.[150] The JSC's argument was that it was under no statutory or constitutional duty to give reasons; that it had in any event provided reasons (those mentioned above); and that because of its secret voting procedure it was not possible to give reasons other than those it had given.[151]

143 *National Lotteries Board* para 27.
144 *National Lotteries Board* para 28.
145 De Ville (2005) 294 fn 67.
146 *National and Overseas Modular Construction (Pty) Ltd v Tender Board, Free State Provincial Government and Another* 1999 (1) SA 701 (O); *Liquor Web (Edms) Bpk v Voorsitter, Drankraad en 'n Ander* 2001 (1) SA 1069 (T); and *Grinaker LTA Ltd and Another v Tender Board (Mpumalanga) and Others* [2002] 3 All SA 336 (T).
147 Currie (2007) 147.
148 2013 (1) SA 170.
149 *JSC v CBC* para 38.
150 *JSC v CBC* para 38.
151 *JSC v CBC* para 42.

The court was not convinced. First, it reasoned, there was an implied duty on the JSC to provide reasons because of the constitutional duty on it 'to exercise its powers in a way that is not irrational or arbitrary', and due to the constitutional values of accountability and transparency.[152] Consequently, the court held that the JSC is, 'as a general rule, obliged to give reasons for its decision not to recommend a particular candidate if properly called upon to do so'.[153]

As for the 'reasons' provided by the JSC, the court held that these were inadequate because they did 'not serve any of the purposes for which reasons should be given'.[154] At first glance, the argument relating to procedure seems compelling, but the court, bearing in mind that the procedure is not imposed upon the JSC, but that the JSC has the power to determine its own procedure, reasoned that the JSC's chosen procedure must, 'as a matter of principle, enable the JSC to comply with its constitutional and legal obligations'.[155] If the procedure does not allow the giving of cogent reasons, so the argument goes, then the JSC must change its procedure to allow it to do so. The court fortified this finding with the observation that the JSC was required to give reasons for a recommendation of an appointment to the Constitutional Court, and if this was possible, then it ought to be possible to do so for other appointments as well.

The absence of adequate reasons in this particular case, consequently, led the court to conclude that the JSC's decision was irrational. This judgment cannot be faulted and it is interesting that the courts have relied on the basic principle of rationality as a component of legality in order to find that, in certain circumstances, rationality requires procedural fairness[156] and, in the case just discussed, the duty to provide reasons as well.

## THIS CHAPTER IN ESSENCE

Section 5 of PAJA gives effect to the right to reasons in section 33(2) of the Constitution. It does this by providing for a 'request-driven' process: the affected individual does not have a right to be provided reasons immediately but may request reasons from the decision-maker within the stipulated time period. The decision-maker must then provide such reasons within a further stipulated time period. These reasons must be in writing and they must be adequate, allowing the affected person to decide how to proceed with her matter. There are several prerequisites for the adequacy of reasons, discussed in some detail and set out clearly in this chapter. Where these prerequisites are not absolute, several factors must be taken into account in determining the adequacy of the reasons. These are also discussed and set out in the chapter.

## FURTHER READING

- Hoexter, C (2012) *Administrative Law in South Africa* (2nd ed) Cape Town: Juta Chapter 8
- Quinot, G (2011) The Right to Reasons for Administrative Action as a Key Ingredient of a Culture of Justification *Speculum Juris* 25:32–47

152 *JSC v CBC* para 43.
153 *JSC v CBC* para 45.
154 *JSC v CBC* para 46.
155 *JSC v CBC* para 47.
156 See *Albutt*.

# Chapter 10

# Administrative justice and drafting empowering provisions

*Geo Quinot*



## 10.1 Introduction

As we have noted throughout the preceding chapters, administrative law in South Africa has historically been dominated by the control mechanism of judicial review. Our very conception of what administrative law is and its role within the overall legal and public administration systems have been largely determined by this reactive, control perspective. We have also, however, noted at various points in the preceding chapters that administrative law has a more proactive role to play in guiding the administration of the state. In Chapter 2, we noted this dual nature of administrative law.[1] As we noted there, administrative law can be described as aiming on the one hand to restrict public power and on the other hand to enable and facilitate the exercise of public power. This dual nature of administrative law was famously described by Harlow and Rawlings in terms of a traffic light metaphor as the 'red light theory' and 'green light theory' of administrative law.[2] One of the key differences between these two

1 See Chapter 2 section 2.6.1.
2 Harlow, C & Rawlings, R (2009) *Law and Administration* (3rd ed) Ch 1.

views on administrative law, is the lesser role assigned to adjudication in green light theory. While red light theorists placed primary emphasis on the role of courts to control administrative decision-making, green light theorists placed less emphasis on adjudication and more emphasis on other forms of control, such as the rules within which administrative decisions must be taken.[3] In Chapters 4 and 5, we also noted these different types of control, what we called judicial and non-judicial regulation of administrative action. Another way of looking at these different forms of control is as external and internal controls.[4] External controls are mostly imposed retrospectively by assessing an administrative decision that has already been taken. Judicial review is the prime example. Internal controls are often imposed prospectively by informing an administrative decision while it is being taken. A prime example of this type of control is the empowering provision that grants the power to take the administrative action. That empowering provision is already an important instrument to control the actions of the administrator in determining what the administrator can and cannot do and how they must do it. It is accordingly important to consider the implications of administrative law for the drafting of legislation that will empower administrators to take decisions. The rules of administrative law should also serve to guide the drafting of empowering provisions in a way aimed at achieving administrative justice.

Another important reason for focusing on the implications of administrative law for the drafting of empowering provisions is the realisation that many of the provisions that empower administrative decision-making in the modern state are not found in primary legislation. Rather, a range of further instruments are used today to empower administrators to take decisions. This is, for example, reflected in the broad definition of 'empowering provision' in the Promotion of Administrative Justice Act (PAJA),[5] which defines an empowering provision as 'a law, a rule of common law, customary law, or an agreement, instrument or other document in terms of which an administrative action was purportedly taken'.[6] Many of these instruments are created by the administration itself, for example regulations made by a Minister under a primary statute. An instrument of increasing relevance is contractual mechanisms. The state administration is increasingly entering into contractual arrangements with private parties to fulfil public functions. In such instances, the various contractual instruments used to set up the relationship between the public entity and the private supplier constitute the empowering provisions in terms of which administrative actions may be taken. This does not only refer to the contract entered into between the parties, but also the tender invitation issued by the public entity to solicit bids that will lead to the conclusion of a contract. For example, in *Allpay Consolidated Investment Holdings (Pty) Ltd and Others v Chief Executive Officer of the South African Social Security Agency and Others*[7] the Constitutional Court measured the administrator's decision against the request for proposals to determine whether there was material non-compliance with a mandatory condition of the empowering provision.

In a sense, administrative law has a double function in respect of such instruments. On the one hand, the creation of the instrument, for example the drafting and publication of the regulation, contract or invitation to tender, may itself be an administrative action and

3 Harlow & Rawlings (2009) 38.
4 Harlow & Rawlings (2009) 37.
5 3 of 2000.
6 PAJA section 1(vi), see Chapter 3 section 3.7.4.
7 2014 (1) SA 604 (CC) para 62.

administrative law would thus apply to that action.[8] On the other hand, the instrument in turn would empower further administrative action, which would be subject to administrative law. In other words, an action that is itself subject to administrative law becomes the instrument (empowering provision) to empower further administrative action. This perspective is illuminated by the useful depiction of administrative law as law *for* the administration, law *of* the administration and law *against* the administration.[9]

In South Africa, not much attention has been given to this dimension of administrative law.[10] That is, the role of administrative law in guiding the drafting of empowering provisions. The elevation of administrative law to the status of supreme constitutional rules by means of the right to administrative justice in section 33 of the Constitution, has, however, made this role more important than before. Administrative law largely amounted to the control of administrative decision-making *in terms of* the statutory mandate granted by the supreme Parliament prior to constitutionalisation in South Africa, which meant that administrative-law controls largely depended on the empowering provision. In contrast, under the supreme Constitution and as part of the constitutional guarantee of administrative justice, the position is now largely reversed. Administrative justice is now part of the supreme normative framework introduced by the Constitution to which all legislation must adhere.

The Constitutional Court has recognised this dimension of administrative justice in its judgment in the *Dawood* case.[11] In this matter, the court declared that the possibility of administrative action being judicially reviewed for compliance with the Constitution does not absolve the legislature from also aiming to protect the right to administrative justice in its work, that is when drafting legislation. The court thus declared:

> The fact, however, that the exercise of a discretionary power may subsequently be successfully challenged on administrative grounds, for example, that it was not reasonable, does not relieve the legislature of its constitutional obligation to promote, protect and fulfil the rights entrenched in the Bill of Rights. In a constitutional democracy such as ours the responsibility to protect constitutional rights in practice is imposed both on the legislature and on the executive and its officials.[12]

This chapter considers the implications of the principles of administrative justice as set out in section 33 of the Constitution and PAJA for the drafting of empowering provisions.

## 10.2 Lawfulness

As noted in Chapter 6, lawfulness involves at its core the requirement that all administrative action must be authorised. This is the basis for the very requirement that an empowering provision must exist for every administrative action. Furthermore, the requirement of lawfulness entails that the administrative action must be taken in terms of the authorisation, that is, the administrative action must fall within the boundaries of the empowering provision.

8 See Chapter 3 section 3.7.1 on the question of whether rule-making amounts to administrative action in South African law.

9 Schlössels, RJN & Zijlstra, SE (2010) *Bestuursrecht in de Sociale Rechstaat* 11–12.

10 A notable exception is the PhD study of Bednar-Giyose, J (2018) *Legislative Drafting and the Appropriate Delineation of Administrative Power* (University of the Witwatersrand).

11 *Dawood and Another v Minister of Home Affairs and Others; Shalabi and Another v Minister of Home Affairs and Others; Thomas and Another v Minister of Home Affairs and Others* 2000 (3) SA 936 (CC).

12 *Dawood* para 48.

Lawfulness therefore gives expression to the core constitutional requirement of legality as part of the rule of law, which the Constitutional Court in *Fedsure Life Assurance Ltd and Others v Greater Johannesburg Transitional Metropolitan Council and Others*[13] formulated as follows:

> It seems central to the conception of our constitutional order that the Legislature and Executive in every sphere are constrained by the principle that they may exercise no power and perform no function beyond that conferred upon them by law.

These basic requirements of lawfulness hold important implications for the drafting of empowering provisions.

### 10.2.1 Certainty

If administrative action is limited to the boundaries of the empowering provision, it is of prime importance that those boundaries be stated as clearly as possible. Without clarity on the exact content and scope of the powers granted, an administrator will always be at risk of stepping outside of those boundaries and hence acting unlawfully.

While clarity is always an objective in legislative drafting,[14] it takes on an added importance in the case of empowering provisions given the requirement of lawfulness. In *Affordable Medicines Trust and Others v Minister of Health and Others*[15] the Constitutional Court thus declared that 'delegation must not be so broad or vague that the authority to whom the power is delegated is unable to determine the nature and the scope of the powers conferred'.

There are numerous general techniques of legislative drafting that can be employed to enhance clarity and hence certainty about the scope of the administrative powers. One such technique is to bear the readership of the provision in mind. As McLeod rightly reminds us, the meaning of any written text depends as much on the reader as on the writer, which is equally true in the case of legislative drafting.[16] When drafting empowering provisions, it is accordingly important to bear in mind who the administrator is that will have to interpret that provision to formulate an administrative action within the boundaries of the provision. The empowering provision should be framed in such a way to make sense within the relevant administrative context and to the particular administrators in that context.

**PAUSE FOR REFLECTION**

**Whose interpretation?**

One of the most vexing questions in administrative law is whose interpretation of empowering provisions should be definitive of the meaning of a particular provision. This question arises when an administrative action is challenged in judicial review on the basis of an error of law. As noted in Chapter 6, PAJA section 6(2)(*d*) allows a court to review an administrative action if the action was materially influenced by an error of law.[17] This will be the case if the administrator adopted an interpretation of the

CONTINUED >>>

13 1999 (1) SA 374 (CC) para 58.

14 McLeod, I (2009) *Principles of Legislative and Regulatory Drafting* 3; *Dawood* para 47; *Investigating Directorate: Serious Economic Offences and Others v Hyundai Motor Distributors (Pty) Ltd and Others: In Re Hyundai Motor Distributors (Pty) Ltd and Others v Smit NO and Others* 2001 (1) SA 545 (CC) para 24.

15 2006 (3) SA 247 (CC) para 34.

16 McLeod (2009) 4.

17 Chapter 6 section 6.3.2.

empowering provision that the court subsequently disagrees with and upon the interpretation that the court adopts, the administrator would have taken a different decision.[18]

The difficult question, however, is why the courts' interpretation should necessarily trump that of the administrator, especially in instances where the administrator's interpretation is a feasible one. This is especially problematic given that courts are only meant to review an administrative action and not to determine its correctness, which would be a matter of appeal. When a court rules that an administrative action should be set aside because the administrator adopted an *incorrect* interpretation of the empowering provision, this distinction between review and appeal, which South African courts insist on as we noted in Chapters 1[19] and 5,[20] becomes distinctly blurred.[21]

The challenges raised by review for error of law have played an important role in the development of the notion of deference in many common-law jurisdictions.[22] Particularly in Canadian administrative law, Dyzenhaus has engaged with the notion of deference as part of the question of how courts should deal with administrative interpretation of the law.[23] That is, should courts defer to the administrator's interpretation of the empowering provision given that the provision was primarily enacted with the view that the relevant administrator would be the one to implement it?

Of course, the issues raised by review for error of law is closely linked to the extent to which the empowering provision allows for significantly different interpretations.

Another important mechanism to enhance certainty in empowering provisions and thus facilitate lawful administrative action, is the inclusion of appropriate definitions. While it is a fairly standard practice to define the key terms used in the particular enactment in primary legislation, it is far less common in other types of empowering provisions such as regulations, instructions etc. For example, the dispute in *Tseleng v Chairman, Unemployment Insurance Board and Another*[24] regarding the calculation of the period of unemployment, which determined the applicant's entitlement to unemployment benefits, could have been avoided if the term 'application' had been defined in the empowering provision so that there could be no uncertainty regarding the calculation of the period of unemployment in terms of the statutory prescript that stated that 'a period of unemployment shall not be deemed to have commenced until the contributor has lodged an application'.

Apart from the need to define key terms, it is also important for those terms to be consistently used with that meaning throughout the instrument.

18 *Johannesburg Metropolitan Municipality v Gauteng Development Tribunal and Others* 2010 (6) SA 182 (CC) para 91.
19 See Chapter 1 section 1.3.5.
20 See Chapter 5 section 5.2.
21 Hoexter, C (2012) *Administrative Law in South Africa* 288; Burns, Y & Henrico, R (2020) *Administrative Law* 447.
22 On deference, see Chapter 5 section 5.4.
23 Dyzenhaus, D 'The politics of deference: judicial review and democracy' in Taggart, M (Ed) *The Province of Administrative Law* (1997) 279.
24 1995 (3) SA 162 (T).

### 10.2.2 Guiding discretionary powers

The limitation imposed by the lawfulness requirement on discretionary decision-making, which is a hallmark of public administration,[25] requires empowering provisions to include boundaries when granting discretionary powers.

In *Dawood*, the Constitutional Court has noted that the obligation of the legislature to protect constitutional rights, by implication including the right to administrative justice, requires the legislature to 'take care when legislation is drafted to limit the risk of an unconstitutional exercise of the discretionary powers it confers'.[26]

In a key passage in its *Dawood* judgment, the Constitutional Court noted the importance of providing guidance to administrators in the exercise of discretionary powers:

> We must not lose sight of the fact that rights enshrined in the Bill of Rights must be protected and may not be unjustifiably infringed. It is for the legislature to ensure that, when necessary, guidance is provided as to when limitation of rights will be justifiable. It is therefore not ordinarily sufficient for the legislature merely to say that discretionary powers that may be exercised in a manner that could limit rights should be read in a manner consistent with the Constitution in the light of the constitutional obligations placed on such officials to respect the Constitution. Such an approach would often not promote the spirit, purport and objects of the Bill of Rights. Guidance will often be required to ensure that the Constitution takes root in the daily practice of governance. Where necessary, such guidance must be given. Guidance could be provided either in the legislation itself, or where appropriate by a legislative requirement that delegated legislation be properly enacted by a competent authority.[27]

In the *Dawood* matter, the court found the empowering provision wanting in failing to set out the factors that the administrators should take into account when exercising the broad discretionary powers granted to them. From this and other judgments of the Constitutional Court, it is clear that drafters of empowering provisions are obliged to provide guidance to administrators when granting (wide) discretionary powers.[28]

### 10.2.3 Purpose

The need to limit discretionary administrative power requires empowering provisions to be explicit about the purposes for which power is granted. This is because even though the particular action may be authorised, it will still be unlawful if that action is taken for a reason not authorised,[29] an ulterior purpose or motive.[30] This requirement can put an administrator at considerable risk in the absence of a clear declaration of purpose in the empowering provision.

25 See Chapter 1 section 1.3.3.
26 *Dawood* para 48.
27 *Dawood* para 54 (footnotes omitted).
28 *Janse van Rensburg and Another v Minister of Trade and Industry and Another* 2001 (1) SA 29 (CC) para 25; *Justice Alliance of South Africa v President of Republic of South Africa and Others, Freedom Under Law v President of Republic of South Africa and Others, Centre for Applied Legal Studies and Another v President of Republic of South Africa and Others* 2011 (5) SA 388 (CC) para 51; *Lawyers for Human Rights v Minister of Home Affairs and Others* 2017 (5) SA 480 (CC) paras 48–49.
29 PAJA section 6(2)(*e*)(i).
30 PAJA section 6(2)(*e*)(ii).

**EXAMPLE**

There are many ways in which the purpose of an empowering provision and accordingly powers granted in that provision can be made clear.

The Border Management Authority Act[31] provides examples of the three most common ways in which purpose is indicated in legislation.

The first is in the so-called long title of the Act, which is the text immediately below the name of the statute. The long title of the Border Management Authority Act reads as follows:

**To provide for the establishment, organisation, regulation, functions and control of the Border Management Authority; to provide for the appointment, terms of office, conditions of service and functions of the Commissioner and Deputy Commissioners; to provide for the appointment and terms and conditions of employment of officials; to provide for the duties, functions and powers of officers; to provide for the establishment of an Inter-Ministerial Consultative Committee, Border Technical Committee and advisory committees; to provide for delegations; to provide for the review or appeal of decisions of officers; to provide for certain offences and penalties; to provide for annual reporting; to provide for the Minister to make regulations with regard to certain matters; and to provide for matters connected therewith.**

The second way to indicate the purpose of an empowering provision is to include a preamble in the statute. The Border Management Authority Act starts with the following:

**PREAMBLE**

**RECOGNISING** that border management is exercised by multiple organs of state with the purpose of securing the borders of the Republic and protecting national interest;

**RECOGNISING FURTHER** that there is a need for integrated and co-ordinated border management in accordance with the Constitution, international and domestic law, in order to–

1. contribute to the socio-economic development of the Republic;
2. ensure effective and efficient border law enforcement functions at ports of entry and the border;
3. contribute to the facilitation of legitimate trade and secure travel;
4. contribute to the prevention of smuggling and trafficking of human beings and goods;
5. prevent illegal cross-border movement;
6. contribute to the protection of the Republic's environmental and natural resources; and
7. protect the Republic from harmful and infectious diseases, pests and substances;

**ACKNOWLEDGING** that the circumstances of modern travel and trade require a single Authority to be responsible for ports of entry and the control of the borders of the Republic and the need to balance the facilitation of legitimate trade and travel with security; and

**ACKNOWLEDGING FURTHER** the constitutional responsibility of the South African National Defence Force to defend and protect the Republic, its territorial integrity and its people.

CONTINUED >>>

31 2 of 2020.

Thirdly, a statute may contain a distinct objects clause. In the Border Management Authority Act, section 3 reads as follows:

> 3. Object of Act.–The object of this Act is to establish and empower the Authority to achieve–
>
> (*a*) integrated border law enforcement within the border law enforcement area and at ports of entry; and
>
> (*b*) co-operation on and co-ordination of border management matters in general.

When discretionary power must subsequently be exercised under this Act, for example an officer must decide whether to search any person, goods, premises or vehicle at a port of entry in terms of the power granted in section 18 of the Act, that officer should rely on the purpose statements above to determine whether their intended actions are lawful, that is whether such search will be aimed at achieving any of these purposes.

The purpose of powers granted in an empowering provision may also be stated more specifically within an empowering provision, typically when the relevant administrator is created or the relevant powers granted. For example, the Border Management Authority Act creates an Inter-Ministerial Consultative Committee in section 24 with the following purpose statement in subsection (1):

> The Inter-Ministerial Consultative Committee is hereby established to–
>
> (*a*) consult on–
>
> (i) the designation, determination, appointment or prescription, and withdrawal or cancellation of a port of entry;
>
> (ii) the proposed amendment of any legislation that may affect border management;
>
> (iii) any international agreement or protocol that affects the Authority;
>
> (iv) the advice and reports of the Border Technical Committee referred to in section 25 (3) and (4); and
>
> (v) any other matter referred to it by any of the Cabinet members referred to in subsection (3) (*b*) or (*c*); and
>
> (*b*) consider and discuss the Commissioner's reports on the performance of the Authority in terms of section 11 (2) (*j*).

Any administrative action taken by this committee can consequently be measured against these provisions to determine its lawfulness in terms of purpose.

Apart from purpose as a distinct basis upon which administrative action may be tested for lawfulness, purpose has also become important to determine compliance with procedures prescribed in the empowering provision. In the important judgment of the Constitutional

Court in *Allpay Consolidated Investment Holdings (Pty) Ltd and Others v Chief Executive Officer, South African Social Security Agency and Others*,[32] the court held that:

> The proper approach is to establish, factually, whether an irregularity occurred. Then the irregularity must be legally evaluated to determine whether it amounts to a ground of review under PAJA. This legal evaluation must, where appropriate, take into account the materiality of any deviance from legal requirements, by linking the question of compliance to the purpose of the provision, before concluding that a review ground under PAJA has been established ... the central element is to link the question of compliance to the purpose of the provision.

It is evident from this statement that an explicit formulation of the purpose of the empowering provision will be of particular value in determining compliance and hence lawfulness of administrative action.

While we have focused in this section on the role of the purpose statement in an empowering provision to promote lawful administrative decisions, it is important to note that purpose also plays an important role in achieving rational administrative decisions. In providing the test for determining the rationality of administrative decisions, PAJA requires in section 6(2)(*f*)(ii)(*bb*) that there must be a rational connection between the administrative decision and the purpose of the empowering provision. This requirement further emphasises the importance of a clear statement of purpose in an empowering provision.

## 10.2.4 Duty to act

A key consideration for the drafting of empowering provisions from a lawfulness perspective is whether a particular provision imposes a duty to act or whether it only grants a power to act. This distinction between duty and power is a common issue in legislative drafting in many legal systems and in particular in those where the distinction may have vastly different consequences in the application of administrative law.[33] The same is true in South Africa. For example, PAJA includes in its definition of administrative action, 'any failure to take a decision'.[34] It consequently provides for a ground of review of administrative action on the basis that 'the action concerned consists of a failure to take a decision'.[35] This immediately raises the question of when an omission by an administrator will qualify as an administrative action open to challenge. In *Offit Enterprises (Pty) Ltd and Another v Coega Development Corporation and Others*[36] the Supreme Court of Appeal explained that a failure that would be relevant under PAJA:

> refers to a decision that the administrator in question is under some obligation to take, not simply to indecisiveness in planning on policy issues. It is directed at dilatoriness in taking decisions that the administrator is supposed to take ...

To distinguish between instances of 'indecisiveness' and 'obligation', the drafting of the particular empowering provision will be of primary importance. The standard approach to distinguish between a duty and a power is to differentiate between the use of the words 'may' and 'shall'/'must' in an empowering provision. As a point of departure, the use of the word

32 2014 (1) SA 604 (CC) paras 28 and 30.
33 McLeod (2009) 103–113.
34 PAJA section 1(i), see Chapter 3 section 3.7.1.
35 PAJA section 6(2)(*g*), see Chapter 6 section 6.2.1.2.
36 2010 (4) SA 242 (SCA) para 43.

'may' in relation to authorisation denotes a power to act, but not a duty to act. In contrast, the use of the words 'shall' or 'must' denote a duty to act.

For example, the Public Finance Management Act[37] states in section 76(1)(*b*) that the 'National Treasury must make regulations or issue instructions applicable to departments, concerning ... the recovery of losses and damages', whereas it states in section 76(2)(*c*) that the 'National Treasury may make regulations or issue instructions applicable to departments, concerning ... the establishment of and control over trading entities'. The sole difference between the authorisation granted in subsection (1) and subsection (2) of section 76 lies in the use of the word 'must' in the former and 'may' in the latter. The clear intention of this drafting is to convey that the former imposes a duty on the National Treasury whereas the latter does not. In terms of administrative law, one would thus be able to challenge a failure on the part of National Treasury to issue regulations or instructions in relation to the matters listed in section 76(1) as an unlawful administrative action, but one would not be able to do the same in relation to a failure on National Treasury's part to issue any regulation or instruction in respect of the matters listed in section 76(2).

However, the matter is not always as clear as in this example. The purpose of the empowering provision is again an important consideration in interpreting the words used in order to determine whether a duty or power is granted. Thus, in *Steenkamp and Others v EDCON Ltd*,[38] the Constitutional Court held that:

> The approach that the use of the word 'shall' in a statutory provision means that anything done contrary to such a provision is a nullity is neither rigid nor conclusive. The same can be said of the use of the word 'must'. Many factors must be considered to determine whether a thing done contrary to such a provision is a nullity ... the proper approach is to ascertain what the purpose of the legislation is in this regard ... In each case the legislation will need to be construed properly to establish its purpose.

It is clear that while the use of the words 'may' and 'shall'/'must' provide some guidance on whether the empowering provision creates a duty or a power, the purpose of the provision will also play a role. When drafting empowering provisions it is accordingly important to provide clear and explicit guidance on whether a particular authorisation amounts to a power or a duty, given the differences in how those will be treated in administrative law.

A final consideration regarding a duty to act, is the timeframe within which the duty must be exercised. PAJA provides that an omission will amount to a failure to act when a duty to act has not been exercised within the stated timeframe or, in the absence of a stated timeframe, within a reasonable time.[39] It may not always be easy to determine exactly what would be a reasonable time, which may create undue pressure on administrators to take premature decisions. It is thus desirable that empowering provisions state a timeframe within which a duty to act must be exercised.

### 10.2.5 Consolidated versions

Empowering provisions are quite often amended from time to time. This is especially true of primary legislation, where amendment acts are common. The amendment of empowering provisions creates potential risk for an administrator acting in terms of such empowering

37 1 of 1999.
38 2016 (3) SA 251 (CC) para 182.
39 PAJA section 6(3).

provision in that the administrator may not be relying on the up-to-date version of the provision. This risk can be greatly reduced if amendments are always incorporated in the main text of the empowering provision so that the administrator always has access to the current consolidated version of the empowering provision when taking action.

Unfortunately, amendments to primary legislation are not routinely incorporated into the main text in South Africa and no consolidated versions are officially published. In most cases, only the specific amendments are published in the relevant amendment act. It is accordingly up to the reader to piece the original text and all amendment acts together in order to work with the up-to-date consolidated version of the relevant empowering provision. This problem is exacerbated by the absence of an official statutory code in South Africa, that is an official publication containing all statutes in consolidated form. Within this context, the danger of working with the wrong version of the empowering provision looms large. For example, the Merchant Shipping Act,[40] which provides for the control of merchant shipping in South Africa and *inter alia* empowers the South African Maritime Safety Authority to take a range of decisions in this respect, has been amended by 32 different amendment acts.

While a number of non-governmental organisations, like the Southern African Legal Information Institute (SAFLII)[41] and the Oliver R Tambo Law Library at the University of Pretoria,[42] have launched projects to create freely available consolidated versions of statutes, these projects do not yet cover all statutes. The only comprehensive sources of consolidated legislation in South Africa at present are the legal databases of commercial publishers, which require subscription. This is an unfortunate state of affairs, which should ideally be resolved by an official publication of consolidated statutory law, either by the Department of Justice and Constitutional Development or Parliament.

**PAUSE FOR REFLECTION**

In Chapter 6, we looked at the following hypothetical example of an empowering provision to engage with the requirement of lawfulness.

**Western Cape Disasters Act**

> 5(1) The Premier must by notice in the *Gazette* designate land, owned or leased by the state, for the purpose of constructing temporary shelter to house people who have been left without shelter due to a natural disaster in the province.

Having now considered the implications of lawfulness for the drafting of empowering provisions, what changes would you recommend to this provision to assist administrators in taking lawful administrative action under this provision?

Consider the following issues:

- Is it clear in which *Gazette* the notice must be published? Should this perhaps be clarified by adding a qualifier such as *Government* or *Provincial* to make it clear, or should a definition of the word 'Gazette' perhaps be added to the enactment?

CONTINUED >>>

40 57 of 1951.

41 See the SAFLII database of South African legislation at http://www.saflii.org.

42 See the library's database at http://www.lawsofsouthafrica.up.ac.za/.

- What does the word 'state' mean in this context? Should it be interpreted widely to refer literally to any land in public ownership regardless of what level of government? That is, does this provision empower the Premier to authorise land owned by a national department or a municipality or SANPARKS? Should the word 'state' not be replaced with a more specific word or defined?
- The condition that the power may only be exercised when people have been left without shelter due to a natural disaster in the province is quite narrow. Should the purpose of the power not be stated a bit more broadly?
- Linked to the previous point, does it really matter that the disaster is a natural one? Could this not create unnecessary uncertainty in exercising power under this provision, that is to first determine whether the relevant disaster is indeed a 'natural' one as opposed to man-made? Would it not be better to omit the word 'natural'?
- What does the qualifier 'in the province' refer to, the disaster or the people? Grammatically one would think it relates to the disaster, that is the disaster must have been in the province. But does that really make sense? Does it really matter whether the disaster was in the province or not? Does it not rather matter that the people without shelter are in the province? If so, what drafting steps can be taken to clarify the meaning of the qualifier 'in the province'?

## 10.3 Procedural fairness

The principle of procedural fairness in essence entails that a person to be affected by an administrative action should have an opportunity to participate in that decision, primarily by having the opportunity to make representations to the administrators. It follows, as a basic point, that when an empowering provisions is drafted that authorises an administrator to take a decision that will impact on a person, attention should be given to how the affected persons will be allowed to participate in the decision-making process.[43]

There are a number of lessons to be drawn from the requirement of procedural fairness in administrative law for the drafting process.

A first point relates to when an affected party should be allowed to participate. In *Earthlife Africa (Cape Town) v Director-General: Department of Environmental Affairs and Tourism and Another*[44] the court held that an affected party must have an opportunity to make representations on the final materials to be considered by the decision-maker in order for participation to be fair. In this matter, new materials had been placed before the decision-maker after affected parties had an opportunity to make representations. The court held that it was not 'procedurally fair to take administrative action based on "substantially different" new matter on which interested parties have not had an opportunity to comment'.[45] The implication of this ruling is that participation in decision-making must be carefully timed in order to allow affected parties to comment on the final considerations that will determine the outcome. This should thus be taken into account when designing participatory processes in empowering provisions.

43 Crabbe, V (1993) *Legislative Drafting* 68.
44 2005 (3) SA 156 (C) para 64.
45 *Earthlife Africa* para 61.

A second relevant point is who should be afforded an opportunity to participate when designing participatory processes. While section 33(1) of the Constitution grants 'everyone' the right to procedurally fair administrative action, PAJA narrows that entitlement down in sections 3 and 4. Under PAJA section 3, it is only persons who will be individually, materially and adversely affected by the decision that are entitled to an individualised opportunity to participate in such decision.[46] Under section 4, public participatory processes must be implemented when the public or a class or group of the public stands to be affected by the decision.[47] When these provisions are met, an administrative action will be considered procedurally fair, also in terms of the Constitution. It follows that empowering provisions providing for participation in decision-making do not have to grant opportunities to participate to a wider group than these.

A third important point is to bear the contextual nature of procedural fairness in mind. It has long been established in South African administrative law, and confirmed in section 3(2)(*a*) of PAJA, that procedural fairness is a contextual requirement.[48] That is, the exact procedural steps to be taken in a given instance of administrative action to make it procedurally fair will depend on the circumstances of that case. It is generally not possible to formulate an exact blueprint for a procedurally fair administrative action in abstract terms, that is, outside of the context of a particular scenario. While this is particularly important for procedural requirements within general administrative law, that is the rules applicable to all types of administrative action regardless of sphere of public administration or context, it is also important to bear in mind when formulating empowering provisions for administrative decision-making in particular areas. It will certainly be possible to be more specific regarding what procedural steps will be appropriate in an empowering provision applying to particular instances of decision-making only, but flexibility will have to be maintained even in such formulations of participatory processes. If an empowering provision is too strict in the procedures that it prescribes, it runs the risk of losing the quality of fairness in specific contexts. In such a case, the administrator will be faced with the dilemma of having to adhere to the prescribed procedures in the empowering provision (as a matter of lawfulness), but will also have to supplement those procedural steps with further procedure drawn from general administrative law in order to achieve the flexibility inherent in procedural fairness. It is accordingly advisable to ensure that procedures prescribed in empowering provisions retain a measure of flexibility.

### 10.3.1 PAJA as supplementary

One of the important innovations of PAJA is the formulation of an explicit framework of steps that will constitute procedurally fair decision-making in sections 3 and 4. While these must still be applied in a flexible manner in adherence to the contextual nature of procedural fairness and are formulated in a manner to be flexible in content (for example, requiring '*adequate* notice' and a '*reasonable* opportunity to make representations'),[49] they do provide an extremely useful set of default rules for both individualised participation[50] and public participation[51] in decision-making.

46 See Chapter 7 section 7.3.1.1.

47 See Chapter 7 section 7.3.2.1.

48 *Zondi v MEC for Traditional and Local Government Affairs and Others* 2005 (3) SA 589 (CC) paras 113–114; *Joseph and Others v City of Johannesburg and Others* 2010 (4) SA 55 (CC) para 56.

49 *Joseph* paras 56, 59.

50 PAJA section 3.

51 PAJA section 4.

The implication of this function of PAJA is that empowering provisions do not necessarily have to include participatory procedures in order to achieve procedural fairness in the exercise of the powers granted in such provisions. PAJA fulfils an important supplementary function to empowering provisions in this respect. The Constitutional Court confirmed this role of PAJA in *Zondi v MEC for Traditional and Local Government Affairs and Others*[52] in the following terms:

> All decision-makers who are entrusted with the authority to make administrative decisions by any statute are therefore required to do so in a manner that is consistent with PAJA. The effect of this is that statutes that authorise administrative action must now be read together with PAJA unless, upon a proper construction, the provisions of the statutes in question are inconsistent with PAJA.

In this matter, the court accordingly held that the empowering provision's silence on requiring the decision-maker to notify the affected party of the proposed administrative action did not result in the provision being unconstitutional for a failure to adhere to the requirement of procedurally fair administrative action. This was because the provision had to be read in conjunction with PAJA, which imposed the necessary procedural steps on the decision-maker to achieve a procedurally fair administrative action.

### 10.3.2 Fair but different

The converse of the supplementary function of PAJA discussed in the previous section is also true. That is, empowering provisions may adopt a completely different set of procedural steps to achieve procedural fairness compared to those set out in PAJA. The procedural steps outlined in sections 3 and 4 of PAJA are thus only default rules and may be displaced by alternative procedures created in the empowering provision.

PAJA itself provides for this possibility in sections 3(5) and 4(1)(*d*) respectively. In both these sections, PAJA mandates an administrator to adopt a procedure that is 'fair but different' from the steps set out in PAJA itself to achieve procedural fairness, but, importantly, only if such alternative procedure is contained in an empowering provision. In this way PAJA thus creates scope for drafters of empowering provisions to craft procedures that are suitable to the circumstances in which the provision will apply. The only restriction is that such procedures must still be fair.[53]

The courts have held that even though PAJA section 3(5) implies a power rather than a duty to follow the fair but different procedure set out in the empowering provision ('the administrator *may* act in accordance with that different procedure'), an administrator will not be able to avoid following the alternative procedure if such procedure is more extensive than the default steps set out in PAJA.[54] Thus, if the empowering provision 'is more extensive in its procedural protections than the PAJA', the administrator will be bound to follow those instead of PAJA's procedures.[55] In this way, the drafter of an empowering provision may bind an administrator to a higher level of procedure than the default steps set out in PAJA.

52 2005 (3) SA 589 (CC) para 101.

53 See Chapter 7 section 7.3.1.2 for an example from the Refugees Act 130 of 1998 of such a 'fair but different' procedure.

54 *Minister of Defence and Military Veterans and Another v Mamasedi* 2018 (2) SA 305 (SCA) para 21; *Police and Prisons Civil Rights Union and Others v Minister of Correctional Services and Others* 2008 (3) SA 91 (E) para 71.

55 Mamasedi para 21.

### 10.3.3 Balancing participation and efficiency

A final consideration in drafting empowering provisions with procedural fairness in mind is the need to maintain a balance between participatory decision-making and administrative efficiency. As we have noted throughout this book and at the start of this chapter as well, administrative justice entails both control and facilitation of administrative decision-making. Placing limitations on administrative power in order to protect citizens is thus as important as enabling administrators to take decisions in pursuit of their constitutional mandate. This dual nature of administrative justice is particularly important in respect of procedural fairness, because there is a real risk that the imposition of inappropriate and overly burdensome procedural requirements on administrative decision-making will undermine the administration's ability to deliver on their mandate. That is, efficiency in public administration can easily be sacrificed in pursuit of procedural fairness. Yet, this is not what the requirement of procedural fairness as part of the constitutional guarantee of administrative justice should entail.

The Constitutional Court has recognised this danger in a number of judgments. In *Premier, Mpumalanga v Executive Committee of the Association of State-Aided Schools, Eastern Transvaal*,[56] the court stated:

> In determining what constitutes procedural fairness in a given case, a court should be slow to impose obligations upon government which will inhibit its ability to make and implement policy effectively (a principle well recognised in our common law and that of other countries). As a young democracy facing immense challenges of transformation, we cannot deny the importance of the need to ensure the ability of the Executive to act efficiently and promptly.

In *Joseph and Others v City of Johannesburg and Others*,[57] the court echoed these sentiments when it stated:

> The spectre of administrative paralysis raised by the respondents is a legitimate concern. Administrative efficiency is an important goal in a democracy, and courts must remain vigilant not to impose unduly onerous administrative burdens on the state bureaucracy.

The Constitutional Court's injunction in these judgments should also be heeded by drafters of empowering provisions. Care should be taken not to focus too much on only one or the other of these two important objectives. That is, empowering provisions should be drafted in a manner that consciously aims to achieve a balance between participatory decision-making and administrative efficiency.

## 10.4 Internal remedies

An important dimension of administrative justice is that those who feel aggrieved at an administrative decision impacting on them should have effective and accessible mechanisms to seek redress. While administrative law traditionally focused narrowly on judicial review of administrative action as the main way of controlling administrative decision-making,

56 1999 (2) SA 91 (CC) para 41.
57 2010 (4) SA 55 (CC) para 29 (footnotes omitted).

administrative justice adopts a wider approach to embrace a range of mechanisms to control and facilitate administrative decision-making.[58]

Internal controls or internal remedies form an important part of the wider approach to enforcing justice in administrative decision-making. Internal remedies refer to those mechanisms within the administration aimed at addressing administrative failures.

We noted in Chapter 4 that internal remedies hold much promise in providing effective relief to persons that feel aggrieved at an administrative action. As the Constitutional Court recognised in *Koyabe and Others v Minister for Home Affairs and Others (Lawyers for Human Rights as Amicus Curiae)*:[59]

> Internal remedies are designed to provide immediate and cost-effective relief, giving the executive the opportunity to utilise its own mechanisms, rectifying irregularities first, before aggrieved parties resort to litigation. Although courts play a vital role in providing litigants with access to justice, the importance of more readily available and cost-effective internal remedies cannot be gainsaid ... Internal administrative remedies may require specialised knowledge which may be of a technical and/or practical nature. The same holds true for fact-intensive cases where administrators have easier access to the relevant facts and information.

PAJA supports this focus on internal remedies by requiring in section 7(2)(*a*) that all internal remedies 'provided for in any law' must first be exhausted before a court may entertain a judicial review application. This duty to exhaust internal remedies is much more strict under PAJA than it was under common law, in keeping with the shift to administrative justice under the Constitution and PAJA.

South African law does not contain a comprehensive, coordinated approach to internal remedies. Everything depends on whether an internal remedy is provided for in a law within each case. The empowering provision, specifically in the form of legislation, is thus determinative in whether the duty under section 7(2) of PAJA applies in any case. The activation of this duty is thus fully in the hands of the drafter of the (statutory) empowering provision.

Given the significant advantages of internal remedies, both for the aggrieved person and the administrator, it is of particular value for drafters to pay close attention to the creation of internal remedies within empowering provisions. The requirements that have emerged from case law regarding the activation of the section 7(2) duty, provide important insights for the drafting of empowering provisions containing internal remedies.

In *Reed and Others v Master of the High Court of South Africa and Others*[60] the court held that an internal remedy 'connote an administrative appeal – an appeal, usually on the merits, to an official or tribunal within the same administrative hierarchy as the initial decision-maker – or, less common, an internal review'. Furthermore, the court noted that a 'distinctive feature of internal remedies is that they are extra-curial'.[61] In *Koyabe*, the court added that the internal remedy must be effective.[62] This means that the remedy must offer the claimant effective relief, must be 'objectively implemented', must 'be readily available and it must be

58 See Chapter 1 section 1.2.1.3.
59 2010 (4) SA 327 (CC) paras 35, 37.
60 2005 2 All SA 429 (E) para 25.
61 *Reed* para 26.
62 *Koyabe* para 44.

possible to pursue without any obstruction, whether systemic or arising from unwarranted administrative conduct'.

COUNTER POINT

**Local government procurement appeals**

One of the most controversial internal control mechanisms in South African law is section 62 of the Local Government: Municipal Systems Act[63] and in particular its application in the case of public procurement disputes.

Section 62 reads (in relevant part) as follows:

> **62. Appeals.–**
>
> (1) A person whose rights are affected by a decision taken by a political structure, political office bearer, councillor or staff member of a municipality in terms of a power or duty delegated or sub-delegated by a delegating authority to the political structure, political office bearer, councillor or staff member, may appeal against that decision by giving written notice of the appeal and reasons to the municipal manager within 21 days of the date of the notification of the decision.
>
> ...
>
> (3) The appeal authority must consider the appeal, and confirm, vary or revoke the decision, but no such variation or revocation of a decision may detract from any rights that may have accrued as a result of the decision.

On the face of it, section 62 seems like an effective internal appeal mechanism that would qualify as an internal remedy for purposes of section 7(2) of PAJA. It allows an appeal to a higher authority within the same administrative hierarchy (the municipality) and potentially offers effective relief to a complainant, that is to have the decision varied or revoked. The Supreme Court of Appeal has recognised section 62 as an internal remedy for purposes of PAJA under particular circumstances.[64]

In the context of public procurement decisions at local government level, that is municipal decisions to award a tender to a private entity, the interaction between sections 62 and 7(2) has become particularly problematic with conflicting judgments.[65]

Some courts have adopted the view that section 62 offers an aggrieved bidder an appeal against the award of the bid to its competitor and that it thus constitutes an internal remedy for purposes of section 7(2) of PAJA.[66] The effect is that the appeal under section 62 must be lodged before a judicial review application under PAJA may be brought.

CONTINUED >>>

63 32 of 2000.

64 *City of Cape Town v Reader and Others* 2009 (1) SA 555 (SCA).

65 Udeh, KT (2016) Viability of Bidder Remedies Under Section 62 of the South African Municipal Systems Act *African Public Procurement Law Journal* 3(2):72.

66 *Groenewald NO v M5 Developments (Cape) (Pty) Ltd* 2010 (5) SA 82 (SCA); *Evaluations Enhanced Property Appraisals (Pty) Ltd v Buffalo City Metropolitan Municipality* [2014] 3 All SA 560 (ECG); *Syntell (Pty) Ltd v The City of Cape Town* [2008] ZAWCHC 120; *Total Computer Services (Pty) Ltd v Municipal Manager, Potchefstroom Local Municipality* 2008 (4) SA 346 (T).

Other courts have held that section 62 does not constitute an internal remedy in the procurement context for purposes of section 7(2).[67] This is because of the effect of section 62(3). Once a bid is accepted by the municipality, a contract comes into being between the municipality and the bidder and rights accordingly vest. The result is that the appeal authority cannot interfere with the award in terms of section 62(3) since it will detract from the contractual rights. It further follows that section 62 would not offer the aggrieved bidder effective relief and thus does not qualify as an internal remedy.

## THIS CHAPTER IN ESSENCE

The dual nature of administrative law, especially as part of the broader notion of administrative justice, implies that the rules of administrative law are equally relevant for the empowerment of administrators to take administrative decisions as they are for the control of such administrative action. In both the enabling and control functions of administrative law, the drafting of empowering provisions play an important role. Administrators obtain all their power to take decisions from empowering provisions, which implies that empowering provisions lie at the heart of facilitating administrative decisions, but also that those same empowering provisions are the first way to control the administrative action. When empowering provisions are drafted, close attention should thus be paid to the principles of administrative justice in order to ensure that those empowering provisions can effectively achieve both functions of administrative law.

## FURTHER READING

- Bednar-Giyose, J (2018) *Legislative Drafting and the Appropriate Delineation of Administrative Power* (PhD dissertation, University of the Witwatersrand)

67 *Loghdey v Advanced Parking Solutions CC* 2009 JDR 0157 (C); *ESDA Properties (Pty) Ltd v Amathole District Municipality* [2014] ZAECGHC 76.

# Chapter 11

# Standing and procedure for judicial review

STEVEN BUDLENDER SC, MFUNDO SALUKAZANA & EMMA WEBBER



## 11.1 Introduction

Chapters 4 and 5 looked at a range of different legal mechanisms aimed at regulating administrative action. That is, mechanisms that can ensure that administrators follow the rules of administrative law. Despite the existence of a variety of mechanisms and the importance of developing an integrated system of administrative-law controls,[1] one mechanism continues to dominate the regulatory landscape, namely judicial review. As has been noted in the preceding chapters, this means that the constraints on administrative law

1 See Hoexter, C (2000) The Future of Judicial Review in South African Administrative Law *SALJ* 117(3):484; Chapter 4 section 4.1 above.

are mostly those that are produced by the grounds of judicial review in section 6(2) of the Promotion of Administrative Justice Act (PAJA).[2]

This chapter looks at when and how an aggrieved person can approach a court to argue that a particular administrative decision falls foul of particular grounds of review.

## 11.2 Standing

Standing is a threshold requirement that a litigant must satisfy before they can persuade a court to engage with the substance of their case. It is the right of a particular person to approach a court of law for relief. Standing might seem a technical issue, but it has a significant impact on the ability of citizens to use administrative law to challenge the use of public power.

### 11.2.1 The concept of standing

Standing is the entitlement to be heard. No judicial process can proceed unless standing has been established. To do so, the claimant must show that he or she has capacity and an interest in the matter. However, any interest in a matter will not do – the claimant may find a matter interesting but nonetheless lack a legally recognised interest in it. The claimant must show an interest that is *sufficient* to entitle him or her to a hearing – they must justify why *this* person should be entitled to pursue *this* claim against *this* defendant.

**PAUSE FOR REFLECTION**

**Standing in two scenarios**

To place the standing debate in context, consider the following scenarios:

**Welfare grants**

Two companies bid for a tender for the distribution of welfare grants in four South African provinces. After a process plagued by irregularities and possible corruption, the tender is awarded to Company A. Company A is in many respects inferior to Company B, the unsuccessful bidder. The distribution process that Company A has proposed would involve significant disruption to the current system – welfare grant-holders would have to travel great distances to re-register for their grants, the distribution would happen at only a few designated offices rather than at post offices and grocery stores (as Company B proposed), grants would be given in cash only and grant-holders would not have the option of receiving their grants as vouchers or bank transfers.

A number of individuals wish to review the decision to grant the tender to Company A.

- Does Company B have standing to seek a review in terms of PAJA?
- Do the individual grant-holders have standing to do so?
- Does ProsperAll, an NGO that assists individuals to apply for welfare grants and monitors the distribution and use of grants, have standing to challenge the decision?
- Citizen M is a resident of Gauteng (one of the provinces not affected by the tender). She has a keen interest in current affairs and has followed the tender process carefully. She is aware of the irregularities in the process and is convinced that the award of the tender was unlawful. Does she have standing to challenge the decision?

CONTINUED >>>

2 3 of 2000.

**Commission of Inquiry**

The President decides to appoint a commission of inquiry into the administration of soccer. This upsets a number of people. In particular, the South African Football Association alleges that they were not given an opportunity to make representations before the Commission was appointed. They wish to challenge and set aside the decision under PAJA. Soccer players and club managers believe that the Commission will harm the reputation of South African soccer.

- Do the Football Association, the players, the club managers or soccer fans have standing to challenge the President's decision?

## 11.2.2 The rationale for a standing requirement

In determining what the criteria for standing in administrative justice claims should be, it is helpful to begin by looking at the rationale that underpins the standing requirement. Why does the law impose restrictions on who should be allowed to bring a matter before court?

A number of justifications for the standing requirement have been offered in the literature and by the South African courts (in both private and public law):

- First, state resources are scarce and the court system is over-burdened. Precious resources would be wasted on the adjudication and defence of claims if mere busybodies could challenge every minor or alleged infraction by the state or private persons.[3] Without a standing requirement the floodgates will open, inundating the courts with vexatious litigation and unnecessary court disputes.[4]
- Second, by requiring that litigants have a sufficient interest in a matter, the law ensures that the court is presented with concrete disputes, rather than abstract or hypothetical cases.[5] In this regard, Chaskalson P stressed that:

> The principal reasons for this objection are that in an adversarial system decisions are best made when there is a genuine dispute in which each party has an interest to protect. There is moreover the need to conserve scarce judicial resources and to apply them to real and not hypothetical disputes.[6]

- Third, the requirement ensures that the person who is best-placed to litigate the issue is the one who appears in court. Individuals who have a clear interest in a matter will have greater access to relevant information. They are better able to place all pertinent facts before the court.[7] Without a standing provision, it is more likely that flimsy cases will be litigated and decided, resulting in poor precedents.[8]
- Finally, the requirement of standing provides the judiciary with a means to protect its independence and to maintain its legitimacy. On occasion, judges use the rules of standing in order to give effect to the notion of justiciability – that is, the idea that it is not appropriate for certain matters to be adjudicated by a court of law.[9] Judges use the rules of standing to shield themselves from matters that are politically loaded or that

3 De Ville, JR (2005) *Judicial Review of Administrative Action in South Africa* (revised 1st ed) 399.
4 Baxter, L (1984) *Administrative Law* 645.
5 Baxter (1984) 645.
6 *Ferreira v Levin NO and Others; Vryenhoek and Others v Powell NO and Others* 1996 (1) SA 984 (CC) para 164. See also *Zantsi v Council of State, Ciskei and Others* 1995 (10) BCLR 1424 (CC) para 7.
7 Baxter (1984) 645.
8 Hoexter, C (2012) *Administrative Law in South Africa* (2nd ed) 490.
9 Hoexter (2012) 490.

would draw courts into issues of policy. In *Ferreira v Levin*, Chaskalson P noted that, when considering standing, courts in the United States have regard to 'the need to prevent courts from being drawn into unnecessary conflict with coordinate branches of government'.[10] With few or no restrictions on standing, litigants would have unlimited opportunities to challenge government action via the courts. This would expand the policing role of the courts in relation to the other branches of government.[11] This, in turn, would threaten the legitimacy of the courts.

These justifications give some insight into the role and importance attributed to standing. However, in order to properly engage in the debate about standing in administrative law, more analysis is necessary. Two questions must be answered:

- First, what is the purpose of judicial review in administrative law? Is it to police unlawful conduct by public officials? Is it to redress injustice and vindicate the rights of a particular claimant? Can a litigant review conduct purely for the first purpose – to uphold the rule of law? If so, any person who alleges that a public official has acted unlawfully would be entitled to institute a review of that conduct. If not, only individuals who can show that they have suffered an injustice will be entitled to institute proceedings.[12]
- Second, what is the relationship between standing and the purposes of judicial review?[13]

With these questions in mind, we enter into the debate about the standing requirement in South African administrative law.

### 11.2.3 Standing under the common law

Prior to 1994, the common-law approach to standing was restrictive. Any person who approached a court was required to show a sufficient, direct and personal interest in the matter (as well as the capacity to sue).

With regard to a 'personal' interest, Innes CJ stated that 'no man can sue in respect of a wrongful act, unless it constitutes the breach of a duty owed to *him* by the wrongdoer, or unless it causes *him* some damage in law'.[14] In addition, the litigant was required to show that some legal right or recognised interest was at stake.[15] A 'sufficient' interest included a proprietary or pecuniary interest or an interest in personal liberty.[16] The requirement of 'directness' meant the conduct challenged must directly affect the complaint. As Baxter puts it, 'this requirement is aimed at ensuring a personal nexus between the complainant and the act complained of'.[17]

10 *Ferreira* para 164.
11 De Ville (2005) 399.
12 Endicott, T (2011) *Administrative Law* (2nd ed) 405, 409.
13 Endicott (2011) 405, 409.
14 *Dalrumple and Others v Colonial Treasurer* 1910 TS 372 at 379, as cited in Baxter (1984) 651.
15 Baxter (1984) 652.
16 Baxter (1984) 653, citing *Riddelsdell v Hall* (1883) 2 SC 356; *Wood and Others v Ondangwa Tribal Authority and Another* 1975 (2) SA 294 (A) 310.
17 Baxter (1984) 654. See also *Johannesburg City Council v Administrator, Transvaal and Another* 1969 (2) SA 72 (T).

### 11.2.4 Standing under section 38 of the Constitution

In the post-apartheid era, a generous and expanded approach to standing was adopted in the public law context. As a result, the categories of persons who are granted standing to seek relief are far broader than our common law has ever permitted.[18]

The generous approach is encapsulated in section 38 of the Constitution, which provides as follows:

> Anyone listed in this section has the right to approach a competent court, alleging that a right in the Bill of Rights has been infringed or threatened, and the court may grant appropriate relief, including a declaration of rights. The persons who may approach a court are—
> (*a*) anyone acting in their own interest;
> (*b*) anyone acting on behalf of another person who cannot act in their own name;
> (*c*) anyone acting as a member of, or in the interest of, a group or class of persons;
> (*d*) anyone acting in the public interest; and
> (*e*) an association acting in the interest of its members.

Section 38 is a radical departure from the standing requirements of the pre-apartheid period. It expressly allows court proceedings by individuals or organisations acting in the public interest. Public interest standing is given in addition to the standing that is granted to individuals or organisations acting on behalf of other persons or on behalf of a class. Justice Kate O'Regan noted that this approach to standing is particularly important in our country, where a large number of people have had scant educational opportunities and may not be aware of their rights.[19]

We briefly expand on the different section 38 grounds for standing below.

### 11.2.5 Standing under PAJA

Importantly, section 38 applies when a right in the Bill of Rights is infringed or threatened. Where, then, does PAJA fit in?

PAJA does not contain an explicit standing provision. During the drafting process, a clause similar to section 38 was inserted in the Bill, only to be removed soon after.[20] The parliamentary committee responsible for the draft did not give clear reasons for its choice to remove the clause.[21] In its final inculcation, PAJA's only reference to standing is contained in section 6(1), which provides that *any person* may institute proceedings in a court or tribunal for the judicial review of administrative action.

What, then, is the standing requirement for litigants instituting administrative-law proceedings? There were notionally three approaches that could have been taken.

- The courts could have held that the narrow common-law approach to standing continued to apply to PAJA litigation.
- The courts could have held that the broader approach of section 38 of the Constitution applied to PAJA litigation.
- The courts could have read section 6 of PAJA literally to provide that 'any person' could institute proceedings – without any requirement of standing.

18 *Ferreira* para 229.
19 *Kruger v President of the Republic of South Africa and Others* 2009 (1) SA 417 (CC) para 22.
20 Hoexter (2012) 494; De Ville (2005) 401.
21 Hoexter (2012) 494; De Ville (2005) 401.

Unsurprisingly the Constitutional Court adopted the second of these approaches. It has held that section 38 of the Constitution does apply to PAJA litigation. It did so in the case of *Giant Concerts*:

> PAJA, which was enacted to realise [the right to administrative justice in] section 33 [of the Constitution], confers a right to challenge a decision in the exercise of a public power or the performance of a public function that 'adversely affects the rights of any person and which has a direct, external legal effect.' PAJA provides that 'any person' may institute proceedings for the judicial review of an administrative action. The wide standing provisions of section 38 were not expressly enacted as part of PAJA. Hoexter suggests that nothing much turns on this because 'it seems clear that the provisions of section 38 ought to be read into the statute.' This is correct.[22]

Since *Giant Concerts*, it is clear that:

- There is a standing requirement under PAJA.
- This standing requirement is the same as that set by section 38 of the Constitution.

This approach is very sensible. It ensures that the advantages of a standing requirement (set out above) are achieved, but also ensures that judicial review proceedings are encouraged and rendered more practical by means of the generous approach under section 38. Moreover, given that the broad standing regime of section 38 applies to review on the basis of the principle of legality,[23] the approach adopted avoided an illogical and unnecessary disjuncture on this issue between PAJA and the principle of legality.

In *Giant Concerts*, the court also helpfully made clear that the question of the standing of a litigant to bring a PAJA review is not the same as the question of whether the PAJA review is sustainable on the merits. Questions of standing and merits must be kept separate:

> [I]n determining Giant's standing, we must assume that its complaints about the lawfulness of the transaction are correct. This is because in determining a litigant's standing, a court must, as a matter of logic, assume that the challenge the litigant seeks to bring is justified. As Hoexter explains:
>
> > The issue of standing is divorced from the substance of the case. It is therefore a question to be decided *in limine* [at the outset], before the merits are considered.[24]

The court correctly explained that this had two implications.

First, it means that the standing enquiry does not focus on whether the decision challenged was unlawful or invalid. Rather, in demonstrating 'own interest' standing,[25] the applicant must focus on the 'interests that confer standing to bring the challenge' and the 'impact the decision' has.[26]

---

22 *Giant Concerts CC v Rinaldo Investments (Pty) Ltd and Others* 2013 (3) BCLR 251 (CC) para 29.

23 See *Democratic Alliance and Others v Acting National Director of Public Prosecutions and Others* 2012 (3) SA 486 (SCA) paras 38–47.

24 *Giant Concerts* para 32.

25 That is standing conferred by section 38(*a*) of the Constitution.

26 *Giant Concerts* para 33.

Second, it means that there may be occasions where an unlawful decision is left in existence – simply because the applicant has failed to make out a case for own interest standing. The court explained that this 'is not illogical':

> standing determines solely whether this particular litigant is entitled to mount the challenge: a successful challenge to a public decision can be brought only if 'the right remedy is sought by the right person in the right proceedings'.[27]

The court did emphasise though that there might be exceptions to this approach and that there may be cases where the interests of justice or the public interest might compel a court to scrutinise action even if the applicant's standing is questionable. As it explained, 'when the public interest cries out for relief, an applicant should not fail merely for acting in his or her own interest'.[28]

In our view, the practical implication of this is that an applicant for judicial review would be well advised to rely not merely on 'own interest' standing under section 38(*a*), but also where possible public interest standing under section 38(*d*). That maximises the possibility of ensuring that the court reaches the merits of the judicial review.

Finally, we point out that since the Constitutional Court's judgment of *State Information Technology Agency SOC Ltd v Gijima Holdings (Pty) Ltd*,[29] an organ of state seeking to review its own decision does *not* have standing under PAJA. In *Gijima*, the court found that since the right to administrative action that is lawful, reasonable and procedurally fair is a fundamental right that is only bestowed on private persons, only they can vindicate the right.[30] Similarly, since PAJA was enacted to give content to section 33, it, too, is exclusive to private persons.[31] The decision therefore makes clear – for the first time – that an organ of state seeking to review its own decision may do so only under the constitutional principle of legality, not PAJA.

### 11.2.6 Standing in practice

In what follows, we briefly expand upon the section 38 grounds for standing in the context of PAJA with reference to practical examples:

a) **Anyone acting in their own interest**
   Section 38(*a*) reflects the common law but goes beyond it.[32] Rather than showing a direct, personal and sufficient interest, the applicant need only show that he or she has been directly affected by the conduct complained of.[33] To illustrate this point, the Constitutional Court has referred to the Canadian case of *Morgentaler*. There, a male doctor was entitled to challenge the constitutionality of legislation dealing with abortion under which he was liable to be prosecuted. He was granted standing despite the fact that the rights upon which the constitutional challenge were based were the rights of pregnant women, which did not and could not vest in the male doctor.[34]
   This 'own interest' type of standing is used in virtually all judicial review applications under PAJA. Examples include people who have been denied refugee permits or social grants, companies that have failed in tender awards, and people seeking to challenge planning approvals granted to their neighbours.

---

27 *Giant Concerts* para 34.
28 *Giant Concerts* para 34.
29 2018 (2) SA 23 (CC).
30 *Gijima* paras 19–29.
31 *Gijima* paras 30–32.
32 Hoexter (2012) 495.
33 *Ferreira* para 166.
34 *Ferreira* para 166, citing *R v Morgentaler, Smoling and Scott* [1988] 31 CRR 1 (SCC).

An interesting application of own interest standing emerged in the matter of *WDR Earthmoving Enterprises & Another v The Joe Gqabi District Municipality*.[35] There, the applicant was a company that had been disqualified from a tender process on the grounds that its bid was found to be non-responsive. It sought to review an organ of state's decision to award the tender to another bidder.

The Full Court of the Eastern Cape Division of the High Court held that the company lacked standing, because it had been disqualified and only a compliant bidder acquires a right to challenge a decision to award a tender.[36]

However, the Supreme Court of Appeal disagreed. It found that the applicant's standing had to be determined by considering whether the decision of the organ of state would have a direct effect upon the interests or potential interests of the applicant. The applicant's interest in the decision was that if the decision was set aside, the applicant would be entitled to participate once the tender process re-commenced.[37] This interest was sufficient to clothe the applicant with standing to review the decision in terms of PAJA.

b) **Anyone acting on behalf of another person who cannot act in their own name**
In *Ngxuza and Others v Permanent Secretary, Department of Welfare, Eastern Cape Provincial Government and Another*,[38] the applicants were grant-holders whose disability grants and social benefits had been discontinued. They sought a declaration that the suspension or cancellation of the grants was unlawful. However, the discontinuation of grants affected thousands of people other than the applicants. Hence, the declaration was also sought on behalf of other grant-holders who were in the same position as the applicants. Froneman J recognised that many grant-holders were poor, did not have access to legal representation and would have difficulty in obtaining legal aid.[39] As a result, they would be unable personally to challenge the unlawful cancellation of their grants.[40] Consequently, the court held that the applicants had standing under section 38(*b*) on the basis that they were acting on behalf of others who could not act in their own names.[41] This case took place before the advent of PAJA, but would now likely be brought in terms of PAJA.

c) **Anyone acting as a member of, or in the interest of, a group or class of persons**
As its name suggests, a 'class action' is a case brought by one or more litigants on behalf of a larger group of persons (the class). Class actions were not part of our law prior to the enactment of the present Constitution in 1997. However, they are now being used more frequently – especially in damages claims relating to a wide range of issues, such as silicosis on mines, pension fund disputes, the failure by government to pay teacher's salaries and price-fixing by bread manufacturers.

There has not yet been a class action brought in terms of PAJA. However, the *Ngxuza* judgment already referred to demonstrates how such a class action would occur. In that case, decided before PAJA was enacted, the applicants were also granted standing in terms of section 38(*c*) on the basis that they were acting for members of a

35 [2018] ZASCA 7.
36 *WDR Earthmoving Enterprises* para 34
37 *WDR Earthmoving Enterprises* para 16.
38 2001 (2) SA 609 (E).
39 *Ngxuza* at 622J–623A.
40 *Ngxuza* at 624F–G.
41 In addition, it held that the applicants were acting in the public interest, thus had standing in terms of section 38(*d*).

class of persons affected by the unlawful decisions of the government in relation to social grants.

Where a class action is brought against private parties, those bringing the class action must seek certification of the class action from the courts.[42] However, it appears that this need for certification does not apply where the class action is brought in an effort to enforce constitutional rights against the state.[43] The same would likely apply to a class action brought in terms of PAJA.

d) **Anyone acting in the public interest**

Section 38(*d*) is the broadest ground for standing, allowing a person to bring a claim in the public interest.[44] The South African Law Commission has provided a lucid and concise definition of a public interest action:

> A public interest action is one brought by the plaintiff who, in claiming the relief he or she seeks, is moved by a desire to benefit the public at large or a segment of the public. The intention of the plaintiff is to vindicate or protect the public interest, not his or her own interest, although he or she may incidentally achieve that end as well.[45]

A clear illustration of standing granted in the public interest is the Limpopo textbooks case.[46] In this case, the applicants (including the NGO 'Section27') challenged the government's protracted failure to deliver textbooks to schools in the Limpopo province for the 2012 academic year. The absence of broad-standing provisions may have prevented vindication of the rights of the learners concerned in this matter. Section27 would have been precluded from participating as a litigant because it does not have a sufficient direct interest in the matter. Only schools or learners themselves could have litigated the issue. However, these learners or schools would not have had a sufficient direct interest in the provision of textbooks to other schools. As a consequence, most schools and learners in Limpopo would have received no relief.

The Constitutional Court has stressed that a person seeking standing in terms of section 38(*d*) must genuinely be acting in the public interest. The following factors are relevant to this determination:

- whether there is another reasonable and effective manner in which the challenge can be brought,
- the nature of the relief sought, and the extent to which it is of general and prospective application, and
- the range of persons or groups who may be directly or indirectly affected by any order made by the court and the opportunity that those persons or groups have had to present evidence and argument to the court,[47]
- the degree of vulnerability of the people affected,
- the nature of the right said to be infringed, and

---

42 On the factors to be taken into account regarding whether to grant certification, see *Trustees for the time being of Children's Resource Centre Trust and Others v Pioneer Food (Pty) Ltd and Others* 2013 (2) SA 213 (SCA) at paras 23 to 28; and *Mukaddam v Pioneer Foods (Pty) Ltd and Others* 2013 (5) SA 89 (CC) at paras 34 to 39.

43 *Mukaddam* para 40.

44 Subsection 38(*d*) connotes an action on behalf of people on a basis wider than the class actions contemplated in the section. See *Lawyers for Human Rights and Another v Minister of Home Affairs and Another* 2004 (4) SA 125 (CC) para 15.

45 South African Law Reform Commission Report (1998) *The Recognition of Class Actions and Public Interest Actions in South African Law* (Project 88); Hoexter (2012) 505.

46 *Section27 and Others v Minister of Education and Another* 2013 (2) SA 40 (GNP) para 9.

47 *Ferreira* (per O'Regan J) para 234; *Lawyers for Human Rights* paras 16–17.

- the consequences of the infringement of the right.[48]

In the context of PAJA, public interest standing will arise relatively frequently. Examples include an organisation of schools reviewing regulations dealing with school admissions and public interest organisations reviewing decisions of government to close refugee reception offices.

In *Afriforum v University of the Free State*,[49] Afriforum, a civil organisation, brought a review application to set aside the respondent's (the University of the Free State) decision to institute a language policy adopting English as the only language of instruction – the University had had both English and Afrikaans as its languages of instruction up until that point. Although the University of the Free State did not dispute the Afriforum's standing, the Supreme Court of Appeal found that Afriforum did not have standing: it was not acting on behalf of the students who were the people that would be adversely affected by the University of the Free State's decision to adopt the new language policy. The Constitutional Court disagreed. It held that Afriforum was acting in the public interest because Afriforum was acting on behalf of Afrikaans-speaking people seeking to assert their children's rights to be instructed in Afrikaans.[50]

e) **An association acting in the interest of its members**

The prerequisites for an association to sue on behalf of its members are the following (i) capacity to sue (the association must have legal personality); and (ii) a sufficient interest to sue.[51] In the context of PAJA, associations relatively frequently make use of this provision to review and set aside decisions affecting their members – for example, decisions of bodies regulating an industry or decisions by municipalities affecting associations of residents.

In *Afriforum*, the Constitutional Court found that a trade union, Solidarity, that had a mandate to advance its members' interests in the labour sphere, did not have standing to act on behalf of students of the University of the Free State who wanted to assert their right to be taught in the language of their choice (Afrikaans) because neither the students nor their parents were members of the trade union.[52] Accordingly, the trade union did not have any interest in the proceedings.

## 11.3 Procedure for judicial review

As has been noted in Chapter 5, judicial review is a mechanism to regulate administrative action. In order to successfully engage in judicial review the litigant establishes the necessary standing to do so (as explained above) and must establish a particular ground of review set out in section 6(2) of PAJA (as explained in Chapter 5).

The litigant must also comply with the procedural requirements applicable to judicial review. Some of these are the same as ordinary civil procedure requirements, but there are also important additional procedural requirements that apply to judicial review of administrative action. In this section we deal with these specific requirements that apply to judicial review of administrative action.

48 *Lawyers for Human Rights* para 18.
49 2018 (2) SA 185 (CC).
50 *Afriforum* para 26.
51 For more detail see De Ville (2005) 428–433 and Hoexter (2012) 508–511.
52 *Afriforum* para 27.

Before a party can proceed with his or her review application, PAJA creates two procedural hurdles that the applicant will have to overcome, namely the duty to exhaust all internal remedies and a prescribed time frame.

### 11.3.1 Duty to exhaust internal remedies

In Chapter 4 above we noted in detail the relationship between internal remedies and judicial review.[53] We saw that section 7(2) of PAJA contains a strict procedural rule that all internal remedies must be exhausted before a court can entertain a judicial review. The rule is, however, not absolute and an applicant can proceed with judicial review despite not having exhausted all internal remedies if he or she can convince a court that there are exceptional circumstances and it is in the interest of justice to proceed with the review immediately. An applicant will have to bring a proper application to the court in terms of section 7(2)(*c*) for an exemption from the duty to exhaust internal remedies before he or she will be allowed to proceed.

### 11.3.2 Time to institute judicial proceedings

Section 7(1) of PAJA sets a time frame within which judicial review applications must be launched. This is without unreasonable delay *and* within 180 days.

PAJA sets out different dates on which the 180 days will start running. It is evident that the existence of an internal remedy will again play a key role in this second hurdle for an applicant to surmount before being able to argue the merits of his or her review before court.

If there is an internal remedy, the 180-day period will only start running *after* all proceedings under the internal remedy have been concluded.[54]

If there is no internal remedy the 180-day period will start running on the date:

- on which the person concerned became aware of the action and the reasons for it, or
- on which the person concerned might reasonably have been expected to have become aware of the action and the reasons.[55]

It is important to note that the time frame under PAJA is not simply 180 days, but – depending on the facts of the case – may indeed be much shorter than that. This is by virtue of the fact that PAJA also requires reviews to be instituted 'without unreasonable delay'. The 180-day period is therefore simply the maximum period, beyond which the applicant will undoubtedly need an extension from the court,[56] as we explain below.

PAJA thus retains the common-law rule against unreasonable delay.[57] This rule is said to serve two purposes:

> First, the failure to bring a review within a reasonable time may cause prejudice to the respondent. Secondly, there is a public interest element in the finality of administrative decisions and the exercise of administrative functions.[58]

53 See Chapter 4 section 4.3.

54 PAJA section 7(1)(*a*).

55 PAJA section 7(1)(*b*).

56 *Opposition to Urban Tolling Alliance and Others v The South African National Roads Agency Ltd and Others* [2013] 4 All SA 639 (SCA) para 26 cited with approval in *Buffalo City Metropolitan Municipality v Asla Construction (Pty) Limited* 2019 (4) SA 331 (CC) para 49.

57 *Chairperson, Standing Tender Committee and Others v JFE Sapela Electronics (Pty) Ltd and Others* 2008 (2) SA 638 (SCA) para 28.

58 *Associated Institutions Pension Fund and Others v Van Zyl and Others* 2005 (2) SA 302 (SCA) para 46.

In judging whether a particular delay in bringing a review application was unreasonable, a court will have to make a value judgment on the facts before it, that is, a court will have to decide what it considers reasonable under the circumstances.[59] Even after finding that the delay was factually unreasonable, the court at common law still had a discretion to condone the delay, taking into account:

- the extent of the prejudice that the respondent (administrator) and other third parties may suffer from instituting the review after the delay,[60]
- the explanation offered for the delay,[61]
- the nature of the decision, particularly relating to the prejudice that may follow from setting aside this type of decision following a delay, and[62]
- the complexity of the factual and legal matrix of the challenged administrative action.[63]

In *South African National Roads Agency v Cape Town City*,[64] the Supreme Court of Appeal found that the merits of the review application are also a critical factor when a court considers whether to condone delay. Navsa JA stated:

> It is true that in [*Opposition to Urban Tolling Alliance*] this Court considered it important to settle the court's jurisdiction to entertain the merits of the matter by first having regard to the question of delay. However, it cannot be read to signal a clinical excision of the merits of the impugned decision, which must be a critical factor when a court embarks on a consideration of all the circumstances of a case in order to determine whether the interests of justice dictate that the delay should be condoned. It would have to include a consideration of whether the non-compliance with statutory prescripts was egregious.[65]

This was affirmed in *City of Cape Town v Aurecon South Africa (Pty) Limited*,[66] where the Constitutional Court held that '... due regard must also be given to the importance of the issue that is raised and the prospects of success'.[67]

The 180-day maximum period to launch review proceedings may be extended in terms of section 9 of PAJA either by way of agreement between the parties (which is of course highly unlikely) or by the court. If agreement cannot be reached with the respondent administrator, the applicant will have to apply to court showing that it is in the interest of justice for the 180-day period to be extended.[68] The factors used to determine whether such extension is in the interest of justice will be largely similar to those listed above in determining whether to condone an unreasonable delay.[69] Since a refusal to grant an extension may lead to an

59 *Wolgroeiers Afslaers (EDMS) BPK v Munisipaliteit van Kaapstad* 1978 (1) SA 13 (A); *Camps Bay Ratepayers' and Residents' Association v Harrison* [2010] 2 All SA 519 (SCA) para 61.

60 *Department of Transport v Tasima (Pty) Limited* 2017 (2) SA 622 (CC) para 170; *Buffalo City* para 54; *Gqwetha v Transkei Development Corporation Ltd and Others* 2006 (2) SA 603 (SCA) para 23; *PG Bison Ltd (in liquidation) and Others v Johannesburg Glassworks (Pty) Ltd (in liquidation)* 2006 (4) SA 535 (W) para 12.

61 *Gqwetha* para 24.

62 *Gqwetha* para 24.

63 *Buffalo City* para 55; *Khumalo and Another v Member of the Executive Council for Education: KwaZulu Natal* 2014 (5) SA 579 (CC) para 57; *Sasol Oil (Pty) Ltd and Another v Metcalfe NO* 2004 (5) SA 161 (W) para 7; *Spier Properties (Pty) Ltd and Another v Chairman, Wine and Spirit Board, and Others* 1999 (3) SA 832 (C) at 844–845.

64 2017 (1) SA 468 (SCA).

65 *SANRAL* para 81.

66 2017 (4) SA 223 (CC).

67 *Aurecon* para 49.

68 PAJA section 9(2).

69 *Camps Bay Ratepayers' and Residents' Association* para 54.

invalid administrative action remaining in force, because the applicant brought the review out of time, a court will also consider the imperatives of legality against finality in deciding upon what is in the interest of justice in the particular case.

In *Gijima*[70] and *Buffalo City*,[71] the Constitutional Court held that even an unreasonable delay should not preclude a court reaching the merits and declaring a decision invalid where it was '*clearly unlawful*'. The court preferred instead to use delay mainly as an issue that went to the question of an appropriate remedy.[72] In *Buffalo City* it held:

> [T]his matter is on the same footing as *Gijima* where the decision maker had failed to provide a satisfactory explanation for the delay and, for the reasons outlined, I am unable to find any basis upon which this delay may be overlooked.
> ... However, this is not the end of the enquiry. On the authority of *Gijima*, this Court must, having established that the Reeston contract was clearly unlawful on undisputed facts, declare it invalid in terms of the provisions of section 172(1)(*a*) and set it aside. The unlawfulness of the Reeston contract cannot be ignored and this Court is obliged, as it did in *Gijima*, to set aside a contract it knows to be unlawful. Even on a restrictive interpretation of the *Gijima* principle, bearing in mind the need to hold the state to the procedural requirements of review, as explained above, I can see no reason to depart from it in this matter.[73]

This approach - that a court may (and must) still declare a decision invalid even after concluding that there has been unreasonable delay in the bringing of the review application and even without condonation being granted or justified - is a substantial and, in our view, regrettable departure from long-standing principles of administrative law.

However, the principles concerned were articulated by the Constitutional Court in the context of legality reviews brought by organs of state in respect of their own decisions. We would thus hope that they are confined to this area and are not extended to PAJA reviews or indeed legality reviews brought by private parties.

### 11.3.3 The courts with jurisdiction in respects of judicial review proceedings

Until recently, judicial review proceedings could only be brought before a High Court and magistrates' courts had no jurisdiction regarding judicial reviews.

However, the definition of 'court' in PAJA contemplated the designation of magistrates' courts by the Minister of Justice as an additional forum with jurisdiction over judicial review applications.

This occurred for the first time in late 2019.[74] With effect from 1 October 2019, district[75] and regional[76] magistrates' courts with jurisdiction to decide civil matters also have the jurisdiction to decide applications for judicial reviews.

70 *Gijima* para 52
71 *Buffalo City* paras 99–100
72 *Gijima* paras 53–54; *Buffalo City* para 105
73 *Buffalo City* paras 99–100
74 Designation of Magistrates' Courts under the Definition of 'Court' in the Promotion of Administrative Justice Act 3 of 2000 – GN 1216 in *GG* 42717 of 19.19.2019.
75 Paragraph (a)(i) of the Designation.
76 Paragraph (a)(ii) of the Designation.

The definition of 'court' in PAJA contemplates both High Courts and magistrates' courts having jurisdiction over judicial review applications[77] and does not determination which matters are to proceed in the High Court and which in the magistrates' courts. The applicant for judicial review is therefore entitled to elect whether to proceed in the High Court or magistrates' court.

The definition of 'court' in PAJA and the designation of magistrates' courts by the Minister make clear that a number of different High Courts and magistrates' courts may have jurisdiction to determine a particular judicial review application:

- The High Court or magistrates' court within whose area of jurisdiction the administrative action occurred – that seems to refer to where the impugned decision was taken,
- The High Court or magistrates' court within whose area of jurisdiction the administrator has its principal place of administration,
- The High Court or magistrates' court within whose area of jurisdiction the party whose rights have been affected is domiciled or ordinarily resident, or
- The High Court or magistrates' court within whose area of jurisdiction the adverse effect of the administrative action was, is or will be experienced.

The applicant for judicial review is entitled to elect which of these courts to proceed in.

Allowing the applicant for judicial review the election regarding whether to proceed in the High Court or magistrates' court, and (if there is more than one such court with jurisdiction) which High Court or magistrates' court, is a sensible and laudable approach.

## 11.3.4 The rules applicable to judicial review proceedings

### 11.3.4.1 An overview

Judicial review proceedings are invariably brought by way of application – not action. In other words, the evidence is placed before the court by means of affidavit, not oral evidence, and there is generally no cross-examination.

However, judicial review proceedings normally take place via a special application procedure.

For ordinary applications (governed by Rule 6 of the High Court Rules),[78] the procedure is as follows:

- The applicant files a Notice of Motion and founding affidavit, in which their entire case must be made out,
- The respondents then file answering affidavits, and
- The applicant then files a replying affidavit.

By contrast, in review applications, applicants generally make use of the special procedure applicable to review proceedings (governed by Rule 53 of the High Court Rules). It provides for a procedure as follows:

- The applicant files a Notice of Motion and founding affidavit.

77 The definition of 'court' also contemplates the Constitutional Court having jurisdiction to hear judicial review applications under its 'direct access' jurisdiction but this appears never to have been used. Given the Constitutional Court's general reluctance to grant direct access, it would require the most extraordinary circumstances to persuade the court to hear a judicial review application under PAJA on a direct access basis. See *Bruce v Fleecytex Johannesburg CC* 1998 (2) SA 1143 (CC) at paras 7–8 and the many cases following it.

78 Also known as the Uniform Rules of Court.

- The decision-maker whose decision is being subjected to judicial review is then required to file the **record** of their decision. We explain what that means below, but in essence it means all the documents that were before the decision-maker at the time of the decision. The decision-maker can and often must file the **reasons** for the decision.
- The applicant is then entitled to file a further affidavit and amend their notice of motion, in light of the Rule 53 record and reasons. This includes an entitlement to add to or subtract from the grounds of review.[79]
- Only thereafter do the respondents file answering affidavits.
- The applicant then files a replying affidavit.

This special procedure for reviews has a number of important advantages for applicants for judicial review, some of which we mention below.

It is important to note that the founding affidavit of the applicant (under Rule 6) or the founding and supplementary affidavits of the applicant (under Rule 53) must set out both the facts relied on by the applicant and the grounds of review relied on.[80] It is, in general, impermissible to raise a ground of review for the first time in a replying affidavit.[81]

### 11.3.4.2 The current position and how it evolved

Prior to the enactment of PAJA, the rules applicable to judicial review proceedings were contained in the Uniform Rules of Court, which regulate proceedings in the High Court.

When PAJA came into force, sections 7(3) and (4) dealt with the rules of procedure for judicial review. Section 7(3) required that the Rules Board[82] enact rules of procedure for judicial review and provided that these rules had to be approved by the Minister of Justice. Until then the High Court Rules would continue to operate.

The Rules Board enacted a set of rules for judicial review in 2009. In a number of key respects these were a radical departure from the High Court Rules and would have put those seeking to challenge administrative action at a substantial disadvantage relative to the position under the High Court Rules. The 2009 PAJA Rules were the subject of a successful constitutional challenge before the High Court, which declared them invalid.[83]

Eventually, on 4 October 2019, a new set of PAJA Rules was enacted.[84] The new PAJA Rules in essence preserve the applicability of the High Court Rules, including Rule 53, for reviews launched in the High Court.

They provide that:

- Where a review application is to be brought in the High Court and no record or an incomplete record has been furnished in advance of the proceedings, the applicant then has the election regarding whether to proceed in terms of Rule 6 or Rule 53.[85]

---

79 *Helen Suzman Foundation v JSC* 2018 (4) SA 1 (CC) para 26.

80 See *Telcordia Technologies Inc v Telkom SA Ltd* 2007 (3) SA 266 (SCA) para 32; *Helen Suzman Foundation* para 26.

81 *Tao Ying Metal Industry (Pty) Ltd v Pooe NO and Others* 2007 (5) SA 146 (SCA) para 98.This flows from the general principle that an applicant's cause of action may not be made out in reply. However, a court has a discretion to allow new matter in a replying affidavit in exceptional circumstances – for example where facts alleged in the respondent's answering affidavit reveal the existence or possible existence of a further ground for the relief sought by the applicant. See *Finishing Touch 163 (Pty) Ltd v BHP Billiton Energy Coal SA* Ltd 2013 (2) SA 204 (SCA) at para 26.

82 The Rules Board is established by the Rules Board for Courts of Law Act 107 of 1985. It is the body that is responsible for making rules for the Supreme Court of Appeal, High Court and magistrates' courts. It includes judges, practitioners, a representative of the Department of Justice and others.

83 *Lawyers for Human Rights v Rules Board for Courts of Law and Another* [2012] 3 All SA 153 (GNP).

84 Promotion of Access to Information Rules and Administrative Review Rules, 2019 – GN R1284 in *GG* 42740 of 04.10.2019.

85 Administrative Review Rules, rule 2(1).

- Where a review application is to be brought in the High Court and a record has been furnished in advance of the proceedings, the applicant shall proceed in terms of Rule 6.[86]
- Where a review application proceeds in terms of Rule 6, the applicant must make the record (or portions of the record it has) available to any respondent opposing the relief sought.[87]
- Where a review application is to be brought in a magistrates' court with jurisdiction, much the same position applies. The applicant may make use of Rule 53 of the High Court Rules or Rule 55 of the Magistrates' Court Rules (which is similar to Rule 6 of the High Court Rules).

The position under the 2019 Rules is a sensible one. It preserves the advantages of Rule 53 and ensures that the principles laid down by the courts over many years regarding what that procedure entails continue to apply in the High Court and are now extended to magistrates' courts with jurisdiction.

#### 11.3.4.3 The value of the Rule 53 record

The fact that Rule 53 requires the decision-maker to make available the record to the applicant is a crucial part of the judicial review proceedings. Our courts have repeatedly made this clear.

For example, in *Jockey Club of SA v Forbes*,[88] the Appellate Division emphasised the need for the Rule 53 record as flowing from the fact that *applicants* for judicial review will often be 'in the dark' as to what occurred before the decision-maker and the reasons for its decision. The provision of the Rule 53 record seeks to prevent this:

> Not infrequently the private citizen is faced with an administrative or quasi-judicial decision adversely affecting his rights, that has not access to the record of the relevant proceedings nor any knowledge of the reasons found in such decision. Were it not for rule 53 he would be obliged to launch review proceedings in the dark and, depending on the answering affidavit(s) of the respondent(s), he could then apply to amend his notice of motion and to supplement his founding affidavit. Manifestly the procedure created by the Rule is to his advantage in that it obviates the delay and expense of an application to amend and provides him with access to the record.

In *Forbes*, the SCA held that because the advantages of Rule 53 were primarily for the benefit of the applicant, it was the applicant who could choose whether to proceed by way of Rule 53 or instead make use of the ordinary application procedure under Rule 6 – where no record would be provided.

The *Forbes* decision, however, took place in the context of a case where the only respondent was the administrative decision-maker itself. Later decisions of the SCA have emphasised the value of the Rule 53 record to *private respondents* in review proceedings. For example, where a decision to award a tender or a broadcasting licence is challenged in review proceedings, the private party who received the tender or broadcasting licence will have to be cited as one of the respondents. However, that private party too will be 'in the

86 Administrative Review Rules, rule 3(1).
87 Administrative Review Rules, rules 2(3)(a) and 3(2)(a).
88 1993 (1) SA 649 (A).

dark' as to the proceedings of the administrative decision-maker and the reasons for its decision. If the private party is to be properly able to exercise its right to seek to defend the administrative decision, it is essential that it has access to the Rule 53 record. This was explained by the SCA in *Stanton Woodbrush*:[89]

> If, as is the usual case, the proceedings are between the applicant and the organ of State involved, the latter can always, in answer to an ordinary application, supply the record of the proceedings and the reasons for its decision. On the other hand, as in this instance, if the rights of another member of the public are involved, and the organ of State, hiding behind a parapet of silence, adopts a supine attitude towards the matter since the order sought will not affect it (no costs were sought against the Registrar if the latter were to remain inactive), the position is materially different. Stanton was entitled to have the full record before the Court and to have the Registrar's reasons for the impugned decisions available. As a respondent in an ordinary application it does not have those rights.

The main benefit of the Rule 53 record is thus to allow the parties and the court to consider whether, in light of the information actually before the administrative decision-maker and the process actually followed, the requirements of PAJA were satisfied. This is to the benefit of the litigants (applicants and respondents) and also the court, as the Constitutional Court has explained:

> Undeniably, a rule 53 record is an invaluable tool in the review process. It may help: shed light on what happened and why; give a lie to unfounded *ex post facto* (after the fact) justification of the decision under review; in the substantiation of as yet not fully substantiated grounds of review; in giving support to the decision-maker's stance; and in the performance of the reviewing court's function.[90]

To provide a few practical examples, the production of the record might reveal that:
- The decision-maker adopted a procedure whereby it invited submissions from some parties, but not others.
- The decision-maker was not properly authorised or quorate when taking the decision.
- The decision-maker had a wealth of information before it, but failed to take account of that information.
- The decision-maker proceeded on an understanding of the facts that was not correct.

Whether and to what extent these give rise to reviewable irregularities will of course depend on the facts of the case. However, the record allows the parties and the court to be aware of the process that was followed and the information available to the decision-maker and thus to properly apply PAJA.

Thus while an applicant for judicial review in proceedings not involving private respondents is still in principle permitted to proceed under Rule 6 (that is, without a complete record) rather than Rule 53, this is not normally the prudent approach to adopt. Indeed, as the Constitutional Court has explained:

> An essential purpose of [the obligation to furnish a Rule 53 record]... is to enable a court to perform its constitutionally entrenched review function. This gives effect

89 *South African Football Association v Stanton Woodrush (Pty) Ltd t/a Stan Smidt & Sons and Another* 2003 (3) SA 313 (SCA) para 5. See also *SACCAWU and Others v President, Industrial Tribunal, and Another* 2001 (2) SA 277 (SCA) para 7.

90 *Turnbull-Jackson v Hibiscus Court Municipality and Others* 2014 (6) SA 592 (CC) para 37.

> to the rights of the parties under s 34 of the Constitution to have justiciable disputes decided in fair public hearings with all the issues being ventilated. It also safeguards parties' ability to enforce their rights under s 33 of the Constitution to administrative action that is lawful, reasonable and procedurally fair. The record was essential to enable the reviewing applicants to understand what occurred during the investigation that led to the impugned remedial action and to equip the court to ensure the proper administration of justice in the case.[91]

### 11.3.4.4 The content of the Rule 53 record

The question of what is in the 'record of proceedings' requires some elaboration. The most frequently cited description of the record is that of the court in *Johannesburg City Council v The Administrator, Transvaal and Another*.[92] There the court held as follows:

> The words record of proceedings cannot be otherwise construed, in my view, than as a loose description of the documents, evidence, arguments and other information before the tribunal relating to the matter under review, at the time of the making of the decision in question. It may be a formal record and dossier of what happened before the tribunal, but it may also be a disjointed indication of the material that was at the tribunal's disposal. In the latter case it would, I venture to think, include every scrap of paper throwing light, however indirectly, on what the proceedings were, both procedurally and evidentially....[93]

This '*every scrap of paper*' approach is now well entrenched in our law and has been expressly endorsed by the Constitutional Court.[94]

Indeed, where the Constitutional Court has diverged from the *Johannesburg City Council* approach, it has broadened – rather than narrowed – the scope of what is to be included in the record of proceedings. In *Johannesburg City Council*, the court held that the 'every scrap of paper' approach would not include a record of the deliberations of the body concerned:

> A record of proceedings is analagous to the record of proceedings in a court of law which quite clearly does not include a record of the deliberations subsequent to the receiving of the evidence and preceding the announcement of the court's decision. Thus the deliberations of the Executive Committee are as little part of the record of proceedings as the private deliberations of the jury or of the Court in a case before it. It does, however, include all the documents before the Executive Committee as well as all documents which are by reference incorporated in the file before it.[95]

In *Helen Suzman Foundation*, the majority of the Constitutional Court rejected this approach. After a careful discussion of the issue, Madlanga J concluded for the majority:

> In sum, I can think of no reason why deliberations as a class of information ought generally to be excluded from a rule 53 record. For me, the question is whether deliberations are relevant, which they are, and whether – despite their

91 *Public Protector v SA Reserve Bank* 2019 (6) SA 253 (CC) para 185 .
92 1970 (2) SA 89 (T).
93 At 91G–H.
94 *Public Protector* para 185.
95 At 91H–92B.

> relevance - there is some legally cognisable basis for excluding them from the record. This approach to what a record for purposes of rule 53 should be better advances a review applicant's right of access to court under section 34 of the Constitution. It thus respects the injunction in section 39(2) of the Constitution that courts must interpret statutes in a manner that promotes the spirit, purport and objects of the Bill of Rights.[96]

It is thus now established that a Rule 53 record will generally include a record of deliberations on the decision at issue.

A remaining issue is whether Rule 53 means that even the President can be required to supply a Rule 53 record where the decision being reviewed is his decision to dismiss a cabinet minister. This arose in the matter of *Democratic Alliance v President*,[97] where the DA sought to compel President Zuma to provide a Rule 53 record in its review application (under the principle of legality) challenging the decision to dismiss Minister Pravin Gordhan and Deputy Minister Mcebisi Jonas. The High Court concluded that the decision did fall within Rule 53, properly interpreted, and compelled production of the record. The matter then came before both the SCA[98] and Constitutional Court,[99] but both courts dismissed the President's appeal on the grounds of mootness, and made clear that they were not expressing a view on the correctness of the High Court's conclusion. The issue has therefore not yet been finally resolved.

## THIS CHAPTER IN ESSENCE

Judicial review of administrative action remains the most important mechanism to enforce administrative law in South Africa.

In order to bring such an application for review before a court, a person will have to fall within one of the categories of persons enjoying standing under section 38 of the Constitution to enforce a provision of the Bill of Rights.

PAJA creates two procedural hurdles for applicants to surmount before a review can be heard. These are that all internal remedies must be exhausted first and that the review must be brought without unreasonable delay and not later than 180 days after concluding the internal remedies or after becoming aware of the administrative action and reasons.

Judicial review is generally brought on motion proceedings following the special court procedure created by Rule 53 of the High Court Rules. One of the most important aspects of Rule 53 is that the full record of the administrative decision must be filed with the court by the administrator once a review application has been launched.

## FURTHER READING


- Plasket, C (2002) The Exhaustion of Internal Remedies and Section 7(2) of the Promotion of Administrative Justice Act 3 of 2000 *SALJ* 119(1):50
- Quinot, G (2010) New Procedures for the Judicial Review of Administration Action *SA Public Law* 25:646


96 At para 27.

97 *Democratic Alliance v President of the Republic of South Africa* 2017 (4) SA 253 (GP).

98 *President of the Republic of South Africa v Democratic Alliance and Others* (664/17) [2018] ZASCA 79 (31 May 2018).

99 *President of the Republic of South Africa v Democratic Alliance and Others* 2020 (1) SA 428 (CC).

# Chapter 12

# Remedies in judicial review proceedings

*Janice Bleazard, Steven Budlender SC & Meghan Finn*

## 12.1 Introduction

Once a court has decided that an administrative action is invalid (on one or more grounds of review), what happens next? This chapter discusses the different remedies that a court may grant if the application for judicial review is successful.

The chapter starts with a discussion of the nature and purpose of remedies on judicial review: what are review remedies, and why are they needed? This is followed by a description of the two-staged approach to judicial review proceedings that the Constitutional Court has adopted, in line with section 172 of the Constitution. The two-staged approach sets out that, at the first stage, if the court finds that the administrative action is unlawful or falls short of what the Constitution, the Promotion of Administrative Justice Act[1] (PAJA) and the common law requires, the court must declare the action invalid. At the second stage, the court then has discretion to order a just and equitable remedy. The two-staged approach now informs how the courts address remedies.

The chapter then discusses the main remedies on judicial review, which are set out in PAJA, and include:

- setting aside the irregular administrative action,
- remittal to the administrative decision-maker for a new decision to be taken,
- substitution of the correct decision by the court,
- a declaration of rights,
- the award of compensation to affected parties, and
- interdicts.

After this, the chapter considers the remedies for an unlawful failure to take administrative action. The chapter concludes with a discussion of other common law or statutory remedies that may be applied by the courts, and the approach to costs orders in judicial review proceedings.

1 3 of 2000.

## 12.2 The nature and purpose of judicial review remedies

A party whose right to just administrative action in section 33 of the Constitution has been breached is entitled to 'appropriate relief' within the meaning of section 38 of the Constitution.[2] Section 38, the provision in the Bill of Rights on standing, provides that:

> Anyone listed in this section has the right to approach a competent court, alleging that a right in the Bill of Rights has been infringed or threatened, and the court may grant appropriate relief, including a declaration of rights.

In *Fose v Minister of Safety and Security*,[3] Ackermann J emphasised that the entitlement to appropriate relief must mean 'an effective remedy'. Ackermann J explained that:

> ... without effective remedies for breach, the values underlying and the right entrenched in the Constitution cannot properly be upheld or enhanced. Particularly in a country where so few have the means to enforce their rights through the courts, it is essential that on those occasions when the legal process does establish that an infringement of an entrenched right has occurred, it be effectively vindicated. The courts have a particular responsibility in this regard and are obliged to 'forge new tools' and shape innovative remedies, if needs be, to achieve this goal.

The Constitutional Court has also explained that appropriate relief for breaches of section 33 generally takes the form of public-law remedies, as opposed to private-law remedies.[4] This takes place via a remedy granted in terms of PAJA when PAJA is being applied or via a remedy granted in terms of section 172 of the Constitution when the constitutional principle of legality is being applied.

Unlike a private-law remedy, which is ordinarily concerned only with compensating a private person for harm or loss suffered, a public-law remedy is required to balance and protect a broader range of affected interests, including accountability and the public interest. The purpose of judicial review remedies, as stated by Moseneke DCJ in *Steenkamp NO v Provincial Tender Board, Eastern Cape*, is 'to pre-empt or correct or reverse an improper administrative function', and ultimately, 'to afford the prejudiced party administrative justice, to advance efficient and effective public administration compelled by constitutional precepts and at a broader level, to entrench the rule of law'.[5]

To achieve its multifaceted purpose, the remedy for a breach of section 33 must be carefully crafted to fit the injury, and must take into account all affected interests and broader public interest considerations. The Constitutional Court has stated that:

> The remedy must be fair to those affected by it and yet vindicate effectively the right violated. It must be just and equitable in the light of the facts, the implicated constitutional principles, if any, and the controlling law.[6]

---

2 *Steenkamp NO v Provincial Tender Board, Eastern Cape* 2007 (3) SA 121 (CC) para 22.
3 1997 (3) SA 786 (CC) para 69.
4 *Steenkamp* para 29.
5 *Steenkamp* paras 29–30. See also *Allpay Consolidated Investment Holdings (Pty) Ltd and Others v Chief Executive Officer, South African Social Security Agency and Others* 2014 (4) SA 179 (CC) (remedy judgment) ('*Allpay (remedy)*') paras 29–34.
6 *Steenkamp* para 29.

Depending on the circumstances, the court may set aside (or annul) the irregular decision and either remit (send) the matter to the decision-maker for a new decision to be taken or, in exceptional cases, substitute its own decision for that of the administrator. The court may direct the administrator to act in an appropriate manner or prohibit him or her from acting in a particular manner, and may even order the administrator to pay compensation to affected parties. In other cases, the court may be constrained by practical considerations, or by the public interest, to suspend a declaration of invalidity or confine itself to a declaration of rights while leaving the irregular decision intact.

Overall, in determining the appropriate remedy, the approach of the South African courts is flexible, context-sensitive and pragmatic. The South African law on remedies is thus relatively simple and unencumbered by technicalities. This is reflected in the provision on remedies under PAJA. Section 8 of PAJA affords the court a 'generous jurisdiction' to craft appropriate remedies and incorporates the overriding constitutional standard that the remedy must be 'just and equitable'.[7] It provides that the court 'may grant *any order* that is just and equitable' and provides an open list of the type of orders that the court may grant.[8] The court's approach to the remedy of compensation under section 8(1)(*c*)(ii)(*bb*) of PAJA is an exception, however. There, the courts have adopted an unusually technical approach, which limits the reach of that remedy.

## 12.3 The two-staged approach to remedies

The Constitutional Court has outlined a two-staged approach to remedies in judicial review proceedings (whether based on PAJA or the constitutional principle of legality). This approach flows from and accords with the court's powers and obligations in deciding constitutional matters under section 172(1) of the Constitution,[9] which provides that:

> 172(1) When deciding a constitutional matter within its power, a court-
> (*a*) must declare that any law or conduct that is inconsistent with the Constitution is invalid to the extent of its inconsistency; and
> (*b*) may make any order that is just and equitable, including-
> (i) an order limiting the retrospective effect of the declaration of invalidity; and

---

7 *Steenkamp* para 30; *Bengwenyama Minerals (Pty) Ltd and Others v Genorah Resources (Pty) Ltd and Others* 2011 (4) SA 113 (CC) para 83.

8 Section 8(1) of PAJA provides:

> (1) The court or tribunal, in proceedings for judicial review in terms of section 6(1), may grant any order that is just and equitable, including orders-
> (*a*) directing the administrator-
> (i) to give reasons; or
> (ii) to act in the manner the court or tribunal requires;
> (*b*) prohibiting the administrator from acting in a particular manner;
> (*c*) setting aside the administrative action and-
> (i) remitting the matter for reconsideration by the administrator, with or without directions; or
> (ii) in exceptional cases-
> (*aa*) substituting or varying the administrative action or correcting a defect resulting from the administrative action; or
> (*bb*) directing the administrator or any other party to the proceedings to pay compensation;
> (*d*) declaring the rights of the parties in respect of any matter to which the administrative action relates;
> (*e*) granting a temporary interdict or other temporary relief; or
> (*f*) as to costs.

9 *Bengwenyama Minerals* paras 81–85; *Allpay Consolidated Investment Holdings (Pty) Ltd and Others v Chief Executive Officer, South African Social Security Agency and Others* 2014 (1) SA 604 (CC) (merits judgment) ('*Allpay (merits)*') para 56; *Allpay (remedy)* para 31.

(ii) an order suspending the declaration of invalidity for any period and on any conditions, to allow the competent authority to correct the defect.

As discussed in Chapters 5 and 11, judicial review of public power is invariably 'a constitutional matter', under the constitutional principle of legality and PAJA which gives effect to section 33 of the Constitution.[10] Section 172(1) of the Constitution thus applies to all judicial review proceedings brought under PAJA and the principle of legality.[11]

At the first stage, section 172(1)(*a*) compels the court to declare any irregular administrative action – as 'conduct that is inconsistent with the Constitution' – to be constitutionally invalid to the extent of its inconsistency. The court has no discretion at this stage: if the court finds that administrative action is irregular, it must declare it to be constitutionally invalid.

Thereafter, the court may make any order that is just and equitable, in accordance with section 172(1)(*b*) of the Constitution and section 8 of PAJA (if applicable). At this second stage, the court has a discretion to grant further relief that is just and equitable. In exercising this discretion, the court must consider the effects of the declaration of invalidity on parties or persons to whom the order applies and whether further relief is required to regulate the consequences flowing from the declaration of constitutional invalidity.

Figure 12.1 below illustrates the two-staged approach and the court's remedial options following a declaration of constitutional invalidity.

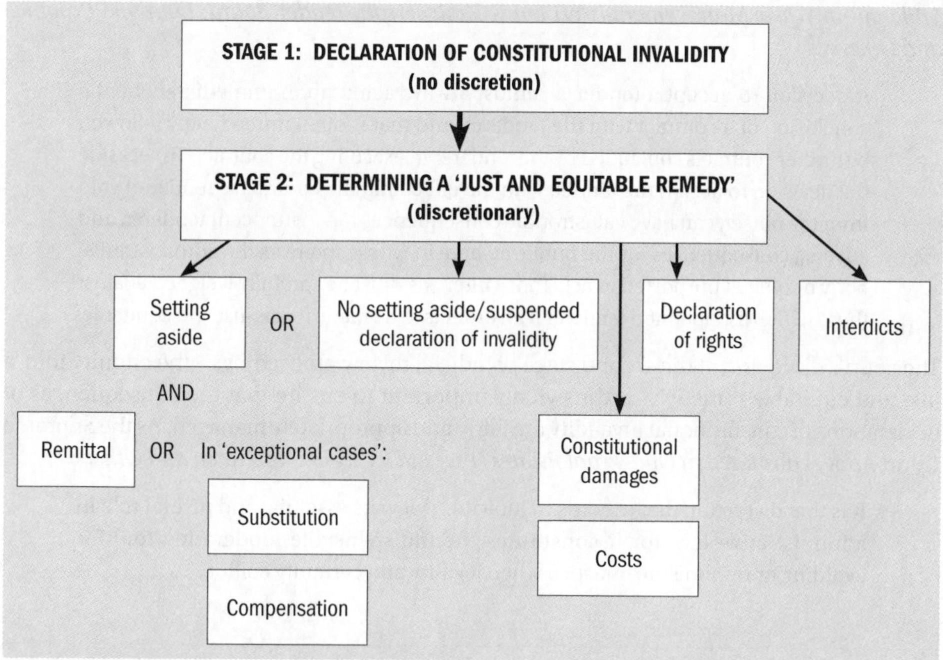


*Figure 12.1 The Constitutional Court's two-staged approach to remedies on judicial review*

10 See *Pharmaceutical Manufacturers Association of SA and Another: In Re Ex Parte President of the Republic of South Africa and Others* 2000 (2) SA 674 (CC) paras 44–45 and 51; *Bato Star Fishing (Pty) Ltd v Minister of Environmental Affairs and Others* 2004 (4) SA 490 (CC) para 22.

11 As discussed in Hoexter, C (2012) *Administrative Law in South Africa* (2nd ed) at 127–131, it remains a matter of some debate whether the judicial review of private power is a constitutional matter or involves only the application of the common law. However, the judicial review of private power is rare, and so is not considered further in this chapter.

## 12.4 Declarations of constitutional invalidity

### 12.4.1 The retrospective operation of declarations of constitutional invalidity

Once an administrative act is declared invalid by the court (but only once the court makes its order), the act will be invalid from the moment the administrative decision was taken. This occurs automatically by virtue of the declaration, unless the court orders otherwise (for example, by suspending the declaration of invalidity).[12] Even an unlawful administrative act can produce legally valid consequences, for as long as the unlawful act is not set aside.[13]

However, once an administrative act is declared to be invalid by the court, it not only ceases to have legal effect but is treated as if it never existed. This means that any subsequent legal acts taken in reliance on the administrative action, and which depend for their own validity on the validity of the administrative action, will also be rendered void.[14] A declaration of invalidity of administrative action can thus have serious and far-reaching consequences for persons who have relied and acted upon the administrative action by the time it is brought under review and declared to be invalid.

The problem of subsequent reliance on invalid administrative action commonly arises in the tender context. This has been helpfully explained by the Supreme Court of Appeal in *Millennium Waste Management (Pty) Ltd v Chairperson, Tender Board: Limpopo Province and Others*:[15]

> A decision to accept a tender is almost always acted upon immediately by the conclusion of a contract with the tenderer, and that is often immediately followed by further contracts concluded by the tenderer in executing the contract. To set aside the decision to accept the tender, with the effect that the contract is rendered void from the outset, can have catastrophic consequences for an innocent tenderer, and adverse consequences for the public at large in whose interests the administrative body or official purported to act. Those interests must be carefully weighed against those of the disappointed tenderer if an order is to be made that is just and equitable.

The court's discretion at the second stage of judicial review proceedings – the enquiry into 'a just and equitable remedy' – is thus vitally important to ensure that the consequences of declarations of constitutional invalidity are fairly and appropriately managed. As the Supreme Court Appeal observed in *Oudekraal Estates (Pty) Ltd v City of Cape Town and Others*:[16]

> It is that discretion that accords to judicial review its essential and pivotal role in administrative law, for it constitutes the indispensable moderating tool for avoiding or minimising injustice when legality and certainty collide.

12 This follows from section 172(1) of the Constitution and the doctrine of objective constitutional invalidity. See the discussion box at section 12.4.3 below for an explanation of the doctrine of objective constitutional invalidity. See also *Ferreira v Levin NO and Others; Vryenhoek and Others v Powell NO and Others* 1996 (1) SA 984 (CC) paras 27–28; *Ex Parte Women's Legal Centre, In Re Moise v Greater Germiston Transitional Local Council* 2001 (4) SA 1288 (CC) paras 11–13.

13 *Oudekraal Estates* para 26; *MEC for Health, Eastern Cape and Another v Kirland Investments (Pty) Ltd t/a Eye and Lazer Institute* 2014 (3) SA 481 (CC) para 100.

14 *Kirland* para 102, fn 74; *Seale v Van Rooyen NO and Others; Provincial Government, North West Province v Van Rooyen NO and Others* 2008 (4) SA 43 (SCA) paras 13–14; *Corruption Watch NPC and Others v President of the Republic of South Africa and Others; Nxasana v Corruption Watch NPC and Others* 2018 (10) BCLR 1179 (CC) paras 31–34.

15 2008 (2) SA 481 (SCA) para 23.

16 2004 (6) SA 222 (SCA) para 36.

We discuss how courts have balanced the competing interests in the leading tender cases at section 12.5.3 below.

### 12.4.2 Subsequent acts that are not affected by declarations of invalidity

As we have explained above, once an administrative act is declared to be invalid by the court, subsequent legal acts taken in reliance on the administrative action, and which depend for their own validity on the validity of the administrative action, will also be rendered void - unless the court orders otherwise in the exercise of its remedial discretion.

However, not all subsequent acts are invalidated by an order declaring prior administrative action invalid. Certain acts may follow which do not depend for their validity on the lawfulness (or legal validity) of the prior administrative action, but only on its factual existence. The validity of these subsequent acts will remain intact notwithstanding a declaration of invalidity of the prior administrative action.

An example of this appears in *Oudekraal Estates*,[17] where administrative acts were taken by various functionaries, including the Surveyor-General and Registrar of Deeds, after a decision of the Administrator to approve the establishment of a township. When interpreting the empowering provisions for the subsequent administrative acts, the court found that they depended only on the *factual existence* of the Administrator's decision to approve the township, and not on the *legal validity* of that decision. The administrative acts of the Surveyor-General and Registrar of Deeds thus remained intact, and of full force and effect, despite the invalidity of the Administrator's decision. The court reasoned that:

> On a proper construction of the Ordinance the validity of each of those steps was not dependent on the legal validity of the Administrator's approval but merely upon the fact that it was given. The legislature could not have expected the Surveyor-General first to satisfy himself that the Administrator's approval was valid before he approved the general plan. It also could not have intended the Registrar of Deeds first to satisfy himself that the approval was valid before he opened a township register. And it could not have expected the township owner and the public at large to enquire into the validity of the Administrator's approval before they relied upon the notification in the Provincial Gazette that the township had been approved. In our view the functionaries were authorized to act as they did merely upon the fact of the Administrator's approval and their acts were accordingly lawful...[18]

In assessing what constitutes a just and equitable remedy, the courts must consider the consequences of the irregular administrative action, particularly its impact on subsequent administrative actions that may have been taken. An irregular administrative action or decision may have consequences that make it undesirable, or even impossible, to set it aside or to declare it invalid without suspending the declaration of invalidity or limiting its

17 We discuss this case in more detail below at 12.5.1.

18 *Oudekraal Estates* para 39. To explain this effect, the SCA quoted and relied on Christopher Forsyth, 'The Metaphysic of Nullity: Invalidity, Conceptual Reasoning and the Rule of Law' in *Essays on Public Law in Honour of Sir William Wade QC* at 141. The following passage by Forsyth (at 159) is quoted at paragraph 29 of the *Oudekraal Estates* judgment, and neatly sums up the principle:

> [I]t has been argued that unlawful administrative acts are void in law. But they clearly exist in fact and they often appear to be valid; and those unaware of their invalidity may take decisions and act on the assumption that these acts are valid. When this happens the validity of these later acts depends upon the legal powers of the second actor. The crucial issue to be determined is whether that second actor has legal power to act validly notwithstanding the invalidity of the first act ...

retrospective effect. These considerations must be properly weighed by the court in determining whether to grant further relief upon a declaration of constitutional invalidity. In the remainder of this chapter, we discuss the types of orders that the court may grant to regulate the consequences of a declaration of constitutional invalidity.

### 12.4.3 Pre-existing rights are not affected by declarations of invalidity

In *Magnificent Mile Trading 30 (Pty) Ltd v Charmaine Celliers NO,*[19] the Constitutional Court was called on to address the impact of a declaration of invalidity of the decision to grant a prospecting right on another, pre-existing right to prospect. Madlanga J, writing for the majority, found that a pre-existing right which does not owe its existence to a later, unlawful administrative act is not invalidated simply because the later administrative act is declared invalid and set aside. Madlanga J explained that this was consistent with the *Oudekraal* principle. He observed:

> To say the later unlawful Magnificent Mile award could effectively wipe out the pre-existing limited real right would be turning the *Oudekraal* rule on its head. *Oudekraal* says no more than that if you want to nullify, or even avert consequences that owe, or would owe, their existence to an initial unlawful administrative act, that initial act must be set aside. It is one thing to say – but for an unlawful administrative act – something would never have come about and that, once it has come about, it continues to exist for as long as the unlawful administrative act to which it owes its existence has not been set aside. It is quite another to say that an unlawful administrative act – through the simple facility of applying the *Oudekraal* rule – can have the effect of obliterating a pre-existing right which does not owe its existence to the unlawful administrative act. Indeed, *Smith, Oudekraal, Kirland* and all other related cases do not suggest so.[20]

**PAUSE FOR REFLECTION**

**The doctrine of objective constitutional invalidity**

The doctrine of objective constitutional invalidity applies to laws and conduct (including administrative action) and informs section 172(1) of the Constitution.

In *Ferreira v Levin NO,*[21] the Constitutional Court explained the doctrine of constitutional invalidity, and its retrospective operation to the date of commencement of the Constitution, as follows:

> [27] The Court's order does not invalidate the law; it merely declares it to be invalid. It is very seldom patent, and in most cases is disputed, that pre-constitutional laws are inconsistent with the provisions of the Constitution. It is one of this Court's functions to determine and pronounce on the invalidity of laws, including Acts of Parliament. This does not detract from the reality that pre-existing laws either remained valid or became invalid upon the provisions of the Constitution coming into operation. In this sense laws are objectively valid or invalid depending on whether they are or are not inconsistent with the Constitution. The fact that a

CONTINUED >>>

19 *Magnificent Mile Trading 30 (Pty) Limited v Charmaine Celliers NO and Others* 2020 (1) BCLR 41 (CC).
20 *Magnificent Mile* para 43.
21 1996 (1) SA 984 (CC).

> dispute concerning inconsistency may only be decided years afterwards, does not affect the objective nature of the invalidity. The issue of whether a law is invalid or not does not in theory therefore depend on whether, at the moment when the issue is being considered, a particular person's rights are threatened or infringed by the offending law or not.
>
> [28] A pre-existing law which was inconsistent with the provisions of the Constitution became invalid the moment the relevant provisions of the Constitution came into effect. The fact that this Court has the power in terms of section 98(5) of the [interim] Constitution to postpone the operation of invalidity and, in terms of section 98(6), to regulate the consequences of the invalidity, does not detract from the conclusion that the test for invalidity is an objective one and that the inception of invalidity of a pre-existing law occurs when the relevant provision of the [interim] Constitution came into operation ...

*Ferreira v Levin NO* was decided under the interim Constitution, but the principles apply equally to the final Constitution.[22]

The effect of the doctrine for laws promulgated after the commencement of the Constitution was described in *Mvumvu and Others v Minister for Transport and Another*:[23]

> [44] Ordinarily an order of constitutional invalidity has a retrospective effect unless its operation is suspended. In terms of the doctrine of objective constitutional invalidity, unless ordered otherwise by the court the invalidity operates retrospectively to the date on which the Constitution came into force. But if the legislation in question was enacted after that date, as was the present Act, the retrospective operation of invalidity goes back to the date on which the legislation came into force ...

While the above judicial pronouncements are made in respect of legislation, the principles apply equally to conduct that is declared to be constitutionally invalid.

22 *Kruger v President of the Republic of South Africa and Others* 2009 (1) SA 417 (CC) para 52.
23 2011 (2) SA 473 (CC).

## 12.5 Setting aside unlawful administrative action

Following a declaration of invalidity, the courts have a discretion whether or not to 'set aside' irregular administrative action.[24] An order setting aside irregular administrative action, as Hoexter has put it, 'is simply a way of saying that the decision no longer stands'.[25] The remedy is derived from the common law and is provided for in section 8(1) of PAJA.[26]

The Constitutional Court has recognised what it terms 'the corrective principle' in administrative law, which recognises that the 'default position' requires the consequences of invalidity to be corrected or reversed where they can no longer be prevented.[27] What this means in practice is that once the decision is declared invalid (as a court must do), usually the decision must also be set aside and remitted (or sent back) to the decision-maker to correct. The court will depart from this approach only if it would be unjust or inequitable to do so in the circumstances.

The reach and effect of the corrective principle still remains uncertain and largely untested, however. This includes, for instance, the question whether a successful tenderer who has performed under the contract, must repay all the profits it has earned under the contract when it is set aside. Debate on this question was prompted by a statement made by the Constitutional Court in the *Allpay* case, which involved the review of a national tender to administer the payment of social grants. The Constitutional Court found that the award of the tender to Cash Paymasters was unlawful, and declared the contract Cash Paymaster had concluded as a result of the award to be invalid. The Constitutional Court described the effect of the invalidation of Cash Paymaster's contract as follows:

> It is true that any invalidation of the existing contract as a result of the invalid tender should not result in any loss to Cash Paymaster. The converse, however, is also true. It has no right to benefit from an unlawful contract. And any benefit that it may derive should not be beyond public scrutiny.[28]

The court's statement that Cash Paymaster had 'no right to benefit from an unlawful contract' generated considerable debate in the litigation saga that ensued, and was dubbed by some of the parties as 'the no profit principle'.

Whether the 'no profit principle' is in fact a principle in our law; whether it is a manifestation of the corrective principle, and thus a default principle; and in what circumstances its application is just and equitable, remains unclear. Much of this uncertainty flows from the fact that, despite setting aside Cash Paymaster's contract, the Constitutional Court did not direct Cash Paymaster to repay the profits it earned under the contract (but

---

24 *Oudekraal Estates* para 36:

> [A] court that is asked to set aside an invalid administrative act in proceedings for judicial review has a discretion whether to grant or to withhold the remedy.

25 Hoexter (2012) 545.

26 See, for example, *Johannesburg Consolidated Investment Co v Johannesburg Town Council* 1903 TS 111 at 115, where Innes CJ held:

> Whenever a public body has a duty imposed on it by statute, and disregards important provisions of the statute, or is guilty of gross irregularity or clear illegality in the performance of the duty, this Court may be asked to review the proceedings complained of and set aside or correct them. This is no special machinery created by the Legislature; it is a right inherent in the Court, which has jurisdiction to entertain all civil causes and proceedings arising ...

See further, Baxter, L (1984) *Administrative Law* 678.

27 *Allpay (remedy)* para 30. See also *Steenkamp* para 29:

> The purpose of a public-law remedy is to pre-empt or correct or reverse an improper administrative function...

28 *Allpay (remedy)* para 67.

only to report to the court on its profits). Also, had the Constitutional Court meant to adopt such a far-reaching and novel principle, one would have expected a more considered discussion of the basis and implications of the principle (like the debate that ensued in *Steenkamp NO v Provincial Tender Board, Eastern Cape,*[29] over a tenderer's entitlement to claim delictual damages for out-of-pocket expenses incurred in reliance on a tender award, discussed in 12.8.1 below). But the Constitutional Court did no more than make the passing remark quoted above, supported by an oblique footnote.

Despite the uncertain import of the Constitutional Court's dictum in *Allpay*, the 'no profit principle' has gained traction. In another case involving Cash Paymaster and its contract to administer social grants, the High Court set aside an extension of that same contract, and directed Cash Paymaster to pay back the full amount it had received under the invalid extension.[30] The High Court's order was upheld by the Supreme Court of Appeal,[31] and leave to appeal to the Constitutional Court was refused for lack of prospects of success.

### 12.5.1 Invalid administrative action has legal effect until declared invalid and set aside by a court of law

Until it is declared to be invalid and set aside by a court, irregular administrative action, however defective it may be, is presumed to be and is treated as though it is valid.[32] However anomalous it may seem, an irregular administrative act or decision has legal effect, and must be observed as if it is lawful, unless and until it is declared to be invalid and set aside by a court. This has been confirmed by the Supreme Court of Appeal in *Oudekraal Estates (Pty) Ltd v City of Cape Town*[33] and by the Constitutional Court in *MEC for Health, Eastern Cape and Another v Kirland Investments (Pty) Ltd.*[34]

In both cases, the court recognised that reliance on administrative action, and the presumption of its validity until declared otherwise by a court, is fundamental to the functioning of a modern bureaucratic state. If an administrative act could simply be ignored without proceeding to court, then 'chaos and not law would rule'.[35] If a public official believes that a decision is irregular, he or she must follow the correct legal process, and approach the courts to have the decision set aside, as '[t]he courts alone, and not public officials, are the arbiters of legality'.[36]

The Supreme Court of Appeal explained in *Oudekraal Estates* that the 'proper functioning of a modern state would be considerably compromised if all administrative acts could be given effect to or ignored depending upon the view the subject takes of the validity of the act in question'.[37] In *Kirland*, Cameron J (writing for the majority of the Constitutional Court) similarly remarked that: 'The clarity and certainty of governmental conduct, on which we all rely in organising our lives, would be imperilled if irregular or invalid administrative acts could be ignored because officials consider them invalid.'[38]

---

29 2007 (3) SA 121 (CC).

30 *Corruption Watch (NPC) (RF) v Chief Executive Officer of the South African Social Services and Others* [2018] ZAGPPHC 7.

31 *Cash Paymaster Services (Pty) Ltd v Chief Executive Officer of the South African Social Security Agency and Others* [2019] 4 All SA 327 (SCA).

32 Under the common law, the rebuttable presumption of validity of administrative acts is expressed in the common-law maxim *omnia praesumuntur rite esse acta*. See Baxter (1984) 355ff.

33 See *Oudekraal Estates* para 26.

34 *Kirland* paras 65–66 and 100–103.

35 *Magnificent Mile* para 50.

36 *Kirland* para 103.

37 *Oudekraal Estates* para 26.

38 *Kirland* para 103.

The facts in *Oudekraal Estates* and *Kirland* illustrate the prejudice and disruption that can occur when government officials ignore administrative decisions that they consider to be irregular but which have not been declared to be invalid and set aside by a court.

In *Oudekraal Estates*, the owner of undeveloped land sought the court to grant declaratory orders confirming his rights to develop the land. Some decades previously, the Provincial Administrator had approved the establishment of a township on the land. Thereafter, various administrative steps had been taken by the previous owner to ready the land for development, including obtaining approval of the general plan by the Surveyor-General and registering its incorporation at the Registrar of Deeds. However, when the new owner applied to the City Council for approval of an engineering services plan for the proposed development, the City refused to consider the application. Defending its refusal in court, the City argued that the Administrator's approval of a township development on the land was unlawful, because the Administrator had failed to consider the existence of Muslim graves and *kramats* on the land, which would be desecrated in the development. The Supreme Court of Appeal accepted that the Administrator's decision was unlawful, as the Administrator had failed to take into account material information (namely, the cultural and religious significance of the Muslim burial sites). However the Supreme Court of Appeal held that, notwithstanding the unlawfulness of the Administrator's decision, the City was not entitled to disregard the decision and not comply with its public functions merely because it believed that the Administrator's decision was unlawful. The Supreme Court of Appeal held that:

> Until the Administrator's approval (and thus also the consequences of the approval) is set aside by a court in proceedings for judicial review it exists in fact and it has legal consequences that cannot simply be overlooked ... It follows that for so long as the Administrator's approval (and the extensions) continues to exist in fact the township owner has been permitted to develop the township and the Cape Metropolitan Council was not entitled simply to ignore that when deciding whether or not to carry out its public functions.[39]

In *Kirland*, the appellant (Kirland) sought to establish private hospitals in the Eastern Cape province and applied to the Head of the Provincial Department of Health (the HoD) for approval. The HoD decided that he would refuse the application but never signed off his refusal or communicated the decision to Kirland. Before he could do so, the HoD was involved in a motor-vehicle accident and took sick leave. During his absence, an Acting HoD approved Kirland's applications on the instructions of the MEC. Kirland was informed of the decision, and it duly submitted building plans for approval and later sought to increase the capacity of the proposed hospitals. By that stage, the HoD had returned from sick leave and resumed his duties. He declined to approve Kirland's new applications and informed Kirland that the approval by the Acting HoD of the private hospitals was withdrawn. Kirland challenged the HoD's withdrawal of the approval on review. In the Constitutional Court, Cameron J held (for the majority) that even though the approval decision of the Acting HoD appeared to be defective (due to unlawful dictation by the MEC), the HoD had erred in purporting to withdraw the decision at his own accord and without applying formally to court to set aside the defective decision. Cameron J explained that, unless specifically authorised otherwise by statute, government must be held to 'the pain and duty' of applying to a court to set aside a defective decision. This is necessary to enable the court properly to

39 *Oudekraal Estates* paras 26 and 40.

assess the effects of the defective decision on those subject to it, and to ensure that setting it aside is just and equitable. Cameron J reasoned as follows:

> When government errs by issuing a defective decision, the subject affected by it is entitled to proper notice, and to be afforded a proper hearing, on whether the decision should be set aside. Government should not be allowed to take shortcuts. Generally, this means that government must apply formally to set aside the decision. Once the subject has relied on a decision, government cannot, barring specific statutory authority, simply ignore what it has done. The decision, despite being defective, may have consequences that make it undesirable or even impossible to set it aside. That demands a proper process, in which all factors for and against are properly weighed.[40]

In a minority judgment Jafta J dissented, and reasoned that it is inconsistent with the rule of law for the court to allow constitutionally invalid administrative action to stand 'on the technical basis that there was no application to have it reviewed and set aside'.[41] The implication of this approach is that an administrative act that is patently or obviously unlawful can simply be ignored by public officials.

The majority and minority judgments in *Kirland* track a divide in the Constitutional Court. Broadly speaking, there are two camps on the question of whether a court must always be approached to declare invalid and set aside unlawful administrative action. The majority camp maintains that, for reasons of legal certainty and due process, a court must be approached, and that an official cannot simply ignore a decision, even if it considers the decision to be unlawful. The minority view (most emphatically expressed by Jafta J) is that the rule of law dictates that an administrative act that is inconsistent with the Constitution is invalid, and cannot be treated as valid and enforced.

The majority position has consistently prevailed in a line of cases, where this same divide is evident.[42] The position in our law therefore remains that a public official must approach a court of law to set aside an administrative act, even if that act is clearly unlawful. Until the court has set that act aside, it exists and has legal consequences.

### 12.5.2 The collateral or reactive challenge

While in general, legal certainty requires that irregular administrative acts be observed by all until set aside by a court of law, there is one pertinent exception. A fundamental incident of the rule of law is that no public authority may infringe upon a person's rights or liberty without statutory authority. This means that unlawful administrative action may be ignored with impunity, and resisted if necessary, by those coerced by the decision.[43] This is known as a 'collateral or reactive challenge' or defence to administrative action, which was described in *Oudekraal Estates* as follows:

> It is in those cases – where the subject is sought to be coerced by a public authority into compliance with an unlawful administrative act – that the subject may be entitled to ignore the unlawful act with impunity and justify his conduct by raising

40 *Kirland* para 65.

41 *Kirland* paras 40–44, 46, 60–61.

42 See, for example, the majority judgments of the Constitutional Court in *Kirland*; *Magnificent Mile*; *Merafong City Local Municipality v AngloGold Ashanti Limited* 2017 (2) SA 211 (CC); and *Department of Transport v Tasima (Pty) Limited* 2017 (2) SA 622 (CC).

43 The 'collateral challenge' is discussed in *Oudekraal Estates* paras 32–36; see also Baxter (1984) 359. More recently, see *Merafong* and *Tasima*.

> what has come to be known as a 'defensive' or a 'collateral' challenge to the validity of the administrative act.[44]

Where a person is required by an administrative authority to do or not to do a particular thing, that person may, if he or she doubts the lawfulness of the administrative act, choose to treat it as invalid and await developments. If the administrative authority involved wishes to compel compliance, it will have to go to court to bring enforcement proceedings, at which point the individual will be able to raise the unlawfulness and invalidity of the underlying administrative act as a defence.[45] The challenge is called a collateral or reactive one because it is only raised once another party has initiated court proceedings to enforce the decision.

When a collateral challenge is raised, the court has no discretion to allow or disallow the raising of that defence. As the Supreme Court of Appeal explained in *Oudekraal Estates*:

> the right to challenge the validity of an administrative act collaterally arises because the validity of the administrative act constitutes the essential prerequisite for the legal force of the action that follows and *ex hypothesi* the subject may not then be precluded from challenging its validity.[46]

Classically, a collateral or reactive challenge is brought by an individual threatened with coercive action by a public authority. However, in *Merafong*, the courts had to decide whether a collateral challenge can be brought by an organ of state, as a defence against the enforcement of another organ of state's coercive decision. AngloGold, a mining company operating within the Merafong municipality, required water to operate its mines. The Merafong municipality charged the mine an additional surcharge for its supply of water. AngloGold objected to the surcharge, and appealed to the Minister of Water Affairs. The Minister ruled that the municipality could not levy a surcharge on the payment, but the municipality ignored this ruling. AngloGold proceeded to court to attempt to enforce the Minister's ruling, and in response, Merafong municipality sought to raise a collateral challenge. It contended that the Minister's ruling was unlawful, and so could not be enforced against it and must be set aside.

The High Court found against Merafong municipality, and held that an organ of state cannot raise a collateral challenge. The Supreme Court of Appeal agreed. It found that an organ of state has a duty to proceed to court itself to have an administrative act – including one taken by another organ of state – reviewed and set aside if it considers it to be unlawful; it cannot wait and only dispute the lawfulness of that act as a defence when the decision is sought to be enforced against it.

The Constitutional Court disagreed. Writing for the majority, Cameron J found that South African law has always recognised some flexibility in reactive challenges to coercive action, and that categorical exclusions should be avoided. It held that neither doctrine nor practical reason warrants categorically barring organs of state from raising collateral or reactive challenges.[47] The majority noted that, as a matter of 'good constitutional citizenship', Merafong municipality should have proceeded to court to challenge the Minister's ruling and not waited. However, the fact that the municipality did not do so did not necessarily bar it from raising a reactive challenge – this would depend on factors like the reasons for the

44 *Oudekraal Estates* para 32.

45 *Oudekraal Estates* para 34.

46 *Oudekraal Estates* para 36.

47 *Merafong* paras 26–30, 55. The minority (per Jafta J) agreed on this point, and found there was no reason of principle to preclude the state from raising a collateral challenge where it faces a claim that it must comply with an illegal decision: paras 100–106.

delay and prejudice.[48] The Constitutional Court remitted (sent back) the matter to the High Court to decide whether Merafong's delay in challenging the Minister's ruling disqualified the challenge and, if it did not, whether the Minister's ruling was valid.

In *Tasima*, the Constitutional Court followed the approach adopted in *Merafong*. An official in the Department of Transport had unlawfully extended a contract between the Department and a company, Tasima, for the provision of IT services. The Department acknowledged that the extension was unlawful, and so refused to pay Tasima under the contract. When Tasima approached the court to enforce the extended contract, the Department raised a reactive challenge and sought to have the extension of the contract declared invalid and set aside. The majority of the Constitutional Court (per Khampepe J) again held that an organ of state is permitted to raise a reactive challenge, even when the decision is sought to be enforced by a private company (rather than another organ of state).[49] The majority emphasised, however, that the organ of state must have sound reasons for raising the challenge reactively (instead of proceeding to court itself to have the decision set aside) and must account for any delay.[50] The majority found that, in this case, the Department had delayed unreasonably, but that the delay should be overlooked in the interests of justice. It reasoned that the Department's delay was not in bad faith; the decision to extend the contract was blatantly unlawful (so that the merits of the reactive challenge were compelling); the extension had a significant adverse effect on state resources; and Tasima would not be prejudiced by setting aside the decision at that late stage (as the contract extension had already expired).[51]

It is clear from these cases that the Constitutional Court has endorsed a flexible and permissive approach to collateral or reactive challenges. When an individual raises a collateral or reactive challenge, he or she generally does not need to justify his or her delay in calling the coercive action into question. However, when an organ of state raises a collateral or reactive challenge it is required to justify its delay in challenging the coercive action. This is because organs of state have a general duty (and the resources) to obtain legal certainty from the courts when they consider conduct to be unlawful, and not to resort to self-help; and to act diligently and without delay in rectifying unlawfulness when they are faced with it.[52]

### 12.5.3 When will courts decline to set aside unlawful administrative action?

The courts exercise their discretion not to set aside – and so in effect, to uphold – an irregular decision in circumstances where the effluxion (passage) of time and intervening events renders it impracticable, overly disruptive, or otherwise unjust and inequitable to do so. These circumstances typically arise in the context of tenders where the successful tenderer has already begun performing the tender by the time the tender award is reviewed by the court.

We discuss a line of these tender cases to illustrate how the courts weigh up the competing considerations to decide whether or not to set aside irregular administration action. As these cases demonstrate, context is all-important in this determination. And, as

48 *Merafong* paras 59–61, 76–77.
49 *Tasima* para 140.
50 *Tasima* para 150.
51 *Tasima* paras 163–171.
52 Section 237 of the Constitution. *Merafong* paras 59–61; *Khumalo and Another v Member of the Executive Council for Education: KwaZulu Natal* 2014 (5) SA 579 (CC) para 46.

the case of *Allpay* vividly illustrates, the impact on the provision of public services (in that case, the payment social grants) is a key consideration.

In *Chairperson, Standing Tender Committee and Others v JFE Sapela Electronics (Pty) Ltd and Others,*[53] the Supreme Court of Appeal declined to set aside tender awards for engineering work at prisons. It did so on the basis that the amount of repair work that had already been done by the time the review was heard, and which was irreversible, rendered it impracticable to start a new tender process for the little work that remained outstanding under the tender.

A useful counterpoint to *Sapela* is the case of *Eskom Holdings Ltd and Another v New Reclamation Group (Pty) Ltd.*[54] Here, the Supreme Court of Appeal confirmed an order setting aside a tender award by Eskom, even though the two-year contract had less than three months to run by the time the appeal was heard. The critical factor was the nature of the particular contract, which involved the *ad hoc* removal of scrap material from Eskom sites and its subsequent processing and sale. The terms of the contract provided that each instruction given by Eskom to the successful tenderer to collect scrap material would 'constitute a separate independent disposal agreement incorporating the terms of [this] agreement'. In view of the nature of this contract – which was not an indivisible contract such as an engineering contract – the court found that it was not impracticable to set it aside.[55] The court's decision was also informed by the fact that the successful tenderer was, at least in part, to blame for the tainted award because its tender was flawed.[56]

The question of the divisibility of the tender contract also arose in *Moseme Road Construction CC and Others v King Civil Engineering Contractors (Pty) Ltd and Another.*[57] In that case, an unsuccessful tenderer (King) challenged the award of a tender to construct a dual carriageway on a highway. King was the highest scoring bidder, but was disqualified from the tender as a result of an error by the responsible department. By the time the review was heard, the successful tenderer (Moseme) had begun construction work on the highway. The High Court found that it was just and equitable to set aside the tender award and contract because the construction contract was 're-measurable' – meaning that payment could be divided according to the work done by Moseme and the new contractor. The High Court's order was overturned however by the Supreme Court of Appeal, which upheld the unlawful tender award. It found that even though the contract was 're-measurable', this measuring exercise was more difficult than the High Court suggested as 'each tenderer will weight and price different items differently' and preliminary and establishment costs are incurred which provide no value to the department but for which each contractor is entitled. It found that the High Court had also underestimated the adverse consequences of setting aside the tender award. These included that Moseme may have an enrichment claim against the department for its performance under the revoked contract, the department would lose any contractual claim it may have against Moseme for defective workmanship, and King may even have a claim for damages against the department for loss of profit on the executed part of the contract because it has now become contractually entitled to the whole contract.[58] The Supreme Court of Appeal also factored in that the successful tenderer, Moseme, was innocent and that the irregularity in the tender process was relatively minor: it did not entail

53 2008 (2) SA 638 (SCA).
54 2009 (4) SA 628 (SCA).
55 *New Reclamation Group* para 16.
56 *New Reclamation Group* para 14.
57 2010 (4) SA 359 (SCA).
58 *Moseme* para 20.

any fraud, but only administrative error by the Department. The court held that '[n]ot every slip in the administration of tenders is necessarily to be visited by judicial sanction'.[59] It accordingly declined to set aside the tender award.

In *Millennium Waste Management (Pty) Ltd v Chairperson, Tender Board: Limpopo Province and Others*,[60] the court was concerned not to interrupt the performance of the tender because of the critical nature of the services being provided under the tender - being the removal, treatment and disposal of health care waste material from hospitals. In assessing whether setting aside the tender was just and equitable, the Supreme Court of Appeal adopted a useful structure of analysis. It identified four interests that had to be factored in: the interests of the disqualified bidder, the successful tenderer, the public and the public purse (that is, the cost to the fiscus). In evaluating these interests, the court emphasised the following factors:[61]

- The loss to Millennium Waste, the disqualified bidder, from the unfair tender process 'was no more than the loss of the opportunity to have its tender considered'. It was by no means clear that it would win the tender upon a fresh evaluation of the bids. Accordingly, effective redress for Millennium Waste meant no more than having its bid fairly evaluated.
- The successful tenderer was an innocent party and not complicit in the exclusion of Millennium Waste from the tender process.
- The successful tenderer had already incurred considerable costs in performing on the contract (by purchasing vehicles and equipment, hiring employees, leasing premises and constructing a waste treatment plant).
- The risk of harm to the public if the medical waste-removal services were interrupted by the termination of the contract.
- The potential benefits for the public purse of setting aside the contract. There was a vast price differential between the two bids, with the successful bidder providing the service at a fee seven times higher than Millennium Waste's bid. With 29 months remaining on the contract, the potential cost savings were significant.[62]

In weighing up these considerations, the court's overriding concern was the uncertainty that would result from setting aside the tender. Jafta JA stated:

> I do not think we should make an order that creates uncertainty - with no promise of gain but instead the potential for loss and chaotic disruption - when that can be avoided.

The court accordingly declined to set aside the tender award without more. However, unlike in *Sapela* and *Moseme*, the court did not simply preserve the *status quo*. It crafted a creative, middle-path remedy. The court declared the tender award to be invalid and remitted the matter to the tender board for a re-evaluation of the parties' bids and granted a setting aside order that was conditional on the tender board reaching a different decision on re-evaluating the bids. Thus the order set aside the tender award only if, on the re-evaluation of the bids,

59 *Moseme* para 21.
60 2008 (2) SA 481 (SCA).
61 *Millennium Waste* paras 25–30.
62 The court acknowledged, however, that it was unable to assess why the differential in bidding price was so large, and it was left to speculate as to whether setting aside the contract at that stage would result in cost savings.

the tender board decided to award the tender to Millennium Waste.[63] In this way, the court left the evaluation of the risks and consequences of appointing a new tenderer or concluding a new tender to the tender board, while vindicating Millennium Waste's right to just administrative action by requiring that the tender board evaluate its bid fairly.[64]

Another case involving the provision of critical public services, which could not be interrupted by the unqualified setting aside of a tender award is *Allpay*.[65] This was the first case in which the Constitutional Court considered the merits of a tender review and the question of a just and equitable remedy in this context.[66] The matter raised difficult questions of remedy – so much so that the Constitutional Court held a second hearing dedicated to determining what would be a just and equitable remedy, and directed all the parties to file further affidavits and written argument on this issue alone. The case concerned the award of a tender by the South African Social Security Agency (SASSA) for the countrywide payment of social grants to beneficiaries. An unsuccessful tenderer (Allpay) brought the review application for the setting aside of the tender award. The scale of the tender was significant: it involved the appointment of a sole service provider for payment of social grants across the entire country – that is, the payment of about fifteen million social grants to about ten million recipients each month, for five years. The successful tenderer (Cash Paymaster) contended that it had invested R1,3 billion to roll out the tender. The remedy sought by Allpay was an order setting aside the tender award and directing SASSA to issue a fresh tender for the same contract period of five years.

The Supreme Court of Appeal had found that the irregularities in the tender process would not have changed the ultimate outcome of the decision under review, and for this reason the decision should not be declared invalid or set aside. The Constitutional Court departed from this, finding that the 'no difference' approach of the Supreme Court of Appeal – that if the irregularities made no difference to the outcome, then the decision is not invalid – impermissibly conflated the merits of a review with the remedy.[67] The Constitutional Court held that the impact of the irregularities on the outcome may have a bearing on the court's remedy, but not on the prior determination of the merits (that is, whether there are reviewable irregularities). The merits enquiry turns on whether the irregularities committed are material – that is, whether the irregularities undermine the purpose of the statutory or prescribed requirements. Applying this purposive test for materiality, the Constitutional Court found that there were indeed reviewable irregularities in the tender process, and it declared the tender award invalid.

---

63 Jafta JA explained the effect of the order at paragraph 32 as follows:

> [It] vindicates the appellant's rights to the full while it prevents the potential for disruption to the service, and it avoids unwarranted loss to the public purse. It might end up that the consortium suffers loss – that will occur only if appellant's tender is accepted and even then commercial considerations that minimise the loss might come into play – but that is inevitable if we are to accommodate the potential loss to the public purse. It seems to me that such an order promises no loss to the public purse and an uninterrupted service. And if it turns out that the consortium has indeed been profiteering excessively and loses the contract as a result, then any loss that it might suffer does not weigh heavily with me. The order envisaged here maintains a balance between the parties' conflicting interests while taking into account the public interest.

64 There is a conceptual problem with the order. While the court declared the tender award to be invalid, it did not suspend the declaration of invalidity. However, this was clearly the intent, as the court made the setting aside of the tender award conditional on the re-evaluation of the bids resulting in a different decision. A suspension of the declaration of invalidity must thus be taken to be implied in the order.

65 *Allpay (merits)*; *Allpay (remedy)*.

66 The only tender case previously before the Constitutional Court, *Steenkamp*, concerned a delictual claim following the setting aside of a tender award. The Constitutional Court did consider the merits of the review nor whether the setting aside of that tender was just and equitable.

67 *Allpay (merits)* paras 23–27.

In turning to determine a just and equitable remedy, the Constitutional Court's foremost concern was the risk of any disruption in the payments of social grants, upon which millions of children, elderly and the poor rely for their livelihood. SASSA, Cash Paymaster and one of the friends of the court (the Centre for Child Law), all argued that if the tender award was set aside, disruptions in the payment of social grants were inevitable. They contended that the only just and equitable remedy, and the only way to ensure the uninterrupted payment of social grants, would be to suspend the declaration of invalidity until the contract concluded between SASSA and Cash Paymaster had run its course.[68] The court did not accept this approach, however. It noted that the likelihood of a disruption of payments to beneficiaries upon the award of a new tender was disputed by the parties, and would have to be evaluated by the responsible administrator, SASSA. The Constitutional Court thus adopted a middle-path approach, similar to that adopted in *Millennium Waste*: it remitted the matter to SASSA for a fresh tender process, but it did not attempt to impose a final solution on SASSA. The court left it to SASSA to decide, on an evaluation of the new tender, whether or not to award the new tender to any of the bidders. It thus remained open to SASSA to decide, after re-running the tender process, not to contract with any bidder or to in-source the services.[69] In the event that SASSA chose not to award a new tender, the court order suspended the declaration of invalidity of the contract concluded between SASSA and Cash Paymaster until the completion of that contract period, thereby ensuring that it remained in full force and effect (so that payment of grants to beneficiaries would not be disrupted). The court also found that, to the extent that it performs the public function of administering social grants, Cash Paymaster is not an ordinary private entity. Instead, for the purposes of its performance of those functions it is an organ of state (in terms of section 239 of the Constitution), and so could not simply walk away from the contract.

As noted, the order in *Allpay* was similar to that in *Millennium Waste* — the court remitted the matter to the administrator without annulling the unlawful decision, and made any annulment of the unlawful tender award conditional on the outcome of the administrator's decision. However, the *Allpay* order differed in that the Constitutional Court directed the administrator not merely to re-evaluate the existing bids (as in *Millennium Waste*), but to re-run a fresh tender process in its entirety. Thus, SASSA was required to issue a new tender, followed by a new bidding process, and the evaluation and adjudication of the new bids. This order is considerably more onerous on the administrator than that of *Millennium Waste*.

---

68 *Allpay (remedy)* para 37.

69 Froneman J explained the 'practical approach' adopted in the order at para 40:

> We acknowledge that we are not in a position to determine what the effect of making a new tender award will be on a number of interests. These include: the ability of other potential tenderers to make truly competitive bids; whether a new system will necessarily disrupt existing payments; whether SASSA will be able to run the administration and payment of social grants independently at the time envisaged; and what advantages Cash Paymaster may derive from its incumbency. A new tender process will make it possible for SASSA to have more information available to it when it makes a decision whether to award a new tender at the end of the process. It is true that this will come at some cost, between R5 million and R10 million at current estimates, but in the context of the vast sums involved, and considering the potential for a more cost-effective solution, this is a justifiable price to pay to ensure that the rule of law and the demands of transparency and accountability are met.

### 12.5.4 Remedial discretion in self-reviews

The Constitutional Court has, in recent years, been confronted with several cases in which state parties have applied to review their own unlawful decisions – what has become known as a 'state self-review'.[70] These cases have proven particularly difficult for the court where the state party has delayed unreasonably in instituting the review. In such circumstances, the court is called upon to balance the rule of law concern of declaring and correcting unlawful decisions, with the importance of expeditious and diligent compliance with constitutional duties (including the duty of state litigants to rectify unlawful decisions) so as to ensure certainty and finality for the parties relying on such decisions.

As exemplified in *State Information Technology Agency SOC Limited v Gijima Holdings (Pty) Limited*[71] and *Buffalo City Metropolitan Municipality v Asla Construction (Pty) Limited*,[72] the Constitutional Court has sought to balance these concerns by declaring the unlawful conduct invalid (and overlooking unreasonable delay by the applicant state party), and protecting the rights of the party that relied on the decision through novel orders aimed at protecting vested contractual rights. The court's approach in these cases is fraught with conceptual difficulties, and has attracted unusually severe academic criticism.[73]

In *Gijima*, the State Information Technology Agency (SITA) applied to court to review and set aside its own decision to conclude a contract with the IT company, Gijima. Although the contract did not comply with SITA's own procurement procedures, SITA had provided assurances to Gijima that there were no irregularities. SITA then took its own decision on review, 22 months after the contract was concluded. On appeal, the Constitutional Court found SITA had delayed unreasonably in instituting the review of its own decision. While the court found that there was no good reason to overlook the delay in this case, it nevertheless declared the contract invalid under section 172(1)(*a*). It did so on the basis that section 172(1)(*a*) of the Constitution obliged the court to declare SITA's award of the contract invalid. The court thus departed from the established approach of refusing to grant any substantive relief (including declarations of invalidity) where the circumstances do not warrant the court overlooking the unreasonable delay.

The court then sought to ameliorate the prejudice that the declaration of invalidity would cause to the contractor, Gijima by granting an extraordinary order, using its wide remedial power to grant a just and equitable order. The court exercised its remedial discretion under section 172(1)(*b*) of the Constitution, and not PAJA, because it found that an organ of state cannot review its own decisions under PAJA; it must proceed under the constitutional principle of legality.[74] The court ordered that 'the order of constitutional invalidity ... does not have the effect of divesting the respondent [Gijima] of any rights it would have been

70 *Khumalo; Kirland; Tasima; City of Cape Town v Aurecon South Africa (Pty) Ltd* 2017 (4) SA 223 (CC); *State Information Technology Agency SOC Limited v Gijima Holdings (Pty) Limited* 2018 (2) SA 23 (CC); and *Buffalo City Metropolitan Municipality v Asla Construction (Pty) Limited* 2019 (4) SA 331 (CC).

71 2018 (2) SA 23 (CC).

72 2019 (4) SA 331 (CC).

73 Boonzaier, L (2018) A Decision to Undo *SALJ* 135(4):642; De Beer, MN (2018) A New Role for the Principle of Legality in Administrative Law *SALJ* 135(4):613; Quinot, G & van der Sijde, E (2019) Opening at the Close: Clarity from the Constitutional Court on the Legal Cause of Action and Regulatory Framework for an Organ of State Seeking to Review its Own Decisions? *TSAR* 2:324.

74 This finding, in particular, has been criticised. See Chapter 11 section 11.2.5.

entitled to under the contract, but for the declaration of invalidity'. The court explained the basis for this order as follows:

> Overall, it seems to us that justice and equity dictate that, despite the invalidity of the award of the DoD agreement, SITA must not benefit from having given Gijima false assurances and from its own undue delay in instituting proceedings. Gijima may well have performed in terms of the contract, while SITA sat idly by and only raised the question of the invalidity of the contract when Gijima instituted arbitration proceedings. In the circumstances, a just and equitable remedy is that the award of the contract and the subsequent decisions to extend it be declared invalid, with a rider that the declaration of invalidity must not have the effect of divesting Gijima of rights to which – but for the declaration of invalidity – it might have been entitled. Whether any such rights did accrue remains a contested issue in the arbitration, the merits of which were never determined because of the arbitrator's holding on jurisdiction.[75]

There are at least two unusual aspects to the Constitutional Court's approach to remedy in *Gijima*. First, in an effort to protect Gijima's contractual rights against SITA, the court introduced a 'rider' to its declaration of invalidity, rather than following the simpler (and conceptually neater) approach of exercising its remedial discretion not to set aside the contract. As discussed in 12.5 above, review courts have always retained the discretion to decline to set aside an unlawful contract, even if it is declared invalid. Second, unreasonable delay typically operates as a threshold enquiry to determine whether the court grants a decision and relief on the merits at all, including whether it grants a declaration of invalidity. However in *Gijima*, delay informed the court's determination of the consequences that flowed from declaring the impugned contract invalid. This oddity flows from the court's finding that it was obliged under section 172(1)(*a*) of the Constitution to declare SITA's decision to award the contract to Gijima invalid – irrespective of unreasonable delay by the reviewing state party.

In *Buffalo City*, the Constitutional Court was confronted with another case of 'self-review' by an organ of state that delayed unreasonably in instituting the review. A majority of the Constitutional Court followed the approach adopted in *Gijima* and found that, notwithstanding the municipality's unreasonable delay in instituting the review, section 172(1)(*a*) of the Constitution compelled the court to declare invalid the municipality's award of an unlawful contract. It reasoned that:

> *Gijima* dictates that where the unlawfulness of the impugned decision is clear and not disputed, then this Court must declare it as unlawful. This is notwithstanding an unreasonable delay in bringing the application for review for which there is no basis for overlooking. Whether an impugned decision is so clearly and indisputably unlawful will depend on the circumstances of each case.[76]

The majority of the Constitutional Court sought to soften the inequities that flowed from the declaration of invalidity with a variation of the order that had been granted in *Gijima*. It declared the municipality's contract invalid, but did not set it aside so as to preserve the rights that the respondent (the contractor) might have been entitled to under the contract. The majority held that 'such an award preserves rights which have already accrued but does

75 At para 54.

76 At para 66.

not permit a party to obtain further rights under the invalid agreement'.[77] In crafting this remedy, the majority addressed the first anomaly we noted in the *Gijima* order, and adopted the simpler route of declaring the contract invalid, while exercising its discretion not to set the contract aside. The second anomaly was, however, repeated by the majority in *Buffalo City*. It again held that section 172(1)(*a*) of the Constitution obliged the court to declare unlawful state conduct constitutionally invalid, irrespective of unreasonable delay in the institution of the review; with the result that delay informed the determination of remedy (as opposed to operating as a threshold enquiry). However on this finding, this time, there was a dissenting minority.

Writing in the minority, Cameron and Froneman JJ reasoned that it was not in the interests of justice for the court to pronounce on the unlawfulness of the municipality's decision to contract, given the unexplained delay and the absence of any manifestly serious unlawfulness in the decision sought to be reviewed. In these circumstances, they stated, section 172(1)(*a*) of the Constitution did not oblige the court to declare the contract invalid and come to the municipality's aid.[78] Cameron and Froneman JJ held:

> In the absence of adequate explanation for unreasonable delay, courts should not intervene to inquire into a final and determinative holding into unlawfulness, unless the seriousness of the unlawfulness at issue warrants overlooking the manifest deficiencies in the state actor's case.[79]

The minority also cautioned that the court's approach in *Gijima* (and of the majority in *Buffalo City*) was open to abuse by state-litigants seeking to avoid the consequences of their unlawful conduct by approaching the court to have their own unlawful decisions set aside. The minority stated:

> A court should be vigilant in ensuring that state self-review is not brought by state officials with a personal interest in evading the consequences of their prior decisions. It should scrutinize the conduct of the public body and its candour in explaining that conduct to ensure, in the public interest, open, responsive and accountable government. Where there is glaring arbitrariness and opportunism – that is, where the government actor's efforts to correct the suspected unlawful decision serve the antithesis of the rule of law – the interests of justice weigh against giving it a free pass by overlooking an unreasonable delay.[80]

Notwithstanding the dissent in *Buffalo City*, the prevailing legal position (following the unanimous decision in *Gijima* and the majority decision in *Buffalo City*) is that:

i) Section 172(1)(a) of the Constitution obliges the court to declare unlawful state conduct invalid, and for this purpose to overlook unreasonable delay in the review of such conduct (at least under the constitutional principle of legality).
ii) Delay may, however, be relevant determination of a just and equitable remedy under section 172(1)(*b*) of the Constitution.
iii) Where an organ of state has unreasonably delayed in instituting a review of its own decision, this may have the consequence that a just remedy is to preserve the other party's rights, notwithstanding that the decision vesting those rights is

77 At para 105.
78 See especially paras 129–133; 147–149.
79 At para 127.
80 At para 139.

declared invalid. This may be achieved by the exercise of the court's remedial discretion to decline to set aside an invalid decision.

**PAUSE FOR REFLECTION**

**The Constitutional Court's decisions in *Allpay v SASSA* and *MEC for Health, Eastern Cape v Kirland Investments***

1. In *Allpay (remedy)*, was the Constitutional Court correct to find that Cash Paymaster was an organ of state when it provided services under its contract with SASSA? What are the consequences of this finding for Cash Paymaster's constitutional and contractual obligations to perform the services under the tender? Consider the Constitutional Court's reasoning at paragraphs 49–67. Is the court's reference at para 65 to *Juma Musjid*, which describes the constitutional obligations of private parties relevant or misplaced?
2. Does the Constitutional Court suggest that a private company like Cash Paymaster, which contracts with the state to provide public services, is not entitled to profit from a contract that it concluded with the state? Would this be fair in *Allpay*, considering that Cash Paymaster is obliged to continue performing under the contract and when the tender process was unlawful through no fault of its own (that is, it was an innocent tenderer)? Consider paragraphs 67 and 70 of the remedy judgment.
3. What are the implications of the Constitutional Court's approach to remedy in *Allpay* for tenders generally? Does it pose a genuine risk that private companies who have the capacity to provide services which the state needs but cannot itself provide, may choose not to tender because of the costs that they incur when tenders are reviewed? Does it threaten to undermine competitiveness in public procurement, which is essential to ensuring cost-effectiveness for the state? Is the court's insistence on public accountability by administrators and tenderers necessary and appropriate? Consider paragraphs 68 to 71 of the *Allpay* remedy judgment.
4. In *MEC for Health, Eastern Cape v Kirland Investments*, do you agree that the state was required to institute a review to set aside its own unlawful administrative action as the majority of the Constitutional Court found (per Cameron J et al)? Or was Jafta J correct to contend that the issue of the validity of the Acting Head of Department's decision was before the court and should have been decided by it, notwithstanding that it was not specifically brought on review? Did the majority judgment place form over substance? Who, if any, might have been prejudiced by Jafta J's approach?
5. Consider *Gijima* and the majority and minority judgments in *Buffalo City*. Do you think the Constitutional Court in *Gijima* is correct in its approach to section 172(1)(*a*) of the Constitution – that is, that it always requires unlawful state conduct to be declared invalid, regardless of unreasonable delay in the institution of the review? Do you think the minority's 'pragmatic' and 'purpose-driven approach' in *Buffalo City* to section 172(1)(*a*) and unreasonable delay is workable and appropriate? Is the minority correct that the case is distinguishable from *Gijima*, to justify a different approach in the application of section 172(1)(*a*)?

## 12.6 Remittal

When a court reviews and sets aside administrative action it almost always sends the matter back, or remits it, to the decision-maker to enable it to reconsider the matter afresh and make a new decision. Occasionally, and only in exceptional cases, the court does not give the administrator a further opportunity. Instead the court makes the decision itself – this is termed 'substitution'.

Remittal can thus be understood as the default remedy upon the setting aside of administrative action. The exercise of this remedy is a manifestation of judicial deference in judicial review, which is required by the constitutional separation of powers and the institutional limitations of courts. The reviewing court will ordinarily remit the matter to the administrator, so that the court does not usurp the decision-making powers that the legislature has delegated to the administrator, and because the court may lack the expertise or the information necessary to make the decision. These two considerations were recognised in *Gauteng Gambling Board v Silverstar Development*, where Heher JA explained that:[81]

> An administrative functionary that is vested by statute with the power to consider and approve or reject an application is generally best equipped by the variety of its composition, by experience, and its access to sources of relevant information and expertise to make the right decision. The court typically has none of these advantages and is required to recognise its own limitations. That is why remittal is almost always the prudent course.

Similarly, in *Intertrade Two (Pty) Ltd v MEC for Roads and Public Works, Eastern Cape and Another*,[82] Plasket J emphasised that the separation of powers principle meant that:

> [C]ourts, when considering the validity of administrative action, must be wary of intruding, even with the best of motives, without justification into the terrain that is reserved for the administrative branch of government. These restraints on the powers of the courts are universal in democratic societies such as ours and necessarily mean that there are limits on the powers of the courts to repair damage that has been caused by a breakdown in the administrative process.

The remedy of remittal is also important for maintaining the functional distinction between appeals and reviews. Unlike an appellate court, which exercises a standard of correctness over a lower court's decision, a reviewing court is concerned only with determining whether a reviewable error was committed in the decision-making process.[83] Thus, the role of the reviewing court is not to 'second-guess' the administrator, or to determine the correct decision, but rather to remedy the defect in the decision-making process. The Supreme Court of Appeal discussed this distinction in *MEC for Environmental Affairs and Development Planning v Clairison's CC*,[84] and criticised the High Court for failing to appreciate the nature of judicial review:

> It bears repeating that a review is not concerned with the correctness of a decision made by a functionary, but with whether he performed the function with which

81 *Gauteng Gambling Board v Silverstar Development Ltd and Others* 2005 (4) SA 67 (SCA) para 29. See also *Bato Star Fishing* paras 46–49; *Logbro Properties CC v Bedderson NO and Others* 2003 (2) SA 460 (SCA) para 21; *Trencon Construction (Pty) Ltd v Industrial Development Corporation of South Africa Limited* 2015 (5) SA 245 (CC) paras 43–46.

82 2007 (6) SA 442 (Ck) para 46.

83 *Allpay (merits)* para 42.

84 2013 (6) SA 235 (SCA).

> he was entrusted. When the law entrusts a functionary with a discretion it means just that: the law gives recognition to the evaluation made by the functionary to whom the discretion is entrusted, and it is not open to a court to second-guess his evaluation. The role of a court is no more than to ensure that the decision-maker has performed the function with which he was entrusted.[85]

Strictly construed, the wording of section 8(1)(*c*)(i) of PAJA suggests that remittal may only be ordered upon the setting aside of administrative action.[86] But the courts have adopted a more flexible approach and have, on occasion, ordered remittal without an order setting aside the decision. This is done where the court is unable properly to assess the consequences of setting aside an irregular decision, or where it deems the decision-maker to be better placed to make this assessment. In these circumstances, the court has remitted the matter to the decision-maker for redetermination, with the setting aside order made conditional on the decision-maker reaching a different decision. This approach was adopted, for example, in the tender cases of *Millennium Waste* and *Allpay*, discussed above.

The court may also couple an order remitting a matter for redetermination with further instructions. For example, in *Allpay*, the Constitutional Court gave detailed directions to the administrator regarding when the decision had to be taken, the composition of the new decision-making body and additional conditions for the fresh tender to provide for, to protect the interests of social grant beneficiaries.

In redetermining a matter remitted to it, can the administrator take into account new information or a change of circumstances since the original decision? This question arose in *Logbro Properties CC v Bedderson NO and Others*.[87] In that case, the High Court had set aside a tender award for the sale of provincial property on the basis that the successful tenderer had failed to comply with the tender conditions. The High Court remitted the matter to the provincial assets committee for redetermination, directing the committee to reconsider the tenders that had complied with the tender conditions. However, by the time the committee reconsidered the matter, two years had passed since its original decision, and the property value had increased. The committee took into account the change in property values and decided not to award the tender to any of the tenderers. Instead, it recommended a call for fresh tenders. One of the compliant tenderers challenged the new decision, contending that the committee had not taken into account the change in property values and ought to have awarded the tender to one of the compliant tenderers. This argument was rejected. In the Supreme Court of Appeal, Cameron JA found that, in reconsidering a matter upon remittal it is appropriate for the decision-maker to take into account all relevant considerations. It was thus appropriate for the committee to have had regard to supervening considerations, including the public benefit to be derived from obtaining a higher price by re-advertising the property.

---

85 *Clairison's* para 18.

86 Section 8(1)(*c*)(i) provides for orders

> (*c*) setting aside the administrative action *and*–
>
> (i) remitting the matter for reconsideration by the administrator, with or without directions. (Emphasis added).

87 2003 (2) SA 460.

Cameron JA pointed out that it was precisely because of the complexity of the committee's mandate, that the matter had been remitted to it for redetermination.[88]

## 12.7 Substitution

Instead of remitting a matter to the administrator, the court has the power to substitute its own decision for that of the administrator, or it may vary the administrative action or correct a defect resulting from the administrative action.[89] However, under both the common law and section 8(1)(*c*)(ii)(*aa*) of PAJA, the exercise of this interventionist remedial power is justified only in 'exceptional cases'.[90] In view of the constitutional separation of powers and the functional distinction between reviews and appeals, substitution is considered to be an extraordinary remedy in judicial review. Thus the courts have held that the remedy is to be 'exercised sparingly, in exceptional circumstances', and only when a court is persuaded that a decision to exercise a power should not be left to the designated functionary.[91]

As the Constitutional Court has stated, 'remittal is still almost always the prudent and proper course'.[92] The Constitutional Court has also emphasised that even where there are exceptional circumstances, a court must be satisfied that it would be just and equitable, and fair to the implicated parties, to grant an order of substitution.[93] In making this determination, the court must have regard to all the relevant facts and circumstances.[94]

### 12.7.1 The test for substitution

There is no closed list of situations in which a court may be justified in substituting its own decision, and section 8 of PAJA does not offer any guidelines as to what constitutes 'exceptional cases' justifying substitution. However, a number of guidelines have crystallised through the cases. The following four factors, discerned by Baxter, have prompted the courts to substitute the decision rather than remit the matter to the original decision-maker.[95] These are:

i) where the court is as well qualified as the original authority to make the decision,[96]
ii) where the end result is a foregone conclusion, and it would be a waste of time to remit the decision to the original decision-maker,[97]

88 *Logbro Properties* paras 20–21. Cameron JA went on to find (at paras 23–25) that procedural fairness required the committee to afford the compliant tenderers an opportunity to make written representations on the significance of the change in property value before the committee decided to recommend re-advertisement. On this basis, Cameron JA set aside the decision to re-advertise and remitted the matter to the committee to allow for such representations to be made before a new decision was taken.

89 Section 8(1)(*c*)(ii)(*aa*) of PAJA.

90 For a discussion of the common-law position, see Baxter (1984) 681–685 and *Trencon Construction v IDC* paras 36–39.

91 *Silverstar* paras 28–29.

92 *Trencon Construction v IDC* para 42.

93 *Trencon Construction v IDC* paras 35, 47, 53.

94 *Trencon Construction v IDC* para 47.

95 Baxter (1984) 681–685. See also Hoexter (2012) 553–557. See these same guidelines recognised in *University of the Western Cape and Others v Member of Executive Committee for Health and Social Services and Others* 1998 (3) SA 124 (C) at 131D–J; *Ruyobeza and Another v Minister of Home Affairs and Others* 2003 (5) SA 51 (C) at 64G.

96 *M v Minister of Home Affairs and Others* (6871/2013) [2014] ZAGPPHC 649 (22 August 2014) paras 177–179; *Silverstar* paras 38–39; *Theron en Andere v Ring van Wellington van die NG Sendingkerk in Suid-Afrika en Andere* 1976 (2) SA 1 (A).

97 See, for example, *Hangklip Environmental Action Group v MEC for Agriculture, Environmental Affairs and Development Planning, Western Cape and Others* 2007 (6) SA 65 (C); *Silverstar* paras 38–39.

iii) where further delay would cause unjustifiable prejudice to the applicant or another affected person, and[98]

iv) where the original decision-maker has exhibited bias or incompetence to such a degree that it would be unfair to ask the applicant to submit to its jurisdiction again.[99]

In *Trencon Construction (Pty) Ltd v Industrial Development Corporation of South Africa Limited,*[100] the Constitutional Court held that the first two institutional factors hold greater weight in the substitution enquiry as a result of the separation of powers doctrine.[101] It explained that these factors ought to be considered first, and cumulatively. Thus in conducting the substitution enquiry, the court must first consider whether it is in as good a position as the administrator to make the decision, and then consider whether the result is a foregone conclusion. Thereafter, if the court is satisfied that it has the institutional competence to take the decision, the court must weigh up the equitable considerations and other relevant factors (such as bias, incompetence of the administrator, delay).[102]

Plasket J advanced a similar approach to the substitution enquiry in *Intertrade Two (Pty) Ltd v MEC for Roads and Public Works, Eastern Cape and Another.*[103] Plasket J explained the reason for first determining the court's institutional competence as follows:

> The availability of proper and adequate information and the institutional competence of the Court to take the decision for the administrative decision-maker are necessary prerequisites that must be present, apart from 'exceptional circumstances', before a court can legitimately assume an administrative decision-making function. This, it seems to me, is a minimum requirement of rational decision-making, a fundamental requirement of the rule of law. In this case, because of the absence of proper estimates, because of the flaws in the evaluations of the tenders and because of the unknown consequences on the tenders of the inexcusable passage of time, both prerequisites are absent ...[104]

Where the court is satisfied that it is able to make the decision, then the overriding principle, and the common thread in the equitable factors, is 'fairness to both sides'.[105]

98 *M v Minister of Home Affairs and Others* paras 175–176; *ICS Pension Fund v Sithole and Others NNO* 2010 (3) SA 419 (T) para 97; *Head, Western Cape Education Department and Others v Governing Body, Point High School and Others* 2008 (5) SA 18 (SCA) para 17; *Ruyobeza* at 65D–H.

99 *M v Minister of Home Affairs and Others* paras 170–174; *Mlokoti v Amathole District Municipality and Another* 2009 (6) SA 354 (E) at 380I–381B; *Tantoush v Refugee Appeal Board* 2008 (1) SA 232 (T) para 127; *Minister of Local Government and Land Tenure v Inkosinathi Property Developers (Pty) Ltd and Another* 1992 (2) SA 234 (TkA); *Mahlaela v De Beer NO* 1986 (4) SA 782 (T) at 794–795; *Essack v Durban City Council* 1953 (4) SA 17 (N) at 23.

100 2015 (5) SA 245 (CC).

101 *Trencon Construction v IDC* para 47.

102 *Trencon Construction v IDC* paras 47–51.

103 2007 (6) SA 442 (Ck).

104 *Intertrade Two* para 43.

105 See Baxter (1984) 684; *Commissioner, Competition Commission v General Council of the Bar of South Africa and Others* 2002 (6) SA 606 (SCA) para 15; *Minister of Trade and Industry v Sundays River Citrus Company (Pty) Ltd* [2020] 1 All SA 635 (SCA) paras 23–27. See also *Masamba v Chairperson, Western Cape Regional Committee, Immigrants Selection Board* 2001 (12) BCLR 1239 (C) at 1259H–1260E; and *Ruyobeza* at 65F–H.

### 12.7.2 Applying the test: illustrative cases

A number of cases illustrate how courts apply the above factors, and weigh up the competing considerations, to determine whether fairness between the parties requires substitution.

In *Gauteng Gambling Board v Silverstar Development Ltd*,[106] the Supreme Court of Appeal found that the High Court had correctly substituted its decision for that of the Gauteng Gambling Board to award a casino licence to Silverstar. Heher JA was satisfied that the High Court was in as good a position as the Board to make the decision because the relative merits and demerits of Silverstar's application had received exhaustive ventilation during the court proceedings, and there were no unresolved issues or objections raised by the Board in respect of its application. Heher JA also reasoned that, if remitted, the result of the Board's decision was a foregone conclusion, since the only other prospective licensee had been disqualified (for failure to obtain an environmental approval) and there was no evidence of any other prospective licensees. As a result, Silverstar was the only remaining applicant for the casino licence for the area in question. Heher JA concluded that 'the Court *a quo* was not merely in as good a position as the Board to reach a decision but was faced with the inevitability of a particular outcome if the Board were once again to be called upon fairly to decide the matter'.[107] Turning to considerations of fairness, Heher JA noted that nothing would be gained by remittal and that there was no reasonable possibility of prejudice to the Board or the public in the event of non-remittal. On the other hand, equitable considerations supported an order of substitution in favour of Silverstar: the delay in the determination of its licence application 'had reached substantial proportions', and the Board had demonstrated an 'unswerving opposition' to Silverstar on dubious grounds, such that Silverstar had 'well-founded grounds for believing that the Board [had] lost its objectivity'. For all these reasons, Heher JA concluded that this was an exceptional case and that the court *a quo* did not err when it declined to remit to the Board and substituted its decision.

In *Trencon Construction v IDC*, the Constitutional Court similarly considered whether substitution of a decision to award a tender was just and equitable. The Constitutional Court overturned the Supreme Court of Appeal to find that the substitution order granted by the High Court was appropriate in the circumstances. The Constitutional Court found that the court was in as good a position as the administrator (the Industrial Development Corporation, (IDC)) to award the tender to Trencon, since the entire tender process had been completed and Trencon had been recommended as the preferred bidder by the procurement committee. The administrator had declined to award the tender to Trencon only as a result of an error of law committed at the final stage of the procurement process. The Constitutional Court explained that 'It is on the basis of the technical and administrative recommendations and processes that had already been completed that this Court finds itself in as good a position as the IDC to decide whether to award the tender to Trencon'.[108]

The Constitutional Court was also satisfied that the correct decision was a foregone conclusion, and that remittal would therefore serve no purpose. On this issue, the Constitutional Court overruled the Supreme Court of Appeal. The Supreme Court of Appeal had found that remittal was appropriate because the IDC was not obliged to award the tender to the lowest bidder or at all. Further, as a result of the litigation, some two years had elapsed since the beginning of the tender process so that the information upon which the tenders were evaluated was dated and supervening circumstances (such as price increases)

106 *Silverstar* paras 38–39.
107 *Silverstar* para 39.
108 *Trencon Construction v IDC* para 58.

would have to be considered by the administrator.[109] The Constitutional Court rejected this reasoning. It noted that procurement legislation obliged the IDC to award the tender to the highest point earner, unless there were 'objective criteria' or 'justifiable reasons' for not doing so. No such criteria or reasons were advanced by the IDC or apparent on the papers - the only reason for the IDC's refusal to award Trencon the tender was an error of law.[110] Similarly, the IDC was obliged under the governing legislation to award the tender save in certain specified instances, none of which were applicable.[111] As regards the two-year delay since the tender process began, the Constitutional Court held that the Supreme Court of Appeal erred in taking this into account because no new facts on supervening circumstances were introduced into evidence on appeal, and ordinarily the substitution enquiry on appeal must be based on the facts that were before the court of first instance.[112] The Constitutional Court also found that the Supreme Court of Appeal had failed to take into account the impact on the public purse of the further delay occasioned by remittal, and the public interest in having procurement disputes involving organs of state resolved expediently. It thus concluded that 'considerations of fairness' also pointed towards the granting of an order of substitution.[113]

In contrast, in *Westinghouse*, [114] the Supreme Court of Appeal set aside a tender award by Eskom but declined to substitute one of the bidders, Westinghouse, as the successful bidder. The court found that it was not a foregone conclusion that Westinghouse would be awarded the contract on remittal, particularly because Eskom had awarded the contract to another bidder (even if unlawfully so and for strategic reasons that were not part of the bid criteria). The successful bidder had also already begun to perform under the contract, so that the consequences of substitution were uncertain. The Supreme Court of Appeal thus remitted the matter to Eskom, to allow it to reconsider the tender and, if it wished, to start the tender process again with revised bid criteria (to include the strategic considerations it regarded vital but had omitted from the tender).[115]

Substitution has been granted in several reviews of decisions refusing asylum-seeker and refugee status, often because of the systemic dysfunction and prejudicial delays in the claims process. One such case is *M v Minister of Home Affairs and Others*,[116] which concerned the review of a refusal by a Refugee Status Determination Officer to grant the applicant ('M') refugee status and asylum, as well as of the Standing Committee on Refugee Affairs' decision to uphold the refusal on internal appeal. The High Court found both decisions to be unlawful, and declined to remit the matter to the Standing Committee. Instead it substituted its decision to grant M refugee status. The High Court considered that it was in as good a position to make a determination on the applicant's eligibility for refugee status, as M met the statutory requirement for refugee status on the uncontested facts. The High Court found further that, in contesting the review application, the Standing Committee had demonstrated a biased attitude against the applicant and an 'intractable belief' that it was entitled to reject the application regardless of the facts before it. The court concluded that there was no point in remitting the matter to the Standing Committee for redetermination, as it would be unlikely to consider the matter with an open and independent mind. An additional

109 *Industrial Development Corporation of South Africa Limited v Trencon Construction (Pty) Ltd* [2014] 4 All SA 561 (SCA) paras 18–19.
110 *Trencon Construction v IDC* paras 62–65.
111 *Trencon Construction v IDC* paras 68–71.
112 *Trencon Construction v IDC* para 73.
113 *Trencon Construction v IDC* para 74.
114 *Westinghouse Electric Belgium Societe Anonyme v Eskom Holdings (Soc) Ltd and Another* 2016 (3) SA 1 (SCA).
115 *Westinghouse* paras 76–78
116 *M v Minister of Home Affairs and Others* paras 170–176.

consideration was the protracted delay in the determination of M's asylum application (with almost five years having passed since the initial refusal of her application), and the risk of further delay on remittal. The court considered the prejudice that such delays had caused to M and to M's five-year-old daughter, who remained stateless and undocumented as a result of her mother's uncertain status, and noted that any further delay would adversely affect M and be severely detrimental to the interests of M's daughter.[117]

A similar case is *Tshiyombo v Refugee Appeal Board and Others*,[118] where the High Court substituted the decision of the Refugee Appeal Board to grant refugee status to the applicant. In that case, the Refugee Appeal Board had failed to file any answer to the review of its decision, with the result that the applicant's version was unchallenged. The High Court considered that, on the applicant's uncontroverted version, it was a foregone conclusion that the applicant should be given refugee status and that the court was in as good a position as the administrator to take this decision. The court emphasised that the processing of Mr Tshiyombo's status application had taken inordinately long, and that Mr Tshiyombo had, in the meantime, put down roots in South Africa (with two children born to him in that time). The court found that the adverse effect on the applicant's family's sense of security of further extending the delay in determining their right to live in the country would be unjust.[119] The court also noted that the Standing Committee on Refugee Affairs was vested with the statutory power to withdraw refugee status. This meant that, even if the applicant's version should subsequently be shown to be false, a substitutive order granting him refugee status would not prejudice the state.[120]

### 12.7.3 Alternatives to full substitution orders

In *Silverstar* and *M v Minister of Home Affairs and Others*, a concern of bias on the part of the administrator was a factor that informed the court's decision to substitute. However, where bias or incompetence of the original decision-maker is a concern, the court may, rather than substitute its own decision, choose to remit the decision to another competent decision-maker, or require the decision-making body to be reconstituted. This was done, for example, in *Allpay*, where the Constitutional Court ordered that the Bid Evaluation Committee and Bid Adjudication Committee be re-established to decide the fresh tender. The court reasoned that the involvement of the Bid Evaluation Committee and Bid Adjudication Committee in the first bid 'may make it difficult for them to bring an independent assessment to bear on a new tender process', and required that new members to be appointed to those committees.[121]

Section 8(1)(*c*)(ii)(*aa*) expressly contemplates that the court may be able to remedy irregular administrative action by varying only a part of the decision, rather than substituting an entirely new decision. This remedy would be applicable, for instance, where an administrator fails to attach a necessary condition to the granting of a licence. Where there is otherwise no dispute over the granting of the licence, the court may vary the administrative action by reading in the necessary condition to the administrator's decision.

117 *M v Minister of Home Affairs and Others* paras 170–179.

118 *Tshiyombo v Refugee Appeal Board and Others* 2016 (4) SA 469 (WCC) at para 46.

119 At paras 43–45.

120 At para 46. See further: *Ruyobiza and Another v Minister of Home Affairs and Others* 2003 (5) SA 51 (C) at 65C–H; *Tantoush v Refugee Appeal Board* 2008 (1) SA 232 (T). See also *Jose and Another v The Minister of Home Affairs and Others* 2019 (4) SA 597 (GP), where the High Court ordered the Minister of Home Affairs to grant the applicants citizenship; and *Gavri v Refugee Status Determination Officer, Cape Town and Others* 2019 (1) SA 21 (CC), where the Constitutional Court substituted a decision of the Refugee Status Determination Offer to refuse an application for refugee status.

121 *Allpay (remedy)* para 68.

## 12.8 Compensation

Judicial review is generally an inappropriate means for an individual to seek recovery of loss suffered as a result of unlawful administrative action. Judicial review is directed primarily at the pre-emption, correction or reversal of improper administrative acts, rather than at compensating people by way of damages.[122] The Rule 53 motion procedure for judicial review is thus not designed to resolve complex and often contested factual disputes over the quantification of damages or the causation of loss. Accordingly, a person seeking compensation for monetary loss caused by irregular administrative action would ordinarily proceed by instituting an action for contractual or delictual damages. Constitutional damages may also be sought under section 38 of the Constitution to vindicate the breach of constitutional rights arising from irregular administrative action where there are no other appropriate remedies available.[123]

Section 8(1)(*c*)(ii)(*bb*) of PAJA does, however, empower the court in judicial review proceedings to award compensation upon setting aside an irregular administrative act, but only 'in exceptional cases'. In such cases, the court may direct 'the administrator or any other party to the proceedings to pay compensation'.

Compensation under section 8 of PAJA is a public-law remedy, which must be distinguished from private-law damages. As Moseneke J noted in *Steenkamp*, the considerations that it attracts differ from those that inform whether a breach of an administrative duty can give rise to private-law delictual damages.[124] Nevertheless, in applying section 8(1)(*c*)(ii)(*bb*), the courts have had regard to the practical and policy concerns that have informed the courts' approach to delictual damages for irregular administrative action.[125]

Since PAJA's promulgation, there have been very few cases on section 8(1)(*c*)(ii)(*bb*), and it is very rare for courts to award compensation. In practice, it is also difficult to claim compensation for delictual damages, particularly because courts have tended to find that irregularities in administrative law are not necessarily wrongful (in the delictual sense).

In this section, we accordingly begin by discussing the courts' approach to claims for delictual damages caused by unlawful administrative action. We also examine the role of the law of unjustified enrichment as a cause of action for compensation. Thereafter, we discuss the remedy of compensation under section 8 of PAJA and constitutional damages.

### 12.8.1 Delictual damages for malperformance of statutory functions

The courts have adopted a cautious approach to awarding delictual damages against public bodies for negligent conduct in the performance of statutory functions. This caution reflects what is regarded as a proper balancing of the policy considerations that inform whether a public body has acted wrongfully (in the delictual sense) when performing an administrative function.[126]

---

122 Hoexter (2012) 520ff. See also *Steenkamp* paras 29–30.

123 Whether constitutional damages can be sought for an infringement only of the right to just administrative action is open to contestation. See discussion at section 12.9.3 below.

124 *Steenkamp* para 31. See, more recently, *Home Talk Developments (Pty) Ltd v Ekurhuleni Metropolitan Municipality* 2018 (1) SA 391 (SCA), and *Odifin (Pty) Ltd v Reynecke* 2018 (1) SA 153 (SCA) – two cases where the Supreme Court of Appeal dismissed delictual claims for pure economic loss on the basis that the breaches of statutory duties were wrongful (in the delictual sense).

125 See *Darson Construction (Pty) Ltd v City of Cape Town and Another* 2007 (4) SA 488 (C) at 504I–505E; *De Jong and Others v The Trustees of the Simcha Trust and Another* 2014 (4) SA 73 (WCC) para 25.

126 *De Jong* para 25.

Thus, the courts have found that an unsuccessful tenderer, or a successful tenderer whose contract is subsequently set aside on review, generally has no claim in delict for pure economic loss resulting from irregularities in the tender process, where the irregularities fall short of fraud or dishonesty by the public officials concerned. *Bona fide* administrative errors, incompetence or even negligence by public officials will ordinarily not found a delictual claim for an unsuccessful tenderer.[127]

In *Olitzki Property Holdings v State Tender Board and Another*[128] (a case decided under the interim Constitution and before PAJA was enacted) an unsuccessful tenderer claimed damages to recover profits that it lost on account of not being awarded a contract following an irregular tender. It founded its delictual claim on the breach of the constitutional provisions on procurement administration and the right to administrative justice.[129] Cameron JA declined to award the unsuccessful tenderer damages for loss of profits on either basis. Cameron JA found that there were 'powerful reasons of policy' pointing away from awarding damages for loss of profits for tender irregularities, either as delictual or constitutional damages. One consideration was the windfall that the plaintiff would obtain by being awarded damages for lost profits in circumstances where the plaintiff did not seek the setting aside and re-allocation of the tender to itself: the plaintiff would thus obtain profits for no work. A further concern was the impact of such awards, which could be substantial indeed, on the public purse. The effect of the claim was 'a double imposition on the State', which would have to pay the successful tenderer the tender amount in contract while paying the same sum in delict to the aggrieved plaintiff.[130] This was an especially important consideration:

> in a country where there is a great demand generally on scarce resources, where the government has various constitutionally prescribed commitments which have substantial economic implications and where there are 'multifarious demands on the public purse and the machinery of government that flow from the urgent need for economic and social reform'.[131]

A third consideration was the availability of other remedies, including that the plaintiff could have interdicted the award of the tender. While Cameron JA was careful to state that he did not decide that lost profits could never be claimed as constitutional damages to vindicate the right to administrative justice, he held that in the circumstances of the case before him, it was not an appropriate remedy.[132]

In *Steenkamp NO v Provincial Tender Board, Eastern Cape*[133] (another pre-PAJA case), the Constitutional Court confirmed the principles articulated in *Olitzki Property Holdings*. The court considered whether a successful tenderer whose tender award was subsequently set aside by a court on review, was entitled to claim delictual damages for out-of-pocket

---

127 *South African Post Office v De Lacy and Another* 2009 (5) SA 255 (SCA) para 4; *Minister of Finance and Others v Gore NO* 2007 (1) SA 111 (SCA) para 10; *Steenkamp* para 56; *Telematrix (Pty) Ltd t/a Matrix Vehicle Tracking v Advertising Standards Authority SA* 2006 (1) SA 461 (SCA) para 26.

128 2001 (3) SA 1247 (SCA).

129 Sections 187 and 24 of the interim Constitution respectively. Cameron JA considered delictual damages as a form of 'appropriate relief' under section 7(4)(*a*) of the interim Constitution (the predecessor to section 38 of the final Constitution) for breach of the right to administrative justice. Section 7(4)(*a*) empowered the court to grant 'appropriate relief' for an infringement or threat to any fundamental right under Chapter 3 of the interim Constitution.

130 *Olitzki Property Holdings* para 30.

131 *Olitzki Property Holdings* para 41, citing Ackermann in *Fose* at para 72. See also the endorsement of Cameron JA's reasoning on this point by the Constitutional Court in *Steenkamp* per Moseneke DCJ at para 40 and per Langa CJ and O'Regan J at paras 79–81.

132 *Olitzki Property Holdings* para 42.

133 2007 (3) SA 121 (CC).

expenses incurred in reliance on the award. It was not disputed that the tender board had acted in good faith, but that the tender was procedurally unfair.

Writing for the majority, Moseneke DCJ found that public policy considerations did not justify permitting delictual claims for the out-of-pocket losses of disappointed successful tenderers. The key considerations that informed this finding were that:[134]

i) A successful tenderer has alternative remedies to mitigate any losses that may be occasioned by the tender award being subsequently set aside.[135]
ii) Tender boards, which make decisions in the public interest, ought to be immune from damages claims in respect of negligent but honest decisions. They must not be 'bogged down' with fear of damages claims, which could compromise their independence.[136]
iii) The purpose of tender legislation is to ensure a fair tendering process in the public interest, rather than to protect participants in the tender process.
iv) Numerous claims by successful tenderers whose tenders are set aside would have a chilling effect on the tender process, resulting in 'a spiral of litigation likely to delay, if not to weaken the effectiveness of or grind to a stop the tender process'.[137]
v) The limited resources of the state treasury, against the background of vast public needs, means that the fiscus can ill-afford to recompense by way of damages disappointed or initially successful tenderers and still remain with the need to procure the same goods or service.

In a forceful dissenting judgment, Langa CJ and O'Regan J reasoned that normative factors favoured permitting the successful tenderer to claim damages for out-of-pocket expenses. They drew on the following countervailing considerations in support of this position:

i) The purpose of procurement legislation governing the tender board was not only to protect the public interest, but also to protect the right to administrative justice of those engaged in tender processes.[138]
ii) A claim for out-of-pocket expenses is a far more modest claim than that for loss of profits: it does not constitute a 'windfall' claim, but only the recovery of money

134 At paras 42–55.

135 The reliance that Moseneke DCJ placed on the availability of alternative remedies (at paras 48–50) was strongly contested in the dissenting judgment of Langa CJ and O'Regan J. Moseneke DCJ found that the successful tenderer had alternative remedies as it could re-tender upon remittal and the running of a fresh tender and, upon the tender award, it could have negotiated that the right to restitution of out-of-pocket expenses upon a setting aside of the tender was included in its contract. Langa CJ and O'Regan J disputed both proposed alternative remedies, at paras 88–89. In respect of the first, they observed that unlike the unsuccessful tenderer, the successful tenderer 'cannot challenge the tender award by way of judicial review nor may it seek to have its validity confirmed'. Moreover, if the tender is repeated, while the successful tenderer may enter the race for the tender again, even if the successful tenderer is again successful, 'it still may not receive reimbursement for out-of-pocket expenses incurred the first time around'. And if it is unsuccessful in the next round, 'it certainly will not have those expenses reimbursed'. As regards the second proposed alternative remedy, Langa CJ and O'Regan J noted that there was no evidence led on this issue, and expressed skepticism as to whether a successful tenderer is indeed able to demand terms in its contract with government which protect its interests in the event of the tender award being set aside.

136 *Steenkamp* at para 55(a), citing *Telematrix* at paras 13–14. *Telematrix* concerned a delictual claim against an incorrect decision by the Advertising Standards Authority. The Supreme Court of Appeal further described the public policy considerations requiring immunity of adjudicators at paras 26–28:

> [P]ublic policy considerations require that adjudicators of disputes are immune to damages claims in respect of their incorrect and negligent decisions. The overriding consideration has always been that, by the very nature of the adjudication process, rights will be affected and that the process will bog down unless decisions can be made without fear of damages claims, something that must impact on the independence of the adjudicator. Decisions made in bad faith are, however, unlawful and can give rise to damages claims.

137 *Steenkamp* paras 42 and 55 (citing the SCA judgment *a quo*).

138 *Steenkamp* para 75.

actually spent by it in good faith pursuance of contractual obligations.[139] Out-of-pocket expenses are also limited to those expenses proved to have been incurred as a direct result of the contract arising from the tender award; ordinary running expenses of businesses will not be included.[140]

iii) The inability to recover out-of-pocket expenses may well render smaller and less financially viable tenderers at risk of liquidation. Government procurement is one of the key mechanisms for ensuring that those previously locked out of economic opportunity by the policies of apartheid, are given an opportunity to participate. By definition such companies and individuals are often new, small and not financially robust.[141]

iv) It would be an undesirable consequence for the performance of government contracts, if successful tenderers are anxiously looking over their shoulders in case their contract should subsequently be declared void. A successful tender applicant should not hesitate before performing in terms of the contract, in case a challenge to the tender award is successfully brought. This would undermine the constitutional commitments to efficiency and the need for delivery which are of immense importance to both government and citizens alike.[142]

v) Holding the Tender Board liable will enhance its accountability.[143]

*Olitzki Property Holdings* and *Steenkamp* concerned *bona fide* and innocent irregularities in the tender process. However, where unsuccessful tenderers have suffered loss as a result of dishonest or fraudulent conduct by public officials, the Supreme Court of Appeal has not hesitated to award delictual damages. Thus, in *Transnet Ltd v Sechaba Photoscan (Pty) Ltd*[144] the Supreme Court of Appeal awarded delictual damages to an unsuccessful tenderer for loss of profits, where the tender process was vitiated by fraud. Similarly, in *Minister of Finance and Others v Gore NO*,[145] the fraudulent and corrupt conduct of certain officials in charge of the tender process was held to found an unsuccessful tenderer's claim against them for damages, for which their employer was vicariously liable. Cameron and Brand JJA reasoned:

> In our view, speaking generally, the fact that a defendant's conduct was deliberate and dishonest strongly suggests that liability for it should follow in damages, even where a public tender is being awarded. In *Olitzki* and *Steenkamp*, the cost to the public purse of imposing liability for lost profit and for out-of-pocket expenses when officials innocently bungled the process was among the considerations that limited liability. We think the opposite applies where deliberately dishonest conduct is at issue: the cost to the public of exempting a fraudulent perpetrator from liability for fraud would be too high.
>
> [T]he question is: is there any conceivable consideration of public or legal policy that dictates that Louw and Scholtz (and vicariously, their employer) should enjoy immunity against liability for their fraudulent conduct? We can think of

139 *Steenkamp* para 84.
140 *Steenkamp* para 92.
141 *Steenkamp* paras 82 and 94.
142 *Steenkamp* para 83.
143 *Steenkamp* para 86. On this point, see however *Country Cloud Trading CC v MEC, Department of Infrastructure Development, Gauteng* 2015 (1) SA 1 (CC) paras 44–50, where the Constitutional Court declined to impose delictual liability for pure economic loss solely on the basis of a norm of accountability.
144 2005 (1) SA 299 (SCA).
145 2007 (1) SA 111 (SCA).

none. The fact that the fraud was committed in the course of a public-tender process cannot, in our view, serve to immunize the wrongdoers (or those vicariously liable for their conduct) from its consequences. And we find no suggestion in *Olitzki* and *Steenkamp* that the tender process itself must provide government institutions with a shield that protects them against vicarious liability for the fraudulent conduct of their servants.[146]

## 12.8.2 Compensation under section 8(1)(*c*)(ii)(*bb*) of PAJA

The claim for compensation under section 8(1)(*c*)(ii)(*bb*) of PAJA is a relatively untested remedy. Until recently, the courts have resisted defining what constitutes 'exceptional cases' justifying an award of compensation under this subsection, preferring to make case-by-case determinations.[147] However, a discrete body of administrative-law principles is beginning to be developed under this subsection, spearheaded by the judgment of Rogers J in the High Court division of the Western Cape, in *De Jong and Others v The Trustees of the Simcha Trust and Another*.[148] The approach set out by Rogers J is compelling for its structural coherence, and has been endorsed by the Supreme Court of Appeal [149] and the Constitutional Court.

In *De Jong*, the owner of a property (Simcha) claimed compensation from the City after building works that it had begun were interdicted and the City's approval of its building plans was reviewed and set aside by neighbouring owners. In approving the building plans, the City had applied a process that had been declared to be unlawful by the Constitutional Court some four months previously.[150] Simcha based its claim for compensation exclusively on section 8(1)(*c*)(ii)(*bb*) of PAJA; there was no claim in delict nor for constitutional damages directly in terms of section 38 of the Constitution. Simcha argued that the City's disregard for the Constitutional Court's judgment when approving Simcha's plans was so reckless or grossly negligent as to render the present matter an 'exceptional case' justifying the granting of compensation to Simcha in terms of section 8(1)(*c*)(ii)(*bb*).

Interpreting the construction of section 8(1)(*c*) of PAJA,[151] Rogers J made two key findings. First, he held that compensation cannot be granted where the court has remitted the matter for reconsideration by the decision-maker. This follows from the structure of section 8(1)(*c*) of PAJA, which provides that on setting aside a decision, the court may either remit the matter for reconsideration to the administrator under section 8(1)(*c*)(i) '*or*' it may adopt one of the two remedies under section 8(1)(*c*)(ii): it may substitute its decision (section 8(1)(*c*)(ii)(*aa*)) '*or*' it may direct the administrator or any other party to the proceedings to pay compensation

146 *Gore* paras 88 and 90.

147 In *Steenkamp* para 30, Moseneke J stated that '[i]t is unnecessary to speculate on when cases are exceptional. That question will have to be left to the specific context of each case'.

148 2014 (4) SA 73 (WCC).

149 *The Trustees of the Simcha Trust and Another v De Jong and Others* 2015 (4) SA 229 (SCA) paras 27–28.

150 *Walele v City of Cape Town and Others* 2008 (6) SA 129 (CC).

151 Section 8(1)(*c*) reads, with emphasis added:

The court or tribunal, in proceedings for judicial review in terms of section 6(1), may grant any order that is just and equitable, including orders –

...

(*c*) setting aside the administrative action *and* –

(i) remitting the matter for reconsideration by the administrator, with or without directions; *or*

(ii) in exceptional cases –

(*aa*) substituting or varying the administrative action or correcting a defect resulting from the administrative action; *or*

(*bb*) directing the administrator or any other party to the proceedings to pay compensation ...

(section 8(1)(*c*)(ii)(*bb*)). Second, Rogers J accepted that what makes a case exceptional is not the egregiousness of the impugned conduct of the administrator (as Simcha had argued), but instead whether it is appropriate to depart from the usual remedy of remittal. Section 8(1)(*c*) indicates that the primary remedy upon setting aside is remittal, and that it is only 'in exceptional cases', where a remittal to the administrator would not be practical or would not achieve justice, that the alternative remedies of substitution and compensation may apply. Rogers J explained that:

> the two alternative substitute remedies would be reserved for the exceptional cases where (a) it is appropriate for there to be a decision on the administrative application but where it would be unjust or inequitable to remit this to the original decision-maker or (b) it is inappropriate for any further decision to be taken on the administrative application but nevertheless just and equitable that the aggrieved applicant should be compensated for the original decision-maker's unlawful conduct.[152]

Rogers J remarked that the egregiousness of the decision-maker's conduct may have a bearing on whether or not the court remits the matter to the decision-maker for redetermination. However, exceptionality under section 8(1)(*c*) 'is concerned with the choice of remedy, not the quality of the administrator's decision in the abstract. In many cases involving very poor decisions a setting aside and remittal will remain appropriate'.[153]

Rogers J emphasised that his findings did not mean that 'an aggrieved party in review proceedings is entitled to compensation merely because there has been neither a remittal nor a substitute decision by the court'. The holding is simply that 'compensation is not available as a remedy if the usual remedy of remittal has been granted or if exceptionally the court has substituted its own decision for that of the administrator'.[154]

The issue of who may claim compensation under section 8(1)(*c*)(ii)(*bb*) was also raised, but not finally decided, in *De Jong*. The City argued that only an aggrieved applicant and not, as in this case, the respondent, could seek compensation. Rogers J noted that section 8(1)(*c*)(ii)(*bb*) does not, on its terms, limit the range of persons to whom the administrator can be ordered to pay compensation. Moreover, as evidenced in *De Jong*, the party most keenly interested in receiving a favourable decision in a judicial review application may be the respondent, not the applicant. There appeared to be no reason why, as a party to the litigation, the respondent cannot contend for an alternative remedy under section 8(1)(*c*)(ii).[155]

The findings made by Rogers J are consistent with the outcomes reached in two earlier cases dealing with compensation under section 8(1)(*c*)(ii)(*bb*) of PAJA. However, these outcomes were not explained in the same terms.[156]

In the first of these, *Darson Construction (Pty) Ltd v City of Cape Town and Another*,[157] an unsuccessful tenderer claimed compensation for loss of profits and 'out-of-pocket expenses' under section 8(1)(*c*)(ii)(*bb*) of PAJA arising from an unlawful tender award. On the facts, there was no question of remitting the decision to the proper authority for reconsideration, because the period of the contract (that had been put out to tender) had

152 *De Jong* para 19.
153 *De Jong* para 21.
154 *De Jong* para 22.
155 *De Jong* para 23.
156 *De Jong* paras 26–28.
157 2007 (4) SA 488 (C).

already run its course.[158] The court also found that there was no basis for substitution of its own decision for that of the relevant administrator.[159] However Selikowitz J found that the applicant was entitled to compensation for out-of-pocket expenses incurred in tendering.[160] As Rogers J noted in *De Jong*, while Selikowitz J did not analyse the structure of section 8(1)(*c*) or make the legal findings set out in *De Jong*, compensation was awarded to vindicate the applicant's right to administrative justice because neither the remedy of remittal nor a substituted decision was feasible or appropriate.[161]

The second case, *Minister of Defence and Others v Dunn*[162] concerned a challenge of a decision by the Minister of Defence not to promote a member of the South African National Defence Force. The High Court granted compensation to Dunn - again, in circumstances where the court considered that neither a remittal nor a substituted decision was feasible. The High Court found that it would not be just and equitable to set aside or substitute the Minister's decision because another person had already been appointed to the post. Instead, it ordered the SANDF to pay Dunn compensation in the amount of the salary he would have been paid if promoted.[163] On appeal, the Supreme Court Appeal found that there was no basis for reviewing the Minister's decision, but proceeded to deal with the remedy granted by the High Court.[164] Lewis JA found that, even if the Minister's decision had been reviewable, there were no 'exceptional circumstances' to justify an order of compensation. Lewis JA did not specifically address the nature of the 'exceptionality' criterion under section 8(1)(*c*)(ii)(*bb*), but appeared to adopt a broader approach than Rogers J in *De Jong*, considering factors such as the prejudice caused to the applicant. In particular, Lewis JA emphasised that there was no evidence of any prejudice to Dunn since non-promotion was always a possibility where there are competing candidates for a position. Lewis JA held further that compensation was an impermissible order since Dunn had failed to prove any loss justifying a monetary award. The Supreme Court of Appeal underscored that compensation must be used as an alternative remedy to substitution, and not as a form of substitution as the High Court had done by awarding Dunn compensation in the form of the salary he would have received if promoted.[165]

In summary, the following emergent principles can be discerned, but have not been finally determined by the Constitutional Court, in respect of compensation awards under section 8(1)(*c*)(ii)(*bb*):

i) Compensation under PAJA will only be granted in 'exceptional cases', which must be determined in 'the specific context of each case'.[166]

---

158 *Darson Construction* at 502F–G.

159 *Darson Construction* at 502J–503F.

160 Selikowitz J reasoned at 510E–G as follows:

> I am, however, satisfied that applicant is entitled to some compensation for the manner in which first respondent breached its right to administrative justice. Having regard to the facts of this matter it is clear that applicant responded - at a cost - to the invitation to tender, only to have its tender considered by an unauthorised administrator - the Supply Chain Management Committee. Applicant deserved far better from first respondent.

161 *De Jong* para 26.

162 2007 (6) SA 52 (SCA).

163 *Dunn v Minister of Defence and Others* 2006 (2) SA 107 (T). Whether the court *a quo*'s order – of compensation without setting aside – is permitted under section 8(1)(*c*) of PAJA is not clear, however. On the construction of section 8(1)(*c*), as discussed in *De Jong*, an order of compensation may have to follow an order that sets aside unlawful administrative action.

164 *Minister of Defence and Others v Dunn* 2007 (6) SA 52 (SCA) para 33.

165 *Minister of Defence v Dunn* paras 38–40.

166 In *Darson Construction* at 502C–D, Selikowitz J opined that the interpretation and application of the phase 'in exceptional cases' under section 8(1)(*c*)(ii)(*bb*) would require the presence of different factors from that in section 8(1)(*c*)(ii)(*aa*). However, Selikowitz J declined to attempt to define the phrase and expressed the view that it is undesirable to do so as 'each case will need to be assessed on its own facts'.

ii) The remedies of remittal and of a substituted decision or compensation are mutually exclusive so that if the usual remedy of remittal is granted, compensation may not be awarded.[167]
iii) Exceptionality for the purposes of substitution or compensation has to do with the circumstances which exceptionally justify the granting of one or other of these unusual remedies in lieu of the usual remedy of remittal, rather than with circumstances which render the administrative decision exceptionally bad.[168]
iv) A party seeking compensation is required to prove that it has suffered loss as a result of the unfair administrative action.[169]
v) It is impermissible for a court to make an order of compensation which has the effect of substituting the court's decision for that of the administrator.[170]

### 12.8.3 Compensation for unjustified enrichment

An area of nascent development is compensation on the basis of unjustified enrichment – either in terms of PAJA section 8(1)(*c*)(ii)(*bb*), the general rubric of 'just and equitable relief' under section 172(1)(*b*) of the Constitution, or as an independent common-law claim. The law of unjustified enrichment presents a mechanism for some measure of compensation in circumstances where work has been performed under a contract that is declared invalid and set aside. However, the remedy is limited to recovery of the value of whatever the claimant transferred to the party without a lawful basis – in other words, the amount by which the other party benefitted or was 'unlawfully enriched' at the expense of the claimant. It does not, therefore, provide for recovery of lost profits or even recovery of expenses incurred in the performance of an invalid contract.

The Supreme Court of Appeal has commented that when an agreement between a public body and a service provider is void for non-compliance with procurement law, the service provider should, in principle, not be left remediless because it could claim from the public body in unjustified enrichment.[171] This means that when a service provider does something which benefits a public body, and there is no legal ground upon which the public body should have been benefited, then the service provider should be allowed to claim the return of that benefit.

Under South African law, traditionally enrichment claims have only been upheld when a plaintiff wishes to claim the return of money or property. However, in the procurement context, the contractor will often have provided services, and will therefore seek to claim the return of the value of services. In the old Appellate Division case of *Nortje v Pool*, the court held that plaintiffs cannot recover for the value of services unless their services resulted in tangible improvements to the defendant's property.[172] This decision is yet to be expressly overruled. However, English law has been clearly developed to recognise enrichment claims

167 *De Jong* para 24.
168 *De Jong* para 24.
169 *Minister of Defence v Dunn* para 40. See also *Darson Construction* at 509F–510D.
170 *Minister of Defence v Dunn* para 39. However, the SCA's findings on compensation were *obiter*.
171 *City of Tshwane Metropolitan Municipality v RPM Bricks Proprietary Ltd* 2008 (3) SA 1 (SCA) para 25.
172 *Nortje v Pool NO* 1966 (3) SA 96 (A) 134G. See also *Pucljowski v Johnston's Executors* 1946 WLD 1 at 6.

for the provision of services.[173] In *Benedetti v Sawari & Ors*,[174] the UK Supreme Court established the following principles for cases of this kind:

> (i) the starting point for identifying whether a benefit has been conferred on a defendant, and for valuing that benefit, is the market price of the services; (ii) the defendant is entitled to adduce evidence in order subjectively to devalue the benefit, thereby proving either that he in fact received no benefit at all, or that he valued the benefit at less than the market price; but (iii) save perhaps in exceptional circumstances, the principle of subjective revaluation should not be recognised, either for the purpose of identifying a benefit, or for valuing a benefit received.[175]

There are clear signs of movement in the same direction in South African courts. The Supreme Court of Appeal has indicated a willingness to extend the boundaries of enrichment law to include recovery of value of services.[176] In at least three cases, the High Court has recognised the possibility of enrichment actions for the provision of services that extend beyond the narrow terms of *Nortje v Pool*.[177]

In *Mangaung Metropolitan Municipality v Maluti Plant Hire*,[178] a full bench on appeal upheld a High Court order directing payment to a service provider based on unjust enrichment. The High Court held that '[i]f a person is enriched as a consequence of services performed by another, the measure of enrichment is the value of the service'; and that the fact that profits were earned or lost as a consequence of the service provided cannot be added to the enrichment claim.[179] In *Special New Fruit Licensing Limited and Others v Colours Fruit (South Africa) (Pty) Limited and Others*,[180] Hendricks AJ accepted the availability of 'a general action for unjustified enrichment' arising from the provision of services, but found that the facts of the case did not give rise to an enrichment action. In *Rural Maintenance (Pty) Ltd v Maluti a-Phofong Local Municipality*,[181] the High Court found that a municipality was 'unjustly enriched' when a company took over its responsibility of supplying electricity. The court accepted that the 'just and equitable relief' envisaged in section 172(1)(*b*) of the Constitution read with section 8(1)(*c*)(ii)(*bb*) of PAJA could include a claim based on unjust enrichment (but was not necessarily limited to such a claim).[182] However, the court went on to find that the claim, properly characterised, was not an enrichment claim, but a claim based on the *actio negotiorum gestio* (an action for recovery of loss incurred by an agent for work done for its principal). Thus rather than computing the value of the actual enrichment of the municipality, the High Court awarded compensation for the value of the expenses incurred by the plaintiff, acting as the municipality's agent, less the income it received from consumers for its provision of electricity.

---

173 *Benedetti v Sawiris & Ors* [2013] UKSC 50.

174 [2013] UKSC 50.

175 *Benedetti v Sawiris & Ors*, majority judgment per Lord Clarke, at para 34.

176 *McCarthy Retail Ltd v Shortdistance Carriers CC* 2001 (3) SA 482 (SCA) paras 8–10. See also the minority judgment of Ogilvie Thompson JA in *Nortje v Pool*.

177 *Mangaung Metropolitan Municipality v Maluti Plant Hire* 2017 JDR 0401 (FB) paras 33–36 (full bench decision); and *Special New Fruit Licensing Limited and Others v Colours Fruit (South Africa) (Pty) Limited and Others* [2019] ZAWCHC 83 paras 143–147.

178 2017 JDR 0401 (FB).

179 *Mangaung Metropolitan Municipality v Maluti Plant Hire* paras 30–33 and 37.

180 [2019] ZAWCHC 83.

181 *Rural Maintenance (Pty) Ltd v Maluti a-Phofong Local Municipality* [2019] ZAFSHC 186.

182 *Rural Maintenance* at paras 29–30, 36–41.

Most tellingly perhaps, in *Allpay* the Constitutional Court referred to the principles underlying claims for unjustified enrichment in describing the consequences of declaring invalid Cash Paymaster's contract for the provision of social grant payment services.[183] The court stated that 'any invalidation of the existing contract as a result of the invalid tender should not result in any loss to Cash Paymaster. The converse, however, is also true. It has no right to benefit from an unlawful contract'. In support of this statement, the court referred to the restitutionary principles in the law of contract (on rescission or cancellation of a contract) and in claims for unjustified enrichment. In *Shabangu*, the Constitutional Court again stated (albeit *obiter*) that recovery of what was transferred under an invalid agreement may be addressed in an enrichment claim, or as part of a broader claim for just and equitable relief under PAJA and section 172(1)(*b*) of the Constitution.[184]

### 12.8.4 Constitutional damages

Constitutional damages have been awarded by the courts for breaches of constitutional rights other than the right to just administrative action, which are infringed as a result of irregular administrative action.[185] It remains to be decided whether constitutional damages may be granted to vindicate only the section 33 right, and if so, whether such constitutional damages are encompassed in the compensation that may be awarded under section 8(1)(*c*)(ii)(*bb*) of PAJA or are independently derived from section 38 of the Constitution.

*MEC, Department of Welfare, Eastern Cape v Kate*[186] is an example of when an award of constitutional damages for the infringement of another right in the Bill of Rights is appropriate. The Supreme Court of Appeal ordered the Eastern Cape Department of Welfare to pay the respondent constitutional damages for its unreasonable delay in processing her application for a social grant. The court found that the Department's unreasonable delay in considering the respondent's application deprived her for a period of her constitutional right to social assistance, and that an order of constitutional damages was appropriate relief for the deprivation of that constitutional right.[187]

In the *Life Esidimeni* arbitration,[188] retired Justice Moseneke (sitting as an arbitrator) awarded R1 million in constitutional damages to each of the claimants. The claims arose from the death of 144 mental health care patients and mistreatment of many others, after the Gauteng Health Department unlawfully terminated a contract with Life Esidimeni Care Centre and transferred all its health care patients to non-governmental facilities that were not duly licensed and qualified to care for them. The arbitrator found that several constitutional rights had been violated by the state's actions,[189] and that given the extent of suffering and trauma that the patients and their families had to endure, and the complete disregard by government officials of their constitutional duties, vindication of the claimants' constitutional rights required an award of constitutional damages (over and above the

---

183 *Allpay (remedy)* para 67, read with footnote 47.

184 *Shabangu v Land and Agricultural Development Bank of South Africa* 2020 (1) SA 305 (CC) paras 26–28.

185 *MEC, Department of Welfare, Eastern Cape v Kate* 2006 (4) SA 478 (SCA) paras 22–33.

186 2006 (4) SA 478 (SCA).

187 *Kate* para 22.

188 Reported at http://www.saflii.org/images/LifeEsidimeniArbitrationAward.pdf

189 This part of the award read:

> The Government is ordered to pay R1 000 000 (one million rand) to each of the claimants listed in Annexures A, B and C as appropriate relief and compensation for the Government's unjustifiable and reckless breaches of section 1(*a*), (*c*) and (*d*), section 7, section 10, section 12(1)(*d*) and (*e*), section 27(1)(*a*) and (*b*) and section 195(1) (*a*), (*b*), (*d*), (*e*), (*f*) and (*g*) and multiple contraventions of the National Health Act 61 of 2003 and the Mental Health Care Act 17 of 2002 that caused the death of 144 mental health care users and the pain, suffering and torture of 1418 mental health care users who survived and their families.

amount already awarded for emotional shock and trauma). While not binding as a court precedent, the arbitration award is a significant development in this area of law, which has been markedly slow to develop.

In considering whether constitutional damages under section 38 might be awarded for breaches of section 33 alone, a useful starting point is the Constitutional Court's discussion of constitutional damages in *Fose*. There, the Constitutional Court held that there is no reason in principle why constitutional damages should not be awarded in an appropriate case. Ackermann J stated:

> ... there is no reason in principle why 'appropriate relief' should not include an award of damages, where such an award is necessary to protect and enforce chapter 3 rights. Such awards are made to compensate persons who have suffered loss as a result of the breach of a statutory right if, on a proper construction of the statute in question, it was the Legislature's intention that such damages should be payable, and it would be strange if damages could not be claimed for, at least, loss occasioned by the breach of a right vested in the claimant by the supreme law. When it would be appropriate to do so, and what the measure of damages should be will depend on the circumstances of each case and the particular right which has been infringed.[190]

As Conradie JA noted in *Jayiya v MEC for Welfare, Eastern Cape and Another*,[191] the remedies under PAJA may already provide appropriate relief for any breach of section 33 of the Constitution as required under section 38. Conradie JA reasoned that, following the principle of subsidiarity, the courts must first look to apply these statutory remedies in protecting and giving effect to section 33; it is only where the statutory remedies do not provide appropriate relief that the court may grant constitutional damages under section 38 of the Constitution.[192]

Conradie JA's approach is contested, however. For instance, in *Kate*, Nugent JA expressed the view (but did not decide the point) that 'the relief that is permitted by s 38 of the Constitution is not a remedy of last resort, to be looked to only when there is no alternative - and indirect - means of asserting and vindicating constitutional rights'.[193] Nugent JA went on to find that additional considerations informed whether the 'direct s 38 remedy' of constitutional damages was justified. In particular, Nugent JA took into account that there was a direct breach of a substantive constitutional right, which deserved 'direct vindication',

190 *Fose v Minister of Safety and Security* 1997 (3) SA 786 (CC) para 60.

191 2004 (2) SA 611 (SCA).

192 In *Jayiya*, Conradie JA explained at para 9 that:

> As appears from its preamble the Promotion of Administrative Justice Act was passed by Parliament to give effect to the constitutional guarantee of just administrative action. The appellant should accordingly have sought her remedy in this Act. 'Constitutional damages' in the sense discussed in *Fose v Minister of Safety and Security* ... might be awarded as appropriate relief where no statutory remedies have been given or no adequate common-law remedies exist. Where the lawgiver has legislated statutory mechanisms for securing constitutional rights, and provided, of course, that they are constitutionally unobjectionable, they must be used. The Promotion of Administrative Justice Act does not provide for the kind of relief afforded to the appellant in paras 2(*c*) and 3 of the order. Instead, it provides in s 8(1)(*c*)(ii)(*bb*) that a Court may in proceedings for judicial review, exceptionally, direct an administrator to pay compensation.

193 *Kate* para 27.

and that there was 'an endemic breach' of the rights concerned that required 'the clear assertion of their independent existence'.[194]

Whether there is a role for constitutional damages to be awarded solely for breaches of the section 33 right will depend, at least in part, on the courts' approach to compensation under section 8(1)(*c*)(ii)(*bb*) of PAJA – including whether compensation under this section is limited to proven financial loss (as suggested in *Minister of Defence v Dunn*) and whether the relatively restricted approach to exceptionality set out in *De Jong* is endorsed by the highest courts. Clearly, the more liberal the courts' approach to compensation under section 8(1)(*c*)(ii)(*bb*) for breaches of the section 33 right, the more difficult it becomes to conceive of a role for constitutional damages. If compensation awards under section 8(1)(*c*)(ii)(*bb*) of PAJA are confined to compensating complainants for proven loss, and to cases where remittal and substitution is not appropriate, there may be cases where constitutional damages are appropriate – either because a just and equitable remedy requires the award of punitive or exemplary damages, and not merely compensatory damages, or because a just and equitable remedy requires an award of compensation notwithstanding remittal or substitution.

In respect of punitive or exemplary constitutional damages, such awards might be premised on the principle of accountability – our courts have recognised that constitutional damages can play a role in reinforcing accountability and obedience to the Constitution.[195] However, the courts have thus far declined to award punitive constitutional damages on the basis that public policy considerations do not favour the award.[196] Further, the Constitutional Court expressed reservations about punitive constitutional damages in *Fose*. As Ackermann J pointed out, for punitive damages awards to individuals to have a helpful effect on the conduct of public officials they would have to be very substantial, and 'the more substantial they are, the greater the anomaly that a single plaintiff receives a windfall of such magnitude'. In addition to this anomaly, awarding large punitive damages could have a grave impact on the fiscus, which is already over-burdened.[197]

**PAUSE FOR REFLECTION**

1. Consider the court's approach to the compensation remedy under section 8(1)(c)(ii)(*bb*) of PAJA. Do you think the court's understanding of 'exceptional circumstances' in this context is correct? Could the provisions of section 8(1)(c)(ii)(*bb*) of PAJA be interpreted purposively to have a broader application?
2. In the *Allpay (remedy)* judgment, did the Constitutional Court in fact establish a 'no profit principle'? Consider the statement in paragraph 67 of the judgment

CONTINUED >>>

194 *Kate* para 27. However, see the Supreme Court of Appeal's judgment in *Komape v Minister of Basic Education* [2019] ZASCA 192, which considered whether constitutional damages should be awarded to the family of Michael Komape, a five-year-old learner who drowned in a pit latrine at his school in Limpopo. The Supreme Court of Appeal awarded his family delictual damages but not constitutional damages, holding that where claimants have been fully compensated for loss sustained and public funds are better served elsewhere, constitutional damages generally should not be awarded.

195 *Steenkamp* para 39; *Premier, Western Cape v Faircape Property Developers (Pty) Ltd* 2003 (6) SA 13 (SCA) para 40; *Minister of Safety and Security v Van Duivenboden* 2002 (6) SA 431 (SCA) para 21.

196 In this regard, Harms JA observed in *Steenkamp NO v Provincial Tender Board, Eastern Cape* 2006 (3) SA 151 (SCA) at para 39:

> The importance of accountability as a public policy factor serving a constitutional imperative has more than once been underscored by this Court, but, as counsel ruefully mentioned, it has never carried the day by imposing delictual liability.

197 *Fose* paras 71–72; see also *Olitzki Property Holdings* para 41.

and the order granted in that case. What is the import, if any, of the court's suspension of the declaration of invalidity of CPS's contract for the application of such a principle?

3. In the *Allpay (remedy)* judgment, is the Constitutional Court's explanation of the statement that the tenderer, Cash Paymaster 'has no right to benefit from an unlawful contract' in footnote 47 of the judgment satisfactory?
4. Is the position of an innocent successful tenderer, who performs under a contract that is subsequently set aside, adequately protected by the remedies of judicial review under our law?

## 12.9 A declaration of rights

A declaration of rights is a common-law remedy and is specifically provided for under section 8(1)(*d*) of PAJA, which empowers the court to grant an order 'declaring the rights of the parties in respect of any matter to which the administrative action relates'. Section 8(2) of PAJA, which describes the remedies for a failure to take a decision, also allows for an order 'declaring the rights of the parties in relation to the taking of the decision'.[198]

Unlike a declaration of constitutional invalidity under section 172(1)(*a*),[199] the courts are not obliged to grant a declaration of rights but may do so where they consider it to constitute appropriate relief. A declaration of rights is a non-invasive remedy: it clarifies the legal position and allows parties to obtain a determination of their rights. It is, as O'Regan J put it in *Rail Commuters Action Group and Others v Transnet Ltd t/a Metrorail and Others*,[200] 'a flexible remedy which can assist in clarifying legal and constitutional obligations in a manner which promotes the protection and enforcement of our Constitution and its values'.[201] It does so by acknowledging wrongdoing, affirming rights and providing guidance for future conduct. A declaration of rights is thus particularly useful where the court finds irregularities in government processes that are likely otherwise to be repeated or where the responsible authorities deny that they have certain obligations (as occurred in *Rail Commuters*).

A declaration of rights may be accompanied by other orders such as interdicts, but it may also stand on its own. As Hoexter notes, a bare declaration of rights may be 'a rather toothless remedy', as it does not require any action to be taken.[202] It relies instead on the goodwill of officials to act in accordance with the declaration, and to take such steps as they deem necessary in doing so. On the other hand, there is value in this non-prescriptive remedy in a constitutional democracy premised on the separation of powers: it enables courts to declare the law, while leaving to the other arms of government, the executive and the legislature, the decision as to how best the law, once stated, should be observed.[203]

198 On the remedies under section 8(2) of PAJA, see below at section 12.11.

199 On section 172(1)(*a*) of the Constitution, see above at section 12.3. It requires that the court must declare 'any law or conduct that is inconsistent with the Constitution' to be invalid to the extent of its inconsistency. It is a special constitutional provision, different to the common-law rules governing the grant of declaratory orders. For a discussion of the differences between the jurisdiction of the High Court to grant declaratory relief and section 172 of the Constitution, see *Islamic Unity Convention v Independent Broadcasting Authority and Others* 2002 (4) SA 294 (CC) paras 8–12 and *National Director of Public Prosecutions and Another v Mohamed NO and Others* 2003 (4) SA 1 (CC) paras 55–56.

200 2005 (2) SA 359 (CC).

201 *Rail Commuters* para 107.

202 Hoexter (2012) 558.

203 *Rail Commuters* para 108.

## 12.10 Interdicts

### 12.10.1 Prohibitory, mandatory and structural interdicts

An interdict is an order of court directing a person not to do something (prohibitory interdict) or directing a person to take certain action (mandatory interdict). In the administrative-law context, prohibitory interdicts are typically used to prevent the commission of irregular administrative action or to prevent the taking of further steps in reliance on administrative action. Mandatory interdicts are used to get performance when public officials refuse to act, or to direct public officials to remedy a situation brought about by irregular administrative action.

Section 8 of PAJA expressly provides for mandatory and prohibitory interdicts. Section 8(1)(*a*)(ii) empowers the court to grant an order 'directing the administrator to act in the manner the court or tribunal requires', while section 8(1)(*b*) provides that the court may grant an order 'prohibiting the administrator from acting in a particular manner'.

The court may retain supervisory jurisdiction and require public officials to report to court within a specified period on the steps they have taken to comply with a mandatory interdict. This is known as a 'structural interdict', and is an especially powerful and potentially far-reaching remedy available to the reviewing court. It enables the court to monitor and enforce compliance with its order over a period of time.

Structural interdicts are typically granted where socio-economic rights are threatened or undermined, and where there has been a sustained failure by the responsible administrator or department to perform its duties. An example of a detailed structural interdict is the Constitutional Court's order in *Black Sash I* – a further order granted in the social grants saga.[204] This order was prompted by the Social Security Agency of South Africa's (SASSA) failure to appoint a new service provider or itself take-over of the administration of social grants in the time specified in the *Allpay (remedy)* order. In *Black Sash I*, the Constitutional Court extended the declaration of invalidity of CPS's contract to allow CPS to continue to providing grant payment services for another 12 months, and issued a structural interdict against the Minister of Social Development and SASSA. It directed these state parties to file reports on affidavit every three months, setting out how they planned to ensure the payment of social grants after the expiry of the suspended period of invalidity of CPS's contract; what steps they had taken and what further steps they would take, and when they would take each future step, so as to ensure that the payment of all social grants is made when they fall due after the expiry of the 12-month period.

When faced with especially serious and systemic failures in the administration, the courts have also resorted to the extraordinary measure of appointing other persons or bodies to assist the dysfunctional department in complying with the court order, or to assist the court by providing independent or expert reports on progress in the implementation of the court's order. This may take the form, for instance, of an independent expert, a claims administrator, a special master or an independent trust.

In *Black Sash I*, the Constitutional Court also adopted this remedy. It directed that a panel of experts be appointed to, amongst other things, evaluate the steps proposed or taken by SASSA for any bidding process or any other processes aimed at appointing a new contractor, or any steps aimed at SASSA itself administering and paying the grants in the future. The court required the panel to file monthly reports for six months, setting out their evaluation

204 *Black Sash Trust v Minister of Social Development* 2017 (3) SA 335 (CC) ('*Black Sash I*').

method, the results of their evaluations and any recommendations they consider necessary. The court order provided for the parties to submit the names of suitably qualified individuals for appointment 'as independent legal practitioners and technical experts' on the panel.

In *Linkside and Others v Minister of Basic Education and Others,*[205] which concerned the appointment of teachers to vacant posts at public schools in the Eastern Cape and the payment of outstanding teacher salaries, the High Court ordered the appointment of a firm of registered chartered accountants as claims administrators to receive funds from the defendant, assess claims by schools and distribute funds to them.

In *Meadow Glen Home Owners Association and Others v City of Tshwane Metropolitan Municipality and Another,*[206] the Supreme Court of Appeal endorsed the use of special masters and other creative remedial approaches, especially in cases involving socio-economic rights. Wallis JA observed:

> Both this Court and the Constitutional Court have stressed the need for courts to be creative in framing remedies to address and resolve complex social problems, especially those that arise in the area of socio-economic rights. It is necessary to add that when doing so in this type of situation courts must also consider how they are to deal with failures to implement orders; the inevitable struggle to find adequate resources; inadequate or incompetent staffing and other administrative issues; problems of implementation not foreseen by the parties' lawyers in formulating the order and the myriad other issues that may arise with orders the operation and implementation of which will occur over a substantial period of time in a fluid situation. Contempt of court is a blunt instrument to deal with these issues and courts should look to orders that secure on-going oversight of the implementation of the order. There is considerable experience in the United States of America with orders of this nature arising from the decision in *Brown v Board of Education* and the federal court supervised process of desegregating schools in that country. The Constitutional Court referred to it with approval in the TAC (No. 2) case. Our courts may need to consider such institutions as the special master used in those cases to supervise the implementation of court orders.[207]

In *Mwelase and Others v Director-General for the Department of Rural Development and Land Reform and Another,*[208] the Constitutional Court upheld the appointment by the Land Claims Court of a special master to assist the Department of Rural Development and Land Affairs to process a backlog of over nearly 11 000 labour tenant applications for land ownership rights. The court found that this order, while certainly novel, did not constitute judicial overreach in light of the Department's longstanding failure to perform its duties. Writing for the majority, Cameron J stressed the seriousness of the Department's failure:

> [O]ver nearly two decades... the Department has manifested and sustained what has seemed to be obstinate misapprehension of its statutory duties. It has shown unresponsiveness plus a refusal to account to those dependent on its cooperation for the realisation of their land claims and associated constitutional rights. And, despite repeated promises, plans and undertakings, it has displayed a patent incapacity or inability to get the job done.

205 [2014] ZAECGHC 111.
206 2015 (2) SA 413 (SCA).
207 At para 35.
208 2019 (6) SA 597 (CC).

> In this, the Department has jeopardised not only the rights of land claimants, but the constitutional security and future of all. South Africans have been waiting for more than 25 years for equitable land reform. More accurately, they have been waiting for centuries before. The Department's failure to practically manage and expedite land reform measures in accordance with constitutional and statutory promises has profoundly exacerbated the intensity and bitterness of our national debate about land reform. It is not the Constitution, nor the courts, nor the laws of the country that are at fault in this. It is the institutional incapacity of the Department to do what the statute and the Constitution require of it that lies at the heart of this colossal crisis.
>
> The performance of the Department in response to the increasingly focused pressures the applicants applied, has been an object, and abject, case in point. Each time, the Department has temporised. It has done this, each time, with promises of better performance. This time it would get things right. But it never did. It has been a classic case of more-same, more-same. The very course of this litigation, right up to the proceedings in this Court, has shown the Department's inability, in colloquial but apposite terms, to get its act together. While the good faith and good intentions of its promises and undertakings may be accepted, they have repeatedly failed to translate into effective, rights-affirming practical action.[209]

Cameron J described the role of the special master, and addressed the concern that the special master remedy breached the separation of powers, as follows:

> Special masters, often with expertise in specialist areas of government, may assist with either devising a remedial plan or implementing it. In implementing a remedy, the main task of a special master is to oversee and monitor – rather than usurping performance of executive functions, which is closer to the functions of other court-appointed officers (administrators or receivers, whose respective tasks may be to supplement or replace management of a government institution).
>
> ...The Land Claims Court made clear that the special master remains an agent of the Court, and acts in extension of the Court's own supervisory jurisdiction. And the Court alas made plain that the work to be done would alleviate its own capacity constraints in overseeing the output of the Department. The apprehension that the special master would be a complete outsider, reigning at will over the Department with unfettered executive power loses sight of a key fact. This is that the independence of the special master is not merely the detached neutrality of a third party expert unaffiliated with the parties. It is rather an extension of judicial independence, because it derives from appointment as an agent of the court, continuingly subject to court control and authority.
>
> While the powers afforded a special master certainly seem intrusive, this is only because it is the Court itself that is exercising the constitutionally entrusted powers to afford effective relief. It is not the Court authorising an outside, unchecked body to intrude into the executive domain. It is the Court stepping in to ensure that nationally critical land reform and restitution processes make headway, 20 years

209 At paras 40–42.

after they should. In this way, the special master's independence is a product of the independence of the Court, to which he or she remains subordinate.[210]

### 12.10.2 Interim and final interdicts

An interdict can be sought either as a temporary or final order, and there are distinct requirements that must be met for each.[211] While subsection 8(1)(*a*)(ii) and 8(1)(*b*) of PAJA empower the court to grant final mandatory and prohibitory interdicts, section 8(1)(*e*) provides additionally for 'granting a temporary interdict or other temporary relief'.

An interim interdict is directed at preserving or restoring the *status quo* pending the final determination of the rights of the parties, and is often sought on an urgent basis. It is fairly common for parties challenging the validity of administrative action to apply for an interim interdict to prevent actual or threatened harm, and to prevent steps being taken in reliance on the administrative action, pending the outcome of the review application. For instance, an interim interdict may be obtained to prevent mining activity pending the review of the decision to award the mining licence, or to prevent a successful tenderer from implementing a tender pending review of the tender award.[212]

The common-law test for an interim interdict has four requirements. The applicant must establish (i) a *prima facie* right that it seeks to protect; (ii) a reasonable apprehension of irreparable and imminent harm if an interdict is not granted; (iii) that the balance of convenience favours the granting of the interdict; and (iv) that no suitable alternative remedy is available.[213] We provide a brief explanation of each of these requirements:

i) ***Prima facie* right**. This requirement was considered by the Constitutional Court in *National Treasury and Others v Opposition to Urban Tolling Alliance and Others.*[214] The court addressed the question whether an applicant seeking an interim interdict pending judicial review could establish a *prima facie* right simply by relying on its right to just administrative action. The court held that this did not suffice. The court explained that the applicant must show that it has a *prima facie* right that requires protection in the form of an interim interdict. Since every person's right to approach a court to review and set aside irregular administrative action is protected under section 33 of the Constitution, the interim interdict does not serve to protect this right. What the applicant must show is 'a right to which, if not protected by an interdict, irreparable harm would ensue'.[215]

ii) **Apprehension of harm**. This is an objective requirement, meaning that on the basis of the facts presented to it, the court must decide whether the applicant has a reasonable basis for the apprehension of harm.[216] Furthermore, an interdict will only be granted where future or ongoing harm is feared. If the infringement

210 At paras 58–62.

211 The requirements for an interdict are discussed only briefly below. For a full discussion see Cilliers, AC, Loots, C & Nel, HC, *Herbstein & Van Winsen: The Civil Practice of the High Courts of South Africa* (5th ed) Vol 2 at 1456–1482; and Van Loggerenberg, *Erasmus: Superior Courts Practice* (Revision Service 45, 2014), Appendix E8: Interdicts at 1–15.

212 In such cases, a two-part application is typically brought, with Part A setting out the basis for the interim interdict and Part B setting out the grounds for the review. Part A will be heard first, and if granted, the interim interdict will operate pending the outcome of the review application in Part B.

213 *Setlogelo v Setlogelo* 1914 AD 221; *Webster v Mitchell* 1948 (1) SA 1186 (W).

214 2012 (6) SA 223 (CC).

215 *Opposition to Urban Tolling Alliance* para 50. See also the discussion in *Economic Freedom Fighters v Gordhan and Others; Public Protector and Another v Gordhan and Others* [2020] ZACC 10 (29 May 2020) paras 24 and 65.

216 *National Council of Societies for the Prevention of Cruelty to Animals v Openshaw* 2008 (5) SA 339 (SCA) at 347D–E.

complained of is one that *prima facie* appears to have occurred once and for all, the applicant must allege facts to show that the harm is likely to be repeated.[217]

iii) **Balance of convenience.** In assessing where the balance of convenience lies, the courts weigh up the harm or prejudice that would be caused to the applicant if the interim interdict is refused against the prejudice that the respondent will suffer if the interdict is granted. All relevant circumstances must be considered. The weight that the court will place on the balance of convenience, is informed by the applicant's prospects of ultimate success in the pending litigation: the stronger the applicant's prospects of success, the less the need for the balance of convenience to favour him; conversely, the weaker the applicant's prospects of success, the greater the need for the balance of convenience to favour him.[218]

iv) **Suitable alternative remedy**. This requires that there be no other legal remedy available that would be as effective in protecting the applicant against the apprehended harm.

It must be recalled that an interim interdict is a discretionary remedy. This means that even if all four requirements are met, the court may refuse to grant the relief.

Turning to the final interdict, this is an order of permanent force and effect, alterable only on appeal. The applicant must establish three requirements on a balance of probabilities: (i) a clear and definite right that it seeks to protect; (ii) the actual or threatened interference with the right; and (iii) the absence of a suitable alternative remedy. It is a matter of some debate whether the court retains a discretion to refuse to grant a final interdict where all the requirements have been met. In *United Technical Equipment Co (Pty) Ltd v Johannesburg City Council*,[219] Harms J discussed the case authorities at some length, and concluded that, if the discretion exists at all, it is exercised only in exceptional circumstances.[220] In general, the discretion of a court to refuse a final interdict is limited and is bound up with the question whether the rights of the complaining party can be protected by any other ordinary remedy.

### 12.10.3 Interdicts that restrain the exercise of executive and legislative power

By granting an interdict that restrains the exercise of an executive or legislative power authorised under statute or the Constitution, the courts threaten to undermine the separation of powers. For this reason, the courts grant interdicts that restrain the exercise of a statutory or constitutional power only 'in the clearest of cases',[221] where there are 'exceptional circumstances and when a strong case is made out for relief'.[222] While the Constitutional Court has cautioned against defining 'the clearest of cases',[223] it has stated that one of the important considerations is whether the harm apprehended by the claimant amounts to a breach of one or more constitutional rights in the Bill of Rights. Under the common law, the courts have granted interdicts to restrain the exercise of statutory power

217 *Openshaw* at 347E–F.

218 *Olympic Passenger Service (Pty) Ltd v Ramlagan* 1957 (2) SA 382 (D) at 383F–G.

219 1987 (4) SA 343 (T).

220 See *United Technical Equipment* at 346B–G. See further *Transvaal Property & Investment Co Ltd and Reinhold & Co Ltd v SA Townships Mining & Finance Corporation Ltd & the Administrator* 1938 TPD 512 at 521.

221 *Opposition to Urban Tolling Alliance* paras 47 and 66.

222 *Gool v Minister of Justice and Another* 1955 (2) SA 682 (C); Molteno Brothers and Others Appellants v South African Railways and Others Respondents 1936 AD 321 at 329 and 331.

223 *Opposition to Urban Tolling Alliance* paras 47 and 90.

in cases where there are allegations of *mala fides* or where a functionary has acted outside the law.[224]

In *International Trade Administration Commission v SCAW South Africa (Pty) Limited*,[225] the Constitutional Court upheld an appeal against an interim interdict granted by the High Court, on the basis that the interdict infringed the separation of powers. The interim interdict restrained, amongst others, the Minister of Trade and Industry from terminating an existing anti-dumping duty. The Constitutional Court emphasised that the determination and implementation of international trade policy (including anti-dumping duties) 'resides in the heartland of national executive function' and entailed polycentric policy considerations. It held that, by granting the interdict, the High Court had usurped the Minister's discretion to make this decision and had inappropriately intruded on the executive domain. The Constitutional Court cautioned that:

> When a court is invited to intrude into the terrain of the executive, especially when the executive decision-making process is still uncompleted, it must do so only in the clearest of cases and only when irreparable harm is likely to ensue if interdictory relief is not granted. This is particularly true when the decision entails multiple considerations of national policy choices and specialist knowledge, in regard to which courts are ill-suited to judge.[226]

The Constitutional Court noted that, under the common law, interim interdicts that restrain statutory power are regarded as 'exceptional'.[227] The Constitutional Court affirmed that this remained the correct standard under the Constitution. It explained further, while the common-law test for an interim interdict remained applicable under the Constitution, the constitutional separation of powers principle must now inform the 'balance of convenience' requirement:

> The balance of convenience enquiry must now carefully probe whether and to which extent the restraining order will probably intrude into the exclusive terrain of another branch of Government. The enquiry must, alongside other relevant harm, have proper regard to what may be called separation of powers harm. A court must keep in mind that a temporary restraint against the exercise of statutory power well ahead of the final adjudication of a claimant's case may be granted only in the clearest of cases and after a careful consideration of separation of powers harm ...[228]

Another case where the court was found to have overstepped the line by granting an interdict – this time a final interdict – is *National Director of Public Prosecutions and Others v Freedom Under Law*.[229] The Supreme Court of Appeal overturned a final mandatory interdict granted by the High Court, which ordered the National Director of Public Prosecutions (NDPP) to reinstate all the charges against the suspended National Commissioner of Crime Intelligence in the South African Police Service (Mdluli), and to ensure that the prosecution of these charges were enrolled and pursued without delay. The High Court further directed the Commissioner of Police to reinstate disciplinary proceedings against Mdluli and to take all

224 See *Gool*; *Molteno Brothers*; *Opposition to Urban Tolling Alliance* paras 47 and 66.
225 2012 (4) SA 618 (CC).
226 *SCAW* para 101.
227 *SCAW* para 45.
228 *SCAW* paras 47, 63–67.
229 2014 (4) SA 298 (SCA).

steps necessary for the prosecution and finalisation of these proceedings. The Supreme Court of Appeal found that while the High Court had correctly reviewed and set aside the unlawful decisions taken by the NDPP and Commissioner of Police, the High Court 'went too far' and transgressed the separation of powers doctrine in granting the interdictory relief. Writing for a unanimous bench, Brand JA stated that:

> In terms of the Constitution the NDPP is the authority mandated to prosecute crime, while the Commissioner of Police is the authority mandated to manage and control the SAPS ... [T]he court will only be allowed to interfere with this constitutional scheme on rare occasions and for compelling reasons. Suffice it to say that in my view this is not one of those rare occasions and I can find no compelling reason why the executive authorities should not be given the opportunity to perform their constitutional mandates in a proper way. The setting aside of the withdrawal of the criminal charges and the disciplinary proceedings have the effect that the charges and the proceedings are automatically reinstated and it is for the executive authorities to deal with them. The court below went too far.[230]

In contrast, a court could grant an interdict against the exercise of a statutory power if the constitutionality of that statutory power is being challenged. The principles that apply in such cases are set out in the *UDM* 'floor-crossing' case.[231] The UDM, a political party, challenged the constitutionality of new floor-crossing legislation (which allowed members of parliament to defect to another party without the member losing his or her seat) and in the interim, sought to bar any floor-crossing from taking place under the legislation. The Constitutional Court held that this was permissible where –

> ... legislation is impugned as unconstitutional, and it appears that action pursuant to its terms is imminent and is likely to cause serious and irreparable prejudice, in all but the most exceptional cases, interim relief could be designed to prevent such prejudice pending a decision by a court having jurisdiction to decide on the constitutionality of the legislation.[232]

The court set out the following principles applicable to the granting of interim relief in these circumstances:

- A court may grant interim relief designed to maintain the status quo or to prevent a violation of a constitutional right where legislation that is alleged to be unconstitutional in itself, or through action it is reasonably feared might cause irreparable harm of a serious nature.
- Such interim relief should only be granted where it is strictly necessary in the interests of justice.
- In determining the interests of justice, the court must balance the interests of the person seeking interim relief against the interests of others who might be affected by the grant of such relief.
- The interim relief should be strictly tailored to interfere as little as possible with the operation of the legislation.[233]

230 *Freedom Under Law* para 51.
231 *President of the Republic of South Africa and Others v United Democratic Movement* 2003 (1) SA 472 (CC) ('*UDM*').
232 *UDM* para 28.
233 *UDM* para 32.

## 12.11 Remedies for the failure to take a decision

Section 8(2) of PAJA provides for a special class of remedies where the failure to take a decision is reviewed. Section 8(2) provides:

> (2) The court or tribunal, in proceedings for judicial review in terms of section 6(3), may grant any order that is just and equitable, including orders-
> (*a*) directing the taking of the decision;
> (*b*) declaring the rights of the parties in relation to the taking of the decision;
> (*c*) directing any of the parties to do, or to refrain from doing, any act or thing the doing, or the refraining from the doing, of which the court or tribunal considers necessary to do justice between the parties; or
> (*d*) as to costs.

The remedies in section 8(2) of PAJA are not strictly necessary, since the broad remedies for judicial review under section 8(1) of PAJA would suffice. However, as Hoexter has pointed out, the clear statement of these remedies is to be welcomed for their ease of application, and especially seeing that administrative delay is a notorious feature of South Africa's administration.[234]

As is evident from the wording of section 8(2) of PAJA, its remedies only apply once it is established that there is a reviewable failure to take a decision in terms of section 6(3) of PAJA.[235] Section 6(3) provides that a failure to take a decision is reviewable where (i) an administrator has a duty to take a decision; and (ii) where the empowering law does not prescribe any period for the taking of the decision but the administrator has delayed unreasonably in exercising the duty to take the decision (section 6(3)(*a*)), or where the empowering law prescribes a period for the taking of the decision and that period has passed without the administrator having taken the decision (section 6(3)(*b*)).[236]

The first question, then, is whether the impugned administrator has a *duty*, as opposed to a power or a right, to take the decision. This distinction was emphasised by the Supreme Court of Appeal in *Commissioner, South African Revenue Service v Trend Finance (Pty) Limited and Another*.[237] The court found that the empowering provision in question did not impose a duty on the Commissioner to take a decision but only empowered the Commissioner to do so, and held on this basis that the section 8(2) remedies did not apply.[238]

Where the empowering law prescribes the time period in which the decision must be taken, then section 6(3)(*b*) of PAJA *ipso facto* entitles the claimant to a just and equitable remedy under section 8(2) once that period has passed. However, if no period is prescribed for the taking of the decision, the applicant must show that the delay is unreasonable. In this determination context is critical, as is evidenced in the following two cases.

In *Ruyobeza and Another v Minister of Home Affairs and Others*,[239] the High Court found that a three-month delay by the Standing Committee on Refugee Affairs to decide an application for a certificate of indefinite refugee status was unreasonable. Thring J emphasised the following factors: the committee had 'totally ignored' the applicant's request

234 Hoexter (2012) 567.

235 Section 6(3) of PAJA must be read with section 6(2)(*g*) of PAJA, which establishes the ground of review 'that the action concerned consists of a failure to take a decision'.

236 See Chapter 6 section 6.2.1.2 above on omissions as a ground upon which the lawfulness of administrative action can be challenged.

237 2007 (6) SA 117 (SCA).

238 *Trend Finance* para 27.

239 2003 (5) SA 51 (C).

for a certificate for three months, despite a reminder; the committee had given no satisfactory explanation for the delay; and the delay had caused considerable prejudice to the applicant, who was effectively prevented from working as a result.[240]

The case of *Sibiya v Director-General: Home Affairs and Others and 55 Related Cases*[241] provides an instructive contrast to *Ruyobeza*, and demonstrates the importance of establishing a proper factual basis for showing that the administrator's delay is unreasonable. In that case fifty-six matters were brought on review in the High Court in which the applicants sought to compel the Department of Home Affairs to issue each applicant with a bar-coded identity document. The applications were brought on the ground that the Department had a duty to issue bar-coded identity documents, and that a reasonable period of three months had elapsed since the applications were lodged with the Department, without any identity documents having been issued. The period of three months was advanced as being a reasonable period of time on the basis of what the applicants had allegedly been told when their applications had been lodged. However, Wallis J rejected the contention that, in all fifty-six cases, a delay of longer than three months was unreasonable. Wallis J noted that this presupposed that all applications for the issue of an identity document were of precisely the same type involving precisely the same issues, which was patently not the case. Wallis J described the nature of the proper enquiry into unreasonable delay as follows:

> As the question of whether the department has delayed unreasonably in attending to an application is a question of fact in my view if an applicant wishes to satisfy a court that there has been unreasonable delay in dealing with their application they must furnish sufficient particulars of their personal circumstances and the nature of their application, so as to indicate on what basis the reasonable period has been determined. Enough information must be furnished to convey to the court the reasons why they contend that there has been undue delay in dealing with their application and why they allege that the department is in default. In other words their application must be tailored to their own situation. While one must be cautious of applying statements made in the wholly different context of what constitutes a reasonable time for performing a contractual obligation in the different environment of administrative action it has there been held that what is a reasonable time will depend amongst other things on the particular circumstances surrounding the performance of the contractual obligation in question, and the difficulties, obstacles and delays in performing that were actually foreseen or would be foreseen by a reasonable person. It has also been said that one is entitled to expect reasonably prompt and appropriate action and due diligence on the part of the party obliged to perform. Suitably adapted, these seem to me to be appropriate matters to take into account in determining whether a reasonable time has passed after the lodging of an application so that it can properly be contended that the department is in default.[242]

Wallis J concluded that it was not apparent from the affidavits what information had been made available to the Department in support of each application for an identity document, and it was thus not possible for the court to determine what a reasonable time was to

240 *Ruyobeza* at 65B–D.
241 2009 (5) SA 145 (KZP).
242 *Sibiya* para 24.

complete the process in each case. The application was accordingly dismissed as fatally defective.[243]

Where there has been unreasonable delay causing prejudice to the applicant, a just and equitable order may require more than the court directing the administrator to take a decision. For instance, in *Mahambehlala v MEC for Welfare, Eastern Cape and Another*,[244] Leach J ordered the Department of Welfare to retrospectively pay the applicant a social welfare grant. The Department had failed, without explanation, to process the applicant's application for a grant for a period of nine months. The court found that three months was a reasonable period for processing the application, and ordered the Department to pay the applicant the amounts she would have been paid if the grant had been approved in three months – that is, backdated for six months, with interest.[245] While Leach J relied on section 38 of the Constitution in granting this order, Leach J could equally have relied on section 8(2)(*c*) of PAJA which affords the court a generous power to grant orders 'directing any of the parties to do ... any act or thing the doing ... of which the court or tribunal considers necessary to do justice between the parties'.[246] As discussed above, more sustained and systemic failures to act may also attract structural interdicts or other creative remedies (such as, in the most severe cases, the appointment of a special master).

## 12.12 Non-PAJA remedies

### 12.12.1 Severance

Severance is a remedy associated with the correction of illegalities in legislation and subordinate legislation (the latter of which is a species of administrative action).[247] It entails the separation and setting aside of only the invalid portions of the legislation, where this is possible to achieve without affecting the valid portions and objects of the legislation. The requirements for the application of this remedy were stated by Centlivres CJ in *Johannesburg City Council v Chesterfield House (Pty) Ltd*:[248]

> The rule ... is that where it is possible to separate the good from the bad in a Statute and the good is not dependent on the bad, then that part of the Statute which is good must be given effect to, provided that what remains carries out the main object of the Statute ... Where, however, the task of separating the bad from the good is of such complication that it is impracticable to do so, the whole Statute must be declared *ultra vires*. In such a case it naturally follows that it is impossible to presume that the legislature intended to pass the Statute in what may prove to be a highly truncated form ...[249]

243 *Sibiya* paras 18–19, 29.

244 2002 (1) SA 342 (SE).

245 See also *Mbanga v MEC for Welfare, Eastern Cape and Another* 2002 (1) SA 359 (SE), where Leach J made a similar order.

246 A further helpful example is *Road Accident Fund v Duma and Three Similar Cases* 2013 (6) SA 9 (SCA) paras 20–23, where the court explained how such an approach could be used in terms of PAJA when the Road Accident Fund failed to take a decision within a reasonable time.

247 See Chapter 3 section 3.7.1 on rule-making, that is the creation of subordinate legislation, as administrative action.

248 1952 (3) SA 809 (A).

249 *Chesterfield House* at 822D–F. See too *S v Prefabricated Housing Corporation (Pty) Ltd and Another* 1974 (1) SA 535 (A) at 539C–F.

Severance is also applied to remedy illegalities in other documents, such as wills or contracts. As a public law remedy, however, severance enables courts to give effect to the constitutional principle, enshrined in section 172(1)(*a*) of the Constitution, that when deciding a constitutional matter within its power, a court must 'declare any law or conduct that is inconsistent with the Constitution invalid to the extent of its inconsistency'.[250] Whether severance is an applicable remedy only 'in exceptional cases', as a form of varying administrative action under section 8(1)(*c*)(ii)(*aa*) of PAJA, is a question that the courts are yet to consider.

An example of the court's reliance on severance in the administrative-law context appears in *Retail Motor Industry Organisation and Another v Minister of Water and Environmental Affairs and Another*.[251] The Supreme Court of Appeal applied severance to remedy a tyre waste management plan, which was approved and published by the Minister under certain environmental regulations. The court found that the plan unlawfully regulated both solid tyres and pneumatic tyres, but was otherwise consistent with the regulatory framework. To remedy the defect, the court severed and set aside all references to solid tyres in the plan, and left the plan otherwise intact.

Severance can also have appropriate application in the case of specific administrative decisions, where it is possible to separate the bad from the good and achieve the objectives of the decision. An example would be the granting of a licence where some, but not all, of the conditions attached to the licence are invalid.[252]

### 12.12.2 Contempt of court

Contempt of court is a useful common-law remedy which litigants may resort to when confronted with wilful and *mala fide* (bad faith) non-compliance with court orders directing an opponent to do or refrain from doing something (orders *ad factum praestandum*).[253] While a contempt of court order is sought by way of application on notice of motion, contempt of court is a criminal offence, and may be punished by a fine or committal to prison. The object of contempt proceedings is to compel performance in accordance with the court order, as well as to protect the rule of law by vindicating the court's dignity, authority and repute in the face of the non-compliance with its order.[254]

While non-compliance with court orders by certain organs of state has unfortunately become rather commonplace,[255] this is not necessarily the result of wilful and *mala fide* non-compliance. It may be symptomatic of a systemic break-down in the administration, or simply of incompetence on the part of public officials.[256] Neither of these causes for non-compliance suffice to establish contempt of court; what is required is deliberate and intentional (that is, wilful) and *mala fide* non-compliance.[257]

250 Section 172(1)(*a*) of the Constitution.

251 2014 (3) SA 251 (SCA) paras 44–49.

252 Baxter (1984) 679.

253 Contempt of court cannot be invoked for non-compliance with court orders directing only at the payment of monies (orders *in pecuniam solvendam*) – such orders must be enforced by way of execution.

254 *Fakie NO v CCII Systems (Pty) Ltd* 2006 (4) SA 326 (SCA) para 8.

255 See *Pheko and Others v Ekurhuleni Metropolitan Municipality (No 2)* 2015 (5) SA 600 (CC) at para 27, and the cases cited there.

256 Roach, K & Budlender, G (2005) Mandatory Relief and Supervisory Jurisdiction: When is it Appropriate, Just and Equitable? *SALJ* 122(2):325.

257 *Fakie* para 9; *Pheko (No 2)* para 42.

Since criminal punishments can follow upon findings of contempt of court, the courts apply the requirements for contempt orders strictly. The Supreme Court of Appeal considered the nature and requirements of contempt of court in detail in *Fakie NO v CCII Systems (Pty) Ltd*.[258] The court confirmed that there are four requirements for a contempt of court order: (i) the existence of an order of court obliging the respondent to perform an obligation *ad factum praestandum*; (ii) the respondent must have personal knowledge of the court order – this may be established by showing that the respondent received service or notice of the court order; (iii) non-compliance by the respondent with the court order; and (iv) willfulness and *mala fides* (bad faith) in the non-compliance. Each of these requirements must be proved on the criminal standard of proof – that is, beyond a reasonable doubt.[259] Once the applicant has proved the first three requirements (court order, service or notice, and non-compliance), the respondent bears an evidential burden in relation to wilfulness and *mala fides*: If the respondent fails to advance evidence to establish a reasonable doubt that the non-compliance was wilful and *mala fide* (in bad faith), contempt will be taken to have been proved beyond a reasonable doubt.

The approach to contempt of court proceedings set out in *Fakie* was endorsed and applied by the Constitutional Court in *Pheko and Others v Ekurhuleni Metropolitan Municipality (No 2)*.[260] In that case, the Constitutional Court confronted non-compliance by a municipality with two court's orders directing the municipality to file a report on its progress in housing an evicted community. The municipality's excuse for its non-compliance was that it had not been made aware of the court orders by its attorney. The Constitutional Court accepted that the municipality's non-compliance with the orders was not wilful or *mala fide*, and that the municipality had not acted with contempt. The court went on to consider whether the municipality's attorney, Mr Khoza, had acted with contempt. The court held that liability for contempt of court extends 'not only the person named or party to the suit but all those who, with the knowledge of the order, aid and abet the disobedience or wilfully are party to the disobedience'.[261] Mr Khoza's excuse was that he too had not received notice of the court's orders, because his email address, telephone and fax numbers had changed when he relocated his office. While the court accepted that Mr Khoza's explanation meant that contempt was not established, it proceeded to grant a personal costs order (costs *de bonis propriis*) against Mr Khoza for gross negligence and a gross disregard for his professional responsibilities.

Generally, contempt of court applications are brought by way of a *rule nisi* (obtained *ex parte*), calling on the respondent to show cause on the return day why an order of contempt of court should not be granted. This procedure ensures that before a contempt order is granted, the respondent has been given proper notice of the alleged non-compliance. This also secures the attendance of the respondent at court on the return day, to enable an order of committal to be enforced.

258 2006 (4) SA 326 (SCA).

259 However, a declaratory order and other appropriate civil remedies remain available to an applicant if contempt of court is proven only on a balance of probabilities.

260 *Pheko and Others v Ekurhuleni Metropolitan Municipality (No 2)* 2015 (5) SA 600 (CC) paras 25–37.

261 *Pheko (No 2)* para 47.

**PAUSE FOR REFLECTION**

**The practical challenges of obtaining contempt of court orders against senior public officials**

Obtaining contempt of court orders against obstructive senior public officials is difficult for several reasons. First, court orders directing officials to take certain steps seldom specify the officials responsible for performing the particular obligations. Instead, entire departments are often directed to take certain measures. Such orders will not found a contempt order; what is required is non-compliance by a particular respondent with a specific performance obligation under the court order. Second, proving non-compliance with a court order is difficult if the order does not specify timeframes for performance. These two difficulties can be addressed by the careful crafting of the relief sought by applicants. The third difficulty is more intractable. Where senior government officials and government ministers are sought to be held in contempt of court, proving personal knowledge of the court order (that is, by personal service or notice of the order) is notoriously difficult. As the Labour Court noted in *Setshedi v Minister Ndebele*,[262] 'the nature of government bureaucracy, [...] insulates senior government officials and ministers from direct personal interaction with sheriffs responsible for giving effect to service'. This places frustrated litigants, as well as the court, in an invidious position, since it remains the duty of the court to ensure that effective remedial action is taken to ensure compliance with its judgments.[263]

Contempt of court proceedings typically play out as a game brinkmanship. Ultimately, however, the threat of a contempt order and the possibility of imprisonment, does tend to prompt government officials to perform their obligations, albeit belatedly. For this reason, the remedy remains, as Cameron JA put it in *Fakie*, 'a most valuable mechanism'.[264]

## 12.13 Costs

Under section 8(1)(*f*) of PAJA, the court's remedial discretion to make any order that is just and equitable includes 'any order as to costs'. The court thus retains the discretion it enjoys under the common law: the award of costs is wholly in the discretion of the court, provided that the discretion is exercised 'judicially', that is honestly and reasonably.[265]

There are, however, two respects in which the exercise of the court's discretion on costs in judicial review proceedings differs from the general common-law approach.

The first distinguishing feature is that judicial review is a form of constitutional litigation.[266] As a result, the principles on costs that govern constitutional litigation must be applied.[267] The *locus classicus* on costs in constitutional litigation involving the state is the Constitutional Court's judgment in *Biowatch Trust v Registrar, Genetic Resources and Others*.[268]

262 *Setshedi v Minister Ndebele and Another* (2014) 35 ILJ 2861 (LC) para 1.

263 *Setshedi* para 1.

264 *Fakie* para 7.

265 For a general discussion on the principles of costs awards under the common law, see *Herbstein & Van Winsen*, Volume 2, Chapter 36 at 951ff. See too, *Affordable Medicines Trust and Others v Minister of Health and Others* 2006 (3) SA 247 (CC) para 138.

266 Whether instituted under PAJA or on the basis of the constitutional principle of legality, judicial review is directed at protecting and giving effect to the right to just administrative action under section 33 of the Constitution.

267 *Freedom Under Law* para 52; *Bengwenyama Minerals* para 88; *Koyabe and Others v Minister for Home Affairs and Others (Lawyers for Human Rights as Amicus Curiae)* 2010 (4) SA 327 (CC) para 87.

268 2009 (6) SA 232 (CC). See also *Affordable Medicines Trust* para 138.

In that case the Constitutional Court held that, where the state is shown to have failed to fulfil its constitutional and statutory obligations, and where different private parties are affected, the general rule is that: (i) the state should bear the costs of litigants who have been successful against it, and (ii) ordinarily there should be no costs orders against any private litigants who have become involved.[269] The Constitutional Court explained the threefold rationale for this rule as follows:

> ... In the first place it diminishes the chilling effect that adverse costs orders would have on parties seeking to assert constitutional rights. Constitutional litigation frequently goes through many courts and the costs involved can be high. Meritorious claims might not be proceeded with because of a fear that failure could lead to financially ruinous consequences. Similarly, people might be deterred from pursuing constitutional claims because of a concern that even if they succeed they will be deprived of their costs because of some inadvertent procedural or technical lapse. Secondly, constitutional litigation, whatever the outcome, might ordinarily bear not only on the interests of the particular litigants involved, but also on the rights of all those in similar situations. Indeed, each constitutional case that is heard enriches the general body of constitutional jurisprudence and adds texture to what it means to be living in a constitutional democracy. Thirdly, it is the State that bears primary responsibility for ensuring that both the law and State conduct are consistent with the Constitution. If there should be a genuine, non-frivolous challenge to the constitutionality of a law or of State conduct, it is appropriate that the State should bear the costs if the challenge is good, but if it is not, then the losing non-State litigant should be shielded from the costs consequences of failure. In this way responsibility for ensuring that the law and State conduct are constitutional is placed at the correct door.[270]

In relation to constitutional litigation between two private parties, the approach to costs is laid down in *Bothma v Els and Others*.[271] It is to the effect that (i) the general principle is that costs will follow the result; and (ii) in 'exceptional cases', the court will make no order as to costs. In particular, no order as to costs will be made where 'the pursuit of public interest litigation could be unduly chilled by an adverse costs order'.[272]

Secondly, where judicial review concerns the performance of public duties by public officials, the award of costs is informed by the court's concern to promote good governance.[273] Thus, on the one hand, where administrators have performed their duties and litigated in good faith, the courts have expressed reluctance to award costs against the administrator. On the other hand, where administrators have acted *mala fide*, or where gross administrative irregularities or abuse of legal process have been committed, the courts have readily awarded costs against the administrator. In particularly egregious cases, the courts have awarded

269 *Biowatch Trust* para 56.
270 *Biowatch Trust* para 23.
271 2010 (2) SA 622 (CC).
272 *Bothma v Els and Others* paras 91–93.
273 See Hoexter (2012) 574–576.

costs on a punitive scale[274] or costs *de bonis propriis*, meaning that the costs must be paid out of the official's own pocket.[275]

In keeping with the *Biowatch Trust* principles, the courts will not readily award costs against persons who are unsuccessful in seeking to enforce their right to just administrative action. However private parties are not immunised from appropriate sanctions, including punitive costs orders and costs *de bonis propriis*, for litigation that is vexatious, frivolous, professionally unbecoming or in any other similar way abusive of the processes of the court. As Ackermann J noted in *Motsepe*, spurious constitutional challenges 'can neither be in the interests of the administration of justice or fair to those who are forced to oppose such attacks'.[276]

In *Black Sash v Minister of Social Development (No 2)*[277] the Constitutional Court ordered the Minister of Social Development, Bathabile Dlamini, to pay a portion of the costs of the litigation personally. A separate fact-finding inquiry into the Minister's conduct (which had been ordered by the court) had found that Ms Dlamini had not made full disclosure to the court of material facts in her affidavits filed in litigation before it. Based on these findings, the court ordered the Minister to pay 20% of the litigation costs out of her own pocket, for misleading the court. The court emphasised that imposing personal liability for costs on public officials who act contrary to their constitutional obligations is an important tool for ensuring accountability. It rejected the Minister's argument that a personal costs order against her would offend the separation of powers, and reasoned that –

> When courts make costs orders they do not make judgments on the political accountability of public officials. They do so only in relation to how the rights of people are affected by the conduct of a public official who is not open, transparent and accountable and how that impacts on the responsibility to a court by those involved in the litigation.[278]

The Constitutional Court was again called upon to consider a personal costs order against a public official – this time, the Public Protector, Busisiwe Mkhwebane – in the *South African Reserve Bank* matter.[279] The High Court had ordered the Public Protector to pay 15% of the Reserve Bank's costs on a punitive attorney-and-client scale, in her personal capacity, for misleading the court under oath as to her reliance on certain expert evidence, for failing to disclose meetings with the Presidency and the State Security Agency in her investigation, and for obfuscating and failing to give a full and frank account of the steps she took in producing a report that, amongst other things, directed Parliament to change the constitutional mandate of the Reserve Bank. The Public Protector appealed against this order to the Constitutional Court. The majority of the Constitutional Court upheld the costs order granted by the High Court. It applied the principles set out in *Black Sash II*, and confirmed that a decision to impose personal and punitive costs – like all costs awards – entails an exercise of true discretion. As such, an appellate court will not lightly interfere with the

274 See, for example, *Nyathi v MEC for Department of Health, Gauteng and Another* 2008 (5) SA 94 (CC) para 91; *Njongi v MEC, Department of Welfare, Eastern Cape*, 2008 (4) SA 237 (CC) para 85.

275 See cases discussed below. See also: *Moeca v Addisionele Komissaris, Bloemfontein* 1981 (2) SA 357 (O) at 366B–C; *Machi v MEC for Province of KwaZulu-Natal Responsible for Social Welfare and Population Development*, unreported case D&CLD 4392/04 of 8 March 2005, discussed in Hoexter (2012) 575–576.

276 *Motsepe v Commissioner for Inland Revenue* 1997 (2) SA 898 (CC) para 30. See also *Affordable Medicines Trust* para 138.

277 *Black Sash Trust v Minister of Social Development and Others (Freedom Under Law NPC Intervening)* 2018 (12) BCLR 1472 (CC) ('*Black Sash II*').

278 *Black Sash II* para 10.

279 *Public Protector v South African Reserve Bank* 2019 (6) SA 253 (CC).

award. The court also emphasised the constitutional source and purpose of personal costs orders, as follows:

> [T]he source of a court's power to impose personal costs orders against public officials is the Constitution itself. The Constitution requires public officials to be accountable and observe heightened standards in litigation. They must not mislead or obfuscate. They must do right and they must do it properly. They are required to be candid and place a full and fair account of the facts before a court.
>
> The purpose of a personal costs order against a public official is to vindicate the Constitution. These orders are not inconsistent with the Constitution; they are required for its protection because public officials who flout their constitutional obligations must be held to account. And when their defiance of their constitutional obligations is egregious, it is they who should pay the costs of the litigation brought against them, and not the taxpayer.[280]

In making costs awards, the court must also be guided by any special provisions on costs in the applicable legislation. For example, sections 32(2) and (3) of the National Environmental Management Act[281] contain special provisions on costs awards for environmental litigation, and provide that a court may decide not to award costs against unsuccessful litigants who are acting in the public interest or to protect the environment and who had made due efforts to use other means for obtaining the relief.

## 12.14 Appealing decisions on remedy

In *Trencon*,[282] the Constitutional Court held that the determination of a just and equitable remedy is an exercise of 'a true discretion'. A true discretion exists where the lower court has a number of equally permissible options available to it. The significance of this characterisation is that another court on appeal will not second-guess or lightly interfere with the exercise of a true discretion. It will only interfere if the discretion was not exercised judicially, was influenced by wrong principles or a misdirection on the facts, or if the decision reached could not reasonably have been made by a court properly directing itself to all the relevant facts and principles. In other words, there must have been a material misdirection on the part of the lower court in order for an appeal court to interfere; it is not sufficient on appeal simply to show that the lower court's order was wrong. This 'principle of appellant restraint' was described by Moseneke DCJ in *Florence v Government of the Republic of South Africa*:[283]

> Where a court is granted wide decision making powers with a number of options or variables, an appellate court may not interfere unless it is clear that the choice the court has preferred is at odds with the law. If the impugned decision lies within a range of permissible decisions, an appeal court may not interfere only because it favours a different option within the range. This principle of appellate restraint preserves judicial comity. It fosters certainty in the application of the law and favours finality in judicial decision making.

---

280 *South African Reserve Bank* at paras 152–153.
281 107 of 1998.
282 *Trencon* paras 89–90.
283 2014 (6) SA 456 (CC) para 113.

## THIS CHAPTER IN ESSENCE

When a court finds that administrative action is irregular, the court must declare the action invalid, and then has a wide discretion to award appropriate relief. Since administrative law litigation amounts to constitutional litigation, the Constitution's provisions dealing with remedies apply to such instances. These provisions are supplemented by PAJA's provisions on remedies in section 8, which mandates courts to grant any order that is just and equitable.

Administrative law remedies thus operate in two stages:

1. when a decision is inconsistent with demands of the Constitution, PAJA or the common law, a court must declare it invalid; and
2. once a court has declared the decision invalid, the court has discretion to order a 'just and equitable' remedy.

The main remedies that the courts grant are first, declaring the irregular administrative action invalid and, second setting it aside and remitting (or sending it back) to the administrator to take the decision afresh. This is the default approach. However, courts may grant an exceptional remedy such as suspending the declaration of invalidity and declining to set the decision aside; substituting the administrative action (where a court makes the decision itself, instead of remitting it to the administrator); or granting compensation (monetary relief).

## FURTHER READING


- Boonzaier, L (2018) A Decision to Undo *SALJ* 135(4):642
- Cilliers, AC; Loots, C & Nel, HC (2009) *Herbstein & Van Winsen: The Civil Practice of the High Courts of South Africa* (5th ed) Vol 2, 1456–1482
- De Beer, MN (2018) A New Role for the Principle of Legality in Administrative Law *SALJ* 135(4):613
- Forsyth, C 'The Metaphysic of Nullity': Invalidity, Conceptual Reasoning and the Rule of Law in Forsyth C & Hare, I (Eds) (1998) *The Golden Metwand and the Crooked Cord: Essays in Honour of Sir William Wade QC* Oxford: OUP
- Forsyth, C (2006) The Theory of the Second Actor Revisited *Acta Juridica* 209
- Mandlana, W (2008) Effective Remedies and Obedience to Court Orders Central to the Rule of Law: An Examination of the Judicial Approach *Speculum Juris* 22:14
- Plasket, C (2000) Protecting the Public Purse: Appropriate Relief and Cost Orders Against Public Officials *SALJ* 117(1):151
- Quinot, G (2008) Worse than Losing a Government Tender: Winning It *Stellenbosch Law Review* 19:101–121
- Roach, K & Budlender, G (2005) Mandatory Relief and Supervisory Jurisdiction: When is it Appropriate, Just and Equitable? *SALJ* 122(2):325
- Quinot, G & Van der Sijde, E (2019) Opening at the Close: Clarity from the Constitutional Court on the Legal Cause of Action and Regulatory Framework for an Organ of State Seeking to Review its Own Decisions? *TSAR* 2:324
- Taylor, H (2019) Forcing the Court's Remedial Hand: Non-Compliance as a Catalyst for Remedial Innovation *Constitutional Court Review* IX:247
- Van Loggerenberg, DE; Bishop, M & Brickhill, J (2014) *Erasmus: Superior Courts Practice* (Revision Service 45) Appendix E8: Interdicts at 1–15

# Promotion of Administrative Justice Act 3 of 2000

*(English text signed by the President.)*
*(Assented to 3 February 2000.)*

**ACT**

**To give effect to the right to administrative action that is lawful, reasonable and procedurally fair and to the right to written reasons for administrative action as contemplated in section 33 of the Constitution of the Republic of South Africa, 1996; and to provide for matters incidental thereto.**

**PREAMBLE**

WHEREAS section 33 (1) and (2) of the Constitution provides that everyone has the right to administrative action that is lawful, reasonable and procedurally fair and that everyone whose rights have been adversely affected by administrative action has the right to be given written reasons;

AND WHEREAS section 33 (3) of the Constitution requires national legislation to be enacted to give effect to those rights, and to -

* provide for the review of administrative action by a court or, where appropriate, an independent and impartial tribunal;
* impose a duty on the state to give effect to those rights; and
* promote an efficient administration;

AND WHEREAS item 23 of Schedule 6 to the Constitution provides that the national legislation envisaged in section 33 (3) must be enacted within three years of the date on which the Constitution took effect;

AND IN ORDER TO -

* promote an efficient administration and good governance; and
* create a culture of accountability, openness and transparency in the public administration or in the exercise of a public power or the performance of a public function, by giving effect to the right to just administrative action,

BE IT THEREFORE ENACTED by the Parliament of the Republic of South Africa, as follows:—

**Definitions**

**1.** In this Act, unless the context indicates otherwise—

**(i)** **"administrative action"** means any decision taken, or any failure to take a decision, by—

(*a*) an organ of state, when—

(i) exercising a power in terms of the Constitution or a provincial constitution; or

(ii) exercising a public power or performing a public function in terms of any legislation; or

(*b*) a natural or juristic person, other than an organ of state, when exercising a public power or performing a public function in terms of an empowering provision,

which adversely affects the rights of any person and which has a direct, external legal effect, but does not include—

(*aa*) the executive powers or functions of the National Executive, including the powers or functions referred to in sections 79 (1) and (4), 84 (2) (*a*), (*b*), (*c*), (*d*), (*f*), (*g*), (*h*), (*i*) and (*k*), 85 (2) (*b*), (*c*), (*d*) and (*e*), 91 (2), (3), (4) and (5), 92 (3), 93, 97, 98, 99 and 100 of the Constitution;

(*bb*) the executive powers or functions of the Provincial Executive, including the powers or functions referred to in sections 121 (1) and (2), 125 (2) (*d*), (*e*) and (*f*), 126, 127 (2), 132 (2), 133 (3) (*b*), 137, 138, 139 and 145 (1) of the Constitution;

(*cc*) the executive powers or functions of a municipal council;

(*dd*) the legislative functions of Parliament, a provincial legislature or a municipal council;

(*ee*) the judicial functions of a judicial officer of a court referred to in section 166 of the Constitution or of a Special Tribunal established under section 2 of the Special Investigating Units and Special Tribunals Act, 1996 (Act No. 74 of 1996), and the judicial functions of a traditional leader under customary law or any other law;

(*ff*) a decision to institute or continue a prosecution;

(*gg*) a decision relating to any aspect regarding the nomination, selection, or appointment of a judicial official or any other person, by the Judicial Service Commission in terms of any law;

(*hh*) any decision taken, or failure to take a decision, in terms of any provision of the Promotion of Access to Information Act, 2000; or

(*ii*) any decision taken, or failure to take a decision, in terms of section 4 (1);

**(ii)** **"administrator"** means an organ of state or any natural or juristic person taking administrative action;

**(iii)** **"Constitution"** means the Constitution of the Republic of South Africa, 1996;

**(iv)** **"court"** means—

(*a*) the Constitutional Court acting in terms of section 167 (6) (*a*) of the Constitution; or

(*b*) (i) a High Court or another court of similar status; or

(ii) a Magistrate's Court for any district or for any regional division established by the Minister for the purposes of adjudicating civil disputes in terms of section 2 of the Magistrates' Courts Act, 1944 (Act No. 32 of 1944), either generally or in respect of a specified class of administrative actions, designated by the Minister by notice in the Gazette and presided over by a magistrate, an additional magistrate or a magistrate of a regional division established for the purposes of adjudicating civil disputes, as the case may be, designated in terms of section 9A,

within whose area of jurisdiction the administrative action occurred or the administrator has his or her or its principal place of administration or the party whose rights have been affected is domiciled or ordinarily resident or the adverse effect of the administrative action was, is or will be experienced;

**(v)** **"decision"** means any decision of an administrative nature made, proposed to be made, or required to be made, as the case may be, under an empowering provision, including a decision relating to—

(*a*) making, suspending, revoking or refusing to make an order, award or determination;

(*b*) giving, suspending, revoking or refusing to give a certificate, direction, approval, consent or permission;

(*c*) issuing, suspending, revoking or refusing to issue a licence, authority or other instrument;

(*d*) imposing a condition or restriction;

(*e*) making a declaration, demand or requirement;

(*f*) retaining, or refusing to deliver up, an article; or

(*g*) doing or refusing to do any other act or thing of an administrative nature, and a reference to a failure to take a decision must be construed accordingly;

(vi) **"empowering provision"** means a law, a rule of common law, customary law, or an agreement, instrument or other document in terms of which an administrative action was purportedly taken;

(vii) **"failure"**, in relation to the taking of a decision, includes a refusal to take the decision;

(viii) **"Minister"** means the Cabinet member responsible for the administration of justice;

(ix) **"organ of state"** bears the meaning assigned to it in section 239 of the Constitution;

(x) **"prescribed"** means prescribed by regulation made under section 10;

(xi) **"public"**, for the purposes of section 4, includes any group or class of the public;

(xii) **"this Act"** includes the regulations; and

(xiii) **"tribunal"** means any independent and impartial tribunal established by national legislation for the purpose of judicially reviewing an administrative action in terms of this Act.

**Application of Act**

2 (1) The Minister may, by notice in the *Gazette*—

(*a*) if it is reasonable and justifiable in the circumstances, exempt an administrative action or a group or class of administrative actions from the application of any of the provisions of section 3, 4 or 5; or

(*b*) in order to promote an efficient administration and if it is reasonable and justifiable in the circumstances, permit an administrator to vary any of the requirements referred to in section 3 (2), 4 (1) (*a*) to (*e*), (2) and (3) or 5 (2), in a manner specified in the notice.

(2) Any exemption or permission granted in terms of subsection (1) must, before publication in the *Gazette*, be approved by Parliament.

**Procedurally fair administrative action affecting any person**

3 (1) Administrative action which materially and adversely affects the rights or legitimate expectations of any person must be procedurally fair.

(2) (*a*) A fair administrative procedure depends on the circumstances of each case.

(*b*) In order to give effect to the right to procedurally fair administrative action, an administrator, subject to subsection (4), must give a person referred to in subsection (1)—

(i) adequate notice of the nature and purpose of the proposed administrative action;

(ii) a reasonable opportunity to make representations;

(iii) a clear statement of the administrative action;

(iv) adequate notice of any right of review or internal appeal, where applicable; and

(v) adequate notice of the right to request reasons in terms of section 5.

(3) In order to give effect to the right to procedurally fair administrative action, an administrator may, in his or her or its discretion, also give a person referred to in subsection (1) an opportunity to—

(*a*) obtain assistance and, in serious or complex cases, legal representation;

(*b*) present and dispute information and arguments; and

(*c*) appear in person.

(4) (*a*) If it is reasonable and justifiable in the circumstances, an administrator may depart from any of the requirements referred to in subsection (2).

(*b*) In determining whether a departure as contemplated in paragraph (*a*) is reasonable and justifiable, an administrator must take into account all relevant factors, including—

(i) the objects of the empowering provision;

(ii) the nature and purpose of, and the need to take, the administrative action;

(iii) the likely effect of the administrative action;

(iv) the urgency of taking the administrative action or the urgency of the matter; and

(v) the need to promote an efficient administration and good governance.

(5) Where an administrator is empowered by any empowering provision to follow a procedure which is fair but different from the provisions of subsection (2), the administrator may act in accordance with that different procedure.

**Administrative action affecting public**

4 (1) In cases where an administrative action materially and adversely affects the rights of the public, an administrator, in order to give effect to the right to procedurally fair administrative action, must decide whether—

(*a*) to hold a public inquiry in terms of subsection (2);

(*b*) to follow a notice and comment procedure in terms of subsection (3);

(*c*) to follow the procedures in both subsections (2) and (3);

(*d*) where the administrator is empowered by any empowering provision to follow a procedure which is fair but different, to follow that procedure; or

(*e*) to follow another appropriate procedure which gives effect to section 3.

(2) If an administrator decides to hold a public inquiry—

(*a*) the administrator must conduct the public inquiry or appoint a suitably qualified person or panel of persons to do so; and

(*b*) the administrator or the person or panel referred to in paragraph (*a*) must—

(i) determine the procedure for the public inquiry, which must—

(*aa*) include a public hearing; and

(*bb*) comply with the procedures to be followed in connection with public inquiries, as prescribed;

(ii) conduct the inquiry in accordance with that procedure;

(iii) compile a written report on the inquiry and give reasons for any administrative action taken or recommended; and

(iv) as soon as possible thereafter—

(*aa*) publish in English and in at least one of the other official languages in the *Gazette* or relevant provincial *Gazette* a notice containing a concise summary of any report and the particulars of the places and times at which the report may be inspected and copied; and (*bb*) convey by such other means of communication which the administrator considers effective, the information referred to in item (*aa*) to the public concerned.

(3) If an administrator decides to follow a notice and comment procedure, the administrator must—

(*a*) take appropriate steps to communicate the administrative action to those likely to be materially and adversely affected by it and call for comments from them;

(*b*) consider any comments received;

(*c*) decide whether or not to take the administrative action, with or without changes; and

(*d*) comply with the procedures to be followed in connection with notice and comment procedures, as prescribed.

(4) (*a*) If it is reasonable and justifiable in the circumstances, an administrator may depart from the requirements referred to in subsections (1) (*a*) to (*e*), (2) and (3).

(*b*) In determining whether a departure as contemplated in paragraph (*a*) is reasonable and justifiable, an administrator must take into account all relevant factors, including—

(i) the objects of the empowering provision;

(ii) the nature and purpose of, and the need to take, the administrative action;

(iii) the likely effect of the administrative action;

(iv) the urgency of taking the administrative action or the urgency of the matter; and

(v) the need to promote an efficient administration and good governance.

**Reasons for administrative action**

5 (1) Any person whose rights have been materially and adversely affected by administrative action and who has not been given reasons for the action may, within 90 days after the date on which that person became aware of the action or might reasonably have been expected to have become aware of the action, request that the administrator concerned furnish written reasons for the action.

(2) The administrator to whom the request is made must, within 90 days after receiving the request, give that person adequate reasons in writing for the administrative action.

(3) If an administrator fails to furnish adequate reasons for an administrative action it must, subject to subsection (4) and in the absence of proof to the contrary, be presumed in any proceedings for judicial review that the administrative action was taken without good reason.

(4) (*a*) An administrator may depart from the requirement to furnish adequate reasons if it is reasonable and justifiable in the circumstances, and must forthwith inform the person making the request of such departure.

(*b*) In determining whether a departure as contemplated in paragraph (*a*) is reasonable and justifiable, an administrator must take into account all relevant factors, including—

(i) the objects of the empowering provision;

(ii) the nature, purpose and likely effect of the administrative action concerned;

(iii) the nature and the extent of the departure;

(iv) the relation between the departure and its purpose;

(v) the importance of the purpose of the departure; and

(vi) the need to promote an efficient administration and good governance.

(5) Where an administrator is empowered by any empowering provision to follow a procedure which is fair but different from the provisions of subsection (2), the administrator may act in accordance with that different procedure.

(6) (*a*) In order to promote an efficient administration, the Minister may, at the request of an administrator, by notice in the *Gazette* publish a list specifying any administrative action or a group or class of administrative actions in respect of which the administrator concerned will automatically furnish reasons to a person whose rights are adversely affected by such actions, without such person having to request reasons in terms of this section.

(*b*) The Minister must, within 14 days after the receipt of a request referred to in paragraph (*a*) and at the cost of the relevant administrator, publish such list, as contemplated in that paragraph.

**Judicial review of administrative action**

6 (1) Any person may institute proceedings in a court or a tribunal for the judicial review of an administrative action.

(2) A court or tribunal has the power to judicially review an administrative action if—

(*a*) the administrator who took it—

(i) was not authorised to do so by the empowering provision;

(ii) acted under a delegation of power which was not authorised by the empowering provision; or

(iii) was biased or reasonably suspected of bias;

(*b*) a mandatory and material procedure or condition prescribed by an empowering provision was not complied with;

(*c*) the action was procedurally unfair;

(*d*) the action was materially influenced by an error of law;

(*e*) the action was taken—

(i) for a reason not authorised by the empowering provision;

(ii) for an ulterior purpose or motive;

(iii) because irrelevant considerations were taken into account or relevant considerations were not considered;

(iv) because of the unauthorised or unwarranted dictates of another person or body;

(v) in bad faith; or

(vi) arbitrarily or capriciously;

(*f*) the action itself—

(i) contravenes a law or is not authorised by the empowering provision; or

(ii) is not rationally connected to—

(*aa*) the purpose for which it was taken;

(*bb*) the purpose of the empowering provision;

(*cc*) the information before the administrator; or

(*dd*) the reasons given for it by the administrator;

(*g*) the action concerned consists of a failure to take a decision;

(*h*) the exercise of the power or the performance of the function authorised by the empowering provision, in pursuance of which the administrative action was purportedly taken, is so unreasonable that no reasonable person could have so exercised the power or performed the function; or

(*i*) the action is otherwise unconstitutional or unlawful.

(3) If any person relies on the ground of review referred to in subsection (2) (*g*), he or she may in respect of a failure to take a decision, where—

(*a*) (i) an administrator has a duty to take a decision;

(ii) there is no law that prescribes a period within which the administrator is required to take that decision; and

(iii) the administrator has failed to take that decision,
institute proceedings in a court or tribunal for judicial review of the failure to take the decision on the ground that there has been unreasonable delay in taking the decision; or

(*b*) (i) an administrator has a duty to take a decision;

(ii) a law prescribes a period within which the administrator is required to take that decision; and

(iii) the administrator has failed to take that decision before the expiration of that period,
institute proceedings in a court or tribunal for judicial review of the failure to take the decision within that period on the ground that the administrator has a duty to take the decision notwithstanding the expiration of that period.

**Procedure for judicial review**

7 (1) Any proceedings for judicial review in terms of section 6 (1) must be instituted without unreasonable delay and not later than 180 days after the date—

(*a*) subject to subsection (2) (*c*), on which any proceedings instituted in terms of internal remedies as contemplated in subsection (2) (*a*) have been concluded; or

(*b*) where no such remedies exist, on which the person concerned was informed of the administrative action, became aware of the action and the reasons for it or might reasonably have been expected to have become aware of the action and the reasons.

(2) (*a*) Subject to paragraph (*c*), no court or tribunal shall review an administrative action in terms of this Act unless any internal remedy provided for in any other law has first been exhausted.

(*b*) Subject to paragraph (*c*), a court or tribunal must, if it is not satisfied that any internal remedy referred to in paragraph (*a*) has been exhausted, direct that the person concerned must first exhaust such remedy before instituting proceedings in a court or tribunal for judicial review in terms of this Act.

(*c*) A court or tribunal may, in exceptional circumstances and on application by the person concerned, exempt such person from the obligation to exhaust any internal remedy if the court or tribunal deems it in the interest of justice.

(3) The Rules Board for Courts of Law established by section 2 of the Rules Board for Courts of Law Act, 1985 (Act 107 of 1985), must, before 28 February 2009, subject to the approval of the Minister, make rules of procedure for judicial review.

(4) Until the rules of procedure referred to in subsection (3) come into operation, all proceedings for judicial review under this Act must be instituted in a High Court or another court having jurisdiction.

(5) Any rule made under subsection (3) must, before publication in the *Gazette*, be approved by Parliament.

**Remedies in proceedings for judicial review**

8 (1) The court or tribunal, in proceedings for judicial review in terms of section 6 (1), may grant any order that is just and equitable, including orders—

(*a*) directing the administrator—

(i) to give reasons; or

(ii) to act in the manner the court or tribunal requires;

(*b*) prohibiting the administrator from acting in a particular manner;

(*c*) setting aside the administrative action and—

(i) remitting the matter for reconsideration by the administrator, with or without directions; or

(ii) in exceptional cases—

(*aa*) substituting or varying the administrative action or correcting a defect resulting from the administrative action; or (*bb*) directing the administrator or any other party to the proceedings to pay compensation;

(*d*) declaring the rights of the parties in respect of any matter to which the administrative action relates;

(*e*) granting a temporary interdict or other temporary relief; or

(*f*) as to costs.

(2) The court or tribunal, in proceedings for judicial review in terms of section 6 (3), may grant any order that is just and equitable, including orders—

(*a*) directing the taking of the decision;

(*b*) declaring the rights of the parties in relation to the taking of the decision;

(*c*) directing any of the parties to do, or to refrain from doing, any act or thing the doing, or the refraining from the doing, of which the court or tribunal considers necessary to do justice between the parties; or

(*d*) as to costs.

**Variation of time**

9 (1) The period of—

(*a*) 90 days referred to in section 5 may be reduced; or

(*b*) 90 days or 180 days referred to in sections 5 and 7 may be extended for a fixed period,

by agreement between the parties or, failing such agreement, by a court or tribunal on application by the person or administrator concerned.

(2) The court or tribunal may grant an application in terms of subsection (1) where the interests of justice so require.

**Designation and training of presiding officers**

9A (1)(*a*) The head of an administrative region defined in section 1 of the Magistrates' Courts Act, 1944 (Act No. 32 of 1944), or the magistrate at the head of a regional division established for the purposes of adjudicating civil disputes in terms of section 2 of the Magistrates' Courts Act, 1944, must designate in writing any magistrate, additional magistrate or magistrate of a regional division established for the purposes of adjudicating civil disputes, as the case may be, as a presiding officer of the Magistrate's Court designated by the Minister in terms of section 1 of this Act.

(*b*) A presiding officer must perform the functions and duties and exercise the powers assigned to or conferred on him or her under this Act or any other law.

(2) ...

(3) The heads of administrative regions or magistrates at the head of regional divisions established for the purposes of adjudicating civil disputes, must take all reasonable steps within available resources to designate at least one presiding officer for each magistrate's court within his or her area of jurisdiction which has been designated by the Minister in terms of section 1.

(4) ...

(5) The South African Judicial Education Institute established in terms of section 3 of the South African Judicial Education Institute Act, 2008 (Act No. 14 of 2008), must develop and implement training courses for presiding officers with the view to building a dedicated and experienced pool of trained and specialised presiding officers for purposes of presiding in court proceedings as contemplated in this Act.

(6) ...

(7) ...

(8) The provisions of section 12 (6) and (8) of the Magistrates' Courts Act, 1944 (Act No. 32 of 1944), are applicable with the necessary changes required by the context.

**Regulations and code of good administrative conduct**

10 (1) The Minister must make regulations relating to—

(*a*) the procedures to be followed by designated administrators or in relation to classes of administrative action in order to promote the right to procedural fairness;

(*b*) the procedures to be followed in connection with public inquiries;

(*c*) the procedures to be followed in connection with notice and comment procedures; and

(*d*) the procedures to be followed in connection with requests for reasons.

(2) The Minister may make regulations relating to—

(*a*) the establishment, duties and powers of an advisory council to monitor the application of this Act and to advise the Minister on—

(i) the appropriateness of publishing uniform rules and standards which must be complied with in the taking of administrative actions, including the compilation and maintenance of registers containing the text of rules and standards used by organs of state;

(ii) any improvements that might be made in respect of internal complaints procedures, internal administrative appeals and the judicial review by courts or tribunals of administrative action;

(iii) the appropriateness of establishing independent and impartial tribunals, in addition to the courts, to review administrative action and of specialised administrative tribunals, including a tribunal with general jurisdiction over all organs of state or a number of organs of state, to hear and determine appeals against administrative action;

(iv) the appropriateness of requiring administrators, from time to time, to consider the continuance of standards administered by them and of prescribing measures for the automatic lapsing of rules and standards;

(v) programmes for educating the public and the members and employees of administrators regarding the contents of this Act and the provisions of the Constitution relating to administrative action;

(vi) any other improvements aimed at ensuring that administrative action conforms with the right to administrative justice;

(vii) any steps which may lead to the achievement of the objects of this Act; and

(viii) any other matter in respect of which the Minister requests advice;

(*b*) the compilation and publication of protocols for the drafting of rules and standards;

(*c*) the initiation, conducting and co-ordination of programmes for educating the public and the members and employees of administrators regarding the contents of this Act and the provisions of the Constitution relating to administrative action;

(*d*) matters required or permitted by this Act to be prescribed; and

(*e*) matters necessary or convenient to be prescribed in order to—

(i) achieve the objects of this Act; or

(ii) subject to subsection (3), give effect to any advice or recommendations by the advisory council referred to in paragraph (*a*).

(3) This section may not be construed as empowering the Minister to make regulations, without prior consultation with the Minister for the Public Service and Administration, regarding any matter which affects the public service.

(4) Any regulation—

(*a*) made under subsections (1) (*a*), (*b*), (*c*) and (*d*) and (2) (*c*), (*d*) and (*e*) must, before publication in the *Gazette*, be submitted to Parliament; and

(*b*) made under subsection (2) (*a*) and (*b*) must, before publication in the *Gazette*, be approved by Parliament.

(5) Any regulation made under subsections (1) and (2) or any provision of the code of good administrative conduct made under subsection (5A) which may result in financial expenditure for the State must be made in consultation with the Minister of Finance.

(5A) The Minister must, by notice in the *Gazette*, publish a code of good administrative conduct in order to provide administrators with practical guidelines and information aimed at the promotion of an efficient administration and the achievement of the objects of this Act.

(6) The code of good administrative conduct referred to in subsection (5A) must, before publication in the *Gazette*, be approved by Cabinet and Parliament and must be made before 28 February 2009.

**Liability**

10A. No person is criminally or civilly liable for anything done in good faith in the exercise or performance or purported exercise or performance of any power or duty in terms of this Act or the rules made under section 7(3).

**Short title and commencement**

11 This Act is called the Promotion of Administrative Justice Act, 2000, and comes into operation on a date fixed by the President by proclamation in the *Gazette*.

# List of references

## Books


Ackerman, B 'Good-bye, Montesquieu' in Rose-Ackerman, S & Lindseth, PL (Eds) (2010) *Comparative Administrative Law* Cheltenham, UK & Northampton, Mass: Edward Elgar

Baxter, L (1984) *Administrative Law* Cape Town: Juta

Bennett, TW & Corder, H (Eds) (1993) *Administrative Law Reform* Cape Town: Juta

Burns, Y & Henrico, R (2020) *Administrative Law* (5th ed) Durban: LexisNexis

Carr, C (1941) *Concerning English Administrative Law* New York: Columbia University Press

Cilliers, AC; Loots, C & Nel, HC (2009) *Herbstein & Van Winsen: The Civil Practice of the High Courts of South Africa* (5th ed) Cape Town: Juta

Corder, H (1984) *Judges at Work* Cape Town: Juta

Corder, H 'Reviewing Review: Much Achieved, Much More to Do' in Corder, H & Van der Vijver, L (Eds) (2002) *Realising Administrative Justice* Cape Town: Siber Ink

Crabbe, V (1993) *Legislative Drafting* 68 London: Cavendish

Currie, I (2007) *The Promotion of Administrative Justice Act: A Commentary* (2nd ed) Cape Town: Siber Ink

Currie, I & De Waal, J (2001) *The New Constitutional and Administrative Law Vol I Constitutional Law* Cape Town: Juta

Currie, I & Klaaren, J (2001) *The Promotion of Administrative Justice Act Benchbook* Cape Town: Siber Ink

De Ville, JR (2005) *Judicial Review of Administrative Action in South Africa* Durban: LexisNexis

Dicey, AV (1924) *Introduction to the Study of the Law of the Constitution* (8th ed) London: Macmillan & Co

Dugard, CJR (1978) *Human Rights and the South African Legal Order* Princeton, NJ: Princeton University Press

Du Plessis, LM (1999) *An Introduction to Law* (3rd ed) Cape Town: Juta

Du Plessis, LM (2002) *Re-Interpretation of Statutes* Durban: LexisNexis

Du Plessis, LM & Corder, H (1994) *Understanding South Africa's Transitional Bill of Rights* Kenwyn: Juta

Dyzenhaus, D 'The politics of deference: judicial review and democracy' in Taggart, M (Ed) (1997) *The Province of Administrative Law* 279 Oxford: Hart

Ellmann, S (1992) *In a Time of Trouble: Law and Liberty in South Africa's State of Emergency* Oxford: Clarendon Press; New York: Oxford University Press

Endicott, T (2011) *Administrative Law* (2nd ed) Oxford; New York: Oxford University Press

Forsyth, CF (1985) *In Danger for their Talents: A Study of the Appellate Division of the Supreme Court of South Africa from 1950-80* Cape Town: Juta

Forsyth, C 'The Metaphysic of Nullity: Invalidity, Conceptual Reasoning and the Rule of Law' in Forsyth, C & Hare, I (Eds) (1998) *The Golden Metwand and the Crooked Cord: Essays on Public Law in Honour of Sir William Wade QC* Oxford: Clarendon Press; New York: Oxford University Press

Govender, K 'Administrative Appeals Tribunals' in Bennett, TW & Corder, H (Eds) (1993) *Administrative Law Reform* Cape Town: Juta

Gwyn, WB (1965) *The Meaning of the Separation of Powers: An Analysis of the Doctrine from its Origin to the Adoption of the United States Constitution* New Orleans: Tulane University

Harlow, C & Rawlings, R (2009) *Law and Administration* (3rd ed) Cambridge, New York: Cambridge University Press

Hoexter, C (2007) *Administrative Law in South Africa* Cape Town: Juta

Hoexter, C (2012) *Administrative Law in South Africa* (2nd ed) Cape Town: Juta

Hoexter, C 'The Rule of Law and the Principle of Legality in South African Administrative Law Today' in Carnelly, M & Hoctor, S (Eds) (2011) *Law, Order and Liberty: Essays in Honour of Tony Mathews* Scottsville: University of KwaZulu-Natal Press

Hoexter, C with Lyster R, & Currie, I (Eds) (2002) *The New Constitutional and Administrative Law Vol II Administrative Law* J Cape Town: Juta

Jowell, J 'Judicial Review of the Substance of Official Decisions' in Bennett, TW & Corder, H (Eds) (1993) *Administrative Law Reform* Cape Town: Juta

Kerans, RP (1994) *Standards of Review Employed by Appellate Courts* Edmonton, Canada: Juriliber

Liebenberg, S (2010) *Socio-Economic Rights Adjudication under a Transformative Constitution* Cape Town: Juta

Mathews, AS (1986) *Freedom, State Security and the Rule of Law: Dilemmas of the Apartheid Society* Cape Town: Juta

McLeod, I (2009) *Principles of Legislative and Regulatory Drafting* 3 Portland: Hart Publishing

Montesquieu *The Spirit of the Laws* tr Nugent, T (1959) New York: Hafner

Plasket, C 'Administrative Justice in South Africa: A Snapshot Survey of Developments Since 1994' in Kidd, M & Hoctor, S (Eds) (2010) *Stella Iuris: Celebrating 100 Years of Teaching Law in Pietermaritzburg* Claremont: Juta

Quinot, G (2008) *Administrative Law: Cases & Materials* Cape Town: Juta

Rose Innes, LA (1963) *Judicial Review of Administrative Tribunals in South Africa* Cape Town: Juta

Saunders, C 'Appeal or Review: The Experience of Administrative Appeals in Australia' in Bennett, TW & Corder, H (Eds) (1993) *Administrative Law Reform* Cape Town: Juta

Schlössels, RJN & Zijlstra, SE (2010) *Bestuursrecht in de Sociale Rechstaat* 11-12 Deventer: Kluwer

Taitz, J (1985) *The Inherent Jurisdiction of the Supreme Court* Cape Town: Juta

Van Loggerenberg, DE; Bishop, M & Brickhill, J (2014) *Erasmus: Superior Courts Practice* (Revision Service 45) Cape Town: Juta

Vile, MJC (1998) *Constitutionalism and the Separation of Powers* (2nd ed) Indianapolis: Liberty Fund

Wade, HWR & Forsyth, CF (2014) *Administrative Law* (11th ed) Oxford: Oxford University Press

Woolf, H et al (2013) *De Smith's Judicial Review* (7th ed) London: Sweet & Maxwell

## Journal articles

Allan, TRS (2006) Human Rights and Judicial Review: A Critique of 'Due Deference' *Cambridge Law Journal* 65(3):671

Bamford, BR (1967) Race Reclassification *SALJ* 84(1):37

Boonzaier, L (2018) A Decision to Undo *SALJ* 135(4):642

Brand, D & Murcott, M (2014) Administrative Law *Juta's Quarterly Review of South African Law* 1

Budlender, G (1988) Law and Lawlessness in South Africa *SAJHR* 4(2):139

Butterworth D, De Oliviera, JAA & De Moor, CL (2012) Are South African Administrative Law Procedures Adequate for the Evaluation of Issues Resting on Scientific Analysis? *SALJ* 129(3):461

Campbell, J (2003) Legitimate Expectations: The Potential and Limits of Substantive Protection in South Africa *SALJ* 120(2):292

Corder, H (1993) Introduction: Administrative Law Reform *Acta Juridica* 1

Corder, H (2004) Without Deference, With Respect: A Response to Justice O'Regan *SALJ* 121(2):438

Creyke, R (2006) Administrative Justice: Beyond the Courtroom Door *Acta Juridica* 257

Currie, I (2006) What Difference Does the Promotion of Administrative Justice Act Make to Administrative Law *Acta Juridica* 325

Davis, DM (2006) To Defer and Then When? Administrative Law and Constitutional Democracy *Acta Juridica* 23

Davis, DM (2006) Adjudicating the Socio-Economic Rights in the South African Constitution: Towards 'Deference Lite'? *SAJHR* 22(2):301

De Beer, MN (2018) A New Role for the Principle of Legality in Administrative Law: *State Information Technology Agency Soc Ltd v Gijima Holdings (Pty) Ltd SALJ* 135(4):613–630

Du Plessis, M & Scott, S (2013) The Variable Standard of Rationality Review: Suggestions for Improved Legality Jurisprudence *SALJ* 130(3):597

Hoexter, C (2000) The Future of Judicial Review in South African Administrative Law *SALJ* 117(3):484

Hoexter, C (2006) 'Administrative Action' in the Courts *Acta Juricia* 303

Kohn, L (2013) The Burgeoning Constitutional Requirement of Rationality and the Separation of Powers: Has Rationality Review Gone too Far? *SALJ* 130(4):810

Maree, PJH & Quinot, G (2016) A Decade and a Half of Deference (Part I) (2016) *Journal of South African Law* 268–280

Maree, PJH & Quinot, G (2016) A Decade and a Half of Deference (Part II) (2016) *Journal of South African Law* 447–466

Murcott, M (2013) Procedural Fairness as a Component of Legality: Is a Reconciliation between *Albutt* and *Masetlha* Possible? *SALJ* 130(2):260

Murcott, M (2015) A Future for the Doctrine of Substantive Legitimate Expectation? The Implications of *Kwazulu-Natal Joint Liaison Committee v MEC for Education, Kwazulu-Natal PER* (18)1:3133

Mureinik, E (1994) A Bridge to Where? Introducing the Interim Bill of Rights *SAJHR* 10(1):31

Mureinik, E (1993) Reconsidering Review: Participation and Accountability *Acta Juridica* 35

O'Regan, K (2004) Breaking Ground: Some Thoughts on the Seismic Shift in our Administrative Law *SALJ* 121(2):424

Plasket, C (2002) The Exhaustion of Internal Remedies and Section 7(2) of the Promotion of Administrative Justice Act 3 of 2000 *SALJ* 119(1):50

Plasket, C (2016) The Fundamental Principles of Justice and Legal Vacuums: The Regulatory Powers of National Sporting Bodies *SALJ* 133(3):569

Plasket, C (2018) Judicial Review, Administrative Power and Deference: A View from the Bench *SALJ* 135(3):502

Plasket, C (2019) Disproportionality — The Hidden Ground of Review: *Medirite (Pty) Ltd v South African Pharmacy Council & Anoth:r SALJ* 136(1):15

Pretorius, DM (2005) The Origins of the *Functus Officio* Doctrine, With Specific Reference to its Application in Administrative Law *SALJ* 122(4):832

Pretorius, DM (2000) Ten Years After Traub: The Doctrine of Legitimate Expectation in South African Administrative Law *SALJ* 117(3):520

Quinot, G (2004) The Developing Doctrine of Substantive Protection of Legitimate Expectations in South African Administrative Law *SA Public Law* 19:543

Quinot, G (2010) Administrative Law *Annual Survey of South African Law* 41

Quinot, G (2010) New Procedures for the Judicial Review of Administrative Action *SA Public Law* 25(2):646

Quinot, G (2010) Substantive Reasoning in Administrative Law Adjudication *Constitutional Court Review* 3:111

Quinot, G (2011) Administrative Law *Annual Survey of South African Law* 49

Quinot, G & Van der Sijde, E (2019) Opening at the Close: Clarity from the Constitutional Court on the Legal Cause of Action and Regulatory Framework for an Organ of State Seeking to Review Its Own Decisions? *TSAR* 2:324

Taylor, H (2019) Forcing the Court's Remedial Hand: Non-Compliance as a Catalyst for Remedial Innovation *Constitutional Court Review* IX:247

Theophilopoulos, C & De Matos Ala, C (2019) An Analysis of the Public Protector's Investigatory and Decision-Making Procedural Powers *PER / PELJ* 22

Tomkins, A (2002) In Defence of the Political Constitution *Oxford Journal of Legal Studies* 22(1):157

Tsele, M (2019) Rationalising Judicial Review: Towards Refining the "Rational Basis" Review Test(s) *SALJ* 136(2):328 at 359–360

Udeh, KT (2016) Viability of bidder remedies under section 62 of the South African Municipal Systems Act *African Public Procurement Law Journal* 3(2):72

Van Wyk, J (2014) Fracking in the Karoo: Approvals Required *Stellenbosch Law Review* 25(1):34

Venter, R (2017) The Executive, the Public Protector and the Legislature: The Lion, the Witch and the Wardrobe *TSAR* 176–189

Wallis, M (2018) Do We Need Deference? *SAJEI* 1(1):97

## Reports and policy papers

Auditor-General of South Africa (2014) *Consolidated General Report on National and Provincial Audit Outcomes PFMA (2013–2014)* Available at: https://www.agsa.co.za/Documents/Auditreports/MFMAgeneralreportsnational.aspx

Department of Water Affairs and Forestry *Water Supply and Sanitation Policy White Paper: Water – An Indivisible National Asset* November 1994

Public Protector *Secure in Comfort: Report on an Investigation into Allegations of Impropriety and Unethical Conduct Relating to the Installation and Implementation of Security Measures by the Department of Public Works at and in Respect of the Private Residence of President Jacob Zuma at Nkandla in the KwaZulu-Natal Province* Report No. 25 of 2013/2014 Available at: http://www.gov.za/sites/www.gov.za/files/Public%20Protector's%20Report%20on%20Nkandla_a.pdf

South African Law Commission Report (August 1998) *The Recognition of Class Actions and Public Interest Actions in South African Law* (Project 88) Pretoria: South African Law Commission Available at: http://www.justice.gov.za/salrc/reports/r_prj88_classact_1998aug.pdf

The International Commission of Jurists (ICJ) *The Rule of Law in a Free Society: A Report on the International Congress of Jurists*, New Delhi India, 1959. Available at: http://www.icj.org/rule-of-law-in-a-free-society-a-report-on-the-international-congress-of-jurists-new-delhi-india-january-5-10-1959/

The International Commission of Jurists (ICJ) *The Dynamic Aspects of the Rule of Law: A Report on the International Congress of Jurists*, Bangkok Thailand, 1965

White Paper on Transforming Public Service Delivery (Batho Pele- "People First" White Paper on Transforming Public Service Delivery) Dept. of Public Service and Administration 18 Sept 1997, Notice 1459 of 1997 in *GG* 18340 of 1 October 1997 Available at: http://www.dpsa.gov.za/dpsa2g/documents/acts®ulations/frameworks/white-papers/transform.pdf

## Dictionaries

*Concise Oxford Dictionary* (1982) 7th ed Oxford: Oxford University Press

*Oxford English Dictionary OED* (Online) (2015) Oxford University Press Available at: http://www.oed.com/

## Additional reading

Bednar-Giyose, J (2018) *Legislative Drafting and the Appropriate Delineation of Administrative Power* PhD dissertation, University of the Witwatersrand

Craig, PP 'What is Public Power?' in Corder, H & Maluwa, T (Eds) (1997) *Administrative Justice in Southern Africa: Proceedings of the Workshop on Controlling Public Power in Southern Africa Held in Cape Town, South Africa, 8-11 March 1996* Cape Town: Dept of Public Law, UCT

Corder, H (1993) Introduction: Administrative Law Reform *Acta Juridica* 1

Forsyth, C (2006) The Theory of the Second Actor Revisited *Acta Juridica* 209

Forsyth, C & Dring, E 'The Final Frontier: The Emergence of Material Error of Fact as a Ground for Judicial Review' in Forsyth, C et al (Eds) (2010) *Effective Judicial Review: A Cornerstone of Good Governance* Oxford; New York: Oxford University Press

Govender, K 'Administrative Appeals Tribunals' in Bennett, TW & Corder, H (Eds) (1993) *Administrative Law Reform* Cape Town: Juta

Hoexter, C (1994) Administrative Justice and Dishonesty *SALJ* 111(4):700

Hoexter, C 'From *Chirwa* to *Gcaba*: An Administrative Lawyer's View' in Kidd, M & Hoctor, S (Eds) (2010) *Stella Iuris: Celebrating 100 Years of Teaching Law in Pietermaritzburg* Cape Town: Juta

Mandlana, W (2008) Effective Remedies and Obedience to Court Orders Central to the Rule of Law: An Examination of the Judicial Approach *Speculum Juris* 22(1):14

Maree, PJH (2013) *Investigating an Alternative Administrative-Law System in South Africa* Unpublished doctoral dissertation (US) Chapter 2 Available at: http://hdl.handle.net/10019.1/85591

Mureinik, E (1993) Reconsidering Review: Participation and Accountability *Acta Juridica* 35

Pfaff, R & Schneider, H (2001) The Promotion of Administrative Justice Act from a German Perspective *SAJHR* 17(1):59

Plasket, C (2000) Protecting the Public Purse: Appropriate Relief and Cost Orders Against Public Officials *SALJ* 117(1):151

Pretorius, DM (2005) The Origins of the *Functus Officio* Doctrine, With Specific Reference to its Application in Administrative Law *SALJ* 122(4):832

Price, A (2010) The Content and Justification of Rationality Review *SA Public Law* 25:346

Quinot, G (2008) Worse Than Losing a Government Tender: Winning It *Stellenbosch Law Review* 19(1):101

Quinot, G (2011) The Right to Reasons for Administrative Action as a Key Ingredient of a Culture of Justification *Speculum Juris* 25(1):32

Roach, K & Budlender, G (2005) Mandatory Relief and Supervisory Jurisdiction: When is it Appropriate, Just and Equitable? *SALJ* 122(2):325

Saunders, C 'Appeal or Review: The Experience of Administrative Appeals in Australia' in Bennett, TW & Corder, H (Eds) (1993) *Administrative Law Reform* Cape Town: Juta

Thornton, L (1999) The Constitutional Right to Just Administrative Action – Are Political Parties Bound? *SAJHR* 15(3):351

Van Loggerenberg, DE; Bishop, M & Brickhill, J (2014) *Erasmus: Superior Courts Practice* (Revision Service 45) Appendix E8: Interdicts at 1–15 Cape Town: Juta

Williams, RC (2011) The Concept of a 'Decision' as the Threshold Requirement for Judicial Review in Terms of the Promotion of Administrative Justice Act *PER* 14:230

## Internet sources

Department of National Treasury RSA (2015) 'Practice Notes' Available at: http://www.treasury.gov.za/legislation/pfma/practice%20notes/default.aspx

Department of National Treasury RSA (2015) *Information about the Ministry* Available at: http://www.treasury.gov.za/ministry/info.aspx

Department of Public Service and Administration RSA (2013) *Public Service Integrity Management Framework* Available at: http://www.dpsa.gov.za/dpsa2g/documents/misc/Public%20Service%20Integrity%20Management%20Framework.pdf

Department of Water Affairs and Sanitation Available at: http://www.dwaf.gov.za/about.aspx

Eskom: *Powering Your World* (2015) Available at: http://www.eskom.co.za/OurCompany/CompanyInformation/Pages/Legislation.aspx

Maree, PJH (2013) *Investigating an Alternative Administrative-Law System in South Africa* Unpublished doctoral dissertation (US) Chapter 2 Available at: http://hdl.handle.net/10019.1/85591

University of the Free State 'UFS Research Sheds Light on Service Delivery Protests in South Africa' 03/02/2015 *Mail and Guardian* Available at: http://pressoffice.mg.co.za/universityofthefreestate/PressRelease.php?StoryID=255849

# Table of cases

**F**



**G**

## M

**N**

**O**



**P**

# Table of legislation

**R**



**S**



**T**



**U**



**V**



**W**

**FOREIGN LEGISLATION**

**Australia**



**USSR**

# Glossary

**administration** Those public institutions primarily concerned with the implementation of legislation and policy, as such, and created for this very purpose.

**administrative action** Generally administrative action are decisions ostensibly taken under empowering provisions in fulfilling the function of state administration and aimed at consequences outside of the administration. This term is comprehensively and technically defined in section 1(*i*) of the Promotion of Administrative Justice Act 3 of 2000.

**administrative justice** The notion of control over and facilitation of administrative action through a range of mechanisms, primarily based in administrative law, aimed at ensuring state administration in line with constitutional norms.

**alternative dispute resolution (ADR)** A range of processes aimed at resolving a legal dispute between two parties other than by means of courts, including negotiation, mediation and arbitration.

**appeal** A process in terms of which the merits of a decision are assessed to determine whether the correct decision was taken and if not to replace the original decision with a new one.

***audi alteram partem*** The common-law rule that requires an administrator to give a person the opportunity to make representations before taking an action that impacts on that person.

**Auditor-General** One of the state institutions supporting constitutional democracy created in Chapter Nine of the Constitution with the mandate to audit and report on the accounts, financial statements and financial management of organs of state.

**Bill** A draft law that the legislature is discussing and considering. Once the President duly passes and signs the Bill, it becomes an Act of the legislature.

**Bill of Rights** Chapter 2 of the Constitution of the Republic of South Africa, 1996 containing fundamental rights protected under the Constitution.

***bona fide*** Latin term meaning 'good faith'.

**branch of government** The name given in constitutional theory to the three pillars of government usually distinguished from each other when discussing the separation of powers doctrine. These three pillars are the legislature, the executive and the judiciary.

**Cabinet** In terms of section 91 of the Constitution, the Cabinet comprises of the President, Deputy President and Ministers appointed by the President and exercising national executive authority with the President. All members of Cabinet except the President and a maximum of two Ministers must be members of the National Assembly. Deputy Ministers are not members of Cabinet.

**case law** The binding legal principles developed by courts when handing down judgments on the interpretation and application of statutes, common law or customary law.

**Chapter Nine institutions** State institutions supporting constitutional democracy created in Chapter Nine of the Constitution, which includes the Public Protector and Auditor General.

**checks and balances** The concept closely associated with the doctrine of separation of powers which envisages that each of the three branches of government (the legislature, the executive and the judiciary) will act as a check (or brake) on the exercise of power by the other two branches to prevent the abuse of power and to ensure accountable government.

**civil service** Personnel constituting the public administration.

**collateral challenge** Resisting irregular administrative action that has not been declared invalid in proceedings where the action is sought to be enforced against a person, the validity of the administrative action thus forms a defence in the enforcement proceedings and is called a collateral challenge.

**common law** The set of legal rules and principles not contained in legislation duly passed by the legislature, but rather inherited from the colonial powers and which are continuously being developed and enforced by the judiciary.

**compensation** A court order for a party to pay another party an amount of money as appropriate relief following the review of an administrative action.

**Constitution** see final Constitution.

**constitutional damages** Where a court finds that a person or institution has infringed the constitutional rights of an individual and (in the absence of other appropriate remedies) orders the person or institution to pay a sum of money to the aggrieved party to remedy the constitutional infringement.

**constitutional supremacy** The Constitution is the supreme authority in the state and all law and conduct is subject to the Constitution.

**contempt of court** A common-law remedy which litigants may resort to when confronted with wilful and *mala fide* (bad faith) non-compliance with court orders directing an opponent to do or refrain from doing something.

**damages** The sum of money a court orders a person or institution to pay to somebody to compensate for the financial or emotional harm or 'damage' suffered by the aggrieved party because of actions taken by the person or institution ordered to pay the damages.

**declaration of constitutional invalidity** Declaration by a court in terms of section 172 of the Constitution that the decision under scrutiny does not comply with constitutional requirements and accordingly in law never existed.

**declaration of rights** A court order that declares the rights of the parties in respect of the matter before the court.

**deference** The notion that courts should show respect to the constitutionally ordained role of other branches of state when reviewing the actions of those branches.

**delegation** The process in terms of which the authority to take an action is transferred from one administrator to another.

***delegatus delegare non potest*** Latin statement meaning that a person that has been granted power generally cannot delegate that power to another person.

**Director-General** The administrative head of a government department.

**doctrine of objective invalidity** Also referred to as the doctrine of objective unconstitutionality, this is the principle that any legislative provision or action which is in conflict with the Constitution is assumed to be invalid from the moment that the conflict first arose. When a court confirms the unconstitutionality and hence invalidity of the legislative provision or action, it will automatically be invalid retrogressively from the moment the conflict arose unless the court orders otherwise.

**Executive** Executive generally refers to that branch within the separation of powers primarily concerned with the formulation of policy and the implementation of legislation and policy; this term is crucial to the study of administrative law. It is usually understood to include both political officials (Cabinet and Deputy Ministers) and the administration.

***ex parte*** Latin term meaning 'from one side'. In litigation this term refers to instances when a party approaches a court in the absence of a respondent, that is, there is only one party to the case.

**final Constitution (also Constitution)** The Constitution of the Republic of South Africa, 1996 finally adopted by the democratically elected Constitutional Assembly in 1996 in terms of which South Africa has been governed since 1997.

**final interdict** An order of court granting interdictory relief of permanent force and effect, that is directing a person not to do something or to take certain action.

**Freedom Charter** The charter setting out core principles according to which South Africa should be governed, adopted by the Congress of the People in 1955 in Kliptown, Soweto. This Charter formed the normative basis of the liberation struggle in South Africa.

***functus officio*** Doctrine in administrative law that holds that once an administrator has taken a final decision that administrator can, as a general rule, not revoke or vary the decision.

**general administrative law** The principles of administrative law that are applicable to all administrative entities, as opposed to specific administrative law which applies to specific areas such as education, the environment, the police, the revenue service and so on.

**government** The term government is employed in several ways. On occasion, 'government' is synonymous with 'executive' in the wide sense, comprising both politicians and administrators. Sometimes government refers to the high executive, that is, Cabinet, and sometimes the ruling or majority party is referred to as the government.

**grounds of review** The bases or arguments in administrative law upon which a court can interfere with an administrative action. Grounds of review in effect capture the mistakes that administrators can make in law that would render their administrative actions subject to invalidation by a court. These are codified in section 6(2) of the Promotion of Administrative Justice Act 3 of 2000.

**horizontal application** Traditionally, a constitution only binds the state and prohibits it from infringing on the rights of private individuals and institutions (and is said to apply vertically only). The South African Constitution applies horizontally as, in certain cases, it also binds private individuals and institutions and prohibits them from infringing on the rights of others.

**human rights** A set of norms and standards contained in a bill of rights or international human rights treaty aimed at protecting the human dignity and other fundamental interests of individuals, which binds the state (and sometimes other parties) and is usually enforced by independent courts or tribunals.

***in limine*** Literally, 'at the threshold', this Latin term refers to a motion made before a trial begins which asks the court, for example, to rule on a preliminary legal point or on the exclusion of certain evidence.

**interdict** An order of court directing a person not to do something (prohibitory interdict) or directing a person to take certain action (mandatory interdict).

**interim Constitution** The South African Constitution according to which South Africa was governed between 1994 and 1996 while a final Constitution was being negotiated. It contained the 34 Constitutional Principles with which the final Constitution had to comply and prescribed the process for the adoption of the final Constitution.

**interim interdict** An order of court granting temporary relief directed at preserving or restoring the status quo pending the final determination of the rights of the parties.

**internal remedy** A mechanism within the administration aimed at providing effective legal relief to a person aggrieved by an administrative action taken by that administration.

**invalid administrative action** Administrative action that has been declared by a court as inconsistent with the Constitution and thus invalid, meaning that the administrative action never existed in law.

***ipse dixit*** Latin term meaning 'he himself said it' and referring to the situation where a claim is based purely on a person's own statement without any further supporting proof.

**irregular (or unjust) administrative action** Administrative action that does not comply with one or more of the three basic requirements of administrative justice under section 33(1) of the Constitution, namely lawfulness, reasonableness and procedural fairness. Irregular administrative action or unjust administrative action covers unlawful administrative action, unreasonable administrative action and procedurally unfair administrative action.

**judicial authority** The term for the power given to judges that allows them to hear a case and to decide in favour of one party.

**judicial independence** The notion that judges should be free from interference by the other branches of government or private parties and which is achieved by providing institutional safeguards.

**judicial review** The process through which judges review the constitutionality of actions taken by the legislature, executive or private parties and declare such actions invalid if they are in conflict with the Constitution. In administrative law, judicial review refers specifically to judicial scrutiny of administrative action.

**judiciary** One of the three branches of government, staffed by judicial officers and led by the Chief Justice.

**jurisdiction** The legal authority of members of the judiciary to hear and determine judicial disputes in a specific geographical area or on specific subject matter.

**justiciability** Concerns the limits on legal issues over which a court can exercise its judicial authority and thus refers to factual or legal questions capable of being decided by a court.

**justiciable** In constitutional law, a matter is justiciable if courts can apply the Constitution to the factual or legal dispute and can declare invalid action in conflict with the Constitution.

**lawfulness** One of the three pillars of administrative justice in terms of section 33(1) of the Constitution, which requires all administrative action to be taken in terms of a valid legal source and in compliance with that source.

**law-making power** The power of an institution such as a legislature, derived from a constitution, to pass valid law.

**legality** The legal ideal that requires all exercises of public power to be rational, non-arbitrary and authorised by law that is clear, ascertainable and non-retrospective.

**legitimate expectation** An expectation on the part of a person that an administrator will take a certain decision or follow a certain procedure based on a promise made by the administrator or on a long-established practice that the person can reasonably expect to continue.

**limitation of rights** When law or conduct infringes on one or more of the rights protected in the Bill of Rights, this is called a limitation of the right. A limitation can be justified in terms of section 36 (and is then constitutionally valid) or it can be unjustified (and is then unconstitutional).

***mala fide*** Latin term meaning 'in bad faith'.

**Member of the Executive Council (MEC)** This is a person appointed by the Premier of a province from among the members of the provincial legislature to serve in the provincial executive, that is the equivalent of the Cabinet at provincial level and who, along with the Premier, exercises provincial executive authority and heads up the provincial government.

**nation state** A political unit consisting of an autonomous state inhabited predominantly by a people sharing a common history.

**National Assembly** The lower House of the national Parliament of South Africa comprising 400 members elected in a general election through the system of proportional representation to represent the interests of the whole electorate.

**National Council of Provinces** The second House of the national Parliament of South Africa comprising 10 delegates from each province, primarily representing the interests of provinces in the national law-making process.

***nemo judex in sua causa esse debet*** Latin statement that states that no one should be a judge in their own cause/interest.

**norms** Values or principles that direct proper, or in constitutional law, legally permissible behaviour in a society.

**notice and comment procedure** A procedure set out in section 4(3) of the Promotion of Administrative Justice Act 3 of 2000, in terms of which the public or groups of the public can be consulted before administrative action impacting on them is taken and which involves written submissions being invited on the proposed administrative action.

**organ of state** In terms of section 239 of the Constitution, any department of state or administration in the national, provincial or local sphere of government; or any other functionary or institution that exercises a power or performs a function in terms of the Constitution or a provincial constitution; or that exercises a public power or performs a public function in terms of any legislation. However, it does not include a court or a judicial officer.

**ouster clause** A provision in a statute that attempts to prevent a court from scrutinising any action taken in terms of that provision or statute.

**Parliament** In South African constitutional law it is the collective name for the National Assembly and the National Council of Provinces, the two Houses of the national legislature empowered jointly to pass legislation and to fulfil the other duties of the national legislature.

**parliamentary supremacy** This is also called parliamentary sovereignty or legislative supremacy and is a concept in the constitutional law of some parliamentary democracies. With parliamentary sovereignty, a legislative body (usually the democratically elected parliament) has absolute sovereignty, meaning it is supreme to all other government institutions, including the executive and the judiciary. This means that the legislative body may change or repeal any previous legislation and is not constrained by the constitution in what legislation it can pass.

**portfolio committees** The various committees of the National Assembly tasked with processing legislation and overseeing the implementation of legislation relating to the portfolio of each member of the Cabinet.

**Premier** In South Africa, the head of a provincial executive and holder of provincial executive authority. The Premier is elected by the provincial legislature from its members.

**President** In South Africa, the head of state and the head of the national executive, elected by the National Assembly from its own members, but who ceases to be a member of the National Assembly upon election as President. The national executive authority vests in the President.

**principle of subsidiarity** The rule that where legislation gives effect to a constitutional right, a litigant must, where possible, rely on the provisions of the legislation and cannot rely directly on the right concerned.

**procedural fairness** One of the three pillars of administrative justice under section 33(1) of the Constitution, which requires administrative action to be taken in terms of a process that is fair towards all those affected by the action. Procedural fairness encompasses, but is not restricted to, the common-law rules of natural justice.

**proportionality** A legal principle used to decide how the right balance should be struck between conflicting interests to accommodate the various interests optimally, usually in a fair and just manner. In administrative law, proportionality is one standard against which the reasonableness of administrative action can be determined and is taken to encompass the three elements of balance, necessity and suitability.

**public administration** That part of the executive concerned with the implementation of legislation and of policy.

**public inquiry** A procedure set out in section 4(2) of the Promotion of Administrative Justice Act 3 of 2000 in terms of which the public or groups of the public can be consulted before administrative action impacting on them is taken and which involves holding a public hearing to obtain input.

**Public Protector** One of the state institutions supporting constitutional democracy in South Africa created in Chapter 9 of the Constitution with the mandate to investigate and report on any conduct in state affairs, or in the public administration in any sphere of government, that is alleged or suspected to be improper or to result in any impropriety or prejudice and to take appropriate remedial action.

**public service** The collective name for those persons who work for the national and provincial government departments.

**rationality** A standard against which the reasonableness of an administrative action can be tested. Rationality in administrative law requires a link between the administrative decision taken and the purpose of the decision, the purpose of the empowering provision under which the action is taken, the information before the administrator and the reasons given for the decision.

**reasonableness** One of the three pillars of administrative justice under section 33(1) of the Constitution, which tests the substantive fairness of administrative action on a scale between rationality at the one end and proportionality at the other. The particular standard for reasonableness in a given case is determined by the context using factors set out in case law.

**reasons** A statement that adequately explains why the administrator took a particular administrative decision.

**remittal** When a court reviews and sets aside administrative action it may refer the matter back, or remit it, to the decision-maker to enable it to reconsider the matter and make a new decision, which is called remittal.

**retrospective operation** When an action is declared constitutionally invalid that declaration operates from the moment that the action was taken and the action accordingly never existed in law.

**royal prerogative** The powers that the Monarch as Head of State enjoyed and which were traditionally not subject to judicial scrutiny. These powers were transferred to the State President when South Africa became a Republic, but ceased to exist when the interim Constitution came into operation.

***rule nisi*** A temporary order granted by a court requiring the person against whom the order is granted to show by a certain date why the order should not become a permanent order.

**rule of law** An evolving constitutional principle enforceable by courts and closely related to the principle of legality which, at a minimum, requires the legislature and the executive in every sphere only to exercise power and perform functions if authorised to do so by law and then only in a rational manner.

**rules of natural justice** At common law the two rules expressed by the Latin statements *nemo judex in sua causa esse debet* (no one should be a judge in their own cause/ interest) and *audi alteram partem* (hear the other side).

**separation of powers** The principle that there must be some separation of function and, in some cases, personnel of the three branches of government.

**setting aside** An order by a court that the administrative action found to be constitutionally invalid does not exist in law.

**severance** The remedy which allows a court to declare invalid only that part of the action which renders the action unconstitutional to fix the unconstitutionality of the action.

**socio-economic rights** The set of rights that ensures that the basic social and economic needs of individuals are met, such as the right to housing, water, health care and social assistance.

**sources of administrative law** The legal sources that contain the rules of administrative law, primarily the Constitution, Promotion of Administrative Justice Act 3 of 2000 and the common law.

**sources of administrative power** The source of the authority in terms of which an administrator takes administrative action, also known as empowering provisions and which can be a law, a rule of common law, customary law, or an agreement, instrument or other document in terms of which an administrative action was purportedly taken.

**specific administrative law** The principles of law that are applicable to discrete areas of administration, for example education, the environment, the police, the revenue service and so on.

**standing** The right of either an individual or an organisation to bring a case to a specific court and to have that case heard in that court.

**state** An organised political community occupying a certain territory and whose members live under the authority of a constitution. The state is therefore a far broader concept than the government.

**structural interdict** A remedy handed down by a court ordering the government to take certain steps and to report back to the court at regular intervals about the steps taken to comply with the Constitution.

**subsidiarity** See principle of subsidiarity.

**substitution** An order in terms of which a court replaces an invalid administrative decision with a different decision following the review and setting aside of the original decision.

**suspension of an order of invalidity** A remedy in which the court, after declaring an action constitutionally invalid, suspends that order, allowing the action to remain in operation, usually for a set period of time to allow the administrator to fix the invalidity of the action.

***trias politica*** The division of the state into three distinct branches - executive, judicial and legislative - in terms of the traditional doctrine of separation of powers.

***ultra vires*** Describes actions taken by government bodies or private institutions that exceed the scope of power given to them by law.

**values** Important and lasting beliefs or ideals contained in a constitution and/or shared by the members of a culture about what is good or bad and desirable or undesirable.

**Westminster system** Also called a parliamentary system, this system of government is based on the British model in which the members of the executive branch (usually the Prime Minister and his or her Cabinet Ministers) are appointed from among the Members of Parliament and obtain their democratic legitimacy from the Parliament. They are members of, as well as accountable to, that body, meaning that the executive and legislative branches are intertwined.

# Index

Page numbers in *italics* indicate information presented in tables or illustrations.

## N



## O



## P